MAMLEY

see "Evolution and Darwinism"
in the Index

THE CHRISTIAN
VIEW OF GOD
AND THE
WORLD

D1534189

THE CHRISTIAN VIEW OF GOD AND THE WORLD

JAMES ORR

FOREWORD BY VERNON GROUNDS

KREGEL PUBLICATIONS
Grand Rapids, MI 49501

The Christian View of God and the World, by James
Orr. Foreword by Vernon C. Grounds. © 1989 by Kregel Pub-
lications, a division of Kregel, Inc. P. O. Box 2607, Grand
Rapids, MI 49501. All rights reserved.

Cover Design: Brian Fowler
Cover Photo: NASA Audio-Visual Branch

Library of Congress Cataloging-in-Publication Data

Orr, James , 1844-1913.
[Christian view of God and the world as centering in the
incarnation]
    The Christian view of God and the world / by James Orr;
foreword by Vernon C. Grounds.
          p.   cm.
    Reprint. Originally published: The Christian view of God
and the world as centering in the incarnation, 3rd ed. New
York: Scribner, 1887.

    1. Theology, Doctrinal. 2. Incarnation. I. Title.
BT75.07   1989   230—dc20   89-2580
                                                                                CIP

ISBN   0-8254-3370-3 (pbk.)

                  1 2 3 4 5 Printing/Year 93 92 91 90 89

Printed in the United States of America

CONTENTS

Contents

Contents

Contents

INDEX TO NOTES

Chapter 1

Chapter 2

Chapter 3

Chapter 4

Chapter 5

Chapter 6

Chapter 7

NOTE TO THE READER

Because of the unfamiliarity of most of us today with the Roman numeral system, used throughout this book for chapter numbers, the following conversion table may offer welcome assistance to many readers:

i	1	xxii	22
ii	2	xxiii	23
iii	3	xxiv	24
iv	4	xxv	25
v	5	xxvi	26
vi	6	xxvii	27
vii	7	xxviii	28
viii	8	xxix	29
ix	9	xxx	30
x	10	xl	40
xi	11	l	50
xii	12	lx	60
xiii	13	lxx	70
xiv	14	lxxx	80
xv	15	xc	90
xvi	16	c	100
xvii	17	cx	110
xviii	18	cxx	120
xvix	19	cxxx	130
xx	20	cxl	140
xxi	21	cl	150

FOREWORD

Nearly a century ago (1891) James Orr, then professor of Church History at Glasgow University, delivered a series of lectures on *The Christian View of God and the World*. Published two years later, they were enthusiastically acclaimed as a masterful apologetic for biblical faith. But with the ongoing of time and the tremendous changes which have occured scientifically, culturally, philosophically, and theologically, can Orr's once-effective defense and exposition of revelational supernaturalism still prove of value in meeting the more-than-formidable challenge of contemporary unbelief in all of its powerful and protean forms? My own answer to that question is an unhesitating affirmative. Let me explain why.

I look back to the years 1937-40 when I, as a seminarian wrestling with the perennial problems of theology, was deeply concerned about finding an adequate apologetic for the faith I had come to re-embrace following my rejection of Christianity as intellectually untenable. I had entered seminary after a conversion experience that compelled me to acknowledge that Jesus Christ was—or at any rate might be—a living reality. That acknowledgment brought with it of course the need to reconsider the whole case for biblical supernaturalism. Suppose there were no mind-compelling rational and factual support for my experience. Suppose it were merely an emotional reaction to some circumstances. Suppose it could be explained away psychologically? Haunted by such misgivings, I took more than an academic interest in my studies. Existentially involved in them, I was seeking, as the apostle Peter puts it, "a reason for the hope" that had brought light into the darkness of my denial. Far be it from me to disparage what my professors and other books contributed to my increasingly firm conviction that Christianity is indeed the final and definitive truth about reality. Yet it was my reading and re-reading of *The Christian View of God and the World* which dissipated my uncertainty and solidified my commitment. And in my opinion, Orr's skillfully articulated argument, which gave me such tremendous help, can still give the same help to searching minds and questing souls as the twentieth century moves toward its close. But before saying more about the book which was a milestone in my own spiritual pilgrimage, let me briefly sketch Orr's distinguished career.

The son of an engineer, Robert Orr, James was born in Glasgow on April 11, 1844. After graduating from the University in his home city, he studied at the Divinity Hall of the University of Edinburgh from which he received his B.D. Later the University of Glasgow granted him a D.D. simply on examination, an extraordinary feat of scholarship. He served the East Bank Presbyterian Church in Hawick for 17 years, diligently studying while faithfully pastoring. In 1891 he was invited to give the first series of Kerr lectures which were later published under the title, *The Christian View of God and the World*. In 1891 he was also appointed to the chair of Church History at his *alma mater* in Edinburgh. In 1900 he took the chair of Apologetics and Systematic Theology in Glasgow where he remained until his death on September 6, 1913.

To appreciate the breadth and depth of Orr's contribution to biblical supernaturalism at a time when evolution, radical criticism, and comparative religion were threatening to undermine the very foundations of Christianity, we can do no better than listen to Alan P. F. Sell as he details Orr's far-reaching impact:

> He examined in Philosophy for Glasgow University; he lectured on German theology at Chicago in 1895; his Elliot Lectures at Allegheny (1897) were published under the title *The Progress of Dogma* (1901); and three lectures originally given at the Mansfield College Summer School, Oxford, in 1894 were repeated as the Morgan Lectures at Auburn, New York in 1897, and subsequently published under the title *Neglected Factors in the Study of the Early Progress of Christianity* (1899). In 1903 Orr delivered the Stone Lectures at Princeton, which appeared as *God's Image in Man* in 1905, and his book on *The Problem of the Old Testament* (1906),

submitted in proof, won the Bross Prize of Lake Forest College, Illinois, for 1905. In April, 1907 he gave a course of lectures to the Bible Teachers' Training School, New York, and these were published in the same year as *The Virgin Birth of Christ.* . . . we note his contributions on Exodus, Deuteronomy, 2 Kings, and Hosea to *The Pulpit Commentary*; his editorship of the five-volume *International Standard Bible Encyclopaedia* (1914) and his essays in *The Fundamentals.* . . . Among Orr's other contributions were those to *Hasting's Dictionary of the Bible* and *Encyclopaedia of Religion and Ethics*, and to such journals as *The Expositor* and *The Expository Times.**

While I have read with care and profit most of what Orr wrote (and, let me confess, utilized his learning and logic in my own teaching), I regard *The Christian View of God and the World* as the greatest of his books. In it he contends persuasively that "Christian truth forms an *organism*—has a unity and coherence which cannot be arbitrarily disturbed in any of its parts without the whole undergoing injury. Conversely the proof that any doctrine fits in essentially to that organism—is an essential part of it—is one of the strongest evidences we can have of its correctness." He therefore contends that the "Christian apologetic can never be satisfactorily separated from the positive exhibition of the Christian system. . . . Christianity in short is its own best apology." That is why he declares:

> He who with his whole heart believes in Jesus as the Son of God is thereby committed to much else besides. He is committed to a view of God, to a view of man, to a view of sin, to a view of Redemption, to a view of the purpose of God in creation and history, to a view of human destiny, found only in Christianity. This forms a *Weltanschauung*, or "Christian view of the world" which stands in marked contrast with theories wrought out from a purely philosophical or scientific standpoint.

I found and still find Orr's apologetic approach at once the strongest defense of Christianity and the sharpest attack against its nay-sayers. Compare this world-view with any rival *Weltanschauung*. What those non-Christian interpretive schemes conspicuously lack is precisely the architectonic coherence of

---

*   Anyone who wishes to study Orr's life and work more fully is advised to read Alan P. F. Sell's *Defending and Declaring the Faith: Some Scottish Examples 1860-1920*, first published by Paternoster Press and now available in the United States from Helmer and Howard, Colorado Springs, Colorado.

biblical faith. Compare those rival world-views with biblical supernaturalism, and you will be impressed, I am confident, by that difference. You will be impressed, moreover, by the fact that Christianity does justice inclusively to all relevant scientific, historical, and experiential data as rival world-views fail to do.

No doubt in reading Orr today we must substitute new names and take into account the varieties of philosophy and theology which have emerged since the end of the nineteenth century. But Orr's basic argument is like a solidly constructed house that needs only remodeling and redecorating. Nor is that all: his extended Notes, his invaluable Appendices, his analysis of important figures and movements through the centuries—all these are of timeless value.

My debt of gratitude to this towering champion of traditional Christianity prompts me to borrow the tribute paid to him by Dr. D.W. Forrest, who was his successor at Glasgow:

> No one who is acquainted with Dr. Orr's writings can fail to be impressed by the great range of his knowledge, alike in philosophy and theology. There were few systems of thought with which he was not familiar: and his accuracy was as remarkable as his range. Nor did this learning over-weight or suppress his individuality. He possessed a speculative gift and a logical acumen which made him a powerful critic. He was in no sense a traditionalist, if by that is meant one who adheres to accepted doctrine, because it has become consecrated by time. If he kept to the broad lines of the evangelical dogmatic, it was because after the fullest investigation they approved themselves to his own judgment: and the grounds of that judgment he was well able to state. But I may be forgiven if . . . I dwell rather on the fine qualities of his personality, the simplicity of his nature, the absence of all pettiness or pretense, and above all the courage and fidelity with which he applied to all social and national questions the Christian principles of justice and compassion.

VERNON GROUNDS

President Emeritus,
Denver Seminary

PREFACE TO THIRD EDITION

This edition is a reprint of the First and Second Editions, with the exception of a few verbal corrections and alterations, and slight adjustments and curtailments in certain of the Notes. The analysis of Contents also has been abridged. The author is indebted to the Rev. Alexander Mair, D.D., for kindly assisting him in the correction of the proofs.

Edinburgh, July, 1897

PREFACE TO FIRST EDITION

These lectures, the first on the Kerr Foundation, are published in fulfillment of the conditions of the Trust under which they were delivered. Their publication has been delayed owing to the author's appointment to the Chair of Church History in the Theological College of the United Presbyterian Church, at the Synod of May, 1891. They have now been made ready for the press under the burden of labor and anxiety connected with the preparation of a second winter's course. This may excuse the minor oversights which, in handling so large a mass of material, must inevitably occur.

The lectures are printed substantially as delivered in the spring of 1891, the chief exception being that portions of the lectures which had to be omitted in the spoken delivery, through the limits of time, are here restored in their proper connection. Material which could not conveniently be incorporated in the lectures has been wrought into Appendices and Notes. The latter are designed to furnish not simply references to authorities, but illustrations, corroborations, and what may be termed generally "assonances" of thought, drawn from a wide range of literature, which it is hoped will aid the reader who is disposed to pursue his study of the subject further, by guiding him to the best sources of knowlede. Since the lectures were delivered, important books have appeared, dealing with parts or aspects of the field here traversed, as Mr. Gore's valuable Bampton Lectures on *The Incarnation*, Principal Chapman's *Pre-organic Evolution*, Mr. Kennedy's Donnellan Lectures on *Natural Theology and Modern Thought*. Occasional references to these and some other works are likewise included in the Notes.

The author's best thanks are due to the Rev. Professor Johnston, D.D., of the United Presbyterian College, and to the Rev. Thomas Kennedy, D.D., Clerk of Synod, for their kind assistance in the revision of the proofs.

Edinburgh, February, 1893

1
THE CHRISTIAN VIEW OF THE
WORLD IN GENERAL

"Jesus Christ is the center of all, and the goal to which all tends." —Pascal

"If we carry back the antagonisms of the present to their ultimate principle, we are obliged to confess that it is of a religious kind. The way in which a man thinks of God and the world, and their relation to one another, is decisive for the whole tendency of his thought, and even in the questions of the purely natural life." —Luthardt

"The Christian truth, with the certifying of which we have to do, is essentially only one, compact in itself, vitally interconnected,—as such at the same time organic,—and it is therefore not possible one should possess and retain a portion of the same, while yet not possessing, or rejecting, the other portions. On the contrary, the member or portion of the truth, which it had been thought to appropriate or maintain alone, would by this isolating cease to be that which it was or is in itself; it would become an empty form or husk, from which the life, the Christian reality, has escaped." —F. H. R. Frank

"In no case can true reason and a right faith oppose each other." —Coleridge

1

THE CHRISTIAN VIEW OF THE WORLD IN GENERAL

see p 16

I MIGHT briefly define the object of the present Lectures by saying that they aim at the exhibition, and, as far as possible within the limits assigned me, at the rational vindication, of what I have called in the title, "The Christian View of the World." This expression, however, is itself one which calls for definition and explanation, and I proceed, in the first place, to give the explanation that is needed.

A reader of the higher class of works in German theology —especially those that deal with the philosophy of religion—cannot fail to be struck with the constant recurrence of a word for which he finds it difficult to get a precise equivalent in English. It is the word "Weltanschauung," sometimes interchanged with another compound of the same signification, "Weltansicht." Both words mean literally "view of the world," but whereas the phrase in English is limited by associations which connect it predominatingly with physical nature, in German the word is not thus limited, but has almost the force of a technical term, denoting the widest view which the mind can take of things in the effort to grasp them together as a whole from the standpoint of some particular philosophy or theology. To speak, therefore, of a "Christian view of the world" implies that Christianity also has its highest point of view, and its view of life connected therewith, and that this, when developed, constitutes an ordered whole.[1]

To some the subject which I have thus chosen may seem unduly wide and vague. I can only reply that I have deliberately chosen it for this very reason, that it enables me to deal with Christianity in its entirety or as a system, instead

---

[1] See Note A.—The Idea of the "Weltanschauung."

of dealing with particular aspects or doctrines of it. Both
methods have their advantages; but no one, I think,
whose eyes are open to the signs of the times, can fail to
perceive that if Christianity is to be effectually defended
from the attacks made upon it, it is the comprehensive method
which is rapidly becoming the more urgent. The opposition
which Christianity has to encounter is no longer confined to
special doctrines or to points of supposed conflict with the
natural sciences,—for example, the relations of Genesis and
geology,—but extends to the whole manner of conceiving of
the world, and of man's place in it, the manner of conceiving
of the entire system of things, natural and moral, of which we
form a part. It is no longer an opposition of detail, but of
principle. This circumstance necessitates an equal extension
of the line of the defence. It is the Christain view of things
in general which is attacked, and it is by an exposition and
vindication of the Christian view of things as a whole that the
attack can most successfully be met.

Everything here, of course, depends on the view we take of
Christianity itself. The view indicated in the title is that
which has its centre in the Divine and human Person of the
Lord Jesus Christ. It implies the true Divinity as well as
the true humanity of the Christian Redeemer. This is a
view of Christianity, I know, which I am not at liberty to
take for granted, but must be prepared in due course to
vindicate. I shall not shrink from the task which this
imposes on me, but would only at present point out that,
for him who does accept it, a very definite view of things
emerges. He who with his whole heart believes in Jesus
as the Son of God is thereby committed to much else besides.
He is committed to a view of God, to a view of man, to a
view of sin, to a view of Redemption, to a view of the purpose
of God in creation and history, to a view of human destiny,
found only in Christianity. This forms a " Weltanschauung,"
or " Christian view of the world," which stands in marked
contrast with theories wrought out from a purely philosophical
or scientific standpoint.

The idea of the " Weltanschauung " may be said to have
entered prominently into modern thought through the influence
of Kant, who derives what he calls the " Weltbegriff "

from the second of his Ideas of Pure Reason, to which is assigned the function of the systematic connection of all our experiences into a unity of a world-whole (Weltganz).[1] But the thing itself is as old as the dawn of reflection, and is found in a cruder or more advanced form in every religion and philosophy with any pretensions to a historical character. The simplest form in which we meet with it is in the rude, tentative efforts at a general explanation of things in the cosmogonies and theogonies of most ancient religions, the mythological character of which need not blind us to the rational motive which operates in them.[2] With the growth of philosophy, a new type of world-view is developed—that which attempts to explain the universe as a system by the help of some general principle or principles (water, air, number, etc.), accompanied by the use of terms which imply the conception of an All or Whole of things (τὰ πάντα, κόσμος— attributed to the Pythagoreans—*mundus, universum*, etc.).[3] An example from ancient thought may be given from Lucretius, who, in his famous poem, "De Rerum Natura," proposes "to discourse of the most high system of heaven and the gods, and to open up the first-beginnings of things, out of which nature gives birth to all things and increase and nourishment, and into which nature likewise resolves them back after their destruction."[4] The outlines of his system are well known. By the aid of certain first principles—atoms and the void— and of certain assumed laws of motion and development, he seeks to account for the existing universe, and constructs for himself a theory on the lines of Epicurus, which he thinks satisfies his intellectual necessities. This is his "Weltanschauung" —the progeny of which is seen in the materialistic systems of the present day. A modern example may be taken from the philosophy of Comte, which, theoretically one of pure phenomenalism, only the more strikingly illustrates the necessity which thought is under to attempt in some form a synthesis of its experience. Comte's standpoint is that

---

[1] *Kritik d. r. Vernunft*, pp. 302 ff. (Bohn's trans., pp. 256 ff.). The references to Kant throughout are to Erdmann's edition (1884).

[2] Cf. Zeller on Hesiod's Theogony, *Pre-Socratic Philosophy*, pp. 88, 89 (Eng. trans.).

[3] See Note B.—Classification of "Weltanschauungen."

[4] Bk. I. Ll. 54–57 (Munro's trans.). Cf. *Lucretius and the Atomic Theory*, by Professor John Veitch, p. 13.

of despair of absolute knowledge. Yet he recognises the tendency in the mind which prompts it to organise its knowledge, and thinks it possible to construct a scheme of existence which shall give practical unity to life—imagination eking out the deficiencies of the intellect. In the words of a recent interpreter, "Beneath and beyond all the details in our ideas of things, there is a certain *esprit d'ensemble*, a general conception of the world without and the world within, in which these details gather to a head."[1] It would not be easy to get a better description of what is meant by a "Weltanschauung" than in these words. The centre of unity in this new conception of the universe is Man. Knowledge is to be organised solely with reference to its bearings on the well-being and progress of Humanity. A religion even is provided for the satisfaction of the emotional and imaginative wants of man in the worship of the same abstraction—Humanity, which is to be viewed with affection and gratitude as a beneficent providence interposed between man and the hard pressure of his outward conditions. In a moral respect the individual is to find his all-comprehensive end in the "service of Humanity." Thus, again, we have a "Weltanschauung" in which knowledge and action are knit up together, and organised into a single view of life.

The causes which lead to the formation of "Weltanschauungen," that is, of general theories of the universe, explanatory of what it is, how it has come to be what it is, and whither it tends, lie deep in the constitution of human nature. They are twofold—speculative and practical, corresponding to the twofold aspect of human nature as thinking and active. On the theoretical side, the mind seeks unity in its representations. It is not content with fragmentary knowledge, but tends constantly to rise from facts to laws, from laws to higher laws, from these to the highest generalisations possible.[2] Ultimately it abuts on questions of origin, purpose,

---

[1] Caird's *Social Philosophy of Comte*, p. 24.

[2] Cf. Strauss—"We proceed from the isolated circles of phenomena around us, from the stable basis and the elementary forces, to vegetable and animal life, to the universal life of the earth, from this to that of our solar system, and so ever further, till at last we have grasped the entire range of existence in a single representation ; and this is the representation of the universe."— *Der alte und der neue Glaube*, p. 150.

and destiny, which, as questions set by reason to itself, it cannot, from its very nature, refuse at least to attempt to answer.[1] Even to prove that an answer to them is impossible, it is found necessary to discuss them, and it will be strange if, in the course of the discussion, the discovery is not made, that underneath the profession of nescience a positive theory of some kind after all lurks.[2] But there is likewise a practical motive urging to the consideration of these well-worn questions of the why, whence, and whither? Looking out on the universe, men cannot but desire to know their place in the system of things of which they form a part, if only that they may know how rightly to determine themselves thereto.[3] Is the constitution of things good or evil? By what ultimate principles ought man to be guided in the framing and ordering of his life? What is the true end of existence? What rational justification does the nature of things afford for the higher sentiments of duty and religion? If it be the case, as the Agnostic affirms, that light absolutely fails us on questions of origin, cause, and end, what conception of life remains? Or, assuming that no higher origin for life and mind can be postulated than matter and force, what revision is necessary of current conceptions of private morality and social duty?

It is a singular circumstance that, with all the distaste of the age for metaphysics, the tendency to the formation of world-systems, or general theories of the universe, was never more powerful than at the present day. One cause of this, no doubt, is the feeling which modern science itself has done so much to engender, of the unity which pervades all orders of existence. The naïve Polytheism of pagan times, when every hill and fountain was supposed to have its special divinity, is no longer possible with modern notions of the

[1] "As science becomes more conscious of its problems and its goal, it struggles the more strenuously towards the region where physics melt into metaphysics."—Fairbairn, *Studies in the Philosophy of Religion and History*, p. 88.

[2] See Note C.—Unconscious Metaphysic.

[3] "The question of questions for mankind, the problem which underlies all others, and is more deeply interesting than any other, is the ascertainment of the place which man occupies in nature, and of his relation to the universe of things. Whence our race has come, what are the limits of our power over nature, and of nature's power over us? to what goal we are tending? are the problems which present themselves anew, and with undiminished interest, to every man born into the world."—Huxley, *Man's Place in Nature*, p. 57.

coherence of the universe. Everywhere the minds of men are opening to the conception that, whatever else the universe is, it is one—one set of laws holds the whole together —one order reigns through all. Everywhere, accordingly, we see a straining after a universal point of view—a grouping and grasping of things together in their unity.[1] The philosophy of Mr. Spencer, for example, is as truly an attempt at the unification of all knowledge as the philosophy of a Hegel; the evolutionist is as confident of being able to embrace all that is, or ever has been, or will be—all existing phenomena of nature, history, or mind—in the range of a few ultimate formulas, as if he had already seen how the task was to be accomplished; the Comtist urges to an imaginative in default of a real and objective synthesis, and rears on this basis at once a social theory and religion. The mind grows bolder with the advance of knowledge, and hopes, if not to reach a final solution of the ultimate mystery of existence, at least to bring thoroughly under its dominion the sphere of the knowable.[2]

What now, it may be asked, has Christianity to do with theories, and questions, and speculations of this sort? As a doctrine of salvation, perhaps, not much, but in its logical presuppositions and consequences a great deal indeed. Christianity, it is granted, is not a scientific system, though, if its views of the world be true, it must be reconcilable with all that is certain and established in the results of science. It is not a philosophy, though, if it be valid, its fundamental assumptions will be found to be in harmony with the conclusions at which sound reason, attacking its own problems, independently arrives. It is a religion, historical in its origin, and claiming to rest on Divine Revelation. But though

---

[1] Cf. Principal Fairbairn—"The search after causes, both efficient and ultimate, is being conducted with the most daring and unwearied enthusiasm. Science has become as speculative, as prolific of physico-metaphysical theories —as the most bewitched metaphysician could desire. . . . The consequent crop of cosmic speculation has been of the most varied and extensive kind, ranging from theories of the origin of species to theories as to the origin of the universe."—*Studies*, pp. 65, 66.

[2] "No one can enter on a consideration of the subject of Evolution with the expectation of attaining to clear ideas and relatively correct conclusions, unless he first of all thinks of it as cosmic, *i.e.* comprehensive, in its operation, of the entire universe of matter and mind, and throughout all time."—Chapman, *Pre-organic Evolution*, etc., p. 3.

Christianity is neither a scientific system, nor a philosophy, it has yet a world-view of its own, to which it stands committed, alike by its fundamental postulate of a personal, holy, self-revealing God, and by its content as a religion of Redemption—which, therefore, necessarily brings it into comparison with the world-views already referred to.[1] It has, as every religion should and must have, its own peculiar interpretation to give of the facts of existence ; its own way of looking at, and accounting for, the existing natural and moral order ; its own idea of a world-aim, and of that "one far-off Divine event," to which, through slow and painful travail, "the whole creation moves."[2] As thus binding together the natural and moral worlds in their highest unity, through reference to their ultimate principle, God, it involves a "Weltanschauung."

It need not further be denied that between this view of the world involved in Christianity, and what is sometimes termed "the modern view of the world," there exists a deep and radical antagonism.[3] This so-called "modern view of the world," indeed,—and it is important to observe it,—is, strictly speaking, not one view, but many views,—a group of views,—most of them as exclusive of one another as they together are of Christianity.[4] The phrase, nevertheless, does point to a homogeneity of these various systems—to a bond of unity which runs through them all, and holds them together in spite of their many differences. This common feature is their thoroughgoing opposition to the supernatural,—at least of the specifically miraculous,—their refusal to recognise anything in nature, life, or history, outside the lines of natural development. Between such a view of the world and Christianity, it is perfectly correct to say that there can be no kindredship. Those who think otherwise—speculative Theists, *e.g.*, like Pfleiderer—can only make good their contention by fundamentally altering the idea of Christianity itself—robbing it also of its miraculous essence and accompaniments. Whether this is tenable we shall consider after-

---

[1] Cf. Dorner, *Syst. of Doct.* i. p. 155 (Eng. trans.).
[2] Tennyson, *In Memoriam.*
[3] See Note D.—Antagonism of Christian and "Modern" Views of the World.
[4] See Note E.—Internal Conflicts of the "Modern" View.

wards. Meanwhile it is to be noted that this at least is not
the Christianity of the New Testament. It may be an
improved and purified form of Christianity, but it is not the
Christianity of Christ and His apostles. Even if, with the
newer criticism, we distinguish between the theology of Christ
and that of His apostles—between the Synoptic Gospels and
the Gospel of John—between the earlier form of the synoptic
tradition and supposed later embellishments—it is still not
to be disputed that, in the simplest view we can take of it,
Jesus held and acted on a view of things totally different
from the rationalistic conception; while for him who accepts
the view of Christianity indicated in the title of these Lectures, it has already been pointed out that a view of things
emerges with which the denial of the supernatural is wholly
incompatible.

The position here taken, that the question at issue between
the opponents and defenders of the Christian view of the world
is at bottom the question of the supernatural, needs to be
guarded against a not uncommon misconception. A good deal of
controversy has recently taken place in regard to certain statements of Professor Max Müller, as to whether "miracles" are
essential to Christianity.[1] But the issue we have to face is totally
misconceived when it is turned into a question of belief in this
or that particular miracle—or of miracles in general—regarded
as mere external appendages to Christianity. The question is
not about isolated "miracles," but about the whole conception
of Christianity—what it is, and whether the supernatural does
not enter into the very essence of it? It is the general question of a supernatural or non-supernatural conception of the
universe. Is there a supernatural Being—God? Is there a
supernatural government of the world? Is there a supernatural relation of God and man, so that God and man
may have communion with one another? Is there a supernatural Revelation? Has that Revelation culminated in a
supernatural Person—Christ? Is there a supernatural work
in the souls of men? Is there a supernatural Redemption? Is
there a supernatural hereafter? It is these larger questions
that have to be settled first, and then the question of particular

---

[1] Cf. Max Müller, Preface to his Lectures on *Anthropological Religion* (Gifford Lectures), 1892.

miracles will fall into its proper place.   Neander has given
admirable expression to the conception of Christianity which is
really at stake, in the following words in the commencement of
his *History of the Church*—"Now we look upon Christianity
not as a power that has sprung up out of the hidden depths of
man's nature, but as one that descended from above, when
heaven opened itself anew to man's long alienated race; a power
which, as both in its origin and its essence it is exalted above
all that human nature can create out of its own resources, was
designed to impart to that nature a new life, and to change it
in its inmost principles.   The prime source of this power is He
whose power exhibits to us the manifestation of it—Jesus of
Nazareth—the Redeemer of mankind when estranged from God
by sin.   In the devotion of faith in Him, and the appropria-
tion of the truth which He revealed, consists the essence of
Christianity and of that fellowship of the Divine life resulting
from it, which we designate by the name of the Church."[1]   It
is this conception of Christianity we have to come to an understanding with, before the question of particular miracles can
profitably be discussed.

While, from the nature of the case, this side of opposition
of the Christian view of the world to certain "modern" conceptions must necessarily receive prominence, I ought, on the
other hand, to remark that it is far from my intention to represent the relation of Christianity to these opposing systems as
one of mere negation.   This would be to overlook the fact,
which cannot be too carefully borne in mind, that no theory
which has obtained wide currency, and held powerful sway
over the minds of men, is ever wholly false; that, on the contrary, it derives what strength it has from some side or aspect
of truth which it embodies, and for which it is in Providence a
witness against the suppression or denial of it in some counter-
theory, or in the general doctrine of the age.   No duty is more
imperative on the Christian teacher than that of showing that
instead of Christianity being simply one theory among the rest,
it is really the higher truth which is the synthesis and completion of all the others,—that view which, rejecting the error,
takes up the vitalising elements in all other systems and religions, and unites them into a living organism, with Christ as

[1] *History of the Church*, i. p. 2 (Eng. trans.).

head.[1] We are reminded of Milton's famous figure in the
"Areopagitica," of the dismemberment of truth,—how truth
was torn limb from limb, and her members were scattered to
the four winds; and how the lovers of truth, imitating the
careful search of Isis for the body of Osiris, have been engaged
ever since in gathering together the severed parts, in order to
unite them again into a perfect whole.[2] If apologetic is to be
spoken of, this surely is the truest and best form of Christian
apology—to show that in Christianity, as nowhere else, the
severed portions of truth found in all other systems are organically united, while it completes the body of truth by discoveries
peculiar to itself. The Christian doctrine of God, for example,
may fairly claim to be the synthesis of all the separate elements
of truth found in Agnosticism, Pantheism, and Deism, which
by their very antagonisms reveal themselves as one-sidednesses,
requiring to be brought into some higher harmony. If Agnosticism affirms that there is that in God—in His infinite and
absolute existence — which transcends finite comprehension,
Christian theology does the same. If Pantheism affirms the
absolute immanence of God in the world, and Deism His
absolute transcendence over it, Christianity unites the two sides
of the truth in a higher concept, maintaining at the same time
the Divine immanence and the Divine transcendence.[3] Even
Polytheism in its nobler forms is in its own dark way a witness
for a truth which a hard, abstract Monotheism, such as we have
in the later (not the Biblical) Judaism, and in Mohammedanism,
ignores—the truth, namely, that God is plurality as well as
unity—that in Him there is a manifoldness of life, a fulness
and diversity of powers and manifestations, such as is expressed

---

[1] Cf. Baring-Gould — "In every religion of the world is to be found, dis-
torted or exaggerated, some great truth, otherwise it would never have obtained
foothold; every religious revolution has been the struggle of thought to gain
another step in the ladder that reaches to heaven. That which we ask of
Revelation is that it shall take up all these varieties into itself, not that it
shall supplant them; and show how that at which each of them aimed, however dimly and indistinctly, has its interpretation and realisation in the
objective truth brought to light by Revelation. Hence we shall be able to
recognise that religion to be the true one, which is the complement and corrective of all the wanderings of the religious instinct in its efforts to provide
objects for its own satisfaction."—*Origin and Development of Religious Belief*,
ii. Pref., p. 10.

[2] Cf. *Areopagitica*, "English Reprints," p. 56. Clement of Alexandria has
a similar figure, *Strom.* i. 13.

[3] Cf. Eph. iv. 6. Flint, *Anti-Theistic Theories*, p. 339.

by the word Elohim. This element of truth in Polytheism Christianity also takes up, and sets in its proper relation to the unity of God in its doctrine of Tri-unity—the concept of God which is distinctively the Christian one, and which furnishes the surest safeguard of a living Theism against the extremes of both Pantheism and Deism.[1] Optimism and Pessimism are another pair of contrasts—each in abstraction an error, yet each a witness for a truth which the other overlooks, and Christianity is the reconciliation of both. To take a last example, Positivism is a very direct negation of Christianity; yet in its strange "worship of Humanity" is there not that which stretches across the gulf and touches hands with a religion which meets the cravings of the heart for the *human* in God by the doctrine of the Incarnation? It is the province of a true and wise Christian theology to take account of all this, and to seek, with ever-increasing enlargement of vision, the comprehensive view in which all factors of the truth are combined. The practical inference I would draw—the very opposite of that drawn by others from the same premises—is, that it is the unwisest way possible of dealing with Christianity to pare it down, or seek to sublimate it away, as if it had no positive content of its own; or, by lavish compromise and concession, to part with that which belongs to its essence. It is not in a blunted and toned-down Christianity, but in the exhibition of the Christian view in the greatest fulness and completeness possible, that the ultimate synthesis of the conflicting elements in the clash of systems around us is to be found.

This is perhaps the place to point out that, whatever the character of the world-view involved in Christianity, it is not one in all respects absolutely new. It rests upon, and carries forward to its completion, the richly concrete view of the world already found in the Old Testament. As an able expounder of Old Testament theology, Hermann Schultz, has justly said— "There is absolutely no New Testament view which does not approve itself as a sound and definitive formation from an Old Testament germ—no truly Old Testament view which did not

---

[1] Cf. Dorner, *Syst. of Doct.* i. pp. 366, 367 (Eng. trans.). Even Ed. v. Hartmann recognises the deep "metaphysical sense" of the doctrine of the Trinity, and the service done by it in reconciling the Divine immanence and transcendence.—*Selbstzersetzung des Christenthums*, p. 108.

inwardly press forward to its New Testament fulfilment." [1]
This is a phenomenon which, I think, has not always received
the attention it deserves.   What are the <u>main characteristics</u>
of this Old Testament conception?   At its root is the idea of
<u>a holy, spiritual, self-revealing</u> God, the free Creator of the
world, and its continual Preserver.   As correlative to this, and
springing out of it, is the idea of <u>man as a being made in God's</u>
image, and capable of moral relations and spiritual fellowship
with his Maker; but who, through sin, has turned aside from
the end of his creation, and stands in need of Redemption.
In the heart of the history, we have the idea of a Divine
purpose, working itself out through the calling of a special
nation, for the ultimate benefit and blessing of mankind.   God's
providential rule extends over all creatures and events, and
embraces all peoples of the earth, near and remote.   In view
of the sin and corruption that have overspread the world, His
government is one of combined mercy and judgment; and His
dealings with Israel in particular are preparative to the introduction of a better economy, in which the grace already partially
exhibited will be fully revealed.   The end is the establishment
of a kingdom of God under the rule of the Messiah, in which
all national limitations will be removed, the Spirit be poured
forth, and Jehovah will become the God of the whole earth.
God will make a new covenant with His people, and will write
His laws by His Spirit in their hearts.   Under this happy reign
the final triumph of righteousness over sin will be accomplished,
and death and all other evils will be abolished.   Here is a very
remarkable "Weltanschauung," the presence of which at all
in the pages of the Hebrew Scriptures is a fact of no ordinary
significance.   In the comparative history of religions, it stands
quite unique. [2]   Speculations on the world and its origin are seen
growing up in the schools of philosophy ; but on the ground of
religion there is nothing to compare with this.   The lower
religions, Fetishism and the like, have of course nothing of the
nature of a developed world-view.   The rudiments of such
a view in the older nature-religions are crude, confused, polytheistic — mixed up abundantly with mythological elements.
Brahmanism and Buddhism rest on a metaphysical foundation ;

---

[1] *Alttestamentliche Theologie,* p. 48.
[2] See Note F.—Uniqueness of the Old Testament View.

they are as truly philosophical systems as the atomistic or pantheistic theories of the Greek schools, or the systems of Schopenhauer and Hartmann in our own day. And the philosophy they inculcate is a philosophy of despair; they contain no spring of hope or progress. Zoroastrianism, with its profound realisation of the conflict of good and evil in the universe, perhaps comes nearest to the religion of the Old Testament, yet is severed from it by an immense gulf. I refer only to its pervading dualism, its reverence for physical elements, its confusion of natural and moral evil—above all, to its total lack of the idea of historical Revelation.[1] The Biblical conception is separated from every other by its monotheistic basis, its unique clearness, its organic unity, its moral character, and its teleological aim.[2] It does not matter for the purposes of this argument what dates we assign to the books of the Old Testament in which these views are found—whether we attribute them, with the critics, to the age of the prophets, or to any other. These views are at least there many centuries before the Christian age began, and they are found nowhere else than on the soil of Israel. This is the singular fact the critic has to face, and we cannot profess to wonder that, impartially studying it, voices should be heard from the midst of the advanced school itself unhesitatingly declaring, Date your books when you will, this religion is not explicable save on the hypothesis of Revelation![3]

The general drift and object of these Lectures should now, I think, be apparent. From the conditions of this Lectureship I am precluded from directly entering the apologetic field. I feel, however, that it would be useless to discuss any important theological subject at the present day without reference to the thought and speculation of the time. No other mode of thought would enable me to do justice to the Christian position, and none, I think, would be so interesting to those for whom the Lectures are primarily intended. This, however, will be sub-

---

[1] Cf. the sketch of Zoroastrianism in Introduction to the Zendavesta in *Sacred Books of the East.* See also Ebrard's *Christian Apologetics*, ii. pp. 186–232. Some interesting remarks will be found in Lotze's *Microcosmus*, ii. p. 459.

[2] Dr. Dorner says—"Israel has the idea of teleology as a kind of soul."—*Syst. of Doct.* i. p. 274 (Eng. trans.).

[3] See Note G.—Origin of the Old Testament View—Relation to Critical Theories.

Purpose of "book" [handwritten marginal note]

sidiary to the main design of showing that there is a definite
Christian view of things, which has a character, coherence, and
unity of its own, and stands in sharp contrast with counter
theories and speculations, and that this world-view has the
stamp of reason and reality upon itself, and can amply justify
itself at the bar both of history and of experience. I shall
endeavour to show that the Christian view of things forms a
logical whole which cannot be infringed on, or accepted or
rejected piecemeal, but stands or falls in its integrity, and can
only suffer from attempts at amalgamation or compromise with
theories which rest on totally distinct bases. I hope thus to
make clear at least the true nature of the issues involved in a
comparison of the Christian and "modern" views, and I shall
be glad if I can in any way contribute to the elucidation of the
former.

at the threshold/beginning — a legal term [handwritten marginal note]

Two objections may be taken *in limine* to the course I
propose to follow, and it is proper at this stage that I should
give them some attention.

I. The first objection is taken from the standpoint of the
theology of feeling, and amounts to a denial of our right to
speak of a Christian "Weltanschauung" at all ; indeed, to
assume that Christianity has a definite doctrinal content of any
kind.[1] This class of objectors would rule the cognitive element
out of religion altogether. Religion, it is frequently alleged,
has nothing to do with notions of the intellect, but only with
states and dispositions of the heart. Theories and doctrines
are no essential part of it, but, on the contrary, a bane and
injury and hindrance to its free development and progress.
Those who speak thus sometimes do so in the interests of a
theory which would seek the essence of religion in certain
instincts, or sentiments, or emotions, which are supposed to be
universal and indestructible in the human race, and to constitute
the imperishable and undecaying substance of all religions—the
emotions, *e.g.*, of awe or wonder, or reverence or dependence,
awakened by the impression of the immensity or mystery of
the universe ; while the ideas and beliefs connected with these
emotions are regarded as but the accidents of a particular stage
of culture, and as possessing no independent value. They are

[1] See Note H.--Nature and Definition of Religion.

at best the variegated moulds into which this emotional life of the spirit has for the time being poured itself—the envelopes and vehicles through which it seeks for itself preservation and expression. All religions, from this impartial standpoint, *Feeling* Christianity included, are equally Divine and equally human. But even those who recognise a higher origin for the Christian religion sometimes speak of it as if in its original form it was devoid of all definite doctrinal content; or at least as if the doctrinal ideas found in connection with it were only external wrappage and covering, and could be stripped off — altered, manipulated, modified, or dispensed with at the pleasure of the critic—without detriment to the moral and spiritual kernel beneath.[1] Christianity is not given up, but there is the attempt to refine and sublimate it till it is reduced to a simple state of sentiment and feeling; to purge it of the theoretic element till nothing is left but the vaguest residuum of doctrinal opinion. Agreeing with this party in their aversion to doctrine, yet occupying a distinct standpoint, are the ultra-spirituals, whose naturally mystical bent of mind, and fondness for the hazy and indefinite in theological as in other thinking, predispose them to dwell in the region of cloudy and undefined conceptions.

It scarcely falls within my province to inquire how far this theory holds good in its general application to religion, though even on this broad field it might easily be shown that it involves a number of untenable assumptions, and really contradicts the idea of religion. For what is meant by the assertion that religion consists only in sentiment or feeling, and has nothing to do with doctrinal conceptions? Not, surely, that religion can subsist wholly without *ideas*, or cognitive apprehension, of some kind. Religion, in the lowest as well as in the highest of its forms, is an expression of the relation of the soul to something beyond itself; it involves, therefore, not one term, but two; it points to the existence of an object, and implies belief in the reality of that object. The element of idea, therefore,—or, as the Germans would say, "Vorstellung," — is inseparable from it. No religion has ever been found which did not involve some rudiments of an objective view. We may learn here even from the pessimist Hartmann, who, in an acute analysis

---

[1] See Note I.—Undogmatic Religion.

of the elements of religion, says, " How true soever it may be that religious feeling forms the innermost kernel of religious life, nevertheless that only is a true religious feeling which is excited through religious representations having a character of objective (if only relative) truth. Religion cannot exist without a religious 'Weltanschauung,' and this not without the conviction of its transcendental truth." [1]

Nor, again, can it be contended that, while a cognitive element of some kind must be conceded, religion is indifferent to the *character* of its ideas—that these have no influence upon the state of sentiment or feeling. The religion of a Thug, *e.g.*, is a very different thing from the religion of a Christian ; and will any one say that the ideas with which the two religions are associated—the ideas they respectively entertain of their deities — have nothing to do with this difference ? In what *do* religions differ as higher and lower, if not in the greater or less purity and elevation of the ideas they entertain of the Godhead, and the greater or less purity of the sentiment to which these ideas give birth ?

Nor, finally, can it be held that it is a matter of unimportance whether these ideas which are connected with a religion are regarded *as true*—*i.e.* whether they are believed to have any objective counterpart. For religion can as little subsist without belief in the reality of its object, as it can dispense with the idea of an object altogether. This is the weakness of subjective religious theories like Feuerbach's, in which religion is regarded as the projection of man's own egoistic consciousness into the infinite ; or of those poetic and æsthetic theories of religion which regard the ends of religion as served if only it furnishes man with elevating and inspiring ideals, without regard to the question of how far these ideals relate to an actual object. Ideas on this hypothesis are necessary to religion, and may be ranked as higher and lower, but have only a fictitious or poetic value. They are products of historical evolution,—guesses, speculations, dreams, imaginings, of the human mind in regard to that which from the nature of the case is beyond the reach of direct knowledge, probably is unknowable. They are therefore not material out of which anything can be built of a scientific character ; not anything

---

[1] *Religionsphilosophie*, ii. p. 32.

that can be brought to an objective test; not anything verifiable. Their sole value, as said earlier, is to serve as the vehicles and support of religious feeling.[1] But it is obvious that, on this view, the utility of religious ideas can only last so long as the illusion in connection with them is not dispelled. For religion is more than a mere æsthetic gratification. It implies belief in the existence of a real object other than self, and includes a desire to get into some relation with this object. The mind in religion is in too earnest a mood to be put off with mere fancies. The moment it dawns on the thoughts of the worshipper that the object he worships has no reality, but is only an illusion or fancy of his own,—the moment he is convinced that in his holiest exercises he is but toying with the creations of his own spirit,—that moment the religious relation is at an end. Neither philosopher nor common man will long continue bowing down to an object in whose actual existence he has ceased to believe.[2] Nor is the conclusion which seems to follow from this—that the illusion of religion is one which the progress of knowledge is destined to destroy—evaded by the concession that there is some dim Unknowable, the consciousness of which lies at the basis of the religious sentiment, and which the mind can still please itself by clothing with the attributes of God. For what is there in this indefinite relation to an Unknowable, of which we can only affirm that it is not what we think it to be, to serve the purpose of a religion? And what avails it to personalise this conception of the Absolute, when we know, as before, that this clothing with personal attributes is only subjective illusion?

No objection, therefore, can fairly be taken from the side of the general "Science of Religions," to the supposition that a religion may exist which can give us a better knowledge of God than is to be found in the vague and uncertain conjectures

---

[1] See Note J.—Æsthetic Theories of Religion.

[2] Cf. Dorner—" Faith does not wish to be a mere relation to itself, or to its representations and thoughts. That would simply be a monologue; faith desires a dialogue."—*Syst. of Doct.* i. p. 123 (Eng. trans.).

Martineau—" No; if religious communion is reduced to a monologue, its essence is extinct, and its soul is gone. It is a living relation, or it is nothing —a response to the Supreme Reality."—*Ideal Substitutes for God,* p. 19.

Strauss—"None but a book student could ever imagine that a creation of the brain, woven of poetry and philosophy, can take the place of real religion." —In *Kaiser Julian,* p. 12 (quoted by Martineau).

and fancies of minds left to their own groping after the
Divine.   If such a religion exists, furnishing clear and satisfying knowledge of God, His character, will, and ways, His
relations to men, and the purposes of His grace, there is plainly
great room and need in the world for it; and the consideration
of its claims cannot be barred by the assumption that the only
valuable elements in any religion must be those which it has in
common with all religions—which is the very point in dispute.
The only question that can be properly raised is, Whether
Christianity is a religion of this nature ?   And this can only be
ascertained by actual inspection.

   Turning next to those within the Christian pale who would
rule the doctrinal element out of their religion, I confess I
find it difficult to understand on what grounds they can
justify their procedure.   If there is a religion in the world
which exalts the office of teaching, it is safe to say that it
is the religion of Jesus Christ.   It has been frequently
remarked that in pagan religions the doctrinal element is at
a minimum—the chief thing there is the performance of a
ritual.[1]   But this is precisely where Christianity distinguishes
itself from other religions—it does contain doctrine.   It comes
to men with definite, positive teaching; it claims to be the
truth ; it bases religion on knowledge, though a knowledge
which is only attainable under moral conditions.   I do not see
how any one can deal fairly with the facts as they lie before
us in the Gospels and Epistles, without coming to the conclusion that the New Testament is full of doctrine.   The
recently founded science of "New Testament Theology,"
which has already attained to a position of such commanding
importance among the theological disciplines, is an unexception-
able witness to the same fact.   And this is as it should be.
A religion based on mere feeling is the vaguest, most unreliable, most unstable of all things.   A strong, stable, religious
life can be built up on no other ground than that of intelligent
conviction.   Christianity, therefore, addresses itself to the

---

[1] Cf. Professor W. R. Smith's *Religion of the Semites*—"The antique religions
had for the most part no creed ; they consisted entirely of institutions and
practices. . . . In all the antique religions mythology takes the place of
dogma, that is, the sacred lore of priests and people, so far as it does not
consist of mere rules for the performance of religious acts, assumes the form
of stories about the gods ; and these stories afford the only explanation that
is offered of the precepts of religion and the prescribed rules of ritual."—P. 18

intelligence as well as to the heart. It sounds plausible indeed to say, Let us avoid all doctrinal subtleties; let as keep to a few plain, easy, simple propositions, in regard to which there will be general agreement. But, unfortunately, men *will* think on those deep problems which lie at the root of religious belief—on the nature of God, His character, His relations to the world and men, sin, the means of deliverance from it, the end to which things are moving,—and if Christianity does not give them an answer, suited to their deeper and more reflective moods, they will simply put it aside as inadequate for their needs. Everything depends here on what the Revelation of the Bible is supposed to be. If it is a few general elementary truths of religion we are in search of, it may freely be conceded that these might have been given in very simple form. But if we are to have a Revelation such as the Bible professes to convey,—a Revelation high as the nature of God, deep as the nature of man, universal as the wants of the race, which is to accompany man through all the ascending stages of his development, and still be felt to be a power and inspiration to him for further progress,—it is absurd to expect that such a Revelation will not have many profound and difficult things in it, and that it will not afford food for thought in its grandest and highest reaches. "Thy judgments are a great deep." [1] A religion divorced from earnest and lofty thought has always, down the whole history of the Church, tended to become weak, jejune, and unwhole- some ; while the intellect, deprived of its rights within religion, has sought its satisfaction without, and developed into godless rationalism.

Christianity, it is sometimes said by those who represent this view, is a *life*, not a creed; it is a spiritual system, and has nothing to do with dogmatic affirmations. But this is to confuse two things essentially different—Christianity as an inward principle of conduct, a subjective religious experi- ence, on the one hand, and Christianity as an objective fact, or an historic magnitude, on the other. But can even the life be produced, or can it be sustained and nourished, without knowledge? Here I cannot forbear the remark that it is a strange idea of many who urge this objection in the interests

[1] Ps. xxxvi. 6.

of what they conceive to be a more spiritual form of Christianity, that "spirituality" in a religion is somehow synonymous with vagueness and indefiniteness; that the more perfectly they can vaporise or volatilise Christianity into a nebulous haze, in which nothing can be perceived distinctly, the nearer they bring it to the ideal of a spiritual religion.[1] This, it is safe to say, was not Paul's idea of spirituality—he by whom the distinction of "letter" and "spirit" was most strongly emphasised. The region of the spiritual was rather with him, as it is throughout Scripture, the region of the clearest insight and most accurate perception—of full and perfect knowledge (ἐπίγνωσις). His unceasing prayer for his converts was, not that their minds might remain in a state of hazy indistinctness, but that God would give them "a spirit of wisdom and revelation in the knowledge of Him, having the eyes of (their) heart enlightened," that they might grow up in this knowledge, till they should "all attain unto the unity of the faith, and of the knowledge of the Son of God, unto a full-grown man, unto the measure of the stature of the fulness of Christ."[2]

An objection to the recognition of doctrine in Christianity may be raised, however, from the side of Christian positivism, as well as from that of Christian mysticism. Christianity, it will be here said, is a *fact-revelation*—it has its centre in a living in Christ, and not a dogmatic creed. And this in a sense is true. The title of my Lectures is the acknowledgment of it. The facts of Revelation are before the doctrines built on them. The gospel is no mere proclamation of "eternal truths," but the discovery of a saving purpose of God for mankind, executed in time. But the doctrines are the interpretation of the facts. The facts do not stand blank and dumb before us, but have a voice given to them, and a meaning put into them. They are accompanied by living speech, which makes their meaning clear. When John declares that Jesus Christ is come in the flesh, and is the Son of God,[3] he is stating a fact, but he is none the less enunciating a doctrine. When Paul affirms, "Christ died for our sins according to the scriptures,"[4] he is proclaiming a fact, but he

---

[1] Cf. Bartlett's *The Letter and the Spirit* (Bampton Lectures, 1888).
[2] Eph. i. 17, 18 ; iv. 13.   [3] 1 John iv. 2, 15.   [4] 1 Cor. xv. 3.

is at the same time giving an interpretation of it. No writer
has laid more stress on the fact, and less on the doctrine, in
primitive Christianity than Professor Harnack, yet he cannot
help saying, "So far as the God and Father of Jesus Christ is
believed in as the Almighty Lord of heaven and earth, the
Christian religion includes a definite knowledge of God, of the
world, and of the world-aim."[1] This concedes in principle
all that I maintain. It affirms that the facts of Christianity,
rightly understood and interpreted, not only yield special
doctrines, but compel us to develop out of them a determinate
"Weltanschauung." This is precisely the assertion of the
present Lectures.

If I refer for a moment in this connection to Schleiermacher, who may be named as the most distinguished
representative of the theology of feeling, it is because I
think that the position of this remarkable man on the question
before us is frequently misunderstood. Schleiermacher's
earlier views are not unlike some of those we have already
been considering, and are entangled in many difficulties and
inconsistencies in consequence. I deal here only with his
later and more matured thought, as represented in his work,
Der christliche Glaube. In it also piety is still defined as
feeling. It is, he says, neither a mode of knowing, nor a
mode of action, but a mode of feeling, or of immediate self-
consciousness. It is the consciousness of ourselves as absolutely
dependent, or, what comes to the same thing, as standing in
relation with God.[2] In his earlier writings he had defined it
more generally as the immediate feeling of the infinite and
eternal, the immediate consciousness of the being of all that is
finite in the infinite, of all that is temporal in the eternal,
awakened by the contemplation of the universe.[3] But along
with this must be taken into account Schleiermacher's view
of the nature of feeling. According to him, feeling is less the

---

[1] *Grundriss der Dogmengeschichte,* i. p. 1. I have used the word "doctrine" in these discussions, and kept clear of "dogma," which is often used
with a prejudice. "Dogma" I take to be a formulation of doctrine stamped
with some ecclesiastical authority. If there are doctrines, no objection can
reasonably be taken to the formulation of them. It is beyond my purpose to
discuss the wider question of the utility and necessity of creeds for church
purposes. Cf. Lect. VI. in Dr. Rainy's *Delivery and Development of Christian
Doctrine* (Cunningham Lectures).

[2] *Der christ. Glaube,* sects. 3 and 4.

[3] Cf. Pfleiderer's *Religionsphilosophie,* i. p. 308 (Eng. trans.).

opposite of knowledge than that pure, original state of consciousness—prior to both knowledge and action—out of which
knowledge and action may subsequently be developed.[1] In
Christianity this raw material of the religious consciousness
receives, as it were, a definite shaping and content. The
peculiarity in the Christian consciousness is that everything
in it is referred back upon Jesus Christ, and the Redemption
accomplished through Him.[2] This moving back from the
religious consciousness to the Person of the sinless Redeemer
as the historical cause of it is already a transcending of the
bounds of a theology of mere feeling. Theology is no longer
merely a description of states of consciousness, when it leads us
out for an explanation of these states into the region of historic
fact. But an equally important circumstance is that, while
describing the Christian consciousness mainly in terms of
feeling, Schleiermacher does not deny that a dogmatic is
implicitly contained in this consciousness, and is capable of
development out of it. His *Der christliche Glaube* is, on the
contrary, the unfolding of such a dogmatic. His position,
therefore, is not offhand to be identified with that of the
advocates of a perfectly undogmatic Christianity. These
would rule the doctrinal element out of Christianity altogether.
But Scheiermacher, while he lays the main stress in the production of this consciousness of Redemption in the believer on
the Person of the Redeemer, and only subordinately on his
teaching, yet recognises in Christian piety a positive, given
content, and out of this he evolves a clearly defined and
scientifically arranged system of doctrines. It is to be
regretted that in the foundation of his theology—the doctrine
of God—Schleiermacher never broke with his initial assumption that God cannot be known as He really is, but only as
reflected in states of human consciousness, and therefore
failed to lift his theology as a whole out of the region of
subjectivity.

A chief reason probably why many entertain a prejudice
against the admission of a definite doctrinal content in Christianity, is that they think it militates against the idea of
" progress " in theology. How does the matter stand in this
respect? Growth and advance of some kind, of course, there

---

[1] *Der christ. Glaube*, sect. 3. 2.   [2] *Ibid.* sect. 11.

is and must be in theology. It cannot be that the other departments of knowledge unceasingly progress, and theology stands still. No one familiar with the history of theology will deny that great changes have taken place in the shape which doctrines have assumed in the course of their development, or will question that these changes have been determined largely by the ruling ideas, the habits of thought, the state of knowledge and culture, of each particular time. The dogmatic moulds which were found adequate for one age have often proved insufficient for the next, to which a larger horizon of vision has been granted; and have had to be broken up that new ones might be created, more adapted to the content of a Revelation which in some sense transcends them all. I recognise therefore to the full the need of growth and progress in theology.[1] Bit by bit, as the ages go on, we see more clearly the essential lineaments of the truth as it is in Jesus; we learn to disengage the genuine truths of Christ's gospel from human additions and corruptions; we apprehend their bearings and relations with one another, and with new truths, more distinctly; we see them in new points of view, develop and apply them in new ways. All this is true, and it is needful to remember it, lest to temporary points of view, and human theories and formulations, we attribute an authority and completeness which in no way belong to them. But it does not by any means follow from this that, therefore, everything in Christianity is fluent,—that it has no fixed starting-points, no definite basal lines, no sure and moveless foundations, no grand determinative positions which control and govern all thought within distinctly Christian limits,—still less that, in the course of its long history, theology has achieved nothing, or has reached no results which can fairly be regarded as settled. This is the exaggeration on the other side, and so far from being helpful to progress in theology, it is in reality the denial of its possibility. Progress in theology implies that there is something to develop—that some truths at all events, relating to God and to Divine things, are ascertainable, and are capable of scientific treatment. It is easy to speak

[1] Cf. Dr. Rainy's *Delivery and Development of Doctrines* (Cunningham Lectures). On the position criticised see, *e.g.*, Bartlett's *The Letter and the Spirit* (Bampton Lectures, 1888).

of the attempt to "limit infinite truth within definite formulæ"; but, on the other hand, unless some portion at least
of this infinite truth can be brought within range of the human
faculties, theology has nothing to work on. It is a pseudo-
science, and to speak of progress in it is idle.

II. The recent tendency in Continental theology, however,
is not so much to deny the existence of a definite "Weltanschauung" in the Bible, as rather to lay stress on the *distinction
between a "religious" and a "theoretic" view of the world*—
ascribing to Christianity the former, but not the latter. This
is the position of the school of Ritschl, and truth and error are
so intimately blended in it that it is necessary to give it our
careful consideration.[1] That a sound distinction underlies the
terms "religious" and "theoretic" is not to be disputed, and
it is important that its nature should be rightly understood.
But, under the plea of expelling metaphysics from theology, the
tendency is at present to revive this distinction in a form which
practically amounts to the resuscitation of the old doctrine of a
"double truth"—the one religious, the other philosophical;
and it is not held necessary that even where the two overlap
they should always be found in agreement. It is not simply
that the two kinds of knowledge have different spheres, move
in different orbits, and have to do with a different class of
objects; for this Ritschl at least denies.[2] But they set out
from different starting-points, judge by different standards, and
as a consequence frequently lead to different results. Religious
knowledge, Ritschl holds, moves only in the sphere of what he
calls worth- or value-judgments. That is to say, it judges of
things, not according to their objective nature and relations,
but according to their value *for us*—according to their fitness
to meet and satisfy religious necessities.[3] This, logically, would
lead to pure subjectivism, and in the hands of some of Ritschl's
followers actually does so.[4] This tendency is strengthened by
the theory of knowledge to which this school generally has
committed itself—a theory Kantian in its origin—which, denying to the mind any power of knowing things as they are, limits

---

[1] See Note K.—Religious and Theoretic Knowledge.
[2] *Rechtfertigung und Versöhnung*, iii. pp. 185, 193–94 (3rd edit.).
[3] See Ritschl's discussion in *Recht. und Ver.* iii. pp. 192–202 ; and in his
Theologie und Metaphysik.
[4] *E.g.* Bender, of Bonn.

it within the sphere of phenomenal representations. Ritschl
himself tries hard to ward off this reproach of subjectivity from
his system, and makes more than one attempt to find a bridge
from the practical to the theoretic, but with no real success.
He never quits the ground that it is not the objective truth of
things — which would carry us into the region of theoretic
knowledge—which forms the subject-matter of our inquiry in
theology, but solely their subjective aspect as related to our
own states of pleasure and pain, or as helping or hindering the
ends sought in religion. In his doctrines of God and Christ,
of Providence and miracle, of sin and Redemption, as we shall
afterwards see, it is constantly this subjective aspect of things,
which may be very different from our actual or scientific judgment upon them, which is brought into prominence. Religion
requires, for example, that we view the universe from a teleological and not from a causal standpoint, and therefore that we
postulate God and Providence. But these are only practical,
not theoretic notions, and the mechanical and causal view of the
universe may stand alongside of them intact. " Miracle " is the
religious name for an event which awakens in us a powerful
impression of the help of God, but is not to be held as inter-
fering with the scientific doctrine of the unbroken connection
of nature.[1] Not only are the two spheres of knowledge to be
thus kept apart in our minds, but we are not to be allowed to
trace any lines of relation between them. We are not to be
allowed, e.g., to seek any theoretic proof of the existence of
God ; or to ask how special Providence, or the efficacy of prayer,
or supernatural Revelation, or miracle, or even our own freedom,
is to be reconciled with the reign of unbroken natural causation.
All such inquiries are tabooed as a mixing up of distinct spheres
of knowledge, with the result, however, that they are not really
kept apart, but that all in the ideas of Providence, miracle,
prayer, etc., which conflicts with the theoretic view, is explained
away.

It should scarcely require much argument to convince us
that this proposal to divide the house of the mind into two
compartments, each of which is to be kept sacredly apart from
the other, is a perfectly illusory and untenable one. It might

---

[1] Cf. Ritschl's remarks on " Miracle " in his *Unterricht in der christ. Religion*,
pp. 14, 15.

have some meaning in an æsthetic theory of religion, in which
the religious conceptions are avowedly treated as pure ideals,
but it can have none where the speech is of religious "knowledge." There are, indeed, different modes of cognising the
same object, as well as different stages and degrees of real
knowledge. If by "theoretic knowledge" is meant only knowledge gained by the methods of exact science, or by philosophical reflection,[1] then, apart from religion altogether, there are
vast fields of our knowledge which will not come under this
category. The knowledge, for example, which we have of one
another in the common intercourse of life, or the knowledge
which the ordinary man gathers from his experience of the
outward world, is very different in purity of theoretical character from the kind of knowledge aimed at by the psychologist or
metaphysician, or by the student of science in his investigations
of nature. It is as far removed as possible from the disinterested character which Ritschl ascribes to the knowledge he
calls "theoretical." Yet there is no part of this knowledge in
which theoretic activities are not present. The same processes
of thought which are employed in philosophy and science are
implied in the simplest act of the understanding. In like
manner, we may grant that there is a distinction of character
and form—not to speak of origin—between religious and what
may be called theoretic knowledge ; and that thus far the distinction insisted on by Ritschl and his school has a certain
relative justification. Religion, assuredly, is not a theoretical
product. It did not originate in reasoning, but in an immediate
perception or experience of the Divine in some of the spheres
of its natural or supernatural manifestation ; for the reception
of which again a native capacity or endowment must be presupposed in the human spirit. Even Revelation implies the
possession of this capacity in man to cognise the manifestations
of the Divine when they are set before him. Originating in
this way, religious knowledge—at least in its first or immediate
form—is distinguished by certain peculiarities. For one thing,
it is distinguished from strictly theoretic knowledge by the
practical motive which obtains in it. Theoretic knowledge aims
at a representation of objects in their purely objective character

---

[1] This seems the view taken in O. Ritschl's *Ueber Werthurtheile*, but would,
if accepted, reduce the distinction to a truism.

and relations. Religion, on the other hand, seeks to set its
objects before it in those lights, and under those aspects, which
directly subserve religious ends. With this difference of aim
is connected a difference of form. Theoretic knowledge is cool,
clear, and scientifically exact. Religious knowledge is touched
with emotion, and moves largely in the region of figurative
conception, or what the Germans would call "Vorstellung." In
the first place, religion, as having to do with the personal relation of the soul to God, moves in a sphere in which the affections and emotions are necessarily allowed large play. Its
modes of apprehension are therefore warm, lively, impassioned,
intuitive. It groups its material under the influence of the
dominant feeling; lays hold of those sides and relations of the
object which affect itself, and lets the others drop out of view;
leaps over intermediate links of causation, and seeks to grasp
the object at once in its essential reality and inner significance
—in its relation to its ultimate cause and final end. A second
cause which leads to the same result is that the objects with
which religion has to deal are largely transcendental—that is,
they lie beyond the range and conditions of our present experience. A certain amount of figurative representation necessarily
enters into the purest conceptions we are able to form of such
objects.

To the extent now indicated we may agree with Ritschl
that religion moves—if he chooses to phrase it so—in the
sphere of value-judgments, and not in that of scientific apprehension. But this is not to be interpreted as if religion did
not affirm the objective truth of the ideas it entertains—as if
its judgments of value were not at the same time judgments
of truth. Still less is it to be conceded that there is any necessary divorce between the mind in its practical and the mind in
its theoretical activities, so that propositions may be affirmed in
the one sphere which have no relation to, can receive no corroboration from, may even be contradicted by, propositions
affirmed in the other. Thus to tear asunder faith and reason
is to render no service to religion, but is to pave the way for
theoretical scepticism. It is in truth the same reason which
works in both spheres; the results, therefore, must be such as
admit of comparison. If Ritschl would raise a bar against any
such comparison of the results of religious thinking with the

conclusions reached by philosophy and science—leaving each
to work in its own domain—a more just view of the subject
will recognise that this is impossible. We cannot have two
spheres of truth lying side by side in the same mind without
some effort to arrive at an adjustment between them. Still
less is it possible for the mind to find itself in conflict with
itself,—on the one side, for instance, affirming the personality
of God, on the other denying it; on the one side affirming
freedom, Revelation, miracle, on the other unbroken natural
causation,—and not do what it can to annul the discrepancy.
Nor will reason in practice be content to remain in this state of
division with itself. It will insist on its knowledge being
brought to some sort of unity, or, if this cannot be done,
in regarding one or other of the conflicting propositions as
illusive.

Finally, it is not sufficiently recognised by Ritschl and his
school that religion itself, while in the first instance practical,
carries in it also the impulse to raise its knowledge to theoretic
form. Faith cannot but seek to advance to knowledge—that
is, to the reflective and scientific comprehension of its own contents. Just because its propositions are held to be not only
"judgments of value," but to contain objective truth, they must
be capable of being submitted to theoretic treatment. Ritschl
himself recognises the necessity of constructing a theology
which shall be adequate to the contents of the Christian Revelation. Only he would have it move solely within the region of
faith-propositions, or, as he calls them, "judgments of value."
Its task is ended when it has faithfully collected, purely expressed, and internally co-ordinated these religious affirmations.[1]
It is not observed how much theoretic and critical activity is
already implied in this very process of collating, sifting, and
co-ordinating; or how largely, in Ritschl's own case, the results
are dependent on the theoretic presuppositions with which
he sets out in his (metaphysical) doctrine of knowledge, and
his general theory of religion. But, waiving this, it is surely
vain to ask theology to go so far, and then say it is to go no
further. Christian science has many tasks beyond those which
the Ritschlian limitation would prescribe for it. How, for
example, can it refuse the task of investigating its own grounds

---

[1] Cf. Ritschl, *Recht. und Ver.* iii. pp. 14–16.

of certainty? How can it help raising the question of how far these religious conceptions, now brought to expression and co-ordinated, answer to objective truth? How can it avoid asking if this content of the Christian Revelation receives no verification from the laws of man's spiritual life, or in what this verification consists? Can it help going back on its own pre-suppositions, and asking what these are, and what kind of view of God and man they imply? How can it help connecting this truth given in Revelation with truth in other departments? And this investigation is not a mere matter of choice in theology; it is forced on it as a necessity. For in the very process of collation and criticism questions arise which can only be solved by going further down. Antinomies arise within theology itself; the different sides of Biblical truth have to be har monised in a wider conception; unity of view has to be sought in a field where only parts are given, and much is left to be inferred. All this involves a large amount of theoretic treatment in theology, and may—I should rather say must—result in showing that the truths of Revelation have also a theoretic side, and are capable of theoretic verification and corroboration.

I conclude, therefore, that it is legitimate to speak of a Christian "Weltanschauung," and that we are not debarred from investigating its relations to theoretic knowledge.

APPENDIX TO CHAPTER 1
SKETCH OF THE CHRISTIAN VIEW

I T may conduce to clearness if, having indicated the general scope and purport of these Lectures, I now give in this Appendix a brief statement, in propositional form, of what I consider the Christian view of the world to be, and sketch on the basis of this the course to be pursued in the succeeding Lectures.

I. First, then, the Christian view affirms the existence of a Personal, Ethical, Self-Revealing God. It is thus at the outset a system of Theism, and as such is opposed to all systems of Atheism, Agnosticism, Pantheism, or mere Deism.

II. The Christian view affirms the creation of the world by God, His immanent presence in it, His transcendence over it, and His holy and wise government of it for moral ends.

III. The Christian view affirms the spiritual nature and dignity of man—his creation in the Divine image, and destination to bear the likeness of God in a perfected relation of sonship.

IV. The Christian view affirms the fact of the sin and disorder of the world, not as something belonging to the Divine idea of it, and inhering in it by necessity, but as something which has entered it by the voluntary turning aside of man from his allegiance to his Creator, and from the path of his normal development. The Christian view of the world, in other words, involves a Fall as the presupposition of its doctrine of Redemption; whereas the "modern" view of the world affirms that the so-called Fall was in reality a rise, and denies by consequence the need of Redemption in the scriptural sense.

V. The Christian view affirms the historical Self-Revelation of God to the patriarchs and in the line of Israel, and, as brought to light by this, a gracious purpose of God for the salvation of the world, centring in Jesus Christ, His Son, and the new Head of humanity.

VI. The Christian view affirms that Jesus Christ was not mere man, but the eternal Son of God—a truly Divine Person —who in the fulness of time took upon Him our humanity, and who, on the ground that in Him as man there dwells the fulness of the Godhead bodily, is to be honoured, worshipped, and trusted, even as God is. This is the transcendent "mystery of godliness"[1]—the central and amazing assertion of the Christian view—by reference to which our relation is determined to everything else which it contains.

Pausing for a moment on this truth of the Incarnation, we have to notice its central place in the Christian system, and how through its light every other doctrine is illuminated and transformed.

1. The Incarnation sheds new light on the nature of God, and, in conjunction with the work of the Spirit, reveals Him as triune—Father, Son, and Spirit—one God.

2. The Incarnation sheds new light on the doctrine of creation—all things being now seen to be created by Christ as well as for Him.

3. The Incarnation sheds new light on the nature of man, alike as respects its capacity for union with the Divine, its possibilities of perfection, and the high destinies awaiting it in the future.

4. The Incarnation sheds new light on the purpose of God in the creation and Redemption of men—that end being, in the words of Paul, "in the dispensation of the fulness of times to gather together in one all things in Christ, both which are in heaven, and which are on earth, even in Him."[2]

5. The Incarnation sheds new light on the permission of sin by showing the possibility of Redemption from it, and how,

---

[1] 1 Tim. iii. 16.   [2] Eph. i. 10.

through the Revelation of the Divine purposes of mercy, a far grander discovery is made of the Divine character, and far higher prospects are opened up for humanity.

VII. The Christian view affirms the Redemption of the world through a great act of Atonement—this Atonement to be appropriated by faith, and availing for all who do not wilfully withstand and reject its grace.

VIII. The Christian view affirms that the historical aim of Christ's work was the founding of a Kingdom of God on earth, which includes not only the spiritual salvation of individuals, but a new order of society, the result of the action of the spiritual forces set in motion through Christ.

IX. Finally, the Christian view affirms that history has a goal, and that the present order of things will be terminated by the appearance of the Son of Man for judgment, the resurrection of the dead, and the final separation of righteous and wicked,—final, so far as the Scriptures afford any light, or entitle us to hold out any hope.

Beyond this are the eternal ages, on whose depths only stray lights fall, as in that remarkable passage—"Then cometh the end, when He shall have delivered up the kingdom to God, even the Father: . . . then shall the Son also Himself be subject unto Him that put all things under Him, that God may be all in all"[1]—and on the mysterious blessedness or sorrow of which, as the case may be, it is needless to speculate.

I have for clearness' sake exhibited this outline of the Christian view in a series of propositions, but I need hardly say that it is not my intention to attempt to exhaust this outline, or anything like it, in this brief course of Lectures. In the actual treatment of my subject I shall be guided very much by the way in which the main positions of the Christian view are related to current theories and negations.

1. It is plain that the Christian view of the world is Theistic, and as such is opposed, as already said, to all the views

[1] 1 Cor. xv. 24–28.

which deny a living personal God, and also to 'Deism, which denies Revelation.

2. The Christian views of nature and man come into conflict with many current theories. They involve, for example, the ideas of creation, and of the spirituality, freedom, and immortal destiny of man — all of which the thoroughgoing "modern" view of the world opposes.

3. The Christian view of sin is irreconcilable with modern theories, which represent sin as a necessity of development, and nullify its true conception by starting man off at a stage but little removed from that of the brutes. At least I take this to be the case, and shall endeavour to give reasons for my opinion.

The above denials, if logically carried out, involve the rejection of the Christian view as a whole. We reject the Christian view *in toto* if we deny the existence of God, the spiritual nature and immortality of man, or destroy the idea of sin. In what follows we are rather in the region of Christian heresy; at least the total rejection of the Christian view is not necessarily implied, though in its mutilation it is found that neither can that which is preserved be permanently maintained.

4. The assertion of the Incarnation may be met by a lower estimate of Christ's Person than the full Christian doctrine implies; or by the complete denial of the supernatural dignity of His Person.

5. The Christian view may be met by the denial of the need or the reality of Atonement, or by inadequate or unscriptural representations of that great doctrine.

6. There may be unscriptural denials, as well as unwarrantable dogmatisms, in the matter of eschatology.

My course, then, in view of the various antitheses, will shape itself as follows :—

First, keeping in mind that it is the Incarnation which is the central point in the Christian view, I shall look in the second Lecture at the alternatives which are historically presented to us if this doctrine is rejected.

Next, in the third, fourth, and fifth Lectures, I shall consider in order the three postulates of the Christian view—God, Nature and Man, and Sin.

The sixth Lecture will be devoted to the Incarnation itself,

and the seventh to the consideration of some related topics—
the higher Christian concept of God, and the relation of the
Incarnation to the plan of the world.

The eighth Lecture will treat of the Incarnation and Redemption from sin ; and the concluding Lecture will treat of the
Incarnation and human destiny.[1]

---

[1] The original plan embraced a Lecture between Lecture VIII. and what is
now IX.—on "The Incarnation and New Life of Humanity : the Kingdom of
God." The subject is touched on in Lecture IX., and dealt with more fully in
an Appendix.

2
THE CHRISTIAN VIEW AND
ITS ALTERNATIVES

"There has seldom been an age more irreligious than ours, yet it will be difficult to find one in which religious questions have been more profoundly discussed." —Hartmann

"In the history of systems an inexorable logic rids them of their halfness and hesitancies, and drives them straight to their inevitable goal." —Martineau

"Conjecture of the worker by the work:
Is there strength there?—enough: intelligence?
Ample: but goodness in a like degree?
Not to the human eye in the present state,
An isoscele deficient in the base.
What lacks, then, of perfection fit for God
But just the instance which this tale supplies
Of love without a limit? So is strength,
So is intelligence; let love be so,
Unlimited in its self-sacrifice,
Then is the tale true and God shows complete."
R. Browning

2
THE CHRISTIAN VIEW AND
ITS ALTERNATIVES

IT is the fundamental assumption of these Lectures that the central point in the Christian view of God and the world is the acknowledgment of Jesus Christ as a truly Divine Person—the Son of God made flesh. How is this assumption to be vindicated? I do not conceal from myself that the issues involved in such an assertion are very stupendous. The belief in Jesus as the Son of God is not one to be lightly taken up, but when it is taken up, it practically determines, as has already been said, a man's views on everything else in Christianity. No one will dispute that, if Jesus Christ is what the creeds declare Him to be—an Incarnation of the Divine—His Person is necessarily central in His own religion, nay, in the universe. Christianity, on this assumption, is correctly described as the religion of the Incarnation.

On the other hand, this is precisely the view of the Person of Christ which, we are told, the modern view of the world compels us to reject. No doctrine stumbles the modern mind so completely as this. It is flatly pronounced incredible and absurd. That Jesus was the holiest of men—the Divinest of the race, the most perfect exhibition of the god-like in humanity—may well be conceded; but of literal Incarnation it is not permitted to the modern intelligence to speak. Science has to investigate the origin of the dogma; to show how it arose from the powerful impression made by Jesus on His followers; how it was shaped by Hebrew and Hellenic modes of thought; but it cannot for a moment entertain the possibility that the idea which it represents is true. As strenuously is our right resisted to speak of this doctrine as an essential and integral part of Christianity. Short of this conception, it is said, there are many grades of belief in

Christ, and we are not entitled to unchristianise any of them
To identify the essence of Christianity with the Incarnation
is, it is held, to make a particular dogmatic interpretation of
Christianity equivalent to Christianity itself? It is not,
indeed, among the extremer sceptics that we find any
difficulty in getting the acknowledgment that the Incarnation
is central in Christianity. "It is," says Strauss, "certainly
the central dogma in Christianity. Here the Founder is at
the same time the most prominent object of worship; the
system based on Him loses its support as soon as He is
shown to be lacking in the qualities appropriate to an object
of religious worship."[1] "In Him alone," says Feuerbach, "is
concentrated the Christian religion."[2] Quite logically, from
his point of view, Strauss draws the conclusion that, since the
Incarnation is untenable, Christianity falls to the ground with
it. But others will not go thus far. They distinguish between
Christianity and its accidents, and put this doctrine in the
category of the accidents. Nay, it is ostensibly in the interests
of what is supposed to be a purer and more primitive form of
Christianity that in many quarters the demand for the
surrender of this doctrine is made. The cry is, "Back from
Christianity to Christ"—back from the Christianity of the
creeds, from the Christianity even of Paul and John—to the
Christ of the simple Galilean gospel, who never dreamt of
making himself God. As Lessing, in a famous passage, distinguishes between "the religion of Christ" and "the
Christian religion," meaning by the former the religion which
Christ Himself professed and practised, and by the latter the
superstructure of dogma subsequently reared on this,[3] so an
analogous distinction is drawn between the Pauline and
Johannine Christ, with His halo of supernatural attributes,
and the meek and lowly Jesus, so intensely human, of the
Synoptic Gospels.

Nevertheless, the ablest theology of the century will
sustain me in the general assertion, that the central principle
of Christianity is the Person of its Founder. Whatever may
be thought of the great speculative movement in the begin-

---

[1] *Der alte und der neue Glaube*, pp. 43, 44.
[2] *Das Wesen des Christenthums*, p. 147 (Eng. trans.).
[3] Cf. Pfleiderer, *Religionsphilosophie*, i. p. 141 (Eng. trans.).

ning of the century, connected with the names of Fichte and
Schelling and Hegel, it cannot be denied that at least it
rendered an essential service to theology in overcoming the
shallow rationalism of the preceding period, and in restoring
to its place of honour in the Christian system the doctrine of
Christ's Person, which it had become customary to put in the
background. Still more influential in this direction was the
powerful impulse given to theology by Schleiermacher. Since
that time all the best theology in Germany may be said to be
Christological. That Christ sustains a different relation to His
religion from that of ordinary founders of religion to the faiths
they have founded; that in Him there was a peculiar union
of the Divine and human; that His appearance and work
were of decisive importance for the Church and for humanity
—these are thoughts which may be said to be common to all
the greater systems, irrespective of schools. They are found
among theologians as widely separated in dogmatic standpoint
and tendency as Rothe and Dorner, Biedermann and Lipsius,
Beyschlag and Ritschl, Luthardt and Frank. It is only outside
the circles of really influential theology that we find a reversion
to the loose deistic conception of Christ as simply a Prophet or
moral Teacher, like Moses or Confucius or Buddha.[1] It is
indeed a powerful proof of the view that the Person of Christ is
of unique importance in His religion, that whenever a new breath
of life passes over theology, and an attempt is made to gain a
profounder apprehension of Christianity, there is a recurrence
to this idea, and the necessity is felt of doing justice to it;
thus testifying to the truth of Dorner's remark, "A Christian
system which is unable to make Christology an integral part
of itself, has pronounced its own judgment; it has really given
up the claim to the title of Christian."[2]

At the same time, this acknowledgment of the central and
unique place of the Founder of Christianity in His religion
does not settle the question of the precise estimate we are to
take of His Person. Is He merely human, or is He Divine
as well? Or if Divine, in what sense do we attach this
predicate to Him? Is it, as with the Hegelians, the mere
expression of a metaphysical idea—of that identity of the

---

[1] See Note A.—The Central Place of Christ in His Religion.

[2] *Doct. of Person of Christ*, v. p. 49 (Eng. Trans.).

Divine and the human which is as true of all men as it is of
Christ, only that it came first to clear consciousness in Him?
Or is it, as with Ritschl, the mere expression of a value-
judgment of the believer—a predicate denoting the worth
which Christ has for the believing soul as the supreme
Revealer of God's character and purpose? Or is it, as with
others, an ethical Divinity that is ascribed to Christ—such
participation in the Divine nature and life of Sonship as may
be experienced also by the believer?[1] Or shall we hold, in
agreement with the general faith of the Church, that Christ
is more than all this—that in Him the Divine pre-existing
Word truly and personally became incarnate, and made our
nature His own—that therefore He is the Son of God, not
simply as we are, but in a high and transcendental sense,
in which we cannot compare ourselves with Him? This
question, in the present state of controversy, is not so easily
settled as might at first sight appear. It is vain, of course,
to appeal to the great ecclesiastical creeds, for it is they
which are in dispute. It is vain also, at this stage, to
attempt to settle the question by the simple method of
citation of proof texts. The facts of Christ's self-revelation,
and His witness to His own Person, must indeed, in the last
resort, be the ground on which our faith in Him rests, and it
will be necessary at a later stage to examine this self-witness
of Christ, as well as the apostolic doctrine, with considerable
care.[2] But at the outset this method is attended by obvious
disadvantages. It is easy to say—the original documents of
Christianity are before us; let us examine them. But, for
one thing, some of these documents—the Fourth Gospel, *e.g.*,
and some of the Pauline epistles—are themselves in dispute
among our opponents; and, even if genuine, their authority
is not accepted as decisive. In the next place, there is the
question, whether there are not traces of development in the
doctrine of the Person of Christ even within the New Testament—whether all the sacred writers teach the same view.
There are many, as I have already said, who will admit that
Christ's Divinity is taught by Paul and John, who would deny
that it is taught by Christ Himself. These are difficulties
which cannot be satisfactorily met by mere assertion, and the

---

[1] Thus, *e.g.*, Wendt in his *Inhalt der Lehre Jesu.*   [2] Cf. Lecture VI.

question recurs, whether—as a provisional expedient at least—any other course is open to us ?

There is another method which I propose to apply in this Lecture, one which appears to me to have the advantage of dealing with all these issues at once, and at the same time deals with issues of a wider character. It is the method of appeal to history. The individual judgment may err in the opinions it forms, and in the conclusions it deduces from them. It is not given to any man to see all the consequences that follow from his own thinking. He may quite conceivably hold in the scheme of his beliefs propositions that are inconsistent with each other, and, if logically carried out, would destroy each other, and not be aware of the fact. In history things get beaten out to their true issues. The strands of thought that are incompatible with each other get separated; conflicting tendencies, at first unperceived, are brought to light; opposite one-sidednesses correct each other ; and the true consequences of theories reveal themselves with inexorable necessity. As Socrates, in Plato's *Republic*,[1] investigating the nature of Justice, proposes to study it first as "writ large " in the collective magnitude of the State, that thereafter he may return with better knowledge to the study of it in the individual, so the movements of thought are best studied on the broad scale in which they present themselves over large periods of time. It is to this test I propose to bring the great question of Christianity—the same that was proposed by Jesus to the Pharisees eighteen hundred years ago—"What think ye of Christ? Whose Son is He?"[2] I shall ask what aid history affords us in determining the true estimate to be put upon the Person of Christ, and the place held in the Christian system by the doctrine of the Incarnation.

It is one advantage of this method, that, as I have said, it brings all the issues into court at once. The verdict of history is at once a judgment on the answers which have been given to the theological question ; on their agreement with the sum-total of the facts of Christianity ; on the methods of exegesis and New Testament criticism by which they have been supported ; on their power to maintain themselves against

---

[1] Book ii. [2] Matt. xxii. 42.

rival views; on how far the existence of Christianity is dependent on them, or bound up with them.

I. History, then, as it seems to me, presents us with a
series of alternatives of a deeply interesting character, by
studying which we may find our bearings on this question,
"What think ye of Christ?" as we can in no other way.

1. The first essential service which history has rendered
us has been in *the elimination of intermediate views* — in
making it clear as a first alternative that the real issue on
this question is between *a truly Divine Christ and pure
humanitarianism.* Intermediate views on Christ's Person
have from time to time arisen, and still go on arising, in the
Church; but, like the intermediate species of plants and
animals Mr. Darwin tells us of, which are invariably driven
to the wall in the struggle for existence, they have never
been able to survive. There is, *e.g.*, the Arian view, which
has appeared again and again in the history of the Church in
times of spiritual decadence. To find a place for the high
attributes ascribed to Christ in Scripture, a lofty supernatural
dignity is in this view assigned to Him. He was a sort of
supreme angel, God's First-born, His instrument in the creation
of the world, etc. But He was not eternal; He was not
of Divine essence. It is safe to say that this view is now
practically extinct. It would be a shallow reading of history
to attribute the defeat of Arianism in the early Church to the
anathemas of councils, the influence of court favour, or any
other accidental circumstances. It perished through its own
inherent weakness.[1] If the Arians admit all they profess to
do about Christ—that He was pre-existent, God's agent in
the creation of the world, etc.—there need be little difficulty
in admitting the rest. On the other hand, if they stop short
of the higher view to which the Scriptures seem to point,
they entangle themselves in difficulties and contradictions,
exegetical and other, which make it impossible for them to

---

[1] See Note B.—The Defeat of Arianism. Dorner says: "Not merely did it
tend back to Ebionitism; not merely was it unable, with its Docetism and its
doctrine of a created higher spirit, to allow even the possibility of an Incarnation: but, by putting a fantastical under-God between God and man, it
separated the two quite as much as it appeared to unite them."—*Person of
Christ*, ii. p. 261 (Eng. trans.).

remain where they are. In reality, these high-sounding attributes which they ascribe to Christ are an excrescence on the system; for on this theory no work remains for Christ to do which could not have been accomplished equally well by a highly endowed man. Historically, therefore, Arianism has always tended to work round to the Socinian or strictly Unitarian view of Christ, where it has not gone upwards, through semi-Arianism, to the recognition of His full Divinity.

But this Socinian or Unitarian view of the Person of Christ —I refer to the older Unitarianism of the Priestley and Channing type—is another of those intermediate views which history also may now be said to have eliminated. Christ, on this view, is the greatest of inspired teachers, a true Prophet. He had a divine mission ; He wrought miracles in confirmation of His doctrine; He rose from the dead on the third day ; He is expected to return to judge the world. Here also there is a great deal of the halo of the supernatural about Christ. He is supernatural in history, if not in nature, and men saw again that they must either believe more or believe less. The rationalistic leaven, which was already working in the rejection of the higher aspects of Christ's Person and work, made itself increasingly felt. As the miraculous adjuncts were retained only in deference to the representations of Scripture, they were readily abandoned when criticism professed to show how they might be stripped off without detriment to Christ's moral image. Be the cause what it may, it is undeniable that Unitarianism of this kind has not been able to maintain itself. It has constantly tended to purge itself of the remaining supernatural features in the portrait of Christ, and to descend to the level of simple humanitarianism, *i.e.*, to the belief in Christ as simply a great man, a religious genius of the first rank, one in whom the light which shines in all men shone in an eminent degree —but still a *mere* man, without anything supernatural in His origin, nature, or history.[1]

A further example of the difficulty of maintaining an intermediate position on the doctrine of the Person of Christ, may be taken from the long series of intermediate views which have sprung up on the soil of Germany as the result

---

[1] See Note C.—Modern Unitarianism.

of the great intellectual and theological movement inaugurated by Hegel and Schleiermacher in the beginning of the century. Passing by the speculative Christologies—in which, when the veil was stripped off, it was found that the idea was everything, the historical Christ nothing—I may refer here to the Christology of Schleiermacher and his school. Schleiermacher recognises to the full "a peculiar being of God in Christ."[1] He affirms Christ's perfect sinlessness, and the unique significance of His Personality for the Church and for the race. He is the Head, Archetype, Representative, and Redeemer of mankind. Only through Him is redemption from sin and fellowship of life with God possible. But when we come to inquire wherein consists this "peculiar being of God" in Christ, it proves, after all, to be only an exceptionally constant and energetic form of that God-consciousness which exists germinally in all men, and indeed lies at the root of religious experience generally. The difference between Christ and other men is thus in degree, not in kind. In Him this Divine element had the ascendency, in us it has not. He is a miracle, in so far as the Divine dwelt in Him in this unique and exceptional fulness and power, constituting Him the Redeemer and second Adam of the race; but there is no entrance of God into humanity such as we associate with the idea of Incarnation. When, further, we investigate the nature of Christ's saving activity, we find that the exalted, high-priestly functions which Schleiermacher ascribes to Christ shrink, on inspection, into very meagre dimensions. Christ's continued saving activity in His Church is presupposed, but it is not the activity of One who still lives and reigns on high, but rather the perpetuation of a posthumous influence, through the preservation of His image in the Gospels, and the fellowship of the Christian society.[2] Ultimately, therefore, Christ's saving activity is reduced to example and teaching; at most, to the spiritual influence of a great and unique historic Personality.[3] When we have got this length, we are clearly back on the road to simple humanitarianism. Accordingly, none of Schleiermacher's followers have been able to stop exactly where he did. They have felt

---

[1] *Der christ. Glaube*, sect. 94.   [2] Thus also Ritschl.
[3] On Schleiermacher's Christology, cf. Dorner, *Person of Christ*, pp. 174-213.

the inexorable compulsion of the less or more; and while some have gone back to rationalism, the great majority, as Rothe acknowledges,[1] have pressed on to more positive views, and have come into substantial harmony with confessional orthodoxy. A new wave of mediating theology has recently arisen in the school of Ritschl; but the fundamental principle of this school—the denial of the right of the theoretic reason to have anything to do with religion or theology—is not one that can permanently be approved of, and would, if followed out, end in boundless subjectivity. In this school also, accordingly, the necessity of less or more is asserting itself. Already the members of the school have begun to move off on different and irreconcilable lines—some in a more negative, the greater number in a more positive direction. The attempt of Ritschl to bar off all inquiry into the nature of Christ's Person, by resolving His "Godhead" into a mere value-judgment of the believer, is felt not to be satisfactory; and the admission is increasingly made that consistency of Christian thinking demands the acknowledgment of a transcendental basis.[2]

The general verdict of history, therefore, is clearly against the permanence of these attempts at a middle view of Christ's Person, and warns us whither they tend. The liberal school in Germany, Holland, and France are clearly right in saying that the only alternative to Christ's true Divinity is pure humanitarianism; and that, if the former doctrine is rejected, the supernatural view of His Person must be altogether given up. This is a clear issue, and I think it is well to have matters brought to it without shrinking or disguise. I desire now to show that this first alternative soon lands us in a second.

2. The first alternative is between a Divine Christ and a purely human one—the second is between *a Divine Christ and pure Agnosticism.* Many of those who take the humanitarian view of Christ's Person are very far from wishing to deny that a great deal of what Christ taught was true. They do not wish to deny the existence of God, or the fact of a future life, or the essentials of Christian morality. In not a few cases they strongly uphold these truths—maintain them to be the true

---

[1] He says: "Since Schleiermacher's death, the school proceeding from him has generally gone back into the way of the Church doctrine."—*Dogmatik,* ii. p. 162.

[2] See Note D.—Concessions of Ritschlians on the Person of Christ.

natural religion, in opposition to revealed. They account it
Christ's greatest glory that He saw so clearly, and announced
so unambiguously, the Fatherhood of God, the dignity of the
soul, the certainty of immortality, and the dependence of happiness here and hereafter on virtue. It is a plausible view to
take, for it seems to secure to those who hold it all that they
take to be essential in Christianity, while at the same time it
leaves them unbounded liberty to accept or reject what they
like in modern "advanced" views—to get rid of miracles, go
in with progressive theories of science, accept the newest criticism of the Gospels, etc. It is a plausible view, but it is an
illusive one ; for if there is one thing more than another which
the logic of events makes evident, it is, that with the humanitarian view of Christ we cannot stop at simple, abstract Theism,
but must go on to pure Agnosticism. This is indeed what the
larger number of the more logical minds which have rejected
supernatural Christianity in our own day are doing. Nor is
the process which leads to this result difficult to follow. The
Deism of the last century rejected Christianity, and sought to
establish in its place what it called "Natural Religion," *i.e.*
a belief in God, in the future life, in a state of rewards
and punishments, etc., based on reason alone. But however
congruous with reason these doctrines may be in the place
which they hold in the religion of Jesus, it was not really
reason which had discovered them, or which gave assurance
about them ; nor did it follow that reason could successfully
vindicate them, when torn from their context, and presented
in the meagre, abstract form in which they appeared in the
writings of the deists. What the deists did was to pick these
doctrines out of the New Testament, separating them from the
rest of the doctrines with which they were associated, and
denuding them of everything which could make them real and
vital to the minds and consciences of men ; then to baptise this
caput mortuum with the name of "Natural Religion." They
were doctrines that had their roots in the Christian system,
and the arguments from reason with which they were supported were not the real grounds of belief in them. In the
present century men are not so easily satisfied.[1] They see
clearly enough that all the objections which have been levelled

---

[1] See Note E.—The Weakness of Deism.

against the God of Revelation tell just as powerfully against the God of nature ; that to admit Christ's doctrine of a Heavenly Father, of a soul made in God's image, of a special providence, of prayer, of forgiveness of sins, of a future life of happiness and misery, is already to have crossed the line which separates a merely natural from a supernatural view of things ; and that to reject Christ's doctrines on these great questions makes it difficult to retain a Theism of any kind.[1] This is not because a theistic view of the world is in itself less reasonable than a non-theistic view—to admit this would be to give up the whole case on behalf of Christianity. But it is because the kind of Theism that remains after the Christian element has been removed out of it, is not one fitted to satisfy either the reason or the heart. It is a pale, emasculated conception, which, finding no support in the facts or experiences of the spiritual life, can never stand against the assaults made on it from without. It is here that Pantheism has its advantage over Deism. It is indeed more reasonable to believe in a living personal God, who created and who controls the universe, than in the "One and All" of the pantheist ; but it does not follow that it is more reasonable to believe in an abstract Deity—a mere figment of the intellect—who stands in separation from the world, and yields no satisfaction to the religious life. Theism is a reasonable view of the universe, but it must be a living Theism, not a barren and notional one.

If, to avoid this bankruptcy, the attempt is made to deal in earnest with the conception of a personal God, and to reclothe the Deity with the warm, gracious attributes which belong to the Father-God of Christ, then we have indeed a Being whom the soul can love, trust, and hold communion with, but the difficulty recurs of believing Him to be a God who remains self-enclosed, impassive, uncommunicative, towards creatures whom He has dowered with a share of His own rational and moral excellences, who has so shut Himself out by natural law from direct contact with the spirits that seek Him, that He can neither speak to them, answer their prayers, help them in trouble, nor even reach them by inward succours—a *silent* God.

---

[1] This is where not only Deism, but also the so-called Liberal Protestantism, fails, in rejecting supernatural Christianity. See Note F.—Weakness of Modern Liberal Protestantism.

who can no more enter into personal relations with His creatures
than if He were *im*personal.   Such a conception is self-contradictory, and cannot maintain itself.   One feels this incongruity
very powerfully in dealing with the Theism of such writers as
the late Mr. Rathbone Greg, or Dr. Martineau, or the authoress
of *Robert Elsmere*.   None of these writers will admit the possibility of miracle; logically, therefore, they shut out the possibility of direct communication between God and man.   Yet
none of them can rest with the cold abstract God of Deism;
or with the immanent impersonal spirit of Pantheism; or with
the comfortless negation of Agnosticism.   God is with them a
personal Being; His will is ethical; communion with Him is
longed after and believed in.   Let Mr. Greg's own pathetic
words tell how insecure is the Theism thus cut off from positive
Revelation.   "My own conception," he says, "perhaps from
early mental habit, perhaps from incurable and very conscious
metaphysical inaptitude, approaches far nearer to the old current
image of a personal God than to any of the sublimated substitutes of modern thought.   Strauss's *Universum*, Comte's
Humanity, even Mr. Arnold's *Stream of Tendency that makes
for Righteousness*, excite in me no enthusiasm, command from
me no worship.   I cannot pray to the 'Immensities' and the
'Eternities' of Carlyle; they proffer me no help; they vouch-
safe me no sympathy; they suggest no comfort.   It may be
that such a personal God is a mere anthropomorphic creation.
It may be—as philosophers with far finer instruments of thought
than mine affirm—that the conception of such a Being, duly
analysed, is demonstrably a self-contradictory one.   But, at
least in resting in it, I rest in something I almost seem to
realise; at least, I share the view which Jesus indisputably
held of the Father whom He obeyed, communed with, and worshipped." [1]   Surely it need hardly be said that a view which,
even while holding it, one doubts may be only a result of "early
mental habit," "a mere anthropomorphic creation," a "self-
contradictory" conception, cannot long stand as a basis for
life; nor will the trust which Jesus had help much, when
one has already rejected as delusion His doctrine of prayer,
of special providence, of forgiveness of sins, and His own
Messianic claims and expectations.   Already we tremble on

---

[1] *Creed of Christendom*, Introd., 3rd ed., pp. 90, 91.

the verge of Agnosticism, if we have not actually passed its bound.

I think, accordingly, I am justified in saying that when the ground of Divine Revelation is once left behind, we have no logical halting-place short of Agnosticism; not because a theistic view of the world is unreasonable, but because a living Theism requires as its complement belief in Revelation. We have these alternatives: either to revivify our Theism till it approaches in the humane and loving attributes it ascribes to God, the Christian conception of the Heavenly Father—in which case we are back to a supernatural view of the universe; or, if this is thought baseless, to dispense with the idea of God altogether, and try to explain the world without reason, without final cause, without spiritual assumptions of any kind.

3. Agnosticism is, however, far from representing the end of this road along which we had begun to travel in rejecting the Divine in Christ. The final alternative—one which we may trust the world at large will never be called upon to face —is *a Divine Christ or Pessimism.* Agnosticism is not a state in which the mind of an intelligent being can permanently rest. It is essentially a condition of suspense—a confession of ignorance—an abdication of thought on the highest subjects.[1] It is not, in the nature of things, possible for the mind to remain persistently in this neutral, passive attitude. It will press on perforce to one or other of the views which present themselves as alternatives—either to Theism, or to Materialism and dogmatic Atheism.[2] I do not speak, of course, of the individual mind, but of the general historical development. But even Agnosticism has brought with it a train of baleful results. With the loss of certainty on the highest questions of existence there comes inevitably a lowering of the pulse of human endeavour all round—a loosening of certainty about morals, for why should these remain unaffected when everything else is going?—and as we see to-day, in much of the

---

[1] Generally, however, under the surface of professed Agnosticism, there will be found some more or less positive opinions about the origin and nature of things, all of them agreeing in this, that they negate the belief in God.

[2] On the Continent there are fewer agnostics, but more atheists and materialists, than with us. " In Germany," says Karl Peters, "things are come to such a pass that one is obliged to ask a sort of absolution if one does not swim with the prevailing atheistic-monistic stream."—*Willenswelt und Weltwille,* p. 350.

speculative thought of France and Germany, a hopelessness about the future. For, obviously, when this point is reached, the rational ground is taken away even from belief in progress.[1] When the idea of God, which is equivalent to the idea of a reason at the foundation of things, is surrendered—whether in Agnosticism, or in some form of dogmatic denial, makes little difference—it becomes a wholly unwarranted assumption that things must certainly go on from better to better. The opposite may quite as well be the case, and progress, now that a given height is reached, may rather be from better to worse. The analogy of nature shows that this is the law in regard to natural life. The plant blooms, reaches its acme, and dies. So, it may be plausibly argued, it will be with humanity. The fact that some progress has been made in the past does not guarantee that this progress will go on indefinitely; rather, the spur to this progress consisted in what we are now told are illusions, and when these are exploded the motives to progress are gone. A more highly evolved society may lead to an increase of misery rather than of happiness; the growth of enlightenment, instead of adding to men's enjoyments, may result in stripping them successively of the illusions that remain, and may leave them at last sad, weary, disappointed, with an intolerable consciousness of the burden and wretchedness of existence.[2] All this is not fancy. The despairing, pessimistic spirit I am speaking of has already taken hold of extensive sections of society, and is giving startling evidences of its presence. For the first time on European soil we see large and influential systems springing up, and gaining for themselves wide popularity and acceptance, which have for their root-idea exactly this conception of the inherent irrationality and misery of existence. There have always been individual thinkers with a tendency to take a prejudiced

---

[1] See Note G.—Christianity and the Idea of Progress.

[2] Pessimism reverses Pascal's saying that the greatness of man consists in thought. Thought, according to Pessimism, is the fatal gift. "Well for those," Schopenhauer thinks, "who have no consciousness of existence. The life of the animal is more to be envied than that of man; the life of the plant is better than that of the fish in the water, or even of the oyster on the rock. Non-being is better than being, and unconsciousness is the blessedness of what does exist. The best would be if all existence were annihilated."—Cf. Luthardt, *Die mod. Welt.* p. 189. "The height of misery is not that of being man; it is, being man, to despise oneself sufficiently to regret that one is not an animal."—CARO, *Le Pessimisme*, p. 135.

and hopeless view of life, but their reveries have not been much regarded. But here, strange to say, under the very shadow of this boasted progress of the nineteenth century—in the very midst of its enlightenment and civilisation and wealth —we see Pessimism raising its head as a serious, carefully thought-out philosophy of existence, and, instead of being scouted and laughed at as an idle dream, it meets with passionate acceptance from multitudes.[1] The same spirit will be found reflected by those who care to note its symptoms in much of our current literature, in the serious raising and discussion, for example, of the question already familiar to us— Is life worth living? Specially noticeable is the tone of sadness which pervades much of the nobler sceptical thinking of the present day—the tone of men who do not think lightly of parting with religion, but feel that with it has gone the hope and gladness of earlier days. This Pessimism of scepticism is to me one of the saddest and most significant phenomena of modern times.[2] And, granting the premises it starts from, what other conclusion is possible? Deprive the world of God, and everything becomes an insoluble mystery, history a scene of wrecked illusions, belief in progress a superstition, and life in general

> " A tale
> Told by an idiot, full of sound and fury,
> Signifying nothing." [3]

II. The descent from faith in Christ has landed us in the abyss of *Pessimism*. But just at this lowest point, where the light of religious faith might seem utterly extinguished, a return movement is felt to be inevitable. For Pessimism, no more than Theism, can escape the necessity laid upon it of giving to itself some account of things as they are—of constructing a " Weltanschauung"; and the moment it attempts to do this, making naked the principle on which it rests, its own insufficiency as a philosophy of existence and of life stands glaring and confessed. Possibly the attempt to work out Pessimism as a system will never be made with much more thoroughness, or with better chances of success, than has

---

[1] See Note H.—The Prevalence of Pessimism.
[2] See Appendix to Lecture.—The Pessimism of Scepticism.
[3] " Macbeth," act v. scene 5.

already been done in the monumental works of Schopenhauer
and Hartmann. But the very thoroughgoingness of the attempt
is the demonstration of its futility. Of all theories, that which
explains the origin of the universe by a mistake—which accounts
for it by the blind rushing into existence of an irrational force,
call it "Will" or what we please—is surely the most incredible.[1]
How came this irrational will-force to be there? What moved
it to this insensate decision? In what state was it before it
committed this enormous blunder of rushing into existence?
How came it to be possessed of that potential wealth of ideas
which now are realised in the world? Of what use were they
if they were never intended to be called into existence? What
I am at present concerned with, however, is not to refute
Pessimism, but rather to show how, as a first step in an upward
movement back to Christ, by its own immanent dialectic it
refutes itself—inverts, in fact, its own starting-point, and works
itself round into a species of Theism.

Schopenhauer and Hartmann both recognise that there is
in the universe not only "Will," but "Idea," and the manner
in which they deal with this element of "Idea" is one of the
most curious examples of the inversion of an original starting-
point in the history of philosophy. For, in the course of its
development, Pessimism has actually adopted as its leading
principle the thought of a rational teleology in the universe,
and as a consequence, as above remarked, has worked itself
back to Theism. How this comes about it is not difficult to
show. The crucial point for all systems of Pessimism is the
presence of reason in the universe. How, if the basis of the
universe is irrational, does reason come to find a place in it
at all? For, manifestly, account for it as we may, there is

---

[1] These Pessimistic theories are not without their roots in the philosophies of
Fichte, Schelling, and Hegel. Cf. Fichte's view of the Absolute as "Will,"
and Schelling's "irrational" ground of the Divine nature (after Böhme). In
his *Philosophie und Religion* (1804), Schelling boldly describes the creation as
the result of an "Abfall"—the original assertion by the Ego of its independence. "This inexplicable and timeless act is the original sin or primal fall of
the spirit, which we expiate in the circles of time-existence" (cf. Professor
Seth's *From Kant to Hegel*, p. 65). Hegel also, in his own way, speaks of
creation as an "Abfall." "It is in the Son," he says, "in the determination of
distinction, that progressive determination proceeds to further distinction. . . .
This transition in the moment of the Son is thus expressed by Jacob Böhme —
that the first-born was Lucifer, the light-bearer, the bright, the clear one ; but
he turned in upon himself in imagination ; *i.e.* he made himself independent,
passed over into being, and so fell."— *Phil. d. Rel.* ii. p. 251 (*Werke*, vol. xii.)

reason in the universe now.   The universe itself is a law-connected whole; there is order and plan, organisation and system, utility and beauty, means and ends.   Above all, in man himself, if nowhere else, there is conscious reason—the very instrument by which this irrationality of the universe is discovered.   There is evidently more here than blind, purposeless will.   How is its existence to be explained? Schopenhauer postulates "Idea."   In accounting for nature, he has to suppose that in this blind, purposeless will there lies potentially a whole world of ideas, representing all the stages and kingdoms through which nature advances in the course of its history.[1]   Hartmann unites "Will" and "Idea" yet more closely, regarding them as co-ordinate attributes of the Absolute, though still, somehow, the will is supposed to be in itself a purely irrational force.   It is only when the will has made the mistake of rushing into existence that it lays hold on the "Idea" as a means of delivering itself from the unblessedness of its new condition.   To this end the universe is represented as ordered with the highest wisdom, the goal of its development being the production of the conscious agent, man, through whom the Redemption of the world-spirit is to be accomplished.   I do not pursue these "metaphysics of wonderland" further.   I only notice the extraordinary contradictions in which Hartmann involves himself in his conception of the Absolute—"the Unconscious," as he prefers to term it—and the extraordinary transformation it undergoes in his hands.   The absolute is unconscious, and needs to create for itself an organ of consciousness in man before it can attain deliverance from its unblessedness. Yet it knows, plans, contrives, orders everything with consummate wisdom, works out its designs with a precision that is unerring, etc.[2]   The contradiction here is too patent.   For, if unconscious, how can we speak of this Absolute as un-

---

[1] *Die Welt als Wille und Vorstellung*, i. pp. 185, 206 (Eng. trans. pp. 203, 219 ff.).   Karl Peters remarks : " If the Will alone bears in itself the stages of the World-All as eternal ideas—how can Schopenhauer call it an absolutely irrational Will?   And if he conceives of it as a radically blind Will, as an insane and altogether groundless 'Drang,' how can he vindicate for it these eternal ideas ?"— *Willenswelt*, p. 129.

[2] " The Unconscious wills in one act all the terms of a process, means and end, etc., not before, beside, or beyond, but in the result itself."—*Phil. d. Unbewussten*, ii. p. 60 (Eng. trans.).

blessed ?   Or how can we think of it as knowing and
planning ?   Hartmann therefore changes his ground, and
speaks in other places of his Absolute rather as *supra-*
conscious ; [1] elsewhere, again, in terms akin to those of Mr.
Spencer, as an "Unknowable" — incapable of being represented in forms of our intelligence. [2]   But if the Absolute is
supra-conscious, *i.e.* exists in a state *higher* than the ordinary
consciousness, why should it need the latter to help it out of
its misery ?   The climax is reached when, in a later work—
while still holding to the view that the Absolute is not a
self-conscious Personality — Hartmann invests it with most
of the attributes characteristic of Deity, sees in it, *e.g.*, the
ground, not only of a natural, but of a moral order, makes it
the object of religious worship, attributes to it, not simply
omnipotence and wisdom, but righteousness and holiness,
views it as a source of Revelation and grace, expressly names
it God ! [3]   We are here far enough from the original assumption of a primitive, irrational will—in fact, what we see is
Pessimism passing over in all but the name into Theism.   It
remained only that this transition should be explicitly made,
and this has been done by a disciple of the school, Karl
Peters, whose work, *Willenswelt und Weltwille*, is one of the
acutest criticisms of previous Pessimism I know.   With him
we finally leave the ground of the philosophy of the "Unconscious," and come round to a Theism in which we have the
full recognition of God as a self-conscious, wise, good, holy
Personality, whose providence is over all, and whose ends all
things subserve. [4]

The theories of Schopenhauer and Hartmann, though pes-

---

[1] The Unconscious, it now appears, has, after all, a kind of consciousness—
is "a transcendent supra-mundane consciousness," "anything but blind, rather
far-seeing and clairvoyant," "superior to all consciousness, at once conscious
and supra-conscious" (!), its "mode of thinking is, in truth, above consciousness."—*Phil. d. Unbewussten*, pp. 246, 247, 258, etc. (Eng. trans.).

[2] *Phil. d. Unbewussten*, pp. 49, 223, 246, etc. (Eng. trans.).   Schopenhauer
also declares his "Will" to be in itself, *i.e.* apart from its phenomenal manifestations, an Unknowable, possibly possessing "ways of existing, determinations, qualities, which are absolutely unknowable and incomprehensible to us,
and which remain ever as its nature when it has abrogated its phenomenal
character, and for our knowledge has passed into empty nothingness."—*Die
Welt als Wille* (Eng. trans.), ii. p. 408.

[3] *Religionsphilosophie :* Part II., *Phil. des Geistes*, pp. 74–89.

[4] See Note I.—Transition from Pessimism to Theism—Hartmann and Karl
Peters

simistic, might with equal propriety have been classed in the family of pantheistic systems. When dealing at an earlier stage with the downward movement from faith in Christ, through Agnosticism to Pessimism, I purposely reserved this alternative of *Pantheism*. This was not because the subject is in itself unimportant, but because it comes at last to the old dilemma, and can best be treated in its higher aspect as a stage in the upward advance to Theism. Pantheism shares the fate of every incomplete system, in being compelled to pass judgment on itself, and either to sink to something lower, or to pass up to something higher. I refer for proof to Germany, which has given birth to some of its noblest forms, but where also history shows how possible it is to descend at one step from the loftiest heights of overstrained Idealism to gross Materialism. Fichte and Schelling and Hegel were followed by Strauss and Feuerbach.[1] The logic of the process is again not difficult to trace. If universal reason is the all, and the finite in comparison with it nothing, in another point of view it is the finite that is all, and reason that is nothing, seeing that in the finite only it attains to actual existence. Concede the premiss, the Absolute has reality only in the universe, and it is but a short step to the conclusion, the universe only is real.[2] Interpret the universe now, in accordance with the "modern" conception, in terms of matter and motion, and Feuerbach's dictum is reached—"Man is what he eats." The goal of this is the old plunge into Nihilism and Pessimism, in which we have just seen that the mind cannot remain.

The other alternative is, however, possible to Pantheism, by holding fast to the *rational* element contained in it, to correct and purify itself by a return to Theism ; and this is the movement we see taking place in the latter forms of the philosophies of Fichte and Schelling, and in the speculative Theism of the later Hegelians. In judging of these systems, we must not be misled by too narrow a use of the word "Theism." The Theism of the writers I refer to is in many respects imperfect,

---

[1] See Note J.—Materialism in Germany.

[2] "If," says Dorner, "God be once defined as the essence of the world, it is a transposition of subject and predicate logically allowable, when Feuerbach, taking the idea seriously, counted the essence of the world to be a part of the world, made the *world* the subject, and reduced God to a mere predicate of the world. The transition was thus made to Anthropologism, the forerunner of Materialism."—*Person of Christ*, v. p. 160.

and bears throughout the marks of its speculative origin.   Yet,
in principle, the line between Pantheism and Theism is crossed
whenever God is conceived of no longer as an impersonal Force
or Idea, but as a spiritual, self-conscious principle at the basis
of the universe—as a knowing, willing Being, with whom man
can sustain, not only natural, but moral and spiritual relations.
There may be difficulties at this stage as to whether the term
"personal" is a suitable term to apply to the Divine; but it is,
nevertheless, a theistic conception of God which is shaping
itself, and the purgation of the system from remaining pantheistic elements is only a question of time.   What, for instance,
but an approximation to Theism is implied in such words as
Fichte's in his fine apostrophe—"Sublime and Living Will!
named by no name, compassed by no thought!   I may well
raise my soul to Thee, for Thou and I are not divided!   Thy
voice sounds within me, mine resounds in Thee; and all my
thoughts, if they be but good and true, live in Thee also. . . .
Thou art best known to the childlike, devoted, simple mind.
To it Thou art the searcher of hearts, who seest its inmost
depths; the ever-present witness of its truth, who knowest
though all the world know it not.   Thou art the Father who
ever desirest its good, who rulest all things for the best. . . .
How Thou art, I may not know.   But let me be what I ought
to be, and Thy relations to me—the mortal—and to all mortals,
lie open before my eyes, and surround me more clearly than the
consciousness of my own existence.   *Thou workest* in me the
knowledge of my duty, of my vocation in the world of reasonable beings:—*how*, I know not, nor need I to know.   Thou
knowest what I think and what I will:—*how* Thou canst know,
through what act Thou bringest about that consciousness, I
cannot understand. . . . *Thou willest* that my free obedience
shall bring with it eternal consequences:—the act of Thy will
I cannot comprehend, I only know that it is not like mine.
Thou doest, and Thy will itself is the deed; but the way of Thy
working is not as my ways—I cannot trace it."[1]   If this is
Pantheism, are we not all pantheists?   If this is Agnosticism,
is it not an Agnosticism in which we must all share?   The
moment in spiritual Pantheism which impels to this develop-

---

[1] "The Vocation of Man" (*Die Bestimmung des Menschen*) in Fichte's
"Popular Works," p. 365 (Eng. trans.).

ment is of course the recognition of the fact that the universe
has its ground in reason. If this position is to be safeguarded
against the lapse into Materialism, it must free itself from the
internal contradiction of supposing that there can be thought
without a thinker;[1] reason without a subject to which the
reason belongs; rational ends posited and executed without
intelligent and self-conscious purpose; moral order without a
moral will. In the case of Fichte and Schelling, this revolution
in their philosophies is seen taking place within their lifetime;
in the case of Hegel, it is seen in the development of his philosophy, in the hands of his disciples, into a speculative Theism.
In Vatke and Biedermann—two prominent representatives—the
Theism is still very shadowy and incomplete; in I. H. Fichte
and Pfleiderer of Berlin, it attains to full and explicit recognition. The latter writer, in particular, takes strong ground, and
from his own point of view may be regarded as one of the ablest
defenders of theistic positions in recent times. In our own
country we have the Neo-Hegelian movement, best represented
by the late Mr. Green of Oxford, and in him also the speculative spirit is seen allying itself very closely with the spirit of
religion, with the result that his philosophy almost inevitably
passes over into Theism. On the metaphysical side, God is
already to Mr. Green an "Eternal Self-Consciousness"[2]—the
author and sustainer of the system of relations which we call
the universe. But, on the religious side, He is thought of
much more positively as a conscious Being who is in eternal
perfection all that man has it in him to come to be—"a Being
of perfect understanding and perfect love"—an infinite Spirit,
present to the soul, but other than itself, towards whom "the
attitude of man at his highest and completest could still only
be that which we have described as self-abasement before an
ideal of holiness."[3] The metaphysical contradictions which still

---

[1] "In spite of Fichte's imperious tone," says Professor Seth, "and his
warning that we are merely setting the seal to our own philosophic incom-
petency, we must summon up all our hardihood, and openly confess that to
speak of thought as self-existent, without any conscious Being whose the thought
is, conveys no meaning to our minds. Thought *exists* only as the thought of a
thinker; it must be centred somewhere."—*Hegelianism and Personality*, p. 73.
He had formerly expressed himself differently.—*From Kant to Hegel*, p. 76.

[2] *Prolegomena to Ethics*, passim.

[3] Pp. 93, 142 of "Memoir" by Nettleship, in Green's *Works*, vol. iii.
Prof. Green's profound Christian feeling, with his ideological views of Christianity, are well brought out in the same "Memoir," and accompanying works.

inhere in the Neo-Hegelian theory have been well pointed out by one—formerly an ardent Hegelian—who has himself lived through the theory he criticises—Prof. Seth of Edinburgh. In him, in the line of this development, we reach at length a perfectly unambiguous position. "It must not be forgotten," he says, "that if we are to keep the name of God at all, or any equivalent term, subjectivity—an existence of God for Himself, analogous to our own personal existence, though doubtless transcending it infinitely in innumerable ways — is an essential element of the conception. . . . God may be, must be, infinitely more—we are at least certain that He cannot be less—than we know ourselves to be." [1]

The Theism we have thus gained embraces the two notions of God as self-conscious reason, and God as moral will. Once, however, this ground of Theism is reached, we are compelled, in order to secure it, to advance a step further, viz. to the thought of God as *self-revealing*. We have already seen that Theism can only be secured if God is thought of as standing in a living relation to mankind—that is, as interesting Himself in their welfare, and capable of entering into moral and spiritual fellowship with them. How can one earnestly believe in a living, personal God, and, on the other hand, in man as a being constituted for moral ends, and not also believe that it is the will of God that man should know Him, and be guided by Him to the fulfilment of his destiny? It is, accordingly, a most noteworthy fact, that in all the higher theology of the time— even rationalistic theology—the attempt is made to come to a right understanding with this concept of Revelation. Strange as it may sound to many, there is no proposition on which theologians of all schools at the present day are more willing to agree than 'this—that all knowledge of God, and consequently all religion, rests on Revelation ; and that, if the true idea of God is to be maintained, He must be thought of as self-revealing. This truth is emphasised, not in the orthodox systems alone, but in the theologies, *e.g.*, of Biedermann, of Lipsius, of Pfleiderer, of Ritschl—even, as I said before, of the pessimist Hartmann, who, in his book on religion, has, with curious

---

[1] *Hegelianism and Personality*, pp. 222–224. Mr. Green's theory is discussed more fully in Professor Veitch's *Knowing and Being*, which touches many vital points.

irony, his chapters on Faith and Revelation. The point of difference arises when we inquire into the nature of Revelation, and specially when we pass from the sphere of natural to that of supernatural Revelation. Supernatural Revelation the theologians of the liberal school—Pfleiderer, Lipsius, etc.—will not allow us to speak of; or rather, natural and supernatural are with them but different sides of the same process. That which, on the Divine side, is viewed as Revelation, is, on the human side, simply the natural development of man's moral and religious consciousness, and *vice versâ*. In the same way, every truly original moment in the life of a man, every birth-moment of a new truth in his soul, every flash of insight into some new secret or law of nature, is a Revelation. This, which is the subtlest view of Revelation at present in the field, is not to be set aside without an attempt to do justice to what is true in it.[1] I am, for my part, not concerned to deny that there is a side of truth, and a very important one, in this theory. If it sounds deistical to say, "Revelation is only through the natural activities of mind"; it may, on the other hand, be a wholesome corrective to a deistic view to say that God is immanent in these activities, and that through them He mediates His Revelation to the human spirit—that what we call the "natural" development of mind involves, when rightly understood, a factor of Revelation. Nor can the line ever be drawn so finely between natural and supernatural Revelation as to enable us to say, "Here precisely the natural ends and the supernatural begins." The theory in question, therefore, I would be disposed to call inadequate, rather than false; or false only as it professes to cover the whole field of Revelation. For in the latter, it must be contended that we have more than can be accounted for by mere natural development. Taken even on its own ground,

---

[1] Cf. on this theory Biedermann, *Christ. Dogmatik*, i. pp. 264–288; Lipsius, *Dogmatik*, pp. 41–68; Pfleiderer, *Religionsphilosophie*, iv. pp. 46–94, specially pp. 64–75 (Eng. trans.), and *Grundriss*, pp. 17–22. H. Schmidt has a good statement and criticism of this theory in his article on "The Ethical Oppositions in the Present Conflict of the Biblical and the Modern Theological View of the World," in the *Studien und Kritiken* for 1876 (3rd part). "The God whom the Scripture from beginning to end preaches," he says, "is a God of supernatural Revelation, who makes Himself known directly, in distinction from the everyday ordering of our lives; the God of rationalism is a God who, if He still as really communicates Himself, yet always remains hidden behind the laws of nature, as behind the natural course of the development of the human spirit, who never manifestly represents Himself to the eye of man in His exaltation over the world."

this theory involves the valuable admission that it is the will
of God to make Himself known to man, and that He has provided in the constitution of things for giving him the knowledge
that is necessary for him.   The only criticism I shall make at
present upon this theory is—and I think it is one which goes
to the heart of the matter—that in some sense the end of the
theory is the refutation of the beginning of it.   The point
from which we start is, that God can be known only through
the natural activities of the mind.   He is present in these
activities as He is present in all the other functions of our
mental, moral, and even physical being ; and He is present in
no other way.   But the peculiarity of this theory is that it ends
in a view of God which affirms the possibility of that with the
denial of which it set out—the possibility of direct communion
between God and the soul.   It is not disputed by any of the
advocates of these views that the highest point in this self-
revelation of God is the Revelation given to men through Jesus
Christ.   But the God and Father of our Lord Jesus Christ is
not a Being who communicates with man only in the indirect
way which this theory supposes.   He is a Being who Himself draws near to man, and seeks fellowship with him ; whose
relations with the spirits He has made are free and personal ;
who is as lovingly communicative as man, on his part, is
expected to be trustfully receptive ; to whom man can speak,
and He answers.   The simply natural is here transcended, and we
are in the region of direct intercourse of spirit with spirit.   And
this view of God is not disputed by the writers I am here
referring to, who deny supernatural Revelation.   Dr. Martineau
says, in words of deep wisdom, "How should related spirits,
joined by a common creative aim, intent on whatever things are
pure and good, live in presence of each other, the one the
bestower, the other the recipient of a sacred trust, and exchange
no thought and give no sign of the love which subsists between
them ? "[1]   Pfleiderer again says, "And why should it be less

---

[1] *Study of Religion*, ii. p. 48.   **Cf.** the following sentences from his *Hours
of Thought* :—"Whatever else may be included in the truth that 'God is
a Spirit,' this at least is implied, that He is free to modify His relations to
all dependent minds in exact conformity with their changes of disposition and
of need, and let the lights and shadows of His look move us swiftly as the
undulating wills on which they fall."—ii. p. 29.
    "Passing by this poor mockery, I would be understood to speak of a direct

possible for God to enter into a loving fellowship with us, than for men to do so with each other? I should be inclined to think that He is even more capable of doing so. For as no man can altogether read the soul of another, so no man can altogether live in the soul of another; hence all our human love is and remains imperfect. But if we are shut off from one another by the limits of individuality, in relation to God it is not so; to Him our hearts are as open as each man's own heart is to himself; He sees through and through them, and He desires to live in them, and to fill them with His own sacred energy and blessedness."[1] True, why not? But if this is admitted, what becomes of the theory that the action of God in Revelation is necessarily bound up within the limits of strict natural law? If the gates of intercourse are thus open between the human soul and God, is it either natural or probable that God will not enter in at them, and that, instead of leaving men simply to feel after Him if haply they may find Him, He will not at some point give them what supernatural light and aid they need to bring them to the true knowledge of Himself, and fit them for the attainment of the highest ends of their existence? Certainly, in light of the above admissions, no *a priori* objection can be raised to the principle of supernatural Revelation.

Pantheism

The legitimate outcome of this theory is, that in addition to general Revelation through reason, conscience, and nature, there is to be expected some special Revelation; and even this, in a certain way, is admitted, for it is conceded by nearly all the writers I have named that in the providential plan of the world a peculiar function was assigned to Israel; that, as the different nations of the world have their several providential tasks (Greece—art, culture, philosophy; Rome—law, government, etc.), to Israel was given the task of developing the idea

---

and natural communion of spirit with spirit, between ourselves and God, in which He receives our affection and gives a responsive breathing of His inspiration. Such communion appears to me as certain of reality as the daily intercourse between man and man; resting upon evidence as positive, and declaring itself by results as marked. The disposition to throw doubt on the testimony of those who affirm that they know this, is a groundless prejudice, an illusion on the negative side as complete as the most positive dreams of enthusiasm."—P. 224.

[1] *Religionsphilosophie*, iii. p. 305 (Eng. trans.). See Note K.—The Reasonableness of Revelation.

of God to its highest perfection in ethical Monotheism.[1]   And, finally, it is conceded that this self-revelation of God reaches its culmination in Jesus Christ, whose Person has world-historical significance, as bearing in it the principle of the perfect relation between God and men—of the absolute religious relation.[2] The line between natural and supernatural Revelation is here, surely, becoming very thin ; and it is therefore, perhaps, not greatly to be wondered at that the latest school in German theology—that of Ritschl—should take the short remaining step, and be marked by precisely this tendency to lay stress on the need and reality of positive Revelation.   The general position of this school may be fairly summed up by saying that God can only be truly known to us by personal, positive Revelation, in which He actually enters into historical relations with mankind ; and that this Revelation has been given in the Person of His Son Jesus Christ.   Through this Revelation alone, but in it perfectly, we have the true knowledge of God's character, of His world-aim in the establishing of a kingdom of God on earth, and of His gracious will of forgiveness and love.[3] Whatever theory of Revelation we adopt, Jesus Christ must be pronounced to be the highest organ of it.   On this point all deep and serious thinkers of our age may be held to be agreed. Thus, then, we are brought back to Christ, are led to recognise in Him the medium of a true Revelation ; and it only remains to ask, What do the facts of this Revelation, and of Christ's own self-testimony, properly construed, imply ?   We have already seen what the verdict of history is on this point, to what alternatives it shuts us up in our treatment of this subject.   We shall afterwards see by examination of the facts themselves how this verdict is justified.

To sum up, we have seen that two movements are to be discerned in history : the one a downward movement leading away from Christ, and resulting from the denial of, or tampering with, His full Divinity ; the other, an upward movement, retracting the stages of the earlier descent, and bringing us back to the confession of Thomas, "My Lord and my

---

[1] Thus, *e.g.*, Kuenen, Wellhausen, Pfleiderer, Martineau (*Seat of Authority*, pp. 116–122).

[2] This is the general position of the higher class of theologians, of whatever schools.

[3] See Note L.—The Ritschlian Doctrine of Revelation.

God."[1] The former movement ends in the gulf of Nihilism and Pessimism; the latter begins from the impossibility of the mind abiding permanently in the denial of a rational basis for the universe. But here, as in the downward movement, the logic of history asserts itself. Belief in a rational basis of the universe can only secure itself through return to Theism; a living Theism can only secure itself through belief in God as self-revealing; belief in Revelation leads historically to the recognition of Christ as the highest organ of God's self-revelation to mankind; belief in Christ as Revealer can only secure itself through belief in His Divinity. "Ye believe in God," said Jesus; "believe also in Me."[2] Belief in God—theistic belief—presses on to belief in Christ, and can only secure itself through it. On the other hand, belief in Christ has for its legitimate outcome belief in God. The two beliefs, as history demonstrates, stand or fall together.

---

[1] John xx. 28.   [2] John xiv. 1.

APPENDIX TO CHAPTER 2
THE PESSIMISM OF SCEPTICISM

ALL the writers on Pessimism dwell on the strangeness of the fact that a century like our own, so marked by mental and material progress, by vigour and enterprise, should witness a revival of this gospel of despair; and bear emphatic testimony to the breadth and depth of the influence which the pessimistic systems are exercising. Apart, however, from the definite acceptance of Pessimism as a creed, it is instructive to note the many indications which literature affords of the sad and hopeless spirit which seems the necessary outcome of the surrender of religious faith. A few illustrations of this Pessimism of scepticism, culled almost at random, will perhaps not be out of place.

Voltaire was not happy. Dr. Cairns writes regarding him: "How little he himself was contented with his own results appears in the gloom shed over his later writings. It is not in *Candide* alone, but in others of them that this sadness comes to light. Thus, in his dialogue, 'Les Louanges de Dieu,' the doubter almost carries it over the adorer—'Strike out a few sages, and the crowd of human beings is nothing but a horrible assemblage of unfortunate criminals, and the globe contains nothing but corpses. I tremble to have to complain once more of the Being of beings, in casting an attentive eye over this terrible picture. I wish I had never been born.' . . . Thus the last utterance of Voltaire's system is a groan." [1]

A deep pessimism lurked in the background of the genial optimism of Goethe. Thus he expresses himself in conversation with Eckermann: "I have ever been esteemed one of fortune's chiefest favourites; nor will I complain or find fault with the course my life has taken. Yet truly there has been

[1] Cairns's *Unbelief in the Eighteenth Century*, p. 141.

nothing but toil and care; and I may say that in all my seventy-five years I have never had a month of genuine comfort. It has been the perpetual rolling of a stone which I have always had to raise anew." His views of the future of the race were not hopeful. "Men will become more clever and more acute, but not better, happier, and stronger in action, or at least only at epochs. I foresee the time when God will have no more joy in them, but will break up everything for a renewed creation."[1] There are numerous such utterances.

Renan writes in the preface to his recently published work, *The Future of Science*, originally composed in the years 1848–49 — "To sum up: if, through the constant labour of the nineteenth century, the knowledge of facts has considerably increased, the destiny of mankind has, on the other hand, become more obscure than ever. The serious thing is that we fail to perceive a means of providing humanity in the future with a catechism that will be acceptable henceforth, except on the condition of returning to a state of credulity. Hence it is possible that the ruin of idealistic beliefs may be fated to follow hard upon the ruin of supernatural beliefs, and that the real abasement of the morality of humanity will date from the day it has seen the reality of things. . . . Candidly speaking, I fail to see how, without the ancient dreams, the foundations of a happy and noble life are to be relaid."[2]

The late Professor Clifford is quoted as saying: "It cannot be doubted that the theistic belief is a comfort to those who hold it, and that the loss of it is a very painful loss. It cannot be doubted, at least by many of us in this generation, who either profess it now, or have received it in our childhood, and have parted from it since with such searching trouble as only cradle-faiths can cause. We have seen the spring sun shine out of an empty heaven to light up a soulless earth; we have felt with utter loneliness that the Great Companion is dead."[3]

Professor Seeley, in the close of his work on *Natural Religion*, thus sums up: "When the supernatural does not come in to

[1] Eckermann's *Conversations of Goethe*, pp. 58, 345 (Eng. trans.). Cf. Lichtenberger's *German Thought in the Nineteenth Century*, p. 269 (Eng. trans.); Martensen's *Christian Ethics*, pp. 172, 173; and Art. "Neo-Paganism," in *Quarterly Review*, April 1891.

[2] *L'Avenir de la Science*, Preface (Eng. trans.). Elsewhere Renan has said, "We are living on the perfume of an empty vase."

[3] Quoted in Harris's *Self-Revelation of God*, p. 404.

overwhelm the natūral, and turn life upside down, when it is admitted that religion deals in the first instance with the known and natural, then we maẏ well begin to doubt whether the known and the natural can suffice for human life.   No sooner do we try to think so than Pessimism raises its head.   The more our thoughts widen and deepen, as the universe grows upon us and we become accustomed to boundless space and time, the more petrifying is the contrast of our own insignificance, the more contemptible become the pettiness, shortness, and fragility of the individual life.   A moral paralysis creeps over us.   For a while we comfort ourselves with the notion of self-sacrifice; we say, What matter if I pass, let me think of others!   But the *other* has become contemptible no less than the self; all human griefs alike seem little worth assuaging, human happiness too paltry at the best to be worth increasing. . . . The affections die away in a world where everything great and enduring is cold; they die of their own conscious feebleness and bootlessness." [1]

Of similar purport is a passage often quoted from *A Candid Examination of Theism*, by "Physicus."   "Forasmuch," this writer says, "as I am far from being able to agree with those who affirm that the twilight doctrine of 'the new faith' is a desirable substitute for the waning splendour of 'the old,' I am not ashamed to confess that, with this virtual negation of God, the universe to me has lost its soul of loveliness; and although from henceforth the precept 'to work while it is day' will doubtless but gain an intensified force from the terribly intensified meaning of the words, 'The night cometh when no man can work,' yet, when at times I think, as think at times I must, of the appalling contrast between the hallowed glory of that creed which once was mine, and the lonely mystery of existence as I now find it, at such times I shall ever feel it impossible to avoid the sharpest pang of which my nature is susceptible.   For, whether it be due to my intelligence not being sufficiently advanced to meet the requirements of the age, or whether it be due to the memory of those sacred associations which, to me at least, were the sweetest that life has given, I cannot but feel that for me, and for others who think as I do, there is a dreadful truth in those words of Hamilton,—

Professor Romanes [handwritten annotation]

[1] *Natural Religion*, pp. 261, 262.

philosophy having become a meditation, not merely of death, but of annihilation, the precept *know thyself* has become transformed into the terrible oracle to Œdipus, 'Mayest thou never know the truth of what thou art.'"[1]

Theodore Jouffroy, the French philosopher, wrote: "Never shall I forget the December evening when the veil which hid my unbelief from mine own eyes was torn away. . . . The hours of the night glided away, and I perceived it not; I anxiously followed my thought, which descended step by step to the bottom of my consciousness, and dissipating, one after another, all the illusions which till then had hid them from my view, rendered its subterfuges more and more visible to me. In vain I clung to my last beliefs, as a shipwrecked sailor to the fragments of his ship; in vain, terrified by the unknown waste in which I was about to float, I threw myself back once more upon my childhood, my family, my country, all that was dear and sacred to me; the inflexible current of my thought was the stronger; parents, family, memories, beliefs—it forced me to leave all. This examination became more obstinate and more severe as it approached the end; nor did it stop till the end was reached. I knew then that at the bottom of myself there was nothing left standing, that all I had believed about myself, about God, and about my destiny in this life and in that to come, I now believed no more. This moment was frightful; and when, towards morning, I threw myself exhausted upon my bed, it seemed to me as if I could feel my former life, so cheerful and complete, die away, and before me there opened up another life, dark and dispeopled, where henceforth I was to live alone, alone with my fatal thought which had just exiled me thither, and which I was tempted to curse."[2]

Here is Professor Huxley's estimate of human progress: "I know," he says, "no study which is so unutterably saddening as that of the evolution of humanity, as it is set forth in the annals of history. Out of the darkness of prehistoric ages man emerges with the marks of his lowly origin strong upon him.

[1] P. 114. It is now known that "Physicus" was the late Professor Romanes, whose happy return to the Christian faith before his death has since been announced. See his *Thoughts on Religion*, edited by Canon Gore.

[2] *Les Nouveaux Mélanges Philosophiques*, by Theodore Jouffroy, pp. 112–115 (cf. Naville's "Christ," p. 16).

He is a brute, only more intelligent than the other brutes; a
blind prey to impulses which as often as not lead him to destruction; a victim to endless illusions, which make his mental
existence a terror and a burden, and fill his physical life with
barren toil and battle. He attains a certain degree of physical
comfort, and develops a more or less workable theory of life, in
such favourable situations as the plains of Mesopotamia or of
Egypt, and then, for thousands and thousands of years, struggles
with varying fortunes, attended by infinite wickedness, blood-
shed, and misery, to maintain himself at this point against the
greed and ambition of his fellow-men. He makes a point of
killing and otherwise persecuting all those who first try to get
him to move on; and when he has moved on a step foolishly
confers post-mortem deification on his victims. He exactly re-
peats the process with all who want to move a step yet further.
And the best men of the best epochs are simply those who make
the fewest blunders, and commit the fewest sins." [1] The passage
is in protest against the Positivist " worship of Humanity."

In further illustration of the Pessimism of scepticism, I may
refer to two instructive magazine articles—one by Emile de Laveleye on " The Future of Religion," in *The Contemporary Review*
for July 1888; and the other by Mr. F. W. H. Myers on " The
Disenchantment of France," in *The Nineteenth Century* for
May 1888. To quote only a sentence or two, M. Laveleye
remarks : " It seems as if humanity could not exist without
religion as a spiritual atmosphere, and we see that, as this
decreases, despair and Pessimism take hold of minds thus
deprived of solace. Madame Ackermann well expresses this
in some lines addressed to Faith, in which she writes—

> ' Eh bien, nous l'expulsons de tes divins royaumes,
>   Dominatrice ardente, et l'instant est venu ;
> Tu ne vas plus savoir où loger tes fantômes,
>   Nous fermons l'Inconnu !

---

[1] " Agnosticism," by Professor Huxley, in *Nineteenth Century*, Feb. 1889,
pp. 191, 192. Mr. Mallock, in his *Is Life Worth Living?* (pp. 128, 171, 172),
quotes other striking sentences of Professor Huxley's. " The lover of moral
beauty," he says, " struggling through a world of sorrow and sin, is surely as
much the stronger for believing that sooner or later a vision of perfect peace
and goodness will burst upon him, as the toiler up a mountain for the belief
that beyond crag and snow lie home and rest." And he adds that, could a
faith like this be placed on a firm basis, mankind would cling to it as " tenaciously as ever drowning sailor did to a hencoop."

Mais ton triumphateur expiera ta défaite,
L'homme déjà se trouble et, vainqueur éperdu,
Il se sent ruiné par sa propre conquête;
En te dépossédant nous avons tout perdu.
Nous restons sans espoir, sans recours, sans asile,
Tandis qu' obstinément le désir qu'on exile
Revient errer autour du gouffre défendu.'

"Incurable sadness takes hold of the man who has no hope of anything better than this life, short as it is, and overwhelmed with trials of all kinds, where iniquity triumphs if it have but force on its side, and where men risk their lives in disputes with each other for a place where there is too little space for all, and the means of subsistence are wholly insufficient. Some German colonies have been founded in America, in which all sorts of Divine worship are proscribed; those who have visited them describe the colonists, the women especially, as appearing exceedingly sad. Life with no hope in the future loses its savour." [1]

Mr. Myers's article on the progress of *disillusionment* in France, "to use the phrase of commonest recurrence in modern French literature and speech," is one, fitted to open many eyes as to the inevitable drift of unbelief to Pessimism. In 1788 France possessed illusions and nothing else,—"the reign of reason, the return to nature, the social contract, liberty, equality, fraternity,—the whole air of that wild time buzzed with new-hatched chimeras"; in 1888 France possesses everything except illusions; and the end is "the vague but general sense of *malaise* or decadence, which permeates so much of modern French literature and life," and of which abundant illustrations are given. Not the least striking of these is a passage from Emile Littré, the once enthusiastic Comtist, who likens his own final mood to that of the Trojan women who *pontum adspectabant flentes !* "Fit epigraph," says Mr. Myers, "for a race who have fallen from hope, on whose ears the waves' world-old message still murmurs without a meaning; while the familiar landmarks fall back into shadow, and there is nothing but the sea." [2]

These illustrations, which might be multiplied indefinitely,

---

[1] *Contemporary Review*, vol. xiv. p. 6. A large number of illustrations from French poetry may be seen in Caro's *Problèmes de Morale Sociale*, pp. 351–380. Cf. also the article next referred to on "The Disenchantment of France."

[2] *Nineteenth Century*, May 1888, p. 676.

sufficiently confirm the words of Mr. Sully in his work on Pessimism [1]: " I am keenly alive to the fact that our scheme of individual happiness, even when taken as including the good of others now living and to live, is no perfect substitute for the idea of eternal happiness presented in religion.   Nobody, I imagine, would seriously contend that the aims of our limited earthly existence, even when our imagination embraces genera- tions to follow us, are of so inspiring a character as the objects presented by religion. . . . Into the reality of these religious beliefs I do not here enter.   I would only say that if men are to abandon all hope of a future life, the loss, in point of cheering and sustaining influence, will be a vast one, and one not to be made good, so far as I can see, by any new idea of services to collective humanity."

---

[1] *Pessimism*, p. 317.

3
THE THEISTIC POSTULATE
OF THE CHRISTIAN VIEW

"For the invisible things of Him since the creation of the world are clearly seen, being perceived through the things that are made, even His everlasting power and Divinity, that they may be without excuse." —Paul

"Let us begin, then, by asking whether all this which they call the universe is left to the guidance of an irrational and random chance, or, on the contrary, as our fathers declared, is ordered and governed by a marvellous intelligence and wisdom." —Plato

"It is easy for the fool, especially the learned and scientific fool, to prove that there is no God, but, like the murmuring sea, which heeds not the scream of wandering birds, the soul of humanity murmurs for God, and confutes the erudite folly of the fool by disregarding it." —J. Service

"It is in the moments when we are best that we believe in God." —Renan

"Atheism is the most irrational form of theology." —Comte

"I have noticed, during my years of self-observation, that it is not in hours of clearness and vigor that this doctrine (Material Atheism) commends itself to my mind; that in the presence of stronger and healthier thought it ever dissolves and disappears, as affording no solution of the mystery in which we dwell, and of which we form a part." —Tyndall

3

THE THEISTIC POSTULATE
OF THE CHRISTIAN VIEW

In entering on the task of unfolding the Christian view of the world under its positive aspects, and of considering its relations to modern thought, I begin where religion itself begins, with the existence of God. Christianity is a theistic system; this is the first postulate—the personal, ethical, self-revealing God.

Volkmar has remarked that of monotheistic religions there are only three in the world—the Israelitish, the Christian, and the Mohammedan; and the last-named is derived from the other two. "So," he adds, "is the 'Israel of God' the one truly religious, the religiously-elect, people of antiquity; and ancient Israel remains for each worshipper of the one, therefore of the true God, who alone is worthy of the name, the classical people. . . . Christianity is the blossom and fruit of the true worship of God in Israel, which has become such for all mankind." [1] This limitation of Monotheism in religion to the peoples who have benefited by the Biblical teaching on this subject, suggests its origin from a higher than human source; and refutes the contention of those who would persuade us that the monotheistic idea is the result of a long process of development through which the race necessarily passes, beginning with Fetishism, or perhaps Ghost-worship, mounting to Polytheism, and ultimately subsuming the multitude of Divine powers under one all-controlling will. It will be time enough to accept this theory when, outside the line of the Biblical development, a single nation can be pointed to which has gone through these stages, and reached this goal. [2]

I should like further at the outset to direct attention to the

---

[1] *Jesus Nazarenus*, p. 5.
[2] See Note A.—Primitive Fetishism and Ghost-Worship.

fact that, in affirming the existence of God as Theism apprehends Him, we have already taken a great step into the supernatural, a step which should make many others easy. Many speak glibly of the denial of the supernatural, who never realise how much of the supernatural they have already admitted in affirming the existence of a personal, wise, holy, and beneficent Author of the universe. They may deny supernatural actions in the sense of miracles, but they have affirmed supernatural Being on a scale and in a degree which casts supernatural action quite into the shade. If God is a reality, the whole universe rests on a supernatural basis. A supernatural presence pervades it; a supernatural power sustains it; a supernatural will operates in its forces; a supernatural wisdom appoints its ends. The whole visible order of things rests on another,—an unseen, spiritual, supernatural order,—and is the symbol, the manifestation, the revelation of it. It is therefore only to be expected that the feeling should grow increasingly in the minds of thoughtful men, that if this supernatural basis of the universe is to be acknowledged, a great deal more must be admitted besides. On the other hand, if the opposition to the supernatural is to be carried out to its logical issue, it must not stop with the denial of miracle, but must extend to the whole theistic conception. This is the secret of the intimate connection which I showed in last Lecture to exist between the idea of God and the idea of Revelation. A genuine Theism can never long remain a bare Theism. At the height to which Christianity has raised our thoughts of God, it is becoming constantly more difficult for minds that reflect seriously to believe in a God who does not manifest Himself in word and deed. This is well brought out in a memorable conversation which Mr. Froude had with Mr. Carlyle in the last days of his life. "I once said to him," says Mr. Froude, "not long before his death, that I could only believe in a God which *did* something. With a cry of pain, which I shall never forget, he said, 'He does nothing.'"[1] This simply means that if we are to retain the idea of a living God, we must be in earnest with it. We must believe in a God who expresses Himself in living deeds in the history of mankind, who has a word and message for mankind, who, having the power and the will to bless man-

---

[1] See the whole passage in Froude's *Carlyle*, ii. pp. 258–263.

kind, does it. Theism, as I contended before, needs **Revelation** to complete it.

Here, accordingly, it is that the Christian view of God has its strength against any conception of God based on mere grounds of natural theology. It binds together, in the closest reciprocal relations, the two ideas of God and Revelation. The Christian doctrine, while including all that the word Theism ordinarily covers, is much more than a doctrine of simple Theism. God, in the Christian view, is a Being who enters into the history of the world in the most living way. He is not only actively present in the material universe,—ordering, guiding, controlling it,—but He enters also in the most direct way into the course of human history, working in it in His general and special providence, and by a gradual and progressive Revelation, which is, at the same time, practical discipline and education, giving to man that knowledge of Himself by which he is enabled to attain the highest ends of his own existence, and to co-operate freely in the carrying out of Divine ends; above all, discovering Himself as the God of Redemption, who, full of long-suffering and mercy, executes in loving deeds, and at infinite sacrifice, His gracious purpose for the salvation of mankind. The Christian view of God is thus bound up with all the remaining elements of the Christian system,—with the idea of Revelation in Christ, with a kingdom of God to be realised through Christ, with Redemption from sin in Christ,—and it is inseparable from them. It is through these elements—not in its abstract character as Theism—that it takes the hold it does on the living convictions of men, and is felt by them to be something real. If I undertake to defend Theism, it is not Theism in dissociation from Revelation, but Theism as completed in the entire Christian view.

It is scarcely necessary that I should prove that Christ's teaching about God embraces all the affirmations commonly understood to be implied in a complete Theism. Christ's doctrine of the Father is, indeed, entirely unmetaphysical. We meet with no terms such as absolute, infinite, unconditioned, first cause, etc., with which the student of philosophy is familiar. Yet all that these terms imply is undeniably recognised by Jesus in His teaching about God. He takes up into His teaching—as the apostles likewise do—all the natural truth about God; He takes up all the truth about God's being, character, perfections, and relations to the world and man, already given in the Old Testament. God, with Jesus, is unquestionably the sole and supreme source of existence; He by whom all things were created, and on whom all things depend; the Lord of heaven and earth, whose power and rule embrace the smallest as well as the greatest events of life; the Eternal One, who sees the end from the beginning, and whose vast counsels hold in their grasp the issues of all things. The attributes of God are similarly dealt with. They are never made by Christ the subject of formal discourse, are never treated of for their own sakes, or in their metaphysical relations. They come into view solely in their religious relations. Yet no one will dispute that all the attributes involved in the highest theistic conception—eternity, omnipotence, omnipresence, omniscience, and the like—are implied in His teaching. God, in Christ's view, is the all-wise, all-present, all-powerful Being, at once infinitely exalted above the world, and active in every part of it, from whose eyes, seeing in secret, nothing can be hid, laying His plans in eternity, and unerringly carrying them out. It is the peculiarity of Christ's teaching, however, that the natural attributes are always viewed in subordination to the moral. In respect of these, Christ's view of God resembles that of the Old Testament in its union of the two ideas of God's unapproachable majesty and elevation above the world as the infinitely Holy One; and of His condescending grace and continued action in history for the salvation and good of men. The two poles in the ethical perfection of God's character are with Him, as with the prophets of the old covenant, righteousness and love—the former embracing His truth, faithfulness, and justice; the latter His beneficence, compassion, long-suffering, and mercy. Ritschl, indeed, in his treatment of this subject, will recognise no attribute but love, and makes all the others, even the so-called physical attributes, but aspects of love. Righteousness, e.g., is but the self-consistency of God in carrying out His purposes of love, and connotes nothing judicial.[1] Righteousness, however, has its relatively independent place as an attribute of God in both Old and New Testaments, and cannot thus be set aside. It has reference to indefeasible

---

[1] Cf. his *Recht. und Ver.* ii. pp. 102–112.

distinctions of right and wrong—to moral norms, which even love must respect. Out of righteousness and love in the character of God, again, issues wrath — another idea which modern thought tries to weaken, but which unquestionably holds an important place in the view of God given us by Christ. By wrath is meant the intense moral displeasure with which God regards sin—His holy abhorrence of it—and the punitive energy of His nature which He puts forth against it. So regarded, it is not opposed to love, but, on the contrary, derives its chief intensity from the presence of love, and is a necessary element in the character of an ethically perfect Being.[1] While, however, Christ's teaching about the character of God is grounded on that of the Old Testament, yet in the purity and perfection with which He apprehends this ethical perfection of God,— above all, in the new light in which He places it by His trans- forming conception of the Divine Fatherhood, we feel that we are carried far beyond the stage of the Old Testament. God, as ethical Personality, is viewed by Christ, *first*, as in Him- self the absolutely Good One—"There is none good but one, that is, God";[2] *second*, as the perfect Archetype of goodness for man's imitation—"Be ye therefore perfect, even as your Father which is in heaven is perfect";[3] *third*, as the moral Will binding the universe together, and prescribing the law of conduct—"Thy will be done on earth, as it is in heaven";[4] but, *fourth*, pre-eminently as *the Father*. It is in the name Father, as expressive of a special loving and gracious relation to the individual members of His kingdom, that Christ's doc- trine of God specially sums itself up. The Old Testament knew God as the Father of the nation; Christ knew Him as the Father of the individual soul, begotten by Him to a new life, and standing to Him in a new moral and spiritual relation, as a member of the kingdom of His Son.

This, then, without further delineation in detail, is the first postulate of Christianity—a God living, personal, ethical, self- revealing, infinite. We have now to ask—How does this postu- late of the Christian view stand related to modern thought, and to the general religious consciousness of mankind? How far is

---

[1] Cf. on the Divine Wrath, Principal Simon, *The Redemption of Men*, ch. v.; Dale on *The Atonement*, Lecture VIII. ; *Lux Mundi*, pp. 285–289.
[2] Mark x. 18.   [3] Matt. v. 48.   [4] Matt. vi. 10.

it corroborated or negated by modern thought? What is the
nature of the corroboration, and what the worth of the negation? I shall consider the negation first.

I. Dogmatic Atheism has not so many advocates—at least in
this country—as at some former times; but, instead, we have a
wide prevalence of that new form of negation which is called
Agnosticism. I have already referred to this as one of the
alternatives to which the mind is driven in its denial of the
supernatural view of Christ's Person; but it is now necessary
to consider it on its own merits. The thought may occur that
this widespread phase of present-day unbelief is not properly
described as "negation," seeing that all it affirms is, that it
"does not know." It does not say, "There is no God," but only
that it does not know that there is one. Its ground is that of
ignorance, lack of evidence, suspense of judgment—not positive
denial. This plea, however, is on various grounds inadmissible.
It is certainly not the case that thorough-going, reasoned-out
Agnosticism, as we have it, for example, in the works of Mr.
Spencer, is simply the modest assertion that it does not know
whether there is a God or not. It is the dogmatic affirmation,
based on an examination of the nature and limits of human
intelligence, that God—or, in Mr. Spencer's phrase, the Power
which manifests itself in consciousness and in the outward
universe—is unknowable.[1] But in all its forms, even the
mildest, Agnosticism is entitled to be regarded as a negation of
the Christian view, for two reasons. *First*, in affirming that
God is not, or cannot be, known, it directly negates, not only
the truths of God's natural Revelation, which Christianity pre-

---

[1] Prof. Huxley, the inventor of the term, has given us *his* explanation of it.
"Agnosticism," he says, "in fact, is not a creed but a method, the essence
of which lies in the rigorous application of a single principle. . . . Positively,
the principle may be thus expressed: in matters of the intellect, follow your
reason as far as it will take you, without regard to any other consideration.
And, negatively, in matters of the intellect, do not pretend that conclusions
are certain which are not demonstrated or demonstrable. That I take to be
the Agnostic faith, which, if a man keep whole and undefiled, he shall not be
ashamed to look the universe in the face, whatever the future may have in store
for him."—"Agnosticism," in *Nineteenth Century*, Feb. 1889. This, however,
is evidently not a "faith" but, as he says, a "method," which in its application may yield positive or negative results, as the case may be. Behind it, at
the same time, lies, in his case, the conviction that real answers to the greater
questions of religion are "not merely actually impossible, but theoretically
inconceivable."—*Ibid.* p. 182.

supposes, but the specific Christian assertion that God can be and is known through the series of His historical Revelations, and supremely through His Son Jesus Christ. "The only begotten Son, which is in the bosom of the Father, He hath declared Him." [1] And, *second*, if God exists, it is impossible in the nature of things that there should not be evidence of His existence, and therefore the denial of such evidence is actually tantamount to the denial of His existence. Why do I say this? It is because the truth about God differs from every other truth in just this respect, that if it is truth it must be capable of a certain measure of rational demonstration. For God is not simply one Being among others. He is the necessary Being. He is the Being whose existence is necessarily involved in the existence of every other being. The whole universe, ourselves as part of it, stands in a relation of necessary dependence upon Him. God, therefore, is unlike every other being our thought can take account of. Other beings may exist, and we may have no evidence of their existence. But it is rationally inconceivable that such an all-comprehending Reality as we call God should exist, and that through Him the whole material and spiritual universe should come into being, and yet no trace be found connecting this universe with its Author—so vast an effect with its cause. If even man, for however short a space of time, sets foot on an uninhabited island, we expect, if we visit his retreat, to find some traces of his occupation. How much more, if this universe owes its existence to infinite wisdom and power, if God is unceasingly present and active in every part of it, must we expect to find evidence of the fact? Therefore, I say that denial of all evidence for God's existence is equivalent to the affirmation that there is no God. If God is, thought must be able, nay, is compelled, to take account of His existence. It must explore the relations in which He stands to us and to the world. An obligation rests on it to do so. To think of God is a duty of love, but it is also a task of science.

Mr. Spencer is so far in agreement with the views just expressed, that he maintains that our thought is compelled to posit the existence of an absolute Being as the ground and cause of the universe, though of the nature of this ultimate reality he holds that we can form no conception. The reason given is,

[1] John i. 18.

that our minds, being finite and conditioned in their thinking, cannot form a conception of an existence which lies outside these conditions.[1] The question, however, is pertinent—If the mind is thus hemmed up within the limits of its finitude, how does it get to know even that an Absolute exists? Or if we can so far transcend the limits of our thought as to know that the Absolute exists—which is a disproof of the position that thought is restricted wholly to the finite—why may we not also have some knowledge of its nature? It is not difficult to show that, in his endeavours to extricate himself from these difficulties, Mr. Spencer involves himself in a mass of self-contradictions. He tells us, *e.g.*, in every variety of phrase, that we cannot know the Absolute, but almost in the same breath he tells us that we have an idea of the Absolute which our minds are compelled to form,[2]—that it is a *positive*, and not, as Sir William Hamilton and Mr. Mansel held, a merely *negative* conception,[3]—nay, that we have not only a conception, but a direct and immediate consciousness of this Absolute, blending itself with all our thoughts and feelings, and recognisable by us as such.[4] Again, if we ask, What is meant by the Absolute? it is defined as that which exists out of all relations, and for this reason the possibility of a knowledge of it is denied.[5] But if we inquire further what ground we have for affirming the existence of such an Absolute, existing out of all relations, we find that the only ground alleged is the knowledge we have of it as standing *in* relations.[6] For this, which Mr. Spencer names the

---

[1] Cf. *First Principles*, pp. 74, 75, 110.   [2] *First Principles*, p. 88.

[3] *First Principles*, pp. 87–92. "Still more manifest," he says, "will this truth become when it is observed that our conception of the Relative itself disappears, if our conception of the Absolute is a pure negation. . . . What, then, becomes of the assertion that 'the Absolute is conceived merely by a negation of conceivability,' or as 'the mere absence of the conditions under which consciousness is possible'? If the Non-relative or Absolute is present in thought only as a mere negation, then the relation between it and the Relative becomes unthinkable, because one of the terms of the relation is absent from consciousness. And if this relation is unthinkable, then is the Relative itself unthinkable, for want of its antithesis ; whence results the disappearance of all thought whatever."—P. 91.

[4] *First Principles*, pp. 89, 91, 94–97. Cf. *Nineteenth Century*, July 1884, p. 24.

[5] *First Principles*, pp. 78, 79, 81. This is qualified in other places by such phrases as "possible existence out of all relation" (Mansel), and "of which no necessary relation can be predicted," pp. 39, 81. But this qualification seems unnecessary, for it is only as out of relation that by definition it is the Absolute.

[6] Even in the passage above quoted, we have the *contradictio in adjecto* of "the relation between it (*i.e.* the Non-Relative) and the Relative."—P. 91.

Absolute, is simply the Infinite Power which he elsewhere tells us manifests itself in all that is—in nature and in consciousness—and is a constituent element in every idea we can form. The Absolute, therefore, stands in relation to both matter and mind—has, so far as we can see, its very nature in that relation. It is not, it turns out, a Being which exists out of all relations, but rather, like the Christian God, a self-revealing Power, manifesting itself, if not directly yet indirectly, in its workings in the worlds of matter and of mind. How strange to speak of a Power thus continually manifesting itself in innumerable ways, the consciousness of which, on Mr. Spencer's own showing,[1] constantly wells up within us, as absolutely unknown or unknowable!

But, after all, as we by and by discover, this Inscrutable Power of Mr. Spencer's is *not* absolutely unknowable. It soon becomes apparent that there are quite a number of affirmations we are able to make regarding it, some of them almost of a theistic character. They are made, I admit, generally under a kind of protest,[2] yet it is difficult to see why, if they are not seriously meant—if they do not convey some modicum of knowledge—they should be made at all. According to Mr. Spencer, this ultimate reality is a Power: it is a force, the nearest analogue to which is our own will;[3] it is infinite, it is eternal, it is omnipresent;[4] it is an infinite and eternal Energy from which all things proceed;[5] it is the Cause of the universe, standing to it in a relation similar to that of the creative power of the Christian conception.[6] Numerous other statements might be quoted all more or less implying knowledge,

---

[1] *Eccles. Instit.* p. 839. [2] E.g. *Eccles. Instit.* p. 843.

[3] *First Principles*, p. 189 ; cf. *Eccles. Instit.* p. 843.

[4] *First Principles*, p. 99.

[5] *Eccles. Instit.* p. 843. "But one truth," he says, "must grow ever clearer —the truth that there is an Inscrutable Existence everywhere manifested, to which he can neither find nor conceive either beginning or end. Amid the mysteries which become the more mysterious the more they are thought about, there will remain the one absolute certainty that he is ever in presence of one Infinite and Eternal Energy, from which all things proceed."

[6] "I held at the outset, and continue to hold, that this Inscrutable Existence which science, in the last resort, is compelled to recognise as unreached by its deepest analysis of matter, motion, thought, and feeling, stands towards our general conception of things in substantially the same relation as does the Creative Power asserted by Theology."—*Nineteenth Century*, July 1884, p. 24. Mr. Spencer tells us that the words quoted in the last note were originally written—"one Infinite and Eternal Energy by which all things are created and sustained."—*Ibid.* p. 4.

—as, *e.g.*, that "the Power manifested throughout the Universe
distinguished as material, is the same Power which in ourselves
wells up under the form of consciousness"; while the "necessity we are under to think of the external energy in terms of
the internal energy gives rather a spiritualistic than a materialistic aspect to the Universe."[1]   This, I take leave to say, so
far from being Agnosticism, would more correctly be described
as a qualified Gnosticism.[2]   Mr. Spencer's so-called Agnosticism
is not an agnostic system at all, but a system of non-material
or semi-spiritual Pantheism.   If we know all that these statements imply about the Absolute, there is no bar in principle to
our knowing a great deal more.   A significant proof of this is
the development which the system has received in the hands of
one of Mr. Spencer's disciples, Mr. Fiske, who in his *Cosmic
Philosophy*, and still more in his book on *The Idea of God*, has
wrought it out into a kind of Theism.   He discards the term
"Unknowable," and writes : "It is enough to remind the reader
that Deity is unknowable, just in so far as it is not manifested
to consciousness through the phenomenal world ; knowable, just
in so far as it is thus manifested ; unknowable, in so far as
infinite and absolute ; knowable, in the order of its phenomenal
manifestations ; knowable, in a symbolic way, as the Power
which is disclosed in every throb of the mighty rhythmic life of
the universe ; knowable, as the eternal Source of a Moral Law,
which is implicated with each action of our lives, and in
obedience to which lies our only guaranty of the happiness
which is incorruptible, and which neither inevitable misfortune
nor unmerited obloquy can take away.   Thus, though we may
not by searching find out God, though we may not compass

---

[1] *Eccles. Instit.* pp. 839, 841.

[2] Mr. Spencer, when pressed in controversy by Mr. Harrison, takes great
pains to show how *positive* his conception of the "Unknowable" is.   He is
astonished that his opponent should assert that "none of the positive attributes
which have ever been predicated of God can be used of this Energy"; maintains
that, instead of being an Everlasting No, Agnosticism is "an Everlasting
Yea"; denies that Agnosticism is "anything more than silent with respect to
personality," seeing that "duty requires us neither to affirm nor deny personality"; holds that the Unknowable is not an "All-nothingness" but the "All-
Being," reiterates that this Reality "stands towards the universe and towards
ourselves in the same relation as an anthropomorphic Creator was supposed to
stand," and "bears a like relation with it not only to human thought, but to
human feeling," etc.—*Nineteenth Century*, July 1884, pp. 5–7, 25.   Mr.
Harrison has no difficulty in showing in what contradictions Mr. Spencer
entangles himself by the use of such language.—*Ibid.* Sept., pp. 358, 359.

infinitude, or attain to absolute knowledge, we may at least know all that it concerns us to know, as intelligent and responsible beings."[1]

It has not been left for Mr. Spencer to discover that, in the depths of His absolute Being, as well as in the plenitude of the modes of His revealed Being, there is that in God which must always pass our comprehension,—that in the present state of existence it is only very dimly and distantly, and by large use of "symbolic conceptions," that we can approximate to a right knowledge of God. This is affirmed in the Bible quite as strongly as it is by the agnostic philosophers. "Canst thou by searching find out God?"[2] "O the depth of the riches, both of the wisdom and knowledge of God! how unsearchable are His judgments, and His ways past finding out!"[3] "Now I know in part."[4] In this sense we can speak of a Christian Agnosticism.[5] This incomprehensibility, however, is held in Scripture to arise, not from any inherent or incurable defect in the human faculties, but simply from the vastness of the object, in the knowledge of which, nevertheless, the mind may continually be growing. The universe itself in its immeasurable extent vastly transcends our present powers of knowledge; how much more the Author of the universe? This, accordingly, is not the point we have in dispute with Mr. Spencer. The point is not whether, in the depths of His absolute existence, there is much in God that must remain unknown to us; but whether He cannot be known by us in His revealed relations to ourselves, and to the world of which we form a part; whether these relations are not also in their measure a true expression of His nature and character, so that through them we come to know *something* of Him, even of His absolute Being—though we cannot know all? When, now, the Agnostic tells us that knowledge of this kind is impossible to us, see in what contradiction he lands himself. Here is a man who says, "I know nothing of God; He is absolutely beyond my ken; I cannot form the faintest conception of what He is." And yet he

---

[1] *Cosmic Philosophy*, ii. p. 470; *Idea of God*, Pref. p. 28.

[2] Job xi. 7.   [3] Rom. xi. 33.   [4] 1 Cor. xiii. 12.

[5] "God," says Augustine, "is more truly thought than He is uttered, and exists more truly than He is thought."—*De Trinitate*, Book vii. ch. 4. "Not the definitely known God," says Professor Veitch, "not the unknown God, is our last word, far less the unknowable God, but the ever-to-be-known God."—*Knowing and Being*, p. 323.

knows so much about God as to be able to say beforehand that
He cannot possibly enter into relations with human beings by
which He might become known to them.   This is a proposition
of which the Agnostic, on his own showing, can never have
any evidence.   If God is unknowable, how can we know this
much about Him—that He cannot in any mode or form enter
into relations with us by which He might be known?   Only on
one supposition can this be maintained.   If, indeed, as Mr.
Spencer thinks, the nature of God and the intelligence of man
are two things absolutely disparate—if, as Spinoza said, to
speak of God taking on Him the nature of man is as absurd as
to speak of a circle taking on it the nature of the square,[1]—then
not only is God unknowable, but the whole Christian system is
a priori ruled out of consideration.   This, however, is a proposition which can never be proved, and we have seen that the
attempt to prove and work with it only entangled Mr. Spencer
in a mass of difficulties.   There is really, on his own principles,
no reason why he should not admit the possibility of a relative
knowledge of God, as true in its way as the knowledge which
we have of space, time, matter, force, or cause,—all which
notions, as well as that of the Absolute, he tells us are prolific
of intellectual contradictions.[2]   Why, for instance, should we
more hesitate to speak of God as Intelligence than to speak of
Him as Power; why shrink from attributing to Him the attribute of Personality any more than that of Cause?[3]   The whole
objection, therefore, falls to the ground with the intellectual
theory on which it is founded.   For once grant that the nature
of God and the intelligence of man are not thus foreign to each
other, as Spencer supposes; grant that man is made in the
image of God, and bears in some measure His likeness—then
man's mind is *not* wholly shut up within the limits of the finite
—there is an absolute element in it, kindred with the absolute
reason of God, and real knowledge both of God and of the nature
of things without us is possible.

II. The *a priori* bar with which Agnosticism would block
the way to the knowledge of God being thus removed, we may

---

[1] Letter to Oldenburg, *Epist.* xxi.   [2] *First Principles*, pp. 159–171.
[3] Cf. Fiske, *Idea of God*, Pref. p. 15; and Chapman's *Pre-Organic Evolution*, p. 254.

proceed to inquire how it stands with the theistic postulate of the Christian view, in respect of the positive evidence in its behalf. It has been shown that, if the Christian view be true, it must, up to a certain point, admit of verification by reason. The doctrine of God's existence must be shown to be in accord with reason, and to be in harmony with and corroborated by the facts of science and of the religious history of mankind. Science, indeed, has not for its object the determination of anything supernatural. Yet in its inquiries — dealing as it does with laws and forces, and with the widest generalisations of experience — it must come to a point at which the questions with which religion and philosophy deal are forced upon it, and it has to take up some attitude to them. The facts which it brings to light, the interpretations which it gives of these facts, cannot but have some bearing on the hypotheses we form as to the ultimate cause of existence. If it does not cross the borderland, it at least brings us within sight of truths which do not lie within its proper sphere, and points the way to their acceptance.

1. I may begin with certain things in regard to which it is possible to claim a large measure of agreement. And—

(1) It may be assumed with little fear of contradiction, that if the idea of God is to be entertained, it can only be in the form of *Monotheism*. The Agnostic will grant us this much. Whatever the power is which works in the universe, it is one. "As for Polytheism," says a writer in *Lux Mundi*, "it has ceased to exist in the civilised world. Every theist is, by a rational necessity, a monotheist."[1] The Christian assumption of the unity and absoluteness of God — of the dependence of the created universe upon Him—is thus confirmed. It is to be remembered that this truth, preached as a last result of science and of the philosophy of evolution, is a first truth of the Biblical religion. It is the Bible, and the Bible alone, which has made Monotheism the possession of the

---

[1] *Lux Mundi*, p. 59. J. S. Mill has said: "The reason, then, why Monotheism may be accepted as the representative of Theism in the abstract is not so much because it is the Theism of all the more improved portions of the human race, as because it is the only Theism which can claim for itself any footing on a scientific ground. Every other theory of the government of the universe by supernatural beings is inconsistent either with the carrying on of that government through a continual series of natural antecedents, according to fixed laws, or with the interdependence of each of these series upon all the rest, which are two of the most general results of science."—*Three Essays on Religion*, p. 133.

world. The unity of God was declared on the soil of Israel
long before science or philosophy had the means of declaring
it.[1] Through Christianity it has been made the possession of
mankind. On the soil of paganism we see reason struggling
towards this idea, striking out partial glimpses of it, sometimes
making wonderful approximations to it, but never in its own
strength lifting itself clear away from Polytheism to the pure
conception of the one spiritual God, such as we find it in
Christianity, still less making this the foundation of a religion
It is through Christianity, not through philosophical speculation, that this truth has become the support of faith, a light
to which the investigations of science themselves owe much, and
a sustaining principle and power in the lives of men.[2]

(2) This Power which the evolutionist requires us to recognise as the origin of all things is the source of *a rational order.*
This is a second fact about which there can be no dispute.
There is a rational order and connection of things in the universe. Science is not only the means by which our knowledge
of this order is extended, but it is itself a standing proof of the
existence of this order. Science can only exist on the assumption that the world is not chaos, but cosmos—that there is
unity, order, law, in it—that it is a coherent and consistent
whole of things, construable through our intelligence, and
capable of being expressed in forms of human speech. And
the more carefully we examine the universe, we find that this
is really its character. It is an harmonious universe. There
is orderly sequence in it. There is orderly connection of part
and part. There is that determinable connection we call
law. There is the harmonious adjustment of means to
ends, which again are embraced in higher ends, till, in
the nobler systems, the teleological idea is extended to the
whole system.[3] In many ways does Mr. Spencer express in
his writings his trust that this Power of which he speaks—
inscrutable as he proclaims it to be—may be depended on not

---

[1] See Note B.—Old Testament Monotheism.

[2] Cf. Naville's *Modern Physics*—" The Philosophy of the Founders of Modern
Physics," pp. 154–243 (Eng. trans.); Fairbairn's *Studies in the Phil. of Rel.
and Hist.*—" Theism and Scientific Speculation," pp. 66–71; and an article
by Dr. Alex. Mair, on " The Contribution of Christianity to Science," in *Presbyterian Review*, Jan. 1888.

[3] So Mr. Spencer speaks of " the naturally-revealed end towards which the
Power manifested throughout Evolution works."—*Data of Ethics*, p. 171.

to put him, as the authors of the "Unseen Universe" phrase it, "to intellectual confusion."[1]   To give only one instance—he bids the man who has some highest truth to speak, not to be afraid to speak it out, on the ground that "it is not for nothing that he has in him these sympathies with some principles, and repugnance to others. . . . He, like every other man," he says, "may properly consider himself as one of the myriad agencies through whom works the Unknown Cause; and when the Unknown Cause produces in him a certain belief, he is thereby authorised to profess and act out that belief.   For to render in their highest sense the words of the poet—

> ' Nature is made better by no mean,
> But Nature makes that mean; o'er that art
> Which you say adds to Nature, is an art
> Which Nature makes.'

Not as adventitious, therefore, will the wise man regard the faith that is in him."[2]   Who does not see in these remarkable sentences that, notwithstanding his reiteration of the words "Unknown Cause," "Unknowable," Mr. Spencer's latent faith is that this Power which works in the world and in men is a Power working according to rational laws and for rational ends —is on this account an object of trust—we might almost add, a source of inspiration?   But now, if this is so, can the conclusion be avoided that the Power on which we thus depend rationally is itself rational?   It is knowable at least thus far, that we know that it is the source of a rational order—of an order construable through our intelligence.   If now it is asserted that the source of this rational order is not itself rational, surely the proof rests, not on him who affirms, but on him who denies.[3] If Mr. Spencer replies, as he does reply, that it is an "erroneous assumption that the choice is between personality and something lower than personality, whereas the choice is rather between personality and something higher," and asks—"Is it not just possible that there is a mode of being as much transcending intelligence and will, as these transcend mechanical motion?"[4]—the answer (not to dwell on the utterly disparate character of the things compared) is ready—this higher mode of being cannot at least be *less* than conscious.   It may be a

---

[1] *Unseen Universe*, 5th ed., p. 88.   [2] *First Principles*, p. 123.
[3] Cf. Chapman's *Pre-Organic Evolution*, pp. 226, 227, 251, 282.
[4] *First Principles*, p. 109

higher kind of consciousness, but it cannot be higher than consciousness. Nor is there the slightest ground for the assumption
that there *can* be anything higher than self-conscious intelligence
or reason.[1] If we find in the universe an order congruous to
the reason we have in ourselves, this is warranty sufficient for
believing, till the contrary is proved, that the Power which
gives rise to this order is not only Power, but Intelligence and
Wisdom as well.

(3) Again, this Power which the evolutionist compels us to
recognise is the source of *a moral order*. Butler, in his *Analogy*,
undertook to prove that the constitution and course of things are
on the side of virtue. His argument is sometimes spoken of as
obsolete, but it is not so much obsolete as simply transformed.
It is a new-fashioned phrase which Matthew Arnold uses when
he speaks of a "Power not ourselves that makes for righteousness," but it means just what Butler meant, that the make and
constitution of things in the universe are for righteousness, and
not for its opposite. Righteous conduct works out good results
for the individual and for society; vicious conduct works out
bad results. But what I wish to point out at present is the new
support which this view receives from the theory of agnostic
evolution, which is supposed by many to overthrow it. No
philosophy, which aims at completeness, can avoid the obligation
resting on it of showing that it is capable of yielding a coherent
theory of human life. The construction of a system of ethics,
therefore, Mr. Spencer justly regards as that part of his work to
which all the other parts are subsidiary. The theological basis
of ethics is rejected; utilitarianism also is set aside as inadequate;
and in room of these the attempt is made to establish the rules
of right conduct on a scientific basis by deducing them from the
general laws of evolution. You find a Power evolving itself in
the universe. Study, says Mr. Spencer, the laws of its evolution: find "the naturally revealed end towards which the Power
manifested throughout evolution works"; then, "since evolution has been, and is still, working towards the highest life, it

---

[1] Prof. Seth has justly said: "Nothing can be more certain than that all
philosophical explanation must be explanation of the lower by the higher, and
not *vice versâ*; and if self-consciousness is the highest fact we know, then we are
justified in using the conception of self-consciousness as our best key to the
ultimate nature of existence as a whole."—*Hegelianism and Personality*,
p. 89.

follows that conforming to these principles by which the higher
life is achieved, is furthering that end."[1]   And when a system
is constructed on this basis, what is the result?   Why, that we
are simply back to the old morality—to what Mr. Spencer himself calls "a rationalised version of the ethical principles" of the
current creed.[2]   The ethical laws which are deduced from the
observations of the laws of evolution are identical with those
which Christian ethics and the natural conscience of man in the
higher stages of its development have always recognised.[3]
What is the inference?   These principles were not originally
gained by scientific induction.   They were the expressions of
the natural consciousness of mankind as to distinctions of right
and wrong, or were promulgated by teachers who claimed to
have received them from a higher source.   In either case, they
were recognised by man as principles independently affirmed by
conscience to be right.   And now that the process of evolution
comes to be scientifically studied, we are told that the principles
of conduct yielded by it, in light of the end to which evolution
naturally works, absolutely coincide with those which spring
from this "work of the law" written in men's hearts.   What
else can we conclude, assuming that the evolutionist is right in
his deduction, but that the universe is constructed in harmony
with right ; that the laws which we have already recognised as
of binding authority in conscience are also laws of the objective
world ; that the principles of right discovered in conscience, and
the moral order of society based on these principles, are productions of the óne great evolutionary cause, which is the Force
impelling and controlling the whole onward movement of
humanity?   There is certainly nothing here to conflict with,
but everything to support the view that the Power which is
above all, and through all, and in all things, is not only Intelligence and Wisdom, but also an Ethical Will.   At least, to
most persons who dispassionately study the subject, I think it
will appear reasonable that a Power which has an ethical end
must be an ethical Power.   If, further, this ethical end embraces,
as Mr. Spencer seems to believe, the highest perfection and
happiness of man,[4] it is still more difficult to conceive how it

---

[1] *Data of Ethics*, p. 171.   [2] *Data of Ethics*, p. 257.
[3] Cf. article by Professor Laidlaw on "Modern Thought in relation to
Christianity and the Christian Church," *Presbyterian Review*, 1885. p. 618.
[4] *Data of Ethics*, pp. 253–257.

should have a place in the nature of things unless the Supreme
Power were itself benevolent and good. It is not, it should
be remembered, as if this ethical end were an after-thought
or accident. It is, according to the theory, the final and
supreme goal to which the whole process of evolution for countless millenniums has been working up, and only when it is
reached will the ripest fruit of the whole development be
gathered. But how is this possible, except on a teleological
view of things; and what teleology can yield a moral result
which does not postulate at the other end a moral cause? Mr.
Spencer may deprecate as he will the imposing of moral ideas
generated in our consciousness upon the Infinite which transcends consciousness. But it is only his own arbitrary denial of
consciousness to the Absolute, and his arbitrary assumption that
there can be no kindredship between that absolute consciousness and our own, which prevents him from drawing the natural
conclusion from his own premises. But if to Mr. Spencer's
definition of the Absolute, as "an Infinite and Eternal Energy
from which all things proceed," we add, as I think we are
entitled to do, the predicates of infinite Intelligence and of
Wisdom, and of Ethical Will, we have all the fundamental
theistic positions affirmed.

If the First Cause of the universe is proved by its manifestations to be at once rational Intelligence and Ethical Will, there
should be no excess of scrupulosity in applying to it the term
"Personal." I have thus far reasoned on the assumptions of
Mr. Spencer, and have spoken of his Ultimate Reality as he
does himself, as "Power," "Force," "Cause," etc. But I cannot leave this part of the subject without remarking that Mr.
Spencer is far from having the field of thought all to himself on
this question of the nature of the Ultimate Existence. It was
shown in last Lecture how, starting from a different point of
view, the higher philosophy of the century—the Neo-Kantian
and Neo-Hegelian—reaches, with a very large degree of certainty,
the conclusion that the ultimate principle of the universe must
be self-conscious. It is well known that the Personality of God
was a point left in very great doubt in the system of Hegel.[1]

---

[1] On this ambiguity in Hegel's doctrine, see Prof. Seth, *Hegelianism and
Personality*, Lect. V.; and the criticism in Dorner, *Person of Christ*, v. pp
147–162 (Eng. trans.).

God was conceived of as the Absolute Reason, but the drift of the system seemed to point rather to an impersonal Reason which first becomes conscious of itself in man, than to a self-consciousness complete and perfect from the beginning. Whatever its other defects, the later Hegelianism has shaken itself clear of this ambiguity, and affirms with emphasis that the principle at the basis of the universe is self-conscious.[1] The other line of development—the Neo-Kantian—is, in the person of its chief representative, Hermann Lotze, explicitly theistic. I only notice here, that after a careful discussion of all the arguments against ascribing Personality to the Divine Being, on the ground that personality implies the limitation of the finite, Lotze arrives at this conclusion, diametrically the opposite of Mr. Spencer's—"Perfect personality is reconcilable only with the conception of an infinite Being; for finite beings only an approximation to this is attainable."[2] It is interesting, further, to notice that even Neo-Spencerianism—if I may coin such a term—has come round, in the person of Mr. Fiske, to a similar affirmation. "The final conclusion," he says, "is, that we must not say that 'God is Force,' since such a phrase inevitably calls up those pantheistic notions of blind necessity, which it is my express desire to avoid; but always bearing in mind the symbolic character of the words, we may say that 'God is Spirit.' How my belief in the personality of God could be more strongly affirmed without entirely deserting the language of modern philosophy and taking refuge in pure mythology, I am unable to see."[3]

2. It is now necessary to come to closer quarters, and to ask whether the ordinary proofs for the existence of God, which have been so much assailed since the time of Kant, still retain their old cogency, and if not, what modifications require to be made on them. The time-honoured division of these proofs—which have recently received so able a re-handling at the

---

[1] See Lecture II. p. 59. The Neo-Hegelian theory, however, is far from satisfactory from the point of view of Theism in other respects.

[2] *Outlines of the Phil. of Religion,* p. 69 (Eng. trans.). See the whole discussion (chap. iv.), and the fuller treatment in the *Microcosmus,* ii. pp. 659–688. Lotze's closing words in the latter are: "Perfect Personality is in God only, to all finite minds there is allotted but a pale copy thereof; the finiteness of the finite is not a producing condition of this Personality, but a limit and a hindrance to its development." Cf. Ritschl, *Recht. und Ver.* iii. pp. 220 ff.

[3] *Idea of God,* p. 117. Cf. the instructive treatment of this subject of Personality in Professor Iverach's *Is God Knowable?* pp. 7, 12–37, 223, 233.

instance of Dr. Hutchison Stirling in his "Gifford Lectures"—
is into the cosmological, the teleological, and the ontological, to
which, as belonging to another category, falls to be added the
moral.   Besides these, Kant thinks, there are no others.[1] This,
however, must be taken with qualification, if the remark is
meant to apply to the old scholastic forms in which these proofs
have customarily been put.   Not only is there no necessity for
the proofs being confined to these forms—some of which are
clearly inadequate—but they are capable of many extensions,
and even transformations, as the result of advancing knowledge,
and of the better insight of reason into its own nature.   I may
add that I do not attach much importance in this connection to
objections to these proofs drawn from Kant's peculiar theory of
knowledge.[2] If it can be shown that in the exercise of our
reason as directed on the world in which we live—or on its own
nature—we are compelled either to cease to think, or to think
in a particular way,—if we find that these necessities of thought
are not peculiar to individuals here and there, but have been
felt by the soundest thinkers in all ages, and among peoples
widely separated from each other,—we may be justified in
believing that our reason is not altogether an untrustworthy
guide, but may be depended on with considerable confidence to
direct us to the truth.

Neither shall I waste time at this stage by discussing in what
sense it is permissible to speak of "proof" of so transcendent a
reality as the Divine existence.   We remember here the saying
of Jacobi, that a God capable of proof would be no God at all;
since this would mean that there is something higher than God
from which His existence can be deduced.   But this applies
only to the ordinary reasoning of the deductive logic.   It does
not apply to that higher kind of proof which may be said to
consist in the mind being guided back to the clear recognition
of its own ultimate pre-suppositions.   Proof in Theism certainly
does not consist in deducing God's existence as a lower from a
higher; but rather in showing that God's existence is itself the
last postulate of reason—the ultimate basis on which all other
knowledge, all other belief rests.   What we mean by proof of

---

[1] *Kritik d. r. Vernunft*, p. 416 (Eng. trans. p. 363).
[2] See an acute criticism of Kant's Theory of Knowledge in Stählin's *Kant,
Lotze, und Ritschl*, pp. 6–83 (Eng. trans.).

God's existence is simply that there are necessary acts of thought by which we rise from the finite to the infinite, from the caused to the uncaused, from the contingent to the necessary, from the reason involved in the structure of the universe to a universal and eternal Reason, which is the ground of all, from morality in conscience to a moral Lawgiver and Judge. In this connection the three theoretical proofs constitute an inseparable unity—"constitute together," as Dr. Stirling finely declares, "but the three undulations of a single wave, which wave is but a natural rise and ascent to God, on the part of man's own thought, with man's own experience and consciousness as the object before him." [1]

(1) Adopting the usual arrangement, I speak first of the *cosmological* proof, which, from the contingency and mutability of the world,—from its finite, dependent, changeful, multiple character,—concludes to an infinite and necessary Being as its ground and cause. That this movement of thought is necessary is shown by the whole history of philosophy and religion. Kant, who subjects the argument to a severe criticism, nevertheless admits—" It is something very remarkable that, on the supposition that something exists, I cannot avoid the inference that something exists necessarily." [2] The question then arises —Is the world this necessary Being? The cosmological proof on its various sides is directed to showing that it is not,—that it is not sufficient for its own explanation,—that, therefore, it must have its ground and origin in some other being that *is* necessary. Whatever exists has either the reason of its existence in itself, or has it in something else. But that the world has not the reason of its existence in itself—is not, in Spinoza's phrase, *causa sui*, is not a necessarily existing being—is shown in various ways.

i. *By the contingency of its existence.*—A necessary Being as Kant himself defines it, is one the necessity of whose existence is given through its possibility, *i.e.* the non-existence of which cannot be thought of as possible.[3] But the world is

---

[1] *Philosophy and Theology*, p. 45. On the theistic proofs generally, and Kant's criticism of them, cf. Dr. J. Caird's *Philosophy of Religion*, pp. 133–159; Prof. E. Caird's *Philosophy of Kant*, ii. pp. 102–129 ; and Dr. Stirling's work cited above.

[2] *Kritik*, p. 431 (Eng. trans. p. 378). See Note C.—Kant on the Cosmological Argument.

[3] *Kritik*, p. 102 (Eng. trans. p. 68).

not an existence of this character. We can think of *its* non-existence without contradiction—as, *e.g.*, we cannot think of the non-existence of space and time. We think away all the contents of space and time, but we cannot think away space and time themselves.

ii. *By the dependency of its several parts.* — It is made up of finite parts, each of which is dependent on the others, and sustains definite relations to them; its parts, therefore, have not the character of self-subsistence. But a world made up of parts, none of which is self-subsistent, cannot as a whole be self-subsistent, or the necessary Being.[1]

iii. *By its temporal succession of effects.* — The world is in constant flux and change. Causes give birth to effects, and effects depend on causes. Each state into which it passes has determining conditions in some immediately preceding state. This fact, apart from the general proof of contingency, suggests the need of conceiving not only of a necessary ground, but likewise of a First Cause of the universe. The alternative supposition is that of an eternal series of causes and effects—a conception which is unthinkable, and affords no resting-place for reason. What can be more self-contradictory than the hypothesis of a chain of causes and effects, each link of which hangs on a preceding link, while yet the whole chain hangs on nothing?[2] Reason, therefore, itself points us to the need of a First Cause of the universe, who is at the same time a self-existing, necessary, infinite Being.

It is, since Kant's time, customarily made an objection to this argument, that it only takes us as far as some necessary being—it does not show us in the least degree what kind of a being this is—whether, *e.g.*, in the world or out of it, whether the world-soul of the Stoics, the pantheistic substance of Spinoza, the impersonal reason of Hegel, or the personal God of the theist. This may be, and therefore the cosmological

---

[1] Cf. Dr. Stirling, in *Phil. and Theol.* p. 126.

[2] Dr. Stirling says, replying to Hume: "No multiplication of parts will make a whole potent if each part is impotent. You will hardly reach a valid conclusion where your every step is invalid. . . . It will be vain to extract one necessity out of a whole infinitude of contingencies. Nor is it at all possible for such infinitude of contingencies to be even conceivable by reason. If each link of the chain hangs on another, the whole will *hang*, and only *hang*, even in eternity, unsupported, like some stark serpent, unless you find a hook for it. Add weakness to weakness, in any quantity, you will never make strength."—*Phil. and Theol.* p. 262.

argument may need the other arguments to complete it. It will be found, however, when we go more deeply (in the ontological argument) into the conception of necessary being, that there is only one kind of existence which answers to this description, and with this more perfect conception the cosmological argument will then connect itself.

As thus presented, the cosmological argument is a process of thought. I cannot leave it, however, without pointing out that it stands connected with a direct fact of consciousness, which, as entering into experience, changes this proof to some extent from a merely logical into a real one. Not to speak of the immediate impression of transitoriness, finitude, contingency, vanity, which, prior to all reasoning, one receives from the world,[1] and which finds expression, more or less, in all religions, there is, at the very root of our religious consciousness, that "feeling of absolute dependence" which Schleiermacher fixes on as the very essence of religion;[2] and which reappears in Mr. Spencer's philosophy in a changed form as the immediate consciousness of an absolute Power on which we and our universe alike depend. This feeling of dependence, so natural to man, and interweaving itself with all his religious experiences, is the counterpart in the practical sphere of the cosmological argument in the logical. Both need their explanation in something deeper than themselves, namely, in the possession by man of a rational nature, which makes him capable of rising in thought and feeling above the finite. And as, in the theoretic sphere, the cosmological argument presses forward to its completion in another and a higher, so in the religious sphere the rational nature of man forbids that this sense of dependence should remain a mere feeling of dependency on a blind Power. Religion must free, bless, inspire, strengthen men. From the first, therefore, the soul is at work, seeking in its depths, and in obedience to its own laws, to change this relation of dependence into a free and personal one.

(2) The second argument for the Divine existence is the *teleological*, — better known simply as the design argument. Kant speaks of this oldest and most popular of the theistic

---

[1] Cf. Caird, *Phil. of Religion*, p. 135.
[2] *Der christ. Glaube*, secs. 3 and 4.

arguments with great respect; and the objections which he
makes to it affect more its adequacy to do all that is expected
from it than its force so far as it goes. It does not, he thinks,
prove a Creator, but only an Architect, of the world; it does
not prove an infinite, but only a very great Intelligence, etc.[1]
I may remark, however, that if it proves even this, it does a
great deal; and from an intelligence *so* great as to hold in its
ken the plan and direction of the universe, the step will not be
found a great one to the Infinite Intelligence which we call
God. But the argument, in the right conception of it, does
more than Kant allows, and is a step of transition to the final
one—the ontological.

A new argument against design in nature has been found
in recent times in the doctrine of evolution. The proof we are
considering turns, as every one knows, on the existence of ends
in nature. In Kant's words: "In the world we find everywhere clear signs of an order which can only spring from design
—an order realised with the greatest wisdom, and in a universe
which is indescribably varied in content, and in extent infinite."[2]
In organisms particularly we see the most extraordinary adaptations of means to ends—structures of almost infinite complexity
and wonderful perfection—contrivances in which we have precisely the same evidence of the adjustment of the parts to produce
the ends as in human works of art.[3] From this the inference is
drawn, that a world so full of evidences of rational purpose can
only be the work of a wise and intelligent mind. But this argument is broken down if it can be shown that what look like ends
in nature are not really such, but simply results—that the appearance of apparently designed arrangements to produce certain
ends can be explained by the action of causes which do not
imply intelligence. This is what evolution, in the hands of
some of its expounders, undertakes to do. By showing how
structures may have arisen through natural selection, operating
to the preservation of favourable variations in the struggle for
existence, it is thought that the aid of intelligence may be dis-

---

[1] See Note D.—Kant on the Teleological Argument.

[2] *Kritik*, p. 436 (Eng. trans. 384).

[3] No recent school has done more to elaborate the proof of teleology in
Nature than that from which the opposite might have been expected—the
pessimistic school. Cf. Schopenhauer's *Die Welt als Wille und Vorstellung*
(Book ii. chap. 26, "On Teleology"), and Hartmann's *Phil. d. Unbewussten*,
dassim.

pensed with, and that a deathblow is given to teleology.[1]   The eye, for example, may have resulted from the gradual accumulation of small variations, each of them accidental, and arising from unknown laws in the organism, but each, as it arises, giving to its possessor some slight advantage in the struggle for existence.   It is a simple case of the survival of the fittest. Instead of the advantage resulting from a designed arrangment, the appearance of arrangement results from the advantage.   In reality, the facts of evolution do not weaken the proof from design, but rather immensely enlarge it by showing all things to be bound together in a vaster, grander plan than had been formerly conceived.   Let us see how the matter precisely stands.

On the general hypothesis of evolution, as applied to the organic world, I have nothing to say, except that, within certain limits, it seems to me extremely probable, and supported by a large body of evidence.   This, however, only refers to the fact of a genetic relationship of some kind between the different species of plants and animals, and does not affect the means by which this development may be supposed to be brought about. On this subject two views may be held.[2]   The first is, that evolution results from development from within ; in which case, obviously, the argument from design stands precisely where it did, except that the sphere of its application is enormously extended.   The second view is, that evolution has resulted from fortuitous variations, combined with action of natural selection, laying hold of and preserving the variations that were favourable.   This is really, under a veil of words, to ask us to

---

[1] Thus, *e.g.*, Strauss, Haeckel, Helmholtz, G. Romanes ("Physicus").   Helmholtz, as quoted by Strauss, says : "Darwin's theory shows how adaptation of structure in organisms can originate without any intermixture of intelligence, through the blind operation of a natural law."—*Der alte und der neue Glaube*, p. 216.   Mr. Romanes says : "If [plants and animals] were specially created, the evidence of supernatural design remains unrefuted and irrefutable, whereas if they were slowly evolved, that evidence has been utterly and for ever destroyed."—*Organic Evolution*, p. 13.   On the bearings of evolution on design, and on the design argument generally in its present relations to science, see Janet's *Final Causes* (Eng. trans.); Stirling's *Philosophy and Theology* ; Kennedy's *Natural Theology and Modern Thought* (1891); Row's *Christian Theism* (1890); Martineau's *Study of Religion* (i. pp. 270–333); Flint's *Theism* ; Mivart's *Lessons from Nature* ; Conder's *Basis of Faith* ; Murphy's *Habit and Intelligence* ; Ebrard's *Christian Apologetics*, ii. pp. 1–56 (Eng. trans.); Argyll's *Reign of Law*, etc.   On Kant's views on evolution and on final causes as connected therewith, cf. Caird's *Phil. of Kant*, ii. 495–499.

[2] See Note E.—Schools of Evolutionists.

believe that accident and fortuity have done the work of mind.
But the facts are not in agreement with the hypothesis. The
variations in organisms are not absolutely indefinite. In the
evolution of an eye, for example, the variations are all more or
less in the line of producing the eye. When the formation of
an eye has begun, the organism keeps to that line in that place.
It does not begin to sprout an ear where the eye is being developed. There is a ground plan that is adhered to in the
midst of the variations. Could we collect the successive forms
through which the eye is supposed to have passed in the course
of its development, what we would see (I speak on the hypothesis of the theory) would be a succession of small increments
of structure, all tending in the direction of greater complexity
and perfection of the organ—the appearance of new muscles,
new lenses, new arrangements for adjusting or perfecting the
sight, etc. But the mere fact that these successive appearances
could be put in a line, however extended, would throw no light
on how the development took place, or how this marvellously
complex organ came to build itself up precisely after this
pattern.[1] The cause invoked to explain this is natural selection. Now the action of natural selection is real, but its influence may be very easily overrated. It is never to be forgotten
that natural selection *produces* nothing. It acts only on organisms already produced, weeding out the weakest, and the least
fitted structurally to survive, and leaving the better adapted in
possession of the field.[2] It is altogether to exaggerate the influence of natural selection, to attribute to it a power to pick out
infallibly on the first appearance the infinitesimal variations in
an organism which are to form the foundations of future useful
organs, though, in their initial stage, they cannot be shown to
confer any benefit on their possessors, and may be balanced or
neutralised by fifty or sixty other variations in an opposite
direction, or by differences of size, strength, speed, etc., on the
part of the competitors in the struggle; and still more a power
to preserve each of these slight variations till another and yet
another of a favourable kind is added to it after long intervals,

---

[1] Cf. Jevons, *Principles of Science*, ii. p. 462; J. S. Mill, *Three Essays on
Religion*, p. 171. Mill concludes that "the adaptations in Nature afford
a large balance of probability in favour of creation by intelligence."—P.
174.
See passages in Note E.

in a contest in which numbers alone are overwhelmingly against the chance of its survival.[1] Taking the facts of evolution as they really stand, what they seem to point to is something like the following :—

i. An inner power of development of organisms.

ii. A power of adjustment in organisms adapting them to environment.

iii. A weeding out of weak and unfit organisms by natural selection.

iv. Great differences in the rate of production of new species. Ordinarily, species seem to have nearly all the characters of fixity which the old view ascribed to them. Variation exists, but it is confined within comparatively narrow limits. The type persists through ages practically unchanged. At other periods in the geological history of the past there seems to be a breaking down of this fixity. The history of life is marked by a great inrush of new forms. New species crowd upon the scene. Plasticity seems the order of the day.[2] We may call this evolution if we like, but it is none the less creation,—the production out of the old of something new and higher. All that we are called upon to notice here is that it in no way conflicts with design, but rather compels the acknowledgment of it.

[1] Mr. Spencer shows that Natural Selection fails as an explanation in proportion as life grows complex. "As fast," he says, "as the faculties are multiplied, so fast does it become possible for the several members of a species to have various kinds of superiority over one another. While one saves its life by higher speed, another does the like by clearer vision, another by keener scent, another by quicker hearing, another by greater strength, another by unusual power of enduring cold and hunger, another by special sagacity, another by special timidity, another by special courage, and others by other bodily and mental attributes. Now it is unquestionably true that, other things being equal, each of these attributes giving its possessor an extra chance of life, is likely to be transmitted to posterity. But there seems no reason to suppose that it will be increased in subsequent generations by natural selection. . . . If those members of the species which have but ordinary shares of it nevertheless survive by virtue of other superiorities which they severally possess, then it is not easy to see how this particular attribute can be developed by natural selection in subsequent generations," etc.—*Principles of Biology*, sec. 166. Cf. Alfred W. Bennett in Martineau's *Study of Religion*, i. 280–282.

[2] Cf. Dawson, *Modern Ideas of Evolution*, pp. 106, 107 ; *The Chain of Life in Geol. Time*, p. 229. "The progress of life," he says, "in geological time has not been uniform or uninterrupted. . . . Evolutionists themselves, those at least who are willing to allow their theory to be at all modified by facts, now perceive this ; and hence we have the doctrine advanced by Mivart, Le Conte, and others, of 'critical periods,' or periods of rapid evolution alternating with others of greater quiescence."—*Mod. Ideas*, pp. 106, 107. See in both works the examples given of this "apparition of species.'

The chief criticism I would be disposed to make upon the design argument, as an argument for intelligence in the cause of the universe, is that it is too narrow. It confines the argument to final causes—that is, to the particular case of the adaptation of means to ends. But the basis for the inference that the universe has a wise and intelligent Author is far wider than this. It is not the marks of purpose alone which necessitate this inference, but everything which bespeaks order, plan, arrangement, harmony, beauty, rationality in the connection and system of things. It is the proof of the presence of *thought* in the world—whatever shape that may take.[1] As we saw in a former part of the Lecture, the assumption on which the whole of science proceeds—and cannot but proceed—in its investigations is, that the system it is studying is intelligible,—that there is an intelligible unity of things. It admits of being reduced to terms of thought. There is a settled and established order on which the investigator can depend. Without this he could not advance one step. Even Kant's objection, that this argument proved only an architect of the universe, but not a creator of its materials, is seen from this point of view to be invalid.[2] The very materials of the universe—the atoms which compose it—show by their structure, their uniformity, their properties, their mathematical relations, that they must have a Creator; that the Power which originated them, which weighed, measured, and numbered them, which stamped on them their common characters, and gave them their definite laws and relations, must have been intelligent. I admit, however, that as the design argument presupposes the cosmological, to give us the idea of an infinite and necessary Being at the basis of the

---

[1] Principal Shairp says : "To begin with the outward world, there is, I shall not say so much the mark of design on all outward things as an experience forced in upon the mind of the thoughtful naturalist that, penetrate into nature wherever he may, thought has been there before him ; that, to quote the words of one of the most distinguished, 'there is really a plan, which may be read in the relations which you and I, and all living beings scattered over the surface of our earth, hold to each other.'"—*Studies in Poetry and Philosophy*, p. 367. Cf. also on this aspect of the subject, M'Cosh, *Method of Divine Government*, pp. 75-151 ; and on the argument from Beauty and Sublimity in Nature, Kennedy's *Natural Theology and Modern Thought*, Lecture IV. (Donnellan Lectures).

[2] Cf. Lecture IV. on Creation. It may be asked, besides, if it is so certain, as Kant assumes, that only a finite power is needed to create—I do not say a universe, but even an atom ; whether there are not finite effects, such as creation, to which only Omnipotence is competent. The point is not that it is an atom, but that it is *created*.

universe, so both of these arguments need the ontological, to show us in the clearest and most convincing manner that this Being and Cause of the universe is infinite, self-conscious Reason.

(3) I come, accordingly, in the third place, to the *ontological* argument—that which Kant, not without reason, affirms to be at the foundation of the other two, and to be the real ground on which the inference to the existence of a necessary and infinitely perfect Being rests. It is an argument which in these days, owing largely to his criticism upon it, has fallen much into disrepute, though a good deal has also been done by able thinkers to rehabilitate it, and to show its real bearings. It must further be admitted that in the form in which it was wont to be put in the schools, the strictures which Kant makes on it are in the main just.[1] In the earlier form, it is an argument from the idea of God as a necessary idea of the mind, to His real existence. I have, reasons Anselm, the idea of a most perfect Being. But this idea includes the attribute of existence. For if the most perfect Being did not exist, there could be conceived a greater than He,—one that did exist,—and therefore He would not be the most perfect. The most perfect Being, therefore, is one in the idea of whom existence is necessarily included. In this form the argument seems little better than a logical quibble, and so Kant has treated it. Kant grants the necessity of the idea—shows how it arises—names it *The Ideal of Pure Reason*—but argues with cogency that from an idea, purely as such, you cannot conclude to real existence. It would be strange, however, if an argument which has wielded such power over some of the strongest intellects were utterly baseless; and Dr. Hutchison Stirling has well shown that when we get to the kernel of Anselm's thought, as he himself explains it, it has by no means the irrational character which might at first sight appear to belong to it.[2] Anselm's form of the argument, however, it must now be observed, is neither the final nor the perfect one. Kant himself has given the impulse to a new development of it, which shows more clearly than ever that it is not baseless, but is really the deepest and most comprehensive

---

[1] *Kritik,* pp. 417-424 (Eng. trans. pp. 364-370). See Note F.—Kant on the Ontological Argument.

[2] *Phil. and Theol.* pp. 182-193,

of all arguments—the argument implied in both of the two
preceding.

The kernel of the ontological argument, as we find it
put, for example, by Prof. Green, is the assertion that
thought is the necessary *prius* of all else that is—even of
all possible or conceivable existence. This assertion is not
arrived at in any *a priori* way, but by the strict and sober
analysis of what is involved in such knowledge of existence as
we have. If we analyse the act of knowledge, we find that in
every form of it there are implied certain necessary and universal conditions, which, from the nature of the case, must be
conditions of experience also, otherwise it could never be
experience for us at all. Thus, any world we are capable of
knowing with our present faculties must be a world in space
and time,—a world subject to conditions of number and quantity,
—a world apprehended in relations of substance and accident,
cause and effect, etc. A world of any other kind—supposing it
to exist—would be in relation to our thought or knowledge
unthinkable. These conditions of knowledge, moreover, are not
arbitrary and contingent, but universal and necessary. They
spring from reason itself, and express its essential and immutable
nature. Thus we feel sure that there is no world in space or
time to which the laws of mathematics do not apply; no world
possible in which events do not follow each other according to
the law of cause and effect; no world in which the fundamental
laws of thought and reasoning are different from what they are
in our own. Mr. J. S. Mill, indeed, thought there might be
worlds in which two and two do not make four; or in which
events succeed each other without any causal relation. But in
this he will get few to agree with him. In like manner, there
are moral principles which our reason recognises as universally
and unconditionally valid. We cannot conceive of a world in
which falsehood would really be a virtue, and truth-speaking a
vice. We hold it, therefore, for certain that reason is the source
of universal and necessary principles which spring from its
essence, and which are the conditions of all possible knowledge.
But this, its own essential nature, reason finds reflected back
from the world around it. A world does exist, constituted
through these very principles which we find within ourselves,—
in space and time, through number and quantity, substance and

quality, cause and effect, etc.,—and therefore knowable by us, and capable of becoming an object of our experience. We arrive, therefore, at this—that the world is constituted through a reason similar to our own; that, in Mr. Green's words, "the understanding which presents an order of nature to us is in principle one with an understanding which constitutes that order itself."[1] And that such a reason not only does, but *must* exist, I see not simply by inference from the existence of the world, which is the higher form of the cosmological argument, but by reflection on the necessary character of the principles of reason themselves. For whence these laws of thought—these universal and necessary conditions of all truth and knowledge— which I discover in myself; which my own reason neither makes nor can unmake; which I recognise to be in me and yet not of me; which I know must belong to every rational being in every part of the universe? They are necessary and eternal in their nature, yet they have not the ground of their existence in my individual mind. Can I conclude otherwise than that they have their seat and ground in an eternal and absolute Reason—the absolute *Prius* of all that is, at once of thought and of existence? It is but a further extension of the same argument when I proceed to show that thought is only possible in relation to an I, to a central principle of self-consciousness, which unifies and connects all thinking and experience.

This argument, which has been called that of "Rational Realism," is one which in varied forms has been accepted by the deepest thinkers, and finds widespread acknowledgment in literature.[2] It is not liable to the objection made to the Anselmic form, of involving an illicit inference from mere idea to real existence; but it has this in common with it, that the existence of an Eternal Reason is shown to be involved in the very thinking of this, or indeed of any thought. In the very act of thinking, thought affirms its own existence. But thought can perceive, not only its own existence, but the necessity of its existence—the necessity of its existence, even, as the *prius* of everything else. What is affirmed, therefore, is not simply my thought, but an Absolute Thought, and with this the existence of an Absolute Thinker; in the words of Dr. Harris, who has

[1] *Prol. to Ethics*, p. 23.
[2] See Note G.—Rational Realism.

done much to give popular expression to this argument, of "an Absolute Reason energising in perfect wisdom and love" in the universe.[1] I cannot but maintain, therefore, that the ontological argument, in the kernel and essence of it, is a sound one, and that in it the existence of God is really seen to be the first, the most certain, and the most indisputable of all truths.

We saw in connection with the cosmological argument that there was a direct fact of consciousness which turned the logical argument into a real one,—which translated, if I may so speak, the abstract proof into a living experience. It is worth our while to inquire, before leaving these theoretic proofs, whether there is anything of the same kind here ; anything in actual religious consciousness which answers to that demonstration of a rational element in the world which is given in the two remaining arguments. I think there is. I refer to that very real perception which mankind have at all times manifested of a spiritual presence and power in nature, which is the effect of the total unanalysed impression which nature in its infinite variety and complexity, its wondrous grandeur, order, beauty, and fulness of life and power, makes upon the soul. The more carefully facts have been examined, the more narrowly the history of religions has been scrutinised, the clearer has it become that underlying all the particular ideas men have of their deities,—underlying their particular acts of worship to them,—there is always this sense of something mysterious, intangible, infinite,—of an all-pervading supernatural Presence and Power,—which is not identified with any of the particular phenomena of nature, but is regarded rather as manifested through them.[2] It is this which Paul speaks of when he says that "the Eternal Power and Divinity" of God are manifested since the creation of the world in the things that are made.[3] It

---

[1] *The Phil. Basis of Theism*, p. 3 ; cf. pp. 82, 146, 560, etc.
[2] This is true of the lowest as well as of the highest religions,—cf. Waitz on *The Religion of the Negroes*, in Max Müller's Hibbert Lectures, pp. 106, 107,—but is much more conspicuous in the oldest forms of natural religion, *e.g.* in the Vedic, Babylonian, and Egyptian religions. On the general facts, cf. Max Müller's works, Réville's *Hist. of Religions*, Sayce's Hibbert Lectures on *The Religion of the Ancient Babylonians*, Renouf's Hibbert Lectures on *The Religion of Ancient Egypt*, Fairbairn's *Studies*, Loring Brace's *The Unknown God*, Pressensé's *The Ancient World and Christianity* (Eng. trans.), etc.; and see Note F. to Lecture V.
[3] Rom. i. 20.

is Max Müller's "perception of the infinite," Schleiermacher's "consciousness of the infinite in the finite," the *sensus numinis* of the older writers, Wordsworth's "sense of something **far** more deeply interfused"—

> "Whose dwelling is the light of setting suns,
> And the round ocean, and the living air,
> And the blue sky, and in the mind of man."[1]

Such a sense or perception of the Divine is the common substratum of all religions, and the theory of religion which fails to take account of it is like the play of Hamlet with Hamlet left out.

But how is this sense of the Divine in nature—which is the stronghold of the theology of feeling—to be accounted for? It is certainly not the result of logical argument, and goes beyond anything that logical argument could yield. Yet it may easily be shown that rational elements are implicit in it, and that the rational elements involved are precisely those which the fore going arguments have sought explicitly to unfold. To understand the impression of the Divine which nature makes on man, we have to remember how much the mind of man has already to do with nature. We have to do here with nature, not primarily as an objectively existing system of laws and forces, but as it exists for man as an object of actual knowledge and experience. And how has it come to be this to him? Not without help from the thinking mind which collates and connects the separate impressions made on it through the senses, and gradually reads the riddle of the universe by the help of what it brings to it out of its own resources. We speak of the immaturity of the savage mind, but there is an intense mental activity in the simplest conception which the savage (or the child) can form of the existence of nature, or of a world around him. He sees changes, but he finds the interpretation of these changes in the idea of causality which he brings to it from his own mind. He groups attributes and forms objects, but he does this through the mental law of substance and accident. He perceives the operation of vast forces in nature, but whence does he get the idea of force? He gets it from the consciousness of power within himself, and through this puts meaning into the scene of change and movement which he finds around him.

---

[1] Wordsworth's *Tintern Abbey*.

Is it wonderful, then, that man, who has put so much of himself into nature, even when constructing it as an object of thought, should again receive back the reflection of his own spiritual image from nature—receive it back on a grander, vastly enhanced scale, proportionate to the greatness and immensity of the universe on which he looks, and should be filled with awe and reverence in presence of this Other-Self, and Higher-than-Self, as that of a Reason, Power, and Will essentially akin to his own, though infinitely greater? Reason does not create this sense of the Divine; it can only follow in its train, and seek to lay bare and analyse—as is done in the theoretic proofs—the rational elements which it involves.

III. There remains the *moral* argument, which deserves a place by itself, and which I must briefly consider before I close. The theoretic proofs, as Kant rightly said, can give us no knowledge of God as a moral Being—as a Being who sets before Him moral ends, and governs the world with reference to these ends. For this we are dependent on the Practical Reason, which shows us not what *is*, but what *ought to be*, and is the source of laws of moral conduct which we recognise as of binding force for every rational agent. The way in which Kant works out his argument from this point is one of the most interesting parts of his system. Nature in itself, he thinks, knows nothing of a highest end. This is given only in the Practical Reason, which sets before us ends of unconditioned worth, and requires us, if our view of the world is to be consistent, to regard these as supreme, *i.e.* to view the world as a moral system, in which natural ends are everywhere subordinated to moral. But such a moral teleology is only possible if there is one principle of the natural and of the moral order, and if nature is so arranged as to secure a final harmony of natural and moral conditions; in other words, if the world has a moral as well as an intelligent cause. God, therefore, is a postulate of the Practical Reason.[1] I quote, in further illustration of this argument, Professor Caird's fuller statement of it, in his excellent exposition of the *Critique of Judgment*, in which he follows

[1] Cf. *Kritik d. r. Vernunft*, pp. 548-557, on "The Ideal of the Highest Good as a Determining Ground of the last end of Pure Reason" (Eng. trans. pp. 487-496); and the *Kritik d. praktischen Vernunft*, Part II. 5—"The Being of God as a Postulate of the Pure Practical Reason."

Kant. "The principle of moral determination in man," he says, "carries with it the idea of a highest end, after which he should strive; in other words, the idea of a system in which all rational beings realise their happiness *through* their moral perfection, and in proportion to it. But such realisation of happiness through morality is no *natural* sequence of effect on cause; for there is nothing in the connection of physical causes that has any relation to such an end. We are forced, therefore, by the same moral necessity which makes us set before us such an end, to postulate outside of nature a cause that determines nature, so as finally to secure this result; and from this follows necessarily the idea of an all-wise, all-powerful, all-righteous, all-merciful God. We have a 'pure moral need' for the existence of such a Being; and our moral needs differ from physical needs in that they have an absolute claim to satisfaction. . . . Furthermore, we are to remember that the principle which leads us to postulate God is a *practical* principle, which does not give us, strictly speaking, a knowledge of God, but only of a special relation in which He stands to us and to nature; while, therefore, in order to find in God the principle which realises the highest good, we are obliged to represent Him as a rational Being, who is guided by the idea of an end, and who uses nature as means to it, we are to remember that this conception is based on an imperfect analogy. . . . 'All that we can say is that, *consistently with the nature of our intelligence*, we cannot make intelligible to ourselves the possibility of such an adaptation of nature to the moral law and its object as is involved in the final end which the moral law commands us to aim at, except by assuming the existence of a Creator and Governor of the world, who is also its moral Legislator.'"[1]

It is to this view of God as a postulate of the Practical Reason, and as satisfying a "pure moral need," that the Ritschlian theology specially attaches itself; but it must be remarked that such an origin of the idea of God, abstracted from direct experience of dependence on Him, would furnish no adequate explanation of the religious relation. We may, however, accept all that Kant says of God as a postulate of the moral consciousness, and yet carry the argument a good deal further than he does. God is not only a postulate of the moral nature in the sense that His

---

[1] *Philosophy of Kant,* ii. pp. 504, 505.

existence is necessary to secure the final harmony of natural and moral conditions, but it may be held that His existence is implied in the very presence of a morally legislating and commanding Reason within us,—just as an eternal self-conscious Reason was seen to be implied in the universal and necessary principles of the theoretic consciousness. That moral law which appears in conscience—the " categorical imperative " of duty for which Kant himself has done so much to intensify our reverence —that ideal of unrealised goodness which hovers constantly above us, awakening in us a noble dissatisfaction with all past attainments,—these are not facts which explain themselves. Nor are they sufficiently explained as products of association and of social convention. Moral law is not comprehensible except as the expression of a will entitled to impose its commands upon us. The rules and ideals of conduct which conscience reveals to us, and which bind the will with such unconditional authority, point to a deeper source in an eternal moral Reason. The ethical ideal, if its absolute character is to be secured, points back to an eternal ground in the Absolute Being. It takes us back to the same conception of God as the ethically perfect Being, source and ground of moral truth, fountain of moral law, which we found to be implied in Christianity.[1]

And let me observe, finally, that here also we have more than logical argument—we have experience. The moral consciousness is one of the most powerful direct sources of man's knowledge of God. In the earliest stages in which we know anything about man, a moral element blends with his thought. There grows up within him—he knows not how—a sense of right and wrong, of a law making its presence felt in his life, prescribing to him moral duties, and speaking to him with a " thou shalt " and " thou shalt not " in his soul which he dare not disregard. His thoughts, meanwhile, accuse or else excuse each other. This law, moreover, presents itself to him as something more than a mere idea of his own mind. It is a real judging power in his soul, an arbiter invested with legislative, but also with judicial functions. It has accordingly from the

[1] Cf. on the moral argument, Conder's *Basis of Faith*, pp. 383–431; Martineau's *Study of Religion*, ii. pp. 1–42; Kennedy's *Natural Theology and Modern Thought*, Lecture VI., " Kant and the Moral Proof "; and M'Cosh's *Divine Government*, Book i. chap. 3.

first a sacred character. It is a power not himself making for righteousness within him. He instinctively connects it with the Power he worships, whose existence is borne in on him from other sources. As conscience develops, his deities come to be more invested with a moral character, and are feared, honoured, or propitiated accordingly. It is the moral consciousness particularly which safeguards the personality of God—the Divine tending to sink back into identity with nature in proportion as the ethical idea is obscured.

The conclusion we reach from the various arguments and considerations advanced in this Lecture is, that the Christian view of a personal and holy God, as the Author of the universe, and its moral Legislator and Ruler, is the only one in which the reason and the heart of man can permanently rest. I do not say that reason could have reached the height of the Christian conception for itself; I do not even think it can hold to it unless it accepts the fact of Revelation and the other truths which Christianity associates with it. But I do say that, with this view as given, reason is able to bring to it abundant corroboration and verification. It is not one line of evidence only which establishes the theistic position, but the concurrent force of many, starting from different and independent standpoints. And the voice of reason is confirmed by the soul's direct experiences in religion. At the very least these considerations show—even if the force of demonstration is denied to them—that the Christian view of God is not *un*reasonable; that it is in accordance with the highest suggestions of reason applied to the facts of existence; that there is no bar in rational thought or in science to its full acceptance. And this is all that at present we need ask.

APPENDIX TO CHAPTER 3
GOD AS RELIGIOUS POSTULATE

If we are to speak of God as a postulate of the soul, we must speak of Him as a postulate for the *whole* need of the soul—for its religious and its rational, not less than for its moral need. We must speak of Him also in such a way as to show that this postulate is not an arbitrary one, but springs necessarily from the soul's rational and moral constitution, and so as to explain the conviction of its truth by which it is accompanied. But this can only be done by showing that there are laws of man's spiritual nature which imperatively demand such and such an object, and by making it clear what these are. In like manner I would lay it down as a first principle, as against all psychological and empirical theories of religion, which propose to account for men's religious ideas and beliefs from natural causes (hopes and fears, animism, ghosts, etc.), without raising the question of how far they correspond with any outward reality, that no theory of religion can be adequate which does not cast light on the deepest ground of the soul's movement towards God, and on the nature of the object which alone can adequately satisfy it. This again assumes that there are laws of the spiritual nature which determine beforehand what the character of the object must be which alone can satisfy the religious necessity, and which impel the soul unceasingly to a search after that object. This, however, is precisely what I consider the truth about religion to be, as a survey of its manifestations in history reveals its nature to us. Religion is not an arbitrary product of the soul. Even in the lowest and poorest religions we see something struggling into consciousness,—a want, a desire, a need,—which is not measured by the extent of its actual knowledge of the Divine. Religion we might define from this point of view as the search of the soul for an adequate spiritual

object to rest in, combined with the consciousness that there
is such an object, and with the impulse to seek after it,
and when found, to surrender itself to it. Now what kind
of object is it which the soul thus demands? This can
only be determined by the study of its laws, as these spring
from its essential nature, and are exhibited on the field
of historical religion. And here, I think, we are warranted
to say—

1. That the soul, as itself personal, demands for the satisfaction of its religious need, a *personal* object. From whatever
source it derives its idea of the Divine (sense of dependence,
outward impressions of nature, moral consciousness), it invariably
personalises it. Over against its "I" it seeks a "Thou," and will
rest satisfied with nothing less.

2. That the soul, as thinking spirit, demands an *infinite*
object. This is a proposition of some importance, and requires
more careful consideration. We cannot err in seeking with
Hegel the deepest ground of man's capacity for religion in his
possession of the power of thought. The power of thought is
not the whole of religion, but it is that which gives man his
capacity for religion. The lower animals are irrational, and
they have no religion. Thought, in this connection, may be
described as the universalising principle in human nature. It
is that which leads us to negate the limits of the finite. It is
that which impels man from fact to principle, from law to wider
law, from the collection of facts and laws in the universe to the
principle on which the whole depends. It is the element of
boundlessness in imagination, of illimitableness in desire, of
insatiableness in the appetite for knowledge. On the side of
religion we see it constantly at work, modifying the idea of the
object of religion, and bringing it more into harmony with what
it is felt that an object of worship ought to be. One way in
which this is done is by the choice of the grander objects of
nature — the sky, sun, mountains, etc. — as the embodiments
and manifestations of the Divine. Another way is by the mere
multiplication of the objects of idolatry—the mind seeking in
this way, as it were, to fill up the gap in its depths. Another
way is physical magnitude—hugeness. "Nebuchadnezzar the
king made an image of gold, whose height was threescore cubits,
and the breadth thereof six cubits ; he set it up in the plain of

Dura."[1]   This love of the colossal is seen in most oriental
religions (*e.g.* Egyptian, Assyrian).   Another way is by what
Max Müller calls Henotheism—fixing on one special deity, and
treating it for the time being as if it was alone and supreme.
Another way is by creating a "system," placing one deity at
the head of the Pantheon, and making the rest subordinate.
We have examples in the position held by Zeus and Jupiter in
the Greek and Roman religions—a position described by Tiele
as one of "Monarchism allied to Monotheism."   Another way
is by tracing back the origin of the gods, as in Hesiod, to some
uncreated principle ; or by placing behind them a fate, necessity,
or destiny, which is a higher power than they.   Finally, in the
philosophical schools, we have reasoned Theism, or Pantheism,
or some cosmic theory in which the universe itself becomes
God.   Through all, the search of the soul for an infinite is
clearly discernible.

3. That the soul, as itself ethical, demands an *ethical* object.
It does this in all the higher forms of religion.   It may be
observed that, once the idea of an ethical God has been brought
home to the mind, no lower conception of the Deity can be
accepted.   The agnostic himself — strongly as he protests
against the knowableness of God — will yet be the first to
maintain that it is impossible to entertain, even as hypothesis,
any idea of God which represents Him as false, cruel, tyrannical,
revengeful, unjust.   He knows enough about God, at any rate,
to be sure that He is not *this*.

4. I may add that the soul, as itself an intelligence, demands
a *knowable* object.   It has previously been shown that, for
purposes of religion, an unknowable God is equivalent to no
God at all.   Religion seeks not only a knowledge of its object,
but such a knowledge as can be made the basis of communion.
Here, again, we are led by the very idea of religion, to the
expectation of Revelation.

The bearing of all this on the Christian view is very obvious.
It gives us a test of the validity of the Christian view, and it
explains to us why this view comes home to the spirit of man
with the self-evidencing power that it does.   It comes to the
spirit as light—attests its truth by its agreement with the laws
of the spirit.   The worth of this attestation is not weakened

---

[1] Dan. iii. 1.

by the fact that the Christian religion itself mostly creates the very capacity by which its truth can be perceived—creates the organ for its own verification. It makes larger demands upon the spirit, calls forth higher ideas than any other; but, in doing so, reveals at the same time the spirit to itself. Brought to the foregoing tests, it discovers to us a God personal, infinite, ethical, and knowable, because self-revealing, and in this way answers the demands of the religious spirit.

4
THE POSTULATE OF THE
CHRISTIAN VIEW OF THE WORLD
IN REGARD TO NATURE AND MAN

"By faith we understand that the worlds have been framed by the Word of God, so that what is seen hath not been made out of things which do appear." —Epistle to the Hebrews

"Man is neither the master nor the slave of nature; he is its interpreter and living word. Man consummates the universe, and gives a voice to the mute creation." —Ed. Quinet

"He who believes in God must also believe in the continuance of man's life after death. Without this there could be no world which would be conceivable as a purpose of God."

—Rothe

"I trust I have not wasted breath;
 I think we are not wholly brain,
 Magnetic mockeries; not in vain,
Like Paul with beasts, I fought with Death;

Not only cunning casts in clay:
 Let Science prove we are, and then
 What matters Science unto men,
At least to me? I would not stay."

Tennyson

"Does the soul survive the body? Is there
 God's self, no or yes?"

R. Browning

4

THE POSTULATE OF THE CHRISTIAN VIEW OF THE WORLD IN REGARD TO NATURE AND MAN

THE Christian doctrine of God as personal, ethical, and self-revealing, carries with it a second postulate as to the nature of man. The Christian doctrine of God and the Christian doctrine of man are in fact correlatives. For how should man know that there is a personal, ethical, self-revealing God,—how should he be able to frame the conception of such a Being, or to attach any meaning to the terms employed to express His existence, —unless he were himself rational and moral—a spiritual personality? The two views imply each other, and stand or fall together. We may express this second postulate of the Christian view in the words, Man made in the image of God.[1]

This truth of a natural kinship between the human spirit and the Divine is at once the oldest declaration in the Bible about man, and is implied in every doctrine of the Christian system. It is implied, as already said, in the knowledge of God, and in the call to fellowship with Him in holiness and love. It is implied in the Christian view of sin; for sin in the Christian view derives its tragic significance from the fact that it is a revolt of the creature will against the Divine will, to which it is by nature bound, that it cuts the soul off from its true life and blessedness in union with God. It is implied in regeneration, and in the capacity of the soul to receive the Spirit of God. For the Spirit of God does not enter the soul as something foreign and extraneous to it. He enters it as the principle of its true life. What, on the one side, we call the operations of the Spirit, or the presence of the Spirit in the

---

[1] Gen. i. 27. Dorner says truly : " The absolute personality of God, and the infinite value of the personality of man, stand and fall with each other."— *Person of Christ*, v. p. 155.

soul, we call, on the other, the new life itself. The Divine
and human here are but one and the same thing on two different sides. It is implied also in the call of man to a Divine
sonship. It is the case, no doubt,—and the fact is one to be
carefully considered,—that in Christ's teaching God is not called
the Father of all men indiscriminately, nor is the title "son of
God" given to all men indiscriminately. It is used only of
those who are the subjects of spiritual renewal, and who bear
in some measure the moral and spiritual likeness of the Father.[1]
It does not denote a merely natural or physical relationship, but
a moral bond as well. Deliberate and hardened transgressors
are spoken of, not as children of God, but rather as children of
the devil.[2] But this is only because these wicked persons have
turned their backs on their own true destination. As made by
God, and as standing in his normal relation to Him, man is
without doubt a son. Hence, in the Gospel of Luke, though
not by Christ Himself, Adam is called "the son of God,"[3] and
Paul does not scruple to quote the saying of the heathen poet,
"For we also are His offspring."[4] The fact that the title "son
of God" should belong to *any*, already implies a natural kinship
between God and man, else the higher relationship would not
be possible. If there were not already a God-related element
in the human spirit, no subsequent act of grace could confer
on man this spiritual dignity.[5]

Not only in the Christian view in general, but specially in
the great central doctrine of the Incarnation, is this truth of
man made in the image of God seen to be implied. I have
already referred to certain services which the German speculative movement in the beginning of the century rendered to
Christianity, in laying stress on the essential kinship which
exists between the human spirit and the Divine, a thought
never since lost sight of in theology. So long as the world is
conceived of in deistic separation from God, it is inevitable that
the Divine and human should be regarded as two opposed

---

[1] Matt. v. 9, 45 ; John i. 12, 13. Cf. Schmid's *Theol. of the New Testament*,
p. 101 (Eng. trans.).
[2] Matt. xxiii. 15 ; John viii. 44.
[3] Luke iii. 38. Yet only through the context—'Αδὰμ, τοῦ Θεοῦ.
[4] Acts xvii. 28.
[5] On the nature of man's sonship, cf. Candlish's *1 atherhood of God*, and Dr.
Crawford's work in reply (same title) ; Bruce's *Kingdom of God*, chaps. iv.
and v. ; Wendt's *Die Lehre Jesu*, ii. pp. 145-151, 453-464.

essences, between which true union is impossible. Once this point of view is overcome, and it is seen that the bond between God and man is inner and essential—that there is a God-related element in the human spirit which makes man capable of receiving from the Divine, and of becoming its living image— a great step is taken towards removing objections to the Incarnation. A union between the Divine and human is seen to be possible, to the intimacy of which no limits can be set,—which, indeed, only reaches its perfection when it becomes personal. The Incarnation has not only this doctrine of man as its presupposition—it is, besides, the highest proof of its truth. Christ, in His own Person, is the demonstration of the truth of the Bible doctrine about man. To get a knowledge of the true essence of anything, we do not look at its ruder and less perfect specimens, but at what it is at its best. Christ is the best of humanity. He is not only the Revelation of God to humanity, but the Revelation of humanity to itself. In Him we see in perfect form what man in the Divine idea of him is. We see how man is made in the image of God, and how humanity is constituted the perfect organ for the Revelation of the Divine.

It is evident that in the Christian view the doctrine of man links itself very closely with the doctrine of nature—of creation. It is not merely that man is related to nature by his body, but he is in Scripture, as in science, the highest being in nature. He is, in some sense, the final cause of nature, the revelation of its purpose, the lord and ruler of nature. Nature exists with supreme reference to him ; is governed with a view to his ends ; suffers in his fall ; and is destined to profit by his Redemption.[1] I propose to begin with the natural basis—the doctrine of creation.

I. The Bible affirms, and perhaps it is the only book that does so, that all things, visible and invisible, have originated from God by a free act of creation.[2] The Bible doctrine of creation is something more than the Mosaic cosmogony. For my present purpose it is indifferent how we interpret the first chapter of Genesis—whether as the result of direct Revelation,

---

[1] See pp. 193–196.
[2] Gen. i. 1 ; John i. 2 ; Col. i. 16 ; Heb. xi. 3, etc.

or as the expression of certain great religious truths in such forms as the natural knowledge of the age admitted of. I believe myself that the narrative gives evidence of its Divine original in its total difference of character from all heathen cosmogonies, but this is a view I need not press.[1] The main point is the absolute derivation of all things from God, and on this truth the Scripture as a whole gives no uncertain sound. Discussions have been raised as to the exact force of the Hebrew word (*bārā*) used to express the idea of creation,[2] but even this is of subordinate importance in view of the fact, which none will dispute, that the uniform teaching of Scripture is that the universe had its origin, not from the fashioning of pre-existent matter, but directly from the will and word of the Almighty.[3] "He spake, and it was done; He commanded, and it stood fast."[4]

Not only is this doctrine of creation fundamental in Scripture, but it is of great practical significance. It might be thought, of what practical importance is it to us to know how the world originated? Is not this a question of purely speculative interest? But a moment's reflection will convince us that it is not so. The vital thing in religion is the relation of dependence. To feel that we and our world, that our human life and all that we are and have, absolutely depend on God,—this is the primary attitude of religion. For if they do not thus depend,—if there is anything in the universe which exists out of and independently of God,—then what guarantee have we for the unfailing execution of His purposes, what ground have we for that assured trust in His Providence which Christ inculcates, what security have we that all things will work together for good? But to affirm that all things depend on God is just in another way to affirm the creation of all things by God. They would not depend on Him if He were not their Creator. They do depend on Him, because they are created by Him. The doctrine of

---

[1] Note A.—The Creation History.

[2] Cf. Delitzsch's *Genesis*, ch. i. 1, and Schultz's *Alt. Theol.* pp. 570, 571.

[3] "Creation out of nothing," says Rothe, " is not found in express words in Holy Scripture. . . . The fact itself, however, is expressed in Scripture quite definitely, since it teaches throughout, with all emphasis, that, through His word and almighty will alone, God has called into being the world, which before did not exist, and this not merely in respect of its form, but also of its matter."—*Dogmatik*, i. 133.

[4] Ps. xxxiii. 9.

creation, therefore, is not a mere speculation. Only this conviction that it is "the Lord that made heaven and earth"[1]—that "of Him, and through Him, and to Him, are all things"[2]—that He has created all things, and for His pleasure they are and were created,[3]—can give us the confidence we need in a holy and wise government of the universe, and in a final triumph of good over evil.

If the doctrine of creation is the only one which meets the wants of our religious nature, it may now further be affirmed that it is a doctrine consonant with reason, and consistent with all true knowledge. It is opposed, first, to all forms of dualism ; secondly, to a merely logical derivation of the universe ; and thirdly, to the atheistic assertion of the self-subsistence and eternity of the universe. Let us glance briefly at these various oppositions.

1. Partly on metaphysical, partly on moral grounds, some have revived the old Platonic doctrine of an eternal matter, or other independent principle, which exists alongside the Deity, and conditions and limits Him in His working. Thus Dr. Martineau holds that, in order to afford an objective field for the Divine operations, we must assume something to have been always there, a primitive *datum*, eternal as God Himself ;[4] while the late J. S. Mill thought the difficulties of the universe could be best explained by supposing the Creator hampered by the insufficiency and intractableness of the materials He had to work with.[5] Karl Peters, a disciple of the pessimistic school already mentioned, sets up space as a second eternal principle beside God ;[6] and others have held similar views. Philosophically, these theories are condemned by the fact that they set up two absolutes in the universe, which, if they really were absolutes, could never be brought into any relation to each other, much less be embraced in a single act of knowledge. Suppose this eternal matter to exist outside of God, how could it ever get to be known by God, or how could He ever act upon it, seeing that it has its being utterly apart from Him ?

[1] Ps. cxxi. 2.   [2] Rom. xi. 36.
[3] Rev. iv. 11. Revised Version reads : "For Thou didst create all things ; and because of Thy will they are and were created."
[4] *Study of Religion*, pp. 405–408 ; *Seat of Authority*, pp. 32, 33.
[5] *Three Essays on Religion*, pp. 178, 186. Cf. Plato, *Timæus*, p. 51 (*Marg.* Jowett's *Plato*, iii.).
[6] *Willenswelt*, pp. 335–341.

Or, if it is not out of relation to His intelligence, by what middle term is this relation brought about? This, which applies to *two* absolutes, applies, of course, much more to a theory which starts from an infinity of independent atoms— that is, from an infinite of absolutes. But these theories are weighted with difficulties of another kind. An absolutely qualityless matter, or ὕλη, such as Plato supposes,[1] is unthinkable and impossible. Plato himself is compelled to describe it as a μὴ ὄν, or nothing. It is a mere abstraction.[2] Is Dr. Martineau's eternal matter, which has no properties of any kind till the Creator bestows them upon it, in any better case? When, again, Mr. Mill identifies this eternal element, not with naked matter, but with the matter and force which we know— with constituted matter, clothed with all its existing properties and laws—are we not in the new predicament of having to account for this matter? How came it there? Whence this definite constitution? Whence these powers and properties and laws which, in their marvellous adjustments and interrelations, show as much evidence of design as any other parts of the universe? To suppose that "the given properties of matter and force, working together and fitting into one another"[3] —which is Mr. Mill's own phrase—need no explanation, but only the uses subsequently made of them, is to manifest a strange blindness to the fundamental conditions of the problem.

2. If the Scripture view of creation is opposed to dualism in all its forms, it is not less opposed to every theory of a mere logical derivation of the universe—whether, with Spinoza, the universe is supposed to flow, with logical necessity, from an absolute substance;[4] or with Hegel, to be the development of

---

[1] Cf. his *Timæus*, pp. 27, 35, 50, 51.

[2] Dr. Stirling says: "A substance without quality were a non-ens, and a quality without a substance were but a fiction in the air. *Matter*, if to be, must be permeated by *form*; and equally *form*, if to be, must be realised by *matter*. Substance takes being from quality; quality, actuality from substance. That is metaphysic; but it is seen to be as well physic,—it is seen to have a physical existence; it is seen to be *in rerum natura*."—*Phil. and Theol.* p. 43.

[3] *Three Essays*, p. 178. I may refer for further development of this argument to two articles by myself in *The Theological Monthly* (July and August, 1891), on "John Stuart Mill and Christianity."

[4] Cf. Spinoza's *Ethics*, Part I. Prop. 29.—"Nothing in the universe is contingent, but all things are conditioned to exist and operate in a particular manner by the necessity of the Divine nature." Prop. 33.—"Things could not have been brought into being by God in any manner or in any order different from that which has in fact obtained."

an impersonal Reason; or with Green, to arise from a Reason
that is self-conscious.   It is this doctrine of a necessary derivation of the universe which takes the place in modern times of
the old theories of emanation; but I shall only make two remarks
on it. (1) It involves an amazing assumption. The assumption
is that this universe, which exhibits so much evidence of wise
arrangement, and of the free selection of means to attain ends,
is the only universe possible, and could not, by any supposition,
be other than it is.   Such a theory may be the only one open
to those who hold the ground of the universe to be impersonal;
but it is not one which a true Theism can sanction, and it is
unprovable.   Why should infinite wisdom not choose its ends,
and also freely choose the means by which they are to be accomplished? Which is the higher view—that which regards the
Divine Being as bound down to a single system—one, too,
which wisdom, love, and freedom have no share in producing,
but which flows from the nature of its cause with the same
necessity with which the properties of a triangle flow from the
triangle; or that which supposes the universe to have originated
in a free, intelligent act, based on the counsels of an infinite
wisdom and goodness?[1]   (2) As in this theory no place is left
for freedom in God, so logically it leaves no place for freedom
in man.   Freedom implies initiative, control, a choice between
possible alternatives.   But, on this theory we are considering,
freedom can never be more than a semblance.   Whether the
individual recognises it or not, all that he sees around him, and
all that takes place within him, is but the working out of an
immanent logical necessity.[2] Things are what they are by a
necessity as stringent as that which obtains in mathematics,
and as little room is left for human initiative as on the most
thorough-going mechanical or materialistic hypothesis. History,
too, shows that the step from the one kind of determinism to
the other is never difficult to take.   The consciousness of

[1] Cf. Veitch's *Knowing and Being*, pp. 290, 291.
[2] Lotze discusses "the conception of the world as 'a necessary, involuntary,
and inevitable development of the nature of God,'" and says regarding it: "It
is wholly useless from the religious point of view, because it leads consistently
to nothing but a thorough-going determinism, according to which not only is
everything that must happen, in case certain conditions occur, appointed in
pursuance of general laws; but according to which even the successive occur-
rence of these conditions, and consequently the whole of history with all its
details, is predetermined."—*Outlines of the Philosophy of Religion*, pp. 71, 72
(Eng. trans.).

freedom, however, is a fact too deeply rooted in our personality ; too many interests depend on it to admit of its being thus put aside at the bidding of any theory, metaphysical or other; and so long as human freedom stands, this view of the origin of the universe can never gain general acceptance.

3. In the third place, the doctrine of creation is opposed to the atheistic assertion of the self-subsistence and eternity of the universe. I may here point out the indications which science itself gives that the universe is neither self-subsistent nor eternal. Science, indeed, cannot prove the creation of the world, but it may bring us to that point at which we are compelled to assume creation.

(1) In the analysis of nature, science compels us to go back to primordial elements. The atomic constitution of matter seems one of the surest results of science,[1] and it is not yet suggested that these primordial elements are developed from one another by any process of evolution, or that their homogeneous structure and identical properties are to be accounted for by natural selection or any similar cause. Here, then, is one limit to evolution, and it is important that those who are disposed to regard evolution as all-embracing should take notice of it. But science not only tells us that the universe is built up of atoms, it finds that each of these atoms is a little world in itself in intricacy and complexity of structure ;[2] and the fact that all atoms of the same class are exactly alike, perfect copies of each other in size, shape, weight, and proportion, irresistibly suggests the inference that they have a common cause. "When we see a great number of things," says Sir John Herschel, "precisely alike, we do not believe this similarity to have originated except from a common

---

[1] Professor Clifford said : "What I wish to impress upon you is this, that what is called 'the atomic theory'—that is just what I have been explaining —is no longer in the position of a theory, but that such of the facts as I have just explained to you are really things which are definitely known, and which are no longer suppositions."—Manchester Science Lecture on "Atoms," Nov. 1872. Cf. art. "Atom" in *Ency. Brit.*, and Stallo's *Concepts of Modern Physics*, pp. 28, 29.

[2] The authors of *The Unseen Universe* say : "To our minds it appears no less false to pronounce eternal *that aggregation we call the atom*, than it would be to pronounce eternal *that aggregation we call the sun*."—P. 213. Cf. p. 139. Professor Jevons believes that "even chemical atoms are very complicated structures ; that an atom of pure iron is probably a vastly more complicated system than that of the planets and their satellites."—*Principles of Science*, ii. p. 452.

principle independent of them." Applying this to the atoms, he observes, "the discoveries alluded to effectually destroy the idea of an eternally self-existent matter, by giving to each of its atoms the essential characters at once of a manufactured article and a subordinate agent."[1] This reasoning, I think, will command general assent, though fastidiousness may be offended with the phrase "manufactured article" as applied to a work of Deity.

(2) Science compels us to go back to a beginning in time. No doctrine comes here more powerfully to our support than the doctrine of evolution, which some suppose to be a denial of creation. If the universe were a stable system,—*i.e.* if it were not in a condition of constant development and change,—it might with some plausibility be argued that it had existed from eternity. But our knowledge of the past history of the world shows us that this is not its character; that, on the contrary, it is progressive and developing.[2] Now it lies in the very thought of a developing universe that, as we trace it back through narrower and narrower circles of development, we come at last to a beginning,—to some point from which the evolution started.[3] The alternative to this is an eternal succession of cycles of existence, a theory which has often recurred, but which brings us back to the impossible conception of a chain without a first link, of a series every term of which depends on a preceding, while yet the whole series depends on nothing.[4] Science can give no proof of an eternal succession, but so far as it has any voice on the subject points in an opposite direction, by showing that when the universe has parted with its energy, as it is in constant process of doing, it has no means of restoring it again.[5]

---

[1] Quoted in Hitchcock's *Religion of Geology*, p. 105, and endorsed by Professor Clerk-Maxwell—art. "Atom," *Ency. Brit.*; and by the authors of *The Unseen Universe*. The latter say: "Now, this production was, as far as we can judge, a sporadic or abrupt act, and the substance produced, that is to say, the atoms which form the substratum of the present universe, bear (as Herschel and Clerk-Maxwell have well said), from their uniformity of constitution, all the marks of being manufactured articles."—P. 214.

[2] This does not necessarily mean acceptance of the nebular theory of development. See Note B.—Evolution in Inorganic Nature—The Nebular Hypothesis.

[3] Professor Clerk-Maxwell says: "This idea of a beginning is one which the physical researches of recent times have brought home to us, more than any observer of the course of scientific thought in former times would have had reason to expect."—Address to Math. and Phys. Sect. of Brit. Assoc., 1870.

[4] See Note C.—The Hypothesis of Cycles.

[5] See passages quoted in Note C.

(3) Finally, it is the view of many distinguished evolutionists, that the course of evolution itself compels us to recognise the existence of breaks in the chain of development, where, as they think, some new and creative cause must have come into operation.   I may instance Mr. Wallace, a thoroughgoing evolutionist, who recognises three such "stages in the development of the organic world, when some new cause or power must necessarily have come into action," viz. (a) at the introduction of life, (b) at the introduction of sensation or consciousness, (c) at the introduction of man.[1]   With the view I hold of development as a process, determined from within, I do not feel the same need for emphasising these as "breaks."   We have, indeed, at the points named, the appearance of something entirely new, but so have we, in a lesser degree, with every advance or improvement in the organism, e.g., with the first rudiment of an eye, or of a new organ of any kind.   The action of the creative cause is spread along the whole line of the advance, revealing itself in higher and higher potencies as the development proceeds.   It only breaks out more manifestly at the points named, where it founds a new order or kingdom of existence.[2]

While thus advocating, as part of the doctrine of creation, a beginning of the world in time, I am not insensible to the enormous difficulties involved in that conception.   Prior to that beginning we have still, it may appear, to postulate a beginningless eternity, during which God existed alone.   The Divine purpose to create was there, but it had not passed into act. Here arises the difficulty.   How are we to fill up in thought these blank eternal ages in the Divine life ?   The doctrine of

---

[1] Darwinism, pp. 474–476.

[2] Mr. Gore has said: "The term supernatural is purely relative to what at any particular stage of thought we mean by nature.   Nature is a progressive development of life, and each new stage of life appears supernatural from the point of view of what lies below it."—The Incarnation (Bampton Lectures), p. 35.   Lange has expanded the same thought.   "Each stage of nature," he says, "prepares for a higher ; which in turn may be regarded as above nature, as contrary to nature, and yet as only higher nature, since it introduces a new and higher principle of life into the existent and natural order of things. . . . Thus the chemical principle appeared as a miracle in the elementary world, as introducing a new and higher life ; similarly the principle of crystallisation is a miracle with reference to the lower principle of chemical affinity ; the plant, a miracle above the crystal ; the animal, a miracle in reference to the plant ; and man, over all the animal world.   Lastly, Christ, as the Second Man, the God-Man, is a miracle above all the world of the first man, who is of the earth earthy."—Com. on Matt. p. 152 (Eng. trans.)..

the Trinity, with its suggestion of an internal Divine life and love, comes in as an aid,[1] but, abstracting from the thought of the world, of the universe afterwards to be created, we know of nothing to serve as a content of the Divine mind, unless it be the so-called "eternal truths." So that here we are in presence of a great deep. A yet greater difficulty arises when we ask, Since God purposed to create, why was creation so long delayed? Why was a whole eternity allowed to elapse before the purpose was put into execution?[2] If it was a satisfaction to love and wisdom to produce a universe, why was creation not as eternal as the purpose of it? Why an eternity's quiescence, and then this transient act? Or rather, since in eternity no one moment is indistinguishable from another, why this *particular* moment chosen for creation? The very mentioning of these difficulties suggests that somehow we are on a wrong track, and that the solution lies—since solution there must be, whether we can reach it or not—in the revisal of the notions we set out with as to the relations of eternity to time.

First, some have sought to cut this knot by the doctrine of an Eternal Creation. God, it is thought, did not wait through a solitary eternity before He called the world into existence— the act of creation is coeval with His Being, and the world, though a creature and dependent, is eternal as Himself. This was the doctrine of Origen in the early Church, of Erigena in the Middle Ages, and has been revived by Rothe, Dorner, Lotze, and many others in modern times. It is carefully to be distinguished from the doctrine of a pre-existent eternal matter formerly referred to. But I do not think it solves the difficulty. It is either only the doctrine of an eternal series of worlds in another form, and is exposed to all the difficulties of that assumption; or it seeks to evade these difficulties by the hypothesis of an undeveloping spiritual world, standing, as Dorner says, in the light of eternity, antecedent to the existing

---

[1] Cf. Professor Flint, in *Anti-Theistic Theories*, pp. 438, 439. He remarks: "Although Omnipotence cannot express itself fully in the finite world to which we belong, the Divine nature may be in itself an infinite universe, where this and all other attributes can find complete expression. . . . The Divine nature must have in itself a plenitude of power and glory, to which the production of numberless worlds can add nothing."

[2] This objection was early urged against the doctrine of creation. Cf. Origen, *De Principiis*, Book iii. 5; Augustine, *De Civitate Dei*, Book xi. 5.

one—an hypothesis which leaves the origin of the temporal and developing world precisely where it was. Besides, how is the purpose of God ever to be summed up into a unity, if there is literally no beginning and no goal in creation ?[1]

Secondly, another form of solution is that of the speculative philosophers, who would have us regard the distinction of time and eternity as due only to our finite standpoint, and who bid us raise ourselves to that higher point of view from which all things are beheld, in Spinoza's phrase, *sub specie æternitatis*.[2] The meaning of this is, that what exists for our consciousness as a time-development exists for the Divine consciousness as an eternally complete whole. For God, temporal succession has no existence. The universe, with all its determinations, past, present, and future, stands before the Divine mind in simultaneous reality. Language of this kind is found in Spinoza, Fichte, Hegel, Green,[3] and is to be met with sometimes in more orthodox theologians. It is, however, difficult to see what meaning can be attached to it which does not reduce all history to an illusion.[4] For, after all, time-development is a reality. There is succession in our conscious life, and in the events of nature. The things that happened yesterday are not the things that are happening to-day. The things that are happening to-day are not the things that will happen to-morrow. The past is past; the future is not yet come. It is plain that if time is a reality, the future is not yet present to God, except ideally.

---

[1] See Note D.—"Eternal Creation."

[2] Spinoza's *Ethics*, Part II. Prop. 44, Cor. ii.—"It is the nature of reason to perceive things *sub quadam æternitatis specie*."

[3] A good illustration is afforded by Mr. Green in a fragment on Immortality. "As a determination of thought," he says, "everything is eternal. What are we to say, then, to the extinct races of animals, the past formations of the earth? How can that which is extinct and past be eternal? . . . The process is eternal, and they *as stages in it* are so too. That which has passed away is only their false appearance of being independent entities, related only to themselves, as opposed to being stages, essentially related to a before and after. In other words, relatively to our temporal consciousness, which can only present one thing to itself at a time, and therefore supposes that when A follows B, B ceases to exist, they have perished; relatively to the thought which, as eternal, holds past, present, and future together, they are permanent; their very transitoriness is eternal."—*Works*, iii. p. 159.

[4] Hegel, indeed, says: "Within the range of the finite we can never see that the end or aim has really been secured. The consummation of the infinite aim, therefore, consists merely in removing the illusion which makes it seem yet unaccomplished. . . . It is this illusion under which we live. . . . In the course of its process the Idea makes itself that illusion, by setting an antithesis to confront it; and its action consists in getting rid of the illusion which it has created."—Wallace's *Logic of Hegel*, p. 304.

The events that will happen to-morrow are not yet existent. Else life is a dream; all, as the Indian philosophers say, is *Maya*,—illusion, appearance, seeming. Even if life *is* a dream, there is succession in the thoughts of that dream, and time is still not got rid of. I cannot see, therefore, that without reducing the process of the world to unreality, this view of it as an eternally completed fact can be upheld. In an ideal sense the world may be, doubtless is, present to the Divine mind; but as regards the parts of it yet future, it cannot be so actually.[1]

What other solution, then, is possible? The solution must lie in getting a proper idea of the relation of eternity to time, and this, so far as I can see, has not yet been satisfactorily accomplished. The nearest analogy I can suggest is that of the spiritual thinking principle within ourselves, which remains a constant factor in all the flux of our thoughts and feelings. It is in the midst of them, yet it is out of the flux and above them. It is not involved in the succession of time, for it is the principle which itself relates things in the succession of time— for which, therefore, such succession exists. I would only venture to remark, further, that even if the universe were conceived of as originating in an eternal act, it would still, to a mind capable of tracing it back through the various stages of its development, present the aspect of a temporal beginning. Before this beginning, it would be possible for the mind to extend its vision indefinitely backwards through imaginary ages, which yet had no existence save as its own ideal construction. But God's eternity is not to be identified with this thought of an indefinitely extended time. Eternity we may rather take to be an expression for the timeless necessity of God's existence; and time, properly speaking, begins its course only with the world.[2]

A few words before leaving this part of the subject on the motive and end of creation. If we reject the idea of metaphysical necessity, and think of creation as originating in a free, intelligent act, it must, like every similar act, be conceived of

---

[1] Cf. Veitch's *Knowing and Being*, chap. vii.; Seth's *Hegelianism and Personality*, pp. 180–184; Pfleiderer, *Religionsphilosophie*, iii. pp. 293–295 (Eng. trans.); Lotze, *Microcosmus*, ii. p. 711 (Eng. trans.); and see Note D. to Lect. III.

[2] See Note E.—Eternity and Time.

as proceeding from a motive, which includes in it at the same
time a rational end.   And if God is free, personal Spirit, who
is at the same time ethical Will, what motive is possible but
goodness or love, or what end can be thought of but an ethical
one ?   In this way it may be held that, though the universe is not
the product of a logical or metaphysical necessity, it arises from
the nature of God by a *moral* necessity which is one with the
highest freedom, and thus the conception of creation may be
secured from arbitrariness.   It is an old thought that the motive
to the creation of the world was the goodness of the Creator.
Plato expresses this idea in his *Timæus*,[1] and points to a yet
more comprehensive view when, in the *Republic*, he names
" the Good " as the highest principle both of knowledge and of
existence.[2]   Since the time of Kant, philosophy has dealt in
very earnest fashion with this idea of " the Good "—now conceived of as ethical good, but likewise as including in it the
highest happiness and blessedness—as at once the moving cause
and end of the world.   Start from the postulate of Kant, that
moral ends are alone of absolute worth, and the inference is
irresistible that the world as a whole is constituted for moral
ends, and that it has its cause in a Supreme Original Good,
which produces the natural for the sake of the moral, and is
guiding the universe to a moral goal.[3]   Hence, from his principles, Kant arrives at the notion of an ethical community or
" Kingdom of God," having the laws of virtue as its basis and
aim, as the end to which creation tends.[4]   Lotze takes up the
same thought of a world ordered in comformity with the idea of
" the Good," and having its source in a Highest-Good Personal,
and from him chiefly it has entered into Ritschlian theology.[5]
But Christian theology from its own standpoint arrives at a
similar result.   We have but to ask, with Dorner, What is the
relation of the ethical nature of God to the other distinctions
we ascribe to Him ? to see that " the non-ethical distinctions in

[1] *Timæus*, p. 29—" Let me tell you, then, why the Creator created and made
the universe.   He was good, and no goodness can ever have any jealousy of
anything.   And being free from jealousy, He desired that all things should be
as like Himself as possible."—Jowett's *Plato*, iii. p. 613.
[2] *Republic*, Bk. vi.   [3] See last Lecture, pp. 108–109.
[4] In his *Religion innerhalb der Grenzen der blossen Vernunft*, Bk. iii.   Cf.
Seth's *From Kant to Hegel*, pp. 123, 124 ; Caird's *Philosophy of Kant*,
pp. 611–613.
[5] Cf. *Microcosmus*, ii. p. 723 (Eng. trans.); *Outlines of Metaphysic*, pp.
151, 152 (Eng. trans.).

the nature of God are related to the ethical as means to an end; but the absolute end can only lie in morality, for it alone is of absolute worth."[1] In the graduated system of ends of which the universe consists, the moral, in other words, must be presumed to be the highest. And this is precisely what Christianity declares when it teaches that Christ and the kingdom of God are the consummation of God's world-purpose; that the government of the world is carried on for moral ends; and that "all things work together for good to them that love God."[2]

II. From the point now reached, the transition is easy to the Scripture doctrine of the nature of man, and of his position in creation. I may begin here with man's place in creation, which of itself is a testimony which nature bears to the meaning and purpose of God in that creation. Assuming that final cause is to be traced in the world at all, we can get no better clue to it than by simply observing whither the process of development tends—what, as Mr. Spencer says, is "the naturally revealed end" towards which evolution works.[3] Here is a process of development, of evolution, going on for millenniums—what, as a matter of fact, do we find to be the outcome of it? At the base of the scale is inorganic matter; then we rise to organic life in the vegetable world; as a next round in the ladder of ascent we have animal and sentient life; we rise through all the gradations of that life—through insect, fish, reptile, bird, mammal—till at length, at the close of the long line of evolution, we find—What? Man, a self-conscious, personal, rational moral being; a being capable of entering not only into moral relations with his fellow-men, but, infinitely higher, into spiritual and moral relations with his invisible Creator. Man's creation, it is true, is only the starting-point of a new line of evolution, but that evolution is one of moral life. So far as the teaching of evolution goes, then, man is the crown and masterpiece of this whole edifice of creation, and this also is the teaching of the Bible. I have been frequently struck with this in reading the works of Mr. Spencer and of other evolutionists, that none of them supposes that evolution is ever to reach a higher being than man; that whatever future development there is to be

---

[1] *Christian Ethics*, p. 65 (Eng. trans.).   [2] Rom. viii. 28.
[3] *Data of Ethics*, p. 171.

will not be development beyond humanity, but development within humanity. In this it is implied that man is the end of nature, and that the end of nature is a moral one. In man, if we may so speak, mute and unintelligent nature attains to consciousness of itself, gains the power of reading back meaning into its own blind past, and has a prophecy of the goal to which its future tends. At the summit of nature's gradations—of her inorganic kingdom and plant kingdom and animal kingdom—there stands a being fitted for the kingdom of God.

The agreement of Scripture and science up to this point is patent and incontestable. In the original picture in Genesis we have, as in nature, a gradually ascending series of creations. We have man at the top of the scale; man as the latest being of all, and distinguished from all by the fact that he alone bears his Creator's image; man set at the head of the lower orders of creatures, as God's rational vicegerent and representative. Science corroborates all this. It gives to man the same place in the ascending series of creations as Scripture gives him; declares him to be the last and final product of nature; links him intimately with the past through his physical organisation, in which the whole of nature, as physiology shows, recapitulates itself; and at the same time acknowledges that he stands alone, and far removed from the other creatures, in his powers of thought and language, in his capacity for a self-regulated moral life under general rules, in his religious nature, in his capability of progress, and of boundless productivity in arts, sciences, laws, and institutions. Nay, looking at creation as a whole, from the vantage-ground which our present knowledge gives us, we can feel that its plan would have remained incomplete, its pyramid would have lacked a summit, had man not appeared upon the scene. For man not only stands at the head of creation, but, in virtue of his rational nature, he occupies a position in relation to it different from every other. The animal, however high in the scale of development, is a mere creature of nature; man has a life above nature. He is a being of "large discourse, looking before and after."[1] He is capable of reflection on himself; on the meaning and causes of things in the world around him; on the ends of his own existence. He can rise above momentary impulse and passion, and

---

[1] *Hamlet*, act iv. scene 4

guide his life by general principles of reason, and so is capable of morality. For the same reason he is capable of religion, and shows his superiority over nature through the thoughts he cherishes of God, of infinity, of eternity. Till a mind of this kind appeared, capable of surveying the scene of its existence, of understanding the wisdom and beauty displayed in its formations, and of utilising for rational purposes the vast resources laid up in its treasuries, the very existence of such a world as this is remained an inexplicable riddle : an adequate final cause—an end-for-self—was not to be found in it.[1]

It would indeed be an exaggeration to view creation solely from the standpoint here taken. The position that man is the final cause of creation must obviously be held with certain qualifications. Were we to attempt to maintain that the world exists solely for man's use and benefit, we would be met by unanswerable objections. Because man is the supreme end of nature, it does not follow that there are not lower ends—the happiness of the sentient creatures, *e.g.*, and many others that we do not know. This world, again, is part of a wider system, and there may be not only lower ends, but wider ends, than those prescribed by man's existence. There is a delight which creative wisdom has in its own productions, which is an end in itself. God saw the works that He had made, and behold they were good ; though not till man appeared upon the scene were they declared " very good." [2] But this in no degree militates against the position that the main use and end of nature is to subserve the purposes of man's existence. Is not this to a thinking mind implied in its very dispositions and arrangements, in its distribution of land and sea, in its river plains and ocean communication, in its supplies of mineral and other wealth stored up in its recesses, in the forces it puts at man's disposal for the accomplishment of his purposes, in the very obstacles it interposes in the way of his advancement, stimulating his mental activity, summoning forth his powers to contend with difficulties, and in this way rousing him up to further conquests ? There are yet higher teleological relations which nature sustains to man, on which I cannot now dwell—the part, *e.g.*, which natural conditions play, as in Greece, in the development of the character and spirit of peoples ; the food which the

---

[1] See Note F.—Man the Head of Creation.　　　　[2] Gen. i. 31.

study of nature affords to his intellect; the beauty which delights, and the sublimity which awes him, both speaking to his spirit of things higher than themselves; the suggestions it gives of the infinite and eternal, etc. Taking it all in all, we may rest in the view that man, as nature's highest being, is the key to the understanding of the whole development; that nature does not exist for its own sake, but supremely for the sake of the moral; that its chief end is to furnish the means for such a development as we now see in the mental and moral history of mankind.[1]

As a compound being, made up of body and of spirit, man is the link which• unites the natural and the spiritual worlds.[2] The direct link between man and nature is the body, which in its erect posture, its highly evolved brain, its developed limbs, and its countenance lifted up to the heavens, bears witness, as already Ovid reminds us,[3] to the dignity of the soul within. As Materialism ignores the rights of the spirit, and would reduce thought, feeling, and will, to functions of matter; so an ultra-spirituality is too apt to ignore the rights of the body, and to regard it as a mere accident of man's personality. Materialism quite rightly protests against this one-sidedness; and the whole tendency of modern inquiry is to draw the two sides of man's nature—the material and the spiritual, the physical and the metaphysical, the physiological and the mental—more closely together. The Bible avoids both extremes. Materialism gets all its rights in the Bible doctrine of the body. The abstract spirituality of a Plotinus, or of a hyper-refined idealism, which regards the body as a mere envelope of the soul, dropped off at death without affecting its entirety, is quite foreign to it. I do not dwell on this now, as I shall have occasion to refer to it in the following Lectures. Enough to remark that the Bible history of man's creation; the remarkable honour its ·places on the body as God's workman-

---

[1] On the teleological relations of nature to man, see Kant, *Kritik d. Urtheilkraft*, sect. 83—"Of the last end of nature as a teleological system," and sect. 84—"Of the final end of the existence of a world, *i.e.* of the creation itself"; and cf. Caird, *Philosophy of Kant*, ii. pp. 545–557.

[2] See this thought worked out in Herder's *Ideen zur Phil. d. Gesch. der Menschheit* (cf. Book v. 6, quoted in Note F.).

[3] *Metamorphoses*, i. 2:

> " Pronaque quum spectent animalia cetera terram,
> Os homini sublime dedit, cœlumque tueri
> Jussit, et erectos ad sidera tollere vultus."

ship and the temple of the Holy Ghost; its doctrines of sin, with death as the penalty; of the Incarnation—"forasmuch as the children are partakers of flesh and blood, He also Himself likewise took part of the same";[1] of Redemption, which includes "the Redemption of the body";[2] of the future life in a glorified corporeity—all warn us against an undue depreciation of the body.

I go on to remark that if the Bible gives its rightful place to the body, much more does it lay stress on the possession by man of a spirit, which is the true seat of his personality, and the link which unites him with the spiritual world, and with God. Psychological questions would be here out of place, and I can only enter into a very brief examination of the Biblical terms used to express the different aspects of man's spiritual nature, relegating the further discussion of these to their proper sphere in Biblical theology or psychology.[3] I would first remark that the Biblical usage of psychological terms can only be understood if we keep strictly to the Biblical point of view. In the Old Testament, it is the unity of the personality which is the main fact, and not the distinction of an immaterial and a material part, as in our modern usage. *Nephesh* or soul does not, in the Old Testament, stand opposed to body, but is rather the principle of "life," which manifests itself on the one hand in the corporeal functions ("the life is in the blood"[4]), and on the other in the conscious activities of the mind. The real contrast in the Old Testament is between "flesh" (*bāsār*) and "spirit" (*rûach*), and the "soul" is the middle term between them, the unity of them.[5] This does not mean that "soul" and "spirit" are separable elements in the same way that "soul" and "body" are, but it means that the "soul," as inbreathed by God, is the source or seat of a double life. On the one side, it is the animating principle of the body; the source of all vital functions. It is its presence in the body which

---

[1] Heb. ii. 14.   [2] Rom. viii. 23.
[3] Cf. on this subject the works of Delitzsch and Beck on Biblical Psychology; Oehler and Schultz on Old Testament Theology; Wendt's *Inhalt der Lehre Jesu*; Heard on the *Tripartite Nature of Man*; Laidlaw's *Bible Doctrine of Man*; Dickson's *Flesh and Spirit* (Baird Lectures), etc.
[4] Lev. xvii. 11.
[5] Another word for spirit is *Neshāmāh*—used twice in the Old Testament, once in a noteworthy passage for the principle of self-consciousness (Prov. xx. 27), as in 1 Cor. ii. 11.

constitutes the latter "flesh." On the other side, it is the principle of self-conscious life. Various names are employed to denote the kinds of these self-conscious activities; but they may be grouped generally under the name "spirit." More explicitly, all the activities of the "spirit" belong to the "soul"; but the converse is not true, that all the activities of the "soul" belong to the "spirit." For the vital functions of the body, with the appetites, desires, impulses, etc., which belong to this side of our nature, likewise are traceable to it as their source. It is only the higher activities of the "soul"—those which we still denominate "spiritual"—I speak of general usage, for probably there is no distinction we can make which has not some exception—which are described by the term "spirit." Thus we read of a spirit of wisdom, of knowledge, of understanding, of an upright spirit, a free spirit, a contrite spirit, etc.[1] That the "soul," *essentially* considered, is also spiritual, is implied in its origin from the Divine Spirit. In the New Testament we have a distinction of "soul" and "body" much more akin to our own, though the influence of Old Testament usage is still very marked. "Soul" ($\psi\nu\chi\acute{\eta}$) still includes a higher and a lower life; and the higher life is still denoted by the term "spirit" ($\pi\nu\epsilon\hat{\nu}\mu\alpha$); while the implication of a body is still always conveyed in the term "soul." There is no "soul" which is not intended to animate a "body"; there are incorporeal spirits (angels, demons), but they are not called by the name "souls." On the other hand, the "soul" is recognised as spiritual in its essence, and in its disembodied state is classed among "spirits," *e.g.* "the spirits in prison."[2] I need not discuss the cognate terms heart ($\kappa\alpha\rho\delta\acute{\iota}\alpha$), mind ($\nu o\hat{\upsilon}s$), understanding ($\delta\iota\acute{\alpha}\nu o\iota\alpha$), etc., but content myself with saying that, except in the sense above explained, I do not see how a trichotomous view of man's nature can be maintained. The distinction of "soul" and "spirit" is a distinction within the one indivisible spiritual nature; and the antithesis "soul" and "body" really covers all the facts of man's personal life. The highest functions of the "spirit" are in the New Testament ascribed also to the "soul";[3] and the "soul" in turn is used

---

[1] Isa. xi. 2; Ps. li. 10–12. Some of the references are to the Divine Spirit, but as the source of spiritual powers in man

[2] 1 Pet. iii. 19.   [3] *E.g.* Matt. xxii. 27; Luke i. 46.

by Jesus as a name for man's highest imperishable life. "He that hateth his life (ψυχή) in this world shall keep it unto life eternal."[1]

From this digression I return to the fact that it is in his "soul" or "spirit" that man peculiarly bears the Divine image. In a threefold respect is man the personal image of his Maker.

1. He bears first of all the *rational* image of God. We have a proof of this in the fact formerly referred to, that man can understand the world God has made. How is science possible, except on the assumption that the reason we find in ourselves is the same in kind as the reason which expresses itself in the universe? The argument is the same as if we were set to translate a book written in a foreign language. The first condition of success in that attempt—the postulate with which we set out—is similarity of intelligence between the man who wrote the book, and ourselves who seek to decipher its meaning. If his reason were of a totally different kind from ours, the attempt to understand him would be hopeless. Precisely the same condition applies to the possibility of our knowledge of the world. Reason in man and the reason expressed in nature must be the same in kind, or no relation between them could be established. Christian theology expresses this by saying that the world is created by the Logos, a term which means at once reason and word.

2. Man bears God's *moral* image, not now in the possession of actual righteousness, but in the possession of the indestructible elements of a moral nature. (1) He is a being with the power of moral knowledge; reason, in other words, is the source to him, not only of principles of knowledge, but of laws of duty. The idea of the good, and with it the moral "ought" or ethical imperative, is part of his constitution. His moral ideal may vary with the degree of his development and culture; but, throughout, man is a being who distinguishes good and evil, and who recognises the obligation to obey the good and to eschew the evil. In this he proclaims himself a subject of moral law, and a being with a moral destiny. (2) He is a free, spiritual cause, *i.e.* he has moral freedom. I speak again not of man as at present he actually is, with

[1] John xii. 25.

his freedom sadly impaired through sin, but of man in the constitutive elements of his nature. And as a free, spiritual, self-determining cause, standing at the summit of nature, man is again in a very marked sense the image of his Maker. It is this power of will and self-decision in man which most of all constitutes him a person. Through it he stands out of and above nature's sequences, and can react on and modify them. He is, as some have chosen to regard him, a supernatural cause in the order of nature.[1] It is surely of little use to deny the possibility of miracle, when every human volition is a species of miracle—a new, hyperphysical cause interpolated in the chain of physical events, and giving them a new direction. (3) Man is a being with moral affections. Without these he would not be a true image of the God who is love. Summing up these points, we recognise in man a conscience which reveals moral law, a will which can execute moral purposes, and affections which create a capacity for moral love. This relates only to formal attributes; but it is now to be remarked that the bearing of God's moral image in the full sense implies not only the possession of these attributes, but an actual resemblance to God in character, in holiness and love. In the primeval state—the *status integritatis* of the Biblical account [2]—this possession of the image of God by man can only be viewed as potentiality, though a pure potentiality, for the perfected image could not be gained except as the result of self-decision and a long process of development, if even then without the appearance of the second Adam from heaven.[3] It is Christ, not the first Adam, who is the ideal here, the model after which we are to be renewed in the image of Him who created us. Only in Christ do we see what a humanity perfectly conformed to the Divine idea of it is.

3. Man bears the image of God in his deputed *sovereignty* over the creatures, a sovereignty which naturally belongs to him in virtue of the attributes just enumerated, and of his place at the head of creation already adverted to. To the

---

[1] Cf. Bushnell, *Nature and Supernatural*, pp. 23–25.

[2] See next Lecture.

[3] This is a view already enunciated with great clearness by Irenæus. Cf. Dorner, *Person of Christ*, i. pp. 314–316; Art. "Irenæus" in *Dict. of Christ. Biog.* vol. iii.; and Harnack, *Dogmengeschichte*, i. p. 499.

reality of this sovereignty, all man's conquests over material conditions, his achievements in art and civilisation, his employment of nature's laws and forces for his own ends, his use of the lower creatures for service and food, etc., abundantly testify.[1]

I might add one other mark of the possession of the Divine image by man, likewise involved in his self-conscious personality. I refer to what may be called the *potential infinitude* of his nature. It has often been remarked that man could not even know himself to be finite, if he were not able in thought to transcend the finite, and frame an idea of the Infinite. It is the strange thing about him, yet not strange once we realise what is implied in the possession of a thinking nature, that though finite, hedged round on every side by the limitations of the finite, he yet shows a constant impulse to transcend these limitations, and ally himself with the Infinite. Through this peculiarity of his nature, there is none of God's infinite attributes which does not find a shadow in his soul. How else could Carlyle, *e.g.*, fill his pages with references to the eternities, the immensities, etc., in which man's spirit finds its awful home? Is a being who can form the idea of eternity not already in affinity with the Eternal, in a sense His image? Man is not omnipresent, but is there not a shadow of God's omnipresence in those thoughts of his that roam through space, and find a satisfaction in the contemplation of its boundlessness? He is not omniscient, but is not his desire for knowledge insatiable? The same spurning of bounds, the same illimitableness, is seen in all his desires, aims, ideals, hopes, and aspirations. This shows the folly of the contention that because man is finite, he is cut off from the knowledge of the Infinite. The objection seems to turn on the thought that there is a physical bigness in the idea of infinity which prevents the mind from holding it. It might as well be contended that because the mind is cooped up within the limits of a cranium only a few inches in diameter, it cannot take account of the space occupied, say by the solar system, or of the distance between the earth and the sun!

In thus affirming the spiritual nature and dignity of man,

---

[1] On the whole subject of the image of God in man, cf. Laidlaw's *Bible Doctrine of Man*, Lect. III. (Cunningham Lectures).

and a sonship to God founded thereon, it was inevitable that the Christian view should meet with keen opposition from the modern anti-supernaturalistic tendency, which regards with extreme disfavour any attempt to lift man out of the ranks of nature, and the prevailing bias of which is strongly towards Materialism.   In this spirit Professor Huxley has told us that "anyone who is acquainted with the history of science will admit that its progress has, in all ages, meant, and now more than ever means, the extension of the province of what we call matter and causation, and the concomitant banishment from all regions of human thought of what we call spirit and spontaneity."[1]   The materialistic hypothesis has wide currency at the present day, though it is difficult to see how any sober mind, reflecting on the patent difference between mental and physical phenomena, could ever suppose that it was adequate, or could imagine that by its aid it had got rid of "spirit."   As involving the denial of the existence of a spiritual principle in man, distinct from the body, this hypothesis is manifestly in contradiction with the Biblical doctrine just explained, and on this account claims a brief consideration.

The great fact on which every theory of Materialism strikes is, of course, the fact of consciousness.   Life, unattended by sensation, presents a great enough difficulty to the theorist who would explain everything on mechanical principles,[2] but when consciousness enters the difficulty is insuperable.[3] It is, at the same time, no easy matter to bind down the advocates of the materialistic theory to a clear and consistent view.

[1] *Lay Sermons*, "On the Physical Basis of Life," p. 156.

[2] Kant has said that the attempt to explain the world on mechanical principles is wrecked on a caterpillar.

[3] Du Bois-Reymond, who himself favours Materialism, specifies, in his *Die Sieben Welträthsel* (The Seven Enigmas of the World), seven limits to the materialistic explanation of Nature.   These are :
  1. The Existence of Matter and Form.
  2. The Origin of Motion.
  3. The Origin of Life.
  4. The Appearance of Design in Nature.
  5. The Existence of Consciousness.
  6. Intelligent Thought and the Origin of Speech.
  7. The Question of Free-Will.
See the account of this work in Kennedy's *Natural Theology and Modern Thought*, from which I take the list (p. 52).   Enigmas 1, 2, and 5 Du Bois-Reymond regards as insoluble.

1. There is the crass, thorough-going Materialism which literally identifies brain with mind, and the movements of the brain with the thoughts and feelings of which we are aware in consciousness. Brain action, on this hypothesis, *is* thought and feeling. "The brain," says Cabanis, "secretes thought, as the liver secretes bile." This is the crude theory of writers like Moleschott, Vogt, and Büchner, but it is too manifestly absurd—it too palpably ignores the striking differences between mental and physiological facts—to be accepted by more cautious scientists without qualification. Brain movements are but changes of place and relation on the part of material atoms, and, however caused, are never more than motions; they have nothing of the nature of thought about them. "It is absolutely and for ever inconceivable," says the distinguished German physiologist, Du Bois-Reymond, "that a number of carbon, hydrogen, nitrogen, and oxygen atoms should be otherwise than indifferent to their own positions or motions, past, present, or future. It is utterly inconceivable how consciousness should result from their joint action."[1] There is, accordingly, general agreement among scientific thinkers that the physical changes and the mental phenomena which accompany them are two distinct sets of facts, which require to be carefully kept apart. "The passage from the physics of the brain to the corresponding facts of consciousness," says Professor Tyndall, "is unthinkable."[2] "I know nothing, and never hope to know anything," says Professor Huxley, "of the steps by which the passage from molecular movement to states of consciousness is effected."[3] "The two things are on two utterly different platforms," says Professor Clifford; "the physical facts go along by themselves, and the mental facts go along by themselves."[4] So far as this goes, it is clearly

---

[1] Lecture on *Die Grenzen des Naturerkennens.* Leipsic, 1872.

[2] *Fragments of Science,* "Scientific Materialism," p. 121. In the sixth edition the words are—"is inconceivable as a result of mechanics" (vol. ii. p. 87). He goes on to say that, could we "see and feel the very molecules of the brain; were we capable of following all their motions, all their groupings, all their electric discharges, . . . the chasm between the two classes of phenomena would still remain intellectually impassable."

[3] Article on "Mr. Darwin's Critics," in *Contemporary Review,* Nov. 1871, p. 464. Mr. Spencer expresses himself similarly: "Can the oscillation of a molecule," he says, "be represented in consciousness side by side with a nervous shock, and the two be recognised as one? No effort enables us to assimilate them."—*Principles of Psychology,* i. sec. 62.

[4] "Body and Mind," in *Fortnightly Review,* December 1874.

in favour of spiritualism, and would seem in consistency to require the abandonment of Materialism.[1]

2. An escape, however, may seem to be afforded from this dilemma, by consenting to regard matter as itself but the phenomenal manifestation of some unknown power, as therefore not the ultimate reality, but only a form or appearance of it to our senses. This is the view held by Strauss, Lange, Haeckel, Spencer, and the scientific professors whose words I have just quoted. "I have always," says Strauss, "tacitly regarded the so loudly proclaimed contrast between Materialism and Idealism (or by whatever terms one may designate the view opposed to the former) as a mere quarrel about words. They have a common foe in the dualism which has pervaded the view of the world (Weltansicht), through the whole Christian era, dividing man into body and soul, his existence into time and eternity, and opposing an eternal Creator to a created and perishable universe."[2] But whatever the change in the theoretic groundwork, this view in practice comes to very much the same thing as the other. It will not be disputed that it does so with Strauss and his German allies, whose Materialism is most pronounced.[3] But our English savants also, while disclaiming the name "materialists," while maintaining in words the distinction between the two classes of facts (mental and physical), while careful to show that a strict interpretation of the *data* would land us rather in a subjective Idealism than in Materialism,[4] none the less proceed constantly upon the hypothesis that mental facts admit of being translated (as they call it) into terms of matter, and that thus only are they capable of being treated by science.[5]

---

[1] Cf. Herbert's *Modern Realism Examined*, pp. 89–94; Kennedy's *Natural Theology and Modern Thought*, pp. 64–66.

[2] *Der alte und der neue Glaube*, p. 212.

[3] Strauss declares his thorough agreement with Carl Vogt in his denial of any special spiritual principle, p. 210.

[4] Thus, *e.g.*, Huxley: "For, after all, what do we know of this terrible 'matter,' except as a name for the unknown and hypothetical cause of states of our own consciousness?" ("On the Physical Basis of Life"). . . . "It follows that what I term legitimate Materialism . . . is neither more nor less than a shorthand Idealism."—"On Descartes," *Lay Sermons*, pp. 157, 374. On the relation of extreme Materialism to Idealism, cf. Kennedy's *Natural Theology*, pp. 64–66.

[5] At least this terminology is held to be preferable. Prof. Huxley says: "In itself it is of little moment whether we express the phenomenon of matter in terms of spirit, or the phenomenon of spirit in terms of matter. . . . But, with a view to the progress of science, the materialistic terminology is in every way to be preferred."—*Lay Sermons*, "On the Physical Basis of Life," p. 160.

Thus, Professor Huxley speaks of our thoughts as "the expression of molecular changes in that matter of life which is the source of our other vital phenomena,"[1] of consciousness as "a function of nervous matter, when that matter has attained a certain degree of organisation."[2] This is carried out so far as to deny the existence of any freedom in volition, or indeed of any influence exercised by consciousness at all upon the train of physical events.

One advantage of this materialistic-idealistic form of the theory is, that it enables the theorist to play fast and loose with language on matter and mind, and yet, when called to account, to preserve an appearance of consistency by putting as much or as little meaning into the term "matter" as he pleases. Professor Tyndall is eloquent on the "opprobrium" which we, in our ignorance, have heaped on matter, in which he prefers to discern "the promise and potency of every form of life."[3] But he has to admit that, before he can do this, he has to make a change in all ordinarily received notions of matter. "Two courses and two only are possible," he says. "Either let us open our doors freely to the conception of creative acts, or, abandoning them, let us radically change our notions of matter."[4] To which Dr. Martineau very justly replies, "Such extremely clever matter, matter that is up to everything, even to writing Hamlet, and finding out its own evolution, and substituting a moral plebiscite for a Divine government of the world, may fairly be regarded as a little too modest in its disclaimer of the attributes of mind."[5] My chief objection to Dr. Tyndall, however, is that practically he does *not* change his notion of matter, but, ignoring his own admission of the "chasm intellectually impassable"[6] between the two classes of phenomena, persists in treating mind as if it were capable of being adequately represented by molecular changes of matter, in the

---

[1] *Lay Sermons*, "On the Physical Basis of Life," p. 152. In the same essay he tells us: "As surely as every future grows out of past and present, so will the physiology of the future extend the realm of matter and law, till it is co-extensive with knowledge, with feeling, and with action."—P. 156.

[2] Article on "Mr. Darwin's Critics," in *Contemporary Review*, Nov. 1871, p. 464. In his Lecture on "Descartes," he says: "Thought is as much a function of matter as motion is."—*Lay Sermons*, p. 371.

[3] "Belfast Address," *Fragments of Science*, ii. p. 193.

[4] *Ibid.* ii. p. 191.

[5] *Religion as Affected by Modern Materialism*, pp. 14, 15.

[6] *Fragments of Science*, ii. p. 87.

ordinary acceptation of the word. Instead, however, of supporting the view that molecular changes and mental functions are convertible terms, science, with its doctrine of the "conservation of energy," has furnished, as we shall now see, a demonstration of the opposite.

There are three points at which, in the light of modern science and philosophy, the argument for Materialism is seen utterly to break down.

1. The first is that which I have just alluded to, the impossibility of accounting for the phenomena of consciousness in consistency with the scientific doctrine of the "conservation of energy." As already remarked, none but the very crassest materialists will maintain that the molecular changes in the brain are themselves the thoughts and feelings which we are aware of in consciousness. What the physicist will say is, that these changes are *attended* by certain conscious phenomena as their concomitants. You have the motions, and you have the conscious fact—the thought or feeling—alongside of it. This is the way in which the matter is put by writers like Huxley and Tyndall, who frankly confess, as we have seen, the unbridgeable gulf between the two classes of phenomena. But, once this is admitted, the assertion that mental phenomena are *products* of cerebral changes is seen to come into collision with the scientific law of conservation. If mental phenomena are produced by material causes, it can only be at the expense of some measure of energy. This, indeed, is what is affirmed. Physical energy, it is supposed, is transformed into vital energy, this again into thought and feeling. But this, it can be shown to demonstration, is precisely what does *not* take place. Every scientific man admits that energy in all its active forms is simply some kind of motion; and that what is called "transformation of energy" (heat into light or electricity, etc.) is merely change from one kind of motion into another. What, then, becomes of the energy which is used when some change takes place in the matter of the brain, accompanied by a fact of sensation? It is all accounted for in the physical changes. No scientific man will hold that any part of it disappears, passes over into an "unseen universe." With keen enough senses you could track that energy through every one of its changes, and see its results in some physical effect produced. The circuit is closed within

the physical. Motions have produced motions, nothing more, and every particle of energy present at the beginning is accounted for in the physical state of the brain at the end. There has been no withdrawal of any portion of it, even temporarily, to account for the conscious phenomenon.[1] This is a new outside fact, lying beyond the circle of the physical changes, a surplusage in the effect, which there is nothing in the expenditure of energy to explain. It is a fact of a new order, quite distinct from physical motions, and apprehended through a distinct faculty, self-consciousness. But, apart from the *nature* of the fact, there is, as I say, no energy available to account for it. What energy there is, is used up in the brain's own motions and changes, and none is left to be carried over for the production of this new conscious phenomenon. If this is true of the simplest fact of consciousness, that of sensation, much more is it true of the higher and complex activities of self-conscious life.[2]

2. The second point on which Materialism breaks down is the impossibility of establishing any relation between the two sets of phenomena in respect of the laws of their succession. The mental facts and the physical facts, we are told, go along together. But it is not held that there is no relation between them. And the relation is, according to Professor Huxley, that the mental order is wholly determined by the physical order; while, conversely, consciousness is not allowed to exercise the slightest influence on the physical series. Consciousness he thinks, in men as in brutes, to be "related to the mechanism of the body simply as a collateral product of its working, and to be as completely without any power of modifying that working as the steam-whistle which accompanies the work of a locomotive

---

[1] "Motion," says Du Bois-Reymond, "can only produce motion, or transform itself into potential energy. Potential energy can only produce motion, maintain statical equilibrium, push, or pull. The sum-total of energy remains constantly the same. More or less than is determined by the law cannot happen in the material universe; the mechanical cause expends itself entirely in mechanical operations. Thus the intellectual occurrences which accompany the material occurrences in the brain are without an adequate cause as contemplated by our understanding. They stand outside the law of causality, and therefore are as incomprehensible as a *mobile perpetuum* would be."—*Ueber die Grenzen des Naturerkennens*, p. 28 (in Kennedy's *Natural Theology*, p. 48).

[2] On this argument, see Herbert's *Modern Realism Examined*, pp. 43, 57; Kennedy's *Natural Theology and Modern Thought*, pp. 48, 49, 79, 80; Harris's *Philosophical Basis of Theism*, pp. 439–442.

engine is without influence upon its machinery."[1] The physical
changes, in other words, would go on precisely as they do, in
obedience to their own laws, were there no such thing as consciousness in existence; and consciousness is simply a bye-
product or reflex of them without any counter-influence.
Similarly, Mr. Spencer says, "Impossible as it is to get immediate proof that feeling and nervous action are the outer and
inner faces of the same change, yet the hypothesis that they
are so harmonises with all the observed facts";[2] and again,
"While the nature of that which is manifested under either
form proves to be inscrutable, the order of its manifestations
throughout all mental phenomena proves to be the same as the
order of its manifestations throughout all material phenomena."[3]
The one point clear in these statements is that in the materialistic hypothesis the order of mental phenomena is identical
with an order of physical phenomena, determined by purely
mechanical conditions.[4] Is this according to fact, or is it not
precisely the point where a materialistic explanation of mind
must for ever break down?   On the hypothesis, the one set of
phenomena follow purely physical (mechanical, chemical, vital)
laws; but the other set, or a large part of the other set (the
mental), follow laws of rational or logical connection.   Suppose
a mind, for example, following out the train of reasoning in one
of the propositions in Euclid—or, better still, think of this
demonstration as it was first wrought out in the discoverer's
own mind.   What is the order of connection here?   Is it not
one in which every step is determined by the perception of its
logical and rationally necessary connection with the step that
went before?   Turn now to the other series.   The laws which
operate in the molecular changes in the brain are purely physical
—mechanical, chemical, vital.   They are physical causes, operating to produce physical effects, without any reference to consciousness.   What possible connection can there be between
two orders so distinct, between an order determined solely by

---

[1] "The Hypothesis that Animals are Automata," in *Fortnightly Review*,
Nov. 1874, pp. 575, 576.   This steam-whistle illustration fails, as his critics
all point out, in the essential respect that a steam-whistle does subtract a
portion of the energy available for working the machinery, while the production of a conscious phenomenon does not.   Cf. Herbert, pp. '46, 47; Kennedy,
p. 79, etc.

[2] *Principles of Psychology*, i. sec. 51.   [3] *Ibid*. i. sec. 273.

[4] See Note G.—Mind and Mechanical Causation

the physical laws, and the foregoing process of rational demonstration? The two orders are, on the face of them, distinct and separate; and not the least light is cast by the one on the other. To suppose that the physical laws are so adjusted as to turn out a product exactly parallel to the steps of a rational demonstration in consciousness, is an assumption of design so stupendous that it would cast all other proof of teleology into the shade. I am far, however, from admitting that, as the materialistic hypothesis supposes, every change in the brain is determined solely by mechanical, chemical, and vital laws. Granting that cerebral changes accompany thought, I believe, if we could see into the heart of the process, it would be found that the changes are determined quite as much by mental causes as by material. I do not believe, for example, that an act of will is wholly without influence on the material sequence. Our mental acts, indeed, neither add to nor take from the energy stored up in the brain, but they may have much to do with the direction and distribution of that energy.[1]

3. A third point on which the materialistic hypothesis breaks down is its irreconcilability with what is seen to be implied in self-consciousness, and with the fact of moral freedom. To constitute self-consciousness, it is not enough that there should be a stream or succession of separate impressions, feelings, or sensations; it is necessary that there should be a principle which apprehends these impressions, and relates them (as resembling, different, co-existent, successive, etc.) to one another and to itself, a principle which not only remains one and the same throughout the changes, but is conscious of its self-identity through them. It is not merely the mental changes that need to be explained, but the consciousness of a persistent self amidst these changes. And this ego or self in consciousness is no hyperphysical figment which admits of being explained away as subjective illusion. It is only through such a persistent, identical self, that knowledge or thought is possible to us; it is implied in the simplest analysis of an act of knowledge. Were we simply part of the stream, we could never know it.[2] As

---

[1] See Note H.—Mind and Cerebral Activity.

[2] Cf. Green's *Prolegomena to Ethics*, Book i.; Lotze's *Microcosmus*, pp. 157, 163; Seth's *Hegelianism and Personality*, pp. 3-5. Lotze puts the point thus: " Our belief in the soul's unity rests not on our appearing to ourselves such a unity, but on our being able to appear to ourselves at all. . . . What

another fact of our conscious life incompatible with subjection to mechanical conditions, I need only refer to the consciousness of moral freedom. In principle, Materialism is the denial of moral freedom, or of freedom of any kind, and with its triumph moral life would disappear.[1]

These considerations are sufficient of themselves to refute Materialism, but the final refutation is that which is given by the general philosophical analysis of the relation of thought to existence, a subject on which I do not enter further than I have already done in the previous Lecture. Thought, as I tried to show there, is itself the *prius* of all things; and in attempting to explain thought out of matter, we are trying to account for it by that which itself requires thought for its explanation. Matter, which seems to some the simplest of all conceptions to work with, is really one of the most difficult; and the deeper its nature is probed, whether on the physical or on the metaphysical side, the more does it tend to disappear into something different from itself; the more, at any rate, is it seen to need for its explanation facts that are spiritual. It was remarked above how, even in the hands of Professors Huxley and Tyndall, matter tends to disappear in a subjective Idealism; the only escape from this is a rational theory of knowledge, which again explains the constitution of the world through rational categories. To explain thought out of matter is, from a philosophical point of view, the crowning instance of a *hysteron proteron*.[2]

III. From the distinction thus shown to exist between the spiritual and the material parts of man's nature, there results the possibility of the soul surviving death, and the foundation is laid for the doctrine of Immortality. The consideration of the Biblical aspect of this subject will more properly be reserved for next Lecture, where I treat of the connection of sin and death. Here I will only ask how far nature and reason have a voice to utter on these two questions: Is man constituted for

a being appears to itself to be is not the important point; if it can appear anyhow to itself, or other things to it, it must be capable of unifying manifold phenomena in an absolute indivisibility of its nature."—*Microcosmus*, p. 157.

[1] Cf. Ebrard's *Christian Apologetics*, ii. pp. 77-98; Dorner's *Christian Ethics*, pp. 105, 106; Kennedy's *Natural Theology*, Lecture V.

[2] Cf. Caird's *Philosophy of Religion*, pp. 94-101.

immortality? And is there a presumption that the soul will survive death? These questions, it ought to be observed, are not identical. The proposition that man, as a being made in God's image, is naturally destined for immortality, is not immediately convertible with the other, that the soul will survive death; for it is no part of the Biblical view, as we shall see afterwards, that death is a natural condition of man. Now, however, that death has supervened, the question arises, Does the soul still survive? To this question also, as I hope to show, both Old and New Testaments give an affirmative answer; but the complete Scripture doctrine of immortality means a great deal more than this.

It is a significant circumstance that the modern unbelieving view of the world has no hope to give us of a life beyond the grave. With the obscuration of the idea of God, and the loss of the sense of the spiritual, there has gone also faith in immortality.[1] Materialism, of course, is bound to deny a future life. The theories of Huxley, Tyndall, and Spencer hold out just as little hope of it,[2] though Mr. Fiske, developing a Theism out of the principles of Mr. Spencer, has developed also a doctrine of immortality, another evidence of the connection of these two beliefs.[3] The hope proposed to us in lieu of individual immortality is that of "corporate immortality," the privilege of joining the "choir invisible" of those who have laboured in the service of humanity, though they live now only in the grateful memory of posterity.[4] Pantheism, likewise,

[1] Renan has said : "No one in business would risk a hundred francs with the prospect of gaining a million, on such a probability as that of the future life."—*Dialogues*, p. 31. Cf. Strauss, *Der alte und der neue Glaube*, pp. 123-134. "In fact," he says, "this supposition is the most gigantic assumption that can be thought of ; and if we ask after its foundation, we meet with nothing but a wish. Man would fain not perish when he dies ; therefore he believes he will not perish."—Pp. 126, 127.

[2] The contrast is again marked with the attitude of the last century "Natural Religion," which regarded the "immortality of the soul" as one of its most certain articles. How little assurance even Theism, apart from Revelation, can give on this subject, is seen in Mr. Greg's statements in *The Creed of Christendom*, chap. xvii. ; and Preface to his *Enigmas of Life*.

[3] Fiske's *Man's Destiny*. Dr. Martineau tells the story that on a report of the arguments of this book being read to an English friend, a Positivist, on its first appearance, his exclamation was : "What? John Fiske say that? Well; it only proves, what I have always maintained, that you cannot make the slightest concession to metaphysics, without ending in a theology !"—Preface to *A Study of Religion*.

[4] "O may I join the choir invisible
    Of those immortal dead who live again

forbids the thought of personal immortality, exalting instead the blessedness of absorption in the Infinite.[1]   We cannot, however, part with the hope of immortality without infinitely lowering the whole pulse and worth even of present existence.[2]

The only *scientific* plea on which the possibility of immortality can be denied to us is based on the fact that mind in this life is so intimately bound up with physiological conditions. Once grant, however, that the thinking principle in man is distinct from the brain which it uses as its instrument, and no reason can be shown, as Bishop Butler demonstrated long ago, why it should not survive the shock of the dissolution we call death.   Death need not even be the suspension of its powers. " Suppose," says Cicero, "a person to have been educated from his infancy in a chamber where he enjoyed no opportunity of seeing external objects but through a small chink in the window shutter, would he not be apt to consider this chink as essential to his vision? and would it not be difficult to persuade him that his prospects would be enlarged by demolishing the walls of his prison? "[3]   It may turn out, as Butler says, that existing and bodily conditions are rather restraints on mind than laws of its essential nature.[4]   Even so rigid a critic of evidence as the late J. S. Mill admits that this argument against immortality from the present dependence of thought and feeling on some action of the bodily organism, is invalid. "There is, therefore," he says, "in science, no evidence against the immortality of the soul, but that negative evidence which consists in the absence of evidence in its favour.   And even the negative evidence is not so strong as negative evidence often is."[5]   It may, at the same time, be questioned, as we have seen, whether there are not

> In minds made better by their presence. . . .
>
>   .   .   .   .   .   .
>   This is life to come,
> Which martyred men have made more glorious
> For us to strive to follow."
>   GEORGE ELIOT, *Jubal, and other Poems*, pp. 301-303.

---

[1] Thus in the Indian systems, but also in modern times. Spinoza's Pantheism has no room in it for personal immortality. In Hegel's system the question was left in the same ambiguity as the question of the Divine personality (cf. Stirling's *Secret of Hegel*, ii. pp. 578-580 ; Seth's *Hegelianism and Personality*, pp. 149, 150).   On Schleiermacher's views, see Note I.—Schleiermacher and Immortality.

[2] Cf. p. 160.

[3] Quoted by Dugald Stewart, *Active and Moral Powers*, i. p. 72 (Collected Works).   Cf. *Tusculan Disputations*, Book i. 20.

[4] *Analogy*, i. chap. 1.   [5] *Three Essays*, p. 201.

limits to the extent to which science has demonstrated the dependence of the higher mental operations on cerebal changes.[1]

Science, therefore, cannot *negative* the idea of immortality, but has reason no positive utterance to give on this great and solemn question of future existence? It is not men of science only, but some believers in Revelation also, who show a disposition to minimise the indications and corroborations which nature affords of man's immortal destiny. Mr. Edward White does this in support of his theory of conditional immortality ;[2] but many others also have held the opinion that this is a question on which reason has little or nothing to say, and which must be determined solely by the light of Revelation. This position seems to me a hazardous one for a believer in Revelation to take up. Just as in speaking of Theism I ventured to say that, if God exists, it is inconceivable that nature should afford no evidence of His existence ;[3] so I would say here that if human immortality be a truth, it is impossible that it should be only, or merely, a truth of Revelation. If, as he came from his Creator's hand, it was man's destiny to be immortal, his fitness and capacity for that destiny must reveal itself in the very make and constitution of his being, in the powers and capabilities that belong to him. If it could really be shown that in man's nature, as we find it, no trace of anything exists pointing to a higher sphere of existence than earth affords, no powers or capabilities for which this earthly scene did not offer full employment or satisfaction, this alone, without any other argument, would be a cogent disproof of immortality. For the same reason, immortality cannot be viewed, as in Mr. White's theory, as a mere external addition to a nature regarded as having originally no capacity or destination for it, a *donum superadditum*. It is impossible that a being should be capable of receiving the gift of immortality, who yet in the make and constitution of his nature gives no evidence that he was destined for immortality. Otherwise immortality loses all moral significance, and sinks to the level of a mere prolongation of existence, just as the life of the brute might be prolonged. Such evidence, if it exists, may not be sufficient to demonstrate man's immortality, but it will show that the make and con-

---

[1] See Professor Calderwood's views in Note H.
[2] In his *Life in Christ*.   [3] Lect. III. p. 81.

stitution of his nature points in that direction, that immortality
is the natural solution of the enigmas of his being, that without immortality he would be a riddle and contradiction to himself and an anomaly in the world which he inhabits.   And are
there not such proofs ?

1. Our minds are arrested here, first, by the fact that *nearly
every tribe and people* on the face of the earth, savage and
civilised, *has held in some form this belief in a future state of
existence*.   This suggests that the belief is one which accords
with the facts of human nature, and to which the mind is
naturally led in its inquiries.   Assume the doctrine to be false,
there is still this fact to be accounted for—that nearly all tribes
and families of mankind have gone on dreaming this strange
dream of a life beyond the grave.[1]   Mr. Spencer, of course,
has a way of explaining this belief which would rob it of all
its worth as evidence.   The hypothesis is a very simple one.
Belief in a future state, according to it, is simply a relic of
superstition.   It had its origin in the fancies of the savage, who,
from the wanderings of his mind in sleep, and supposed appearances of the dead, aided by such facts as the reflection of his
image on the water and the appearance of his shadow, imagined
the existence of a soul, or double, separable from the body, and
capable of surviving death.[2]   Were I discussing this theory at
length, I would like to put in a word for Mr. Spencer's savage.
I would like to ask, first, Is Mr. Spencer so sure that this *is*
the whole explanation of that singularly persistent instinct
which leads even savage minds to cling so tenaciously to the
idea of a future life ?   May it not be, though a philosopher may
not care to take account of them,

> " That even in savage bosoms
> There are longings, yearnings, strivings,
> For the good they comprehend not,"

and that, sometimes at least,

> " The feeble hands and helpless,
> Groping blindly in the darkness,
> Touch God's right hand in that darkness,
> And are lifted up and strengthened ! "[3]

---

[1] Cicero urges the argument in *The Tusculan Disputations*, Book i. 13.   For
modern illustrations, cf. Max Müller's *Anthropological Religion*, Lecture V.;
Dawson's *Fossil Men and their Modern Representatives*, chap. x., etc.
[2] *Eccles. Institutions*, chaps. i., xiv.; Strauss has a similar theory, *Der alte
und der neue Glaube*, p. 124.   [3] Longfellow's *Hiawatha*, Introduction.

And I would like, secondly, to ask, Is the savage, after all, so illogical as Mr. Spencer would make him out to be? Allow that he has crude notions of apparitions and dreams, this is not the essential point. The essential point is that, from the activity of his mind in thinking and dreaming, he infers the working of a power within him distinct from his body. Is he so far wrong in this? I do not think we do justice always to the workings of the savage mind.[1] The savage knows, to begin with, that there is a something within him which thinks, feels, acts, and remembers. He does not need to wait on dreams to give him that knowledge.[2] The step is natural to distinguish this thinking something from his hands and head and body, which remain after its departure.[3] Going further, he peoples nature with spiritual agents after the type of the mind he finds within himself. Here, therefore, we have the clear yet not reasoned out distinction between body and spirit, and this, in connection with other hopes, instincts, and aspirations, readily gives birth to ideas of future continued existence. But, however it may be with the savage, how absurd it is for Mr. Spencer to assume that the mature and thinking portion of mankind have no better foundation for their belief than is implied in these vulgar superstitions which he names! You sit at the feet of a Plato, and see his keen intellect applied to this subject; you listen to the eloquence of a Cicero discoursing on it;[4] you

---

[1] Max Müller says: "We cannot protest too strongly against what used to be a very general habit among anthropologists, namely, to charge primitive man with all kinds of stupidities in his early views about the soul, whether in this life or the next."—*Anthropological Religion*, p. 218.

[2] Cf. Max Müller's discussion of the "shadow" and "dream" theory in *Anthropological Religion*, pp. 218–226. "Before primitive man could bring himself to imagine that his soul was like a dream, or like an apparition, it is clear that he must already have framed to himself some name or concept of soul."—P. 221.

[3] Cf. Max Müller, *Anthropological Religion*, pp. 195, 281, 337, 338. "It was a perfectly simple process: what may almost be called a mere process of subtraction. There was man, a living body, acting, feeling, perceiving, thinking, and speaking. Suddenly, after receiving one blow with a club, that living body collapses, dies, putrefies, falls to dust. The body, therefore, is seen to be destroyed. But there is nothing to prove that the agent within that body, who felt, who perceived, who thought and spoke, had likewise been destroyed, had died, putrefied, and fallen to dust. Hence the very natural conclusion that, though that agent had separated, it continued to exist somewhere, even though there was no evidence to show *how* it existed and *where* it existed."—P. 281. See also Mr. Greg, Preface to *Enigmas of Life*, p. 7; and Fairbairn's *Studies in Philosophy of Religion*, pp. 115 ff.

[4] Plato's *Phædo*, Cicero's *Tusculan Disputations* and *Dream of Scipio*, etc. Cf. Max Müller on *Anthropological Religion*, Lecture XI.

are lifted up by the grand strains of the poets of immortality.
You really thought that it was proof of the greater mental
stature and calibre of these men that they speculated on such
themes at all, and expressed themselves so nobly in regard to
them.   But it turns out you are mistaken.   You and they
have miserably deceived yourselves ; and what seemed to you
rational and ennobling belief is but the survival of superstitions, born of the dreams and ghost fancies of the untutored
savage !

2. But let us leave the savage, and look at this subject in
the light of the higher considerations which have in all ages
appealed with special force to the minds of rational men.   I
pass by here the metaphysical arguments, which at most are
better fitted to remove bars to the acceptance of the doctrine
than to furnish positive proofs of it.   The real proofs are those
which, as already said, show that the make and constitution of
man's nature are not explicable on the hypothesis that he is
destined only for a few short years of life on earth, but are
such as point to a nobler and enduring state of existence.   It
is an interesting circumstance that Mr. J. S. Mill, who, in his
treatment of this question, took evident delight in reducing the
logical evidence to its minimum, yet practically brings all those
arguments which he had thrust out by the door of the head
back by the door of the heart, and uses them to found the duty
of cherishing this-hope of a future life.[1]   What are these indications which point to a fitness for, and are a prophecy of,
immortality in man ?

(1) There is *the fact that the scale of man's nature is too
large for his present scene of existence.*   I have already spoken
of that shadow of infinitude in man which manifests itself in
all his thoughts, his imaginations, his desires, etc.   Look, first,
at his rational constitution.   In the ascent of the mountain of
knowledge, is man ever satisfied ?   Does not every new height
he reaches but reveal a higher height ?   Does not every new
attainment but whet his appetite to attain more ?   Is any thirst
more insatiable than the thirst for knowledge ?   Is it not the last
confession of ripened wisdom that man as yet knows nothing
as he would wish to know ?   Or look at the ideas which man's
mind is capable of containing.   His mind spans the physical

---

[1] In the Essay on "Theism," in *Three Essays on Religion.*   See below.

universe, and ever as the telescope expands the horizon of knowledge, it reaches out in desire for a further flight. But there are greater ideas than even those of worlds and systems. His mind can take in the thought of God, of eternity, of infinity. Is this like the endowment of a creature destined only for threescore years and ten? The same illimitableness attaches to imagination. "The use of this feigned history," says Lord Bacon, speaking of poetry, "is to give some shadow of satisfaction to the mind of man on those points wherein the nature of things doth deny it, the world being in proportion inferior to the soul; by reason whereof there is, agreeable to the spirit of man, a more ample greatness, a more exact goodness, and a more absolute variety than can be found in the nature of things."[1] Finally, there is desire. Give a man all of the world he asks for, and he is yet unsatisfied.

> " I cannot chain my soul; it will not rest
> In its clay prison, this most narrow sphere.
> It has strange powers, and feelings, and desires
> Which I cannot account for nor explain,
> But which I stifle not, being bound to trust
> All feelings equally, to hear all sides.
> Yet I cannot indulge them, and they live,
> Referring to some state of life unknown."[2]

This argument is not met by saying, as Mill does, that there are many things we desire which we never get. This may be true, but the point is that even if we did get all the satisfaction which the earth could give us, our desires would still go beyond that earthly bound.[3]

> " And thus I know the earth is not my sphere,
> For I cannot so narrow me, but that
> I still exceed it."[4]

The argument is further strengthened by comparing man with

---

[1] *Adv. of Learning*, Book ii. 13.

[2] R. Browning, *Pauline*. [The text is somewhat altered in 1889 edition. *Works*, i. p. 27.]

[3] "Man," says Kant, "is not so constituted as to rest and be satisfied in any possession or enjoyment whatsoever."—*Kritik d. Urtheilskraft*, p. 281 (Erdmann's ed.).

[4] Browning, *Pauline*. As revised :—

> " How should this earth's life prove my only sphere?
> Can I so narrow sense but that in life
> Soul still exceeds it?" *Works*, i. p. 29.

the other creatures that tenant the earth. Modern science justly lays stress on the constant relation subsisting between creatures and their environments. Throughout nature you find the most careful adjustment of faculty to environment. If there is a fin, there is water; if there is an eye, there is light; if there is a wing, there is air to cleave, etc. But here is a creature whose powers, whose capabilities, whose desires, stretch far beyond the terrestrial scene that would contain him ! Must we not put him in a different category ?

(2) The same inference which follows from the scale of man's endowments results if we consider life from *the point of view of moral discipline.* Everything which strengthens our view of the world as a scene of moral government, everything which leads us to put a high value on character, and to believe that the Creator's main end in His dealings with man is to purify and develop character, strengthens also our belief in immortality. The only way we can conceive of the relation of nature to man, so as to put a rational meaning into it, is, as Kant has shown, to represent it to ourselves as a means to the end of his culture and morality.[1] Can we believe, then, that God will spend a lifetime in perfecting a character, developing and purifying it, as great souls always are developed, by sharp trial and discipline, till its very best has been evoked, only in the end to dash it again into nothingness ? What would we think of an earthly artist who dealt thus with his works, spending a lifetime, *e.g.*, on a block of marble, evolving from it a statue of faultless proportions and classic grace, only in the end, just when his chisel was putting his last finishing touches on it, to seize his mallet and dash it again to pieces. It would stumble our faith in God —in the "Divine reasonableness"[2]—to believe that such could be His action.

(3) A third consideration which points in the same direction is that frequently insisted on—*the manifest incompleteness* of the present scene of things, both as respects human character and work, and as respects the Divine administration. Here,

---

[1] Cf. Kant on "The Last End of Nature as a Teleological System," *Kritik d. Urtheilskraft*, pp. 280–285 ; and Caird, *Philosophy of Kant*, ii. p. 501.

[2] "For my part," says Mr. Fiske, "I believe in the immortality of the soul, not in the sense in which I accept the demonstrable truths of science, but as a supreme act of faith in the reasonableness of God's work."—*Man's Destiny* p. 116.

again, everything that strengthens our faith in a moral government of the world, that impresses us with the infinite worth of
human personality, that intensifies our sense of justice and
injustice, forces on us the conviction that the present life, with
its abounding anomalies, imperfections, and iniquities, is not
God's last word to us;[1] that there is another chapter to our
existence than that which closes on earth. Here comes in the
consideration which Kant urges of the need of prolonged existence to complete the fulfilment of our moral destiny;[2] the sense
of accountability which we all carry with us, instinctively anti-
cipating a day of final reckoning; the feeling of an unredressed
balance of wrong in the arrangements of life and society; above
all, the sense of incompleteness which so often oppresses us
when we see the wise and good cut down in the midst of their
labours, and their life-work left unfinished. These are the
"enigmas of life" for which it is difficult to see how any
solution is provided if there is not a future state in
which life's mysteries shall be made clear, its unredressed
wrongs rectified, the righteousness of the good vindicated,
and a completion granted to noble lives, broken off prema-
turely here. Our faith in God leads us again to trust Him,
that "He that hath begun a good work"[3] in us will not leave
it unfinished.

(4) Finally, there is the fact which all history verifies, that
only under the influence of this hope do *the human faculties*,
even here, *find their largest scope and play*. This was the
consideration which, more than any other, weighed with the
late J. S. Mill, in inclining him to admit the hope of immortality. "The beneficial influence of such a hope," he says,

---

[1]   " There is no reconciling wisdom with a world distraught,
Goodness with triumphant evil, power with failure in the aim,
If—(to my own sense, remember! though none other feel the same!)—
If you bar me from assuming earth to be a pupil's place,
And life, time,—with all their chances, changes,—just probation-space,
Mine, for me!"   BROWNING, *La Saisiaz*, Works, xiv. p. 178.
[2] It should be noticed that, as Kant grants a doctrinal faith" in the existence
of God, as distinguished from theoretical demonstration on the one hand, and
the moral proof on the other (see note D. to Lecture III.), so he admits also a
"doctrinal faith" in immortality. "In view of the Divine wisdom," he says,
"and having respect to the splendid endowment of human nature, and to the
shortness of life, so inadequate for its development, we can find an equally
satisfactory ground for a doctrinal faith in the future life of the human soul."
—*Kritik d. r. Vernunft*, p. 561 (Eng. trans. pp. 590, 591).
[3] Phil. i. 6.

in words well worth quoting, "is far from trifling. It makes
life and human nature a far greater thing to the feelings, and
gives greater strength as well as greater solemnity to all the
sentiments which are awakened in us by our fellow-creatures,
and by mankind at large.[1] It allays the sense of that irony of
nature, which is so painfully felt when we see the exertions and
sacrifices of a life culminating in the formation of a wise and
noble mind, only to disappear from the world when the time
has just arrived at which the world seems about to begin
reaping the benefit of it. . . . But the benefit consists less in
the presence of any specific hope than in the enlargement of
the general scale of the feelings; the loftier aspirations being
no longer kept down by a sense of the insignificance of human
life—by the disastrous feeling of 'not worth while.'"[2] The
evolutionist, it seems to me, should, beyond all others, respect
these voices of the soul, this natural and unforced testimony of
our nature to a life beyond, which does not disappear (as it
would do were Mr. Spencer's hypothesis correct), but only
grows clearer and more solemn, as the history of humanity
advances.

I think, then, we may conclude that reason does create a
presumption, and that a very strong one, in favour of a future
life. The considerations we have urged prove the possibility
of immortality, and show that the soul of man is naturally
fitted for immortality. We need not claim that they do more,
though they have proved sufficient to inspire many of the
noblest minds of our race, even apart from the gospel, with a
very steady persuasion that there is a life hereafter. They
cannot give absolute certainty. They may not be able, apart
from the light of Revelation, to lift the mind wholly above the

---

[1] Cf. Uhlhorn in his *Christian Charity in the Ancient Church.* "There is
an idea," he says, "which has been again met with in our own day, that men,
when they first clearly come to believe that human life finds its life in this life
alone, would be on that account the more ready to help one another, so that
at least life here below might be made as pleasant to all as possible, and kept
free from evil. But, in truth, the opposite is the case. If the individual man
is only a passing shadow, without any everlasting significance, then reflection
quickly makes us decide: Since it is of no importance whether he exists or
not, why should I deprive myself of anything to give it to him? . . . It was
only when through Christianity it was for the first time made known that
every human soul possessed an infinite value, that each individual existence is
of much more worth than the whole world,—it was only then that room was
found for the growth of a genuine charity."—Pp. 33, 34 (Eng. trans.).

[2] *Three Essays*, p. 249.

suspicion that the law of waste and destruction which prevails here against the body may somewhere else, and finally, prevail against the soul. But, so far as they go, they must be accepted as a powerful corroboration and confirmation, from the side of nature, of the Christian view.

5
THE POSTULATE OF THE CHRISTIAN VIEW IN REGARD TO THE SIN AND DISORDER OF THE WORLD

"Therefore, as through one man sin entered into the world, and death through sin; and so death passed unto all men, for that all have sinned." —Paul

"This is a wonder to which the worshipers of reason have not yet given a name—the story of the fall of the first man. Is it allegory? history? fable? And yet there it stands, following the account of the creation, one of the pillars of Hercules, beyond which there is nothing—the point from which all succeeding history starts. . . . And yet, ye dear, most ancient, and undying traditions of my race—ye are the very kernel and germ of its most hidden history. Without you, mankind would be what so many other things are—a book without a title, without the first cover and introduction." —Herder

"The existence of the two selves in a man, a better self which takes pleasure in the good, and a worse self which makes for the bad, is a fact too plain to be denied."

—F. H. Bradley

"When we speak of primitive man, we do not mean while he was emerging from brutality to humanity, 'while he was losing his fur and gaining his intellect.' We leave that to the few biologists who, undeterred by the absence of facts, still profess a belief in descent of man from some known or unknown animal species." —Max Müller

"Are God and Nature then at strife,
    That Nature lends such evil dreams?
    So careful of the type she seems,
So careless of the single life; . . .

'So careful of the type?' but no.
    From scarpèd cliff and quarried stone
    She cries, 'A thousand types are gone,
I care for nothing, all shall go.'"

Tennyson

5

THE POSTULATE OF THE CHRISTIAN VIEW IN REGARD TO THE SIN AND DISORDER OF THE WORLD

CHRISTIANITY is the religion of Redemption. As such, it has for its third postulate the sin and disorder of the world. The existence of natural and moral evil is one of the darkest, deepest, and most difficult problems that can occupy human thought. It is one which has exercised the hearts of men in all ages, one which is often raised in Scripture, and which should warn us off from light and superficial views of the Divine character and purposes. Its presence is the great difficulty' in the way of a belief on natural grounds in the perfect justice and goodness of God, the obstacle we immediately encounter when we try to persuade ourselves that the universe is created and ordered by a supremely good Being. So grave is this difficulty, even in respect to natural evil, that Mr. J. S. Mill declares "the problem of reconciling infinite benevolence and justice in the Creator of such a world as this" to be "impossible"; and adds, "The attempt to do so not only involves absolute contradiction in an intellectual point of view, but exhibits in excess the revolting spectacle of a jesuitical defence of moral enormities."[1] From the natural point of view, the assurance of God's perfect goodness must always be, to some extent, an act of faith, based on the postulate of our own moral consciousness; and even this will often find it difficult to sustain itself, since Christianity alone imparts the moral consciousness in sufficient strength to uphold the faith required.

It is important to observe that, though this problem meets us in connection with the Christian view of the world, it is not

[1] *Three Essays on Religion*, pp. 186, 187. Cf. pp. 24–41, 112, etc. See Note A.—Defects in Creation: an Argument against Theism.

Christianity that makes this problem. Natural and moral evil is there as a fact in the universe, and would be there though Christianity had never been heard of. Christianity intensifies the problem by the stronger light it casts on the character of God, and the higher view it gives of man, but it does not create the problem. What it professes to do is to help us to solve it. But the problem is there all the while, and has to be taken account of by every system, whether Christian or not. It is a difficulty of philosophy, not less than of theology.

While, however, in naturalistic systems moral evil is apt to fall behind natural evil, in Christianity it is the other way —the moral evil is throughout placed in the forefront, and natural evil is looked at mainly in the light of it. This is as it should be; for while, as we shall see, natural evil presents an independent problem, there can be no doubt that its existence is deeply implicated with the existence of moral evil.[1] If we subtract from the sum of suffering in the world all that is directly or indirectly caused by sin—by the play and action of forces that are morally evil—we shall reduce the problem to very manageable dimensions indeed. It is the existence of moral evil which is the tremendous difficulty from a theistic point of view. I might go further, and say that it is only for a theistic system that the problem of moral evil properly exists.[2] Materialism and Pantheism may acknowledge natural evil— misfortune, pain, sorrow, misery—but it is only by an inconsistency they can speak of sin. Both are systems of determinism, and leave no place for moral action. There is, besides, in either system, no question of a theodicy, for there is to them no God. Things are as they are by a necessity of nature, which we can neither account for nor get behind. If we could, indeed, really get rid of the problem of sin by adopting either of these systems, there would be some reason for accepting them. But unfortunately the problem of moral evil is one which refuses to be thus summarily got rid of. Sin is there; the feeling of responsibility and of guilt is there; and neither the heart nor the reason of humanity will allow us to treat them as nonentities. Nor does the denial of God's existence really

---

[1] This is a point which Mr. Mill overlooks.
[2] Cf. Ott's *Le Problème du Mal*, pp. 1–5, 98, 99

mitigate the difficulty. Dark as the problem of evil is, it would be immeasurably darker if we were compelled to believe that there is no infinite righteousness and love behind, through which a solution of the problem may ultimately be hoped for. I proceed to consider more narrowly what the Christian view of sin is, and how it stands related to modern theories and speculations.

I. It is in their respective relations to the sin and disorder of the world, perhaps more than at any other point, that the Christian and "modern" views of the world come to a direct issue. On the one hand, there are certain respects in which the Christian view finds unexpected support from the modern view of the world; on the other, there are certain respects in which it is fundamentally at variance with it. Let us briefly consider both.

There are three respects, in particular, in which the modern view of the world comes to the support of the Christian view of sin.

1. The modern view of things is marked by a stronger sense than in former times of the *reality* and *universal presence* of evil—both of natural evil and of moral evil, though moral evil, as was to be expected, is regarded more from its side of error, misery, and bondage, than from its side of guilt. The modern view has disposed of the superficial optimism of earlier times. The days of a flimsy optimism, when men demonstrated to their own satisfaction that this was the best of all possible worlds, and made light of the facts which contradicted their pleasing hypothesis, are over, and everywhere there is an oppressive sense of the weight of the evils which burden humanity, and of the unsatisfactoriness of natural existence generally. The strain of modern thought is pessimistic rather than optimistic. Its high-water mark is not optimism, but what George Eliot prefers to call "meliorism."[1] Herbert Spencer, indeed, still looks for an "evanescence of evil," as the result of the working of natural and necessary laws of evolution,[2] but I do not find that this represents the general temper of the age. Schopenhauer and Hartmann have at least this merit, that they raise

---

[1] Cf. Sully's *Pessimism*, p. 399. He adopts the term.
[2] *Social Statics*, p. 79.

the question of the good or evil of existence in a form which
makes it impossible ever again to ignore it, or bury it out of
sight. Pessimism, as Professor Flint has said, "like Macbeth,
has murdered sleep."[1] All this is a gain to the Christian view.
Hartmann even goes so far as to find the merit of Christianity
in the fact that it is a system of Pessimism.[2] Both systems
take for granted the facts of existence, and both look them
boldly in the face. But there is this difference—Christianity
looks on the world in a spirit of hope; Pessimism looks on it
in a spirit of despair.

2. It is an extension of the same remark to say that the
modern view of the world has disposed effectually of the shallow
Rousseau view of the *inherent goodness of human nature*, and
of the eighteenth-century illumination dreams of a perfectibility
of man based on education, and on altered social and political
conditions.[3] The optimistic and Pelagian views of human
nature are as completely discredited as the optimistic view of
the world generally. Kant struck this deeper keynote when,
in opposition to the preceding Rationalism, he acknowledged
the presence of a "radical evil" in human nature, which he
could only account for by an act of the will above time.[4] The
modern evolutionary philosophy goes even beyond Christianity
in its affirmation of the dominance of the brute element in
man's being—of the ascendency of the egoistic over the social
impulses in the natural man;[5] while the moralisation of

---

[1] *Anti-Theistic Theories*, p. 294.

[2] *Selbstzersetzung des Christenthums*, p. 51. Its characteristic mark, he
thinks, is "the pessimistic conviction of the unworthiness of this world to
exist." Schopenhauer's language is similar. "Let no one think," he says,
"that Christianity is favourable to optimism; for in the Gospels world and
evil are used as almost synonymous." "The inmost kernel of Christianity is
identical with that of Brahmanism and Buddhism."—*Die Welt als Wille*, etc.,
i. p. 420; iii. p. 420 (Eng. trans.).

[3] Schopenhauer says: "Indeed, the fundamental characteristic and the πρῶτον
ψεῦδος of Rousseau's whole philosophy is this, that in the place of the Christian
doctrine of original sin, and the original depravity of the human race, he puts
an original goodness and unlimited perfectibility of it, which has only been
led astray by civilisation and its consequences, and then founds upon this his
optimism and humanism."—*Die Welt als Wille*, etc., iii. p. 398.

[4] *Die Religion innerhalb der Grenzen der blossen Vernunft*, Book i.—"On
the Indwelling of the Evil Principle along with the Good, or on the Radical
Evil in Human Nature." Cf. Caird's *Philosophy of Kant*, ii. pp. 566–568.

[5] Mr. Fiske says:—"Thus we see what human progress means. It means
throwing off the brute-inheritance,—gradually throwing it off through ages of
struggle that are by and by to make struggle needless. . . . The ape and the
tiger in human nature will become extinct. Theology has had much to say

humanity which it anticipates, in the sense of a gradual sub-ordination of the former to the latter, is admitted to be yet very imperfect. From the side of modern thought, therefore, there is no hesitation in admitting, what Christianity also affirms, that the animal in man has an undue preponderance over the intellectual and spiritual; that the will, even in the best of men, is hampered and fettered by impulses of the lower nature to a degree which often evokes the liveliest expressions of shame and self-reproach; that society is largely ruled by egoistic passions and aims. The law in the members warring against the law in the mind [1]—in a sense, a natural depravity and " original sin "—has its recognition in modern science and philosophy.

3. In the modern view of the world we have the fullest recognition of the *organic* principle in human life, and of the corollary of this in *heredity*. This, which is the correction of the individualistic view of human nature which prevailed in last century, I take to be one of the greatest gains of modern thought for the right understanding of the Christian doctrines both of sin and of Redemption. The Christian view is one which gives its rightful place alike to the individual, and to the organic connection of the individual with the race; and it is the latter side of the truth which modern thought has done so much to further. Rather, perhaps, I should say that both sides are being brought into strong prominence; for if there never was so much stress laid on the connection of the individual with society, neither was there ever so much said about individual rights. The former idea, at all events, is now thoroughly incorporated into modern habits of thinking, under the name of the " solidarity " of the race.[2] There is an individual life, and there is a social life in which we all share. The race is an organism, and the individual, if we may so speak, is a cell in the tissue of that organism, indissolubly con-

about original sin. This original sin is neither more nor less than the brute-inheritance which every man carries with him, and the process of evolution is an advance towards true salvation."—*Man's Destiny*, p. 103.

> " Arise and fly
> The reeling Faun, the sensual feast ;
> Move upward, working out the beast,
> And let the ape and tiger die."
>
> TENNYSON, *In Memoriam.*

[1] Rom. vii. 23.
[2] The word, I believe, has come from Comte.

nected for good or evil with the other cells in the unity of a
common life.[1] From this follows the conception of heredity,
which plays so important a part in modern theories. Man is
not simply bound up with his fellows through the external
usages and institutions of society. " He has been produced
by, and has become a part of them, . . . he is organically
related to all the members of the race, not only bone of their
bone and flesh of their flesh, but mind of their mind." [2] He
is a bundle of inherited tendencies, and will in turn transmit
his nature, with its new marks of good and evil, to those who
come after him.[3] It is easy to see that this conception of
heredity, and of the organic unity of the race, is but the
scientific expression of a doctrine which is fundamental to the
Scriptures, and which underlies all its teaching about sin and
salvation.

In respect of the points just named, therefore, it may be
affirmed that the modern view of the world is largely in agreement with Christianity. We may not agree with Schopenhauer
and Hartmann that Christianity is a system of Pessimism ; but
we may admit that Pessimism, in so far as it recognises that
the world is in an evil state, is far truer to facts and to
Christianity than the superficial Optimism, the shallow
perfectionism, and the Pelagian denial of original and inherited
sin, which it helped to displace. In the respect last named,
indeed, modern thought is nearer to Christianity than some
Christian systems themselves. Ritschl, for example, teaches
that sin consists only in acts, and not in states and dispositions
of the heart ; that there is no such thing as original or inherited
sin ; that sin is not transmissible by nature, but only through
education, influence, the reciprocal action of individuals in
society, etc.[4] But in maintaining this, he comes into conflict,

---

[1] Cf. Stephen's *Science of Ethics*, chap. iii. sec. 4, "Social Tissue."

[2] Sorley's *Ethics of Naturalism*, pp. 123, 135.

[3] Perhaps the most forcible illustrations of heredity are to be found in
Maudsley's works. "Most certain is it," he says, "that men are not bred well
or ill by accident, little as they reck of it in practice, any more than are the
animals, the select breeding of which they make such a careful study ; that there
are laws of hereditary action, working definitely in direct transmission of
qualities, or indirectly through combinations and repulsions, neutralisations
and modifications of qualities ; and that it is by virtue of these laws determining the moral and physical constitution of every individual that a good result
ensues in one case, a bad result in another."—*Body and Will*, p. 248.

[4] *Recht. und Ver.* iii. pp. 317–332 (3rd ed.). "As a personal propensity in
the life of each individual," he says, "it originates so far as our observation

not merely with texts of Scripture, but with the whole modern conception of the organic union of the race. Universal sin,—sin which does not consist merely in acts, but springs from deep-seated causes in the heart, the effects of which, both bodily and mental, are hereditarily transmitted,—these I take to be conceptions which neither Ritschl nor any other will now be able to overthrow.[1]

When all this is said, however, it must still be granted that the most fundamental difference exists between the two views—the Christian and the modern. The difference is partly one as to the nature of sin, and it runs up into a difference as to its origin. The Christian view of sin is not only infinitely deeper and more earnest than in any current conception apart from Christianity; but it is, as I formerly remarked, profoundly modified by the difference in the views of God and of man. The first thing we have to do here is to secure clearly the Christian idea of sin; then, when we have done this, and asked whether it is verified in conscience and experience, we are prepared to judge of theories of origin.

I lay it down as a first principle that, in the Christian view, sin is that which absolutely *ought not to be*.[2] How that which absolutely ought not to be is yet permitted to exist under the government of a wise and holy God, is a problem we may not be able to solve; but the first thing to do is to hold firmly to the conception of sin itself. Sin, as such, is that which unconditionally ought not to be, which contradicts or infringes upon an unconditional law of right, and therefore can only be understood in the light of that which ought to be—of the moral good.[3]

reaches, out of the sinful desire and action which as such finds its adequate ground in the self-determination of the individual will."—P. 331.

[1] Mr. J. J. Murphy says of Original Sin: " It is not a revealed doctrine, but an observed fact ; a fact of all human experience, and witnessed to as strongly by classical as by Biblical writers, as strongly by heathens and atheists as by Christians."—*Scientific Basis of Faith*, p. 262. Pfleiderer speaks of " the undeniable fact of experience, that, from the very dawn of moral life, we find evil present in us as a power, the origin of which accordingly must be beyond the conscious exercise of our freedom," as " a fact on which indeterminism, Pelagian or rationalistic, must ever suffer shipwreck."—*Religionsphilosophie*, iv. p. 28 (Eng. trans.).

[2] Hegel also uses this formula, but ambiguously. "What ought not to be,' means with Hegel, "what ought to be done away." Cf. Julius Müller, *Christian Doctrine of Sin*, i. p. 322 (Eng. trans.). See on Hegel's views later.

[3] "For how can anything be called evil, unless it deviate from an obligatory good, and be therefore a violation of what ought to be (seinsollendes)—of the holy law."—Dorner, *System of Doctrine*, ii. p. 308 (Eng. trans.).

The Christian view of sin, accordingly, has for its presupposition the doctrine of God as ethical Personality, previously
explained. It is God's perfect nature and holy will which form
the norm of character and duty for man. The law of holiness
requires, not only that the human will subsist in perfect
harmony with the Divine, being surrendered to it in love,
trust, and obedience, but, as involved in this, that there should
be a right state of the affections, a pure and harmonious *inner*
life. The external sphere for obedience is prescribed by our
position in the world, and by our relation to it, to our neighbours,
and to God.

As the negation of this, sin, in the Biblical view, consists in
the revolt of the creature will from its rightful allegiance to
the sovereign will of God, and the setting up of a false independence, the substitution of a life-for-self for life-for-God.[1]
How such an act should ever originate may again be a problem
we cannot solve; but it is evidently included in the possibilities
of human freedom. The possibility of sin arises from the fact
that the creature has necessarily a relative independence; and
that in man, particularly, together with the impulse towards
God, there exists an impulse towards the world, which the will
may be tempted to make an object on its own account.[2] The
false choice made, the spiritual bond between God and the soul
is cut or at least infinitely weakened; the soul enters into
subjection to the world to which it has surrendered itself, and
an abnormal development begins, in which the baneful and
God-negating character of the egoistic principle taken into the
will gradually reveals itself.[3]

While thus spiritual in its origin, as arising from the free act
of a will up to that time pure, sin is anything but spiritual in
its effects. Its immediate result is the subversion of the true
relation of the natural and the spiritual in man's constitution,
making that supreme which ought to be subordinate, and that
subordinate which ought to be supreme. The relation of the
spiritual and psychical in human nature is inverted. The
spiritual is reduced to subjection, can at best make only feeble

---

[1] Exemplified in the Parable of the Prodigal (Luke xv. 11 ff.).
[2] Cf. Martensen's *Christian Ethics*, i. secs. 26–28 (Eng. trans. pp. 94–102).
[3] On the development and forms of sin, see Müller, *Christian Doctrine of Sin*, i. pp. 147–182; Dorner, *System of Doctrine*, ii. pp. 393–397; Martensen, *Christian Ethics*, i. pp. 102–108, etc. (Eng. trans.)

and ineffectual protests ; the natural or psychical is elevated to authority and rule.   Further, the spiritual bond being broken which kept the nature in harmony—reason, conscience, the God-ward affections ruling, while the lower passions and desires observed the bounds which higher law prescribed for them— not only is the psychical nature exalted to undue ascendency, but its own actings are now turbulent and irregular.   It refuses to obey law ; its desires clamour importunately each for its own special gratification ; discord and division take the place of the normal unity.   There is introduced into the soul a state of ἀνομία—lawlessness.[1]   Reason and conscience are still there as indestructible elements of human nature, nor can the sense of its dependence on God, or obligation to Him, ever be entirely lost.   Hence arise, even in the natural man, conflict, struggle, self-condemnation, painful and ineffectual attempts to break the dominion of sin, never truly successful.[2]   For this reason, that carnality preponderates in the nature of man as a whole, and that the most spiritual acts of the natural man betray the signs of its controlling influence, the whole man is spoken of as "in the flesh," though elsewhere Paul distinguishes the flesh from that better self—the νοῦς, or inner man—which protests against its rule.[3]   All this finds its verification in conscience and experience, if not in its totality in every man's conscious- ness, yet in the general consciousness of the race.   What a man's judgment of himself will be depends upon his standpoint, but in proportion to the depth of his self-knowledge he will confess that his heart is not naturally possessed by love to God, and by spiritual affections ; that his inner life is not perfectly pure and harmonious ; that there are principles in his heart at war with what duty and the law of God require ; that he often transgresses the commandment which he recognises as " holy, and just, and good,"[4] in thought and word and deed ; and that, in all this, he lies under his own self-condemnation.   He is conscious that the sin of his heart is such that he would not willingly lay bare its secrets to his closest intimate, and he

---

[1] 1 John iii. 4.   [2] Rom. vii. 13–25.
[3] Rom. vii. 22, 23.   On the various views of the Pauline use of the term σάρξ, with criticism of these, see Dr. Dickson's *St. Paul's Use of the Terms Flesh and Spirit* (Baird Lectures, 1883).   Cf. Dorner, *System of Doctrine*, ii. p. 319 (Eng. trans.).
[4] Rom. vii. 12.

would probably confess also that this state in which he finds himself did not spring wholly, or *de novo*, from his individual will, but that it developed from a nature in which the principle of disorder was already implanted.

Gathering these observations to an issue, I conclude that the cardinal point in the Christian view of sin is, that it is not something natural, normal, and necessary, but, both as actual and as hereditary, something which must find its explanation in a free act of the creature, annulling the original relation of the creature to God.   The Christian view, in other words, cannot be maintained on the hypothesis that man's existing state is his original one,—still less on the assumption that, in a moral respect, it is an advance and improvement on his original one, but only on the supposition that man has wilfully defaced the Divine image in which he was originally made and has voluntarily turned aside to evil.   Apart from express statements on the subject, the underlying presupposition of the Christian view is that sin has a volitional cause, which, as the sin itself is universal, must be carried back to the beginning of the race —that, in other words, the development of the race has not been a natural and normal, but an abnormal and perverted one. And here it is, I admit, that the modern view of the world, with its doctrine of man's original brutishness, and his ascent by his own efforts to civilisation and moral life, comes into the most direct and absolute contradiction with it.   Many attempts —some of them well meant—have been made to gloze over, or get rid of, this contradiction ; but these would-be solutions all break on the fact that they make sin, or what passes for sin, a natural necessity ; whereas, on the Biblical view, it is clearly not man's misfortune only, but his fault—a deep and terrible evil for which he is responsible.

We shall best appreciate the force of this contradiction by looking at some of the theories to which the Christian view is opposed.

1. First, we have a class of theories which seek the ground of evil in *creation*, or in *the original constitution of the world* ; but these I do not dwell upon.   Such is the theory of Buddhism, and of all the pessimistic systems.   "The existence of the world," Schopenhauer holds, "is itself the greatest evil of all, and underlies all other evil, and similarly the root evil of each

individual is his having come into the world"; [1] and Hartmann speaks of the "inexpiable crime" of creation.[2] Such, again, is the hypothesis of two original principles in creation, *e.g.*, the Persian dualism, of which we see some faint attempts at a revival in modern times.[3] Such were the Platonic and Gnostic theories, that evil had its origin in matter. This doctrine also has its modern revivals. Even Rothe has adopted the view which seeks the origin of evil in matter, though why matter should be supposed inimical to goodness it is not easy to see. With him, it is the *non-divine*, the contradictory counterpart to God, opposed in its essence to the Divine, a conception not Biblical, and one which cannot be maintained.[4]

2. We come, second, to a class of theories which seek the explanation of evil in *the nature of man*. It is the characteristic of all these theories that they regard sin as necessarily resulting from the constitution of human nature, in contrast with the Biblical view that it entered the world voluntarily. Of this class of theories, again, we have several kinds.

(1) We have the *metaphysical* theories of sin—that, *e.g.*, of Hegel. Sin is here regarded as a necessary stage in the development of spirit. Hegel is fond of explicating the story of Eden in the interests of his philosophy, and this is how he does it. "Knowledge, as the disannulling of the unity of nature," he says, "is the 'Fall,' which is no casual conception, but the eternal history of spirit. For the state of innocence, the paradisaical condition, is that of the brute. Paradise is a park, where only brutes, not men, can remain. . . . The fall is,

---

[1] Pfleiderer, *Religionsphilosophie*, ii. p. 233 (Eng. trans.). Cf. *Welt als Wille*, etc., i. pp. 452–461 ; iii. pp. 420–454.

[2] That is, on the supposition that the Creator knew what He was about.

[3] See Note B.—Dualistic Theories of the Origin of Evil.

[4] See his theory in *Theologische Ethik*, 2nd ed., i. secs. 40, 104–130. Cf. his *Still Hours* (Eng. trans.), pp. 185, 186. He says : "The development of man passes through stages of sin. . . . If sin is a necessary point in human development, it is not on that account merely negative. . . . Evil in the course of development, or sin, is not in itself a condition of the development of the good ; but it belongs to the idea of creation, as a creation out of nothing, that the created personality cannot detach itself from material nature otherwise than by being clothed upon with matter, and being in this way altered, rendered impure or sinful. This is the necessary commencement of the creation of man, but only its mere commencement, which comes to a close in the Second Adam. . . . The necessity of a transition through sin is not directly an ethical, but rather a physical necessity." The theory is criticised by Müller, i. pp. 146, 147 (Eng. trans.) : and Dorner, *System of Doctrine*, ii. pp. 375–380 (Eng. trans.).

therefore, the eternal mythus of man, in fact the very transition by which he becomes man." [1] Sin, in brief, is the first step of man out of his naturalness, and the only way in which he could take that step. It is the negation of the immediate unity of man with nature, and of the innocence of that pristine state, but only that the negation may be in turn negated, and the true destination of spirit realised. [2]

(2.) We have the *ethical* and *would-be Christian* forms of these theories, in which the subject is looked at from the religious point of view. Such, *e.g.*, is the theory of Schleiermacher, who derives sin from a relative weakness of the spirit as compared with sense. [3] Such, again, is the theory of Lipsius, who explains it from the fact that man is at first a naturally conditioned and self-seeking being, while his moral will is only gradually developed. [4] Such is the theory of Ritschl, who connects it with man's ignorance. With him also man starts as a purely natural being, the subject of self-seeking desires, while his will for good is a "growing" quantity. [5] Sin, therefore, is an inevitable stage in his development.

(3) We have the *evolutionary* theories, in which man begins only a shade removed from the brutes, and his subsequent moralisation is the result of slow development. This theory may be held in a more naturalistic or in a more philosophical form. In the former, the genesis of our moral ideas, from which the sense of sin arises, is sought in causes outside of the moral altogether—in the possession by man of social as well as egoistic impulses, in the perception of the advantage that would accrue from the subordination of the latter to the former, in the gradual accumulation of the results of experience in the organism through heredity, in the strengthening of the bonds of society through custom, law, etc. [6] What this theory fails

[1] *Philosophy of History* (Eng. trans.), p. 333.   Cf. *Religionsphilosophie*, ii. pp. 264–266.
[2] See Note C.—Hegel's Doctrine of Sin.
[3] *Der christ. Glaube*, secs. 66–69. Cf. Müller, i. pp. 341–359, on "Schleiermacher's View of the Essence and Origin of Sin"; and Dorner, *System of Doctrine*, iii. pp. 34–38 (Eng. trans.).
[4] *Dogmatik*, pp. 374, 375.
[5] Cf. his *Unterricht*, 3rd ed. p. 26. This, according to him, creates only "a possibility and probability" of sin ; but it is a possibility which, as shown below, in the early stages of man's history, cannot fail to be realised.
[6] Cf. for different forms of the evolution theory, Darwin's *Descent of Man*, Stephen's *Science of Ethics*, Spencer's *Data of Ethics*; and see criticism in Sorley's *Ethics of Naturalism*, chaps. v. to viii.

to show is how this idea of the advantageous becomes converted into the perfectly distinct conception of the morally obligatory. A clearly perceived duty lays an obligation on the will quite distinct from a perceived advantage; and even supposing the discovery made that a larger good would accrue through every individual devoting himself to the common weal, a distinct notion is involved when it is perceived that duty requires us to adopt this for our end.[1] The higher form of the evolutionary theory, accordingly, makes a more promising beginning, in that it grants to man from the first his rational nature, and recognises that his ideas of moral truth and obligation spring directly from a rational source. It is held, however, as in the theories already considered, that at first it is the instinctive impulses, in which the self-regarding desires are necessarily preponderant, which hold the field, and that man comes to the knowledge of his true nature only gradually. Man, indeed, only begins to be a moral being when, through the awakening of his moral consciousness, he makes the discovery that he is not what, in the true idea of his personality, he ought to be— when he forms an ideal. It is this impulse to realise his true nature, to attain to moral freedom, and bring the self-seeking impulses into harmony with moral law, which, on this theory, constitutes the mainspring of all development and progress.[2]

Taking this class of theories together, I contend that it is impossible to derive out of them conceptions of sin and guilt adequate to the Christian view. In the first place, it is evident that, in all these theories, sin is made something necessary— not simply something that might be, or could be, but an absolute necessity. In every one of them, the original condition of man is supposed to be such that sin could not but

---

[1] Mr. Stephen substitutes the "health" for the "happiness" of society as the moral end (p. 366). But the health is in order to the happiness, and it is presumed that the two tend to coincide (pp. 82, 83). "Morality is a statement of the conditions of social welfare," "the sum of the preservative instincts of society," "virtue is a condition of social welfare," etc. (p. 217). Strong in his criticism of the ordinary utilitarianism, Mr. Stephen is weak in his attempt to provide a substitute, or show how the moral can possibly arise out of the non-moral. See Mr. Sorley's criticism, *Ethics of Naturalism*, chap. viii.

[2] Cf. with this general sketch Bradley's *Ethical Studies* (see pp. 261–265 on "The Origin of the Bad Self": and Green's *Prolegomena to Ethics*, Book iii., on "the Moral Ideal and Moral Progress." Green finds the moral end in rational "self-satisfaction,"—a conception into which it is difficult to avoid importing a subtle kind of hedonism; Bradley less objectionably finds it in "self-realisation."

result from it.   This, it seems to me, is practically to empty the
idea of sin of its real significance, and to throw the responsibility of it directly back on the Creator.   It is probably a feeling
of this kind which leads many who favour the view we are
considering to disclaim the word "necessity."   Hegel, even,
tells us that sin is not necessary ; that man can will evil, but is
not under compulsion to will it.   But this is a mere evasion,
arising from an ambiguous use of terms.   In a multitude of
other places Hegel tells us that sin arises from the highest
logical and speculative necessity.[1]   Schleiermacher, in like
manner, disclaims the view that sin is a necessary law of
human development.[2]   He could not do otherwise, and hold,
as he does, the sinlessness of Christ.   But he holds at the same
time that the development through sin—or what we subjectively
regard as sin—is the form of growth ordained for us by God,
with a view to the ultimate Redemption, or perfecting, of the
race in Christ.[3]   Lipsius will have it that sin is at once
necessary and free and avoidable.[4]   Ritschl holds, in the same
way, that a necessity of sinning can be derived neither from
the outfit of human nature, nor from the ends of moral life, nor
from a design of God.[5]   Yet he grants, and starting off with
man as he does as a merely natural being, he could not do
otherwise, that sin is an apparently unavoidable product of the
human will under the given conditions of its development.[6]
All these theories in fact, therefore, however they may evade
the use of the name, do make sin a necessity.   In the evolutionary theories this is very obvious.   There is here no pretence
that a sinless development is possible.   How is it conceivable
that a being beginning at the stage of lowest savagery should
avoid sin ; and what responsibility can be supposed to attach
to the acts of such a being, in whom brute passions and desires
have full ascendency, while reason and conscience are yet a
glimmer—a bare potentiality ?

One immediate effect of these theories, accordingly, is to
weaken, if not entirely to destroy, the idea of *guilt*.   How can

---

[1] Cf. the references to *Phil. des Rechts*, sec. 139, in Müller, p. 392, and see
Note C.

[2] *Der christ. Glaube*, sec. 68, 3.   [3] *Der christ. Glaube*, secs. 80, 81.

[4] *Dogmatik*, pp. 376, 377, secs. 475–477.

[5] *Unterricht*, p. 26 ; and *Recht. und Ver.* iii. p. 358.

[6] *Recht. und Ver.* iii. 3rd ed. p. 360.

man be held responsible for acts which the constitution of his nature and his environment—without the intervention of moral causes of any kind, such as is involved in the idea of a "Fall" —make inevitable? In all these theories I have named, accordingly, it will be found that there is a great weakening down of the idea of guilt. That man attributes his acts to himself, and feels guilty on account of them, is, of course, admitted; but instead of guilt being regarded as something objectively real, which God as well as man is bound to take account of, it comes to be viewed as something clinging only to the subjective consciousness,—a subjective judgment which the sinner passes on himself, to which nothing actual corresponds. Redemption thus becomes, in theories that admit Redemption, not the removal of guilt, but of the consciousness of guilt; and this, not by any real Divine pardon, but by the sinner being brought to see that his guilty fears misrepresented the actual state of God's mind towards him. Thus it is in the theories of Schleiermacher, of Lipsius, and of Ritschl—in that of Ritschl most conspicuously. According to Schleiermacher, this subjective consciousness of guilt is a Divinely ordained thing to serve as a spur to make men seek Redemption, *i.e.* to be taken up into the perfect life of Christ.[1] Ritschl regards all sins as arising so much from ignorance as to be without real guilt in the eyes of God. God does not impute guilt on account of the ignorance in which we now live. The reason, therefore, why sins are pardonable is, that though the sinner imputes them to himself as offences, they are not properly sins at all, but acts done in ignorance. The guilt attaching to these acts is but a feeling in the sinner's own consciousness, separating him from God, which the revelation of God's Fatherly love in the Gospel enables him to overcome.[2] But I ask, Does this harmonise with the moral experience of the race—not to say with the statements of the Bible? Is it not the universal feeling of mankind that guilt is a terrible and stern reality, carrying with it objective

---

[1] *Der christ. Glaube*, secs. 80, 81. Cf. Müller, pp. 355, 356. The views of Lipsius may be seen in his *Dogmatik*, secs. 768–771. "Justification," he says, "in respect of human sin, is the removal of the consciousness of guilt as a power separating from God, . . . the certainty awakened in him by the Spirit of God present in man of his fellowship in life and love with God, as something graciously restored in him by God Himself."—P. 690.

[2] *Recht. und Ver.* iii. pp. 46, 52, 56, 83; 306, 307; 356–363, etc. See Note D.—Ritschl's Doctrine of Guilt.

and lasting effects, that it is as real as the "ought" is real, and that conscience, in passing judgment on our state, is but reflecting the judgment of God, to whom, ultimately, we are accountable? This weakening down and subjectivising of the idea of guilt is to me a strong condemnation of any theory from which it springs.

These theories contradict the Christian view of sin, not simply in respect of its nature and of the degree of guilt attaching to it, but in the accounts they give of its *origin*. They regard that as a normal state for man in the beginning of his history, which the Christian view can only regard as an abnormal one. This is, indeed, the primary difference on which all the others depend. With minor differences, these theories all agree in regarding man's original condition as one but little removed from the brute; the animal impulses are powerful and ungoverned. Is this a state which, from the Christian point of view, can ever be regarded as normal? It may be a normal state for the animal—can it be a normal state for a moral personality? In such a being, even from the first, the moral law asks for a subordination of the animal impulses to reason and conscience, for unity, and not for disorganisation and lawlessness. It asks for this, not as something to be attained through ages of development, but as something which ought to exist *now*, and counts the being in a wrong moral state who does not possess it. What, according to these theories themselves, is the judgment which the individual, when moral consciousness awakes, passes on himself? Is it not that he is in a wrong moral state, a state in which he condemns himself, and feels shame at the thought of being in it? Else whence this sense of moral dissatisfaction, which it is acknowledged that he feels, and feels the more keenly in proportion as his moral perceptions become more acute? It is not simply that he has an ideal which he has not reached: this is an experience to be found in every stage of development, even when the conscience implies no blame. But the contrast is between the idea of the "is" and of the "ought to be," even in his present state, and this awakens the feeling of blame.[1] On what ground,

---

[1] Dorner truly says: "Evil does not consist in man's not yet being initially what he will one day become; for then evil must be called normal, and can only be esteemed exceptionable by an error. Evil is something different from mere development. . . . Evil is the discord of man with his idea, as, and so

further, must it be held that man must have commenced his career from this low and non-moral, if not positively immoral point? Is it a necessary part of a law of development, that a man can only reach that which he ought to be by passing through that which he ought not to be? Then evil has a relative justification, and the judgment which the immediate consciousness passes on it must be retracted or modified from a higher point of view.[1] We have only to compare the Christian estimate of sin with that to which this theory leads us, to see how profound is the difference between them. On this theory of development, when a man has reached the higher moral standpoint, he judges of his former state more leniently than he did at first; he ceases to pass condemnatory judgments on himself on account of it. In the Christian view, on the other hand, the higher the stage which a Christian man has reached, the evil and guilt of his former state will appear in a deeper dye; the more emphatically will he condemn it as one of lostness and shame. Which estimate is the more just? I do not think there is any difficulty, at least, in seeing which is most in accord with the idea of the moral.

I cannot, therefore, think that the picture sometimes given us of man's primeval state—that of a miserable, half-starved, naked wretch, just emerged from the bestial condition, torn with fierce passions, and fighting his way among his compeers with low-browed cunning—is one in harmony with the Christian view. And the adversaries of the Christian faith not only admit the discrepancy between their view and ours, but glory in it. Christianity, they say, requires you to accept one view of man's origin, and science gives quite another. As it is sometimes put, the doctrine of Redemption rests on the doctrine of the Fall; and the doctrine of the Fall rests on the third chapter of Genesis. But science has exploded the third chapter of Genesis, so the whole structure falls to the ground. I acknow-

---

far as, that idea should be realised at the given moment. . . . Sin is not being imperfect at all, but the contravention of what ought to be at a given moment, and of what can lay claim to unconditioned worth."—*System of Doctrine*, iii. pp. 36, 37.

[1] Dorner says: "If evil is supposed to consist only in development, which God has willed in His character as Creator, then its absolute wrongfulness must come to an end. The non-realisation of the idea cannot be blameworthy in itself, if the innate law of life itself prescribes progressiveness of development."—*System of Doctrine*, p. 264.

ledge the issue, but it is not rightly put to say that the doctrine
of the Fall rests on the third chapter of Genesis. The Christian
doctrine of Redemption certainly does not rest on the narrative
in Gen. iii., but it rests on the reality of the sin and guilt of
the world, which would remain facts though the third chapter
of Genesis never had been written. It would be truer to say
that I believe in the third chapter of Genesis, or in the essential
truth which it contains, because I believe in sin and Redemption, than to say that I believe in sin and Redemption because
of the story of the Fall.[1] Put the third chapter of Genesis
out of view, and you have the facts of the sin and disorder
of the world to be accounted for, and dealt with, all the same.

The question, however, arises, and it is a perfectly fair one to
raise, Whatever we may say of the relation to the Christian
view, is not this doctrine of man's origin, which implies a pure
point of beginning in the history of the race, expressly contradicted by the facts of anthropology? Do not the facts of
modern science compel us to adopt a different view? Must we
not conclude, if regard is had to the evidence, that man did
begin as a savage, but a few degrees removed from the brutes,
and has only gradually worked his way upwards to his present
condition? In answer I would say, I certainly do not believe
that this theory has been proved, and, expressing my own
opinion, I do not think it is likely to be proved. If it were
proved, I admit that it would profoundly modify our whole
conception of the Christian system. Negatively, evolutionists
have not proved that this was the original state of man. The
missing link between man and brute has long been sought for,
but as yet has been sought in vain. The oldest specimens of
men known to science are just as truly men as any of their
successors.[2] At the same time, we need not reject the hypo-

---

[1] Cf. the suggestive remarks in Auberlen's *The Divine Revelation*, pp.
175–185 (Eng. trans.).

[2] Professor Dana said, in 1875: "No remains of fossil man bear evidence to
less perfect erectness of structure than in civilised man, or to any nearer
approach to the man ape in essential characteristics. . . . This is the more
extraordinary, in view of the fact that from the lowest limits in existing man
there are all possible gradations up to the highest'; while below that limit there
is an abrupt fall to the ape level, in which the cubic capacity of the brain is
one-half less. If the links ever existed, their annihilation, without trace, is so
extremely improbable that it may be pronounced impossible. Until some are
found, science cannot assert that they ever existed."—*Geology*, p. 603.
Virchow said, in 1879: "On the whole, we must readily acknowledge that

thesis of evolution within the limits in which science has really rendered it probable. The only theory of evolution which necessarily conflicts with the Biblical view is that which supposes evolution to proceed by slow and gradual modifications— "insensible gradations," as Mr. Spencer puts it—and this is a view to which many of the facts of science are themselves opposed. Evolution is not opposed to the appearance, at certain points in the chain of development, of something absolutely new, and it has already been mentioned that distinguished evolutionists, like Mr. Alfred Russel Wallace, freely recognise this fact.[1] The "insensible gradation" theory, as respects the transition from ape to man, has not a single fact to support it. With man, from the point of view of the Bible, we have the rise of a new kingdom, just as truly as when life first entered,— the entrance on the stage of nature of a being self-conscious, rational, and moral, a being made in the image of God,—and it is arbitrary to assume that this new beginning will not be marked by differences which distinguish it from the introduction of purely animal races.

The evidence which is adduced from other quarters of the originally savage state of man is equally inconclusive. There is no reason to believe that existing savage races represent the earliest condition of mankind ; rather there is evidence to show that they represent a degradation from a higher state. The traces of early man which geology has disinterred show, indeed, the existence in various parts of the world of races in a comparatively rude and uncivilised state ; but they are found

all fossil type of a lower human development is absolutely wanting. Indeed, if we take the total of all fossil men that have been found hitherto, and compare them with what the present offers, then we can maintain with certainty that among the present generation there is a much larger number of relatively low-type individuals than among the fossils hitherto known. . . . We cannot designate it as a revelation of science that man descended from the ape or any other animal."—*Die Freiheit der Wissenschaft*, pp. 29, 31.

No new facts have been discovered since, requiring a modification of these statements.

[1] Not only in respect of his mind, but in respect also of his body, Mr. Wallace has contended that the appearance of man cannot be explained on Darwinian principles. He argues from the brain of primitive man as having a development beyond his actual attainments, suggesting the idea of " a surplusage of power ; of an instrument beyond the wants of its possessor " ; from his hairless back, " thus reversing the characteristics of all other mammalia " ; from the peculiar construction of the foot and hand, the latter "containing latent capacities and powers which are unused by savages " ; from the " wonderful power, range, flexibility, and sweetness of the musical sounds producible by the human larynx," etc.—*Natural Selection*, pp. 332, 330.

mostly in outlying regions, far from the original centres of distribution, and afford no good evidence of what man was when
he first appeared upon the earth.[1]   On the other hand, when
we turn to the regions which tradition points to as the cradle
of the race, we find great empires and civilisations which show
no traces of those gradual advances from savagery which the
modern theory requires, but which represent man as from the
earliest period as in possession of faculties of thought and
action of a high order.[2]   The theory, again, that man began
with the lowest Fetishism in religion, and only gradually raised
himself through Polytheism to Monotheism, finds no support
from the history of religions.[3]   There is not the slightest proof,
e.g., that the Vedic religion was developed out of fetish worship,
or ghost worship, but many indications that it was preceded by
a purer faith, in which the sense of the unity of God was
not yet lost.   The same may be said of the religions of the
most ancient civilised peoples,—that while all, or nearly all, in
the form in which we know them, are polytheistic and idolatrous,
there is not any which does not show a substratum of monotheistic truth, and from which we cannot adduce many proofs
of an earlier purer faith.[4]

Another side from which the Christian view is contested,
and the hypothesis of an originally savage condition of man is
supposed to be supported, is the evidence that has been accumu-
lated of an extreme antiquity of the human race.   I am not
aware that the Bible is committed to any definite date for the
appearance of man upon the earth ; but it will be generally felt
that if the extreme views which some advocate on this subject,
carrying back man's appearance some hundred thousand or two
hundred thousand years, were accepted, it would, taken in connection with the comparatively recent origin of civilisation,
militate against the view which we defend.   I am free further
to admit that, did no religious interest enter, and were the facts
of science the only ones to be regarded, we would probably have
been found yielding a ready assent to the hypothesis of a great
antiquity.   The religious interests at stake lead us, while of

---

[1] See Note E.—Alleged Primitive Savagery of Mankind.
[2] Cf. Canon Rawlinson's *Origin of Nations*, Part I., " On Early Civilisations ";
and the same author's " Antiquity of Man Historically Considered," in *Present
Day Tracts*, No. 9.
[3] Cf. Note A. to Lecture III.   [4] See Note F.—Early Monotheistic Ideas.

course acknowledging that whatever science really proves must be accepted as true, to be a little more careful in our examination of the proofs. And it is well we have been thus cautious; for, if we take the latest testimony of science as to what has been really proved, we find that the recent tendency is rather to retrench than to extend the enormous periods which were at first demanded; and that, while some geologists tell us that one or two hundred thousand years are needed, others, equally well informed, declare that ten thousand years would cover all the facts at present in evidence.[1] Professor Boyd Dawkins has said in a recent Address :—"The question of the antiquity of man is inseparably connected with the further question, Is it possible to measure the lapse of geological time in years? Various attempts have been made, and all, as it seems to me, have ended in failure. Till we know the rate of causation in the past, and until we can be sure that it is invariable and uninterrupted, I cannot see anything but failure in the future. Neither the rate of the erosion of the land by sub-aërial agencies, nor its destruction by oceanic currents, nor the rate of the deposit of stalagmite, or of the movement of the glaciers, have as yet given us anything at all approaching to a satisfactory date. We have only a sequence of events recorded in the rocks, with intervals the length of which we cannot measure. It is surely impossible to fix a date in term of years, either for the first appearance of man, or for any event outside the written record."[2]

I claim, then, that so far as the evidence of science goes, the Bible doctrine of a pure beginning of the race is not overturned. I do not enter into the question of how we are to interpret the third chapter of Genesis,—whether as history or allegory or myth, or, most probably of all, as old tradition clothed in oriental allegorical dress,—but the truth embodied in that narrative, viz. the fall of man from an original state of purity, I take to be vital to the Christian view. On the other hand, we must beware, even while holding to the Biblical account, of putting into the original state of man more that the narrative warrants. The picture given us of the first man in the Bible is primitive

---

[1] See Note G.—The Antiquity of Man and Geological Time.
[2] Report of Address to British Association, Sept. 6, 1888. Professor Dawkins is himself an advocate of man's great antiquity.

in every way.   The Adam of the book of Genesis is not a being
of advanced intellectual attainments, or endowed with an
intuitive knowledge of the various arts and sciences.   If his
state is far removed from that of the savage, it is equally far
removed from that of the civilised man.[1]   The earliest steps in
what we call civilisation are of later date, and are duly recorded,
though they belong, not to the race of Seth, but to that of Cain.[2]
It is presumed that man had high and noble faculties, a pure
and harmonious nature, rectitude of will, capability of understanding his Creator's instructions, and power to obey them.
Beyond that we need not go.   The essence of the Biblical view
is summed up in the words of the Preacher: "God made man
upright; but they sought out many inventions."[3]

II. I pass to the consideration of the connection of moral
with natural evil, reserving for discussion in a succeeding
section a special aspect of that connection—the relation of sin
to death.   I begin by a brief consideration of the problem of
natural evil, as such.   It is not sin only, but natural evil—the
existence of pain and suffering in the world—which is made the
ground of an impeachment of God's justice and goodness.
Everyone will remember Mr. J. S. Mill's terrible indictment of
nature on this score;[4] and Pessimism has given new voice to
the plaints which have always been heard of the misery and
suffering bound up with life.   On the general question, I would
only like again to emphasise what I said at the outset of the
extent to which this problem of natural evil is bound up with
that of sin.   Apart from all theological prepossessions, we have
only to cast our eyes abroad to see how large a part of the total
difficulty this connection with moral evil covers.   Take away
from the history of humanity all the evils which have come on
man through his own folly, sin, and vice; through the follies
and vices of society; through tyranny, misgovernment, and
oppression; through the cruelty and inhumanity of man to
man; and how vast a portion of the problem of evil would
already be solved!   What myriads of lives have been sacrificed

---

[1] Cf. Dawson, *Modern Science in Bible Lands*, iv., "Early Man in Genesis."
[2] Gen. iv. 16–22.   [3] Eccl. vii. 29.   Cf. Delitzsch, *in loc.*
[4] *Three Essays*, pp. 29–31: "In sober truth, nearly all the things which men
are hanged or imprisoned for doing to one another, are Nature's everyday
performances," etc.

at the shrines of Bacchus and of lust; what untold misery has been inflicted on the race, to gratify the unscrupulous ambitions of ruthless conquerors; what tears and groans have sprung from the institution of slavery; what wretchedness is hourly inflicted on human hearts by domestic tyranny, private selfishness, the preying of the strong upon the weak, dishonesty and chicanery in society! If great civilisations have fallen, to what has the result been commonly due, if not to their own vices and corruptions, which sapped and destroyed their vigour, and made them an easy prey to ruder and stronger races?[1] If society witnesses great volcanic eruptions like the French Revolution, is it not when evil has reached such a height through the long-accumulating iniquities of centuries that it can no longer be borne, and the explosion effects a remedy which could not otherwise be achieved? If all the suffering and sorrow which follow directly or indirectly from human sin could be abstracted, what a happy world, after all, this would be! Yet there seem to be natural evils which are independent of sin, and we must endeavour to look the problem suggested by them fairly in the face.

First of all, I would say that this problem of natural evil can hardly be said to meet us in the *inorganic* world at all, *i.e.* regarding it merely as such.[2] We see there what may appear to us like disharmony and disorder; convulsion, upheaval, the letting loose of titanic forces which work havoc and destruction; but except in relation to sentient existences, we cannot properly speak of these as evil. We may wonder why they should be, but when we see what ends are served in the economy of nature by this apparently lawless clash and conflict of forces, we may reconcile ourselves to it as part of a system, which, on the whole, is very good.[3]

Neither does this problem properly meet us in connection with the *organic* world, so far as it is not sentient, *e.g.*, in connection with the law of decay and death in the vegetable world. When it is said that, according to the Bible, there was no death before Adam, it is to be remembered that the Bible speaks of a vegetable creation, which was evidently intended to be perish-

---

[1] Cf. Martineau, *Study of Religion*, ii. pp. 131–135 (Book ii. chap. iii.).

[2] Cf. Ott, *Le Problème du Mal*, p. 18; Naville, do., p. 50 (Eng. trans.).

[3] These disturbances, however, present a very different aspect when viewed in relation to man. See below.

able,[1]—which, in fact, was given for food to animals and men
We feel no difficulty in this. The plants are part of nature.
They flower, seed, decay. They fall under the law of all finite,
merely natural existences, in being subject to corruptibility and
death.

When we rise to *animal* life, the problem does appear, for
here we have sentiency and suffering. Yet abstracting for a
moment from this sentiency, the same thing applies to animals
as to plants. They are finite, merely natural creatures, not ends
in themselves, but subserving some general use in the economy
of nature, and, by the law of their creation, exposed to corruption and death. How is this modified by the fact of sentiency?
I think we have only to look at the matter fairly to see that it
is not modified in any way which is incompatible with the
justice and goodness of the Creator. Leaving out of reckoning
the pain of human life, and the sufferings inflicted on the
animal world by man, we might fairly ask the pessimist to face
the question, Is the world of sentient beings an unhappy one?
Look at the fish in the stream, the bird in the air, the insect on
the wing, the creatures of the forest,—is their lot one of greater
pleasure or pain? I do not think it is unhappy. We speak of
"the struggle for existence," but is this necessarily pain? The
capacity for pleasure, indeed, implies as its counterpart the
susceptibility of pain, but whereas the avenues for pleasure are
many, the experience of pain is minimised by the suddenness
with which death comes, the absence of the power of reflection,
the paralysis of feeling through fascination or excitement, etc.[2]
I have been struck with observing the predominatingly optimistic way in which the Bible, and especially Jesus, all through
regard the natural and sentient world, dwelling on its brightness,
its beauty, its rejoicing, the care of Providence over the creatures,
their happy freedom,[3]—in striking contrast with the morbid

---

[1] Gen. i. 11, 12 (seed producing).

[2] We may exaggerate, too, the power of sensibility in the lower species of
animals. See on this, Mivart, *Lessons from Nature*, pp. 368, 369. "Though,
of course, animals *feel*, they do not *know* that they feel, nor reflect upon the
sufferings they have had, or will have to endure. . . . If a wasp, while enjoy-
ing a meal of honey, has its slender waist suddenly snipped through and its
whole abdomen cut away, it does not allow such a trifle for a moment to interrupt its pleasurable repast, but it continues to rapidly devour the savoury food,
which escapes as rapidly from its mutilated thorax."—P. 369.

[3] *E.g.* the Sermon on the Mount, Matt. vi. 26. Another note as respects
creation as a whole is struck by Paul in Rom. viii. 19-22.

brooding over the aspects of struggle in nature which fill our modern treatises.[1] The thing which strikes us most as a difficulty, perhaps, is the universal preying of species on species —"nature red in tooth and claw"[2]—which seems so strange a feature in a government assumed to have for its motive beneficence. But the difficulty is modified by the consideration that food in some way must be provided for the creatures; and if sentiency is better than insentiency, greater beneficence is shown in giving the bird or insect its brief span of life than in with holding existence from it altogether. The present plan provides for the multiplication of sentient creatures to an extent which would not be possible on any other system; it provides, too, since death must rule over such organisms, for their removal from nature in the way which least pollutes nature with corruption.[3]

The real question which underlies the problem in relation to the natural world is,—Is there to be room in the universe for any grades of existence short of the highest? In nature, as the evolutionist is fond of showing, we find every blank space filled —every corner and niche that would be otherwise empty occupied by some form of life. Why should it not be so? If, in addition to the higher orders of being, lower grades of sentient existence are possible, enhancing the total sum of life and happiness, why should they not also be created? Why—to give our thoughts for a moment the widest possible range—if there is in the universe, as Dorner supposes, "a world standing in the light of eternity, a world of pure spirits, withdrawn from all relation to succession"[4] (the angelic world), should there not be also a material and time-developing world? Why, in this

---

[1] Cf. for an example of this a passage quoted from De Maistre by Naville, p. 54: "In the vast domain of living Nature open violence reigns, a kind of fury which arms all creatures *in mutua funera*," etc.

[2] Tennyson, *In Memoriam*, lv.

[3] Martineau says: "I will be content with a single question, How would you dispose of the dead animals? . . . If no creature would touch muscular fibre, or adipose tissue, or blood, and all animated nature had to be provided with cemeteries like ours, we should be baffled by an unmanageable problem; the streams would be poisoned, and the forests and the plains would be as noisome as the recent battlefield. Nature, in her predatory tribes, has appointed a sanitary commission, and in her carrion-feeders a burial board, far more effective than those which watch over our villages and cities."—*Study of Religion*, ii. p. 95. See his whole treatment of this problem.

[4] *System of Doctrine*, ii. pp. 33–99 (Eng. trans.). Dorner mentions the idea of Aquinas of "a complete world, exhibiting without a break all possible forms of life."—P. 99.

temporal world, should there be only the highest creature, man, and not also an infinity of creatures under him, stocking the seas, rivers, plains, forests, and taking possession of every vacant opening and nook which present themselves ?   Or, in a developing world, could the highest be reached except through the lower—the spiritual except through the natural?   Is not this the law of Scripture, as well as of nature—"that was not first which is spiritual, but that which is natural, and afterwards that which is spiritual"?[1]   The mere fact that in a world of this kind the denizens would be finite and perishable—exposed to incidental pains, as well as constituted for pleasures—would not be a reason for not creating it, unless the pains were a predominant feature, and constituted a surplusage over the pleasures. But this we do not acknowledge to be the case.   The pleasures of the animal world we take to be the rule ; the pains are the exception.[2]

It is when we rise from the animal world to the consideration of natural evil in relation to *man*, that we first meet with the problem in a form which constitutes it a formidable difficulty.   For man, unlike the animals, is an end to himself ; pain means more to him than it does to them ; death, in particular, seems a contradiction of his destiny ; and it is not easy to understand why he should be placed in a world in which he is naturally, nay necessarily, exposed to these evils.   The natural disturbances which we formerly noticed—floods, hurricanes, earthquakes, volcanoes, and the like—now assume a new aspect as elements in a world of which man is to be the inhabitant, and where he may be called upon to suffer through their agency.[3]   This is really a serious problem, and we have to ask whether the Biblical view affords any clue to the solution of it, and whether that solution will sustain the test of reason and of fact?

It is scarcely an adequate solution of this problem of natural

---

[1] 1 Cor. xv. 46.

[2] The difficulty is "modified," as said, but not altogether removed, by these considerations, especially when the world is viewed in its teleological relations to man, and where stress is laid, not only on the mere fact of the preying of one creature on another, but on some of the *kinds* of creatures with which the earth is stocked, and on the *manner* of their warfare ; on their hideousness, repulsiveness, fierceness, unnecessary cruelty, etc.   See a powerful statement in Martensen's *Jacob Böhme*, pp. 217–222 (Eng. trans.).

[3] To a certain extent these disturbances affect animals also, but in these cases the question is subordinate.

evil and death as it affects man, though, no doubt, a profound element in the solution, to point to the disciplinary and other wholesome uses which misfortune and suffering are fitted to subserve in the moral education of man. This is the line followed by most earnest thinkers in trying to explain the mystery of suffering in the world, and it rests on the true thought that there is a Divinely ordained connection between the pains we are called upon to suffer and the ends of our highest life.[1]   Without trials and difficulties, it is urged, where were progress? without checks to self-will, where were the lessons of submission to a higher will? without experience of resistance, where were the stimulus to effort? without danger and misfortune, where were courage, manhood, and endurance? without pain, where were sympathy?[2] without sorrow and distress, where would the opportunity for self-sacrifice be? This is quite true, but does it go to the root of the matter? Does it explain all? Because suffering and death, as existing in the world, have an educating and purifying effect; because, as may be freely granted, they have a power of developing a type of character greater and nobler than could have been developed without them (a glimpse of theodicy in the permission of evil at all); because they serve for purposes of test and trial where character is already formed, and aid its yet ampler growth[3]—does it follow that a world such as this, with its manifold disorders, would have been a suitable abode for an unfallen race; or that it would have been righteous to expose such a race to these calamities; or that, in the case of pure beings, less violent and painful methods of education would not have sufficed?[4] Of course, if this method of arguing were admitted, the existence of moral evils would have to be justified on the same ground, for in conflict with these, even more than

---

[1] Thus Rothe, Pfleiderer, Martineau, Ott, etc.

[2] Cf. Browning, *Ferishtah's Fancies*—" Mihrab Shah."

[3] The theodicy in Job takes this form.

[4] Cf. Lotze, *Outlines of Philosophy of Religion* (Eng. trans.), pp. 124, 125; and Browning, *La Saisiaz*, Works, xiv. p. 181 :—

> "What, no way but this that man may learn and lay to heart how rife!
> Life were with delights would only death allow their taste to life?
> Must the rose sigh ' Pluck—I perish !' must the eve weep ' Gaze—I fade !'
> —Every sweet warn ''Ware my bitter !' every shine bid ' Wait my shade ' ?
> Can we love but on condition that the thing we love must die?
> Needs there groan a world in anguish just to teach us sympathy—
> Multitudinously wretched that we, wretched too, may guess
> What a preferable state were universal happiness ? "

with outward misfortune, is the highest type of character developed. It will be observed, also, that the argument rests largely, though not wholly, on the assumption of fault in human nature to be corrected (self-will, selfishness, etc.), and thus already presupposes sin; it does not, for instance, tell what a world would have been into which no sin had entered. But do even the advocates of this explanation of natural evil abide by their own thesis? Pain, it is said, begets tenderness and sympathy; suffering engenders philanthropy; the presence of evils in the world awakens noble self-sacrificing efforts for their removal—summons man, as Pfleiderer puts it, to fellowship with "the aim of God Himself, viz. to advance goodness, and to overcome evil in the world."[1] Then these *are* evils, and, notwithstanding their advantages, we are to treat them as things which would be better absent, and do our utmost to remove them. A concrete case in this connection is worth a good deal of argument, and I take it from Naville. He tells of a letter he received, written from Zurich, at a time when the cholera was ravaging the city. "My correspondent," he says, "told me that he had seen sad things—the results of selfishness and fear; but he also told me that so much courage, devotedness, and regard for the good of others had been brought out under the pressure of the malady, that different ranks of society had been so drawn together by the inspiration of generous sentiments, that he would not for the world have been absent from his native place, and so have missed witnessing such a spectacle."[2] Shall we then, because of these salutary effects, wish for the prevalence of cholera? Or because wars bring out noble examples of heroism, shall we desire to see wars prevail? The question has only to be asked to be answered, and it shows that this mode of justifying natural evil leaves much yet to be accounted for.

It has just been seen that even this mode of explaining the existence of natural evil, and the use made of it in the moral government of God, presupposes, to some extent, the existence of *sin*. This yields a point of transition to the Biblical view, in which this solidarity of man with his outward world, and the consequent connection of natural with

---

[1] *Religionsphilosophie*, iv. p. 63 (Eng. trans.).
[2] *Problem of Evil*, p. 65 (Eng. trans.).

moral evil, is a central and undeniable feature. We are not, indeed, at liberty to trace a strict relation between the sins of individuals and the outward calamities that befall them; but Christ's warning on this subject by no means contradicts the view that there is an intimate connection between natural and moral evils, and that the former are often used by God as the punishment of the latter. It is one of the most deeply ingrained ideas in the Bible, that physical evils are often used by God for the punishment of individual and national wickedness, and Christ Himself expressly endorses this view in His own predictions of the approaching judgments on Jerusalem.[1] He warns us only that the proposition,—Sin is often punished with physical evils—is by no means convertible with the other, —All physical evils are the punishment of individual sins. Nor is this teaching of Scripture to be explained away, as it is by Lipsius, Pfleiderer, and Ritschl, as meaning merely that the evil conscience subjectively regards these visitations as retributive, though objectively they have no such character, but simply flow from the natural course of events.[2] Similarly, the expression, "All things work together for good to them that love God,"[3] is explained as meaning that things work together for good to the believer, because, whatever the course of events, he is sure to profit by them. This is not the Biblical view, and it is not a reasonable one for those to take, who, like the above-named writers, admit a government of the world for moral ends. Once allow a relation between the natural and the moral in the government of God, and it is difficult to avoid the conclusion that the course of outward events is directed with a regard to the good and evil conduct of the subjects of that government.

A deeper question, however, which lies behind this immediate one, of the place of natural evils in the moral government of God is, Is nature itself in a normal condition? The Bible, again, undeniably answers this question in the negative, and it is important for us to ascertain in what sense precisely it does so. The most explicit passage in the New Testament is perhaps

---

[1] Matt. xxiii. 35; cf. John v. 14: "Sin no more, lest a worse thing come unto thee."

[2] Cf., e.g., Ritschl, *Recht. und Ver.* iii. p. 334; Pfleiderer, *Religionsphilosophie*, iv. pp. 42–44.

[3] Rom. viii. 28.

that in Rom. viii. 19–23, where the Apostle Paul expressly declares, "For the earnest expectation of the creation waiteth for the revealing of the sons of God. For the creation was subjected to vanity, not of its own will, but by reason of Him who subjected it, in hope that the creation itself also shall be delivered from the bondage of corruption into the liberty of the glory of the children of God. For we know that the whole creation groaneth and travaileth in pain together until now." The plain implication of this passage is that nature is a sufferer with man on account of sin; that, as I expressed it above, there is a solidarity between man and the outward world, both in his Fall and his Redemption. So far the passage is an echo of the statement of Genesis, that the earth lies under a curse on account of human sin. Is this view scientifically tenable, or is it not a baseless dream, directly contradicted by the facts already conceded of physical disturbance, decay, and death in the world, long ere man appeared in it? I do not think it is. This implication of creation in the effects of human sin, though science certainly cannot prove it, is an idea by no means inadmissible, or in contradiction with known facts.

1. The view has often been suggested—is maintained, *e.g.*, by Dorner and Delitzsch [1]—that the constitution of nature had from the first a teleological relation to sin; that sin did not enter the world as an unforeseen accident, but, as foreseen, was provided for in the arrangements of the world; that creation, in other words, had from the beginning an anticipative reference to sin. This view would explain many things that seem mysterious in the earlier stages of creation, and falls in with other truths of Scripture, to which attention will subsequently be directed. [2]

---

[1] Dorner, *System of Doctrine*, ii. p. 67 (Eng. trans.); Delitzsch, *New Commentary on Genesis*, i. p. 103 (Eng. trans.). "The whole of the six days' creation," says the latter, "is, so to speak, supralapsarian, *i.e.* so constituted that the consequences of this foreseen fall of man were taken into account."

[2] This theory is ingeniously argued out in an interesting chapter in Bushnell's *Nature and the Supernatural*, chap. vii., "Anticipative Consequences." Cf. also Hugh Miller's *Footprints of the Creator*, pp. 268 ff.; "Final Causes; their Bearing on Geologic History"; and Hitchcock, *Religion of Geology*, Lecture III. I have not touched on another theory, beginning with Böhme, which connects the present state of creation with yet earlier, *i.e.* dæmonic evil. The most striking statement of this theory is perhaps in Martensen, *Jacob Böhme* (Eng. trans.), pp. 217–222—a passage already referred to. See the theory criticised in Reusch's *Nature and the Bible*, Book i. chap. xvii. (Eng. trans.).

2. I do not feel, however, that I need to avail myself of this hypothesis. All that is essential in the Apostle's statement can be conserved without going back to pre-Adamic ages, or to vegetable decay, and animal suffering and death. We gain the best key to the passage if we keep to the meaning of his own word "vanity" ($\mu\alpha\tau\alpha\iota\acute{o}\tau\eta s$)—profitlessness—as expressive of that to which creation was subjected. "It is not said," remarks Bishop Ellicott, "that the creation was subject to death or corruption, though both lie involved in the expression, but to something more frightfully generic, to something almost worse than non-existence,—to purposelessness, to an inability to realise its natural tendencies, and the ends for which it was called into being, to baffled endeavour and mocked expectations, to a blossoming and not bearing fruit, a pursuing and not attaining, yea, and as the analogies of the language of the original significantly imply, to a searching and never finding."[1]   Thus interpreted, the apostle's words convey the idea that nature is in a state of arrested development through sin, is frustrated of its true end, and has a destiny before it which sin does not permit it to attain.   There is an arrest, delay, or back-putting through sin, which begets in the creature a sense of bondage, and an earnest longing for deliverance.[2]   This certainly harmonises sufficiently well with the general impression nature makes upon us, which has found expression in the poetry and literature of all ages.

3. The earth is under "bondage to corruption" in another way,—in the very presence of man and his sin upon it; in being the abode of a sinful race; in being compelled, through its laws and agencies, to subserve the purposes of man's sin; in being perverted from its true uses in the service of his lusts and vices; in the suffering of the animal creation through his cruelty; in the blight, famine, earthquake, etc., to which it is subjected in consequence of his sin, and as the means of punishment of it.   For it by no means follows that because

---

[1] *Destiny of the Creature*, p. 7.

[2] Thus also Dorner: "So far, then, as sin retards this perfection, it may certainly be said that Nature is detained by sin in a state of corruption against its will, as well as that it has been placed in a long-enduring state of corruptibleness, which, apart from sin, was unnecessary, if the assimilation of Nature by spirit could have been accomplished forthwith."—*Syst. of Doct.* ii. p. 66.

these things were found in the world *in the making*, they were intended to be, or continue, in the world *as made*, or would have been found had sin not entered it. Science may *affirm*, it can certainly never prove, that the world is in a normal state in these respects, or that even under existing laws a better balance of harmony could not be maintained, had the Creator so willed it.

III. This whole discussion of the connection of natural with moral evil sums itself up in the consideration of one special problem, in which the contending views may be said to be brought to a distinct and decisive issue—I mean the relation of sin to death. Is human death—that crowning evil, which carries so many other sorrows in its train—the result of sin, or is it not? Here, again, it is hardly necessary for me to say, there is a direct contradiction between the Biblical and the "modern" view, and it is for us very carefully to inquire whether the Pauline statement, "Through one man sin entered into the world, and death through sin; and so death passed unto all men, for that all have sinned,"[1] enters into the essence of the Christian view, or whether, as some seem to think, it is an excrescence which may be stripped off.

Now, so far from regarding this relation of human death to sin as a mere accident of the Christian view, which may be dropped without detriment to its substance, I am disposed to look on it as a truth most fundamental and vital—organically connected with the entire Christian system. Its importance comes out most clearly when we consider it in the light of the Christian doctrine of Redemption. The Bible, as we shall immediately see, knows nothing of an abstract immortality of the soul, as the schools speak of it; nor is its Redemption a Redemption of the soul only, but of the body as well. It is a Redemption of man in his whole complex personality—body and soul together. It was in the body that Christ rose from the dead; in the body that He has ascended to heaven; in the body that He lives and reigns there for evermore. It is His promise that, if He lives, we shall live also;[2] and this promise includes a pledge of the resurrection of the body. The truth which underlies this is, that death for man is an effect of sin.

---

[1] Rom. v. 12 (R.V.).   [2] John xiv. 19.

It did not lie in the Creator's original design for man that he should die,—that these two component parts of his nature, body and soul, should ever be violently disrupted and severed, as death now severs them. Death is an abnormal fact in the history of the race; and Redemption is, among other things, the undoing of. this evil, and the restoration of man to his normal completeness as a personal being.

That man was originally a mortal being neither follows from the fact of death as a law of the animal creation, nor from its present universality. It is, no doubt, an essential part of the modern anti-Christian view, that man is a dying creature, and always has been. This goes with the view that man is simply an evolution from the animal, and falls under the same law of death as the rest of the animal creation. But I have shown some reasons for not admitting the premiss,[1] and therefore I cannot assent to the conclusion. There is not a word in the Bible to indicate that in its view death entered the animal world as a consequence of the sin of man. But, with the advent of man upon the scene, there was, as remarked in an earlier part of the Lecture, the introduction of something new. There now appeared at the head of creation a moral and spiritual being—a being made in God's image—a rational and accountable being—a being for the first time capable of moral life, and bearing within him infinite possibilities of progress and happiness; and it does not follow that because mere animals are subject to a law of death, a being of this kind must be. More than this, it is the distinction of man from the animals that he is immortal, and they are not. He bears in his nature the various evidences that he has a destiny stretching out far into the future—into eternity; and many even, who hold that death is not a consequence of sin, do not dispute that his soul is immortal. But here is the difficulty in which such a view is involved. The soul is not the whole of the man. It is a false view of the constitution of human nature to regard the body as a mere appendage to the soul, or to suppose that the human being can be equally complete whether he has his body, or is deprived of it. This is not the Biblical view, nor, I venture to say, is it the view to which the facts of modern psychology and physiology point. If

---

[1] Cf. last Lecture.

anything is evident, it is that soul and body are made for each other, that the perfect life for man is a corporeal one; that he is not *pure* spirit, but incorporated spirit. The soul is capable of separation from the body; but in that state it is in an imperfect and mutilated condition. Thus it is always represented in the Bible, and heathen feeling coincides with this view in its representations of the cheerless, sunless, joyless, ghost-like state of Hades. If, then, it is held that man was naturally constituted for immortality, how can it be maintained, with any show of consistency, that he stood originally under a law of death? That the animal should die is natural. But for the rational, moral agent, death is something *un*natural— abnormal; the violent rupture, or separation, or tearing apart, so to speak, of two parts of his nature which, in the Creator's design, were never intended to be sundered. There is, there- fore, profound truth in the Biblical representation, "In the day that thou eatest thereof thou shalt surely die "—" Dust thou art, and unto dust thou shalt return." [1] Some other way of leaving the world, no doubt, there would have been—some Enoch or Elijah-like translation, or gradual transformation of a lower corporeity into a higher, but not death as we know it. [2]

The true Biblical doctrine of immortality, then, I think, includes the following points :—

1. It rests on the Biblical doctrine of human nature. According to the Bible, and according to fact, man is a compound being—not, like God and the angels, a pure spirit, but an embodied spirit, a being made up of body and of soul. The soul, it is true, is the higher part of human nature, the seat of personality, and of mental, moral, and spiritual life. Yet it is intended and adapted for life in the body, and body and soul together make the man—the complete human being.

2. It was no part of the Creator's design for man in his ideal constitution that body and soul should ever be separated. The immortality man was to enjoy was an immortality in which the body was to have its share. This is the profound truth in the teaching of the Bible when it says that, as

---

[1] Gen. ii. 16, iii. 19.
[2] See further on this subject, Note H.—The Connection of Sin and Death.

respects man, death is the result of sin. Had sin not entered we must suppose that man—the complete man—would have enjoyed immortality; even his body, its energies replenished from vital forces from within, being exempt from decay, or at least not decaying till a new and more spiritual tenement for the soul had been prepared. With the entrance of sin, and departure of holiness from the soul, this condition ceased, and the body sank, as part of general nature, under the law of death.

3. The soul in separation from the body is in a state of imperfection and mutilation. When a human being loses one of his limbs, we regard him as a mutilated being. Were he to lose all his limbs, we would regard him as worse mutilated still. So, when the soul is entirely denuded of its body, though consciousness and memory yet remain, it must still be regarded —and in the Bible is regarded—as subsisting in an imperfect condition, a condition of enfeebled life, diminished powers, restricted capacities of action—a state, in short, of deprivation. The man whose life is hid with Christ in God will no doubt with that life retain the blessedness that belongs to it even in the state of separation from the body—he will " be with Christ, which is far better";[1] but it is still true that so long as he remains in that disembodied state, he wants part of himself, and cannot be perfectly blessed, as he will be after his body, in renewed and glorified form, is restored to him.

4. The last point, therefore, in the Biblical doctrine is, that true immortality is through Redemption, and that this Redemption embraces the Resurrection of the body.[2] It is a complete Redemption, a Redemption of man in his whole personality, and not simply of a part of man. This is a subject which will be considered afterwards. It is enough for the present to have shown that the Biblical doctrines of man's nature, of the connection of sin and death, of Redemption, and of the true immortality, cohere together and form a unity— are of a piece.

---

[1] 2 Cor. v. 8; Phil. i. 23; Rev. xiv. 13, etc.
[2] Rom. v. 11, viii. 23.

APPENDIX TO CHAPTER 5
THE OLD TESTAMENT DOCTRINE
OF IMMORTALITY

THE views advanced in the Lecture have an important bearing on the much discussed question of the Old Testament doctrine of immortality. The statement is often made that the Old Testament, especially in the older books, has no distinct doctrine of Immortality. Many explanations have been offered of this difficulty, but I would humbly suggest that the real explanation may be that we have been looking for evidence of that doctrine in a wrong direction. We have been looking for a doctrine of "the immortality of the soul" in the sense of the schools, whereas the real hope of patriarchs and saints, so far as they had one, was, in accordance with the Biblical doctrine already explained, that of restored life in the body.[1]

The early Hebrews had no manner of doubt, any more than we have, that the soul, or spiritual part of man, survived the body.[2] It would be strange if they had, for every other ancient people is known to have had this belief. The Egyptians, *e.g.*, taught that the dead descended to an under-world, where they were judged by Osiris and his forty-two assessors.[3] The Babylonians and Assyrians conceived of the abode of the dead as a great city having seven encircling walls, and a river flowing round or through it.[4] A name they gave to this city is believed

---

[1] The view defended in this Appendix will be found indicated in Hofmann's *Schriftbeweis*, iii. pp. 461–477 ; and Dr. P. Fairbairn's *Typology of Scripture*, 3rd ed. i. pp. 343–359.

[2] Cf. Max Müller, *Anthropological Religion*, on "Belief on Immortality in the Old Testament," pp. 367, 377.

[3] Cf. Renouf, Hibbert Lectures, pp. 195, 196 ; Budge, *Dwellers on the Nile* ("By-Paths of Bible Knowledge" Series), chap. ix. ; Vigoroux's *La Bible et les Découvertes modernes*, iii. pp. 133–141.

[4] Cf. the *Descent of Ishtar*, in Sayce's Hibbert Lectures, Lecture IV.; Budge's *Babylonian Life and History* ("By-Paths of Bible Knowledge" Series), pp. 140–142 ; Vigoroux, *La Bible et les Découvertes modernes*, iii. pp. 123–132.

by some to have been "Sualu,"[1] the same word as the Hebrew
Sheol, which is the name in the Old Testament for the place of
departed spirits.   It is one of the merits of the Revised Version
that it has in many places (why not in all?) printed this word in
the text, and tells the reader in the preface that "Sheol," sometimes in the Old Version translated "grave," sometimes "pit,"
sometimes "hell," means definitely "the abode of departed spirits,
and corresponds to the Greek 'Hades,' or the under-world," and
does *not* signify "the place of burial."   But the thought of
going to "Sheol" was no comfort to the good man.   The gloomy
associations of death hung over this abode; it was figured as a
land of silence and forgetfulness; the warm and rich light of
the upper-world was excluded from it;[2] no ray of gospel light
had as yet been given to chase away its gloom.   The idea of
"Sheol" was thus not one which attracted, but one which
repelled, the mind.   Men shrank from it as we do from the
breath and cool shades of the charnel-house.   The saint, strong
in his hope in God, might believe that God would not desert
him even in "Sheol"; that His presence and fellowship would
be given him even there; but it would only be in moments of
strong faith he could thus triumph, and in hours of despondency the gloomiest thoughts were apt to come back on him.
His real trust, so far as he was able to cherish one, was that
God would not leave his soul in "Sheol," but would redeem
him from that state, and restore him to life in the body.[3]   His
hope was for resurrection.

To illustrate this state of feeling and belief, in regard to the
state of the separate existence of the soul, it may be well to
cite one or two passages bearing on the subject.   An indication
of a belief in a future state of the soul is found in an expression
several times met with in Genesis—"gathered to his people"
—where, in every instance, the gathering to the people (in
"Sheol") is definitely distinguished from the act of burial.[4]

---

[1] Thus F. Delitzsch, and Boscawen in British Museum Lecture on *Sheol,
Death, the Grave, and Immortality*.   But the identification is held by others
to be conjectural (Schrader, *Keilinschriften*, ii. p. 80 [Eng. trans.]; Budge,
Babylonian Life and History, p. 140, etc.; Vigouroux, iii. p. 125).   The
Assyrian gives the name as Aralu.

[2] Thus also in the Babylonian and Greek conceptions.   Cf. Sayce, Hibbert
Lectures, p. 364; Fairbairn, *Studies*, "The Belief in Immortality," pp.
190, 191.

[3] See passages discussed below.   [4] Gen. xxv. 8, 9, xxxv. 29, xlix. 29, 31, 33.

Other evidences are afforded by the belief in necromancy, the narratives of resurrection, etc. What kind of place "Sheol" was to the popular imagination is well represented in the words of Job—

> " I go whence I shall not return,
> Even to the land of darkness and the shadow of death,
> A land of thick darkness, as darkness itself,
> A land of the shadow of death, without any order,
> And where light is as darkness." [1]

There was not much cheer in looking forward to an abode like this, and it is therefore not surprising that even good men, in moments of despondency, when it seemed as if God's presence and favour were taken from them, should moan, as David did—

> " Return, O Lord, deliver my soul ;
> Save me for Thy loving kindness' sake,
> For in death there is no remembrance of Thee,
> In Sheol who shall give Thee thanks ? " [2]

or with Hezekiah—

> " Sheol cannot praise Thee, death cannot celebrate Thee :
> They that go down into the pit cannot hope for Thy truth.
> The living, the living, he shall praise Thee, as I do this day." [3]

It is not, therefore, in this direction that we are to look for the positive and cheering side of the Old Testament hope of immortality, but in quite another. It is said we have no doctrine of Immortality in the Old Testament. But I reply, we *have* immortality at the very commencement—for man, as he came from the hands of his Creator, was made for immortal life. Man in Eden was immortal. He was intended to live, not to die. Then came sin, and with it death. Adam called his son Seth, and Seth called his son Enoch, which means "frail, mortal man." Seth himself died, his son died, his son's son died, and so the line of death goes on. Then comes an interruption, the intervention, as it were, of a higher law, a new inbreaking of immortality into a line of death. "Enoch walked with God, and he was not ; for God took him." [4] Enoch did not die. Every other life in that record ends with the statement, "and he died" ; but Enoch's is given as an exception. He did not die, but God "took" him, *i.e.* without death. He

---

[1] Job x. 21, 22. Cf. description in *Descent of Ishtar*, Hibbert Lectures.
[2] Ps. vi. 4, 5.   [3] Isa. xxxviii. 18, 19.   [4] Gen. v. 24.

simply "was not" on earth, but he "was" with God in another
and invisible state of existence.[1] His case is thus in some
respects the true type of all immortality, for it is an immortality
of the true personality, in which the body has as real a share
as the soul.   It agrees with what I have advanced in the Lecture, that it is not an immortality of the soul only that the
Bible speaks of — that is left for the philosophers — but an
immortality of the whole person, body and soul together.   Such
is the Christian hope, and such, as I shall now try to show, was
the Hebrew hope also.

It is a current view that the doctrine of the Resurrection of
the dead was a very late doctrine among the Hebrews, borrowed,
as many think, from the Persians, during, or subsequent to, the
Babylonian exile.   Dr. Cheyne sees in it an effect of Zoroastrian influence on the religion of Israel.[2]   My opinion, on the
contrary, is that it is one of the very oldest doctrines in the
Bible, the form, in fact, in which the hope of immortality was
held, so far as it was held, from the days of the patriarchs
downward.[3]   In any case, it was a doctrine of very remote
antiquity.   We find traces of it in many ancient religions outside the Hebrew, an instructive testimony to the truth of the
idea on which it rested.   The Egyptians believed, *e.g.*, that
the reanimation of the body was essential to perfected existence ; and this, according to some, was the thought that under-
lay the practice of embalming.[4]   The ancient Babylonians and
Assyrians also had the idea of resurrection.   One of their hymns
to Merodach celebrates him as the

> " Merciful one among the gods,
>   Merciful one, who restores the dead to life." [5]

---

[1] So, later, Elijah.

[2] *Origin of Psalter*, Lecture VIII.; and papers in *The Expository Times*
(July and August 1891) on "Possible Zoroastrian Influences on the Religion of
Israel."

[3] Thus also Hofmann : "Nothing can be more erroneous than the opinion
that the resurrection from the dead is a late idea, first entering through human
reflection, the earliest traces of which, if not first given by the Parsees to the
Jews, are to be met with in Isaiah and Ezekiel."—*Schriftbeweis*, iii. p. 461.
Cf. on this theory of Parsic influence, Pusey's *Daniel*, pp. 512–517.

[4] "There is a chapter with a vignette representing the soul uniting itself to
the body, and the text promises that they shall never again be separated."—
Renouf, Hibbert Lectures, p. 188.   "They believed," says Budge, "that the
soul would revisit the body after a number of years, and therefore it was
absolutely necessary that the body should be preserved, if its owner wished to
live for ever with the gods."—*Dwellers on the Nile*, p. 156.

[5] Cf. Boscawen, British Museum Lecture, pp. 23, 24 ; Sayce, pp. 98–100 ;

The belief was probably also held by the Persians, though it is still a disputed question whether it is found in the older portions of the Zend-Avesta. That question is not so easily settled as Dr. Cheyne thinks;[1] but in any case the older references are few and ambiguous, and are totally inadequate to explain the remarkable prominence which this doctrine assumed in the Old Testament.[2] The Bible has a coherent and consistent doctrine of its own upon the subject, and is not dependent on doubtful allusions in Zoroastrian texts for its clear and bold statements of the final swallowing up of death in victory. Let me briefly review some of the lines of evidence.

I have referred already to the case of Enoch in the beginning of the history, as illustrative of the Biblical idea of immortality. As respects the patriarchs, the references to their beliefs and hopes are necessarily few and inferential,—a fact which speaks strongly for the early date and genuineness of the tradition. The New Testament signalises them as men of "faith," and certainly their conduct is that of men who, accounting themselves "strangers and pilgrims" on the earth, look for a future fulfilment of the promises as of something in which they have a personal interest.[3] Not improbably it was some hope of resurrection which inspired (as with the Egyptians) their great care for their dead, and prompted the injunctions left by Jacob and Joseph regarding the interment of their "bones" in the land of promise.[4] It is significant that the Epistle to the Hebrews connects Abraham's sacrifice of Isaac with his faith in a resurrection. "By faith Abraham, being tried, offered up Isaac . . . accounting that God is able to raise up, even from the dead;

Cheyne, *Origin of Psalter*, p. 392. There is no evidence, however, of a general hope of resurrection.

[1] Cf. Pusey, pp. 512–517; and Cheyne's own citations from recent scholars, *Origin of Psalter*, pp. 425, 451. M. Montet formerly held that the germs of the doctrine came from Zoroastrianism, but "in 1890, in deference, it would seem, to M. Harlez, and in opposition not less to Spiegel than to Gelder, he pronounces the antiquity of the resurrection doctrine in Zoroastrianism as yet unproven."—Cheyne, p. 451. Cf. Schultz, *Alttest. Theol.* p. 762.

[2] Anyone can satisfy himself on this head by consulting the passages for himself in the Zend-Avesta, in *Sacred Books of the East*. The indices to the three volumes give only one reference to the subject, and that to one of a few undated "Miscellaneous Fragments" at the end. Professor Cheyne himself can say no more than that "Mills even thinks that there is a trace of the doctrine of the Resurrection in the Gathas. . . . He (Zoroaster) may have had a vague conception of the revival of bodies, but not a theory."—*Origin of Psalter*, p. 438.

[3] Heb. xi. 13.   [4] Gen. i. 5, 25; Ex. xiii. 19; Heb. xi. 22.

from whence also he did in a parable receive him back."[1] The Rabbis drew a curious inference from God's word to Abraham, "I will give *to thee*, and to thy seed after thee, the land wherein thou art a stranger."[2] "But it appears," they argued, "that Abraham and the other patriarchs did not possess that land; therefore it is of necessity that they should be raised up to enjoy the good promises, else the promises of God should be vain and false. So that here we have a proof, not only of the immortality of the soul, but also of the foundation of the law— namely, the resurrection of the dead."[3] If this be thought fanciful, I would refer to the teaching of a greater than the Rabbis. Reasoning with the Sadducees, Jesus quotes that saying of God to Moses, "I am the God of Abraham, and the God of Isaac, and the God of Jacob," adding, "God is not the God of the dead, but of the living."[4] The point to be observed is that Jesus quotes this passage, not simply in proof of the continued subsistence of the patriarchs in some state of being, but in proof of the resurrection of the dead. And how does it prove that? Only on the ground, which Jesus assumes, that the relation of the believer to God carries with it a *whole* immortality, and this, as we have seen, implies life in the body. If God is the God of Abraham and Isaac and Jacob, this covenant relation pledges to these patriarchs not only continuance of existence, but Redemption from the power of death, *i.e.* resurrection.

It is, however, when we come to the later books—the Book of Job, the Psalms, the Prophets—that we get clearer light on the form which the hope of immortality assumed in the minds of Old Testament believers; and it may be affirmed with considerable confidence that this light is all, or nearly all, in favour of the identification of this hope with the hope of resurrection. I take first the Book of Job, because, whenever written, it relates to patriarchal times, or at least moves in patriarchal conditions. The first remarkable passage in this book is in chapter xiv. This chapter raises the very question we are now dealing with, and it is noteworthy that the form in which it does so is the possibility of bodily revival. First,

---

[1] Heb. xi. 17–19; cf. Hofmann, pp. 461, 462.
[2] Gen. xvii. 8.   [3] Quoted in Fairbairn, i. p. 353.
[4] Matt. xxii. 23.

Job enumerates the appearances which seem hostile to man's living again (vers. 7–12). Then faith, rising in her very extremity, reasserts herself against doubt and fear—

> "Oh that Thou wouldest hide me in Sheol,
>   That Thou wouldest keep me secret, till Thy wrath be past,
>   That Thou wouldest appoint me a set time, and remember me!
>   If a man die, shall he live again?
>   All the days of my warfare would I wait,
>   Till my release should come.
>   Thou shouldest call, and I would answer Thee,
>   Thou wouldest have a desire to the work of Thy hands." [1]

There seems no reasonable room for question that what is before Job's mind here is the thought of resurrection. Dr. A. B. Davidson explains : "On this side death he has no hope of a return to God's favour. Hence, contemplating that he shall die under God's anger, his thought is that he might remain in Sheol till God's wrath be past, for He keepeth not His anger for ever; that God would appoint him a period to remain in death, and then remember him with returning mercy, and call him back again to His fellowship. But to his mind this involves a complete return to life again of the whole man (ver. 14), for in death there is no fellowship with God (Ps. vi. 5). Thus his solution, though it appears to his mind only as a momentary gleam of light, is broader than that of the Psalmist, and corresponds to that made known in subsequent revelation." [2]

The second passage in Job is the well-known one in chapter xix., translated in the Revised Version thus—

> "But I know that my Redeemer liveth,
>   And that He shall stand up at the last upon the earth [Heb. *dust*].
>   And after my skin hath been thus destroyed,
>   Yet from my flesh shall I see God:
>   Whom I shall see for myself,
>   And mine eyes shall behold, and not another." [3]

I do not enter into the many difficulties of this passage, but

---

[1] Job xiv. 13–15 (R.V.). The margin translates as in A.V., "Thou shalt call," etc. As remarked, the form in which the question is put in this passage is as significant as the answer to it. It implies that revived existence in the body is the only form in which the patriarch contemplated immortality. Life and even sensation in Sheol are presupposed in ver. 22.

[2] *Com. on Job, in loc.* (Cambridge Series). I can scarcely agree that Job's solution is broader than that of the Psalmist's. See below.

[3] Job xix. 25–27.

refer only to the crucial line, "Yet from my flesh shall I see God." The margin gives as another rendering, "without my flesh," but this is arrived at only as an interpretation of the word "from," which is literally the one used. The natural meaning would therefore seem to be, "Yet from (or out of) my flesh shall I see God," which implies that he will be clothed with flesh.[1] Dr. Davidson allows the admissibility of this rendering, and says: "If therefore we understand the words 'from my flesh' in the sense of *in* my flesh, we must suppose that Job anticipated being clothed in a new body after death. Something may be said for this view. Undoubtedly, in chapter xiv. 13 *seq.*, Job clearly conceived the idea of being delivered from Sheol and living again, and fervently prayed that such a thing might be. And what he there ventured to long for, he might here speak of as a thing of which he was assured. No violence would be done to the line of thought in the book by this supposition." Yet he thinks "it is highly improbable that the great thought of the resurrection of the body could be referred to in a way so brief," and so prefers the rendering "without."[2] I think, however, this is hardly a sufficient reason to outweigh the tremendously strong fact that we have already this thought of resurrection conceded in chapter xiv., and, further, that the thought of living again in the body seemed the only way in which Job there could conceive the idea of immortality. If that is so, it may explain why more stress is not laid upon resurrection here. The hope which absorbs all Job's thought is that of "seeing God," and the fact that, if he does so at all, he must do it "in" or "from" the flesh, is taken for granted as a thing of course.[3]

The question of the testimony of the Psalms is greatly simplified by the large concessions which writers like Dr. Cheyne are now ready to make, in the belief that in the references to resurrection doctrine they have a proof of "Zoroastrian influences." The passages, however, are happily of an order that speak for themselves, and need no forcing to yield us their meaning. A conspicuous example is Ps. xvi.

---

[1] Cf. Pusey, p. 508, and Vigoroux, iii. pp. 172–180.

[2] *Commentary on Job*, Appendix on chap. xix. 23–27, p. 292.

[3] Dr. Davidson's remark, "On Old Testament ground, and in the situation of Job, such a matter-of-course kind of reference is almost inconceivable" (p. 292), involves the very point at issue.

8–11, cited in the New Testament as a prophecy of the resurrection of Christ—

> "I have set the Lord always before me :
> Because He is at my right hand, I shall not be moved.
> Therefore my heart is glad, and my glory rejoiceth ;
> My flesh also shall dwell in safety (or *confidently*),
> For Thou wilt not leave my soul to Sheol ;
> Neither wilt Thou suffer Thine Holy One to see corruption (or *the pit*).
> Thou wilt show me the path of life :
> In Thy presence is fulness of joy ;
> In Thy right hand there are pleasures for evermore." [1]

Another passage is in Psalm xvii. 15, where, after describing the apparent prosperity of the wicked, the Psalmist says—

> "As for me, I shall behold Thy face in righteousness :
> I shall be satisfied, when I awake, with Thy likeness."

The "awakening" here, as Delitzsch says, can only be that from the sleep of death.[2] Yet more distinct is Ps. xlix. 14, 15—

> "They (the wicked) are appointed as a flock for Sheol :
> Death shall be their shepherd :
> And the upright shall have dominion over them in the morning ;
> And their beauty shall be for Sheol to consume, that there be no habitation for it.
> But God will redeem my soul from the power (hand) of Sheol :
> For He shall receive me."

There is here again, it is believed, clear reference to the "morning" of the resurrection. The passage is the more significant that in the last words, as well as in Ps. lxxiii. 24, there is direct allusion to the case of Enoch. "'God,' says the Psalmist, 'shall redeem my soul from the hand of Hades, for He shall take me,' as He took Enoch, and as He took Elijah, to Himself."[3] Ps. lxxiii. 24 reads thus—

> "Nevertheless I am continually with Thee :
> Thou hast holden my right hand.
> Thou shalt guide me with Thy counsel,
> And afterward receive me to glory.

---

[1] See Acts ii. 24–31. Cf. Delitzsch, *in loc.* ; and Cheyne, *Origin of the Psalter*, p. 431.

[2] *Com., in loc.* Thus also Pusey, Perowne, Cheyne, Hofmann, etc. "The awakening," says Cheyne, "probably means the passing of the soul into a resurrection body."—*Origin of Psalter*, p. 406.

[3] Perowne, *in loc.* Thus also Pusey, Delitzsch, Cheyne, etc. "The 'dawn,'" says Cheyne, "is that of the resurrection day."—*Expository Times*, ii. p. 249 ;

> Whom have I in heaven but Thee ?
> And there is none on the earth that I desire beside Thee.
> My flesh and my heart faileth :
> But God is the strength of my heart and my portion for ever."

These, and a few others, are the passages usually cited in favour of the doctrine of Immortality in the Book of Psalms, and it will be seen that in all of them this hope is clothed in a form which implies a resurrection.[1]

I need not delay on the passages in the prophetic books, for here it is usually granted that the idea of resurrection is familiar. Not only is the restoration of the Jewish people frequently presented under this figure, but a time is comimg when, for the Church as a whole, including the individuals in it, death shall be swallowed up in victory. We have a passage already in Hosea, which is beyond suspicion of Zoroastrian influence—

> "After two days will He revive us:
> On the third day He will raise us up, and we shall live before Him."

And again—

> "I will ransom them from the power of Sheol ;
> I will redeem them from death :
> O death, where are thy plagues ?
> O grave, where is thy destruction ?"[2]

The climax of this class of passages is reached in Isa. xxv. 6–8, xxvi. 19. Cf. also Ezek. xxxvii. 1–10, the vision of the dry bones.[3]

---

cf. *Origin of Psalter*, pp. 382, 406, 407. Delitzsch, in note on Ps. xvi. 8–11, says : "Nor is the awakening in xlix. 15 some morning or other that will very soon follow upon the night, but the final morning, which brings deliverance to the upright, and enables them to obtain dominion."

[1] Or if not resurrection, then immortality in the body without tasting of death, as Enoch. But this is a hope the Old Testament believer could hardly have cherished for himself. The view of deliverance *from* death seems therefore the more probable in Ps. xlix. 15, etc. A very different view is taken by Schultz in his *Alttestamentliche Theologie*, pp. 753–758. Schultz not only sees no proof of the resurrection in the passages we have quoted, but will not even allow that they have any reference to a future life. So extreme a view surely refutes itself. It is at least certain that if these passages teach a future life, it is a life in connection with the body.

[2] Hos. vi. 2, xiii. 14. Cf. Cheyne, p. 383.

[3] On the passages in Isaiah, Cheyne remarks : "Instead of swallowing up, Sheol in the Messianic period shall itself be swallowed up. And this prospect concerns not merely the church-nation, but all of its believing members, and indeed all, whether Jews or not, who submit to the true King, Jehovah."— *Origin of Psalter*, p. 402. Cf. *Expository Times*, ii. p. 226. In Ezekiel, the subject is national resurrection, but "that the power of God *can*, against all

The last Old Testament passage I will quote is an undisputed one, and has the special feature of interest that in it for the first time mention is made of the resurrection of the wicked as well as of the just. It is that in Dan. xii. 2—"And many of them that sleep in the dust of the earth shall awake, some to everlasting life, and some to shame and everlasting contempt." This needs no comment.

From the whole survey I think it will be evident that I was entitled to say that from the first the manner in which the hope of immortality was conceived by holy men in Israel was that of a resurrection. Yet, when all is said, we cannot but feel that it was but a *hope*—not resting on express revelation, but springing out of the consciousness of the indissoluble relation between God and the believing soul, and the conviction that God's Redemption will be a complete one. Life and immortality were not yet brought to light as they are now by Christ in His gospel.[1] The matter is unexceptionably stated by Dr. A. B. Davidson in the following words, with which I conclude: "The human spirit is conscious of fellowship with God; and this fellowship, from the nature of God, is a thing imperishable, and, in spite of obscurations, it must yet be fully manifested by God. This principle, grasped with convulsive earnestness in the prospect of death, became the Hebrew doctrine of Immortality. This doctrine was but the necessary corollary of religion. In this life the true relations of men to God were felt to be realised; and the Hebrew faith of immortality—never a belief in the mere existence of the soul after death, for the lowest superstition assumed this—was a faith that the dark and mysterious event of death would not interrupt the life of the person with God, enjoyed in this world. . . . The doctrine of Immortality in the Book (of Job) is the same as that of other parts of the Old Testament. Immortality is the corollary of religion. If there be religion—that is, if God be—there is immortality, not of the soul, but of the whole personal being of man (Ps. xvi. 9). This teaching of the whole Old Testament is expressed by our Lord with a surprising incisiveness in two

---

human thought and hope, reanimate the dead, is the general idea of the passage, from which consequently the hope of a literal resurrection of the dead may naturally be inferred."—Oehler, *Theology of Old Testament*, ii. p. 395 (Eng. trans.). Oehler does more justice to these passages than Schultz.

[1] 2 Tim. i. 10.

sentences—'I am the *God* of Abraham. God is not the God of the dead but of the *living*.'"[1]

Note to Third Edition.—Believing that the tendency at present is to find too little rather than too much in the Old Testament, I leave this Appendix as it is. The recent work of Professor S. D. F. Salmond on Immortality—which for long will be the classic work on this subject—does not go so far in finding a doctrine of Resurrection in the Psalms as is done here, but it may be said at least that it lays down the premisses in its doctrines of God, and of man's origin, constitution, and destiny, which justify such an interpretation, and might easily have gone farther without inconsistency, or violation of sound exegesis. Accepting it as the Old Testament doctrine that man was created for immortality in body and soul in fellowship with God, that death is a penalty of sin, that fellowship with God contains the pledge of preservation from Sheol, or of rescue from it, which hopes are allowed to find expression in at least certain of the Psalms and in Job, and to take definite shape in the doctrine of Resurrection in the prophets, Professor Salmond's position does not differ very widely in principle from that indicated above. Enoch and Elijah are viewed as the type of immortality in Ps. xlix. and lxxiii., etc. It is difficult to see in what way this "postulate of faith" could shape itself, however vaguely, if not as a faith in a revived life in the body. If the Psalms came after the prophets, according to the modern theory, it is still more difficult to see how this hope should have shaped itself in the prophetic books, and not have exercised any influence upon the Psalms. Even the writer of the 16th Psalm can hardly have anticipated permanent exemption from death; his confidence, therefore, that in fellowship with God "soul and flesh, himself in his entire living being, shall continue secure" everlastingly, becomes unintelligible if his hope did not stretch beyond death, and carry in it the assurance of a resurrection. Cf. specially pp. 193–197, 217–220, 238–255, 258 ff.

---

[1] *Commentary on Job*, Appendix, pp. 293–295.

6
THE CENTRAL ASSERTION OF THE CHRISTIAN VIEW—THE INCARNATION OF GOD IN CHRIST

"With historical science, the life of Jesus takes its place in the great stream of the world's history; He is a human individual, who became what He was, and was to be, through the living action of ideas and the circumstances of His time, and He, as a mighty storm-wave which has arisen through the conflict of forces, is destined to sink once more into the smooth sea, in the restless whirl of earthly things, quietly subsiding from the general life of humanity, in order to make room for new and stronger throes and creations. Here, in the Church, He is the rock which rules over the flood, instead of being moved by it. . . . He, the pillar, the Son of God, will survey humanity, however far and wide it may extend, permitting it only to hold fast by Him, or to wreck itself against Him." —Keim

"But Thee, but Thee, O Sovereign Seer of time,
But Thee, O Poet's Poet, wisdom's tongue,
But Thee, O man's best Man, O love's best Love,
O perfect life in perfect labour writ,
O all men's Comrade, Servant, King, or Priest,—
What if or yet, what mole, what flaw, what lapse,
What least defect or shadow of defect
What rumor, tattled by an enemy,
Of inference loose, what lack of grace
Even in torture's grasp, or sleep's, or death's—
Oh, what amiss may I forgive in Thee,
Jesus, good Paragon, thou crystal Christ?"

Sidney Lanier

6

THE CENTRAL ASSERTION OF
THE CHRISTIAN VIEW—THE
INCARNATION OF GOD IN CHRIST

In the second Lecture I conducted an historical argument intended to show that there is really no intermediate position in which the mind can logically rest between the admission of a truly Divine Christ and a purely humanitarian view. This argument I have now to complete, by showing that the necessity which history declares to exist arises from the actual state of the facts in the Christian Revelation. We have seen what the alternative is, and we have now to ask why it is so.

Why is it that we cannot rest in a conception of Christ as simply a prophet of a higher order? or as a God-filled man in whom the Divine dwelt as it dwells in no other? or as the central Personage of our race, at once ideal man and the Revelation to us of the absolute principles of religion? These views seem plausible; they are accepted by many; they seem at first sight to bring Christ nearer to us than on the supposition of His true God-manhood; why cannot the mind of the Church rest in them? Must not the explanation be that, taking into account the sum-total of the facts of Christianity, they refuse to square with any subordinate view, but compel us to press up to the higher conception? This is what I affirm, and I propose in this Lecture to test the question by an examination of the facts themselves.

There is, I know, in some minds, an insuperable objection, *a priori*, to the acceptance of the fact of the Incarnation, arising from the lowliness of Christ's earthly origin and condition. Can we believe, it is said, that in this historical individual, Jesus of Nazareth—this son of a carpenter—God actually became incarnate; that in this humble man, so poor in all His earthly surroundings, there literally dwelt the fulness of the

Godhead bodily? Is the thought not on the face of it incredible?
The appeal here is to our powers of imagination—of conceiving
—to our sense of the likelihood or unlikelihood of things; and
to enable us to judge fairly of that appeal, and of its nature as
an objection to the Incarnation, a great many things would have
to be taken into account, both before and after.

I would only say that, as regards a certain class who make
that objection—the higher class of liberal theologians especially
—the question seems only one of degree. If Christ is, in any
case, as most of them affirm, the central, typical, religiously
greatest individual of the race; if the principle of the absolute
religion is manifested in Him, as Pfleiderer allows;[1] if He is
the ideally perfect man in whom the God-consciousness finds its
fullest expression, as Schleiermacher declares;[2] if He is alone
the sinless Personality of the race, as even Lipsius will grant,[3]
—these are already remarkable claims, and, as compared with
His lowly appearance and mean historical environment, create
almost as great a feeling of strangeness as on the supposition of
His true Divinity. Or let us suppose that the objection comes
from the evolutionist. Then contrast the strangeness he
speaks of with that of his own views. His objection is, that
he cannot believe that in this lowly Man of Nazareth there
should reside all the potentialities of Divinity. But what does
he ask *us* to believe? He goes back to the primitive state of
things, and there, in that little speck of jelly at the first dawn
of life,—in that humble drop of protoplasmic matter buried in
some oozy slime,—he bids us believe that there lies wrapped
up, only waiting for development, the promise and potency of
the whole subsequent evolution of life. In that first germ-cell
there lies enfolded—latent—not only the whole wealth of
vegetable existence, not only the long procession of future races
and species of lower and higher animals, with their bodily
powers and mental instincts, but, in addition, the later possibilities of humanity; all that has now come to light in human
development—the wealth of genius, the riches of civilisation,
the powers of intellect, imagination, and heart, the treasures of
human love and goodness, of poetry and art—the genius of
Dante, of Shakespeare, of Milton—the spiritual greatness and

---

[1] Cf. his *Grundriss*, secs. 128, 129.   [2] *Der christl. Glaube*, ii. secs. 93, 94.
[3] *Dogmatik*, sec. 651

holiness of Christ Himself;—all, in a word, that has ever come out of man, is supposed by the evolutionist to have been potentially present from the first in that little primitive speck of protoplasm![1] I confess that, putting his assertion alongside the Christian one, I do not feel that there is much to choose between them in point of strangeness. But evolution, he would tell us, is not deprived of its truth by the strangeness at first sight of its assertion—neither is the Christian view. The question is not one to be settled *a priori*, but to be brought to the test of facts.

I. Godet has said, "Christianity is entirely based upon Christ's consciousness of Himself, and it is the heroism of faith to rest upon the extraordinary testimony which this Being gave to Himself."[2] This must be so, for the reason which Christ Himself gives, that He alone has the knowledge which qualifies Him to give a true estimate of Himself. "For I know," He said to the Jews, "whence I came, and whither I go."[3] I propose, however, to begin at a point further down—that to which our first written documents belong—and to ask, What was the view of Christ's Person held in the apostolic age? The testimony of that age is clearly one of great importance, as throwing light on Christ's own claims. When men say, Buddha also was raised to the rank of Divinity by his followers, though he himself made no such claim, I answer that the cases are not parallel. It was only long centuries after his death, and within limited circles, that Buddha was regarded as Divine; but one short step takes us from the days when Christ Himself lived and taught on earth, into the midst of a Church, founded by His apostles, which in all its branches worshipped and adored Him as the veritable Son of God made manifest on earth for our salvation. If it can be shown that in the apostolic Church a practically consentient view existed of Christ's Person, this,

---

[1] Tyndall carries back this promise and potency to the original fire-mist. "For what are the core and essence of this hypothesis? Strip it naked, and you stand face to face with the notion that not alone the more ignoble forms of animalcular or animal life, not alone the nobler forms of the horse and lion, not alone the exquisite and wonderful mechanism of the human body, but that the human mind itself—emotion, intellect, will, and all their phenomena—were once latent in a fiery cloud."—*Fragments*, ii. p. 132.

[2] *Commentary on John*, ii. p. 315 (Eng. trans.).

[3] John viii. 14.

of itself, is a strong reason for believing that it rested on claims made by Christ Himself, and rose naturally out of the facts of His historical self-manifestation.[1]

I begin with the broad fact which none can dispute, that, in the first age of Christianity, Christ was universally regarded as one who had risen from the dead, who had ascended on high to the right hand of God, who exercised there a government of the world, who was to return again to judge the quick and dead, and who, on these grounds, was the object of worship and prayer in all the churches.[2] This view of Christ is found in every book of the New Testament,—in the Acts, in the Pauline Epistles, in Hebrews, in Peter, in the Book of Revelation, in the Epistles of John, and James, and Jude,—and is so generally acknowledged to be there, that I do not need to delay in quoting special texts. But even so much as this cannot be admitted, without implying that in the faith of the early Church Christ was no mere man, but a supernatural Personage, *i.e.* that the Ebionitic view was not the primitive one. Think only of what is implied in this one claim to be the Judge of the world—the arbiter of the everlasting destiny of mankind.[3] There is no point on which the writers of the New Testament are more absolutely unanimous than this—that Christ shall come again to be our Judge ; and whether the early Christians analysed all that was involved in this belief or not, there can be no doubt in the mind of anyone who has analysed it that it involved the possession of attributes which can belong only to God (*e.g.*, omniscience). Or take the other outstanding fact of worship paid to Christ—such, *e.g.*, as we find in the Book of Revelation. The idea of Divine honours externally conferred on one who is essentially but man is quite foreign to the New Testament ; and the only alternative is, to suppose that Christ was from the first regarded as having a supernatural and Divine side to His Person—as being essentially Divine.

As regards the apostolic testimony, the ground is happily

---

[1] A good summary of the apostolic evidence will be seen in Dr. Whitelaw's *How is the Divinity of Jesus depicted in the Gospels and Epistles ?*

[2] Cf. Weiss's *Bib. Theol. of the New Testament*, pp. 177–181 (Eng. trans.) ; Harnack's *Dogmengeschichte*, i. pp. 66–68.

[3] Cf. Baldensperger, *Das Selbstbewusstsein Jesu*, p. 152. "How does such a claim fit into the frame of a human consciousness ? Such an assumption lies in fact beyond all *our* experience, also beyond the highest religious experience," etc.

cleared in modern times by the large measure of general agreement which exists among impartial exegetes as to the nature of
the doctrines taught in the several books. The old Unitarian
glosses on passages which seemed to affirm the Divinity of
Christ are now seldom met with ; and it is freely admitted that
the bulk of the New Testament writings teach a doctrine of
Christ's Person practically as high as the Church has ever
affirmed. For instance, it is no longer disputed by any competent authority that, in Paul and John, it is the supernatural
view of Christ's Person that is given. As to John—using that
name at present for the author of the Fourth Gospel and
related Epistles—his doctrine of Christ is of the highest. This
is admitted by the most negative critics, *e.g.*, by Dr. Martineau,
who says that the phrase "Son of God," applied to the pre-
existing Word in the Fourth Gospel, leaves all finite analogies
behind. "The oneness with God which it means to mark is
not such resembling reflex of the Divine thought and character
as men or angels may attain, but identity of essence, constituting Him not god-like alone, but God. Others may be children
of God in a moral sense ; but by this right of elemental nature,
none but He ; He is, herein, the *only* Son ; so little separate,
so close to the inner Divine life which He expresses, that He
is in the bosom of the Father. This language undoubtedly
describes a great deal more than such harmony of will and
sympathy of affection as may subsist between finite obedience
and its infinite Inspirer ; it denotes two natures homogeneous,
entirely one ; and both so essential to the Godhead that
neither can be omitted from any truth you speak of it. . . . It
was one and the same Logos that in the beginning was with
God, who in due time appeared in human form, and showed
forth the Father's pure prefections in relation to mankind, who
then returned to His eternal life, with the spiritual ties unbroken which He brought from His finished work."[1] In this
Gospel, therefore, the question is not so much as to the doctrine
taught, but as to whether the evangelist has given us an
authentic record of what Christ said and did. On this question,
so far as it is affected by the Christology, it will be well to

---

[1] *Seat of Authority*, pp. 428, 429. Biedermann, Lipsius, Pfleiderer, Reuss,
Réville, etc., all agree in their estimate of John's doctrine. Wendt (*Die Lehre
Jesu*, ii. pp. 450–476) seems to go back, and to explain the expressions in John
only of an ethical Sonship. Cf. Appendix to Lecture.

reserve our judgment till we see whether the other writings of
the apostolic age do not give us—or yield by implication—
quite as high a view of Christ's Person as that which creates
offence in John.

To aid us in determining this question, there lie first to hand
the writings, above alluded to, of the Apostle Paul. Here,
again, it is not seriously doubted that in Paul's undisputed
Epistles we have as clear and strong an assertion of Christ's
Divine dignity as we could well desire. That, in Paul's theology,
Christ had a heavenly pre-existence;[1] that the title "Son of
God" applies to Him in this pre-existent state; that He was a
being of Divine essence; that He mediated the creation of the
world; that in the fulness of time He took on Him human
nature; that now, since His death and resurrection, He has
been exalted again to Divine power and glory—all this the most
candid exegetes now admit. A new turn, however, has been
given in recent years to this theology of Paul, by the fancy of
some theologians that this heavenly, pre-existent essence of
the earlier Pauline Epistles—the "Son of God" who became
incarnate in Christ—is not a second Divine Person, as we
understand that expression, but a pre-existent "heavenly man,"
a being apparently of subordinate rank, at once the perfect
spiritual image of God and the heavenly prototype of humanity
—a conception easier to state than to make intelligible. This
"heavenly man" theory, as we may call it, has been seized on
with avidity by many as the true key to the Pauline Christology.[2] Beyschlag of Halle adopts it as the basis of his own
theory,—in this, however, differing from the others, that he
attributes only an *ideal* pre-existence to this heavenly principle,[3]
while the majority admit that what Paul had in view was a
real and personal pre-existence. This whole hypothesis of the
"heavenly man" I can only regard as a new-fangled conceit

[1] See Note A.—The Doctrine of Pre-Existence.

[2] It goes back to Baur, and to Ritschl, *Entstehung*, p. 80 (1857), and has
been adopted by Holsten, Hilgenfeld, Biedermann, Lipsius, Pfleiderer, etc.
Biedermann states it succinctly thus:—"The Person, the I of Christ, has
already, before His appearance in the earthly corporeity, in the flesh, pre-
existed in a pre-earthly condition with God as the εἰκὼν Θεοῦ, as the human
image of God, and consequently as the archetypal pattern of humanity; thus
is He the Son of God. . . . The appearance of Christ in the world, sent by
God in love, is not a becoming *man*, but a coming of the heavenly, pneumatic
Man in the *flesh*."—*Dogmatik*, ii. pp. 93, 97.

[3] *Christologie*, pp. 225, 226, 243.

of exegesis, resting practically on one passage—that in which
Paul speaks of "the second man from heaven,"[1]—and in
diametric opposition to the general teaching of the Epistles.
It is an hypothesis, therefore, which finds no countenance from
more sober expositors like Meyer, Weiss, or Reuss, all of whom
recognise in Paul's "Son of God" a Being truly Divine.[2]
Christ indeed, in Paul's view, has humanity, but it is not a
humanity which He brought with Him from heaven, but a
humanity which He assumed when He came to earth.

The argument for the "heavenly man" theory completely
breaks down if we take into account the later Epistles—especially Philippians, Ephesians, and Colossians, the genuineness of
which there are no good grounds for disputing.[3]   Pfleiderer,
who advocates this theory, admits the genuineness of the
Epistle to the Philippians, but there we have the strongest
assertion of Christ's pre-existent Divinity.   The whole argument in chap. ii. 5–11 turns on Christ's original condition of
Divine glory—"being in the form of God"—and His voluntary
abdication of it to take upon Him "the form of a servant"—
"being made in the likeness of men"—"being found in fashion
as a man."[4]   As to the teaching of the Epistles to the Colossians
and the Ephesians, there is no dispute, even among the friends
of this theory.   In these Epistles, says Lipsius, "Christ, as
the image of God and the first-born of the whole creation, is an
essentially Divine Personality, and the Mediator of the creation
of the world."[5]   Pfleiderer sees, or imagines he sees, in them
the same influence of the Philonic Logos doctrine as is traceable in the Gospel of John[6]—an indirect witness that between
the theology of Paul in these Epistles and that of the Fourth
Gospel there is no essential difference.   But though the
Christology of the later Epistles is admittedly more developed
than that of the earlier Epistles, the doctrine of Christ in both
is substantially one.[7]   In both, Christ was "the Son of God,"
eternally pre-existing in a state of glory with the Father, who,

---

[1] 1 Cor. xv. 47 (R.V.).
[2] See Weiss's criticism in *Biblical Theology*, i. pp. 410–412, and ii. p. 100 ;
Meyer on 1 Cor. xv. 47 ; Dorner, *System of Doctrine*, iii. pp. 175, 176.
[3] Renan, Reuss, Sabatier, Weiss, etc., accept them all as Pauline.
[4] Cf. Bruce's *Humiliation of Christ* (Cunningham Lectures), pp. 21–28,
403–411.
[5] *Dogmatik*, p. 453.   [6] *Urchristenthum*, pp. 676, 695.
[7] Cf. Schmid, *Bib. Theol. of New Testament*, pp. 469–478 (Eng. trans.).

in the fulness of time, moved by love, became incarnate for our
salvation.[1]   In both—as also in John—He existed before the
creation of the world, and was the agent in its creation.[2]   That
He is the centre of the Divine purpose, and therefore the One
for whom all things as well as by whom all things, are made, is
a doctrine as clearly taught in the Epistles to the Romans and
the Corinthians as in those to the Colossians and the Ephesians.[3]
In both, the Divine name Κύριος is freely given to Him; passages
applied in the Old Testament to Jehovah are applied to Him
also; Divine honour is paid to Him; He is exalted to a Divine
sovereignty of the world;[4] His name is constantly joined with
that of the Father as the source of grace and peace in the
introductions to the Epistles,[5] and again with those of the
Father and of the Spirit in the apostolic benediction;[6] it is
declared of Him that, as Judge, He has the attribute of the
Divine searcher of hearts.[7]   Taking all the facts into account,
and remembering how inconsonant it would have been with
Paul's rigorous Monotheism to attribute Divine honours to a
Being not truly Divine, it seems impossible to doubt that, in
the view of the Apostle, Christ was truly a Divine Person, one
in essence, though distinct in Person from the Father.[8]   But
the most remarkable circumstance of all is—and it is a point
which I desire specially to emphasise—that in propounding
these high views of Christ's Person, Paul in no case speaks or
argues as one teaching a new doctrine, but throughout takes it
for granted that his reader's estimate of the Lord's dignity is
the same as his own.   He gives no indication in these letters
that he preached or contended for a higher view of Christ's

---

[1] 2 Cor. viii. 9; Gal. iv. 4.   [2] 1 Cor. viii. 6.

[3] Cf. Rom. i. 1-4, xvi. 25-27; 1 Cor. viii. 6.   Bishop Lightfoot says: "The
absolute universal mediation of the Son is declared as unreservedly in this
passage from the First Epistle to the Corinthians ('One Lord Jesus Christ;
through whom are all things, and we through Him'), as in any later statement
of the apostle; and if all the doctrinal and practical inferences which it
implicitly involves were not directly emphasised at this early date, it was
because the circumstances did not yet require explicitness on these points."—
Commentary on Colossians, pp. 188, 189.

[4] Cf. on above statements, Weiss, *Biblical Theology*, i. pp. 390–393.

[5] Rom. i. 7; 1 Cor. i. 3; 2 Cor. i. 2; Gal. i. 3.

[6] 2 Cor. xiii. 14.

[7] Rom. ii. 16; 1 Cor. iv. 5.

[8] It is a noteworthy circumstance that nearly all the modern scholars agree
in that interpretation of the strongest passage of all, Rom. ix. 5, "who is over
all, God blessed for ever, Amen," which makes it refer to Christ.   Thus, *e.g.*,
Rothe, Lipsius, Pfleiderer, Ritschl, Schultz, Weiss, etc.

Person than that which was currently received.[1]   He has no
monopoly of this truth, but assumes it as the common possession
of the Church.   He argues at length for the doctrine of justification by faith, but we never find him arguing for the Divinity
of Christ.   Whether writing to his own converts, or to churches
he had never seen, he uses the same language on this subject,
and apparently anticipates no doubt or contradiction on the
part of his readers.   What inference can we draw, but that the
doctrine of Christ's Person in the early Church was anything
but Ebionitic,—that from the first a Divine dignity was ascribed
to Christ?

Paul's Epistles, however, are not the only witnesses on this
point of Apostolic theology.   Essentially the same doctrine we
find in the Epistle to the Hebrews, long attributed to Paul, but
now almost universally assigned to another author.   It has,
therefore, the value of an independent witness.   The Epistle is
further valuable for its early date, most critics unhesitatingly
referring it to the period before the destruction of Jerusalem,
probably about A.D. 66.[2]   But here, though the writer's standpoint is somewhat different from both Paul's and John's, we
find precisely the same doctrine as before,—Jesus, the Divine
Son of God, the effulgence of the Father's glory and very
image of His substance, the creator, upholder, and heir of all
things, who, because the children were partakers of flesh and
blood, Himself likewise partook of the same, and is now again
exalted to the right hand of the Majesty on high.[3]   Further,
in teaching this high Christological view, the author is not
conscious any more than Paul of bringing in a new doctrine.
He stands rather upon the ground of the common Christian
confession, which he exhorts the Hebrews to hold fast.[4]

It is conceded, however, that in the main the Christology of
the Epistle to the Hebrews is of the Pauline type, and the
question arises—Have we anywhere a witness of another type,

[1] Cf. Reuss, *History of Christian Theology*, i. p. 397 (Eng. trans.).   The
passage is quoted below.
[2] Cf. Weiss, *Introduction to New Testament*, ii. p. 31 (Eng. trans.) ; Dr. A.
B. Davidson, *Hebrews*, etc.   A few, like Pfleiderer (who, however, thinks
Apollos may have been the author), date it later.—*Urchristenthum*, p. 629.
[3] Cf. Weiss, ii. pp. 186–190 ; Reuss, ii. pp. 243, 244.   Reuss says : "It is
clear from the figures chosen that the intention of the theology is to establish
at once the Divinity and the plurality of the Persons in the Godhead, side by
side with the monotheistic principle."
[4] Heb. iv. 14.

showing how the Person of Christ was viewed in the distinctively Jewish, as contrasted with the Gentile sections of the Church? The answer is given in another book of the apostolic age, the early date of which is one of the articles of the modern creed, and which is supposed by some—*e.g.*, by Volkmar—to have been written expressly with the view of opposing Paul.[1] I refer to the Apocalypse. By general consent of the modern school of critics, this book was composed immediately after the death of Nero,[2] and its anti-Pauline character is not only admitted, but insisted on. Here, then, we have what may be regarded as a representative early Jewish-Christian writing; and the question is of deep interest, What kind of view of Christ's Person do we find in it? And the answer must be given that the doctrine of Christ in the Apocalypse is as high, or nearly as high, as it is in either Paul or John. Reuss, who is certainly an unprejudiced witness, has some remarks here which are worth quoting as corroborative of the previous line of argument. "We may here observe," he says, "that the writings of Paul, which carry us back, so to speak, into the very cradle of the Church, contain nothing to indicate that their Christological doctrine, so different from that of common Ebionitism, was regarded as an innovation, or gave rise to any disputations at the time of its first appearance. But we have in our hands another book, essentially Judæo-Christian, which gives emphatic support to our assertion. This is the Book of Revelation. . . . It ought unhesitatingly to be acknowledged that Christ is placed in the Revelation on a par with God. He is called the First and the Last, the Beginning and the End, and these same expressions are used to designate the Most High."[3] Professor Pfleiderer is another critic who puts this point so strongly and unambiguously, that I cannot do better than give

---

[1] Pfleiderer shares this view. See it criticised by Reuss, *Christian Theology*, i. pp. 308–312. Pfleiderer thinks, too, that the passage in Matthew, "Whosoever, therefore, shall break one of these least commandments," etc. (Matt. v. 19), is a blow aimed at Paul's antinomianism!—Hibbert Lectures, p. 178.

[2] "It is now pretty generally acknowledged that the date of this book is the year 68–69 A.D."—Pfleiderer, Hibbert Lectures, p. 153. Since the above was written, the hypothesis promulgated by Vischer (1886), and favoured by Harnack, etc., has come into vogue, that the present book is a Christian working-up of an older Jewish Apocalypse, or of several such writings. See the views in Jülicher's *Einleitung*, pp. 181–183. Jülicher takes the date to be about 95 A.D. Dr. C. A. Briggs, who at first opposed this theory, now adopts it.

[3] *History of Christian Theology*, i. pp. 397, 398 (Eng. trans.).

his words. " As, according to Paul," he says, " Christ has been exalted to the regal dignity of Divine dominion over all, so, according to our author, He has taken His seat on the throne by the side of His Father, participating therefore in His Divine dominion and power—He is the Lord of the churches, holds their stars, or guardian angels, in His hand, and is also Ruler of nations and King of kings, the all-wise and almighty Judge of the nations ; indeed, to Him is due a worship similar to that of God Himself. As the author of the Apocalypse, in his apotheosis of Christ as an object of worship, thus almost out-strips Paul, neither does he in his dogmatic definitions of Christ's nature at all fall behind the Apostle. Like Paul, he calls Christ the ' Son of God ' in the metaphysical sense of a godlike spiritual being, and far beyond the merely theocratic significance of the title. . . . As Paul had described the celestial Son of Man as at the same time the image of God, the agent of creation, the head of every man, and finally even God over all, so the Christ of the Apocalypse introduces Himself with the predicates of Divine majesty : ' I am the Alpha and the Omega, saith the Lord God, who is, and who was, and who is to come, the All-powerful ' ; and He is accordingly called also the ' Head of Creation,' and ' the Word of God,' that is, the mediating instrument of all Divine Revelation from the creation of the world to the final judgment. It appears from this that the similarity of the Christology of the Apocalypse to that of Paul is complete ; this Christ occupies the same exalted position as the Pauline Christ above the terrestrial Son of Man."[1]

It is not necessary, after these examples, that I should dwell long on the Christology of the Petrine and minor Epistles. Peter is again a distinct witness, and his testimony is in har-mony with what we have already seen. Christ is, to refer only to the First Epistle, joined with the Father and the Spirit as one of the principals in the work of salvation ;[2] He is the Redeemer, foreordained before the foundation of the world, but manifest in these last times ;[3] His Spirit testified beforehand in the prophets ;[4] He is called Κύριος, and passages used in the Old Testament of Jehovah are applied to Him—remarkably in

---

[1] Hibbert Lectures, pp. 159–161.　　[2] 1 Pet. i. 2.
[3] 1 Pet. i. 20.　　[4] 1 Pet. i. 11.

chap. ii¹. 15, "Sanctify in your hearts Christ as Lord";[1] He has gone into heaven, and is at the right hand of God, angels and authorities and powers being made subject to Him;[2] He is the ordained Judge of quick and dead.[3] He is therefore, as Weiss says, in His exaltation a Divine Being,[4] whether the Epistle directly teaches His pre-existence or not, as, however, Pfleiderer thinks it does.[5] Even James, who barely touches Christology in his Epistle, speaks of Christ as the "Lord of Glory," and the Judge of the world, and prayer is to be made in His name.[6] Not less instructive are the references in the brief Epistle of Jude, who describes Jesus as "our only Master and Lord, Jesus Christ"; who exhorts believers to pray in the Holy Spirit, and keep themselves in the love of God, looking for the mercy of our Lord Jesus Christ; and who concludes his short letter by ascribing to the only God, our Saviour, through Jesus Christ our Lord, glory, majesty, dominion, and power, before all time, and now, and for evermore.[7] If to these sources of evidence we add the popular discourses in the Acts of the Apostles, we shall have a tolerably clear idea of the views of Christ held in the Church in the earliest period of Christianity. These discourses, though, as might be expected, containing little or no dogmatic teaching on the origin or constitution of Christ's Person, yet do not fail to represent Him as possessing a unique dignity;[8] as the holy and sinless One, whom it was not possible for death to hold;[9] as the Prince of Life, exalted to the throne of universal dominion;[10] as the Lord on whose name men were to call, the One in whom alone under heaven there was salvation, and through whom was preached forgiveness of sins to men;[11] as the Giver of the Holy Ghost;[12] as the appointed Judge of the world, whom the heaven must retain till the time of the restitution of all things.[13] These representations, though simpler, are not inconsistent with the more developed Christology of the Epistles, but rather furnish

---

[1] Cf. 1 Pet. i. 5, ii. 13, iii. 12. [2] 1 Pet. iii. 22.
[3] 1 Pet. iv. 5. [4] *Biblical Theology of New Testament*, i. p. 238.
[5] *Urchristenthum*, p. 659. [6] James ii. 1, v. 7–9, 14, 15.
[7] Jude 4, 20, 21, 25 (R.V.).
[8] Acts iii. 13, 25, iv. 27. "Servant," in sense of Isaiah's "Servant of Jehovah."
[9] ii. 24, iii. 14. [10] ii. 36, iii. 15.
[11] i. 21, 38, iii. 26, iv. 10–12, v. 30, 31.
[12] ii. 33. [13] iii. 20, 21.

the *data* or premises from which all the positions of that Christology can be deduced.[1]

The supernatural view of Christ, then, is no late development, but was in all its leading features fully established in the Church in the generation immediately succeeding Christ's death. We find it presupposed in all the apostolic writings, and assumed as well known among the persons to whom these writings were addressed. If there were, as the Tübingen school alleges, Pauline and Petrine parties in the Church, it was held by both of these; whatever other shades of doctrinal opinion existed, this was a common element. But this, it seems to me, is only conceivable on the supposition that the view in question was in harmony with the facts of Christ's own life on earth, with the claims He made, and with the testimony which His apostles had deposited in the various churches regarding Him. We are now to see how far this is borne out by the actual records we possess of Christ's life.

II. We go back then to the Gospels, and ask what they teach. Here I leave out of view the Fourth Gospel, about the teaching of which there can be little possible dispute. Not simply the prologue, but the acts and sayings of Christ recorded in that Gospel, are decisive for anyone who admits it, as I do, to be a truthful record by the beloved disciple of what Christ did and said on earth.[2] It would be out of place here to discuss the question of the genuineness. I would only say that, so far as the objections are drawn from the advanced Christology of the Gospel, and the alleged traces of Alexandrian influence, after what we have seen of the general state of opinion in the apostolic age, very little weight need be attached to them. The

---

[1] Cf. Weiss, i. p. 180: "The Messiah who is exalted to this *κυριότης* must, of course, be a Divine Being, although, for the earliest proclamation, this conclusion gave no occasion for the consideration of the question on how far such an exaltation was rooted in the original nature of His Person."

[2] It is precisely the discourses of Jesus in the Fourth Gospel which Wendt, in his recent *Die Lehre Jesu*, is disposed to attribute to a genuine Johannine source. On the difference of style between the Johannine and the Synoptical discourses, Godet remarks: "The discourses of the Fourth Gospel, then, do not resemble a photograph, but the extracted essence of a savoury fruit. From the change wrought in the external form of the substance, it does not follow that the slightest foreign element has been mingled with the latter."—Introduction to *Commentary*, p. 135 (Eng. trans.). The contrast, however, may be exaggerated, as shown by comparison of passages where the Synoptics and John cross each other.—Cf. Godet, Introduction, pp. 155–157.

Christology of John is not a whit higher than the Christology of Paul, or that of the Epistle to the Hebrews, or even that of the Apocalypse—all lying within the apostolic age; the alleged traces of Philonic influence are as conspicuous in the Epistle to the Hebrews as in the Fourth Gospel. It is not, therefore, necessary to go beyond the apostolic age to account for them. I question, indeed, very much whether, if we except the pro-logue—*i.e.*, if we keep to Christ's own doings and sayings—there is much in John's Gospel at all which would directly suggest the peculiarities of Philo. There is certainly a very exalted doctrine of Christ's Person, but the doctrine is Christian, not Philonic.[1]

It may, however, still be said that at least the Synoptics[2] tell a very different story. Here, it will be maintained, we have the human, the truly historical Christ, in contrast with the idealised and untrustworthy picture of the fourth evangelist. Dr. Martineau makes this his strongest ground for the rejection of the Gospel of John. But is it really so? Certainly it is not so, if we let these Gospels—as it is only fair that in the first instance we should do—speak fully and freely for themselves, and do not, in the interest of theory, curtail any part of their testimony. The picture given us in the Synoptics is not at all that of the humanitarian Christ. We have a true human life, indeed,—the life of One who went in and out among men as a friend and brother, who grieved, who suffered, who was tempted, who was poor and despised,—a true " Son of Man," in every sense of the word. But do we not find more? Does this represent their whole testimony about Christ? On the contrary, does not this lowly Being move as a supernatural Personage throughout, and do not His character and works bear amplest witness to the justice of His claims? Is there, according to the Synoptics, nothing extraordinary in the com-mencement of Christ's life, nothing extraordinary in its close,

---

[1] Harnack expresses himself very decidedly on this subject. " Neither the religious philosophy of Philo," he says, " nor the manner of thought out of which it originated, has exercised a provable influence on the first generation of Christian believers. . . . A Philonic element is also not provable in Paul. . . . The apprehension of the relation of God and the world in the Fourth Gospel is not the Philonic. Therefore, also, the Logos doctrine found there is essentially not that of Philo."—*Dogmengeschichte*, i. p. 99. See Note B.—Philo and the Fourth Gospel.

[2] Matthew, Mark, and Luke.

nothing in keeping with this extraordinary beginning and end
in the career that lies between? It is easy, no doubt, to get rid
of all this by denying the historical character of the Gospels, or
pruning them down to suit; but after every allowance is made
for possible additions to the narrative, there remains a clear
enough picture of Jesus to enable us to determine the great
subjects of His teaching, and the general character of His
claims. In fact, the further criticism goes, the supernatural
character of Jesus stands out in clearer relief. These are not
mere embellishments, mere external additions, obscuring the
picture of a Christ otherwise human. They are not things
that can be stripped off, and the real image of Christ be left
behind, as the writing of a palimpsest might be removed and
the picture below be brought into view. The history *is* the
picture. All fair historical criticism must see that these supernatural features belong to the very essence of the historical
representation of Jesus in the Gospels, and that, if we take them
away, we have no longer a historical Christ *at all*, but only a
Christ of our own imaginings;[1] that we must either take these
features as part of our view of Christ, or say frankly with
Strauss that we really know little or nothing about Him. But
it is just the impossibility of resting in this dictum with any
fair regard to the canons of historical criticism which has
constantly forced even negative critics back to a fuller recognition of the historical reality of the portraiture in the Gospels,
and has again placed them in the dilemma of having to reconsider these claims of the Son of Man.

Let us look at these *claims* of Jesus in the Synoptics a little
more in detail. Even this title "Son of Man"—found only in
Christ's own lips, and never given Him by His followers—has
something unique and exceptional about it. It wells up from
the depths of the consciousness of One who knew Himself to
stand in some peculiar and representative relation to humanity,
and to bear the nature of man in some exceptional way.[2] He
is not simply "*a* Son of Man," but "*the* Son of Man"; just as,

---

[1] Cf. on this, Bushnell's *Nature and the Supernatural*, chap. xii., "Water-
marks on the Christian Doctrine," and Row's *Jesus of the Evangelists*.

[2] Cf. Dorner, *Person of Christ*, i. p. 55 (Eng. trans.), and *System of Doctrine*,
iii. p. 170; Gess, *Christi Person und Werk*, i. p. 212. On the various views as
to the meaning of the title, see Bruce, *Humiliation of Christ*, pp. 474–487
(Cunningham Lecture).

in a higher relation, He is not simply "*a* Son of God," but "*the* Son of God." How high this latter relation is, is brought out in the words—" No one knoweth the Son save the Father; neither doth any know the Father, save the Son, and he to whomsoever the Son willeth to reveal Him." [1] In conformity with the uniqueness of nature implied in these titles, He claims to be the Messiah,[2] the Fulfiller of law and prophets,[3] the Founder of the kingdom of God, the supreme Legislator and Head of that kingdom,[4] He, through faith in whom salvation is to be obtained,[5] the One who demands, as no other is entitled to do, the absolute and undivided surrender of the heart to Himself.[6] He forgives sins with Divine authority,[7] is the giver of the Holy Ghost,[8] ascribes an expiatory virtue to His death,[9] anticipates His resurrection and return in glory,[10] announces Himself as the appointed Judge of the world.[11] This claim of Christ to be the final Judge of the world, found already in the Sermon on the Mount; [12] His repeated declarations of His future return in the glory of His Father, and His own glory, and the glory of the holy angels; [13] the eschatological parables, in which He makes the ultimate destinies of men depend on relation to Himself,[14] are among the most remarkable features in His teaching, and are not to be explained away as mere figurative assurances of the ultimate triumph of His cause. They constitute a claim which must either be conceded, or Christ be pronounced the victim of an extravagant hallucination! We have to add to these claims of Christ, His endorsement of Peter's confession of the unique dignity of His Person — "Thou art the Christ, the Son of the living God"; [15] His solemn words, so fraught with self-consciousness, in answer to the High Priest's adjuration— "Henceforth ye shall see the Son of Man sitting at the right hand of power, and coming in the clouds of heaven"; [16] and such sublime declarations, implying an omnipresent and omni-

---

[1] Matt. xi. 27 (R.V.).   [2] Matt. xi. 1-6; Luke iv. 17-21, etc.

[3] Matt. v. 17.

[4] Matt. xiii. (Parables of Kingdom); Matt. v.–vii. (Sermon on Mount).

[5] Matt. xi. 28; Luke vii. 50.   [6] Matt. x. 37-39.

[7] Matt. ix. 2, 6.   [8] Matt. iii. 11, etc.

[9] Matt. xx. 28, xxi. 26-28, etc.   [10] Matt. xvi. 21, 27, xvii. 23, xx. 19, etc.

[11] Matt. xxv. 31-46, etc.   [12] Matt. vii. 21-23.

[13] Mark viii. 38, etc.   [14] Matt. xxv.; Luke xii. 11-27.

[15] Matt. xvi. 16, 17.   [16] Matt. xxv. 64.

scient relation to His Church, as "Where two or three are gathered together in My name, there am I in the midst of them." [1]

These are stupendous claims of Christ, but we have next to observe that the whole representation of Christ in the Synoptic Gospels is worthy of them. I do not dwell here on the holy majesty with which Christ bears Himself throughout the Gospels in all circumstances, on the tone of authority with which He speaks, on the grace and tenderness which marked His whole relations to men,—I would concentrate attention on the one point that Christ, according to the picture given of Him in the Gospels, is a *sinless* Being—in this respect also standing quite apart from other men. It is the uniform testimony of the apostles and other writers of the New Testament—of Paul, of Peter, of John, of the Epistle to the Hebrews, of the Apocalypse, [2]—that Christ was without sin; and the Synoptic narratives, in the picture they give us of a character entirely God-centred, dominated by the passion of love to men, embracing the widest contrasts, maintaining itself in absolute spiritual freedom in relation to the world, to men and to events, uniformly victorious in temptation, untouched by the faintest stain of base, paltry, or selfish motive, completely bear out this description. So strong is the evidence on this point, that we find the sinlessness of Christ widely admitted, even by the representatives of schools whose general principles, one would imagine, would lead them to deny it—by adherents of the Hegelian school like Daub, Marheineke, Rosenkranz, Vatke; [3] by mediating theologians of all types, like Schleiermacher, [4] Beyschlag, [5] Rothe, [6] and Ritschl; [7] by liberal theologians, like Hase [8] and Schenkel, [9] and so decided

---

[1] Matt. xviii. 20.

[2] *E.g.*, 2 Cor. v. 21; 1 Pet. ii. 22; 1 John iii. 5; Heb. iv. 15; Rev. iii. 14, etc. Cf. on this subject Ullmann's *Sinlessness of Jesus*, and Bushnell's *Nature and the Supernatural*, x.

[3] Cf. Dorner's *Person of Christ*, v. pp. 121–131; *System of Doctrine*, iii. p. 261 (Eng. trans.).

[4] *Der christl. Glaube*, sec. 98 (ii. 78, 83).   [5] *Leben Jesu*, i. pp. 181–191.

[6] *Dogmatik*, ii. pp. 83, 108.   [7] *Unterricht*, p. 19.

[8] *Geschichte Jesu*, p. 248. Hase, however, only recognises the sinlessness of Jesus from His entrance on His public work. It was a sinlessness won by struggle.

[9] In his *Dogmatik*, see sketch in Pfleiderer's *Dev. of Theol.* pp. 177–182. Pfleiderer himself doubts the "psychological possibility" of sinless perfection, and does not ascribe it to Christ.—*Ibid.* pp. 117, 118. In his *Religionsphilo-*

an opponent of the miraculous even as Lipsius.[1] We must contend, however, that if Christ was really the sinless Being which the Gospels represent Him, and His followers believed Him to be, we have a phenomenon in history which is not to be explained out of mere natural grounds, or on any principle of development, but a literal new creation, a true moral miracle, involving further consequences as to the origin and nature of the exceptional Personality to whom these predicates of sinlessness belong.[2]

In keeping with the character and with the claims of Jesus are the *works* ascribed to Him in the Gospels. It is, as the merest glance will show, a supernatural history throughout. The miracles attributed to Jesus are not mere wonders, but deeds of mercy and love—the outflow of just such Divinity as we claim for Him. They are, accordingly, wrought by Jesus in His own name, in the exercise of His own authority,[3] and are suitably spoken of as simply His "works"[4]—*i.e.* standing in the same relation of naturalness to Him, and to His position in the world, as our ordinary works do to us, and to our position in the world. So far from being isolated from the rest of His manifestation, Christ's miracles are entirely of one piece with it,—are revelations of the powers and spirit of His kingdom,[5]—are the works of the kingdom, or, as they are called in John, "signs."[6] The most skilful criticism, therefore, has never been able to excise them from the narrative. Their roots intertwine inseparably with the most characteristic elements of the gospel tradition, — with sayings of Christ,

---

sophie, i. p. 339 (Eng. trans.), he blames Schleiermacher for identifying "this personality so entirely with the ideal principle, that it is exalted to an absolute ideal, and indeed to a miraculous appearance." This affords a good standard for the measurement of Pfleiderer's general Christian position.

[1] *Dogmatik*, sec. 651, p. 569.

[2] Strauss acknowledges this when he says : "A sinless, archetypal Christ is not a hair's-breadth less unthinkable than one supernaturally born, with a Divine and human nature."—*Der Christus des Glaubens und der Jesus der Geschichte*, p. 63. But Strauss himself bears high tribute to the perfection of Jesus. "In the attainment of this serene inward disposition, in unity with God, and comprehending all men as brethren, Jesus had realised in Himself the prophetic ideal of the New Covenant with the Law written in the heart ; He had—to speak with the poet—taken the Godhead into His will. . . . In Him man made the transition from bondage to freedom."—*Leben Jesu*, p. 207 (1864).

[3] *E.g.*, Matt. viii. 3, 7–10, 26.

[4] Matt. xi. 2. "Mighty works," in vers. 20, 21, 23, is literally "powers." "Works" is the favourite term in John.

[5] Matt. xi. 4, 5 ; Luke xi. 20.   [6] John ii. 11, etc.

for example, of unimpeachable freshness, originality, and beauty; and, as part of the history, they produce upon us precisely the same impression of dignity, wisdom, and beneficence, as the rest of the narrative. They are, in short, integral parts of that total presentation of Jesus which produces on us so marked and irresistible an impression of Divinity.[1]

Even this is not the highest point in the Synoptic testimony about Christ. If Christ died, He *rose again* on the third day. Meeting with His disciples, He declares to them, "All authority hath been given unto Me in heaven and on earth"; He commissions them to preach repentance and remission of sins in His name to all the nations; He bids them "make disciples of all the nations, baptizing them into the name of the Father and of the Son and of the Holy Ghost" (one name); He utters for their encouragement this sublime promise, "Lo, I am with you always, even unto the end of the world."[2] There can be no mistake as to the meaning of this Trinitarian formula, which, as Dorner says, does not express a relation to men, but "requires us to regard the Father as the Father of the Son, and the Son as the Son of the Father, and therefore does not signify a paternal relation to the world in general, but to the Son, who, standing between the Father and the Spirit, must be somehow thought of as pertaining to the sphere of the Divine, and therefore denotes a distinction in the Divine itself."[3] Attempts are made to challenge the authenticity of these sayings. But they are at least part of the Synoptic representation of Christ, and must be taken into account when the comparison is between the Synoptic representation and that found in John, and in other parts of the New Testament. When, however, Christ's whole claim is considered, no valid objection can be taken to these sayings, except on principles which imply that the resurrection never took place at all,—a position which works round to the subversion of the claim itself.[4]

Such, then, is the view of Christ in the Synoptic Gospels;

---

[1] Cf. Godet's *Lectures in Defence of the Christian Faith*, iii., "The Miracles of Jesus Christ," p. 124 (Eng. trans.); and Pressensé, *Vie de Jésus*, p. 373 (Eng. trans. p. 277).
[2] Matt. xxviii. 18–20.　　　[3] *System of Doctrine*, i. p. 351 (Eng. trans.).
[4] See Note C.—The Resurrection of Christ and the Reality of His Divine Claim.

and the conclusion I draw is, that it is in keeping with the estimate formed of Christ's Person in the apostolic age. The two things are in harmony. Given such a life as we have in the Gospels, this explains the phenomena of the apostolic age. On the other hand, given the estimate of Christ's Person and work in the apostolic age, this supports the reliableness of the picture of Christ in the Gospels, for only from such a life could the faith of the Church have originated. We have, in this Synoptic picture, the very Being whom the writings of Paul and John present to us; and the forms they use are the only forms which can adequately interpret Him to us. In other words, given the Christ of the Synoptic Gospels, the doctrine of Paul and John is felt to be the only adequate explanation of His character and claims. I agree, therefore, entirely with Dorner when he says, "It may be boldly affirmed that the entire representation of Christ given by the Synoptics may be placed by the side of the Johannine as perfectly identical, inasmuch as faith, moulded by means of the Synoptic tradition, must have essentially the same features in its concept of Christ as John has"; and adds, "Those who reject the Gospel of John on account of its glorifying of Christ, can hardly have set themselves in clear relations with the Synoptic Christology." [1]

I claim, then, to have shown that if we are to do justice to the facts of Christianity, we must accept the supernatural view of Christ's Person, and recognise in Him the appearance of a Divine Being in humanity. The argument I have conducted— if it be correct—goes further than to show that this doctrine is an integral part of Christianity. If this were all, it might still be said, Rather than that this doctrine be accepted, let Christianity go! But if my contention is right, we are not at liberty to let Christianity go. The reason why Christianity cannot be waved out of the world at the bidding of sceptics simply is, that the facts are too strong for the attempt. The theories which would explain Christianity away make shipwreck on the facts. But if Christianity is not to be parted with, its full testimony to itself must be maintained; and we have now seen what this means. Formerly it was shown that the attempts to maintain Christianity, while rejecting the truth of the Incarna-

[1] *Person of Christ*, i. pp. 60, 61,

tion, have uniformly failed.   Now we have seen why it is so.
It was shown also whither the rejection of Christianity led us,
and how the painful steps of return conducted us back through
Theism to Revelation, and through Revelation to belief in
Christ as the supreme Revealer.   But this faith leads us again
to His testimony about Himself, and so once more to the Incarnation.   Thus it is that the Lord stands constantly chal-
lenging the ages to give their answer to His question, "What
think ye of Christ? whose Son is He?"[1] and increasingly it is
shown that it is not in the world's power to put this question
aside.   However silenced for the moment, it soon again asserts
its rights, and will not cease to be heard till humanity, from
one end of the earth to the other, has joined in the devout
acknowledgment—"My Lord and my God!"[2]

III. This fact of the Incarnation being given, how are we
to interpret it?   The full discussion of what, doctrinally, is
involved in the Incarnation, belongs rather to dogmatics than
to the present inquiry; but certain limiting positions may at
least be laid down, which may help to keep our thoughts in
·harmony with the facts we have had before us, and may serve
as a check on modern theories, which, professing to give us a
re-reading of this all-important doctrine more in agreement with
the Christian verity than the old Christological decisions, fall
short of, or go beyond these facts.   The early decisions of the
Church on Christ's Person are not, indeed, to be regarded as
beyond criticism.   It may very well be that reconstruction is
needed in this doctrine as in many others.   Only, we should be
careful not to part with the old formulas till something better
—something at least equally true to the facts of Christianity—
is put in their place; and I confess that most of the modern
attempts at a revised Christology do not seem to me to fulfil
this condition.

Constrained by the evidence of Scripture, many theologians
agree in ascribing "Godhead" to Christ, whose views of the
Person of Christ yet fall short of what the complete testimony
of Scripture seems to require.   Schleiermacher may be included
in this class, though he avoids the term;[3] of more recent theo-

---

[1] Matt. xxii. 42.   [2] John xx. 28.
[3] See Schleiermacher's views in *Der christl. Glaube*, ii. pp. 56, 57, 93.   He

logians, Rothe, Beyschlag, Ritschl, Lipsius, etc., who speak freely of the "Godhead" (Gottheit), "God-manhood" (Gottmenschheit), of Christ, and of the "Incarnation" (Menschwerdung) of God in Him.[1]   But what do these expressions mean?   In all, or most, of these theories, Christ has a high and unique position assigned to Him.   He is the second Adam, or new Head of the race, Son of God in a sense that no other is, archetypal Man, sinless Mediator and Redeemer of mankind.[2] This is a great deal, and must be recognised in any theory of the Incarnation.   All these theories acknowledge, further, a peculiar being or Revelation of God in Christ, on the ground of which these predicates "Godhead" and "God-manhood" are ascribed to Him.   But what is its nature?   In Schleiermacher, as already seen in the second Lecture, it is the constant and energetic activity of that God-consciousness which is potentially present in every man—which constitutes, therefore, an original element in human nature.[3]   In Rothe, it is an ethical union of God with humanity, gradually brought about in the course of the sinless development of Christ, and constituting, when complete, a perfect indwelling of God in man—a perfect unity of the Divine and human.[4]   In Beyschlag, it is the consciousness of a perfect and original relation of Sonship to God, which has its transcendental ground in an impersonal (Divine-human) principle eternally pre-existent in the Godhead.[5]   In Ritschl, the "Godhead" of Christ has a purely moral and religious sense, expressing the fact that in Christ, as the supreme Revealer of God, and Founder of the kingdom of God, there

---

says : "Inasmuch as all the human activity of Christ in its whole connection depends on this being of God in Him, and represents it, the expression is justified that in the Redeemer God became man, in a sense true of Him exclusively ; as also each moment of His existence, so far as one can isolate it, represents a new and similar incarnation of God and state of being incarnate ; since always and everywhere, all that is human in Him proceeds out of that which is Divine."—Pp. 56, 57.   He objects to the term "God-Man" as too definite.—P. 93.

[1] Rothe, *Dogmatik*, ii. pp. 88, 107, etc.; Beyschlag, *Leben Jesu*, p. 191, etc.; Ritschl, *Recht. und Ver.* iii. pp. 364–393 ; *Unterricht*, p. 22 ; Lipsius, *Dogmatik*, p. 457.   Cf. also Schultz, *Lehre von der Gottheit Christi*, pp. 536, 537 ; Herrmann, *Verkehr des Christen mit Gott*, pp. 42–62 ; Nitzsch, *Evangelische Dogmatik*, ii. p. 514, etc.   [Beyschlag's views are further expounded in his *New Testament Theology*, since published and translated.]

[2] Schleiermacher, ii. p. 19 ; Lipsius, sec. 638.

[3] *Der christl. Glaube*, ii. pp. 40, 56.   Cf. Lipsius, p. 492.

[4] *Dogmatik*, ii. pp. 88–97, 165–182.

[5] *Leben Jesu*, i. p. 191 ; *Christologie*, pp. 58, 84, etc.

is perfect oneness of will with God in this world-purpose, and a perfect manifestation of the Divine attributes of grace and truth, and of dominion over the world.[1] In Lipsius, again, and those who think with him, "Incarnation" and "Godhead" denote the realisation in Christ of that perfect relation of Sonship to God (Gottessohnschaft) which lies in the original idea of humanity, and the perfect Revelation of the Divine will of love (Liebewillen) in that Revelation.[2] Now I do not deny that in these theories we have a certain union of the Divine and human, just as believers in Christ, through union with Him and participation in His Spirit, become "sons of God," and "partakers of the Divine nature."[3] I do not deny, further, that these theories secure for Christ a certain distinction from every other, in that they make Him the original type of that relation of Divine Sonship into which others can only enter through Him. It is a thought also which not unnaturally occurs, whether on this idea of a God-filled humanity — a humanity of which it may be truly said that in an ethical respect the fulness of the Godhead dwells in it bodily—we have not all that is of practical value in any doctrine of Incarnation. We must beware, however, of imposing on ourselves with words, and I believe that, if we do not rise to a higher view, it will be difficult, as the second Lecture showed, to prevent ourselves drifting to pure humanitarianism.

Two things are to be considered here—First, whether these theories are tenable on their own merits; and, second, whether they do justice to the facts of Christ's Revelation, and to the *data* of the New Testament generally. I shall offer a few remarks on these points, then add a brief notice of the theories known as Kenotic.

1. There are two classes of these theories—those which do not, and those which do, presuppose a transcendental or metaphysical ground for the predicate "Godhead" applied to Christ,

---

[1] *Unterricht*, p. 22. It will be seen that this is a tolerably complex idea of "Godhead."

[2] *Dogmatik*, pp. 574, 575. Lipsius distinguishes between the "principle" of the Christian religion — which is that of religion absolutely — and the historical revelation of that principle in the Person and Work of Christ.—Pp. 535, 536. Yet this principle is not accidentally or externally bound up with Christ, as if He were only casually the first representative of it, or His work only the external occasion for the symbolical representation of the general activity of this principle in humanity.—Pp. 537, 538.

[3] John i. 12 ; 2 Pet. i. 4.

and as important differences exist between them, it is desirable to distinguish them.

(1) Of the former class are those of Schleiermacher, Ritschl, Lipsius, with many others that might be named. I abstract from other features in these theories, and look only at the grounds on which "Godhead" is ascribed to Christ; and I do not find any which transcend the limits of humanity. Christ is archetypal man, ideal man, sinless man, the perfect Revelation of grace and truth, the central individual of the race, the bearer of the principle of true religion, the Founder of the kingdom of God in humanity, the pre-eminent object of the Father's love,—but He is not more than man. His humanity may be a "God-filled" humanity; still a God-filled man is one thing, and God become man is another. There may be participation in the Divine life—even in the Divine nature—on the part of the ordinary believer; but the man in whom God thus dwells does not on this account regard himself as Divine, does not speak of himself as a Divine person, does not think himself entitled to Divine honours, would deem it blasphemy to have the term "Godhead" applied to him. If, therefore, this is the only account we can give of Christ's Person, it is clear that this predicate "Godhead" can never properly be applied to Him. We might speak of the Divine in Christ, but we could not say that Christ Himself was Divine. We might see in Him the highest organ of Divine Revelation, but we would require to distinguish between the God revealing Himself and the humanity through which He is manifested. It would be blasphemy here also to speak of Christ Himself as God. It would be idolatry to give Him Divine honours. We find, therefore, that Ritschl has to admit that it is only in a figurative and improper sense that the Church can attribute "Godhead" to Christ.[1] This predicate, he says, is not a theoretic truth, but only a judgment of value—an expression of the worth which Christ has for the religious consciousness of the believer. In further carrying out the same idea, both Schleiermacher and Ritschl strip away, as formerly shown, all the eschatological attributes from Christ, and resolve His sitting at the right hand of God, His return to judge the world, etc., into metaphors. The only real sense in which Christ is spiritually

[1] Ritschl, *Recht. und Ver.* iii. p. 378.

present in His Church is through the perpetuation of His image, of His teaching, and of His influence in the community of believers.[1] This is the legitimate consequence of a theory which does not go beyond the bounds of the human in its estimate of Christ; for if the eschatological teaching of Jesus is admitted, it seems impossible to stop short of a much higher view of His Person. This method, however, of simply sweeping aside what is distasteful, is too violent to be long endured; there are besides those utterances of Jesus which bespeak the consciousness of a relation different in kind, and not merely in degree, from that sustained by others to the Father. This class of theories, therefore, naturally passes over to another—that which seeks to do justice to the facts by admitting a deeper ground for Christ's Personality than the earthly one.

(2) Of this second class of theories, I may take those of Rothe and Beyschlag as examples. Rothe thinks he effectually secures the idea of Christ's Godhead by assuming that, in the course of Christ's sinless development, God constantly unites Himself with Him in closer and closer relations, till at length a perfect union both of person and of nature is effected.[2] Beyschlag thinks to do the same by supposing that a Divine impersonal principle—a pre-existent ideal humanity—is somehow incarnated in Christ.[3] But not to speak of the absence of scriptural proof for both of these theories, see the difficulties under which they labour. Can it be seriously said that, if a transcendental ground of Christ's Person is to be admitted, these theories have any advantage in simplicity or intelligibility over the old view? Take Rothe's theory. What are we to make of the supposition of a personality which begins as human, and ultimately and gradually is changed into Divine? Then what is meant by two persons merging into one, and this by moral process? For God is one Person to begin with, and Christ is another, and at length a perfect union is effected of both. Do we really in this theory get beyond the idea of an ethical union, or perfect moral friendship, in which, after all,

---

[1] Ritschl, *Recht. und Ver.* pp. 383, 384, 407, 408. "In any other sense," he thinks, "the formula of the exaltation of Christ to the right hand of God is either without content for us, because Christ as exalted is directly hidden for us; or becomes the occasion of all possible extravagance (Schwärmerei)."— P. 407. Schleiermacher, *Der christl. Glaube*, pp. 84–88, 290–292; Lipsius, *Dogmatik*, pp. 494, 587.

[2] *Dogmatik*, pp. 165–182.   [3] *Christologie*, p. 84, etc.

the two Persons remain distinct, though united in will and love? If this is the character of the union, it is only by a misuse of terms that we can speak of Christ becoming really God. Yet Rothe is perfectly in earnest with this conception of the deification of Christ, so we ask finally—How is this newly constituted Person related to God the Father? For Rothe acknowledges no immanent distinction of Persons in the Godhead, and it is the Father Himself who thus unites Himself with Christ, and confers Godhead upon His Person. Rothe says expressly, "The Incarnation of God in the Second Adam is essentially an incarnation of both in Him—of the Divine personality, and of the Divine nature."[1] But if it is the One absolute Personality whom we call God, who enters into the union with the humanity of Jesus, how can the resultant relation be described as that of Father and Son? Or if a new Divine Person really is constituted, does not Rothe's theory amount to this, that, since the Incarnation, a new Person has been added to the Godhead? But what does the constitution of a new Divine Person mean? Is it not, if the expression is to be taken literally, very like a contradiction in terms? I need not wait long on Beyschlag's rival theory of a pre-existent impersonal humanity, which solves no difficulties, and is loaded with inconceivabilities of its own. For in what sense can this idea of humanity be spoken of as Divine, any more than any other idea of the Divine mind which is realised in time?—the idea, e.g., of the world, or of the believer, or of the Church. What, besides, is meant by a heavenly, ideal humanity? Does it include only the single Person of Christ, or not also all the members of the human race?[2] How, further, is this ideal of humanity, which forms the supernatural principle in Christ, related to His actual humanity of flesh and blood, which came to Him "of the seed of David"?[3] Finally, if Christ's Person was thus peculiarly constituted, even in respect of its humanity, how can it be said of Him that He was made in all things like unto His brethren?[4] It may seem a waste of time to discuss such questions; yet theories like Rothe's and Beyschlag's have

---

[1] *Dogmatik*, ii. p. 172.

[2] Cf. his *Christologie*, p. 58; and *Leben Jesu*, p. 46.   [3] Rom. i. 4.

[4] Heb. ii. 17. Beyschlag would avoid some of these difficulties, if he kept consistently by the position that Christ is but the perfect realisation of the "Ebenbild" of humanity, which is fragmentarily realised in all men,—is, in

their uses; for they aid us, by a process of exclusion, in seeing what the true theory must be, and where we are to look for it.

2. The second question I proposed to ask is already in large measure answered in the course of the above discussion, Do these theories do justice to the facts of Christ's Revelation, and to the data of the New Testament generally? They clearly do not, either in a negative or a positive respect. There is no hint in the Scriptures of either Rothe's gradual incarnation, or of Beyschlag's pre-existent principle of humanity; but there are many passages which directly, or by implication, claim for Christ personal pre-existence, and attribute to Him Divine acts and functions in that state of pre-existence. But, apart from this, all those passages which claim for Christ a unique relation of Sonship to the Father, taken with the sayings which imply His consciousness of the possession of attributes and functions raised above those of humanity, point to a super-earthly and pre-incarnate state of existence. And this brings us back to the fundamental distinction between a true and a false or inadequate doctrine of Incarnation. Incarnation is not simply the endowing of human nature with the highest conceivable plenitude of gifts and graces; it is not a mere dynamical relation of God to the human spirit—acting on it or in it with exceptional energy; it is not simply the coming to consciousness of the metaphysical unity all along subsisting between humanity and God; it is not even such moral union, such spiritual indwelling and oneness of character and will, as subsists between God and the believer; still less, of course, is it analogous to the heathen ideas of sons of the gods, where the relation is that of physical paternity —or of the appearances of gods in human guise—or even of temporary appearances in humanity, as in the case of the Avatars of Vishnu. The scriptural idea of the Incarnation is as unique as is the Biblical conception as a whole. It is not, to state the matter in a word, the union simply of the Divine nature with the human,—for that I acknowledge in the case of every believer through the indwelling Spirit,—but the entrance

---

fact, simply the ideal Man; but he seeks to establish a metaphysical distinction between Christ's humanity and ours, in virtue of which His personality is "originally and essentially" Divine, while ours is not.—*Christologie*, p. 58. See further on Beyschlag's views in Appendix.

of a Divine Person into the human.   That there is an analogy,
and a closer one than is sometimes admitted, between the
believer's relation to God and Christ's relation to the Father
is expressly declared in Christ's own words in John xvii. 21,
where He asks "that they may all be one; even as Thou, Father,
art in Me, and I in Thee, that they may be one in Us."   But
the subject here is moral union,—not union of essence, as in
John i. 1, and perhaps John x. 30, but the mutual ensphering
of personalities in an atmosphere of love, such as obtains in its
highest degree between the Father and the Son.   For "he that
abideth in love, abideth in God, and God abideth in him."[1]
There is this also in Christ.   But the distinction remains—
these personalities of ours are human, and continue so, no
matter how entirely filled, penetrated, possessed, with the light
and love and knowledge of God they may be; but His was a
Personality of a higher rank—a Divine Personality, which
entered into the limitations and conditions of humanity from
above, which was not originally human, as ours is, but became
se.   Here questions deep and difficult, I acknowledge, crowd
thick upon us, to many of which no answer may be possible;
but so much as this, I think, is assuredly implied in the
Christian Incarnation.

3. Before, however, venturing further in this direction, I
must bestow at least a glance on what is known as the question
of the Kenosis.   This word, meaning "emptying," is taken, as
is well known, from Phil. ii. 7, in which passage Christ is said
to have "emptied Himself" (ἑαυτὸν ἐκένωσε), taking the form
of a servant.   The question is, What does this emptying
include?   Did the Son of God—the Eternal Word—literally
lay aside His Divine glory, and, ceasing to be in the form of
God, enter by human birth into the conditions of earthly
poverty and weakness?   Or, if He did not, what is the import
of this remarkable phrase?   The Kenotic theories—represented
in Germany by a long list of honoured names [2]—answer the
former question in the affirmative.   Godet among French
writers advocates the same view.   The Divine Logos, he
thinks, literally laid aside His Divine attributes at the Incarnation, and entered the sphere of the finite as an unconscious

---

[1] 1 John iv. 16.
[2] *E.g.* Thomasius, Gess, Ebrard, Kahnis, Luthardt, etc.

babe.[1] The object of these theories, of course, is to secure the reality of Christ's humanity, and the fact of a true human development, which seemed imperilled by the older view. Notwithstanding, however, the wide support they have received, I cannot think that these theories will ever permanently commend themselves to the judgment of the Church.[2] They seem to me—to come to the heart of the matter at once—to involve an impossibility, inasmuch as they ask us to believe in the temporary suspension of the consciousness, and the cessation from all Divine functions, of one of the Persons of the Godhead! How does this consist with Scripture? Are we not told of the Son, in particular, not only that by Him all things were created, but that in Him all things consist—that He upholdeth all things by the word of His power? Is this relation to the universe not an essential one? and does the Kenotic theory not reduce it to one wholly unessential and contingent? I cannot therefore accept this theory, nor do I think that the reality of the Incarnation requires it. I might appeal here to the analogy of nature. There is an immanent presence of God in nature, but there is also a transcendent existence of God beyond nature. So the Divine Son took upon Him our nature with its human limits, but above and beyond that, if we may so express it, was the vast " over-soul " of His Divine consciousness. Even human psychology, in making us more familiar than we were with the idea of different strata of consciousness even in the same personal being, gives us a hint which need not be lost. The sense of the apostle's words seems sufficiently met by the lowly form of Christ's earthly manifestation—"despised and rejected of men, a man of sorrows, and acquainted with grief."[3]

The result of our inquiry has not been to overthrow the Christological decisions of the early Church, but rather to impress us with the justice and tact of these decisions in guarding the truth against opposite errors. Has all the labour and earnestness of modern investigation on this profound subject, then, been absolutely without result? I do not think

---

[1] Cf. *Commentary on John*, i. 14. Pressensé and Gretillat are other French Kenoticists.

[2] For an able discussion of Kenotic theories see Professor Bruce's *Humiliation of Christ*, Lecture IV. (Cunningham Lectures).

[3] Isa. liii. 3.

so. One remarkable gain has already been adverted to, in the tendency of modern speculation to draw the Divine and the human nearer together, and to emphasise, if not their identity, at least their kindredness, and the capacity of the human to receive the Divine.[1] But many lights and suggestions have been afforded in the treatment of this subject, from Schleier- macher downwards, which in any attempt at a constructive view must always be of great value. This will perhaps become apparent if, in closing this survey, I notice an objection which is sometimes urged against the view of the Incarnation here presented—the ordinary, and as I believe the scriptural one— namely, that in affirming the incarnation of a heavenly and pre-existent Person we seem to impinge on the reality, or at least the integrity, of the human nature which Christ bore. The question is, Had Christ's human nature an independent Personality of its own, or was the Divine the only Personality? To guard against Nestorian error, or the assumption of two persons in Christ, the Church, it will be remembered, affirmed what is called the "impersonality" of the human nature of Christ, and, as might appear, with perfect reason on the prin- ciples of the Logos Christology.[2] But this very consequence is made in modern times the ground of an objection to that Christology, which, it is said, while maintaining the Divinity, impairs the integrity of the humanity, of the Redeemer. For (1) If Christ's human nature had no independent Personality, was not His human nature thereby mutilated? and (2) If it is the Divine Personality that is the subject—the Ego—does not this detract on the other side from the truth of His humanity? For this reason, some are disposed to grant that Christ's humanity also must be conceived of as personal, and that the Incarnation must be thought of, with Rothe, as the union both of person and of nature. Let us see how it stands with this difficulty on closer inspection, and from what point of view it can best be obviated.

1. It would be well if the objector to the ordinary ecclesi-

---

[1] In a practical respect the chief gain is that we begin with the earthly side of Christ's humanity, and rise to the recognition of His Divinity ; more stress is laid on the humanity which manifests the Divinity than formerly. See Kaftan's *Brauchen wir ein neues Dogma ?* p. 54.

[2] Cf. on this subject of the *Anhypostasia*, as it is called, Schaff's *Creeds of Christendom*, pp. 32, 33 ; Dorner's *System of Doctrine*, iii. p. 254 (Eng. trans.); Bruce's *Humiliation of Christ*, pp. 427-430.

astical view—he who admits in any sense an Incarnation—would think out carefully what is implied in the attribution of an independent Personality to Christ's human nature. On both sides there will be agreement that the unity of the Person must in some form be maintained. You cannot have two Egos in Christ's one Divine-human Person—however close the relation between them. If the human Ego retains in any measure its distinction from the Divine, then we have not an Incarnation, but a Nestorian relation of persons. If, therefore, an independent human Ego is to be assumed, it must be supposed to be so incorporated with the Divine Ego—so lost in it, so interpenetrated by it, so absorbed in it—that all sense of separate identity is parted with;[1] while, on the other hand, the Divine Ego so transfuses itself into the human, so limits and conditions itself, so becomes the ruling and controlling force in the human consciousness, as itself practically to become human. There is perhaps no obvious objection to this view, but, at the same time, it is difficult to see what is gained by it. The human Ego, as a distinct Ego, is as entirely lost sight of—is as completely taken up and merged into the Divine—as on the other supposition. For it is of the essence of the true view of Incarnation that the bond of personal identity should remain unbroken between the Son who shared the glory of the Father in eternity, and the human Christ who prayed, "O Father, glorify Thou Me with Thine own self with the glory which I had with Thee before the world was."[2]

---

[1] This was Origen's view in the early Church. The Logos, he thought, united itself with an unfallen soul in the pre-existent state. Cf. *De Principiis*, Book ii. chap. vi. : "But since, agreeably to the faculty of free-will, variety and diversity characterised the individual souls, so that one was attached with a warmer love to the Author of its being, and another with a feebler and weaker regard, that soul, . . . inhering from the beginning of the creation, and afterwards, inseparably and indissolubly in Him, as being the Wisdom and Word of God, and the Truth and the true Light, and receiving Him wholly, and passing into His light and splendour, was made with Him in a pre-eminent degree one Spirit, according to the promise of the apostle to those who ought to imitate it, that 'he who is joined to the Lord is one spirit' (1 Cor. vi. 17). . . . Neither was it opposed to the nature of that soul, as a rational existence, to receive God, into whom, as stated above, as into the Word and the Wisdom and the Truth, it had already wholly entered. And therefore deservedly is it also called, along with the flesh which it had assumed, the Son of God, and the Power of God, the Christ, and the Wisdom of God, either because it was wholly in the Son of God, or because it received the Son of God wholly into itself."—*Ante-Nicene Library* trans. Origen's view may be compared with Rothe's, only that Rothe does not allow a separate personality in the Logos.

[2] John xvii. 5.

2. The other side of the objection — If it is the Divine
Personality which is the subject, does not this detract from the
truth of the human nature, give us only an unreal and doketic
Christ?—raises a much deeper question—that, namely, of the
original relation of the Divine Logos to humanity.   If God can
become man, it can only be on the presupposition of an original
relation between God and humanity, in virtue of which there is
an essential kindredness and bond of connection between them.
This is already implied in the Scripture doctrine of man made
in the image of God, but it receives a deeper interpretation
through the doctrine of the Logos.[1]   When it is objected that
the Divine Logos, even though entering into the nature and
conditions and limitations of humanity, is not truly a human
Person, the question is to be asked, Is the relation between
Personality in the Logos and that in man one of contrariety,-or
is not Personality in the Logos rather the truth of that which
we find in humanity?   Is man's personality in every case not
grounded in that of the Logos?   Is He not the light and life of
all men, even in a natural respect—the light of intelligence, of
conscience, of spirit?   But if man's personality is thus grounded
in the Logos, is there a difference of kind between them, or not
rather one of condition?   Is there not a human side in the
Logos, and a Divine side in man? and is not this the truth
we have to conserve in such theories as Beyschlag's and Hegel's.
There is no denial, therefore, in the doctrine of the Incarnation,
rightly understood, of a true human Personality in Christ,—
what is denied is that the Personality of the Divine Son cannot also become in the incarnate condition a truly human one.
A further question would be, whether the idea of the human
race did not include from the first the idea of an Incarnation,
with the Son Himself as Head—a subject which will be dealt
with in the next Lecture.

I remark, in a word, in closing, that we do not do justice to
this stupendous fact of the Incarnation, if we neglect to look at
it in the light of its revealed ends.   The advantage of taking
the doctrine in this way is, that we see at a glance the inadequacy of all lower theories of the Person of Christ, if the

---

[1] An original relation of the Logos to humanity on the ground of the Incarnation, is already implied in the theology of Irenæus, Clement, and Origen
(cf. Dorner's *History*) ; is made prominent in recent Christological discussions
in Germany ; was the view of Maurice, etc.

ends intended to be accomplished by His appearance were to be attained. If Christ came to do only the work of a prophet, or of a philanthropist, or of a teacher of ethical truth, I admit that the Incarnation would shrivel up into an absurdity. The means would be out of all proportion to the ends. But who will say this of the actual ends for which the Son of God came into the world? Who will affirm that if a world was to be redeemed from sin and guilt, and spiritual bondage—to be renewed, sanctified, and brought into the fellowship of life with God—anyone less than Divine was adequate to the task?[1] Here, again, the Christian view is in keeping with itself. There is a proportion between the Incarnation and the ends sought to be accomplished by it. The denial of the Incarnation of necessity carries with it a lowering of the view of the work Christ came to do for men. He, on the other hand, who believes in that work—who feels the need of it—much more who has experienced the redeeming power of it in his own heart—will not doubt that He who has brought this salvation to him is none other than the "Strong Son of God—Immortal Love."[2]

---

[1] Even Hartmann recognises this. "If one sees in Jesus," he says, "only the son of the carpenter Joseph and of his wife Mary, this Jesus and His death can as little redeem me from my sins as, say, Bismarck can do it," etc.—*Selbst-zersetzung*, p. 92.

[2] *In Memoriam.*

APPENDIX TO CHAPTER 6

THE SELF-CONSCIOUSNESS OF JESUS

IT is a significant circumstance that, in recent years, interest has concentrated itself more and more on the question of Christ's self-consciousness—that is, on what He thought and felt about Himself, and on how He arrived at these convictions. The fact is an illustration of the saying of Godet, quoted in the Lecture, that in the last instance Christianity rests on Christ's witness to Himself. I have noted below some of the chief books which bear upon this subject,[1] and may refer here to a few of their results, only venturing very sparingly upon criticism.

The general subject is the origin and development of Christ's Messianic consciousness, as that may be deduced from the Gospels, and the points chiefly discussed are the following :—

1. What was the fundamental fact in Christ's Messianic consciousness out of which the other elements grew—the consciousness of a perfect religious relation to the Father (Beyschlag, Weiss, Wendt, etc.), or, behind this, of sinlessness? (Baldensperger).

2. When did Christ clearly realise His Messianic calling? —At the Baptism? (Beyschlag, Wendt, Baldensperger, etc.). Or earlier? (Neander, Hase, Weiss, etc.). Or not till a later period? (Renan, Strauss, Schenkel, etc.).

---

[1] Beyschlag's *Das Leben Jesu,* i. pp. 171–244—("Das Selbstbewusstsein Jesu," "Der messianische Beruf," etc.). 1885. [Cf. *his New Testament Theology.*]

Gess's *Christi Person und Werk, nach Christi Selbstzeugniss,* etc., vol. i. (1870).

Hermann Schmidt on "Bildung und Gehalt des messianischen Bewusstseins Jesu," in *Studien und Kritiken* (1889).

Grau's *Das Selbstbewusstsein Jesu im Licht der messianischen Hoffnungen seiner Zeit* (1888, 2nd ed. 1892).

Wendt's *Die Lehre Jesu,* vol. ii. (1890).

Stanton's *The Jewish and Christian Messiah* (1886).

Lives of Christ, by Weiss, Keim, Hase, etc.

Biblical Theology of New Testament,—Weiss, Reuss, etc.

3. Was Christ's "plan" one and the same throughout? (Neander, Schmidt, etc.). Or, did Christ's views change with the course of events? (Beyschlag, Schenkel, Hase, Keim, Baldensperger, etc.). Was it, *e.g.*, only gradually that He realised the necessity of His death? (Beyschlag, Weiss, Baldensperger, Wendt, etc.).

4. The import and origin of the titles "Son of Man" and "Son of God." Does the former represent Christ as "weak, creaturely man"? (Holsten, Wendt). Or as "ideal, typical man"? (Neander, Reuss, Beyschlag, etc.). Or simply as Messiah? (Baldensperger). Was it borrowed from Daniel (as most hold), and to what extent was it a popular, well-known title for Messiah? (Against this, Matt. xvi. 13.)

This title expresses the two ideas that Christ at once belongs to the race of humanity, and sustains a peculiar and unique relation to it. It may be held to denote Christ's consciousness that He is true and perfect Man, that He sustains a universal relation to the race, and that He is the Messiah.

As respects the second title, does it denote an ethical and religious relation (so most of the above), or has it also any metaphysical (or, as I prefer to say, transcendental) implication? (Beyschlag, Reuss, Schmidt, etc.). Is it a title which Christ shares with others (in part Wendt), or uses in a peculiar and exceptional sense of Himself? (Beyschlag, Reuss, Weiss, etc.).

It will help the understanding of the subject if I sketch a little more fully the views of some of the above-named writers.

Beyschlag's view does not hang well together. It begins with a Christ who is unique among men—sinless, the Son of God in an absolute sense, whose nature is grounded in eternity, who works miracles, is raised from the dead, is translated into heavenly power and glory, who has Godhead, who demands worship; but who grows only gradually into the consciousness of His Messiahship, is limited in nature and gifts, makes mistakes, errs in His expectations, etc. Beyschlag's opinions, however, contain many notable elements. On the general subject he says, "First in a Personality in which the Divine nature translates itself so perfectly into the human that it can be said, 'Who sees Me, sees the Father,' can the Divine Revelation

perfect itself." [1]   The God-manhood is "the wonder of all
wonders." [2]   He separates himself from the Church doctrine,
and declares himself in favour of an "anthropocentric" Christology, though only on the ground, as he explains it, of "a
theocentric anthropology," that is, of the view that it is the
image of God which is the essential thing in the nature of man. [3]
He rejects Strauss's view, that the sinlessness of Jesus is "the
death of all true humanity," and contends that "the Christ of
faith" is no impossibility. [4]   The history of the childhood of
Jesus, at the same time, he resolves into poetry, and thinks the
birth from a virgin not essential to sinlessness, or to a new
beginning of humanity. [5]   On the self-consciousness of Jesus,
he holds that the individuality of Jesus had its limitations, but
in respect of the consciousness of a Divine Sonship was clear
and absolute.   "It is not the old Israelitish religious consciousness which lives in Jesus in such all-determining fashion,
but a new, till then in the world unheard of and perfect consciousness, which not only is still unsurpassed but in its inward-
ness and clearness never can be surpassed." [6]   Its central point is
the consciousness of God as Father, to which the name "Son"
corresponds.   "Sonship to God (Gottessohnschaft) is the
peculiar expression of the self-consciousness of Jesus." [7]   This
name represents the highest aim, or ideal, for all men, but still
there is a singularity in its application to Jesus. [8]   God was His
Father in a special sense.   "While He calls God not merely
'His' Father, but names Him also 'the' Father absolutely,
and teaches His disciples to pray 'our Father in heaven,' He
yet never includes Himself with them under an 'our Father,'
but always says 'My Father' or 'your Father,' thus distinguishing His relation from theirs." [9]   This does not mean "that He
is the first who has recognised and realised this destination to
a Divine Sonship."   It means that, while all others become sons
of God through a change of disposition—through conversion,
the new birth, etc.—and not through themselves, but only
through Him—His relation to the Father is original, perfect,
absolute, so that He knows Himself to be the object of God's

---

[1] *Leben Jesu*, i. p. 39.
[2] *Ibid*. i. p. 39.
[3] *Ibid*. i. p. 46.
[4] *Ibid*. i. pp. 50, 56.
[5] *Ibid*. pp. 146, 161, 162.
[6] *Ibid*. i. p. 175.
[7] *Ibid*. i. p. 176.
[8] *Ibid*. i. p. 177.
[9] *Ibid*. i. p. 178.

love absolutely.[1] In this is involved His sinlessness.[2] This is a necessary pre-supposition of Christian faith—the religious, moral absoluteness of Jesus, and the history confirms it.[3] If He has not this absolute greatness, He is no Saviour of others, but stands in need of salvation Himself.[4] This is the "Godhead" of Jesus. "It is never a relative greatness, however exalted and super-excellent it may be, but the absolute which is the appearance of Godhead in humanity; the religiously and morally perfect, and this alone, is in the domain of the human, the truly Divine, in which we can believe, and which admits of and demands worship."[5] But this religious-moral Godhead of Christ does not stand in opposition to a metaphysical. A real being of God in Him lies at the foundation of the consciousness of Christ, that which He expresses in the word, "I am in the Father and the Father in Me"; so that in Him in whom the eternal love has perfectly appeared an essential Godhead also may be recognised.[6] The passages in John which seem to imply personal pre-existence, Beyschlag explains away by predestination, etc. On the Messianic calling, he finds the birth-moment of the Messianic consciousness of Jesus in the baptism.[7] He reviews the opinions of those who would put it earlier or later, and finds them untenable.[8] But though Christ from this moment knew Himself to be the Messiah, He did not know what the course of His Messianic life was to be.[9] He had no foreseen plan. "The public life of Jesus began under quite other stars than the expectation of the death of the Cross."[10] Beyschlag distinguishes three stages in the development of Christ's ideas:[11]—

1. A stage when the kingdom is conceived of as near—standing at the door (early ministry in John).

2. Jesus realises that His people are anything but ready for the kingdom; and sees that its triumph will involve a long-protracted development (Galilean ministry).

3. He foresees His death, and the triumph of the kingdom is now transported into the future, in connection with a second advent. The name "Son of Man," Beyschlag connects with

---

[1] *Leben Jesu*, i. p. 179.
[2] *Ibid*. i. p. 181.
[3] *Ibid*. i. p. 190.
[4] *Ibid*. i. p. 190.
[5] *Ibid*. i. p. 191.
[6] *Ibid*. i. p. 191.
[7] *Ibid*. i. p. 213.
[8] *Ibid*. i. pp. 216, 217.
[9] *Ibid*. i. p. 289.
[10] *Ibid*. i. p. 231.
[11] *Ibid*. i. pp. 233–236.

the Messianic dignity (from Daniel); but holds that Christ knew and felt Himself also as "the heavenly, archetypal (urbildlich) man."[1]   The reality of the resurrection is strongly defended, and the following explanation is given of the ascension. "What, then, was the original thought of the ascent to heaven? What else can it have been than that of the elevation of Jesus above the limits of the earthly life, of His translation into another, supramundane, Divine form of existence,—in a word, of His exaltation or glorification?"[2]

H. Schmidt's article in the *Studien und Kritiken*, on "The Formation and Content of the Messianic Consciousness of Jesus," is an acute criticism of the views of Beyschlag and Weiss, and also an able independent treatment of the subject. He inquires "first as to the time in which Jesus came to the consciousness of His Messianic destination, and then what moments His Messianic consciousness comprehended, and what measure of clearness there was already present in Him as to the nature of His kingdom."[3]   As against Weiss, who seeks to lead from the consciousness of Christ's unique Son-relationship to the consciousness of His Messiahship by way of inference, he argues very powerfully for a peculiarity in the self-consciousness of Jesus other than the mere sense of a perfect religious relation to the Father.[4]   Sonship implies a knowledge of the thoughts and love of God to the individual, not of God's thoughts or purposes for the world.   On the other hand—this against Beyschlag—the consciousness of a unique and sinless Sonship could not exist without the idea of a unique calling connected therewith.[5]   For Jesus to know that He was the only sinless Being in humanity, was already to know that He had a calling beyond that of a Nazarene carpenter.   He strongly presses the point that the appearance of a perfectly sinless Being in the empirical state of the race is scarcely comprehensible by us "without the background of a distinction of essence";[6] and shows that Beyschlag's admission that the peculiarity of Christ's Person, as the absolute moral ideal, involves a permanent distinction between Him and others, and rests on a metaphysical background, is fatal to his "anthropocentric" view, for it means

---

[1] *Leben Jesu*, i. p. 241.   [2] *Ibid*. i. p. 448.
[3] *Stud. und Krit.* 1889, p. 425.   [4] *Ibid*. 1889, 432.
[5] *Ibid*. 1889, p. 433.   [6] *Ibid*. 1889, p. 499.

that the centre of Christ's Person is in the suprahuman—the Divine.[1] He examines the alleged traces of growth in the Messianic consciousness of Jesus during His public ministry, and demonstrates how weak are the grounds on which this view rests.[2] He holds it to have been inconceivable that Jesus should have been in unclearness in regard to, at least, "the constitutive moments" of His kingdom, and therefore in regard to His death.[3] He combats Weiss's view that Jesus thought at first only of Israel, not of a universal kingdom.[4] "If at the entrance on His Messianic course, already the kingdoms of the world and the glory of them were offered to Him, one would think He must have had a wide glimpse into this world."[5] The whole essay deserves careful consideration.

Another critic of current theories is Grau, who thus defines the subject in his preface. "The capital question in this domain," he says, is, "What Jesus has thought about Himself, His vocation, and the significance of His Person?" Another form of the question is, "How is the Christ of the Nicene Creed related to the Christ of the New Testament, and specially to the Christ of the Synoptics"?[6] He criticises very severely the view of H. Schultz, in his work on *The Godhead of Christ*, but along with this, the theories of Beyschlag, etc. He quotes Schultz's criticism on the Socinian writers, that they ascribed "a *become* Godhead" (eine gewordene Gottheit) to Christ, and asks wherein their view differed from his own, as expressed in the following passage :—" If we teach the Godhead of Christ, it is that we are certain that Jesus, *after He has completed His work*, has become perfectly one with the Christ-idea of God. . . . God has made Him Lord and Christ. And so He has also received, as His personal attribute, the Godhead which is proper to the Christ. *The Christ* is for us God. *Jesus has become God* in becoming Christ."[7] The old view, Grau remarks, was that "God became man in Jesus Christ"; now the truth of salvation is expressed by Schultz and his friends in the proposition, "The man Jesus Christ has become God." "This Godhead," he says, "can be no 'true' Godhead, because it is one that has become. So, finally, is this whole

---

[1] *Stud. und Krit.* 1889, p. 435.
[2] *Ibid.* 1889, pp. 448–451.
[3] *Ibid.* 1889, p. 472.
[4] *Ibid.* 1889, p. 490.
[5] *Ibid.* 1889, p. 490.
[6] *Das Selbstbewusstsein Jesu*, Preface, pp. 5, 9.
[7] *Ibid.* Preface, p. 12.

representation nothing else than what it was with the Socinians —a misuse of the name of God." [1] Grau's own book, however, though it goes on original lines, can hardly be recommended as a satisfactory contribution to the subject. He is often far from concise or clear in his statements, and somewhat unmethodical in his treatment. He does not systematically investigate the question of Christ's self-consciousness — its development, relation to current ideas, contents, etc.—but aims rather at proving the thesis that Christ is the one who combines, in His Messianic calling, all the attributes of Jehovah in the Old Testament. An elaborate discussion of the title " Son of Man " sums itself up in the following remark :—" This is the (title) Son of Man, the grasping together and fulfilment of all the offices in the kingdom of God which lie side by side in the Old Testament, and complete each other—those of shepherd, physician, priest (but also of sacrifice), of prophet, of king, and judge." [2]

A much more thorough discussion of the subject is Baldensperger's recent work on *The Self-Consciousness of Jesus in the Light of the Messianic Hopes of His Time*. Baldensperger will have nothing to say to the "ideal man" theory—which he ridicules as an attempt to carry back our nineteenth-century ideas into a period to which they were quite strange—and treats the title " Son of Man " as simply a designation for the Messiah. [3] Yet his general view is exposed to the same objections as Beyschlag's. He makes Jesus first arrive dimly at the feeling that He is Messiah; then, aroused by John's preaching and baptised, He reaches religious assurance (but still expecting, according to the ideas of the time, signs in confirmation of His call); He is perplexed (the Temptation) ; after this, He gains clearness, yet not such absolute certainty as warrants Him in publicly proclaiming Himself ; ultimately he attains to this certainty, and at the same time sees that His victory is only to be secured through death, and now looks for the completion of the kingdom of God through the Parousia and last judgment, etc. [4] It is obvious how much of all this is mere theory, without corroboration in the history. To mention only one objection—according to Baldensperger, Christ did not announce Himself as Messiah till

---

[1] *Das Selbstbewusstsein Jesu*, Preface, p. 13. Cf. the criticism of Schultz in Frank's *Gewissheit*, p. 444 (Eng. trans.).

[2] *Ibid.* p. 215. [3] *Ibid.* p. 137 ; 2nd ed. p. 178.

[4] See Wendt's criticism in his *Die Lehre Jesu*, ii. pp. 307–310.

the time of Peter's confession,[1] while yet the name " Son of Man," which Baldensperger takes to be quite equivalent to Messiah, is on His lips in the Gospels from the first.[2] To avoid this difficulty, the critic has no alternative but arbitrarily to change the order of the sections, and to assume that all those incidents in which this name occurs, took place *after* Peter's confession—a violent and unwarrantable hypothesis.[3] It is a weakness of Baldensperger's theory that it fluctuates between a view according to which Jesus is certain of Himself, and another according to which He is in doubt and perplexity. Surely, if there is one thing clearer in the Gospels than another, it is that Christ is quite certain of Himself from the beginning. Not to build on this expression "Son of Man," can we listen to the tone of authority in the Sermon on the Mount, and doubt it? The hypothesis of a wavering and fluctuating consciousness totally lacks support in the Gospel narrative. Had Christ any doubt of Himself when He answered John's messengers, when He chose the twelve apostles, when He invited the labouring and heavy laden to come to Him for rest, when He said, "All things are delivered to Me of My Father," etc.?[4] One thing which Baldensperger totally fails to show us is, what amount of reliance we are to place in self-beliefs of Christ, arrived at by the psychological methods he indicates, through contact with the apocalyptic notions of the time, etc. In other words, what *objective* value have these beliefs of Christ for us—His beliefs, *e.g.*, about His atoning death, His Parousia, the judgment of the world, etc.? Apparently Baldensperger attaches great religious weight to these beliefs, stripped at least of their immediate form, yet it is not easy to see on what grounds he can do so. He leaves wholly undetermined, besides, Christ's relation to His miracles, to the resurrection, etc., without which, surely, His self-witness is not set in its right light.

I would refer, finally, to the important discussion of these subjects in Wendt's able and exhaustive work on *The Doctrine of Jesus*. In this book Wendt subjects the opinions of

---

[1] *Das Selbstbewusstsein Jesu*, ii. p. 177 ; 2nd ed. p. 246.
[2] *E.g.*, Matt. xi. 6 ; Mark ii. 10, 28. Cf. *Das Selbstbewusstsein Jesu*, ii. p. 179 ; 2nd ed. p. 249.
[3] They are to be regarded as " erratic blocks " in the history, *Das Selbstbewusstsein Jesu*, p. 180 ; 2nd ed. p. 252.
[4] Matt. xi. 27, 28.

Beyschlag and Baldensperger, as to a change in Christ's views of His kingdom, to a careful criticism, and arrives at the conclusion that, in all essential respects, Christ's views of the nature and coming of His kingdom as a present, spiritual, gradually developing reality on earth, remained unchanged during the period of His ministry.[1] He holds, however, that this does not apply to the details of the development; and grants, in agreement with the others, that at the beginning of His work Christ had no thought of the necessity of His death, not to speak of so speedy and frightful a death.[2] The difference of the two views, therefore, resolves itself into one of degree, for unless it is held that Christ's death had no essential relation to the nature of His kingdom, and the manner of its setting up, it is impossible to say that ignorance in regard to that event did not affect the conception of the kingdom. Wendt, like Beyschlag, holds that the baptism was the moment of the miraculous revelation to Christ of His Messiahship, though He finds this prepared for in His previous consciousness of standing in an inner communion of love with His heavenly Father. "In this consciousness was given the psychological pre-supposition for His gaining the certainty of His own Messiahship, and therewith, at the same time, obtaining a new, higher knowledge of the nature and coming of the kingdom of God. But, previously to the baptism, this conclusion from His inner fellowship with God as His Son was to Him still not clear."[3] On the meaning of the name "Son of Man," Wendt argues strongly for the view that this title designates Christ as a weak, creaturely being—member, Messiah though He was, of the weak, creaturely race of humanity.[4] This view, in turn, is ably criticised by Baldensperger in the work noticed above.[5] It cannot be carried through without doing violence to many passages in which this name is evidently used by Christ as a title of dignity; the highest Messianic functions being claimed by him, not (as Wendt's argument would require) despite of His being Son of Man, but because He is Son of Man.[6] In general, Wendt's ideas of Jesus and His teaching are very high. "My interest in the historical treatment of the teaching of Jesus," he says,

[1] *Die Lehre Jesu*, ii. pp. 307–3ᴢ5.　　[2] *Ibid*. ii. pp. 306, 320.
[3] *Ibid*. ii. p. 316.　　　　　　　　　[4] *Ibid*. ii. pp. 442, 443.
[5] *Ibid*. ii. 2nd ed. p. 182, etc.　　　[6] Mark ii. 28 ; John v. 27, etc.

"arises from the conviction that the historical Jesus Christ, in His annunciation, by word and deed, of the kingdom of God, was the perfect Revelation of God to men"; and again, "We recognise in His teaching concerning the kingdom of God the highest and perfect Revelation of God."[1] On the other hand, this high estimate is limited by the admission that on everything but the one peculiar point of His own mission—the founding of the kingdom of God—Jesus simply occupied the standpoint, and used the language, of His contemporaries. His views of the natural world—*e.g.* of the Old Testament, of angels and devils, of the future world, etc.—were simply those of His age, and liable to all the error and imperfection of the time.[2] But then the question cannot help arising, If Jesus is avowedly wrong on all points where a scientific view of the world is concerned, how are we to trust Him when He speaks to us of supernatural and supersensible realities? May not His own words be applied, "If I have told you earthly things and ye believe not, how shall ye believe if I tell you of heavenly things?"[3] There need be no dispute as to what Dr. Wendt says of the religious ideas of Christ, of His spiritual conception of the kingdom of God, of His doctrine of the Divine Fatherhood, of His pure and exalted doctrine of righteousness. The sceptic would admit it all. He would only question whether, with the altered view of the world which has arisen since Christ's time, such doctrines are tenable now as sober, objective truth. And to answer that question satisfactorily, firmer ground must be taken up in regard to Christ's consciousness as a whole. Dr. Wendt's book is, in many respects, a richly instructive one, full of suggestive points, but it lacks the means of guarding Christianity against the subjectivity which would grant to it every kind of moral worth and beauty, but would deny its objective truth as Revelation.

---

[1] Preface to recent Eng. trans. of *Die Lehre Jesu.* Dr. Wendt, however, does not allow anything higher than an ethical Sonship to Jesus, identical in kind with that enjoyed by all the other members of the kingdom of God— "viz. a fellowship of love with God, in which God as the Father bestows His eternal salvation, and man as son trustfully and obediently appropriates and follows the will of God; only that Jesus knows that this relation of Sonship to God is realised in Himself in unique perfection, and on this account regards Himself as the Son of God *κατ' ἐξοχήν.*"—P. 453. He expressly denies to Jesus pre-existence, or a transcendental mode of being, and explains away the sayings in John which seem to teach such higher existence.—Pp. 453–476.

[2] *Die Lehre Jesu*, ii. pp. 113–129.   [3] John iii. 12.

7
THE HIGHER CONCEPT OF GOD INVOLVED IN THE INCARNATION— THE INCARNATION AND THE PLAN OF THE WORLD

"God is one, but not solitary."—Peter Chrysologus

"Christian worship calls men away from the altars of Polytheism, and elevates their souls to the One God, but it does this in a threefold direction; for we know by faith that eternal life streams down to us out of three personal fountains of love—from God the Father, who has created us; from God the Son, who has redeemed us; and from God the Holy Ghost, who sanctifies us and makes us the children of God; —in the Trinity alone do we possess the whole of love." —Martensen

"The conceptions of speculative philosophy, where they are most profound, come nearest to the Christian doctrine; nor need we be anxious lest speculative philosophy should ever reach a height from which it may look down and say that the Christian element is left behind. No thought can transcend the Christian idea, for it is truth in itself." —Braniss (in *Christlieb*)

"For who among men knoweth the things of a man, save the spirit of the man, which is in him? Even so the things of God none knoweth, save the Spirit of God." —Paul

7

THE HIGHER CONCEPT OF GOD INVOLVED IN THE INCARNATION— THE INCARNATION AND THE PLAN OF THE WORLD

THE point reached at the conclusion of last Lecture was that the facts of Christ's Revelation are reconcilable with no lower estimate of His Person than that which we find in the apostolic writings. This conclusion is counterchecked by the circumstance that, in the history of doctrine, no lower estimate of Christ's Person has been found able to maintain itself.

Theories, therefore, like that of Ritschl, which ascribe "Godhead" to Christ only in a figurative way, or like those of Rothe and Beyschlag, which aim at investing Christ with a real Divinity, but deny His personal pre-existence, are none of them in full harmony with Scripture testimony. The former sinks back into humanitarianism; the latter involve themselves in the difficulty that they must suppose a new Divine person to come into existence in the Incarnation. They literally add a new Person to the Godhead. This difficulty is not obviated by taking the predicate "Divinity" in a quasi-ideal sense to denote simply the ethical indwelling of God in Christ. There is no doubt a true presence of the Divine in Christ, just as there is a true presence of God by His Spirit in the heart of every believer; and what is imperfectly true of the believer may be held to be perfectly true of Christ. But no matter how entirely the believer is filled with the Divine life, and in this sense is a partaker of the Divine nature, we do not regard this as a reason for worshipping him. We may worship and glorify the God revealed in him, but we do not worship the believer himself. The worship paid to Christ, therefore, and that from the earliest period, marks a distinction between His Divinity and that of every other. Not simply as the possessor of a communicated Divine nature, but in the root of His own Personality, Christ was Divine.

I. I come now to speak of the higher concept of God involved in this truth of the Incarnation—I mean the concept of God as triune. This is the first of the corollaries of the doctrine of the Incarnation, taken in connection with the related doctrine of the Spirit. It must be evident to any one who thinks upon it, that such a doctrine as that of the Incarnation cannot be seriously entertained without profoundly reacting upon and modifying our concept of God. Necessity is laid on us, as it was laid on the early Church, to reconstruct our concept of God so as to bring it into harmony with the new and higher Revelation which has been given us. The result is the Trinitarian view, which Christendom expresses in the formula— Father, Son, and Spirit, one God; and which is as essentially bound up with Christianity as the Incarnation itself.[1]

Here let me say, to begin with, that it is a mistake to shrink from the triune view of God as if it did nothing else than impose a mysterious burden on our faith,—as if it had no voice to reason, or brought no light into our view of the world, or had no practical relation to Christian life. This doctrine has not been gained indeed by speculation, but by induction from the facts of God's self-revelation,—just, e.g., as the man of science gains his knowledge of the polarity of the magnet by induction from the facts of nature. Yet it is not a doctrine which the Church, having once gained it, could ever again willingly part with. Even from a philosophical point of view, the worth of this doctrine is very great. The more profoundly speculation has occupied itself with the mystery of the Divine existence, the more impossible has it been found to rest in the thought of God as an abstract, distinctionless unity, the more has the triune conception of God been felt to be necessary to secure the life, love, personality,—even the Fatherhood of God. Professor Flint says of this doctrine, that it is "a mystery indeed, yet one which explains many other mysteries, and

---

[1] Kaftan says: "Christian faith in God is faith in the three-one God. That is the expression, alike simple and yet all-comprehending, of the Christian truth of faith."—Das Wesen, etc. p. 387. Most modern theologians, as Schleiermacher, Biedermann, Lipsius, Pfleiderer, etc., express themselves similarly, though each has his own interpretation of the Trinitarian formula.

which sheds a marvellous light on God, on nature, and on man."[1]   Professor Laidlaw says of it, "This doctrine is one of the most prolific and far-reaching among the discoveries of Revelation. Fully to receive it influences every part of our theological system, and of our practical religion. It is the consummation and the only perfect protection of Theism."[2] Martensen has declared, "If Christian dogmatics had not asserted and developed the doctrine of the Trinity, ethics must postulate it in its own interests."[3]   Similar testimonies might be multiplied indefinitely.

It is well to keep clearly in view how this doctrine has originated. It has just been said that the doctrine of the Trinity is not a result of mere speculation,—not a theory or hypothesis spun by theologians out of their own fancies,—still less, as some eminent writers would maintain, the result of the importation of Greek metaphysics into Christian theology.[4]   It is, in the first instance, the result of a simple process of induc tion from the facts of the Christian Revelation. We could know nothing positively of this self-distinction in the nature of God save as He Himself discovers it to us in the facts of His self-revelation; we do not know it through the discovery of Himself as Father, Son, and Spirit. We know it just as, *e.g.*, we know of the existence of reason, memory, imagination, will, etc., in our own minds, through their actual manifestations; or as we know of the various modes of force in nature—light, heat, electricity, chemical force, etc.—through observation of their workings. Our faith in the Trinity does not rest even on the proof-texts which are adduced from the Scriptures in support of the Trinitarian distinction.[5]   These have their value as summaries of the truth we gain from the complex of facts of the New Testament Revelation, and serve to assure us that we are on right lines in our interpretation of these facts, but the fundamental ground on which we rest is the facts themselves. The triune conception of God is justified when it is shown to be the conception which underlies the triune Revelation God

---

[1] *Anti-Theistic Theories*, p. 439.
[2] *Bible Doctrine of Man*, p. 126 (Cunningham Lectures).
[3] *Christian Ethics*, i. 75 (Eng. trans.).
[4] Thus Harnack, Hatch, etc.
[5] *E.g.* Matt. xxviii. 19; 2 Cor. xiii. 14; 1 Cor. xii. 4–6; 1 Pet. i. 2; Rev. i. 4, 5.

has given of Himself, and the triune activity in the work of
Redemption.

For this same reason that the doctrine of the Trinity is one
which properly arises only out of the facts of the completed
Revelation in the New Testament, we do not look, or we look in
vain, for any full discovery of it in the Old Testament. Yet,
if the doctrine be true, we would anticipate that the older
dispensation would not be without at least some foregleams or
intimations of it,—that some facts which point in its direction
would not be wanting,—and this we find to be actually the case.
It is only, I think, a very superficial view of the Old Testament
which will allow us to say that no such traces exist. I do not
lay any stress upon the plural word "Elohim," or on the plural
pronouns sometimes associated with it, though this word is an
indication of the deep feeling which the Hebrews had for that
plurality of powers in the Divine nature, which Polytheism
separated, and worshipped in isolation, or under some visible
manifestation (sky, etc.). It is this which constitutes the
Monotheism of the Bible from the first a living thing, and
keeps it from degenerating into a hard, unspiritual monadism.
More to the purpose is the large place allowed in the Old Testament to ideas and representations which naturally and almost
necessarily suggest—if indeed they do not sometimes formally
express—the thought of self-distinction in the Divine nature.
I might refer here (1) to the remarkable series of facts connected
in the older Scriptures with the appearances and Revelations of
the "Angel of Jehovah."[1] Discussion goes on to this day as
to whether the mysterious Being who bears this designation in
the older narratives of the Bible is to be viewed as a mere
theophany, or as a created angel, or as a distinct hypostasis;[2]
but I think a dispassionate review of all the facts will dispose

---

[1] "Angel of God" in Elohistic sections. Cf. Gen. xvi. 7–13, xviii. 20, 26,
xxii. 11–19, xxiv. 7, 40, xxxi. 11–13, xlviii. 15, 16; Ex. iii. 2–6, xiii. 21,
compared with xiv. 19; xxxii. 14 compared with Isa. lxiii. 9; Josh. v. 14, 15;
Zech. i. 12, iii. 1, 2, etc.

[2] Cf. on this subject Oehler's *Theology of Old Testament*, i. pp. 188–196 (Eng.
trans.); Schultz's *Alttest. Theol.* pp. 600–606; Delitzsch's *New Commentary
on Genesis*, on chap. xvi. 7, etc. Delitzsch founds on Gen. xviii. in support of
his view that the Mal'ach was a created angel, but Schultz shows that this was
not so. Schultz holds a mediating view, but says: "There is certainly in the
Angel of God something of what Christian theology seeks to express in the
doctrine of the Logos," p. 606. Delitzsch also holds that "the angelophanies
of God were a prefiguration of His Christophany," ii. p. 21.

us to agree with Oehler that, judged by his manifestations, the
" Mal'ach " is best described as "a self-presentation of Jehovah,
entering into the sphere of the creature, which is one in essence
with Jehovah, and yet again different from Him."[1]   (2) We
have again the very full development given to the doctrine of
the Spirit.   Ordinarily the Spirit appears only as a power or
energy proceeding from Jehovah, but in function and operation
the tendency is to represent Him as an independent agent, and
there are several passages, especially in the later chapters of
Isaiah, where this view receives distinct expression.   Such, *e.g.*,
is Isa. xl. 13, "Who hath directed the Spirit of the Lord, or,
being His counsellor, hath taught Him ?" where, in Oehler's
words, "The Divine Spirit acting in creation is a consciously
working and intelligent power."[2]   Cheyne observes on the
same passage: "In Isaiah there is a marked tendency to
hypostatise the Spirit : here, for instance, consciousness and
intelligence are distinctly predicated of the Spirit."[3]   (3) There
is in the later books the doctrine of the Divine Wisdom, which
in the Jewish and Alexandrian schools developed into the view
of a distinct hypostasis.   Still, whatever the measure of these
approximations, it was not till the actual appearance of the Son
in the flesh, and till the actual outpouring of the Spirit consequent on Christ's exaltation, that the facts were available which
gave this doctrine a distinct place in the faith of the Church.

The doctrine of the Trinity is first of all a doctrine of
distinctions interior to the Divine essence, and as such it has
frequently been objected to on the ground that it asks us

---

[1] *Theology of Old Testament*, i. p. 193.

[2] *Ibid.* p. 172.

[3] On Isa. xlviii. 16, Cheyne remarks : "I cannot but think with Kleinert
(who, however, makes 'His Spirit' the subject) that we have both here and
in Gen. i. 2 an early trace of what is known as the Christian doctrine of the
Holy Spirit"; and on chap. xliii. 10: "There is an evident tendency in this
book to hypostatise the Holy Spirit (which it mentions no less than seven
times) with special distinctness.   The author has already claimed to have been
sent in special union with the Spirit of Jehovah ; he now employs another
phrase which could not have been used (cf. ver. 14) except of a person."
Delitzsch confirms this view, remarking on chap. xlviii. 16 : "Although 'His
Spirit' is taken as a second object, the passage confirms what Cheyne and
Driver agree in remarking, that in II. Isa. the tendency is evidently to regard
the Spirit of God as a separate personality."   Schultz remarks, in speaking
of Creation :—"The Spirit of God and His Word appear as powers enclosed in
God.   The Spirit appears as very independent, in the manner of an hypostasis."
—*Alttest. Theol.* p. 569.   On the doctrine of the Spirit in the Old Testament,
see Schultz, Oehler, and Kleinert in *Jahrbcüher für deutsche Theologie* for 1867
(referred to by Cheyne).

to accept an intellectual puzzle, or to believe in an intellectual contradiction—that three can be one, and one be three. No objection is more common than this, yet none is more baseless — more narrowly the product of the mere logical understanding.[1]   The objection does not turn peculiarly on the point of the attribution of Personality to the three modes of existence in the Godhead—to call them such for the present —but simply on the formal contradiction of "one and three." But what is there to which the same objection would not apply?   What is there which is not at the same time one and manifold?   Take any object—it can only be conceived of as unity of substance, yet plurality of attributes.   Take mind—it is one, if anything is, yet we distinguish in it a variety of powers—reason, memory, imagination, will, etc.—a plurality of faculties, yet all expressions of the one undivided spiritual self.   Take any form of life—what an unfolding into multiplicity have we there of what is in its principle one.   Is it not the very essence of life to unfold and maintain itself in the play of distinctions?   Take a yet higher view, and the same contradiction meets us—if contradiction it is—in any explanation we may give of the ultimate ground of the universe. However we may choose to conceive of it, the many must in some way have come out of the One,—that One, accordingly, must have in it a plurality of powers, must be thought of as capable of expressing, or unfolding, or differentiating itself into a manifold.   This is as true on the pantheistic hypothesis, or on Mr. Spencer's theory of an Unknowable Power, which manifests itself in matter and mind, or on any of the monistic systems,—Haeckel's or Hartmann's, for example,—as in the Christian doctrine.   It will be remembered how this question was one of the difficulties discussed in the early Greek schools, and what came of the attempts of the Eleatics and others to hold fast the unity of the Absolute in contrast to all distinctions.   From the idea of one absolute distinctionless unity, excluding all plurality, all change, all mobility, all decay, came the relegation of the world of perception to the category of mere seeming, show, unreality, non-being—in brief, the denial of the reality of the existing world, or Acosmism.[2]   It

---

[1] Cf. Hegel, *Religionsphilosophie*, ii. pp. 237–239.
[2] Cf. Zeller on the Eleatics, *Pre-Socratic Philosophy*, i. pp. 533–642.

was in the attempt to overcome this difficulty that philosophy from Plato downwards felt the need of a conception - of God which should embrace the element of self-distinction. Hence the Logos speculations of the Stoics and of Philo, the *nous* of the Neo-Platonists. In like manner, self-diremption, self-distinction in God, is the key to all the higher speculative movements of the present century. Whether these speculative views be held to be satisfactory or not, they have at least served to show that the Trinitarian conception, instead of being the shallow thing it is sometimes represented to be, includes elements of the deepest speculative importance.[1]

It is not, therefore, to the mere fact that Christianity posits self-distinctions in God, but to the nature of these distinctions as personal, that the real objections to the doctrine of the Trinity must be addressed. And this is the point on which, within the Church itself, discussion on the nature of the Trinity really turns. What is the character of this distinction which we must ascribe to God, which exhaustively expresses, or does full justice to, the facts of the Christian Revelation ? Is it a distinction of essence, or only of working ? an immanent distinction, or one only of Revelation ? a personal distinction, or one which is impersonal ? Now, in applying this word "Person" to these distinctions in the Godhead, it is granted that we are conscious of inevitable limitations and drawbacks. The objection commonly made to the word is that it represents the Godhead as constituted by three separate individualities, as distinct from each other as human beings are distinct,—a conception which would, of course, be fatal to the Divine unity. This word Person, it is to be observed, does not occur in Scripture itself.[2] It comes to us from the Latin, while the

---

[1] "In philosophy," says Hegel, "it is shown that the whole content of nature, of spirit, gravitates to this centre as its absolute truth."—*Religionsphilosophie*, ii. p. 229.

[2] Calvin on this ground objected to the term. "Specially was he annoyed by the attacks made on him by one Caroli, who impeached his orthodoxy, and even had him brought before a synod to clear himself of the charge of Arianism. It is curious to see Calvin—hard dogmatist as we are apt to think him—called to account for not using the terms 'Trinity' and 'Person' in his teachings on the Godhead, and having to defend himself for his preference for simple scriptural expressions. When blamed by Caroli for not accepting the ancient creeds, he 'rejoined,' say the Genevese preachers (in a letter to Berne), 'that we have sworn to the belief in One God, and not to the creed of Athanasius, whose symbol a true Church would never have admitted.'"—Lecture on "John Calvin" by the author, in volume on *The Reformers* (1885).

Greek Church employed the term ὑπόστασις, or substance ; se
that, as Augustine says, the Greeks spoke of one essence, three
substances, but the Latins of one substance, three Persons,
while yet both meant the same thing.[1]   The same father even
says, "Three Persons, if they are to be so called, for the
unspeakable exaltedness of the object cannot be set forth by
this term," [2] and he reminds us of what I have just stated, that
Scripture does not anywhere mention three Persons.[3]   Too
much stress, therefore, must not be laid on the mere term.
Yet I do not know any word which would so well express
the idea which we wish to convey, and which the titles Father,
Son, and Spirit seem to imply—the existence in the Divine
nature of three mutually related yet distinct centres of knowledge, love, and will, not existing apart as human individualities
do, but in and through each other as moments in one Divine
self-conscious life.

Using the term "Person," therefore, to denote distinctions
in the Divine nature, properly described as I and Thou and
He, without contradiction of the thought of the comprehension
of these distinctions in a higher unity of essence, we certainly
hold that the distinctions in the Christian Trinity are personal.
This is already implied, as just hinted, in the names given to
the members of the Trinitarian circle—Father, Son, and Spirit
—at least the two former are personal, and for that very
reason the third is presumably so also.   But, apart from this,
all those facts and testimonies which go to show that in Christ
we have the Incarnation of a true Divine Person, distinct from
the Father, establish this truth ; while, finally, all the facts
and testimonies which show that the Holy Spirit, sent forth
by Christ as the Guide, Teacher, Comforter, and Sanctifier of
His disciples, is a Divine Person, distinct from the Father and
the Son, support the same view.   I do not enlarge on this
series of testimonies relating to the Spirit, for the reason that
few who admit a real personal distinction in regard to the Son
are disposed to deny it in regard to the Spirit.   It has, indeed,

---

[1] *De Trinitate*, Book vii. chap. iv. (p. 189, trans. in Clark's series).   Cf.
Book v. chap. v. p. 155.
[2] Quoted by Van Oosterzee, *Dogmatics*, p. 289 (Eng. trans.).   Cf. *De Trinitate*, v. 9 : "When the question is asked, What three ? human language labours
altogether under great poverty of speech.   The answer, however, is given, three
persons, not that it might be spoken, but that it might not be left unspoken."
[3] *De Trinitate* Book iv. chap. iv. sec. 8, p. 192 (Eng. trans.).

been said, and with justice, that in regard to the Son the dispute has not been as to His Personality, but as to His Divinity ;
while in regard to the Spirit the dispute has not been as to His
Divinity but as to His Personality. Yet it is a rare thing to
find those who admit the Personality and Divinity of the Son
denying the Personality of the Spirit ; rather it is felt that if
the distinction of Father and Son is admitted there is a necessity for completing the triad in the Divine life by the acknowledgment of the Spirit also. The other view of a merely
modal or economical Trinity—a Trinity, that is, not of essence,
but only of Revelation — has had many advocates both in
ancient and modern times, but falls to the ground if a true
Incarnation of the Son be admitted.[1] It is, besides, loaded
with difficulties and contradictions of its own, which make it,
whenever the matter is thought out, untenable as an hypothesis.
In the old Sabellian view, for example, we had indeed a Divine
Christ, but the distinction between Father and Son was
abolished, because it was the same being who first appeared
as Father, who afterwards appeared as Son. Modern theories
escape this difficulty by ascribing to Christ only an ethical
Sonship—that is, by denying His true Divinity ; but this in
turn deprives us of even a Trinity of Revelation. We have
now God the Father and God the Spirit, but no longer, in the
proper sense, God the Son. The Son is the bearer or medium
of the Revelation of the Father, but does not Himself belong to
the Divine circle. Or suppose that with Rothe and Beyschlag
we seek to save Christ's Divinity by asserting a "becoming"
Godhead, then we involve ourselves in the old dilemma, that
to complete the Trinitarian circle we add a new Person to
the Godhead, and the Trinity is no longer economical. The
only way of clearing ourselves of these entanglements is to
hold fast to the scriptural idea of the true entrance of a Divine

---

[1] Biedermann and Pfleiderer grant that, with the presupposition of the
Personal Incarnation in Christ, the ontological Trinity is inevitable. "The
Trinity," says Biedermann, "is the specific Christian concept of God, as it
must necessarily develop itself out of the identification of the Divine principle
in Christ with the Ego of Jesus Christ."—*Dogmatik*, ii. p. 600. Pfleiderer
says : "When we observe that dogmatic reflection had to work with the
presuppositions set up by the Pauline and Johannine theology, and with the
notions provided in the philosophy of the age, we can scarcely imagine any
other result to have been possible than that embodied in the decrees of the
councils of Nicæa, Constantinople, and Chalcedon."—*Religionsphilosophie*,
iii. p. 218 (Eng. trans.).

Personal Being — the Eternal Son — into the conditions of humanity; and, in accordance with this, to move back from an economical to an ontological and personal Trinity.[1]

The question is now to be considered, How does this doctrine stand related to rational thought and to experience? It may be thought that at the best this doctrine is one to be received as a mystery of faith, that it can bring no light or help to the intellect, and that in point of simplicity and clearness it compares unfavourably with the Unitarian view. This, however, if the doctrine of the Trinity is true, is most unlikely; and I confess to have a great dislike to doctrines which are supposed to come to us in the form of absolute mysteries, and to have no point of contact with thought through which some ray of rational light may break in upon them. In proof that the Trinitarian view is not without relation to thought, I might appeal to the fact that it is to the influence of philosophical thought on Christianity that many would attribute the rise of such a doctrine in the Church at all. It is certainly not without meaning that, as already remarked, in the attempt to explain the Revelation of God to the world, we should see a Logos doctrine springing up in the schools of Alexandria; should find at a later period the Neo-Platonists developing on Platonic principles something like a doctrine of the Trinity; should find in the deep-reaching speculations of Böhme in the seventeenth century,[2] and in the modern speculative philosophies, the self-diremption of God as an essential feature. These speculative constructions are sometimes far enough removed from the pure Christian view, but they have a value as bringing clearly to light the reality of a threefold pulse or movement, involved in the very nature of thought, and the fact that the life of Spirit only maintains itself through this

---

[1] "The anti-trinitarian movements of recent times have made it perfectly clear that there consequently only remains the choice either to think of God in a Unitarian manner, and in that case to see even in Jesus a mere man, or, if He is supposed to be the God-Man, to hold to eternal distinctions in God, and therefore to undertake to prove that the unity of God is quite consistent with such distinctions."—Dorner, *System of Doctrine*, i. p. 415 (Eng. trans.). But has Dr. Dorner himself a truly immanent Trinity? See Note A.—Recent Theories of the Trinity.

[2] Böhme's "mode of imagining, of thinking," says Hegel, "is certainly somewhat fantastic and wild; he has not raised himself into the pure form of thought, but this is the ruling, the ground tendency of his ferment and struggle—to see the Trinity in everything and everywhere."—*Religionsphilo-sophie*, ii. p. 246.

triple movement of distinction of self from other, and the resolution of this distinction in a higher unity. These thoughts of the speculative philosophy I heartily accept, and believe them to be in deepest harmony with Christian doctrine.[1]

The attempts met with in Augustine and others to find an image of the Trinity in the constitution of the soul, need not detain us here. Augustine's ingenious analysis of the mind's relation to its own knowledge, and of both to its love of itself, —of the relations of memory, understanding, and will,—his comparison of the Divine Word to our own inner and mental word, and of the Holy Spirit to love, — have profounder elements in them than is always recognised ; but he himself is quite conscious of the imperfection of the analogies, and especially of the fact that what they give us is a Trinity of powers and functions in the one Person, and not a Trinity of personal distinctions.[2] If I were disposed to look for a shadow of such distinctions in our own mental life, I am not sure but that I would seek it, as Augustine also hints, in that mysterious power which the soul has of dialogue with itself,—in that indrawn, ideal life of the spirit, when the mind, excluding the outward world, holds converse and argument with itself— divides itself as it were within itself, and holds discussion with itself, putting its questions and answering them, proposing difficulties and solving them, offering objections and repelling them,—all the while remaining, as we may say, in a third

---

[1] "No wonder," says Christlieb, "that philosophy too—and that not only the old mystic theosophical speculation, but also modern idealism, with all the acuteness of its dialectics—has taken up the idea of a Triune God, and endeavoured to comprehend and prove it. . . . Their efforts show us that modern philosophy (from Jacob Böhme onwards) feels that this doctrine is the true solution of the world's enigma. Moreover, these philosophical investigations cast a strong light on the unconscionable superficiality and shortsightedness of those who most reject this fundamental doctrine of the Christian faith untested, without a notion of its deep religious, philosophical, and historical importance."—*Moderne Zweifel*, pp. 273, 274 (Eng. trans.). See Note A.— As above.

[2] Augustine is constantly acknowledging the imperfection of finite analogies to express the ineffable reality of the Godhead. See specially Book xv. The following are some of the headings of chapters : "That it is not easy to discover the Trinity that is God from the trinities we have spoken of." "There is the greatest possible unlikeness between our word and knowledge and the Divine Word and knowledge." "Still further of the difference between the knowledge and word of our mind, and the knowledge and Word of God." "How great is the unlikeness between our word and the Divine Word ! Our word cannot be, or be called, eternal," etc. "We know but in an enigma," and "Who can explain how great is the unlikeness also, in this glass, in this enigma, in this likeness, such as it is ?"—*De Trinitate*, p. 402 (Eng. trans.).

capacity the neutral spectator of itself, taking watchful note of
what is advanced on both sides of the debate, and passing
favourable or unfavourable judgment on the issues. Yet, after
all, this trilogy is only shadow, and, in conjunction with other
elements of our spiritual life, can but faintly suggest to us
what, if the distinction went deeper, Trinity might mean.

We get more help when, leaving the ground of purely
psychological analogies, we proceed to inquire into the conditions under which, so far as our thought can go, self-consciousness, personality, love, are possible. Here we begin to
see the positive philosophical and theological value of this concept of God. There are several points of view from which its
advantage over the Unitarian view of God becomes apparent.

1. First of all, there is the bearing of this doctrine on the
Divine self-consciousness—on knowledge and Personality in
God. The relation of knowledge seems necessarily to imply a
distinction of subject and object. Philosophers have spoken of
a transcendental kind of knowledge which is above this distinction,—in which subject and object melt into one. But
their words convey no idea to the mind. The only kind of
knowledge we are capable of conceiving is one in which the
subject distinguishes himself from some object which is not
himself, and through this distinction returns to knowledge
of himself and of his own states. In our own case, this
knowledge of self is mediated through knowledge of the
outward world, and in the highest degree through intercourse
with our fellow human beings. Seizing on this analogy,
some have thought that the Divine consciousness might be
conceived of as mediated by the idea of the world.[1] The
idea of the world in this view takes the place of the Son
in the orthodox theology. The objections to this are—

(1) It makes God dependent on the world, the idea of which
is necessary for the realisation of His self-consciousness.

(2) The object in this case is an ideal one, and this seems
inadequate to mediate a real self-consciousness. Hegel is
consistent, accordingly, if this theory is to be adopted, in
making not the idea of the world, but the world itself, the
object through which the Divine Spirit attains to self-consciousness.

---

[1] Thus, *e.g.*, Weisse.

(3) The world is a finite object, and cannot be an adequate means for the mediation of an infinite self-consciousness.[1]

(4) Finally, the world is not a personal object. But the true depths of personality are only sounded when the "I" knows itself in contradistinction from and in reciprocal relations with a "Thou"—a counter-self to its own.[2]

The result we reach by this line of thought is that we can only secure the reality of the Divine self-consciousness by regarding it as complete in itself—apart from the idea of the world ; and this can only be done by positing an *immanent* distinction in the Godhead, through which the Divine consciousness carries its object within itself ; and this neither an ideal, nor finite, nor impersonal object, but One in whom God sees His own personal image perfectly expressed,—who, in Scripture language, is "the effulgence of His glory, and the very image of His substance" ($\dot{v}\pi\acute{o}\sigma\tau\alpha\sigma\iota s$).[3] The value of the doctrine of the Trinity from this point of view is very evident. The third moment—that which corresponds to the Holy Spirit—is more difficult to arrive at *à priori*, but one feels the need of it to complete the circle of the Divine life in bringing to light the unity which underlies the previous distinction.[4]

2. A more familiar deduction is that from Divine love. Here, in realising what is involved in Divine love, we feel, quite as strongly as in the case of the Divine Personality, the need of self-distinction. The proof of the Trinity from love— if proof it can be called—is a favourite one with theologians.[5]

---

[1] It is besides only progressively realised, and thus would involve a *growing* self-consciousness.

[2] This objection is not obviated by assuming a world of finite personalities.

[3] Heb. i. 3. Pfleiderer supposes that the Divine self-consciousness is mediated by God's own thoughts ("His changing activities and states")—but thoughts of what ?—*Religionsphilosophie*, iii. p. 282 (Eng. trans.).

[4] Cf. on this argument Dorner, *System of Doctrine*, pp. 422–426 ; Christlieb, *Moderne Zweifel*, pp. 271, 272 (Eng. trans.), etc. Hegel makes it the starting-point of his deduction. "Knowing implies that there is another which is known ; and in the act of knowing, the other is appropriated. Herein it is contained that God, the eternally in-and-for-Himself existing One, eternally begets Himself as His Son, distinguishes Himself from Himself—the absolute act of judgment."—*Religionsphilosophie*, ii. p. 228.

[5] It is developed specially by Sartorius in his *Doctrine of Divine Love* (translated). See also Martensen's *Christian Ethics*, i. p. 73 ; Christlieb's *Moderne Zweifel*, pp. 272, 273 (Eng. trans.) ; Laidlaw's *Bible Doctrine of Man*, pp. 126, 127 ; Murphy's *Scientific Basis of Faith*, p. 377 ; *Lux Mundi*, p. 92, etc.

"God is love."[1]   But love is self-communication to another.
There cannot be love without an object to be loved.   If,
therefore, God is essentially love, this is in other words to
say that He has from eternity an object of His love.   This
object cannot be the world—ideally or really—for the reason
already given, that this would be to make God dependent on
the world,—to make the world, indeed, an essential moment
in God's life,—whereas the true doctrine is that God has love
in its fulness in Himself, and out of that fulness of love, loves
the world.[2]   The world, besides, is a finite object, and could
not be an adequate object for the infinite love of God.   If,
therefore, God is love in Himself—in His own eternal and
transcendent being—He must have in some way within
Himself the perfect and eternal object of His love—which is
just the Scripture doctrine of the Son.   This view of God is
completed in the perfect communion the Divine Persons have
with each other through the Holy Spirit—the bond and
medium of their love.

   To see the importance of this view, we have but to contrast
it with its opposite, and to ask, What can love in God mean
on the supposition of His absolute solitariness?   What can
be the object of God's love throughout eternity, if there is no
triune distinction in God?   What can it be but Himself?
Instead of love, therefore, as we understand it,—affection
going out to another,—what we have in the universe is an
infinite solitary Ego; a Being who loves Himself only, as,
indeed, there is no other to love.   Either, therefore, we must
come back to seek an object for God's love in the finite,
created world, or recognise that God has an infinitely blessed
life of love within Himself, and this brings us to the doctrine
of an immanent Trinity.   The value of the doctrine in an
ethical aspect is seen when we recognise that only through

----

[1] 1 John iv. 16.

[2] This is an important point in the doctrine of Divine Love.   The thought is
already met with in Irenæus.   Cf. Dorner, *Person of Christ*, i. p. 306.
Martensen says : "God's love to the world is only then pure and unmixed
holy affection when God, whilst He is sufficient to Himself and in need of
nothing, out of infinite grace and mercy calls forth life and liberty beyond
His own Being. . . . But this free power of love in the relations of God
to the world presupposes the existence of perfect love realised within
itself, the love of the Father and the Son in the unity of the Holy Spirit."—
Christian Ethics, i. p. 74.   Similarly Dorner in his *Christian Ethics*, p. 94
(Eng. trans.).

the Trinitarian distinction are we brought into communion with a Being who has within Himself a life of communion.

3. Connected with this as a third point of view—though it is really only an extension of the foregoing—is a deduction from the Divine Fatherhood. God is Father. This is Christ's own new name for Him, and expresses His relation to those who stand in moral dependence on Him, and who bear His image. But Father and Son are terms of relation.[1] If, then, God be Father, where shall we find the Son who corresponds with this relation? If we say, men, created angels, creatures of any kind, we are led to this, that Fatherhood in God depended on there being a creation. God is not Father simply as God. Fatherhood is not of His very essence. This could not easily be better put than it has been by Mr. R. H. Hutton, in a well-known essay on the Incarnation in his volume of *Theological Essays*. "If Christ is the eternal Son of God," he says, "God is indeed and in essence a Father; the social nature, the spring of love, is of the very essence of the Eternal Being; the communication of His life, the reciprocation of His affection, dates from beyond time— belongs, in other words, to the very being of God. . . . The Unitarian conviction that God is—as God and in His eternal essence—a single, solitary Personality . . . thoroughly realised, renders it impossible to identify any of the social attributes with His real essence—renders it difficult not to regard power as the true root of all other Divine life. If we are to believe that *the Father* was from all time, we must believe that He was *as a Father*,—that is, that love was actual in Him as well as potential, that the communication of life and thought and fulness of joy was of the inmost nature of God, and never began to be, if God never began to be."[2]

4. Finally, this doctrine of the Trinity has a profound bearing on the relation of God to the world. Not without reason does Scripture connect the Son with the creation, and give His person and His work a cosmical significance. We may conceive of God in two relations to the world—either in

---

[1] This is the mistake of those who, in a Sabellian way, take Father as the name for God as the Creator, etc. The Christian idea of the Father comes to birth only in the Revelation of the Son. The terms are reciprocal. See Note A.

[2] *Theological Essays*, 3rd ed. p. 257.

His absolute transcendence over it, which is the deistic conception, or as immanently identified with it, which is the pantheistic conception. Or we may conceive of Him as at the same time exalted above the world—transcending it, and yet present in it as its immanent sustaining ground, which is the Christian conception. It was to maintain this double relation to the world that, as we have seen, Philo conceived of the Logos as a middle term between God and the creation, and the Neo-Platonists distinguished between God, the νοῦς, and the soul of the world. When a middle term is wanting, we have either, as in the later Judaism and Mohammedanism, an abstract and immobile Monotheism; or, in recoil from this, a losing of God in the world in Pantheism. In the Christian doctrine of the triune God we have the necessary safeguards against both of these errors, and at the same time the link between God and the world supplied which speculation vainly strove to find.[1] The Christian view is, therefore, the true protection of a living Theism, which otherwise oscillates uncertainly between these two extremes of Deism and Pantheism, either of which is fatal to it.[2]

II. It is a special service of the doctrine of the Trinity, from the point of view we have now reached, that it brings creation and Redemption into line, teaching us to look on creation and Redemption as parts of one grand whole, and on Christ, now exalted to supreme dominion in the universe, as at once the first-born of creation and the first-born from the dead.[3] This thought of the Son as the link between God and creation— which is so prominent a thought in the New Testament—forms the transition to the other subject on which I propose to speak in this Lecture—the relation of the Incarnation to the plan of

---

[1] This important aspect of the Trinity, as safeguarding the true idea of God in relation to the world (His immanence and transcendence) against the opposite errors of Deism and Pantheism, is brought out with special fulness by Dorner in his discussion of Sabellianism and Arianism, *Person of Christ*, i. and ii., and his *System of Doctrine*, i. pp. 365–378. Cf. also Martensen's *Dogmatics*, pp. 103–106; Christlieb's *Moderne Zweifel*, pp. 263–265; *Lux Mundi*, pp. 92–102, etc.

[2] A remarkable illustration of how the deeper thought on God runs almost necessarily into a Trinitarian mould, is furnished by an essay of Dr. Martineau's on "A Way out of the Trinitarian Controversy," in his recently published volume of *Essays, Ecclesiastical and Historical*. See Note B.—Dr. Martineau as a Trinitarian.

[3] Col. i. 15–18.

the world. The Revelation of the Trinity is given in the work of Redemption, but once given we can see that it has its bearings also on the work of creation. This is the view of all the leading writers in the New Testament,—of Paul, of John, of the author of the Epistle to the Hebrews,—who go back, or reason back, to an original agency of the Son in the creation of the world.[1] Even the Apocalypse speaks of Christ as "the beginning ($\dot{a}\rho\chi\dot{\eta}$, or principle) of the creation of God."[2] But once started on this line, it is impossible to shut one's eyes to the question which inevitably arises, and which has so frequently been discussed in the history of theology—more keenly than ever in modern theology—Did an Incarnation lie in the original plan of the world? Would there have been an Incarnation had man never fallen? Has the Incarnation any relation to the original ends for which the world was made? Or is the Incarnation connected solely with the entrance of sin and the need of Redemption?

To raise a question of this kind at all may be thought by many to savour of idle and presumptuous speculation. It may be thought that it is one which the Scripture directly and expressly settles in the negative, in connecting the Incarnation so intimately as it does with God's great purpose of salvation to our race—making it, indeed, the crowning proof of His love to sinners that He has sent His only-begotten Son into the world, that the world might live through Him.[3] There are, however, certain considerations which should give us pause before coming too hastily to this conclusion.

1. The first is that this is a question which does rise naturally out of so transcendent a fact as the Incarnation.

2. It is a question which has forced itself on the mind of the Church, and has been deeply and reverently discussed by its ablest thinkers for centuries. It is a view which the late Principal Fairbairn, who reasons against it, admits undoubtedly to include among its defenders "some of the most learned theologians of the present day."[4]

3. But, mainly, the theory referred to is one not unsuggested by certain of the teachings of Scripture. The same objection

---

[1] John i. 3 ; 1 Cor. viii. 6 ; Eph. iii. 9–11 ; Col. i. 15–18 ; Heb. i. 2.
[2] Rev. iii. 14.   [3] 1 John iv. 9.
[4] *Typology of Scripture*, 4th ed. i. p. 118.

which is taken to this—that it lies outside the field of view of Redemption—may be made against the Scripture statements as to the relation of the Son to creation ; but it is the grandeur of the Christian view that, starting with our primary necessities as sinners, it opens up principles and views fertile and far-reaching vastly beyond their original application.

It is unnecessary for my purpose to enter at any length into the history of the question. A sketch of it may be seen in Dorner's *History of the Doctrine of the Person of Jesus Christ*,[1] or in the finely-toned essay on the subject, entitled " The Gospel of Creation," appended to Bishop Westcott's *Commentary on the Epistles of St. John*. These writers, with Archbishop Trench, in his *Cambridge University Sermons*, take the view that the Incarnation was not conditioned by human sin ; and the same view is held by Rothe, Lange, Oosterzee, Martensen, Ebrard, and a large number of other theologians. The opposite view is stated with great temperateness and force by Principal Fairbairn in the *fourth* edition of his valuable work on the *Typology of Scripture*.[2] It may perhaps be found as the result of a brief consideration of the subject, that the truth does not lie exclusively on either side in this profound and difficult controversy, but that a higher point of view is possible from which the opposition disappears.

The strong point in favour of the view that the Incarnation is conditioned solely by human sin, is the fact that in Scripture it is represented invariably in this connection. I need not quote many passages in illustration of this statement. " The Son of Man came to seek and to save that which was lost."[3] " God so loved the world that He gave His only-begotten Son, that whosoever believeth in Him should not perish, but have eternal life."[4] " God sent forth His Son, born of a woman, born under the law, that He might redeem them which were under the law, that we might receive the adoption of sons."[5] " To this end was the Son of God manifested, that He might destroy the works of the devil."[6] These and numerous other Scriptures explicitly associate Christ's coming with man's Redemption

---

[1] *Person of Christ*, iii. pp. 361–369. This view was already involved in the theology of Irenæus. See Dorner, i. p. 316 ; and Article " Irenæus," in *Dictionary of Christian Biography*.
[2] Vol. i. pp. 117–135.   [3] Luke xix. 10.   [4] John iii. 16.
[5] Gal. iv. 4 (R.V.).   [6] 1 John iii. 8.

Christ is the unspeakable gift of God's love to men for their salvation.

On the other hand, it is argued that, while the Scripture thus directly connects the Incarnation with the work of Redemption, it leaves room for, and contains passages which necessarily suggest, a wider view. Such are the passages already referred to, which throw light on the original relation of the Son to creation—which declare that all things were made by Him, that all things consist or hold together in Him, that He is the first-born of all creation—above all, that all things were created for Him—that, in the language of Dr. Lightfoot, "the Word is the final cause as well as the creative agent of the universe"—"not only the ἀρχή but also the τέλος of creation, not only the first but also the last in the history of the universe."[1] These passages I shall advert to again. It is further argued—and this is a point on which great stress is laid—that an event of such tremendous magnitude as the Incarnation cannot be regarded as a mere contingency in the universe; that if it was in view at all, it must have governed the whole plan of creation; and that, in point of fact, it is through it that, according to Scripture, the creation *does* reach its end—not only redeemed humanity, but all things, both in heaven and in earth, being ultimately gathered up into Christ as Head.[2] A plan of such vast extent cannot, it is held, be conceived of as an afterthought,—as something grafted on creation outside its original design,—it must have lain in the original design itself.

It seems to me that the real source of difficulty in thinking on this subject lies in not grasping with sufficient firmness the fact that, however we may distinguish from our human point of view between parts and aspects of the Divine plan, God's plan is in reality one, and it is but an abstract way of thinking which leads us to suppose otherwise. In our human way of apprehension, we speak as if God had first one plan of creation —complete and rounded off in itself—in which sin was to have no place; then, when it was foreseen that sin would enter, another plan was introduced, which vitally altered and enlarged the former. But if we take a sufficiently high point of view, we shall be compelled to conclude, I think, that the plan of the universe is one, and that, however harsh the expression may

---

[1] On Col. i. 16. [2] Eph. i. 10.

sound, the foresight and permission of sin were from the first included in it. An ultra-Calvinist would speak of the fore-ordination of sin; I take lower ground, and speak only of the foresight and permission of sin. Dealing with the question on the largest scale, I do not see how either Calvinist or Arminian can get away from this. It is not a question of how sin historically or empirically eventuated,—that we agree it must have done through human freedom,—but it is the question of fact, that sin is here, and that in the Divine plan it has been permitted to exist—that it has been taken up by God into His plan of the world. His plan included the permission of sin, and the treatment of it by Redemption. In a previous Lecture I referred to the view held by some, that nature, even before the Fall, had a prophetic reference to man's sin, and that in this way is to be explained much that is otherwise mysterious and perplexing in its arrangements. We have only to enlarge our range of vision to see that this way of looking at the sub-ject applies to the whole plan of God. It is idle to speculate whether, had there been no sin, the plan of the universe would have included an Incarnation or not. Had this been different, everything else would have been different also. What we do know is, in that the infinite possibilities of things, God has chosen to create a universe into which it was foreseen that sin would enter ; and the Incarnation is a part of the plan of such a creation. This being so, it may very well be conceived that the Incarnation was the pivot on which everything else in this plan of creation was made to turn. To state my view in a sentence—God's plan is one ; Christ was the Lamb slain from the foundation of the world ;[1] and even creation itself is built up on Redemption lines.

We must, I think, on this question allow great weight to the consideration of the revealed end. The Scriptures speak of an ultimate gathering together in one of all things in Christ—of a summing up of them in Him as Head.[2] It is then to be asked, Is this only the external unification of a universe not originally intended to be so unified, but in regard to which God's original plan was something entirely different? Or did it not lie in its

---

[1] Rev. xiii. 8. Cf. the interesting remarks in Hugh Miller's *Footprints of the Creator*, 23rd ed. p. 289 (1887)

[2] Eph. i. 10.

original destination? The end of a thing, we are to remember, is that which in the Divine plan determines the beginning of it. What a thing is to be it is fitted for being by its original make. To turn it from that end, and superinduce another upon it, would be to some extent to contradict its true nature. If this is so in general, must it not be so in the highest degree when the end we speak of is the end of the universe, and the plan in question is that of gathering together in one all things in the Incarnate Son. If such a destination did not lie in the original plan of creation, was it in the nature of things possible that it could afterwards be externally superinduced upon it? Then what, in this view, becomes of the statement that all things were made for Christ, as well as by Him?[1] Can it be received at all, for such words go deeper than a mere economical adaptation? The longer these questions are pondered, the clearer will it appear that Christ's relation to the universe cannot be thought of as something adventitious and contingent; it is vital and organic. This means that His Incarnation had a relation to the whole plan of the world, and not simply to sin.

Dr. Fairbairn himself really admits all that is here contended for, when he says, "The argument derived from the wonderful relationship, the personal and everlasting union into which humanity has been brought with the Godhead, as if the purpose concerning it should be turned into a kind of afterthought, and it should sink, in a manner derogatory to its high and unspeakably important nature, into something arbitrary and contingent, if placed in connection merely with the Fall;—such an argument derives all its plausibility from the limitations and defects inseparable from a human mode of contemplation. To the eye of Him who sees the end from the beginning,—whose purpose, embracing the whole compass of the providential plan, was formed before even the beginning was effected,—there could be nothing really contingent or uncertain in any part of the process."[2] That is to say, the Incarnation is not to be placed in connection merely with the Fall; but the plan even of creation had from the first a reference to an Incarnation for the sake of Redemption from sin, and the perfecting of humanity.

When, from this point of view, we look back to the

---

[1] Col. i. 16.   [2] *Typology of Scripture*, 4th ed. i. p. 133.

Scriptures, we find them in full harmony with the ideas now indicated.

1. The Scriptures know of only one undivided purpose of God,—that eternal purpose which He purposed in Christ Jesus, and which embraces, apparently, both creation and Redemption.[1]

2. We have the clearest acknowledgment, as has already been shown, of a direct relation of the Son to the work of creation.[2] It does not detract from the suggestiveness of the passages which declare this relation, but immensely adds to it, that, as Dr. Fairbairn says, the subject of the assertions is the historical Christ, He by whom believers have obtained Redemption, and in whom they have forgiveness of sins. For the drift of the passages is evidently to bring these two things more completely into line—the work of creation and the work of Redemption, and to show them to be parts of one Divine plan.

3. Still more significant is the fact already insisted on, that, in some of the above passages, Christ is not only represented as the agent in creation, but as the final cause of creation. "All things have been created through Him, and *unto* Him."[3] He is the Alpha and Omega, the First and the Last.[4] Indirectly suggestive of the same idea are the passages which speak of "the kingdom prepared for (believers) from the foundation of the world";[5] of "the Lamb slain from the foundation of the world";[6] of Christ as "foreknown indeed before the foundation of the world," etc.[7]

4. There are the express statements, also ·already quoted, of the goal to which God's purpose actually tends. I may here again avail myself of the words of Bishop Lightfoot, commenting on the phrase "unto Him."[8] "All things," he says, "must find their meeting-point, their reconciliation, at length in Him from whom they took their rise—in the Word

---

[1] Cf. Weiss, *Biblical Theology of New Testament*, ii. pp. 97–100 (Eng. trans.). On Eph. iii. 9 he says : "If it is said that the mystery of salvation was hid from eternity in God, who created the universe, it is indicated by this characteristic of God, that the purpose of salvation is connected in the closest way with the plan of the world, which began to be realised in creation ; and that purpose, having been formed by the Creator before the creation of the world, was regulative even in its creation."

[2] John i. 3 ; 1 Cor. viii. 6 ; Col. i. 15–18 ; Heb. i. 3.

[3] Col. i. 16.   [4] Rev. i. 8, 17.   [5] Matt. xxv. 34.

[6] Rev. xiii. 8.   [7] 1 Pet. i. 20 (R.V.).   [8] Col. i. 16.

as mediatorial agent, and through the Word in the Father as the primary source. . . . This ultimate goal of the present dispensation in time is similarly stated in several passages. Sometimes it is represented as the birth-throe and deliverance of all creation through Christ—as Rom. viii. 19, sq. Sometimes it is the absolute and final subjection of universal nature to Him — as 1 Cor. xv. 28. Sometimes it is the reconciliation of all things through Him—as below, ver. 20. Sometimes it is the recapitulation, the gathering up in one head, of the universe in Him—as Eph. i. 10. The image involved in this last passage best illustrates the particular expression in the text; but all alike enunciate the same truth in different terms. The Eternal Word is the goal of the universe, as He was the starting-point. It must end in unity, as it proceeded from unity; and the centre of this unity is Christ."

The conclusion I reach is that this question, Would there have been an Incarnation but for sin? is one which rests upon a false abstraction. There is but one plan of God from the creation of the world, and it includes at once the permission of sin and the purpose of Redemption from it. It includes, therefore, the Incarnation as an integral and essential part of that purpose. The Incarnation has, indeed, immediate reference to Redemption; but it has at the same time a wider scope. It aims at carrying through the plan of creation, and conducts, not the redeemed portion of humanity alone, but the universe at large, to its goal. There is, however, another inference which we are entitled to draw—one which remarkably illustrates the unity of the Christian view. If we rightly interpret that view as implying that the Divine plan of the world contemplates an ultimate gathering up of all things into one in Christ, it will readily be seen that this, in turn, reflects back light on the doctrine of Christ's Person. It shows that we are right in ascribing to Him full and proper Divinity, not less than true humanity. For it is manifest that no other than a truly Divine Being is fitted to occupy this position which Scripture, with consentient voice, assigns to Christ. From the new height we have reached, light falls back also on Christ's place in the universe, in remarkable agreement with our previous postulates as to the nature of man, his place in creation, and the law of ascent and development to which God's natural works so strikingly testify. As the inferior stages of existence are summed up in man, who stands at the head of the earthly creation, and forms a first link between the natural and the spiritual, so are all stages of humanity summed up in Christ, who in His Person as God-man links the creation absolutely with God.

8
THE INCARNATION AND REDEMPTION FROM SIN

"In whom we have our Redemption through His blood, the forgiveness of our trespasses, according to the riches of His grace." —Paul

"The faith of the Atonement presupposes the faith of the Incarnation. It may be also said historically that the faith of the Incarnation has usually had conjoined with it the faith of the Atonement. The great question which has divided men as to these fundamental doctrines of the faith has been the relation in which they stand to each other—which was to be regarded as primary, which secondary? Was an Atonement the great necessity in reference to man's salvation, out of which the necessity for an Incarnation arose, because a Divine Saviour alone could make an adequate Atonement for sin?—or, is the Incarnation to be regarded as the primary and highest fact in the history of God's relation to man, in the light of which God's interest in man and purpose for man can alone be truly seen?—and is the Atonement to be contemplated as taking place in order to the fulfilment of the Divine purpose for man which the Incarnation reveals?" —J. M'Leod Campbell

"Fourier's void,
And Comte absurd, and Cabet puerile,
Subsist no rules of life outside of life,
No perfect manners without Christian souls;
The Christ Himself had been no Lawgiver
Unless He had given the Life, too, with the Law."
Mrs. Browning

8

THE INCARNATION AND REDEMPTION FROM SIN

WHATEVER we may think of the Incarnation in its wider relations to the plan of the world and the ends of creation as a whole, it remains the fact that in Scripture it is always brought into immediate connection with sin, and with the purpose of God in Redemption. "He was manifested to take away sins," says John, "and in Him was no sin";[1] and so say all the writers in the New Testament. Christianity is thus distinctively a religion of Redemption, — a great Divine economy for the recovery of men from the guilt and power of sin—from a state of estrangement and hostility to God—to a state of holiness and blessedness in the favour of God, and of fitness for the attainment of their true destination. It is in this light we are to consider it in the present Lecture.

We may, therefore, set aside at once as alien to the true Christian view, or at least as inadequate and defective, all such representations of Christianity as see in its Founder only a great religious teacher and preacher of righteousness; or a great religious and social reformer, such as has often appeared in the history of the world; or a great philanthropist, caring for the bodies and souls of men; or one whose main business it was to inoculate men with a new "enthusiasm for humanity";[2] or a teacher with a new ethical secret to impart to mankind; or even such representations as see in Him only a new spiritual Head of humanity, whose work it is to complete the old creation, and lift the race to a higher platform of spiritual attainment, or help it a stage further onwards to the goal of its perfection. Christ is all this, but He is infinitely more. God's end in His creation indeed stands, as also His purpose to realise it; but, under the

---

[1] 1 John iii. 5 (R.V.).   [2] *Ecce Homo*, chap. 17.

conditions in which humanity exists, that end can only be
realised through a Redemption, and it is this Redemption
which Christ pre-eminently came into the world to affect.

A comparison has sometimes been instituted in this respect
between Christianity and Buddhism, which also is in some
sort a religion of Redemption.   But the comparison only
brings out the more conspicuously the unique and original
character of the Christian system.   For whereas Buddhism
starts from the conception of the inherent evil and misery of
existence, and the Redemption which it promises as the result
of indefinitely prolonged striving through many successive lives
is the eternal rest and peace of non-being; the Christian view,
on the other hand, starts from the conception that everything
in its original nature and in the intent of its Creator is good,
and that the evil of the world is the result of wrong and
perverted development,—holds, therefore, that Redemption
from it is possible by the use of appropriate means.   And
Redemption here includes, not merely deliverance from existing
evils, but restoration of the Divine likeness which has been lost
by man, and the ultimate blessedness of the life everlasting.[1]

The chief point on which the discussion in this subject
turns is the connection of Redemption with the Person and
work of Christ.   Here at the outset it is necessary to guard
against too narrow an idea of Redemption, as if the saving
work of Christ were limited to that doing and suffering which
we call the Atonement.   The ends of Christ's coming into
the world include much more than the making atonement for
sin.   This is recognised when the Church names three offices
which Christ executes as our Redeemer—a prophetic and a
kingly as well as a priestly office.   Yet it is principally on
the question of Atonement, or the manner of the connection
of Redemption with the doing and suffering of Christ, that
discussion has been directed, and it is to this subject I shall
specially address myself.[2]

---

[1] "In Buddhism Redemption comes from below ; in Christianity it is from
above : in Buddhism it comes from man ; in Christianity it comes from God."
—Carpenter, *Permanent Elements of Religion*, Introduction, p. 34.

[2] To prevent ambiguity, it is desirable that I should refer here for a moment
to the meaning of this word "atonement."   It is the equivalent of the New
Testament word καταλλαγή, which is always translated in the Revised Version
"reconciliation," and of the German words "Versöhnung" and "Sühnung."
It is therefore capable of a wider and of a more special sense.   In both cases it

I. It needs no proof that all the New Testament writers who refer to the subject regard the forgiveness of sins and the salvation of men as connected in quite a peculiar way with the death of Christ; and it is not less evident that they do this because they ascribe to Christ's death a sacrificial and expiatory value. They do this further, as every one must feel, not in a mere poetic and figurative way, but with the most intense conviction that they have really been redeemed and reconciled to God by the death of Christ upon the cross. The *how* of this redemptive transaction most of them may not enter into, but Paul, at least, has a theology on this subject, with the main outlines of which the others, judging from the expressions they use, and the propitiatory virtue they ascribe to the shedding of Christ's blood, must be held to agree.[1] Happily we are freed from the necessity of dwelling long on the apostolic testimony on this subject, for the same reason which I gave when speaking of the Person of Christ—namely, that impartial exegesis and Biblical theology practically grant to us all that we assert. Apart from such occasional speculations as, *e.g.*, Holsten's, that, in Paul's view, sin is identical with the body or "flesh" of Christ, and that the slaying of Christ's body or flesh denotes the slaying of sin,[2] it will be found that the descriptions given of the teaching of the Epistles as to the work of Redemption do not differ much from those met with in our ordinary books of theology. The accounts given us, *e.g.*, by Baur or Reuss or Pfleiderer, or even by Martineau[3]—not to speak of an exegete like Meyer,

refers to the "reconciliation" or "making-at-one" of mankind and God, and in New Testament usage implies that this reconciliation is effected through expiation or propitiation. But in the one case it denotes the actual state of reconciliation with God into which believers are introduced through Christ, whose work is then regarded as the means to this end; whereas in the other it denotes the reconciling act itself—mankind being viewed as objectively reconciled to God in the work or death of His Son, which is the sense the term ordinarily bears when we speak of the Atonement. Dr. Hodge would discard this term altogether because of its ambiguity, and substitute for the latter meaning of it the term "satisfaction."—*Systematic Theology*, ii. p. 469. But "satisfaction" is too narrow and exclusively forensic a term to express all that is implied in the reconciling act.

[1] The passages may be seen classified in Dale on *The Atonement*, or in Professor Crawford's *Doctrine of Holy Scripture respecting the Atonement*.

[2] Cf. Weiss, *Biblical Theology of the New Testament*, i. p. 422 (Eng. trans.).

[3] Cf. *Seat of Authority*, pp. 478, 479. Baur's views may be seen in his *Paulus*, pp. 537–547; those of Reuss in his *Hist. of Christ. Theol. in the Apost. Age*, ii. pp. 68–74 (Eng. trans.); those of Lipsius in his *Dogmatik*, p. 498; those of Pfleiderer in his *Urchristenthum*, pp. 222–242.

or a Biblical theologian like Weiss—of the doctrine of Paul
on Redemption, is what, with very slight exception, any of
us could accept. The same is true of the other New Testament witnesses—of the Epistle to the Hebrews, of Peter, of
Revelation, of the Epistles of John. With differences of
standpoint and strong individual characteristics, it is acknowledged that they teach a fundamentally identical doctrine of
Redemption from the guilt and power of sin through Christ,
and particularly that they ascribe to His death a sacrificial
or propitiatory virtue. To get rid of the attribution of this
view to the author of the Fourth Gospel, Dr. Martineau has
to assume, in face of all probability and evidence, that the
First Epistle of John is not by the same author as the
Gospel.[1]

More important is the question which the newer forms of
controversy press upon us—Whether Christ's doctrine on this
subject is the same as that of His apostles? We have a
theology of propitiation in the Epistles—that is admitted;
but have we anything of the same kind in Christ's own
words? Was not the gospel preached in Galilee a much
simpler thing than the theological gospel preached by Paul,
or contained in the Epistle to the Hebrews, and is it not free
from every trace of this cumbrous machinery of Atonement, or
of pardon on the ground of the suffering and death of another?
Where, it is asked, is there any vestige of this doctrine in the
Sermon on the Mount, or in the parable of the Prodigal Son?
Is this doctrine not an aftergrowth, the result of the running
of the Divine thoughts of the Master, and of the impression
produced by His life and death, into the moulds of Jewish
sacrificial conceptions which had no real affinity with them,
and have indeed served to overlay and obscure them to the
apprehension of all subsequent generations?

If the case were as this objection represents it, I grant that
it would have very serious consequences for our faith. If the
apostles of Christ—the very persons chosen by Him to com-
municate His doctrine to the world, and to whom He promised
the illumination of His Spirit for this very end—could so
seriously misunderstand and pervert His doctrine on this
essential point, I do not know what credit we should be able

---

[1] *Seat of Authority*, p. 509.

to attach to them on any point on which they profess to represent the mind of Christ. Dr. Dale has argued this point so strongly in his book on the Atonement,[1] that I do not need to do more than refer to it. It is not for us, it is for the objector to explain how the guides and leaders of the apostolic Church should come with this singular unanimity to shift the centre of gravity in Christ's gospel from where He Himself had placed it, and so to mislead the world as to the essentials of their Master's teaching. But the question remains—Have they done so? And this is certainly not proved from the circumstance that, in Christ's own teaching, the doctrine of Atonement is not brought forward with the same explicitness as it is in the apostolic writings. That Christ took up a central position in relation to the truths which He proclaimed, that he invited men to faith in Himself as the condition of their participation in the blessings of the kingdom, that He promised the fullest satisfaction in the approaching kingdom to the hunger and thirst of the spiritually needy, that He declared that it was by their relation to Him that men would be ultimately judged,—this lies upon the surface of the Gospels. But that He should have preached to the Galilean multitudes truths which, on any hypothesis, could only be intelligible after His death and resurrection had taken place,—that He should have done this before He had even publicly proclaimed Himself to be the Messiah,— this is to ask what in reason we are not entitled to expect. Before there could be any preaching of an Atonement, there must be an Atonement to preach. I grant, however, that if the apostolic gospel really represents the truth about Christ's work, the facts of His early manifestation ought to bear this out. They must be such, at least, that the apostolic gospel is felt to be the natural key to them. In reality they are much more ; for, taken in their entirety, they point unmistakably to just such a view as the apostolic doctrine gives, and explain to us, what else would be a complete enigma, how such a doctrine could arise.

It is significant that the most unbiassed modern inquiry into Christ's teaching recognises that He attributed a redemptive virtue to His death, and connected it directly with the

1 Lecture IV.

forgiveness of sins.[1]   Ritschl also acknowledges that Christ
first, and after Him the oldest witnesses, connect Redemption
or forgiveness, not with His prophetic office, but much more
with the fact of His death.[2]   Taking the testimony of the
Gospels as a whole, I think it is exceedingly strong.   It is
remarkable that in the Gospel of John, the most spiritual of
the four, we have both the earliest and the clearest statements of the fact that Christ's death stood in direct relation
to the salvation of the world.   I refer to such passages as
the Baptist's utterance, "Behold the Lamb of God, which
taketh away the sin of the world";[3] Christ's words to
Nicodemus, "As Moses lifted up the serpent in the wilderness, even so must the Son of Man be lifted up,"[4] etc. ; and the
sayings in chap. vi. about giving His flesh for the life of the
world.[5]   In the Synoptic Gospels, while in one saying at least
of the earlier ministry there is a premonition of the cross,[6] it
was not till after Peter's great confession that Jesus began to
speak explicitly to the disciples of His approaching sufferings
and death.[7]   Then we have many utterances declaring the
necessity of His death, and such a saying throwing light upon
its character as, "For verily the Son of Man came not to be
ministered unto, but to minister, and to give His life a ransom
for many."[8]   On the Mount of Transfiguration it was the
decease which He should accomplish at Jerusalem which was
the subject of discourse.[9]   But the clearest expression of all
prior to His death is His solemn utterance at the institution
of the Supper, when, taking the sacramental bread and wine,
He said, "This is My body ; this is My blood of the Covenant, which is shed for many, unto remission of sins."[10]   To
this must be added the instruction which the disciples are
recorded to have received after the resurrection.   On one
remarkable occasion we read that Christ said to them, "O
foolish men, and slow of heart to believe in all that the

[1] Cf. Baldensperger's *Selbstbewusstsein Jesu*, 2nd ed. pp. 153–155 ; Wendt's
Lehre Jesu, ii. pp. 526–530 ; Schmoller's *Die Lehre vom Reiche Gottes*, pp.
144, 145, etc.

[2] *Unterricht*, p. 36.

[3] John i. 29.   Marg. in R.V., "beareth the sin."   Cf. Dorner, *System of
Doctrine*, iii. p. 415.

[4] John iii. 15.

[5] Vers. 51–56.

[6] Matt. ix. 15.

[7] Mark viii. 31, ix. 12, 31, x. 33, 34.

[8] Mark x. 45 (R.V.).

[9] Luke ix. 31.

[10] Matt. xxvi. 26, 28 (R.V.).

prophets have spoken! Behoved it not the Christ to suffer these things, and to enter into His glory? And beginning from Moses and from all the prophets, He interpreted to them in all the scriptures the things concerning Himself."[1] And at a later meeting with the eleven, "These are My words which I spake unto you, while I was yet with you, how that all things must needs be fulfilled, which are written in the law of Moses, and the prophets, and the psalms concerning Me. Then opened He their mind, that they might understand the scriptures; and He said unto them, Thus it is written, that the Christ should suffer, and rise again from the dead on the third day; and that repentance and remission of sins should be preached in His name unto all the nations, beginning from Jerusalem."[2] These passages are invaluable as giving us a clue to the clearness and decision of the subsequent apostolic doctrine. What these lengthened interpretations of Jesus included we cannot of course tell, but they must have embraced much light on the significance of His death; and for the nature of that light we are entitled to look to the Spirit-guided utterances of the apostles who received it.

The apostolic Church, therefore, was not left without guidance in its construction of the doctrine of Redemption, any more than in its construction of the doctrine of Christ's Person. It had various groups of facts to lead it to a conclusion.

1. It had the objective facts themselves of Christ's death, resurrection, and subsequent exaltation to heaven. Holding fast as it did to the Messiahship and Divine Sonship of Jesus, it could not but find the death of Christ a dark and perplexing problem, till it grasped the solution in the thought of a Divine necessity for that death for the accomplishment of the Messianic salvation. With this had to be taken the fact of Christ's own command, that repentance and remission of sins should be preached in His name to all nations. Behind this again were all the facts of His earthly life, with its revelations of Messianic power and grace, and its not less wonderful self-abasement and sorrow.

2. There were the sayings of Christ, above referred to, which threw light upon the meaning and necessity of His sufferings and death. These, in the new illumination of

---

[1] Luke xxiv. 25–27 (R.V.).   [2] Luke xxiv. 44–47.

the Spirit, would be earnestly pondered, and are sufficient to explain all the forms in which Christ's death came to be regarded by them.

3. There was an earlier Revelation with which the new economy stood in the closest relations, and to which Christ Himself had directed His disciples for instruction regarding Himself. In many ways also this old covenant aided them to a fuller comprehension of the meaning of the sufferings and death of Christ.

(1) There were the prophecies of the Old Testament,— foremost among them that wonderful prophecy of the Servant of Jehovah in Isaiah liii., to whose undeserved sufferings, lovingly and submissively borne, an expiatory virtue is expressly ascribed. "There is no exegete," says Professor G. A. Smith, "but agrees to this: . . . all agree to the fact that by Himself, or by God, the Servant's life is offered an expiation for sin—a satisfaction to the law of God."[1]

(2) There was the work of the law in men's hearts, begetting in them the sense of sin, and, in virtue of its propædeutic character, creating the deep feeling of the need of Redemption. It is with this consciousness of the want of righteousness wrought by the law, and the consequent feeling of the need of Redemption, that Paul's doctrine specially connects itself.

(3) There was the sacrificial system of the Old Testament. This was the remaining key in the hands of the early Church to unlock the significance of Christ's death. If the law created the sense of sin, it was the sacrificial system which created the idea of Atonement. This, in turn, is the thought to which the Epistle to the Hebrews specially attaches itself. When, therefore, exception is taken to the apostles casting their ideas into the moulds of Jewish sacrificial conceptions, we have rather to ask whether the economy of sacrifice was not Divinely prepared for this very end, that it might foreshadow the one and true Sacrifice by which the sin of the world is taken away, and whether this is not in accordance with all the data at our disposal.

II. Assuming, however, that all this is granted,—that it is conceded that the apostles teach Redemption through the death

---

[1] *The Book of Isaiah*, ii. p. 364.

of Christ, and that there is no discrepancy in this respect between their teaching and that of Christ Himself,—we are still far from a solution of the many questions which may be raised in regard to this great cardinal doctrine. Indeed, our real task is only commencing. Those who think that, on the basis of Scripture passages, a ready-made theory of Atonement lies to our hand, have only to consider the slow and gradual process by which the doctrine of the Church has been built up to its present form, to become convinced of the contrary. Christ's death is a sacrifice, but in what sense is it a sacrifice? It is a propitiation for our sins; but what are the elements in it which give it value as a propitiation? It is connected with the remission of sins; but what is the nature of this connection? These are questions as keenly discussed to-day as ever, and we cannot avoid considering them in connection with the deep and difficult problems which they raise.

Now I for one do not think it is the duty of the Church to rest content—as some express it—with the fact of the Atonement, without further inquiring as deeply as we can into its nature. I cannot believe that any doctrine of Scripture—least of all the doctrine of Atonement, which is represented in Scripture as the Revelation of the innermost heart of God to man, the central and supreme manifestation of His love to the world —was ever meant to lie like a dead-weight on our understanding, incapable of being in any degree assimilated by our thought. Certain it is that any doctrine which is treated in this way will not long retain its hold on men's convictions, but will sooner or later be swept out of the way as a piece of useless theological lumber. The Atonement, as Dr. John M'Leod Campbell was fond of putting it, must be capable of being seen in its own light. I grant, indeed, that the fact of the Atonement is greater than all our apprehensions of it. We are here in the very Holy of holies of the Christian faith, and our treatment of the subject cannot be too reverential. The one thing *a priori* certain about the Atonement is, that it has heights and depths, lengths and breadths, greater than any line of ours can fathom or span. It is this which should make us patient of what are called theories of the Atonement. I do not know any one of these theories of which it can justly be said that it is unmixed error,—which has not rather in the heart of it a portion of the truth,—which does not apprehend some side or aspect of the Atonement which other theories neglect, or have thrust into the background. Instead, therefore, of being too keen to scent error in these theories, our wiser plan will be to be ever on the outlook for an enlargement of our knowledge of the truth through them.

If I might indicate in a word what I take to be the tendency of the modern treatment of the Atonement, I would say that it consists in the endeavour to give a spiritual interpretation to the great fact which lies at the heart of our Redemption; not necessarily to deny its judicial aspect,—for that, I take it, will be found impossible,—but to remove from it the hard, legal aspect it is apt to assume when treated as a purely external fact, without regard to its inner spiritual content; and, further, to bring it into harmony with the spiritual laws and analogies which obtain in other spheres. There is the attempt (1) to find spiritual laws which will make the Atonement itself intelligible; and (2) to find spiritual laws which connect the Atonement with the new life which springs from it. I may add that this is a department of the truth in which I think that the theology of our own country has rendered better service to the Christian view than the theology of the Continent.

In accordance with my plan, I am led to study this subject of Atonement through Christ especially from the point of view of the Incarnation. There is an advantage in this method, for as, on the one hand, we see how the Atonement rises naturally out of the Incarnation, so that the Son of God could not appear in our nature without undertaking such a work as this term denotes; so, on the other, we see that the Incarnation is itself a pledge and anticipation of reconciliation. It is evident that such an event could never have taken place had there been no purpose or possibility of salvation; had humanity been a hopelessly ruined and rejected race. In principle, therefore, the Incarnation is the declaration of a purpose to save the world. It is more: it is itself a certain stage in that reconciliation, and the point of departure for every other. In the Incarnation, God and man are already in a sense one. In Christ a pure point of union is established with our fallen and sin-laden humanity, and this carries with it the assurance that everything

else that is necessary for the complete recovery of the world to
God will not be lacking. Theories, therefore, have never been
wanting in the Church which, in one form or another, lay the
stress in Redemption on the simple fact of the Incarnation.
As Dr. Hodge has expressed it, "The Incarnation itself, the
union of the Divine and human natures, was the great saving
act. Christ redeems us by what He is, not by what He does." [1]
Germs of such theories appear in some of the early Church
fathers, *e.g.* in Irenæus.[2] They reappeared in the Middle Ages,
and at the Reformation.[3] They have a modern analogue in the
theories of the Hegelian school, which in the realised unity of
God and humanity in Christ see the prototype of that unity of
God and man which is to be accomplished in the race in general.
The thought of the identity of Incarnation and Redemption
colours modern theology in many other ways.[4] These theories
are obviously defective, if meant to exhaust the whole Scripture
doctrine on the subject; but they have their point of truth in
this, that the perfect union of the Word with humanity is
already a reconciliation of the race with God in principle, and
is, besides, the medium by which a new Divine life is introduced into humanity—a view with which the theology of John
specially connects itself.

In further considering the theories on this subject, it will be
convenient to observe that all theories of Redemption within
Christian limits agree in taking for granted three things as
included under this term :—

1. There is the removal of guilt, or of the consciousness of
guilt, which carries with it the sense of the Divine forgiveness.

2. There is the breaking down of the actual enmity of the

---

[1] *System. Theology*, ii. p. 585.

[2] *E.g.* "To this end the Word of God was made Man, and He who was the
Son of God became the Son of man, that man, having been taken into the
Word, and receiving the adoption, might become the Son of God."—*Iren.* iii.
19. Harnack finds a germ of this doctrine in Justin Martyr. — *Dogmen-
geschichte*, i. p. 459. There are, however, other elements in the teaching on
Redemption of all these Fathers.

[3] *E.g.* Osiander, Schwenkfeld.

[4] *E.g.* in the school of Erskine of Linlathen. Cf. Murphy, *Scientific Basis
of Faith* (a disciple of this school) : "I do not speak of the Incarnation as one
act and the Atonement as another—they are one and the same Divine act,
which in itself is called the Incarnation, and in its results is called the Atonement. The act of the Son of God in becoming a partaker of our nature is the
Incarnation ; the result of this act, in making us partakers of the Divine
nature, is the Atonement or Reconciliation ; though these latter words are
both of them inadequate."—P. 384.

heart and will to God, and the turning of the sinner from dead works to serve the living and true God.

3. There is the taking up of the believer into the positive fellowship of eternal life with Christ, and into the consciousness of a Divine Sonship.

These are the immediate effects, from which others follow in a changed relation to the world, gradual progress in holiness, and deliverance at death and in eternity from all natural and spiritual evils.

Accordingly now as theories relate themselves predominantly to one or other of these points of view, they present a different aspect.

1. Theories which attach themselves by preference to the last point of view—that of fellowship—are apt to regard Christ chiefly as the type of the normal relation of God to humanity, and to subordinate the other aspects of His life and work to this.

2. Theories which attach themselves to the second point of view—the breaking down of the sinner's enmity—regard Christ's work as a great moral dynamic—"the power of God unto salvation,"[1] the effect of which is to break down the natural distrust of the heart towards God, and to melt the sinner into penitence,—"to bring men," as Bushnell expresses it, "out of their sins, and so out of their penalties."[2]

3. Theories which attach themselves to the first point of view—the removal of guilt—lay special stress on the relation of Christ's work to the Divine righteousness, and view it specially as an expiation.

A perfect theory, if we could obtain it, would be one which did justice to all these standpoints, and presented them in their scriptural relations to each other and to the Person and work of the Redeemer.

Without adhering rigidly to the scheme here indicated, which would be indeed impossible, seeing that the different theories cross each other at innumerable points, I shall now glance at the chief standpoints represented in these theories, and try to show that they gradually lead us up to a view which embraces them all, and is in harmony with the full Scripture testimony.

1. We have a class of theories which start from the idea of

---

[1] Rom. i. 16.   [2] *Vicarious Sacrifice*, p. 7.

fellowship, based on the unique relation which Christ sustains
to the race as perfect, archetypal Man—a relation expressed in
the title—"Son of Man." The point on which stress is laid
here is the solidarity between Christ and the race which He
came to save, a true thought in itself, and one which takes the
place in modern theology of the older way of looking at Christ's
relation to the race as purely federal or official. The typical
example of this class of theories is Schleiermacher's. With the
idea of fellowship Schleiermacher combines that of *representation.* The essence of Redemption, in his view, consists in
deliverance from the miserable contradiction of flesh and spirit,
through being taken up into the fellowship of Christ's life of
holiness and blessedness.[1] As standing in this fellowship with
Christ, believers are the objects of the love of God, who looks
upon them in Him. "Christ," he says, "purely represents us
before God in virtue of His own perfect fulfilment of the Divine
will, to which, through His life in us, the impulse is active in
us also, so that in this connection with Him we also are objects
of the Divine good pleasure."[2] In thus speaking of Christ in
His sinless perfection as representing believers before God, it
might appear as if Schleiermacher held a doctrine of imputation,
—indeed, he says this is the true meaning of that much misunderstood phrase, the imputation of the righteousness of
Christ.[3] When, however, we probe the matter a little further,
his meaning is found to be nothing more than this—that God
already sees in the initial stage of the believer's holiness the germ
of his subsequent full perfection,—of that perfection of which
Christ is the pattern or type,—and views him in the light of
that ideal.[4] This thought of a justification through germinal
holiness is a favourite one with writers of a mystical and speculative tendency; but it manifestly shifts the ground of acceptance from Christ for us to Christ in us, and treats objective
reconciliation as unnecessary.[5] In Schleiermacher's theory,
accordingly, as in those of a kindred type, Christ's sufferings
and death have only a very subordinate place. These sufferings
arose from His being in a world where evils are a necessary
result of sin, and from His fellow-feeling for us in our sins.

---

[1] "The Redeemer takes believers up into the fellowship of His untroubled
blessedness, and this is His atoning activity."—*Der christl. Glaube,* sec. 101.
[2] *Ibid.* ii. p. 133.   [3] *Ibid.* ii. p. 133.   [4] *Ibid.* ii. pp. 133, 134.
[5] See Note A.—The Germ Theory of Justification.

They may therefore be called substitutionary, as endured by a sinless Being for the sake of others, but they are in no sense satisfactory or expiatory. They are connected with our Redemption as teaching us to feel that outward evils are not necessarily penal, but chiefly through the Revelation they give us of Christ's constancy and love, and through the moral impression they are fitted to make upon us.[1] Schleiermacher's theory in the end thus passes over into one of moral influence; indeed, it is through the powerful working of Christ's Personality upon us that we are moved to enter into fellowship with Him at all. He is our Redeemer through the exceptional strength of His God-consciousness, by which our own is invigorated to overcome sin. If, then, we ask how, on this theory, the sense of guilt is removed, the answer we get is very curious. In fellowship with Christ, Schleiermacher says, the believer is a new man, and in the new man sin is no longer active. Sin in the believer is but the after-working and back-working of the old man, and as such the believer does not identify himself with it.[2] He is relieved, therefore, from the consciousness of guilt. Something like this is Kant's theory,[3] and in our own days it is the theory of a section of the Plymouth Brethren— so do extremes meet. But it is evident that, on this hypothesis, the doctrine of forgiveness is retained only in name. The old man is not forgiven, and the new man does not need forgiveness. Between the two forgiveness falls to the ground.[4]

2. Schleiermacher, in his treatment of Christ's sufferings, lays special stress on His sympathy or fellow-feeling with us, as a cause of these sufferings. This gives us a point of transition to a second class of theories, the keynote of which may be said to be *sympathy*. The starting-point here is not the thought of Christ's archetypal perfection, but the fitness

---

[1] Cf. on these views, *Der christl. Glaube*, ii. pp. 136–147.

[2] *Der christl. Glaube*, ii. p. 194. What Schleiermacher means by forgiveness of sins is indicated in the following sentence: "The beginning here is the vanishing of the old man, consequently also of the old manner of referring all evil to sin, therefore the vanishing of the consciousness of desert of punishment, consequently the first thing in the moment of reconciliation is the forgiveness of sin."—P. 105.

[3] *Religion innerhalb der Grenzen der bloss. Vernunft*, Book ii. sec. 3.

[4] Ritschl rightly remarks that what Schleiermacher calls reconciliation with God is really reconciliation with evil,—"the reconciliation of man with suffering, with his position in the world, which as sinner he had traced to his guilt." —*Recht. und Ver.* i. p. 470 (Eng. trans.).

of Christianity in a dynamical relation to break down the
enmity of the sinner's heart to God. The best-known type
of this class of theory is Dr. Bushnell's, in his original and
freshest presentation of it in his work on *Vicarious Sacrifice*.
The strong and true point in Dr. Bushnell's theory is in its
insistence on the vicarious element involved in the very nature
of sympathetic love. We speak of Christ's substitutionary
work,[1]—of His standing, suffering, dying for sinners,—but how
often do we apprehend this in a purely external and official
way! It is the merit of Dr. Bushnell's book that, with a
wealth of illustration drawn from every sphere of life in which
a like law of substitution prevails, he makes us feel that it is
something real and vital. When we speak of sympathy, we
are already in a region in which substitutionary forces are at
work. "None of us liveth to himself, and none dieth to himself."[2] We benefit and suffer involuntarily through each other,
but we have it also in our power to enter voluntarily into the
partnership of the world's joys and sorrows, and by bearing the
burdens of others to help to relieve them of their load. From
His unique relation to our race, this law applied in the highest
degree to Christ. In the whole domain of love, Divine and
human, we find substitutionary forces acting; but in Christ's
life we find them acting at a maximum. Christ not only wears
our nature, but in the exercise of a perfect sympathy He truly
identifies Himself with us in our lot, bears our sins and sorrows
on His soul, and represents us to the Father, not as an external
legal surety, but with a throbbing heart of love. This of itself
may not be Atonement—we shall see immediately it is not—
but whatever else there is in Atonement, Scripture warrants
us in saying that at least there is this. "Himself took our
infirmities, and bare our diseases," says Matthew,[3] in a passage
which Dr. Bushnell adopts as the key to his theory. "It behoved Him in all things to be made like unto His brethren,
that He might be a merciful and faithful High Priest in things
pertaining to God, to make propitiation for the sins of the
people."[4]

This, then, is the key which Dr. Bushnell gives us to the

---

[1] Cf. Dorner, *System of Doctrine*, iv. pp. 89–98: "There are substitutionary
forces, and a receptiveness for them in humanity."
[2] Rom. xiv. 8 (R.V.).   [3] Matt. viii. 17.
[4] Heb. ii. 17 (R.V.); cf. v. 12.

vicarious sufferings of Christ—that of sympathetic love; and
so far as the book in question goes, it is the whole key.   If I
were disposed to criticise the theory minutely, I might remark
that, on Dr. Bushnell's own principles, it is too narrow to cover
all the facts.   To get an adequate explanation of Christ's undeserved sufferings, alike as regards their nature, their motive,
and their end, we need a wider view of them than is covered
by this single word—sympathy.   Sympathy, in a pure and holy
nature like Christ's, was necessarily one cause of His sufferings,
but it was not the only cause.   He suffered from natural causes
—as hunger and thirst, from the unbelief of the world, from
the persecutions and malice of His enemies, from temptations of
the devil, from the faithlessness and desertion of disciples, etc.
Deeper and more mysterious causes of suffering are not obscurely
intimated in the Gospel narratives.   Sympathy was only indirectly concerned with all these.   If it be said that it was the
sympathetic entrance into and endurance of these sufferings
which gave them their vicarious character, I would remark that
we need here a wider word than sympathy.   Christ voluntarily
took upon Him abasement, suffering, and death for the salvation
of men; but He did so, not simply from sympathy, but—as Dr.
Bushnell also often recognises, though still generally emphasising the sympathetic aspect—in a spirit of large, self-sacrificing
love.   Love includes sympathy, but is not necessarily exhausted
by it.   We take also too narrow a view when we seek in the
moral influence of sympathy or love the *sole* key to the peculiar
fruitfulness of self-sacrifice.   That self-sacrifice acts as a potent
inspiration to like deeds in others—that it has power to soften
and subdue the obdurate heart—is a great truth.   But it should
not be overlooked that a main part of the secret of the fruitfulness of self-sacrifice lies in the way in which one life is linked
with another, and society is bound together as a whole; so that,
through the labours and sacrifices of one, or of a handful,
martyrs or patriots, benefits accrue to multitudes who never
come within the range of its moral influence.[1]

This leads directly to another remark—namely, that Dr.
Bushnell does not give any clear answer to the question,
What was the distinctive life-task, or vocation, in the fulfil-

---

[1] This is admirably worked out in the section on the fruitfulness of sacrifice
in Bishop Westcott's *The Victory of the Cross*, ii. 23–35.

ment of which these great and heavy sorrows came upon
Christ? This is a point of very great importance. Sympathy, or disinterested love, will lead one person to undertake
labours and undergo sacrifices for another, but the sacrifice is
undergone, not for the mere sake of displaying sympathy, but
always in the prosecution of some independent end. The
mother wears out her strength for her sick child, but it is
in the hope that by her nursing she will aid in its recovery.
The philanthropist will devote life and fortune for the cause
in which he is interested, but it is in carrying out plans and
projects which he thinks will contribute to the success of
his object. If we ask, then, What was the work which Christ
came into the world to do, in the accomplishment of which
He endured such sufferings? it will not do to reply simply,
To manifest sympathy, for the sake of the moral impression to
be produced by it. We must still ask, What was the work
which made submission to this suffering necessary? To this
question Dr. Bushnell gives us no very definite answer, none
which carries us beyond Christ's immediate ministries to soul
and body, or His witness-bearing in word or deed for the
Father. But even this must have for its content some special
declaration of God's character and will, if it is not simply to
point us back to the exhibition of love in the vicarious
suffering. It is on the latter really that Dr. Bushnell lays all
the stress ; the suffering, in his view, is not simply a necessary
incident in the prosecution of some independent task of love,
but is the main, substantial reason of Christ's appearance in
the world.[1] If, on the other hand, we lay the chief weight on
the witness of Christ, and view His sufferings in subordination to this as furnishing occasions for the manifestation of
His patience, steadfastness, and love to men—then is His work
purely declarative. His sufferings add nothing to its content,
and owe their value for redemptive purposes solely to their
power of moral enforcement.

It is obvious that, if Dr. Bushnell's theory be true, vicarious
suffering which has redemptive efficacy, is not confined to

---

[1] The work of Christ he conceives of " as beginning at the point of sacrifice,
vicarious sacrifice, ending at the same, and being just this all through."—
Vicarious Sacrifice, Introduction, p. 35 (1886). On the sense in which he does
regard Christ's work as declarative, *i.e.* as a Revelation of the eternal vicarious
sufferings of the Godhead, see below.

Christ, but runs through the whole spiritual universe. This, indeed, is what he asserts.[1] It points, however, to a clear defect in his view, inasmuch as it removes the work of Christ from that unique and exceptional position which the Scriptures constantly ascribe to it. Even were this difficulty surmounted, there remains the crowning objection, which is the really fatal one—namely, that in resolving the redeeming efficacy of the sufferings of Christ solely into their moral influence, the theory runs directly counter to the explicit and uniform declarations of the New Testament, which put in the foreground their expiatory and propitiatory character. It is the less necessary to ask whether Dr. Bushnell's theory in this respect is adequate, since he himself at a subsequent period was compelled to modify it in favour of the recognition of an objective element in the Atonement. In his later work on *Forgiveness and Law,* he tells us that he had formerly conceived the whole import and effect of Christ's work to lie in its reconciling power on others ; now he has been brought to see that it has a propitiatory effect on God also. The peculiar view which underlies this second work—namely, that God must overcome His repugnance to the sinner by making cost or sacrifice for him, need not detain us here, especially as I do not know of anyone who has ever adopted it.[2] But I cannot refrain from adverting, as most of Dr. Bushnell's critics have done, to the striking evidence which even the earlier volume affords of the necessity of recognising an objective propitiation. There is, perhaps, nothing more curious in literature than the way in which, in the closing chapter of his *Vicarious Sacrifice,* after exhausting all his powers to convince us that the efficacy of Christ's

---

[1] *Vicarious Sacrifice,* pp. 17, 18. "The suffering of Christ," he says, "was vicarious suffering in no way peculiar to Him, save in degree."—P. 68.

[2] In this work Dr. Bushnell develops the idea already suggested in his earlier book (pp. 18, 35, 37), that Christ's sacrifice has its chief significance as a revelation of the eternal sacrifice in God's own nature. "The transactional matter of Christ's life and death," he says, "is a specimen chapter, so to speak, of the infinite book that records the eternal going on of God's blessed nature within. . . . All God's forgiving dispositions are dateless, and are cast in this mould. The Lambhood nature is in Him, and the cross set up, before the Incarnate Son arrives. . . . I have already said that the propitiation, so called, is not a fact accomplished in time, but an historic matter represented in that way, to exhibit the interior, ante-mundane, eternally proceeding sacrifice of the Lamb that was slain before the foundation of the world."—Pp. 60, 61, 74. This, surely, is to give Christ's work something of a docetic character.

sufferings lies solely in their moral efficacy, Dr. Bushnell practically throws the whole theory he has been inculcating to the winds as inadequate for the moral and spiritual needs of men. "In the facts of our Lord's passion," he says, "outwardly regarded, there is no sacrifice, or oblation, or atonement, or propitiation, but simply a living and dying thus and thus. . . . If, then, the question arises, How are we to use such a history so as to be reconciled by it? we hardly know in what way to begin. How shall we come to God by the help of this martyrdom? How shall we turn it, or turn ourselves under it, so as to be justified and set in peace with God? Plainly there is a want here, and this want is met by giving a thought-form to the facts which is not in the facts themselves. They are put directly into the moulds of the altar, and we are called to accept the crucified God-Man as our sacrifice, an offering or oblation for us, our propitiation, so as to be sprinkled from our evil conscience—washed, purged, and cleansed from our sin. . . . So much is there in this, that without these forms of the altar we should be utterly at a loss in making any use of the Christian facts that would set us in a condition of practical reconciliation with God. Christ is good, beautiful, wonderful; His disinterested love is a picture by itself; His forgiving patience melts into my feeling; His passion rends my heart. But what is He for? And how shall He be made to me the salvation that I want? One word—He is my sacrifice—opens all to me ; and beholding Him, with all my sin upon Him, I count Him my offering; I come unto God by Him, and enter into the holiest by His blood."[1] Not a word needs to be added to this self-drawn picture by Dr. Bushnell of the inadequacy of a mere moral influence theory of the Atonement. If the soul, in order to find peace with God, must explicitly renounce that theory, how can it be put forward as in any sense a theory of reconciliation? It fails to satisfy the wants of the awakened conscience ; and it fails to satisfy Scripture, which, as we have seen, demands an objective connection between Christ's work and our forgiveness.

3. Before dealing with theories which recognise an objective element in the Atonement, it may be useful to glance at a

---

[1] *Vicarious Sacrifice*, pp. 460, 461.

theory which really belongs to the subjective class, though its author has done his best to give it an objective form—I mean the theory of Ritschl. As Bushnell's theory turns on the idea of sympathy, so that of Ritschl may be said to turn on the idea of *Vocation*. Ritschl's strong point lies precisely in the answer which he gives to the question which Bushnell failed to meet—namely, What was the work which Christ came into the world to do, which entailed on Him suffering and rejection? What was His vocation, His life-work, His peculiar moral task? It is this thought of Christ's fulfilment of His vocation (Beruf) which is the central thing in Ritschl. He speaks of the solidaric unity of Christ with God.[1] By this he means that Christ adopted God's end in the creation and government of the world (Weltzweck) as His own end, and lived and died to fulfil it. This end is summed up in the establishing of the kingdom of God—that is, of a religious and moral community, in which the members are bound together by love to God and love to man, and act solely from the motive of love ; and in which they attain the end aimed at in all religions, namely, moral supremacy over the world, which is Ritschl's synonym for eternal life.[2] This, it will be allowed, is a somewhat bald scheme, and it does not become richer as we proceed. In what sense, we ask, is Christ a Redeemer? The essential part of the answer seems to be that through His Revelation of God's grace and truth, through His preaching of the kingdom of God, and through His personal devotion to God's world-aim, He influences and enables men to turn from their sins, and leads them to appropriate God's end as their own. The uniqueness of Christ's Person is supposed to be secured by the fact that in Him first the final end of the kingdom of God is realised in a personal life, so that everyone who would undertake the same life-task must do it in dependence on Him.[3] Ritschl, therefore, is able, like Schleiermacher, to speak of Christ as the " Urbild " of humanity in its relation to the kingdom of God,

---

[1] *Unterricht*, pp. 20, 21 ; cf. *Recht. und Ver*. 3rd ed. iii. p. 428.

[2] *Ibid*. pp. 7, 12 ; cf. *Recht. und Ver*. iii. p. 497 : " Therefore is the direct content of eternal life or of blessedness to be recognised in the religious functions ruling the world."—P. 497 (" Eternal Life, or Freedom over the World," title of sec. 54).

[3] *Ibid*. p. 20.

and as such the original object of the love of God, in whom
God beholds and loves those who are embraced in His fellowship.[1] But fellowship here means simply unity of moral aim.
What significance, on this theory, have the sufferings of
Christ? Only this significance, that they are the highest
proof of Christ's fidelity in His vocation—the guarantee of
the reality of that new relation to God which is exhibited in
His Person.[2] Here, as in Schleiermacher, we are plainly back
to the theory of a mere moral influence. Ritschl, like Dr.
Bushnell, would cast his idea of Christ's death in the moulds
of the altar; but this must be connected with his theory of
the Old Testament sacrifices, which, he holds, had no reference
to Atonement for sin, but only served to dispel the creature's
distrust in drawing near to a great and awful God. Christ, in
like manner, by His death, brings us near to God by dispel-
ling distrust of God, and inspiring confidence in His grace.[3]
What, finally, on this theory, becomes of the idea of guilt?
Strictly speaking, guilt is not removed, but God admits us to
fellowship with Himself, and to co-operation with Him in
work for His kingdom, without our guilt, or feeling of guilt,
forming any hindrance thereto.[4] This is what Ritschl under-
stands by justification. It is the easier for him to take this
view, that, as we saw before, guilt with him has little objective
significance, and exists more for our own feeling than for
God.[5] In proportion as this view is adopted, however, the
experience of forgiveness becomes subjective also, and there
remains nothing objective but the actual change of mind and
feeling.[6] It is plain that we have here quite changed the
centre of gravity in the Christian view of Redemption; and
the only remedy is to restore the idea of guilt to its scriptural

---

[1] *Unterricht*, p. 20.   [2] Cf. *ibid*. pp. 36, 37, 38.
[3] Cf. *ibid*. p. 40. Cf. Dorner's criticism of Ritschl on this point, *System of
Doctrine*, iii. 405, 406.
[4] *Ibid*. p. 32.
[5] Ritschl's view of Christ's sufferings and their relation to forgiveness is
expounded at length in his *Recht. und Vers.* 3rd ed. iii. 417-428, 505-533.
Cf. specially pp. 422, 511, 512, 513, 524, 574. "Christ's death, in the view of
the apostles, is the compendious expression for the fact that Christ has
inwardly maintained His religious unity with God and His revelation-position
in the whole course of His life."—P. 511.
[6] It is not remarkable, therefore, that Herrmann, as quoted by Lipsius,
should speak of the forgiveness of sins as "nothing at all particular" (*ganz
nichts besonderes*).—*Die Ritschl'sche Theologie*, p. 12. Herrmann certainly
expresses himself very differently in his *Verkehr*, pp. 39, 40 (2nd ed. p. 103).

importance, which, again, necessitates a changed idea of its treatment.[1]

The theories we are now to consider differ from those we have just had under review, in that they recognise an *objective* element in the Atonement, and in this way come nearer to the manifest teaching of Scripture.   They recognise that Christ's work not only affects us subjectively in the way of moral influence, but is an objective work, on the ground of which God forgives sin, and receives us into fellowship with Himself.   And the question they raise is, What is the nature of this objective element?

4. The first answer which is given to this question is by that group of theories which find the essential feature in the Atonement in the surrender of the holy will of Christ to God.   The idea of Atonement here, then, is the *self-surrender* of the human will to the Divine.   This is Maurice's theory, but essentially also that of Rothe, Pressensé, Bähr, Oehler, and many others.[2] Here, as in previous theories, Christ is regarded as the Head of the race, and as representing in Himself all humanity.   In this humanity He offers up to God the perfect sacrifice of a will entirely surrendered to His service.   As Maurice puts it, "Supposing the Father's will to be a will to all good; supposing the Son of God, being one with Him and Lord of man, to obey and fulfil in our flesh that will by entering into the lowest condition into which men had fallen through their sin; supposing this Man to be, for this reason, an object of continual complacency to His Father, and that complacency to be fully drawn out by the death of the cross; supposing His death to be a sacrifice, the only complete sacrifice ever offered, the entire surrender of the whole spirit and body to God,—is not this, in

---

[1] A kindred view of atonement to Ritschl's is that of F. A. B. Nitzsch in his *Lehrbuch der Evang. Dogmatik*, ii. (1892).   "God," he holds, "could only forgive the sin of humanity if the representative of humanity was able to afford him the security of a moral renewal of the same, the security of a new humanity.   But this Christ did as the Beginner of the new humanity, and as Founder of a community upon which He could take over His own fellowship with God.   We cannot, therefore, say that the doing of Christ first made it possible for God the Father to be graciously disposed to men, but rather that He made it possible for God to reveal His grace."—P. 508.   Christ is therefore a guarantee to God for our future sanctification.   This is not a thought which we find prominent in Scripture, while the scriptural idea that Christ reconciles us to God by removal of our guilt is overlooked.

[2] Cf. Rothe's *Dogmatik*, ii. pp. 265–269 ; Pressensé, *Apostolic Age*, p. 274 (Eng. trans. 4th ed.); Bähr, *Symbolik*, etc.

the highest sense, the Atonement? Is not the true, sinless root
of humanity revealed; is not God in Him reconciled to man?
Is not the cross the meeting-point between man and man, between man and God?"[1] That which, on this view, gives the
sacrifice of Christ its value, is not the suffering, but the perfect
will of obedience expressed in the suffering. When, according
to the Epistle to the Hebrews, sacrifices and offerings, and
whole burnt-offerings and sacrifices for sin, God would not,
neither had pleasure therein, "then hath He said, Lo, I am
come to do Thy will. He taketh away the first, that He may
establish the second. By which will we have been sanctified,
through the offering of the body of Jesus Christ once for all."[2]
This surrender of the will is the only kind of sacrifice God
delights in, and it is the perfect Atonement.[3] The sin of
humanity is its negation of the will of God, and the cross
takes back that negation on behalf of humanity. This is
brought into harmony with the Old Testament sacrifices by the
theory that in these sacrifices it is not the death of the victim
that is the essential thing, but the presentation of the blood.
The death is only the means of obtaining the blood, which, as
the vehicle of the pure life, the offerer presents to God as a
covering for his own sin.[4]

Again, there can be no doubt of the deep spiritual truth
involved in this theory of the sacrifice which Christ offered for
our Redemption. We may again say that, whatever else there
is in the Atonement, there is this in it. Viewing Christ's
death as a sacrifice, we cannot question that the nerve and core
of the sacrifice was the holy will, in which, through the Eternal
Spirit, He offered Himself without spot or blemish to God.[5] It
was not the mere fact of the sufferings, but that which was the
soul of the sufferings,—the holy, loving will in which they were
borne, and the self-surrender to the will of the Father in them,
—which gave them their spiritual value.[6] The only question is,

---

[1] *Theological Essays*, p. 147.   [2] Heb. x. 5–10 (R.V.).
[3] Erskine of Linlathen's theory was akin to this: "The true and proper
sacrifice for *our* sin" is "the shedding out of the blood of *our* will—of that
will which had offended."—*Doctrine of Election*, 2nd ed. p. 156.
[4] Cf. *e.g.*, Oehler, *Theology of Old Testament*, i. p. 411 (Eng. trans.); Bähr,
Symbolik (see his view criticised by Dorner, *System of Doctrine*, iii. pp. 407,
408; and Fairbairn, *Typology*, 3rd ed. ii. pp. 290–297). Thus also Rothe,
Riehm, Nitzsch, Schultz, etc.   [5] Heb. ix. 14, x. 4–10.
[6] This is the point of view emphasised in Bishop Westcott's *The Victory of
the Cross*, which may be classed with this group of theories. The key-words of

Is this the whole of the explanation? Does this exhaust the meaning of Christ's sacrifice? Does this fill up the whole of the scriptural testimony regarding it? And, however fascinated one may be for a time with this theory, it seems impossible permanently to rest in it as adequate. I do not go back on the inadequacy of a theory which lays the whole stress of Atonement on self-sacrifice, without saying sacrifice *for* what, or *in* what, but come at once to the point in which it seems peculiarly to fail. That point is, that the Scriptures appear to assert a direct relation of the sacrifice of Christ to the sin and guilt of men,—a direct expiatory power to remove that guilt,—a relation, not only to God's commanding will, but to His condemning will. Not only the Old and New Testament doctrine of the righteousness and holiness of God, and of His judicial attitude towards sin,—not only the extreme gravity of the scriptural doctrine of guilt, but the deepest feeling of the awakened conscience itself, demands that guilt shall not be simply overlooked, but that it shall be dealt with also in the transacting of Christ with God for man, and that the forgiveness which is sealed in His death shall have placed on it the holy sanction of justice as well as that of love. I go on, therefore—

5. To look at theories which not only affirm the offering up of a holy will of obedience in Christ's sacrifice, but recognise its relation to *guilt*. Such theories include, after all, among their representatives, the great bulk of the ablest and most scriptural theologians—as Dorner, Luthardt, Martensen, Oosterzee, Godet, etc.; and an undesigned testimony is borne to their substantial truth by the approximations often made to them in theories of a different tendency, and by the difficulty felt in avoiding language which would imply the expiatory view, as well as by

the book are Fatherhood, Incarnation, Sacrifice. Sufferings in general are viewed in the light of discipline—" a revelation of the Fatherhood of God, who brings back His children to Himself in righteousness and love."—P. 82. Christ bore these sufferings according to the mind of God as " entering into the Divine law of purifying chastisement," " realising in every pain the healing power of a Father's wisdom."—Pp. 69, 82. But in what sense can we speak of " purifying chastisement" and " healing power" in the case of the Sinless One? Bishop Westcott himself has expressions which recognise a deeper relation of sufferings to sin, as where, *e.g.*, Christ is spoken of as gathering " into one supreme sacrifice the bitterness of death, the last penalty of sin, knowing all it means, and bearing it as He knows"; and His sufferings are held as showing " His complete acceptance of the just, the inevitable sentence of God on the sin of humanity."—Pp. 68, 81. The thoughts of the book are not worked out into perfect clearness.

the studied accommodation of all parties, as far as possible, to the recognised language of the Church. Yet the dislike of many, and these often men of the most spiritual mind, to the forms of the imputation theology, their inability to rest in anything which seems to them to wear an air of legal fiction, suggests to us the necessity of seeking to approach even this side of the subject from within, and of trying to connect it with spiritual laws which will commend it to the conscience and the heart.

I may begin here with a theory which, though it opposes itself directly to the idea of penal sufferings, yet deals with this question of the relation of Atonement to guilt, and has, I think, valuable light to throw upon the subject,—more, perhaps, than is sometimes admitted,—I refer to the theory of Dr. John M'Leod Campbell. Dr. Campbell starts with the Incarnation, and his idea is to see the Atonement developing itself naturally and necessarily out of Christ's relation to men as the Incarnate Son—which is, I think, a sound point of view. Next, he distinguishes in Christ's work two sides—(1) a dealing with men on the part of God, and (2) a dealing with God on the part of men; which, again, I think, is a true distinction. The peculiarity of his theory, and here undoubtedly it becomes artificial and indefensible, lies in the proposal to substitute a vicarious repentance for sins, and confession of sins, for the vicarious endurance of the penalties of transgression.[1] There is here, first, a confusion between repentance for sins and confession of them. The idea that Christ could in any sense repent of the sins of the humanity which He represented, could bring to God " a perfect repentance " for them, is one totally inadmissible, even though his premiss were granted, which it cannot be, that a perfect repentance would of itself constitute Atonement. That Christ should confess our sins in His high-priestly intercession for us with God is, on the other hand, not inadmissible, but is rightly classed as a part of His substitutionary activity for us. It has its analogies in the intercessory confessions of Moses, Daniel, and Nehemiah, and may very well be regarded by us as an element in the Atonement.

When we get behind Dr. Campbell's words, and look at the kernel of his theory, and even at what he means to convey by

---

[1] *The Nature of the Atonement*, 4th ed. p. 117.   [2] *Ibid.* p. 118.

these unfortunate expressions about a perfect repentance, we obtain light on the Atonement which is, I think, valuable. The point of this theory, as I understand it—that on which Dr. Campbell himself constantly insists through all his volume —is, that with the most perfect apprehension of what the sin of man was, on the one hand, and of what the mind of God towards sin, and sin's due at the hands of God, were, on the other, there went up from the depths of Christ's sinless humanity a perfect "Amen" to the righteous judgment of God against sin.   There must, therefore, be recognised, even on Dr. M'Leod Campbell's theory, a certain dealing of Christ with God's wrath —with His judicial condemnation upon sin.   "Christ, in dealing with God on behalf of men," he says, "must be conceived of as dealing with the righteous wrath of God against sin, and as according to it that which was due."[1]   "Let us consider," he says again, "this 'Amen' from the depths of the humanity of Christ to the Divine condemnation of sin.   What is it in relation to God's wrath against sin?   What place has it in Christ's dealing with that wrath?   I answer, He who so responds to the Divine wrath against sin, saying, 'Thou art righteous, O Lord, who judgest so,' is necessarily receiving the full apprehension and realisation of that wrath, as well as of that sin against which it comes forth, into His soul and spirit, into the bosom of the Divine humanity, and so receiving it, He responds to it with a perfect response—a response from the depths of that Divine humanity, and in that perfect response He absorbs it."[2]   If, however, this were all that was in Dr. Campbell's theory, we should still have to say that, valuable as the suggestion is which it contains, it is only a half-truth.   It will be observed that, so far as these quotations go, it is only a vivid mental realisation of God's wrath against sin to which we are to conceive Christ as responding.   He has the perfect realisation of what sin is in man; He has the perfect realisation of God's mind towards sin; but He is Himself in no sense brought under the experience of that wrath, or of its penal effects: it may be thought by many He could not be.   And this might seem to detract from the value of that "Amen" from the depths of Christ's humanity on which all the stress is laid.   To take an analogous case, it is one thing to be patient

---

[1] *The Nature of the Atonement*, 4th ed. p. 117.   [2] *Ibid.* p. 118.

and resigned under a vivid mental realisation of possible trials, another thing to be resigned under actual experience of sorrow. Yet the only resignation which has worth is that which has been actually tested in the fires of trial. In order, therefore, that Christ's "Amen" to the judgment of God against sin might have its fullest content, it would appear to be necessary that it should be uttered, not under a mere ideal realisation of what God's wrath against sin is, but under the actual pressure of the judgment which that wrath inflicts. Is this possible? Strange to say, with all his protests against Christ being thought of as enduring penal evils, it is precisely this view to which Dr. Campbell in the end comes. He is quite awake to the fact of the unique character of Christ's sufferings; quite aware that they involved elements found in no ordinary martyr's death; quite conscious that an "Amen" uttered, as he calls it, "in naked existence,"[1] would have little value. It must be uttered under actual experience of the evils which this judgment of God lays on humanity, especially under the experience of death. The closing period of Christ's life, he says, was one of which the distinctive character was suffering in connection with a permitted hour and power of darkness;[2] while his remarks on our Lord's tasting death are so important and apposite that I cannot forbear quoting one or two of them. "When I think of our Lord as tasting death," he says, "it seems to me as if He alone ever truly tasted death. . . . Further, as our Lord alone truly tasted death, so to Him alone had death its perfect meaning as the wages of sin. . . . For thus, in Christ's honouring of the righteous law of God, *the sentence of the law* was included, as well as *the mind of God* which that sentence expressed. . . . Had sin existed in men as mere spirits, death could not have been the wages of sin, and any response to the Divine mind concerning sin which would have been an Atonement for their sin, could only have had spiritual elements; but man being by the constitution of humanity capable of death, and death having come as the wages of sin, it was not simply sin that had to be dealt with, but an existing law with its penalty of death, and that death as already incurred. So that it was not only the Divine mind that had to be responded to, but also that expression of the

---

[1] *The Nature of the Atonement*, p. 259.   [2] *Ibid.* p. 224.

Divine mind which was contained in God's making death the
wages of sin."[1]　It is evident how nearly in such passages Dr.
Campbell comes to a theory of the Atonement which holds that
Christ, as a member of humanity and the new Head of the
race, really bore in His own Person the penal evils which are
the expression of the wrath of God against the sin of the world.
He maintains, indeed, that for Christ these were not really
penal evils ; but, in the light of the explanations just given,
the difference seems to resolve itself mainly into one of nomenclature.　Whatever sense we may give to that expression,
" Christ bore the wrath of God for us," it is held by no one
to mean that Christ was personally the object of His Father's
anger.　All that is meant is that by Divine ordainment He
passed under the experience of evils which are the expression
of God's wrath against sin, or a judgment laid on humanity on
account of that sin.　The peculiarly valuable idea, as I take
it, which Dr. Campbell brings to the elucidation of Christ's
sufferings as atoning is—that it was not simply the patience
and resignation with which He bore them, not simply the
surrender of His will to God in them, but the perfect acknowledgment, which accompanied His endurance of them, of the
righteousness of God in their ordainment, which made them a
satisfaction for sin.　" By that perfect response in Amen to the
mind of God, in relation to sin," as he himself expresses it, " is
the wrath of God rightly met, and that is accorded to Divine
justice which is its due, and could alone satisfy it."[2]

It is, I own, difficult to frame a theory to which no exception
can be taken, which shall show how the sufferings of Christ,
which were in large part sufferings endured for righteousness'
sake, had at the same time an expiatory value ; yet it is the
clear teaching of Scripture that they possess this character.　As
aids to the apprehension of the subject, the facts remain that
these sufferings of the sinless Son of God were voluntarily undertaken, and (what can be said of no other of the race) wholly
undeserved ; that Christ did enter, as far as a sinless Being

---

[1] *The Nature of the Atonement*, pp. 259–262.　He even says : " The *peace-
making* between God and man, which was perfected by our Lord on the cross,
required to its reality the presence to the spirit of Christ of the *elements of
the alienation* as well as the possession by Him of that eternal righteousness
in which was the virtue to make peace."—Page 250.　The italics in the extracts
are Dr. Campbell's own.　　　　　　　　　　　　　[2] *Ibid.* p. 119.

could, into the penal evils of our state, and finally submitted to death—the doom which sin has brought on our humanity; that He did this with a perfect consciousness and realisation of the relation of these evils to sin; that He experienced the full bitterness of these evils, and, especially in His last hours, was permitted to endure them without even the alleviations and spiritual comforts which many of His own people enjoy; that there were mysterious elements in His sufferings, which outward causes do not seem adequate to explain (*e.g.* the agony in Gethsemane, the awful darkness of His soul on Calvary), which appear related to His position as our Sin-bearer;—finally, that in this mortal sorrow He still retains unbroken His relation to the Father, overcomes our spiritual enemies, so transacts with God for men, so offers Himself to God in substitutionary love on our behalf, so recognises and honours the justice of God in His condemnation of sin, and in the evils that were befalling Himself in consequence of that sin, that His death may fitly be regarded as a satisfaction to righteousness for us—the Redemption of the world, not, indeed, *ipso facto*, but for those who through faith appropriate His sacrifice, die in spirit with Him in His death, and make His righteousness the ground of their hope.

Is exception taken—as it was by the Socinians—to the idea of the innocent satisfying for the guilty? Is it asked, How should the righteous suffer for the guilty? Is it just that they should do so? Or, how can the sufferings of the righteous atone for the unrighteous? I would point out in answer that there are two questions here. The first relates to a matter of fact—the suffering of the righteous for the guilty. We know that they do so. It is the commonest fact in our experience. In the organic relation in which we stand to each other it could not be otherwise. The penalties of evil-doing are probably never confined to the actual wrong-doer, but overflow upon others, and sometimes involve them in untold misery. To impeach the justice of this is to impeach the justice of an organic constitution of the race. Thus far, then, we can say that Christ is no exception to this universal law; nay, He is the highest exemplification of it. Christ could not enter the world without receiving upon Him the brunt of its evils. Just because He was the infinitely pure

and holy One, they fell on Him with greater severity. A
writer like Bushnell here often uses the strongest language.
He speaks of Christ as incarnated into the curse of the world.
"It is," he says, "as if the condemnations of God were upon
Him, as they are on all the solidarities of the race into which
He is come."[1] "It means," he says again, "that He is
incarnated into common condition with us, under what is
called the curse. . . . He must become a habitant with us,
a fellow-nature, a brother; and that He could not be without
being entered into what is our principal distinction as being
under the curse. . . . He has it upon Him, consciously, as the
curse or penal shame and disaster of our transgression."[2] The
question is not, therefore, How should Christ, the sinless One,
suffer for the guilty? but, How can sufferings thus endured
become expiatory or atoning? And this I have tried to
answer by pointing out the unique relation which Christ
sustains to our race, in virtue of which He could become its
Representative and Sin-bearer; and, secondly, by indicating
how in our humanity He must, as Dr. M'Leod Campbell says,
have related Himself to our sins—not only patiently and
lovingly enduring sufferings, not only yielding up to His
Father a will of obedience in them, but viewing them in the
light of their causes, entering fully into God's judgment on
the sin of which they were the consequences, and rendering
to God in our nature a full and perfect and glorifying response
to His justice in them. In this way His sufferings might
well become, like those of the Servant of the Lord in Isaiah
liii., expiatory.

Gathering together, in closing, the various aspects of Christ's
work which have been brought before us, we see, I think, the
truth of a previous remark that the true or full view of
Christ's work in Redemption is wide enough to include them
all—takes up the elements of truth in every one of them.
A complete view of Christ's work will include the fact that
in the Incarnation a new Divine life has entered humanity;
will include the fact that Christ is our perfect Representative

---

[1] *Forgiveness and Law*, p. 155.
[2] *Ibid.* pp. 150, 158. Bushnell will have it that his "penal sanctions" are
"never punitive, but only coercive and corrective."—P. 132. But what does
"penal" mean, if not "punitive"? And can penalties not be "judicial,"
and yet up to a certain point "corrective"?

before God as the new Head of the race, and the wearer of our humanity in its pure and perfect form ; will include the fact of an organic relation of Christ with all the members of the race, in virtue of which He entered, not merely outwardly, but in the most real and vital way, into the fellowship of our sin and suffering, and truly bore us on His heart before God as a merciful and faithful High Priest; will include the idea of a vocation which Christ had as Founder of the kingdom of God on earth, though this vocation will embrace, not only the Revelation of the Father's character and doing His will among men, but also the making reconciliation for the sins of the people; will include the fact of a holy and perfect and continuous surrender of Christ's will to God, as an offering, through the Eternal Spirit, in humanity, of that which man ought to render, but is unable in his own strength to give—the presentation to God in humanity, therefore, of a perfect righteousness, on the ground of which humanity stands in a new relation to God, and is accepted in the Beloved ;— will include, finally, a dealing with God in reference to the guilt of sin, which is not simply a sympathetic realisation of the burden of that guilt as it rests on us, nor yet simply a confession of sins in our name, nor yet simply an acknowledgment in humanity of the righteousness of God in visiting our sins with wrath and judgment, but is a positive entrance into the penal events of our condition, and, above all, into death as the last and most terrible of these evils, in order that in these also He might become one with us, and under that experience might render to God what was due to His judicial righteousness,—an Atonement which, as Dr. M'Leod Campbell says, has in it an " Amen " from the depths of our humanity towards the righteous judgment of God on our sins. So far from this latter aspect of Christ's work—the judicial— being to be thrown into the background, it is, I think, the one which the apostolic theology specially fastens upon as the ground of the remission of sins, and the means by which the sinner is brought into a relation of peace with God—the ground, as Bunyan phrases it, on which God "justly justifies the sinner."

Christ, as the Son of God, incarnate in our nature, is the only one qualified to undertake this work ; and as Son of

God and Son of Man He did it. He alone could enter, on the one hand, into the meaning of the sin of the world; on the other, into a realisation of all that was due to that sin from God, not minimising either the sin or the righteousness, but doing justice to both, upholding righteousness, yet opening to the world the gates of a forgiving mercy. In Him we see that done which we could not do; we see that brought which we could not bring; we see that reparation made to a broken law which we could not make; we see, at the same time, a righteousness consummated we long to make our own, a victory over the world we long to share, a will of love we long to have reproduced in ourselves, a grandeur of self-sacrifice we long to imitate. And, appropriating that sacrifice, not only in its atoning merit, but in its inward spirit, we know ourselves redeemed and reconciled.

9
THE INCARNATION AND
HUMAN DESTINY

"This earth is too small
For Love Divine? Is God not Infinite?
If so, His Love is Infinite. Too small!
One famished babe meets pity oft from man
More than an army slain! Too small for Love?
Was earth too small to be of God created?
Why then too small to be redeemed?"

Aubrey De Vere

"And so beside the silent sea
 I wait the muffled oar:
No harm from Him can come to me
 On ocean or on shore.

"I know not where His islands lift
 Their fronded palms in air,
I only know I cannot drift
 Beyond His love and care."

Whittier

"The last enemy that shall be abolished is death."

Paul

9

THE INCARNATION AND HUMAN DESTINY

EVERY view of the world has its eschatology. It cannot help raising the question of the whither, as well as of the what and the whence? "O my Lord," said Daniel to the angel, "what shall be the end of these things?"[1] What is the end, the final destiny, of the individual? Does he perish at death, or does he enter into another state of being; and under what conditions of happiness or woe does he exist there? What is the end, the final aim, of the great whole; that far-off Divine event to which the whole creation moves? It is vain to tell man not to ask these questions. He will ask them, and must ask them. He will pore over every scrap of fact, or trace of law, which seems to give any indication of an answer. He will try from the experience of the past, and the knowledge of the present, to deduce what the future shall be. He will peer as far as he can into the unseen; and, where knowledge fails, will weave from his hopes and trusts pictures and conjectures.

It is not religions only, but philosophy and science also, which have their eschatologies. The Stoics had their conceptions of world-cycles, when everything, reabsorbed in the primal fire, was produced anew exactly as before. The Buddhists had their kalpas, or world-ages, periods of destruction and restoration, "during which (as in Brahmanism) constant universes are supposed to appear, disappear, and reappear";[2] new worlds, phœnix-like, incessantly rising out of the ruins of the old. The pessimist Hartmann has his eschatology as truly as the New Testament has its.[3] Kant speculated, in his *Theory of the Heavens*, on the birth and death of worlds;

---

[1] Dan. xii. 8.
[2] *Buddhism*, by Professor Monier-Williams, p. 120. Cf. p. 118.
[3] On Hartmann's " Cosmic Suicide," see Caro's *Le Pessimisme*, chap. viii.

and Strauss compares the cosmos to one of those tropical trees on which, simultaneously, here a blossom bursts into flower, there a ripe fruit drops from the bough.[1] How is the science of to-day seen peering on into the future, trying to make out what shall be the end of these things; whither the changes, and transformations, and integrations, and dissolutions of the physical universe all tend; and what fate is in store for the earth, and for the physical system as a whole! Mr. Spencer has his eschatology, and speculates on a boundless space, holding here and there extinct suns, fated to remain thus for ever; though he clings to the hope that, in some way he knows not, out of the ashes of this old universe a new universe will arise.[2] The authors of *The Unseen Universe* say, "What happens to our system will happen likewise to the whole visible universe, which will, if finite, become in time a lifeless mass, if indeed it be not doomed to utter desolation. In fine, it will become old and effete, no less truly than the individual,—it is a glorious garment this visible universe, but not an immortal one — we must look elsewhere, if we are to be clothed with immortality as with a garment."[3]

The Christian view of the world, also, has its eschatology —one too, in its physical issues, not very different from that just described. The Christian view, however, is positive, where that of science is negative; ethical, where it is material; human, where it is cosmogonic; ending in personal immortality, where this ends in extinction and death. The eschatology of Christianity springs from its character as a teleological religion. The highest type of "Weltanschauung" is that which seeks to grasp the unity of the world through the conception of an end or aim. It is only through a conception of the world that is itself unified that man can give a true unity to his life—only in reference to an aim or end that he can organise his life to a consistent whole. On the cycle hypothesis, no satisfactory view of life is possible. All is vanity and vexation of spirit. A truly purposeful view of life is only possible on the basis of a world-view which gathers itself up to a highest definite aim. As giving this, Christianity

---

[1] *Der alte und der neue Glaube*, p. 152.   [2] *First Principles*, pp. 529, 537.
[3] *Unseen Universe*, 5th ed. p. 196.   Cf. pp. 165, 166.

is the teleological religion *par excellence*. It is, says Dorner, the only absolute teleological religion.[1] In one other respect Christianity agrees with the higher speculation—scientific and other—and that is in its breadth and scope, extending in its issues far beyond this little spot called earth, and touching in its influence the remotest regions of creation.

I. Before entering directly on eschatological questions, it may be worth our while, in connection with the fact just mentioned, to glance at the objection sometimes raised to Christianity from the enlargement of our knowledge of the physical universe through modern discoveries—chiefly through astronomy. The enormous expansion of our ideas in regard to the extent of the physical universe brought about through the telescope, and the corresponding sense of the insignificance of our planet, awakened by comparison with the gigantic whole, is supposed by many to be fatal to belief in Christianity. Strauss boldly affirms that the Copernican system gave the death-blow to the Christian view of the world.[2] So long as the earth was believed to be the centre of the universe, and the only inhabited spot in it, so long was it possible to maintain that God had a peculiar love to the inhabitants of our world, and had sent His Son for their Redemption. But when the true relation of the earth to the sun, and to the other planets of the system, was discovered—when, beyond this, the infinite depths of the heavens were laid bare, with their innumerable suns, galaxies, and constellations, to which our own sun, with its attendant planets, is but as a drop in the immeasurable ocean—then the idea that this little globe of ours—this insignificant speck—should become the scene of so stupendous a Divine drama as the Christian religion represents; should be the peculiar object of God's favours, and the recipient of His revelations; that, above all, the Son of God should become incarnate on its surface,—seemed nothing less than incredible. In a universe teeming with worlds, presumably inhabited by intelligences of every order and degree, it is thought preposterous to connect the

[1] *System of Doctrine*, iv. p. 376 (Eng. trans.). Cf. Martensen, *Dogmatics*, pp. 465, 466 (Eng. trans.).
[2] Is fatal even to belief in a personal God. Cf. his *Der alte und der neue Glaube*, pp. 108–110.

Deity in this peculiar and transcendent way with one of the very smallest of them.

Here, first, since the objection is made in the name of science, it might fairly be asked how far the premiss on which it rests — the assumption of innumerable spheres peopled with such intelligences as we have in man (I do not refer to angelic intelligences, for the Christian view has always admitted these, without our thoughts of the greatness of the Christian Redemption being thereby lessened, but corporeal inhabitants of other planets and worlds)—how far this assumption is scientifically established, or is even matter of plausible conjecture. Kant declared that he would not hesitate to stake his all on the truth of the proposition—if there were any way of bringing it to the test of experience —that at least some one of the planets which we see is inhabited;[1] but others may not be prepared to share his confidence. Of direct scientific evidence, of course, there is none, and the argument from analogy is weakened rather than strengthened by the progress of modern discovery. If astronomy has been extending our views of the universe in space, geology has been extending our views of our own world backwards in time, and it has been pointed out that, though preparation was being made through the millions of years of that long past, it is only in quite recent times that man appeared upon its surface, and then under conditions which we have no reason to suppose exist in any other planet of our system.[2] Are there not worlds in the making, as well as worlds already made? Certain it is, that of the seven hundred and fifty-one parts, or thereabouts, into which our solar system[3] can be divided, life, such as we know it, or can conceive of it, is not found in seven hundred and fifty of them, for the sun monopolises that enormous proportion of the whole for himself; and of the remaining one part, it is only an insignificant fraction in which the physical conditions exist which render any of the higher conditions of life possible.[4] If the same proportion prevails through the

---

[1] *Kritik d. r. Ver.* p. 561, Erdmann's ed. (Eng. trans. p. 500).
[2] This is the point specially made in Whewell's *The Plurality of Worlds.*
[3] Sun and planets.
[4] In Mars, and even here, Professor Ball doubts the possibility.—*Story of the Heavens*, p. 190.

universe, the area reserved for rational life will be correspondingly restricted. But, in truth, we know nothing of planets in other parts of the heavens at all, or even whether —except in one or two problematical instances—such bodies exist.[1] What if, after all, our little planet should be the Eden of the planetary system—the only spot on which a place has been prepared for rational life, or in which the conditions favourable to its blossoming forth have been found?[2] It is a singular circumstance that the objection here urged against Christianity is not exclusively applicable to it, but bears as strongly against all those speculative systems— Hegelianism, Schopenhauerism, Hartmannism, etc. — which have been hatched in the full light of the nineteenth century. Here, too, it is assumed that our planet stands alone as the place in which the Absolute has come to consciousness of himself (or itself), and where the great drama of his historical evolution is unfolded—where, in Hegelian phrase, God is incarnate in man ![3]

Apart from such considerations, however, the real reply to this objection to the Christian view of the world is that it is merely a quantitative one. Be the physical magnitude of the universe what it may, it remains the fact that, on this little planet, life *has* effloresced into reason; that we have here a race of rational beings who bear God's image, and are capable of knowing, loving, and obeying Him. This is a fact against which it is absurd to put into comparison any mere quantities of inanimate matter—any number of suns, nebulæ, and planets. Even suppose that there were other inhabited worlds, or any number of them, this does not detract from the soul's value in this world. Mind, if it has the powers we know it has, is not less great because other

---

[1] Professor Ball says : " It may be that, as the other stars are suns, so they too may have other planets circulating round them ; but of this we know nothing. Of the stars we can only say that they are points of light, and if they had hosts of planets these planets must for ever remain invisible to us, even if they were many times as large as Jupiter."—*Story of the Heavens*, p. 95.

[2] " The earth is perhaps at this hour the only inhabited globe in the midst of almost boundless space."—Renan, *Dialogues*, p. 61.

[3] Cf. Renan : " For my part I think there is not in the universe any intelligence superior to that of man, so that the greatest genius of our planet is truly the priest of the world, since he is the highest reflection of it."— *Dialogues*, p. 283. See on Renan's extraordinary eschatology—Note A.

minds may exist elsewhere. Man is not less great, because he is not alone great. If he is a spiritual being,—if he has a soul of infinite worth, which is the Christian assumption,—that fact is not affected though there were a whole universe-ful of other spiritual beings, as indeed the Christian Church has always believed there is. The truth is, what we have underlying this objection is that very anthropomorphism in thinking about God against which the objection is directed. It is thought that, while it might be worthy of God to care for man if he existed alone, it is derogatory to God's greatness to think of him when there are so many other objects in the universe. Or it is thought that God is a Being so exalted that He will lose sight of the individual in the crowd. Those who think thus must have very unworthy ideas of the Being whom they wish to exalt; must forget, too, that the universe can only exist on the condition that God is present in the little as in the great; that His knowledge, power, and care extend, not to things in the mass, but to each atom of matter separately, to each tiniest blade of grass, to each insect on the wing, and animalcule in the drop of water. It is the Bible which gives the true philosophy, when it teaches that the same God who cares for stars cares also for souls; that the very hairs of our head are all numbered; that not even a sparrow falls to the ground without our heavenly Father.[1]

But the question still remains, even if all these bright worlds were inhabited—which they are not,—inhabited by rational beings like to man himself,—are they sinful? Sin retains its awful significance in the universe, no matter how many worlds there may be. If this world alone is sinful, then it is worthy of God to redeem it. Have men's hearts not recognised the Divineness of that parable of Christ about the lost sheep? Is it not the Divinest thing that God can do to seek and to save the lost? Suppose that this universe were as full of intelligent life as the objection represents, but that this world is the one lost sheep of the Divine flock, would it not be worthy of the Good Shepherd to seek it out and save it? Shall its size prevent? Then is the worth of the soul a thing to be weighed in scales?

[1] Ps. cxlvii. 3, 4 ; Matt. x. 29–31.

Mr. Spencer, in one passage of his writings, thinks he has destroyed the case for Revelation, when he asks us if we can believe that "the Cause to which we can put no limits in space or time, and of which our entire solar system is a relatively infinitesimal product, took the disguise of a man for the purpose of covenanting with a shepherd-chief in Syria." [1] He first defines God in terms which put Him infinitely far away from us, and then asks us to combine with this a conception which seems to contradict it. But what if God is not only the "Cause" of all things—the infinitely great Creator of stars and systems—but, as Mr. Spencer's own principles might lead him to hold, One also infinitely near to us—

"Speak to Him, thou, for He hears, and spirit with spirit can meet;
 Closer is He than breathing, and nearer than hands or feet," [2]—

and, beyond this, infinite goodness and love as well,—is it then so strange that He should draw a Syrian shepherd to His side, and should establish a covenant with him which had for its ultimate aim, not that shepherd's personal aggrandisement, but the blessing, through him, of all mankind?

But finally, and this is the complete answer to the objection, if the Christian view is true, the scope of God's purpose is *not* confined to this little planet, but embraces all the realms of creation. [3] The Incarnation is not a fact the significance of which is confined to earth. The Scriptures do not so represent it, but seek rather to impress us with the thought of how wide this purpose of God is, how extensive in its sweep, how far-reaching in its issues. The objection to the Christian scheme with many, I fancy, will rather be, that with its base on earth it rises too high; that when it speaks to us of the bearing of the gospel on different parts of creation, of angels desiring to look into it, of principalities and powers in the heavenly places being instructed by it in the many-sided wisdom of God,—above all, of all things in heaven and in earth being gathered up in Christ, [4]—it presents us with a plan the magnitude of which soars beyond our powers of belief. But if the Divine plan is on a scale of this grandeur, why complain because its starting-

---

[1] *Eccles. Institutions*, p. 704.   [2] Tennyson's *Higher Pantheism*.
[3] This is the argument developed in Chalmers's celebrated *Astronomical Discourses*. See Note B.—The Gospel and the Vastness of Creation.
[4] 1 Pet. i. 12; Eph. ii. 10, i. 10, etc.

point is this physically small globe? The answer to this objection, as to the similar one drawn from the earthly lowliness of
Christ, must be, *Respice finem*—Look to the end!

II. In proceeding now to deal directly with the eschatological
relations of the Christian view, it is to be remembered that it
stands differently with lines of prophecy projected into the
future from what it does with facts already past. In dealing
with the history of God's past Revelations — with the ages
before the Advent, with the earthly life and Revelation of Jesus
Christ, with the subsequent course of God's Providence in His
Church—we are dealing with that which has already been. It
stands in concrete reality before us, and we can reason from it
as a thing known in its totality and its details. But when the
subject of Revelation is that which is yet to be, especially that
which is yet to be under forms and conditions of which we
have no direct experience, the case is widely altered. Here it
is at most outlines we can look for; and even these outlines
will be largely clothed in figure and symbol; the spiritual
kernel will seek material investiture to body itself forth; the
conditions of the future will require to be presented largely
in forms borrowed from known relations.[1] The outstanding
thoughts will be sufficiently apparent, but the forms in which
these thoughts are cast will partake of metaphor and image.

Examples of undue literalism in the interpretation of prophetic language will occur to every one; as an example on the
other side, I may instance Ritschl, who, because of the figurative character of the language employed, sweeps the whole of
the New Testament eschatology on one side, and simply takes
no account of it. This is a drastic method, which makes us
wonder why, if these representations convey no intelligible
representations to the mind, use was made of them at all.
With Ritschl, the sole thing of value is the idea of the kingdom of God, for the realisation of which we are to labour in
this world. The form which the kingdom of God will assume
beyond this life we cannot know, and need not concern ourselves
about. The recoil from this one-sided position of Ritschl is
seen in the further development of his school, particularly in
Kaftan, who precisely reverses Ritschl's standpoint, and trans-

---

[1] Cf. Fairbairn's *Prophecy*, chap. iv. sec. 4.

ports the good of the kingdom of God entirely into the life beyond. "The certainty of an eternal life in a kingdom of God," he says, "which is above the world, which lies to us as yet in the beyond, is the very nerve of our Christian piety." [1] This is an exaggeration on the other side, in opposition to which the truth of Ritschl's view has to be contended for, that there is a kingdom of God to be striven for even in this world. What did Christ come for, if not to impart a new life to humanity, which, working from within outwards, is destined to transform all human relations—all family and social life, all industry and commerce, all art and literature, all government and relations among peoples—till the kingdoms of this world are become the kingdoms of our Lord and of His Christ? [2] Whether more slowly or more rapidly, whether peacefully or, as Scripture seems to indicate, by a succession of crises, surely this grand result of a kingdom of God will be brought about; and it is our duty and privilege to pray and labour for it. What is the reproach which is sometimes brought against Christianity by its enemies, but that of "other-worldliness" —of exclusive devotion to a good beyond this life, to the neglect of interests lying immediately to hand? And what is the remedy for this reproach, but to show that Christianity is a power also for temporal and social salvation, a leaven which is to permeate the whole lump of humanity? It is on this side that a great and fruitful field opens itself up for Christian effort in the present day; on this side that Christianity finds itself in touch with some of the most characteristic movements of the time. The ideals of the day are pre-eminently social; the key-word of Positivism is "Altruism"—the organisation of humanity for social efforts; the call is to a "service of humanity"; [3] the air is full of ideas, schemes, Utopias, theories of social reform; and we who believe that Christianity is the motive power which alone can effectually attain what these systems of men are striving after, are surely bound to put

---

[1] The sentence is quoted from Pfleiderer, *Religionsphilosophie*, ii. p. 206 (Eng. trans.). Cf. Kaftan, *Wesen*, pp. 67, 71, 171, 173, 214, 213, etc.; *Wahrheit*, p. 547, etc.

[2] Rev. xi. 15.

[3] Cf. Cotter Morison's *The Service of Man*. "The worship of deities has passed into 'the Service of Man.' Instead of Theolatry, we have Anthropolatry; the divine service has become human service."—P. 265. As if the truest service of God did not carry in it the service of humanity.

our faith to the proof, and show to men that in deed and in truth, and not in word only, the kingdom of God has come nigh to them. We know something of what Christianity did in the Roman Empire as a power of social purification and reform;[1] of what it did in the Middle Ages in the Christianising and disciplining of barbarous nations; of the power it has been in modern times as the inspiration of the great moral and philanthropic movements of the century;[2] and this power of Christianity is likely to be yet greater in the future than in the past. There is yet vast work to be accomplished ere the kingdom of God is fully come.[3]

This, therefore, may be said to be the nearer aim of Christianity—the coming of the kingdom of God on earth; but beyond this there is, as certainly, another end. Even on earth the kingdom of God does not consist supremely, or even peculiarly, in the possession of outward good, but in the inward life of the Spirit, in righteousness and peace and joy in the Holy Ghost.[4] History, too, moves onward to its goal, which is not simply a transformed society, but a winding-up of all terrestrial affairs, and the transition from a world of time to a new order of things in eternity, in which the good of the kingdom of God will be perfectly realised.

In dealing with the eschatology proper of the Christian view, it will be of advantage to turn our attention first to those aspects of it which stand out distinct and clear. I have said that a truly purposeful life is only possible on the basis of a world-view which has a definite aim. What that aim is in the Christian view, as respects its positive and bright side, is seen in the light of the Incarnation. There are three points here which seem to stand out free from all uncertainty.

1. The aim of God as regards believers is summed up in the simple phrase—conformity to the image of the Son. " Whom He foreknew, He also foreordained to be conformed to the image

---

[1] Cf. Loring Brace's *Gesta Christi* ; Schmidt's *Social Results of Early Christianity* (Eng. trans.) ; Uhlhorn's *Christian Charity in the Early Church* ; Lecky's *History of European Morals*, etc.

[2] Mr. Stead, himself an enthusiast in social work, says : " Most good work is done by Christians. Mrs. Besant herself expressed to me that they did very little indeed, and those who did were only those who, like herself, had been brought up Christians."—*Church of the Future*, p. 9.

[3] See Appendix on " The Idea of the Kingdom of God."

[4] Rom. xiv. 17.

of His Son, that He might be the First-born among many brethren." [1] This is the one absolute light-point in the eternal future. The mists and shadows which rest on other parts of the eschatological problem do not affect us here. We see not yet all things put under humanity, " but we behold Him who hath been made a little lower than the angels, even Jesus, because of the suffering of death crowned with glory and honour," [2] and we know that our destiny is to be made like Him. This is conformity to type in the highest degree. By what processes the result is to be brought about we may not know, but the end itself is clear—the assimilation begun on earth shall be perfected above.

2. This conformity to Christ includes not only moral and spiritual likeness to Christ, but likeness to Him also in His glorious body; that is, the Redemption of the body, life in a glorified corporeity. Difficulties rise here of course in great numbers, and the question will be put, " How are the dead raised, and with what manner of body do they come?" [3] But, first, I would say that there are certain things here also which stand out clear.

(1) First of all, this doctrine of the Redemption of the body is needful for the completion of the Christian view. It is not an accident, but an essential and integral part of it. It is essential to a complete Redemption, as we saw in speaking of immortality, that not the soul only, but man in his whole complex personality, body and soul together, should be redeemed. In the disembodied state, the believer indeed is with Christ, rests in the blessedness of unbroken fellowship with Him, but it is the resurrection which is the perfection of his life. [4]

(2) I say, next, that this doctrine of the Resurrection of the body is not exposed to some of the objections often made to it. How, it is asked, can the same body be raised, when it is utterly decayed, and the particles of which it was composed are scattered to the winds of heaven, or perhaps taken up into other bodies? But the doctrine of the Resurrection does not

---

[1] Rom. viii. 29 (R.V.). [2] Heb. ii. 8, 9 (R.V.). [3] 1 Cor. xv. 35 (R.V.).
[4] The idealistic school, on the other hand, speak slightingly of life in the body. "A renewed 'embodiment,'" says Mr. Green, "if it means anything, would be but a return to that condition in which we are but parts of nature, a condition from which the moral life is already a partial deliverance."—*Works*, iii. p. 206. Was Plotinus then right when he blushed that he had a body?

involve any such belief. The solution lies, I think, in a right conception of what it is which constitutes identity. Wherein, let us ask, does the identity even of our present bodies consist? Not, certainly, in the mere identity of the particles of matter of which our bodies are composed, for this is continually changing, is in constant process of flux. The principle of identity lies rather in that which holds the particles together, which vitally organises ond constructs them, which impresses on them their form and shape, and maintains them in unity with the soul to serve as its instrument and medium of expression. It lies, if we may so say, in the organic, constructive principle, which in its own nature is spiritual and immaterial, and adheres to the side of the soul. At death, the body perishes. It is resolved into its elements; but this vital, immaterial principle endures, prepared, when God wills, to give form to a new and grander, because more spiritual, corporeity. The existence of mystery here I grant: we cannot understand the resurrection from natural causes, but only, as Christ teaches us, from the power of God.[1] It is a miracle, and the crowning act of an economy of miracles. But we need not make the mystery greater than it is by insisting on a material identity between the new body and the old, which is no part of the doctrine of Scripture—indeed, is expressly contradicted by the words of the apostle, touching on this very point. " Thou foolish one," says Paul, " that which thou thyself sowest is not quickened, except it die; and that which thou sowest, *thou sowest not the body which shall be*, but a bare grain, it may chance of wheat, or of some other kind; but God giveth it a body even as it pleaseth Him, and to each seed a body of its own."[2] In the case supposed, we see very clearly, first, that the identity consists only in a very minute degree, if at all—and then only accidentally—in identity of material particles; and, second, that the real bond lies in the active, vital principle which connects the two bodies.

---

[1] Matt. xxii. 29.

[2] 1 Cor. xv. 36–38 (R.V.). Cf. Origen, *De Principiis*, ii. 6: " For him the resurrection is not the reproduction of any particular organism, but the preservation of complete identity of person, an identity maintained under new conditions, which he presents under the apostolic figure of the growth of the plant from the seed : the seed is committed to the earth, perishes, and yet the vital power which it contains gathers a new frame answering to its proper nature."—Westcott in *Dictionary of Christian Biography*, iv. p. 121.

(3) A third point is, that the resurrection contemplated is not a resurrection at death, but a future event connected with the consummation of all things. The opposite view is one which has had many modern advocates,—among them the authors of *The Unseen Universe*;[1] but, though it professes to stay itself on the expressions, "a house not made with hands, eternal in the heavens," "clothed upon with our habitation which is from heaven,"[2] I do not think that this view accords with the general representations of Scripture, which always contemplate the resurrection as future, and regard the believer's state as, till that time, one of being "unclothed." What Scripture does seem to teach is, that meanwhile a preparation for this spiritual body is going on, a spiritual basis for it is being laid, through the possession and working of Christ's Spirit.[3]

3. The doctrine of the Christian consummation carries with it, further, the idea that, together with the perfecting of the believer, or of the sons of God, there will be a perfecting or glorification even of outward nature. This is implied in the possession of a corporeity of any kind, for that stands in relation to an environment, to a general system of things. A new heaven and earth there must be, if there is to be glorified corporeity. Scripture, accordingly, makes clear that nature also, the creation also, will be delivered from the bondage of vanity and corruption under which it is at present held.[4] It is needless for us to attempt to anticipate what changes this may imply; how it is to be brought about, or how it stands related to the changes in the material universe predicted by science. The day alone will declare it.

Connected with these views and anticipations of the consum-

---

[1] *Unseen Universe*, pp. 200–211, and on Swedenborg's views, pp. 63, 64. Thus also Munger in his *Freedom of Faith*: "This change necessarily takes place at death. A disembodied state, or state of torpid existence between death and some far-off day of resurrection, an under-world where the soul waits for the reanimation of its body : these are old-world notions that survive only through chance contact with the Christian system."—P. 309. Then, were Hymenæus and Philetus not right who said that "the resurrection is past already," and in Paul's view overthrew the faith of some? (2 Tim. ii. 18.) Cf. Newman Smyth's *Old Faiths in New Lights*, chap. viii.

[2] 2 Cor. v. 1, 2 (R.V.).

[3] The Scriptures mention also a resurrection of the wicked (John v. 29; Acts xxiv. 15; Rev. xx. 12), likewise, we cannot doubt, connected with Christ's appearance in our nature, but, beyond describing it as a resurrection of condemnation, they throw little light upon its nature.

[4] Rom. viii. 21; 2 Pet. iii. 13.

mation, are certain pictorial and scenic elements in the Christian eschatology, to which attention must now be given. Such are the descriptions of the second Advent and of the general Judgment. Here belong the eschatological discourses and sayings of Christ and His apostles, in regard to which, again, the question is, How are they to be interpreted? Taking, first, those which relate to Christ's personal return to the world, I might quote Beyschlag as a typical example of how these pictorial and scenic elements are treated by many who are indisposed to take a literal view of their import. "Jesus," he says, "grasps up together in the sensible image of His coming again on the clouds of heaven all that which lay beyond His death—the whole glorious reversal of His earthly life and the death on the cross, from His resurrection on till the perfecting of His kingdom at the last day; and the more we keep in view the genuinely prophetic nature of this comprehensive sense-image, and how it shares the essential limits of all prophecy, the more is a solution found of the at first apparently insoluble difficulty of this prophetic part of His doctrine."[1] Now, I think a careful study of the passages will compel us to agree with this writer on one main point, namely, that Jesus does not always speak of His coming in the same sense; that it is to Him rather a process in which many elements flow together in a single image, than a single definite event, always looked at in the same light.[2] Thus, He says to the high priest, with obvious reference to the prophecy in Daniel, "Henceforth," that is, from this time on, "ye shall see the Son of Man sitting at the right hand of power, and coming on the clouds of heaven."[3] He came again to His disciples after the resurrection; He came in the mission of the Comforter; He came in the power and spread of His kingdom, especially after the removal of the limitations created by the existing Jewish polity, which seems to be the meaning in the passage, "There

---

[1] *Leben Jesu*, i. p. 356.

[2] That Jesus did not anticipate His immediate return, but contemplated a slow and progressive development of His kingdom, is shown by many indications in the Gospels. Cf. on this subject, Beyschlag, *Leben Jesu*, i. pp. 354–356; Reuss, *Hist. of Christ. Theol.* i. pp. 217, 218; Bruce's *Kingdom of God*, chap. xii.

[3] Matt. xxvi. 64 (R.V.). Cf. Dan. vii. 13, 14. In Daniel's vision the "one like unto a son of man" comes with the clouds of heaven to receive a kingdom from the Ancient of Days, not to judge the world.

be some of them that stand here which shall in no wise taste of death, till they see the Son of Man coming in His kingdom " ;[1] He has come in every great day of the Lord in the history of His Church ; He will come yet more conspicuously in the events of the future. Yet I cannot agree with Beyschlag when, on these grounds, he would exclude altogether a final, personal advent of Jesus, a visible return in power and glory to the world. It seems to me that Christ's words on this subject, repeated by His apostles, are altogether too explicit and of too solemn an import to be explained away into mere metaphor. I would agree, therefore, with the Church catholic in its confession, "From thence He shall come to judge the quick and the dead." In Beyschlag's case it seems the more arbitrary to deny this, as he fully admits the reality of Christ's resurrection, and, if not of His visible ascent, at least of His actual bodily reception into heaven. His words are, "What then was the original thought of the ascension? What else can it have been than that of the elevation of Jesus above the limits of the earthly life, of His translation into another, supra-mundane, Divine form of existence—in a word, of His exaltation or glorification?"[2] If this be so, there is surely no incogruity in the thought that He who thus went away shall again appear in manifested glory.

It is not otherwise with the pictures we have of a final act of Judgment as the accompaniment of this reappearance of the Lord. Here, also, it is correct to speak of a continuous judgment of the world. The history of the world, as we often hear, is the judgment of the world. Yet the representations which Christ Himself gives us of a gradual ripening of both good and evil to the harvest, then of a final and decisive separation[3]— joined with the similar representations of the apostles[4]—compel us, it seems to me, to speak of a day of reckoning, when God shall judge the secrets of men by Christ Jesus ; which shall be at once a vindication of God's action in the government of the world, and a decision upon the issues of the individual life. From a teleological view of the world, also, as well as

---

[1] Matt. xvi. 28 (R.V.). Mark has "till they see the kingdom of God come with power" (ix. 1); Luke simply, "till they see the kingdom of God" (ix. 27).
[2] *Leben Jesu*, i. p. 448.   [3] Matt. xiii. 30, 49, etc.
[4] Acts xvii. 31 ; Rom. ii. 16 ; 2 Cor. v. 10, etc.

from a survey of its existing imperfections, it is felt that there is an inherent fitness, if not a moral necessity, in the supposition of such a last judgment which shall form, as it were, the *dénouement* of the great drama of universal history.[1] It is manifest, on the other hand, that all the descriptions and pictures which we have of this dread event are so charged with figurative and parabolic elements that we can infer nothing from them beyond the great principles on which the judgment will proceed.

III. By these steps we are led up, in the consideration of the last things, to that which is for us the question of supreme concern, on this subject—the question of individual destiny. I have spoken of this already as regards the believer. But what of the shadow alongside of the light? What of the judgment of condemnation alongside of the judgment of life? What of the wrath of God abiding on the unbeliever, alongside of the blessedness of those who are saved? These questions are not arbitrarily raised, but are forced upon us by the plain statements of Scripture, by the fears and forebodings of the guilty conscience, and by the anxiety and perplexity they are causing to many hearts. To the questions thus raised, three main answers have been given, and are given.

1. The first is that of *dogmatic Universalism*. This was the view of Origen in the early Church,[2] and is the view of Schleiermacher, expressed in the words, "that through the power of Redemption there will result in the future a general restoration of all human souls";[3] the view expressed yet more dogmatically by Dr. Samuel Cox, "While our brethren hold the Redemption of Christ to extend only to the life that now is, and to take effect only on some men, we maintain, on the contrary, that it extends to the life to come, and must take effect on all men at the last";[4] the view breathed as a wish by Tennyson—

> "The wish that of the living whole
> No life may fail beyond the grave."[5]

---

[1] Cf. Martensen, Dorner, Van Oosterzee, Luthardt, for illustrations of this thought.

[2] *De Principiis*, i. 6.

[3] *Der christl. Glaube*, ii. p. 505.

[4] *Salvator Mundi*, 11th ed. p. 225.

[5] *In Memoriam*.

It is a view which, I am sure, we would all be glad to hold, if the Scriptures gave us light enough to assure us that it was true.

2. The second answer is that of the theory of *Annihilation*, or, as it is sometimes called, Conditional Immortality. This is the direct opposite of the universalistic view, inasmuch as it assumes that the wicked will be absolutely destroyed, or put out of existence. Rothe and others have held this view among Continental theologians;[1] in this country it is best known through the writings of Mr. Edward White. A kindred view is that of Bushnell, who, reasoning "from the known effects of wicked feeling and practice in the reprobate characters," expects "that the staple of being and capacity in such will be gradually diminished, and the possibility is thus suggested that, at some remote period, they may be quite wasted away, or extirpated."[2] The service which this theory has rendered is as a corrective to Universalism, in laying stress on those passages in Scripture which appear to teach a final ruin of the wicked.

3. The third answer is that which has been the prevailing one in the Protestant Church, the theory of an *eternal punishment* of the wicked in a state of conscious suffering; a theory, also, with which, in the form in which it has been commonly presented, a strong feeling of dissatisfaction at present exists. A modification of this theory is that which supposes the ultimate fate of the wicked—or of those who are the wicked here—to consist in the punishment of loss, rather than in that of eternal suffering.

Such are the views that are held; what attitude are we to take up towards them? I shall best consult my own feelings and sense of duty by speaking frankly what I think upon the subject. Here, in the first place, I would like to lay down one or two fundamental positions which seem to me of the nature of certainties.

1. I would lay down, as the first and great fundamental certitude, the truth enunciated by the prophet, "Say ye of the righteous, that it shall be well with him; for they shall eat the fruit of their doings. Woe unto the wicked! it shall be ill

---

[1] *Dogmatik*, iii. p. 108. Ritschl, too, teaches that *if* there are any who oppose themselves absolutely to the realisation of the Divine plan, their fate would be annihilation.—*Recht. und Ver.* ii. pp. 129, 140-142. But the case is purely hypothetical, iii. p. 363.

[2] *Forgiveness and Law*, p. 147.

with him ; for the reward of his hands shall be given him " ; [1] in other words, the great and fundamental principle of certain retribution for sin. This is a principle we cannot hold too clearly or too strongly. Whatever tends to tamper with this principle, or to weaken its hold upon the conscience, is alien to the true Christian view. By unalterable laws impressed upon the nature of man and on the universe, righteousness is life, and sin is inevitable misery and death.[2] Omnipotence itself could not reverse this law, that so long as the sinner continues in his sin he must suffer. On the other hand, where this principle is firmly grasped, there ought, I think, to be much room left for difference of views on points which, from the nature of the case, are obscure and tentative.

2. I think, in the next place, a strong distinction ought to be drawn between those things which Scripture expressly teaches, and those things on which it simply gives no light, in regard to which it neither affirms nor denies, but is simply silent. Here our wisdom is to imitate its caution, and refrain from dogmatism. I confess I marvel sometimes at the confidence with which people pronounce on that which must and shall be through the eternities and eternities—the ages and ages—of God's unending life, during which also the soul of man is to exist ; and this in respect of so appalling a subject as the future fate of the lost. There is room here for a wise Agnosticism. I prefer to say that, so far as my light goes, I see no end, and there to stop.

3. I hold it for a certainty that, to deal with all the sides and relations of this difficult subject, we would require a much larger calculus than with our present light we possess. What chiefly weighs with many in creating dissatisfaction with the current Church view is not so much special texts of Scripture, as rather the general impression produced on the mind by the whole spirit and scope of the gospel Revelation. Starting with

---

[1] Isa. iii. 10, 11 (R.V.).

[2] Mr. Greg also has his doctrine of future retribution. " Must not a future world in itself—the condition of 'spiritual corporeity' alone—bring with it dreadful retribution to the wicked, the selfish, and the weak ? In the mere fact of their *cleared perceptions*, in the realisation of their low position, in seeing themselves at length as they really are, in feeling that all their work *is yet to do*, in beholding all those they loved and venerated far before them, away from them, fading in the bright distance, may lie, must lie, a torture, a purifying fire, in comparison with which the representations of Dante and Milton shrivel into baseness and inadequacy."—*Creed of Christendom*, p. 280.

the character of God as Christ reveals it; with the fact of the
Incarnation; with the reality and breadth of the Atonement;
with the glimpses given into the issues of Christ's work,—the
feeling is produced in every thoughtful mind, that the sweep of
this great scheme of Incarnation and Redemption cannot be
exhausted in the comparatively meagre results which we see
springing from it here,—meagre, I mean, in comparison with
the whole compass of the race or even of those who are brought
outwardly within the range of its influence. What, men are
asking with a constantly heavier sense of the burden of the
difficulty, of the untold millions who have never heard of
Christ at all, of the millions and millions who have never even
had the chance of hearing of Him? What, even within the
limits of Christendom, of the multitudes, as they must be
reckoned, in comparison with the really Christ-like in our midst,
who give no evidence of true regeneration, vast numbers of
whom are living openly worldly and godless lives? We feel
instinctively that the last word has not been—cannot be—
spoken by us here. It may be said, and with much truth, that
for those who have the light, there is no excuse. Salvation
has been put within their reach, and they have deliberately
rejected it. But even here, are there not elements we dare not
overlook? Men are responsible for the use they make of light,
but how much here also is not due to the individual will,
which is crossed by influences from heredity, from environment,
from up-bringing, from pressure of events! God alone can
disentangle the threads of freedom in the web of character and
action, and say how much is a man's individual responsibility
in the result, as distinguished from his share in the common
guilt of the race.[1] It is certain, from Christ's own statement,
that, in the judgment of Omniscience, all these things are taken
into account, and that even in the administration of punishment there are gradations of penalty, proportionate to men's
knowledge and opportunities; that, as Paul says, there is a

---

[1] Maudsley says : "When we reflect how much time and what a multitude
of divers experiences have gone to the formation of a character, what a complex
product it is, and what an inconceivably intricate interworking of intimate
energies, active and inhibitive, any display of it in feeling and will means, it
must appear a gross absurdity for anyone to aspire to estimate or appraise all
the component motives of a particular act of will. . . . To dissect any act of
will accurately, and then to recompose it, would be to dissect and recompose
humanity."—*Body and Will*, p. 29. But see below.

distinction made between those who have "sinned without law," and those who have "sinned under law."[1]

These principles being laid down, I proceed to offer a few remarks on the various theories which have been submitted.

1. And, first, I cannot accept the view of *dogmatic Universalism*. There is undoubtedly no clear and certain scripture which affirms that all men will be saved; on the other hand, there are many passages which look in another direction, which seem to put the stamp of finality on the sinner's state in eternity. Even Archdeacon Farrar, so strong an advocate of this theory, admits that some souls *may* ultimately be lost;[2] and it is to be observed that, if even one soul is lost finally, the principle is admitted on which the chief difficulty turns. I am convinced that the light and airy assertions one sometimes meets with of dogmatic Universalism are not characterised by a due sense of the gravity of the evil of sin, or of the awful possibilities of resistance to goodness that lie within the human will. It seems to me plain that deliberate rejection of Christ here means, at the very least, awful and irreparable loss in eternity; that to go from the judgment-seat condemned is to exclude oneself in perpetuity from the privilege and glory which belong to God's sons. Even the texts, some of them formerly quoted, which at first sight might seem to favour Universalism, are admitted by the most impartial expositors not to bear this weight of meaning. We read, *e.g.*, of "a restoration of all things"—the same that Christ calls the παλιγγενεσία—but in the same breath we are told of those who will not hearken, and will be destroyed.[3] We read of Christ drawing all men unto Him;[4] but we are not less clearly told that at His coming Christ will pronounce on some a tremendous condemnation.[5] We read of all things being gathered, or summed up, in Christ, of Christ subduing all things to Himself, etc.; but representative exegetes like Meyer and Weiss show that it is far from Paul's view to teach

---

[1] Rom. ii. 12 (R.V.).

[2] "I cannot tell whether some souls may not resist God for ever, and therefore may not be for ever shut out from His presence, and I believe that to be without God is 'hell'; and that in this sense there is a hell beyond the grave; and that for any soul to fall even for a time into this condition, though it be through its own hardened impenitence and resistance of God's grace, is a very awful and terrible prospect; and that in this sense there may be for some souls an endless hell."—*Mercy and Judgment*, p. 485.

[3] Matt. xix. 28; Acts iii. 21, 23 (R.V.).   [4] John x. 32.

[5] Matt. vii. 23, xxv. 41.

an ultimate conversion or annihilation of the kingdom of evil.[1]
I confess, however, that the strain of these last passages does
seem to point in the direction of some ultimate unity, be it
through subjugation, or in some other way, in which active
opposition to God's kingdom is no longer to be reckoned with.

2. Neither can I accept the doctrine of the *Annihilation of
the Wicked*. In itself considered, and divested of some of the
features with which Mr. White clothes it in his *Life in Christ*,
this may be admitted to be an abstractly possible hypothesis,
and as such has received the assent, as before stated, of Rothe
and others who are not materialistically disposed. There is a
certain sense in which everyone will admit that a man has not
a necessary or inherent immortality, that he depends for his
continued existence, therefore for his immortality, solely on the
will and power of God. Man can never rise above the limits
of his creaturehood. As created, he is, and must remain, a
dependent being. It is, therefore, a possible supposition—one
not *a priori* to be rejected—that though originally made and
destined for immortality, man might have this destiny cancelled.
There is force, too, in what is said, that it is difficult to see the
utility of keeping a being in existence merely to sin and suffer.
Yet, when the theory is brought to the test of Scripture proof,
it is found to fail in evidence.

(1) Stress is laid on those passages which speak of the destruction of the wicked, of their perishing,[2] of their being consumed in fire, as chaff, tares, branches, etc.[3] So far as the last
class of passages is concerned, they are plainly metaphorical,
and, in face of other evidence, it is difficult to put on any of
them the meaning that is asked. For this destruction comes
on the ungodly at the day of judgment, at the day of the Lord.
"Sudden destruction," an apostle calls it;[4] yet it is part of this
theory that the wicked are *not* annihilated at the day of judgment, but live on in suffering for an indefinitely prolonged time,
as a punishment for their offences, the greatest sinners suffering
most. In this respect the theory approximates to the ordinary
view, for it makes the real punishment of the sinner lie in the
period of his conscious existence, and the annihilation which

---

[1] See Note C.—Alleged Pauline Universalism.
[2] Matt. vii. 13; 2 Thess. i. 9; 2 Cor. ii. 15; 2 Pet. ii. 12, etc.
[3] Matt. iii. 12, xiii. 30, 50; John xv. 6, etc.   [4] 1 Thess. v. 3.

comes after is rather a merciful termination of his sufferings than the crowning of his woe. If Mr. White's theory is to be made consistent with itself, it ought to provide for the immediate annihilation of the wicked at death, or at least at the judgment. In reality, however, the "destruction" comes at the judgment, and the "annihilation" not till long after; so that, on his own principles, we cannot argue from the mere word to the fact of annihilation.

(2) Another thing which suggests itself in regard to this theory is that, taken strictly, it seems to shut out all gradations of punishment; the end of all being "death," *i.e.* "annihilation." If, to escape this, reference is made to the longer or shorter period of the suffering before annihilation, this shows, as before, that it is in the conscious sufferings, not in the annihilation, that the real punishment is supposed to lie.

(3) But the crowning objection to this theory—so far as proof from Scripture is concerned—is that in its use of the words "life" and "death," it misses the true significance of these Bible terms. Life is not, in Scripture usage, simple existence; death is not simple non-existence, but separation from true and complete life. This theory itself being witness, the soul survives in the state of natural death. It passes into the intermediate condition, and there awaits judgment. Life, in short, is, in its Scripture sense, a word with a moral and spiritual connotation; a person may not possess it, and yet continue to exist. "He that obeyeth not the Son," we are told, "shall not see life, but the wrath of God abideth on him."[1] But so long as the wrath of God abides (μένει) on him, he must abide. So far as Scripture goes, therefore, this theory is not proved. It must remain a mere speculation, and one which cuts the knot rather than unties it.

It is interesting to mark that Mr. White himself seems little satisfied with his theory, and does his best to relieve it of its harsher features. If the thought is terrible of the countless multitudes who leave this world without having heard of Christ, or without deliberate acceptance of Him, being doomed to endless suffering, it is scarcely less appalling to think of these myriads, after longer or shorter terms of suffering, being swept from existence by the fiat of Omnipotence. Mr. White

---

[1] John iii. 36 (R.V.).

feels the weight of this difficulty, and tries to alleviate it by the thought of a prolonged probation in Hades.[1] Here, he thinks, we find the solution of the problem of the heathen ; and of many more whose opportunities have not been sufficiently great to bring them to clear decision. I have no doubt that Mr. White cherishes in his heart the hope that by far the greater proportion of mankind will thus be saved ; that, in consequence, the finally lost will be comparatively few. In other words, just as in the admission of prolonged periods of penal suffering his theory was seen approximating to that of eternal punishment, so here we see it stretching out hands, as it were, on the other side, towards " the larger hope " of Universalism. It is certainly a curious result that a theory which begins by denying to man any natural immortality—which takes away the natural grounds of belief in a future state—should end by transferring the great bulk of the evangelising and converting work of the gospel over to that future state ; for, assuredly, what is accomplished there must be immense as compared with what, in his view, is done on earth. This brings me—

3. To speak of the ordinary doctrine, and as a proposed alleviation of this, of the theory of a *Future Probation,* a theory which we have just seen is held also by Mr. Edward White. By future probation is meant here probation, not after the judgment, but intermediately between death and judgment. This is a theory which, as is well known, has found wide acceptance among believing theologians on the Continent, and also in America, and is advanced by its adherents as a solution of the difficulties which arise from supposing that all who leave this world without having heard of Christ or having definitely accepted Him necessarily perish. It is the theory held, *e.g.*, by Dorner, Van Oosterzee, Martensen, Godet, Gretillat, and very many others. No one, it is said, will be lost without being brought to a knowledge of Christ, and having the opportunity given him of accepting His salvation. Every man must be brought to a definite acceptance or rejection of Christ, if not here, then hereafter. The theory is believed to be supported by the well-known passages in the First Epistle of Peter which speak of a preaching by Christ to the spirits in prison, and of the gospel being preached to the dead.[2]

---

[1] *Life in Christ*, chap. xxii.   [2] 1 Pet. iii. 18–20, iv. 6.

Yet, when all is said, this theory must be admitted to be based more on general principles than on definite scriptural information. Our own Church is not committed on the subject; indeed, as I have occasion to remember, in framing its Declaratory Act, it expressly rejected an amendment designed to bind it to the position that probation in every case is limited to time. The Synod acted wisely, I think, in rejecting that amendment. All the same, I wish now to say that I do not much like this phrase, "Future Probation." Least of all am I disposed with some to make a dogma of it. There are three facts in regard to the scriptural aspect of this theory which ought, I think, to make us cautious.

(1) The first is the intense concentration of every ray of exhortation and appeal into the present. "*Now* is the acceptable time ; behold, *now* is the day of salvation."[1] This is the strain of Scripture throughout. Everything which would weaken the force of this appeal, or lead men to throw over into a possible future what ought to be done now, is a distinct evil.

(2) The second is the fact that, in Scripture, judgment is invariably represented as proceeding on the matter of this life, on the "deeds done in the body."[2] The state after death is expressly described, in contrast with the present life, as one of "judgment."[3] In every description of the judgment, or allusion to it, it is constantly what a man has been, or has done, in this life, which is represented as the basis on which the determination of his final state depends. There is not a word, or hint, to indicate that a man who would be found on the left hand of the King, or who would pass under condemnation, on the basis of his earthly record, may possibly be found on the other side, and be accepted, on the ground of some transaction in the state between death and judgment. Surely this does not agree well with a "future probation" theory, but would rather require us to suppose that, in principle at least, man is presumed to decide his destiny here.

(3) There is, as the converse of these facts, the silence of Scripture on the subject of probation beyond ; for the passages in 1 Peter, even accepting the interpretation which makes

[1] 2 Cor. vi. 2 (R.V.).
[2] *E.g.* Matt. xxv. 31–46 ; 2 Cor. v 10 · Rev. xx. 12.   [3] Heb. ix. 27.

them refer to a work of Christ in the state of the dead, form surely a slender foundation on which to build so vast a structure. The suggestions they offer are not to be neglected. But neither do they speak of general probation, if of probation at all; nor give information as to the special character of this preaching to the dead, or its results in conversion; least of all do they show that what may apply to the heathen, or others similarly situated, applies to those whose opportunities have been ample. I have spoken of the influences of heredity, etc., as an element to be taken account of in judgment; but we must beware, even here, of forgetting how much responsibility remains. Will is `at work here also; personal volition is interweaving itself with the warp of natural circumstance and of hereditary predisposition. In the sphere of heathenism itself—even apart from the direct preaching of the gospel—there is room for moral decision wider than is sometimes apprehended, and a type of will is being formed on which eternal issues may depend.

I recognise, however, in the light of what I have stated about the need of a larger calculus, that the issues of this life must prolong themselves into the unseen, and, in some way unknown to us, be brought to a bearing there. All I plead for is, that we should not set up a definite theory where, in the nature of things, we have not the light to enable us to do so. This again is a reason for refusing to acquiesce in many of the dogmatic affirmations which are advanced in the name of a doctrine of eternal punishment. Suffering and loss beyond expression I cannot but conceive of as following from definite rejection of Christ; nor do I see anything in Scripture to lead me to believe that this loss can ever be repaired. How this will relate itself to conditions of existence in eternity I do not know, and beyond this I decline to speculate.

The conclusion I arrive at is, that we have not the elements of a complete solution, and we ought not to attempt it. What visions beyond there may be, what larger hopes, what ultimate harmonies, if such there are in store, will come in God's good time; it is not ours to anticipate them, or lift the veil where God has left it drawn! What Scripture wishes us to realise is the fact of probation now, of respon sibility here. We should keep this in view, and, concentrating all our exhortations and entreaty into the present, should refuse to sanction hopes which Scripture does not support; striving, rather, to bring men to live under the impression, "How shall we escape, if we neglect so great salvation?" (Heb. ii. 3).

Here I bring these Lectures to a conclusion. No one is more conscious than myself of the imperfection of the outlines I have sought to trace; of the thoughts I have brought before you in the wide and important field over which we have had to travel. Only, in a closing word, would I state the deepened, strengthened conviction which has come to myself out of the study, often prolonged and anxious enough, which the duties of this Lectureship have entailed on me: the deepened and strengthened conviction of the reality and certainty of God's supernatural Revelation to the world,— of His great purpose of love and grace, centring in the manifestation of His Son, but stretching out in its issues through all worlds, and into all eternities,—of a Redemption adequate to human sin and need, the blessings of which it is our highest privilege to share, and to make known to others. With this has gone the feeling—one of thankfulness and hope—of the breadth of the range of the influence of this new power which has gone out from Christ: not confined, as we might be apt to think, to those who make the full confession of His name, but touching society, and the world of modern thought and action, on all its sides—influencing its life and moulding its ideals; and in circles where the truth, as we conceive it, is mutilated, and even in important parts eclipsed, begetting a personal devotion to Christ, a recognition of His unique and peerless position in history, and a faith in the spread and ultimate triumph of His kingdom, which is full of significance and comfort. I hail these omens; this widespread influence of the name of Jesus. It tells us that, despite of appearances which seem adverse, there is a true kingdom of God on earth, and that a day of gathering up in Christ Jesus is yet to come. I do not believe that the modern world has ceased to need the Christian view, or that in spirit its back is turned against it. The " isms " of the day are numerous, and the denials from many quarters are fierce and vehement. But in the very unbelief of the time there is a serious feeling such as never existed before; and there is not one of these systems but, with all its negations, has its side of light turned towards Christ and His religion. Christ is the centre towards which their broken lights converge, and, as lifted up, He will yet draw them unto Him. I do not, therefore, believe that the Christian view is obsolete; that it is doomed to go down like a faded constellation in the west of the sky of humanity. I do not believe that, in order to preserve it, one single truth we have been accustomed to see shining in that constellation will require to be withdrawn, or that the world at heart desires it to be withdrawn. The world needs them all, and will one day acknowledge it. It is not with a sense of failure, therefore, but with a sense of triumph, that I see the progress of the battle between faith and unbelief. I have no fear that the conflict will issue in defeat. Like the ark above the waters, Christ's religion will ride in safety the waves of present-day unbelief, as it has ridden the waves of unbelief in days gone by, bearing in it the hopes of the future of humanity.

I thank the Principal and Professors, I thank the students, for their unfailing courtesy, and for their generous reception of myself and of my Lectures.

APPENDIX

**THE IDEA OF THE
KINGDOM OF GOD**

APPENDIX

THE IDEA OF THE KINGDOM OF GOD

In the original plan of these Lectures it was my intention to include a Lecture on " The Incarnation and the New Life of Humanity ; the Kingdom of God," which would have found its fitting place between the eighth and what is now the ninth. Such a Lecture is obviously needed to complete the course. After resurrection came exaltation. After Calvary came Pentecost. After the ministry of the Son came the dispensation of the Spirit. The new life proceeding from Christ, entering first as a regenerating principle into the individual soul, was gradually to permeate and transform society. The doctrine of Redemption passes over into that of the kingdom of God. This design has reluctantly had to be abandoned, and all I can here attempt, in addition to the brief allusions in Lecture Ninth, is to give a few notes on the general idea of the kingdom of God.

I. I shall refer first to the place of this idea in recent theology.

This idea has had a prominence accorded to it in recent theology it never possessed before, and the most thorough-going attempts are made to give it application in both dogmatics and ethics. By making it the head-notion in theology, and endeavouring to deduce all particular conceptions from it, it is thought that we place ourselves most in Christ's own point of view, and keep most nearly to His own lines of teaching. Kant here, as in so many other departments, may be named as the forerunner ; and fruitful suggestions may be gleaned from writers like Schleiermacher, Schmid, and Beck. It is the school of Ritschl, however, which has done most to carry out consistently this all-ruling notion of the kingdom of God, making it the determinative conception even in our ideas of sin, of the Person of Christ, etc. Through their influence it has penetrated widely and deeply into current theological thought, and is creating for itself quite an extensive literature.[1]

This being the prevailing tendency, I may not unnaturally be blamed for not making more use of this idea than I have done in these Lectures. If this is the chief and all-embracing, the all-comprehensive and all-inclusive notion of the pure Christian view, it may be felt that the attempt to develop the Christian " Weltanschauung," without explicit reference to it, is bound to be a failure. I may reply that I have not altogether left it out; it is, indeed, the conception I should have wished to develop further, as best fitted to convey my idea of the goal of the Christian Redemption, and of the great purpose of God of which that is the expression. But I have another reason. It is, that I gravely doubt the possibility or desirability of making this the all-embracing, all-dominating conception of Christian theology, except, of course, as the conception of an end affects and determines all that leads up to it. And even here the idea of the kingdom of God is not the only or perfectly exhaustive conception. The following reasons may be given for this opinion :—

1. The kingdom of God is not so presented in the New Testament. In the preaching of Christ in the Synoptic Gospels, this idea has indeed a large place. Christ attaches Himself in this way to the hopes of His nation, and to the doctrine of the prophets. Yet the very variety of the aspects of His doctrine of the kingdom shows how difficult it must be to sum them all up permanently under this single formula. In the Gospel of John, the idea is not so prominent, but recedes behind that of "life." In the Epistles, it goes still more decidedly into the background. Instead of the kingdom, it is Christ Himself who is now made prominent, and becomes

---

[1] Recent works in our own country are Professor Candlish's *The Kingdom of God* (Cunningham Lectures, 1884), and Professor A. B. Bruce's *The Kingdom of God* (1889). A good discussion of the subject is contained in an article by D. J. Köstlin, in the *Studien und Kritiken* for 1892 (3rd part). I may mention also Schmoller's recent work, *Die Lehre vom Reiche Gottes in den Schriften des Neuen Testaments* (1891) ; another by E. Issel on the same subject (1891) ; and a revolutionary essay by J. Weiss, entitled *Die Predigt Jesu vom Reiche Gottes* (1892).

the centre of interest. Harnack notices this in his *Dogmengeschichte*. "It is not wonderful," he says, "that in the oldest Christian preaching 'Jesus Christ' meets us as frequently as in the preaching of Jesus the kingdom of God itself."[1] In 1 Peter the expression is not found ; in James only once. The Pauline theology is developed from its own basis, without any attempt to make it fit into this conception. In the Epistle to the Hebrews, it is other ideas that rule. Where this idea is used in the Epistles, it is generally with an eschatological reference.[2] The Apocalypse is the book of the New Testament which gives it most prominence.

2. The kingdom of God is not a notion which can be treated as a fixed quantity. The greatest possible diversity prevails among the interpreters as to what ideas are to be attached to this expression. Whether the kingdom of God is something set up in this life (Ritschl, Wendt, etc.), or is something which has reference only to the future (Kaftan, Schmoller, J. Weiss, etc.) ; whether it is to be taken in a purely ethical and religious sense (Ritschl, etc.), or is to be extended to embrace all the relations of existence—the family, state, art, culture, etc. (Schleiermacher, Beck, etc.) ; what is the nature of the good which it promises—these and numberless other points are still keenly under discussion. This is not a reason for saying that on Christ's lips the term has no definite signification, but it shows that the time is not yet ripe for making it the one and all-inclusive notion in theology.

3. Even when we have reached what seems a satisfactory conception of the kingdom, it will be found difficult in practice to bring all the parts and subjects of theology under it. In proof of this, appeal might be made to the work of those who have adopted this as their principle of treatment.[3] The older Nitzsch, in his *System of Doctrine*, says of a writer (Theremin) who maintained the possibility of such a deduction, that if he

---

[1] Vol. i. p. 79. Kaftan similarly remarks: "In Paul also the doctrine of the highest good is determined through faith in the risen and exalted Christ who had appeared to him before the gates of Damascus. It can indeed be said that the glorified Christ here fills the place taken in the preaching of Jesus by the super-terrestrial kingdom of God, which has appeared in His Person, and through Him is made accessible as a possession to His disciples."—*Das Wesen*, p. 229.

[2] Not always, however; *e.g.* Rom. xiv. 17. Besides, what Christ meant by the present being of His kingdom is always recognised by these writers.

[3] Cf. article by Köstlin above referred to.

had really applied his general notion of the kingdom of God to a partition and articulation of the Christian doctrinal system, it would have become manifest of itself that this was not the right middle notion to bind the parts together. Schleiermacher, and Beck, and Lipsius, alike fail to carry through this idea in their systems. *Either* the doctrines are viewed only in this relation, in which case many aspects are overlooked which belong to a full system of theology ; *or* a mass of material is taken in which is only connected with this idea in the loosest way. The idea of the kingdom of God becomes in this way little more than a formal scheme or groundwork into which the ordinary material of theology is fitted. Ritschl, indeed, renounces the idea of a perfect unity, when he says that Christianity is an ellipse with *two foci*—one the idea of the kingdom of God, the other the idea of Redemption.[1]

4. The true place of the idea of the kingdom of God in theology is as a teleological conception. It defines the aim and purpose of God in creation and Redemption. It is the *highest* aim, but everything else in the plan and purpose of God cannot be deduced from it. Even as end, we must distinguish between the aim of God to establish a kingdom of God on earth and the *ultimate* end—the unity of all things natural and spiritual in Christ. The fulness of this last conception is not exhausted in the one idea of "kingdom," though this certainly touches the central and essential fact, that God is "all in all."[2]

II. Let us next consider the teaching of Jesus on the kingdom of God. Here,

1. I cannot but agree with those who think that the kingdom of God, in Christ's view, is a present, developing reality.[3] This is implied in the parables of growth (mustard seed, leaven, seed growing secretly) ; in the representations of it, in its earthly form, as a mixture of good and bad (wheat and tares, the net of fishes) ; in the description of the righteousness of the kingdom (Sermon on the Mount), which is to be realised in the ordinary human relations ; as well as in many special sayings. I do not see how anyone can read these passages and doubt that in Christ's view the kingdom was a presently-existing, slowly-

---

[1] *Recht. und Ver.* iii. p. 11.　　　[2] 1 Cor. xv. 28.　　　[3] *E.g.* Wendt.

developing reality,[1] originating in His word, containing mixed elements, and bound in its development to a definite law of rhythm ("first the blade, then the ear," etc.).[2] On the other hand, the idea has an eschatological reference. The kingdom is not something which humanity produces by its own efforts, but something which comes to it from above. It is the entrance into humanity of a new life from heaven. In its origin, its powers, its blessings, its aims, its end, it is supernatural and heavenly. Hence it is the kingdom of heaven, and two stadia are distinguished in its existence—an earthly and an eternal; the latter being the aspect that chiefly prevails in the Epistles.[3]

2. What is the nature of this kingdom of God on earth? In the Lecture, I have spoken of it as a new principle introduced into society which is fitted and destined to transform it in all its relations. This is the view of Schleiermacher, Neander,[4] Beck, of Dorner, Martensen, Harless, in their works on "Christian Ethics," and of most Protestant writers. This view, however, is contested, and has to be considered.

(1) Now, first, it is to be acknowledged that in Christ's

---

[1] Cf. as in earlier note (p. 334), Reuss, *Hist. of Christ. Theol.* i. pp. 217, 218 (Eng. trans.) ; Bruce, *Kingdom of God*, chap. xii.

[2] The kingdom of God, in its simplest definition, is the *reign* of God in human hearts and in society ; and as such it may be viewed under two aspects : (1) the reign or dominion of God Himself ; (2) the sphere of this dominion. This sphere, again, may be (1) the individual soul ; (2) the totality of such souls (the Church invisible) ; (3) the visible society of believers (the Church) ; (4) humanity in the whole complex of its relations, so far as this is brought under the influence of God's Spirit and of the principles of His religion.

It is obvious—and this is one source of the difficulty in coming to a common understanding—that Christ does not always use this expression in the same sense, or with the same breadth of signification. Sometimes one aspect, sometimes another, of His rich complex idea is intended by this term. Sometimes the kingdom of God is a power within the soul of the individual ; sometimes it is a leaven in the world, working for its spiritual transformation ; sometimes it is the mixed visible society ; sometimes it is that society under its ideal aspect ; sometimes it is the totality of its blessings and powers (the chief good) ; sometimes it is the future kingdom of God in its heavenly glory and perfection.

The view that Christ looked for a long and slow process of development and ripening in His kingdom may seem to be opposed by the eschatological predictions in Matt. xxiv. Even here, however, it is possible to distinguish a nearer and a remoter horizon—the one, referring to the destruction of Jerusalem and the dissolution of the Jewish state, and denoted by the expression, "these things" ("this generation shall not pass away, till all these things be accomplished," ver. 34) ; and the other, denoted by the words, "that day and hour" (ver. 36), regarding which Christ says, "Of that day and hour knoweth no one-not even the angels of heaven, neither the Son, but the Father only."

[3] The eschatological view alone is that taken by Kaftan, Schmoller, J. Weiss, etc.

[4] See *History of the Church*, opening paragraphs.

teaching it is the spiritual, or directly religious and ethical, side of the kingdom which alone is made prominent. Those who would identify the kingdom off-hand with social aims and endeavours, such as we know them in the nineteenth century, look in vain in Christ's teaching for their warrant. There the whole weight is rested on the inward disposition, on the new relation to God, on the new life of the Spirit, on the new righteousness proceeding from that life, on the new hopes and privileges of the sons of God. Everything is looked at in the light of the spiritual, the eternal. We read nothing in Christ of the effects of His religion on art, on culture, on philosophy, on politics, on commerce, on education, on science, on literature, on economical or social reform. It is the same with the apostles. Absorbed in the immediate work of men's salvation, they do not look at, or speak of, its remoter social effects. How far this is due in their case to the absence of apprehension of a long period of development of Christ's religion, and to a belief on the impending dissolution of the world, I need not here discuss.[1] The fact remains that, as already stated, while regarding the believer as already *in* God's kingdom and par-taker of its blessings, their conceptions of the kingdom, in its actual manifestation, are mainly eschatological.

(2) But, second, as it is certain that a principle of this kind could not enter into society without profoundly affecting it in all its relations, so we may be sure that Christ did not leave this aspect of it out of account. And when we look a little deeper, we see that Christ, though He does not lay stress on this side, yet by no means excludes it, but, on the contrary, presupposes and assumes it in His teaching. It is to be observed :

(*a*) Christ, in His teaching, presupposes the truth of the Old Testament, and moves in the circle of its conceptions. The Old Testament moves predominatingly in the religious and ethical sphere too, but there is a large material background or frame-work. We have accounts of the creation, of the early history of man, of his vocation to replenish the earth and subdue it, of

---

[1] Paul's large view of the philosophy of history in Rom. xi., of a future "fulness of the Gentiles," etc., is against this supposition. It is too hastily assumed that the Apostle looked for the Lord's return in his own lifetime.— See note by Professor Marcus Dods on 1 Thess. iv. 15 in Schaff's *Popular Commentary on the New Testament.*

the first institutions of society, of the beginnings of civilisation, of the divisions of nations, etc. Christ never leaves this Old Testament ground. The world to Him is God's world, and not the devil's. He has the deepest feeling for its beauty, its sacredness, the interest of God in the humblest of His creatures ; His parables are drawn from its laws ; He recognises that its institutions are the expression of a Divine order. The worlds of nature and society, therefore, in all the wealth and fulness of their relations, are always the background of His picture. We see this in His parables, which have nothing narrow and ascetic about them, but mirror the life of humanity in it amplest breadth—the sower, shepherd, merchant, handicraftsman, the servants with their talents (and proving faithful and unfaithful in the use of them), the builder, the vineyard-keeper, weddings, royal feasts, etc.

(b) The world, indeed, in its existing form, Christ cannot recognise as belonging to His kingdom. Rather, it is a hostile power—"the world," in the bad sense. His disciples are to expect hatred and persecution in it. It is under the dominion of Satan, "the prince of this world." [1] His kingdom will only come through a long succession of wars, crises, sorrows, and terrible tribulations. Yet there is nothing Manichæan, or dualistic, in Christ's way of conceiving of this presence of evil in the world. If man is evil, he is still capable of Redemption ; and what is true of the individual is true of society. His kingdom is a new power entering into it for the purpose of its transformation, and is regarded as a growing power in it.

(c) Christ, accordingly, gives us many indications of His true view of the relation of His kingdom to society. The world is His Father's, and human paternity is but a lower reflection of the Divine Fatherhood. Marriage is a Divine institution, to be jealously guarded, and Christ consecrated it by His special presence and blessing. The State also is a Divine ordinance, and tribute is due to its authorities. [2] The principles He lays down in regard to the use and perils of wealth ; love to our neighbour in his helplessness and misery ; the care of the poor ; the infinite value of the soul, etc., intro-

---

[1] John xii. 31, xvi. 11, etc.
[2] On above see Matt. vii. 11, xix. 3-9 ; John ii. 1-11 (cf. Matt. ix. 15) ; Matt. xxii. 21, etc.

duce new ideals, and involve principles fitted to transform the whole social system. His miracles of healing show His care for the body. With this correspond His injunctions to His disciples. He does not pray that they may be taken out of the world, but only that they may be kept from its evil.[1] They are rather to live *in* the world, showing by their good works that they are the sons of their Father in heaven; are to be the light of the world, and the salt of the earth.[2] Out of this life in the world will spring a new type of marriage relation, of family life, of relation between masters and servants, of social existence generally. It cannot be otherwise, if Christ's kingdom is to be the leaven He says it shall be. The apostles, in their views on all these subjects, are in entire accord with Christ.[3]

(3) We may glance at a remaining point, the relation of the idea of the kingdom of God to that of the Church. If our previous exposition is correct, these ideas are not quite identical, as they have frequently been taken to be. The kingdom of God is a wider conception than that of the Church. On the other hand, these ideas do not stand so far apart as they are sometimes represented. In some cases, as, *e.g.*, in Matt. xviii. 18, 19, the phrase " kingdom of heaven " is practically synonymous with the Church. The Church is, as a society, the visible expression of this kingdom in the world ; is, indeed, the only society which does formally profess (very imperfectly often) to represent it. Yet the Church is not the outward embodiment of this kingdom in all its aspects, but only in its directly religious and ethical, *i.e.* in its purely spiritual aspect. It is not the direct business of the Church, *e.g.*, to take to do with art, science, politics, general literature, etc., but to bear witness for God and His truth to men, to preach and spread the gospel of the kingdom, to maintain God's worship, to administer the sacraments, to provide for the self-edification and religious fellowship of believers. Yet the Church has a side turned towards all these other matters, especially to all efforts for the social good and bettering of mankind, and cannot but interest herself in these efforts, and lend what aid to them she can. She has her protest to utter against social injustice and immorality ; her witness to bear to the principles of conduct

---

[1] John xvii. 15.   [2] Matt. v. 13–16.
[3] *E.g.* Rom. xiii.; 1 Tim. ii. 1, 2 ; Heb. xiii. 4 ; 1 Pet. ii. 13–15.

which ought to guide individuals and nations in the various departments of their existence; her help to bring to the solution of the questions which spring up in connection with capital and labour, rich and poor, rulers and subjects; her influence to throw into the scale on behalf of "whatsoever things are true, whatsoever things are honourable, whatsoever things are just, whatsoever things are pure, whatsoever things are lovely, whatsoever things are of good report" (Phil. iv. 8). A wholesome tone in literature, a Christian spirit in art and science, a healthy temper in amusements, wise and beneficent legislation on Christian principles in the councils of the nation, the spirit of long-suffering, peace, forbearance, and generosity, brought into the relations of men with one another in society, Christian ideals in the relations of nations to one another, self-sacrificing labours for the amelioration and elevation of the condition of the masses of the people,—these are matters in which the Church can never but be interested. Else she foregoes her calling, and may speedily expect to be removed out of her place.

III. Historically, we might have looked, had space permitted, at this kingdom of God as the principle of a new life to humanity. I do not enter into this extensive field, but only remark:

1. The principle of this new life is Christ risen and exalted. It was not by His preaching merely that Christ came to set up the kingdom of God. The foundation of it was laid, not only in His Word, but in His redeeming acts—in His death, His resurrection, His exaltation to heaven, His sending of the Spirit. The new kingdom may be said to have begun its formal existence on the day of Pentecost. This is the mistake of those who would have us confine our ideas of the kingdom solely to what is given in the records of Christ's earthly life— they would have us go behind Pentecost, and remain there. But Christ's teaching on earth could not anticipate, much less realise, what His death, and the gift of His Spirit, have given us. It is not Christ's earthly life, but His risen life, which is the principle of quickening to His Church.[1] He himself bade

---

[1] "In truth the life of the soul hidden with Christ in God is the kernel of the Christian religion."—Kaftan, *Das Wesen*, p. 76. Kaftan has here the advantage over Ritschl, Schleiermacher, etc.

His disciples wait for the coming of the Spirit; and told them that it was through His being "lifted up" that the world would be brought to Him.   The Spirit would complete His mission; supply what was lacking in His teaching; bring to remembrance what He had said to them; and would work as a power convincing of sin, of righteousness, and of judgment in the world.[1]

2. This new life in humanity is (1) a new life in the individual, a regeneration of the individual soul, a power of sanctification and transformation in the nature.   But (2) it is further, as we have seen, a principle of new life in society, exercising there a transforming influence.   What society owes to the religion of Christ, even in a temporal and social respect, it is beyond the power of man to tell.   It is this that enables us, from the Christian standpoint, to take an interest in all labours for the social good of men, whether they directly bear the Christian name or not.   The influence of Christ and His ideals is more apparent in them than their promoters sometimes think. They are not without relation to the progress of the kingdom.

3. The kingdom of God, being the end, is also the centre, *i.e.* it is with ultimate reference to it that we are to read, and are best able to appreciate, the great movements of Providence. We can already see how the progress of invention and discovery, of learning and science, of facilities of communication and interconnection of nations, has aided in manifold ways the advance of the kingdom of God.   It has often been remarked how the early spread of Christianity was facilitated by the political unity of the Roman Empire, and the prevalence of the Greek tongue; and how much the revival of learning, the invention of printing, and the enlargement of men's ideas by discovery, did to prepare the way for the sixteenth century Reformation.   In our own century the world is opened up as never before, and the means of a rapid spread of the gospel are put within our power, if the Church has only faithfulness to use them.   It is difficult to avoid the belief that the singular development of conditions in this century, its unexampled progress in discovery and in the practical mastery of nature, the marvellous opening up of the world which has been the result, and the extraordinary multiplication of the means and

[1] John xii. 32, xiv. 26, xv. 7–15.

agencies of rapid communication, together portend some striking development of the kingdom of God which shall cast all others into the shade,—a crisis, perhaps, which shall have the most profound effect upon the future of humanity.[1] The call is going forth again, "Prepare ye in the wilderness the way of the Lord, make straight in the desert a highway for our God. Every valley shall be exalted, and every mountain and hill shall be made low; and the crooked shall be made straight, and the rough places plain; and the glory of the Lord shall be revealed, and all flesh shall see it together; for the mouth of the Lord hath spoken it."[2]

---

[1] It is curious how this feeling of an impending crisis sometimes finds expression in minds not given to apocalyptic reveries. Lord Beaconsfield said in 1874 : " The great crisis of the world is nearer than some suppose." In a recent number of the *Forum*, Professor Goldwin Smith remarks : " There is a general feeling abroad that the stream of history is drawing near a climax now ; and there are apparent grounds for the surmise. There is everywhere in the social frame an untoward unrest, which is usually a sign of fundamental change within."

[2] Isa. xl. 3, 4 (R.V.)

NOTES TO CHAPTERS

NOTES TO CHAPTER 1

Note A—p. 3

The Idea of the *Weltanschauung*

THE history of this term has yet to be written. I do not know that Kant uses it, or the equivalent term "Weltansicht," at all—it is at least not common with him. The same is true of Fichte, Schelling, and generally of writers till after the middle of this century.[1] Yet Kant above all gave the impulse to its use, both by his theoretic "Idea" of the world, and by his practical philosophy, which results in a "Weltanschauung" under the idea of the moral. Hegel, however, has the word, *e.g.*, "As man, religion is essential to him, and not a strange experience. Still the question arises as to the relation of religion to the rest of his 'Weltanschauung,' and philosophical knowledge relates itself to this subject, and has to do essentially with it."—*Religionsphilosophie*, i. p. 7. Within the last two or three decades the word has become exceedingly common in all kinds of books dealing with the higher questions of religion and philosophy —so much so as to have become in a manner indispensable. Thus we ·read of the "Theistic," "Atheistic," "Pantheistic," "Realistic," "Materialistic," "Mechanistic," "Buddhistic," "Kantian" Weltanschauungen ; and a multitude of similar phrases might be cited.

The best special contribution to the discussion of the idea I have met with is in a book entitled *Die Weltanschauung des Christenthums*, by August Baur (1881), which I regret I did not come across till my own work was finished.[2] In this work the author expresses

[1] But Fichte has the equivalent "Ansicht der Welt," and occasionally "Weltansicht." See especially his *Die Anweisung zum seligen Leben* (1806), Lect. V. "Weltansicht" is Schopenhauer's word.

[2] The headings of the chapters of Baur's book will suffice to show its importance for our subject. They are—

1. The general notion of the "Weltanschauung."
2. Characterisation and criticism of the objections of the modern spirit against religion and the religious "Weltanschauung."
3. Possibility and necessity of an ideal, supersensible "Weltanschauung."
4. The supersensible, ideal "Weltanschauung" according to its essence, and in its transition to the religious "Weltanschauung" generally.
5. The "Weltanschauung" of Christianity.

In theology A. Baur is a follower of Alex. Schweizer, of whom a good notice may be seen in Pfleiderer's *Development of Theology*, pp. 125–130.

his surprise that more has not been done for the elucidation of a term which has become one of the favourite terms of the day; and alludes to the absence of any explanation of it (a fact which had struck myself) in books professedly dealing with the terminology of philosophy and theology, as, *e.g.*, Rud. Eucken's *Geschichte und Kritik der Grundbegriffe der Gegenwart* (1878), and *Geschichte der philosophischen Terminologie* (1879).[1] The same writer has contributed an article on "The Notion and Ground-plan of the 'Weltanschauung' generally, and of the Christian in particular," to the *Jahrbücher d. prot. Theologie*, vol. iii. A valuable examination of the subject is contained also in an able work published in 1887, *Das menschliche Erkennen, Grundlinien der Erkenntnisstheorie und Metaphysik*, by Dr. A. Dorner. I might further refer to Hartmann's *Religionsphilosophie, Zweiter Theil: Die Religion des Geistes*, which, on this particular subject, contains a good deal of most suggestive matter (pp. 1–55). As may be gathered from the remarks in the close of the Lecture, the idea has a large place in the writings of the Ritschlian school. It is discussed with special fulness and care in Herrmann's *Die Religion im Verhältniss zum Welterkennen und zur Sittlichkeit*, the last section of which bears the heading, "The Task of the Dogmatic Proof of the Christian 'Weltanschauung.'" Lipsius also devotes considerable attention to it in the first part of his *Dogmatik* (sects. 16–115).

It is characteristic of the Ritschlian school that it will allow no origin for the "Weltanschauung" but that which springs from religion or morality. Ritschl, *e.g.*, traces the tendency to the formation of general views of the world solely to the religious impulse. Philosophy also, he says, "raises the claim to produce in its own way a view of the world as a whole; but in this there betrays itself much more an impulse of a religious kind, which philosophers must distinguish from their method of knowledge."—*Die christ. Lehre von der Rechtfertigung und Versöhnung*, iii. p. 197 (3rd ed.). This is connected with his view that religion itself originates in the need which man feels of help from a supernatural power to enable him to maintain his personality against the limitations and hindrances of natural existence.[2] Since, however, he allows that philosophy has as part of its task "the aim of comprehending the world-whole in a highest law," and that "the thought of God which pertains to religion is also employed in some form in every philosophy which is not materialistic" (p. 194), what he really contends for would seem to amount to no more than this, that theoretic knowledge alone cannot attain to that highest view of God which is given in the Christian religion, and which is necessary for the completion of a

---

[1] Eucken himself, however, uses it, as when he says, "Böhme strives after an expression for the notion of consciousness and self-consciousness, which has a central place within his 'Weltanschauung'" (*Gesch. der phil. Term.* p. 128); and has recently published an admirable historical and critical work, bearing the kindred title, *Die Lebensanschauungen der grossen Denker* (1890). This work contains a valuable section on "Die christliche Welt and die Lebensanschauungen Jesu" (pp. 154–205).

[2] Cf. *Recht. und Ver.* iii. p. 189.

satisfactory view of the universe as a whole.[1]   The truth is, Ritschl's views vary very widely on these topics in the different editions of his chief work, and it is no easy task to reduce his statements to unity.

In quite a similar spirit to Ritschl, his disciples Herrmann and Kaftan conceive of the "Weltanschauung" as due only to the opera-- tion of the practical or religious motive.[2]   The peculiarity of the Christian "Weltanschauung" Kaftan sums up in the two positions —"that the world is perfectly dependent on God, and that He orders everything in it in conformity with the end of His holy love."[3]

Note B—p. 5

Classification of *Weltanschauungen*

IT is not easy to find a principle of division which will yield a perfectly satisfactory classification of systems which we yet readily recognise as presenting distinct types of world-view. The deepest ground of division, undoubtedly, is that which divides systems according as they do or do not recognise a spiritual principle at the basis of the universe. But when, by the aid of this principle, we have put certain systems on the one side, and certain systems on the other, it does not carry us much further. We must, therefore, either content ourselves with a simple catalogue, or try some other method. In the earliest attempts at a world-view many elements are mixed up together—religious, rational, and ethical impulses, poetic per- sonification of nature, the mythological tendency, etc., and classifica- tion is impossible. The "Weltanschauung" at this stage is rude, tentative, imperfect, and goes little further than seeking an origin of some kind for the existing state of things, and connecting the different parts of nature and of human life in some definite way with particular gods. The interest felt in the soul and its fates enlarge this "Weltanschauung" to embrace a world of the unseen (Sheol, Amenti, etc.). Of reflective "Weltanschauungen," as these appear in history, we may roughly distinguish—

I. The Phenomenalistic and Agnostic—which refuse all inquiry into causes, and would confine themselves strictly to the laws of phenomena. The only pure type of this class which I know is the Comtist or Positivist, which contents itself with a subjective syn-

---

[1] Ritschl's own words, with which we heartily agree, are : "If theoretical thought is ever to solve the problem of the world as a whole, it will have to fall back on the Christian view of God, of the world, and of human destiny" (2nd ed. p. 210).

[2] With the Ritschlian theologians religion and morality sustain only an external relation to each other. The deepest impulse is not religion, but self- maintenance (Herrmann), or self-satisfaction (Kaftan). Religion is but a means to this end.

[3] *Das Wesen d. christ. Religion*, p. 393.

thesis.[1] (Mr. Spencer's system, though called Agnostic, is really a system of Monism, and falls into the third class. See Lecture III.)

II. The Atomistic and Materialistic (Atheistic). The systems of Democritus, Epicurus, Lucretius, and materialistic systems generally, are of this class. As no spiritual principle is recognised, the unity can only be sought in a highest law of the elements—in the order of the universe—in the way in which things cohere. (But many modern systems of Materialism, again, are really monisms, e.g., Haeckel, Strauss.)

III. Pantheistic systems—and these constitute a vast family with a great variety of forms. Here the universe is conceived as dependent on a first principle or power, but one within itself, of which it is simply the necessary unfolding, and with which, in essence, it is identical. The systems differ according to the view taken of the nature of this principle, and of the law of its evolution. The principle may be conceived of :

1. Predominatingly as physical—in which case the system is allied to Materialism (Materialistic Pantheism).

2. As the vital principle of an organism (Hylozoistic).

3. As an intelligent world-soul (Stoicism—analogous to fire).

4. Metaphysically—as Being (Eleatics), Substance (Spinoza), etc.

5. Spiritually—as impersonal Reason, or Spirit (Hegel), or Will (Schopenhauer, etc.).

Thus, while on its lower side Pantheism is indistinguishable from Materialism and Atheism, on its higher side it approaches, and often nearly merges into, Theism (as with the Neo-Hegelians).

IV. Systems which recognise a spiritual, self-conscious Cause of the universe: Here belong :

1. Deism—which views God predominatingly as Creator, but denies present communication and Revelation, and practically separates God from the world.[2]

2. Theism—which views God as the Living Creator, Immanent Cause, and Moral Ruler of the world and of man.

3. Christian Trinitarianism—a higher form of Theism.

[The division of systems as Optimistic and Pessimistic has reference to another standpoint—not to the first principle of the system, but to its ethical character and end. As combined with the others, it would form a cross-division.]

There is yet another division of types of world-view (equally important for our subject), based, not on their objective character, but on the mental attitude of the observer, and on the activities employed in their formation. Three main types of world-view may be here distinguished, answering to three distinct standpoints of the human spirit, from each of which a " Weltanschauung " necessarily results. These are :

---

[1] A more extreme type of view still is the denial of the reality of the world altogether—Acosmism.

[2] On the definition of terms, cf. Lipsius's *Dogmatik*, pp. 88, 89 ; and Flint's *Anti-Theistic Theories*, pp. 339, 441–445.

1. The "Scientific"—in which the standpoint of the observer is in the objective world, and things are viewed, as it were, wholly from without. Abstraction is made from the thinking mind, and only external relations (co-existence, succession, cause and effect, resemblance, etc.) are regarded. The means employed are observation and induction, and the end is the discovery of laws, and ultimately of a highest law, under which all particular phenomena may be subsumed.

2. The "Philosophical"—which precisely inverts this relation. The standpoint here is the thinking Ego, and things are regarded from within in their relations to thought and knowledge. It starts from the side of the thinking mind, as science from the side of the world as known, in abstraction from the mind knowing it. From the philosophical standpoint the world assumes a very different aspect from that which it presents to empirical science, or to the ordinary irreflective observer. All higher philosophy may be described as an attempt to conclude in some way from the unity of reason to the unity of things. The resultant world-view will assume two forms, according as the point of departure is from the theoretical or the practical reason : (1) a theoretical (as in the Absolutist attempts to deduce all things from a principle given through pure thought) ; (2) a moral (*e.g.* the Kantian).

3. The "Religious"—which views everything from the standpoint of the consciousness of dependence upon God, and refers all back to God. It starts from the practical relation in which man stands to God as dependent on Him, and desiring His help, support, and furtherance in the aims of his life (natural, moral, distinctively religious aims). The nature of the religious "Weltanschauung" and its relation to theoretic knowledge is discussed later.

At no time, however, can these points of view be kept perfectly distinct, and the claim of either science or philosophy to produce a self-sufficing world-view must be pronounced untenable. Insensibly, even in the pursuit of science, the standpoint changes from science to philosophy ; but this, in turn, cannot dispense with the material which the sciences and the history of religions furnish to it ; and it is equally unable, out of its own resources, to produce an adequate and satisfying world-view. It cannot therefore take the place of religion, or furnish a "Weltanschauung" satisfying to the religious consciousness. It is a well-recognised truth that philosophy has founded systems and schools, but never religions.[1] The religious world-view is better capable of independent existence than the others, for here at least the mind is in union with the deepest principle of all. But that principle needs to develop itself, and in practice it is found ·that religion also is largely influenced in the

---

[1] "A religion," says Réville, "may become historical, but no philosophy has ever founded a religion possessing true historical power."—*History of Religions*, p. 22 (Eng. trans.) ; cf. Strauss, *Der alte und der neue Glaube*, p. 103 ; Hartmann, *Religionsphilosophie*, p. 23 ; A. Dorner, *Das menschl. Erkennen*, p. 239.

construction of its world-views by the state of scientific knowledge
and the philosophy of the time. The Indian religious systems are
metaphysical throughout. The early Greek fathers of the Church
were largely influenced by Platonism ; the mediæval schoolmen by
Aristotelianism ; modern theologians by Kant, Hegel, etc. The
type of world-view freest from all trace of foreign influence is that
found in the Old Testament, and completed in the New. This
unique character belongs to it as the religion of Revelation.

Note C—p. 7

Unconscious Metaphysic

SCHOPENHAUER has remarked that each man has his metaphysic.

" The man," says Zeller, " who is without any philosophic standpoint is not on that account without any standpoint whatever ; he
who has formed no scientific opinion on philosopical questions has
an unscientific opinion about them."—*Pre-Soc. Phil.* p. 23.

Principal Fairbairn observes : " Professor Tyndall's presidential
address is memorable enough, were it only as an instance of sweet
simplicity in things historical, and the most high-flying metaphysics
disguised in scientific terms."—*Studies*, p. 65.

Regarding Mr. Spencer : " Just as the term force revolutionises
the conception of the Unknowable, so it, in turn, transmuted into
forces, beguiles the physicist into the fancy that he is walking in
the, to him, sober and certain paths of observation and experiment,
while in truth he is soaring in the heaven of metaphysics."—*Ibid.*
p. 97.

Professor Caird remarks of Comte : " Hence, while he pretends
to renounce metaphysics, he has committed himself to one of the
most indefensible of all metaphysical positions. . . . It is a residuum
of bad metaphysics, which, by a natural Nemesis, seems almost invariably to haunt the minds of those writers who think they have
renounced metaphysics altogether."—*Soc. Phil. of Comte*, p. 121.

Note D—p. 9

Antagonism of Christian and *Modern* views of the World— Antisupernaturalism of the Latter

I ADD some illustrations of the remarks made on this subject in the
text.

Principal Fairbairn puts the matter thus : " The scientific and
religious conceptions of the world seem to stand at this moment in
the sharpest possible antagonism. . . . There is one fact we cannot
well overrate—the state of conflict or mental schism in which every

devout man, who is also a man of culture, feels himself compelled more or less consciously to live. His mind is an arena in which two conceptions struggle for the mastery, and the struggle seems so deadly as to demand the death of the one for the life of the other, faith sacrificed to knowledge, or knowledge to faith."—*Studies in the Philosophy of Religion and History*, pp. 61, 62.

The uncompromising character of the conflict and the nature of the issues involved are well brought out in the following extracts from Mr. Wicksteed's pamphlet on *The Ecclesiastical Insitutions of Holland.*

"The religious movement," he says, "known in Holland as that of the 'Modern School,' or 'New School,' or sometimes the 'School of Leiden,' is essentially a branch of that wider religious movement extending over the whole of Europe and America, which is a direct product upon the field of religion of the whole intellectual life of the nineteenth century.

"This Modern School, in the larger sense, is in fact essentially the religious phase of that undefinable 'Zeit-Geist,' or spirit of the age, sometimes called on the Continent 'modern consciousness,' the most characteristic feature of which is a profound conviction of the *organic unity*, whether spiritual or material, of the universe.

"This modern consciousness can make no permanent treaty of peace with the belief which takes both the history and the philosophic science of religion out of organic connection with history and philosophical science in general. No compromise, no mere profession of a frank acceptance of the principles of the modern view of the world, can in the long-run avail. The Traditional School cannot content the claims of the 'Zeit-Geist' by concessions. Ultimately, it must either defy it or yield to it unconditionally. . . .

"The task of modern theology, then, is to bring all parts of the history of religion into organic connection with each other, and with the general history of man, and to find in the human faculties themselves, not in something extraneous to them, the foundations of religious faith."—Pp. 55, 56.

The venerable Dr. Delitzsch, from the standpoint of faith, recognises the same irreconcilable contrast, and in *The Deep Gulf between the Old and Modern Theology; a Confession* (1890), gives strong expression to his sense of the gravity of the situation. "It is plain," he says, "that the difference between old and modern theology coincides at bottom with the difference between the two conceptions of the world, which are at present more harshly opposed than ever before. The modern view of the world declares the miracle to be unthinkable, and thus excluded from the historical mode of treatment; for there is only one world system, that of natural law, with whose permanence the direct, extraordinary interferences of God are irreconcilable.[1] . . . When the one conception of the world

---

[1] Similarly Max Müller finds the kernel of the modern conception of the world in the idea "that there is law and order in everything, and that an unbroken chain of causes and effects holds the whole universe together,"—a conception which reduces the miraculous to mere seeming.—*Anthropological Religion*, Preface, p. 10.

is thus presented from the standpoint of the other, the mode of statement unavoidably partakes of the nature of a polemic. The special purpose, however, with which I entered on my subject was not polemical. I wished to exhibit as objectively as possible the deep gap which divides the theologians of to-day, especially the thoughtful minds who have come into contact with philosophy and science, into two camps. An accommodation of this antagonism is impossible. We must belong to the one camp or the other. We may, it is true, inside the negative camp, tone down our negation to the very border of affirmation, and inside the positive camp we may weaken our affirmation so as almost to change it to negation ; the representation by individuals of the one standpoint or the other leaves room for a multitude of gradations and shades. But to the fundamental question—Is there a supernatural realm of grace, and within it a miraculous interference of God in the world of nature, an interference displaying itself most centrally and decisively in the raising of the Redeemer from the dead?—to this fundamental question, however we may seek to evade it, the answer can only be yes or no. The deep gulf remains. It will remain to the end of time. No effort of thought can fill it up. There is no synthesis to bridge this thesis and antithesis. Never shall we be able, by means of reasons, evidence, or the witness of history, to convince those who reject this truth. But this do we claim for ourselves, that prophets and apostles, and the Lord Himself, stand upon our side ; this we claim, that while the others use the treasures of God's Word eclectically, we take our stand upon the whole undivided truth."—Translation in *Expositor*, vol. ix. (3rd series), pp. 50, 53.

See also Hartmann's *Die Krisis des Christenthums in der modernen Theologie* (1888), and his *Selbstzersetzung des Christenthums* (1888). "From whatever side," he declares, "we may consider the ground-ideas of Christianity and those of modern culture, everywhere there stands out an irreconcilable contradiction of the two, and it is therefore no wonder if this contradiction comes to light more or less in all derivative questions."—*Selbstzersetzung des Christenthums*, p. 30.

Note E—p. 9

Internal Conflicts of the *Modern* View

AN internecine warfare is waged among the representatives of the "modern" view, quite as embittered and irreconcilable as that which they unitedly wage against Christianity. A "Kampf der Weltanschauungen" is going on here also. Deists, Pantheists, Agnostics, Pessimists, Atheists, Positivists, and liberal theologians, unceasingly refute each other ; and were their respective opinions put to the vote, out of a dozen systems, each would be found in a minority of one, with the other eleven against it. If escape were sought in a theoretical scepticism, which despairs of truth altogether, this would but add another sect to the number, which would en-counter the hostility of all the rest.

Not without justice, therefore, does Dr. Dorner, after reviewing the systems, speak of the attempt to set up a rival view to Christianity as ending in a " screaming contradiction."—*System of Christian Doctrine*, i. pp. 121, 122 (Eng. trans.).

"The atheistic systems of Germany," says Lichtenberger, "have raised the standard, or rather the 'red rag' of Radicalism and Nihilism ; and have professed that their one and only principle was the very absence of principles. The one bond which unites them at bottom is their hatred of religion and of Christianity."—*History of German Theology in the Nineteenth Century*, p. 370 (Eng. trans.).

"It is not here our business," says Beyschlag, "philosophically to arrange matters between the Christian theistic 'Weltanschauung' on the one side, and the deistic, or pantheistic, or materialistic, on the other, which latter have first to fight out their mortal conflict with one another."—*Leben Jesu*, i. p. 10.

A few examples *in concreto* will point the moral better than many general statements.

The columns of the *Nineteenth Century* for 1884 witnessed an interesting controversy between Mr. Herbert Spencer and Mr. Frederick Harrison, in which some pretty hard words were bandied to and fro between the combatants. Mr. Spencer had written a paper ("Religious Retrospect and Prospect," January 1884), developing his theory of the origin of religion from ghost-worship, and expounding his own substitute for decaying religious faith. To this Mr. Harrison replied in a vigorous article (July 1884), ridiculing Mr. Spencer's proposed substitute as "The Ghost of Religion," and scoffing at his " Unknowable " as " an ever-present conundrum to be everlastingly given up." Extending his attack to certain modern Theisms, he said, "The Neo-Theisms have all the same mortal weakness that the Unknowable has. They offer no kinship, sympathy, or relation whatever between worshippers and worshipped. They, too, are logical formulas begotten in controversy, dwelling apart from men and the world." "Tacitly implying," retorts Mr. Spencer, in a later round of the controversy, "that Mr. Harrison's religion supplies this relation " (November 1884), which, as he shows at great length, it does not ("Retrogressive Religion," July 1884). Sir James Stephen also had offended Mr. Spencer by describing his "Unknowable" (June 1884) as "like a gigantic soap-bubble, not burst, but blown thinner and thinner till it has become absolutely imperceptible"; and Mr. Harrison also returns to the attack ("Agnostic Metaphysics," September 1884).

In a subsequent controversy, Mr. Harrison fares as badly at the hands of Professor Huxley as he did at those of Mr. Spencer. Replying to an article of his on "The Future of Agnosticism," Professor Huxley says : "I am afraid I can say nothing which shall manifest my personal respect for this able writer, and for the zeal and energy with which he ever and anon galvanises the weakly frame of Positivism, until it looks more than ever like John Bun-

yan's Pope and Pagan rolled into one. There is a story often
repeated, and I am afraid none the less mythical on that account,
of a valiant and loud-voiced corporal, in command of two full
privates, who, falling in with a regiment of the enemy in the dark,
orders it to surrender under pain of instant annihilation by his
force; and the enemy surrenders accordingly. I am always reminded
of this tale when I read the Positivist commands to the forces of
Christianity and of science; only, the enemy shows no more signs
of intending to obey now than they have done any time these forty
years."—" Agnosticism," in *Nineteenth Century*, February 1889.[1]

Mr. Samuel Laing, author of *Modern Science and Modern Thought*,
probably regards himself as quite a typical representative of the
modern spirit. The "old creeds," he informs us, "must be transformed or die." Unfortunately, not content with assailing other
people's creeds, he undertook the construction of one of his own,[2]
concerning which Professor Huxley writes : "I speak only for myself, and I do not dream of anathematising and excommunicating
Mr. Laing. But when I consider his creed, and compare it with the
Athanasian, I think I have, on the whole, a clearer conception of
the meaning of the latter. 'Polarity,' in Art. viii., for example,
is a word about which I heard a good deal in my youth, when
'Natur-philosophie' was in fashion, and greatly did I suffer from it.
For many years past, whenever I have met with 'polarity' anywhere but in a discussion of some purely physical topic, such as
magnetism, I have shut the book. Mr. Laing must excuse me if
the force of habit was too much for me when I read his eighth
article."—*Nineteenth Century*, February 1889. Mr. Laing's own book
is a good example of how these "modern" systems eat and devour
one another. See his criticisms of theories in chap. vii., etc.

Mr. Rathbone Greg is another writer who laboured hard to
demolish "the creed of Christendom," while retaining a great
personal reverence for Jesus. His concessions on this subject, however, did not meet with much favour on his own side. Mr. F. W.
Newman, in an article on "The New Christology," in the *Fortnightly
Review* (December 1873), thus speaks of his general treatment : "He
has tried and proved the New Testament, and has found it wanting,
not only as to historical truth, but as to moral and religious wisdom;
yet he persists in the effort of hammering out of it what shall be a
'guide of life.' In *fact*, he learns by studying the actual world of
man ; but in his *theory* he is to discover a fountain of wisdom, by

---

[1] Mr. Harrison complains (*Fortnightly Review*, October 1892) that Mr.
Huxley, in this article, has held him up "to public ridicule as pontiff,
prophet, general humbug, and counterpart of Joe Smith the Mormon," and
tries to show how much agreement, mostly in negations, underlies their
differences.

[2] "It appears that Mr. Gladstone, some time ago, asked Mr. Laing if he
could draw up a short summary of the negative creed ; a body of negative
propositions which have so far been adopted on the negative side as to be what
the Apostles' and other accepted creeds are on the positive ; and Mr. Laing at
once kindly obliged Mr. Gladstone with the desired articles—eight of them.'
—Professor Huxley, as above.

penetrating to some 'essence' in a book which he esteems very defective and erroneous. This is 'to rebuild the things he has destroyed.' To sit in judgment on Jesus of Nazareth, and convict Him of glaring errors, as a first step, and then, as a second, set Him on a pedestal to glorify Him as the most Divine of men and the sublimest of teachers, a perpetual miracle,—is a very lame and inconsequent proceeding. . . . Mr. Greg, as perhaps all our Unitarians, desires a purified gospel. Why, then, is not such a thing published? No doubt, because it is presently found that nearly every sentence has to be either cut out or rewritten."

Mr. Greg and Mr. Newman are Theists. The latter even writes : "The claim of retaining a belief in God, while rejecting a Personal God, I do not know how to treat with respect." Mr. Fiske also, author of *Cosmic Philosophy*, is in his own way a Theist. But "Physicus," another representative of the "modern" view, in his *Candid Examination of Theism*, can see no evidence for the existence of a God, and speaks thus of Mr. Fiske's attempt to develop Theism out of Mr. Spencer's philosophy : "I confess that, on first seeing his work, I experienced a faint hope that, in the higher departments of the philosophy of evolution as conceived by Mr. Spencer, and elaborated by his disciple, there might be found some rational justification for an attenuated form of Theism. But on examination I find that the bread which these fathers have offered us turns out to be a stone. . . . We have but to think of the disgust with which the vast majority of living persons would regard the sense in which Mr. Fiske uses the term 'Theism,' to perceive how intimate is the association of that term with the idea of a Personal God. Such persons will feel strongly that, by this final act of purification, Mr. Fiske has simply purified the Deity altogether out of existence."—*Candid Examination*, essay on "Cosmic Theism," pp. 131, 138, and throughout.[1]

Thus the strife goes on. Strauss, in his *Old Faith and the New*, refutes Pessimism ; but Hartmann, the Pessimist, retorts on Strauss that he has "no philosophic head," and shows the ridiculousness of his demand that we should love the Universe. "It is a rather strong, or rather naïve claim, that we should experience a sentiment of religious piety and dependence for a 'Universum' which is only an aggregate of all material substances, and which threatens every instant to crush us between the wheels and teeth of its pitiless mechanism."—*Selbstzer. des Christ.* Pref. and p. 81.

Hartmann may as well speak of the "Selbstzersetzung" and "Zersplitterung" of unbelief, as of the disintegration of Christianity.

---

[1] It has already been noted that the author, Mr. G. J. Romanes, returned later to the Christian faith. See his *Thoughts on Religion*, edited by Canon Gore (1895).

Note F—p. 14

Uniqueness of the Old Testament View

IT may be confidently affirmed that the drift of modern criticism and research has not been to lower, but immensely to exalt, our conceptions of the unique character of the Old Testament religion. The views of the critics of the earlier stages of the religion of Israel are low and poor enough, but, as if in compensation, they exalt the "Ethical Monotheism" and spiritual religion of the prophets and psalms, till one feels, in reading their works, that truly this religion of Israel is something unexampled on the face of the earth, and is not to be accounted for on purely natural principles. Schleiermacher and Hegel spoke disparagingly of the Old Testament, but this is not the more recent tendency. The following are some testimonies from various standpoints.

Lotze, in his *Microcosmus*, bears a noble testimony to the uniqueness of the Old Testament religion, and to the sublimity and unparalleled character of its literature. "Among the theocratically governed nations of the East," he says, "the Hebrews seem to us as sober men among drunkards" (vol. ii. p. 267, Eng. trans.). See his spirited sketch of the Old Testament view (pp. 466–468), and his eulogy of the literature (pp. 402–404).

Dr. Hutcheson Stirling says: "The sacred writings of the Hebrews, indeed, are so immeasurably superior to those of every other name, that, for the sake of the latter, to invite a comparison is to undergo instantaneous extinction. Nay, regard these Scriptures as a literature only, the literature of the Jews—even then, in the kind of quality, is there any literature to be compared with it? Will it not even then remain still the sacred literature? A taking simpleness, a simple takingness, that is Divine—all that can lift us out of our own week-day selves, and place us, pure then, holy, rapt, in the joy and the peace of Sabbath feeling and Sabbath vision, is to be found in the *mere nature* of these old idylls, in the full-filling sublimity of these psalms, in the inspired God-words of these intense-souled prophets."—*Phil. and Theol.* (Gifford Lectures), pp. 18, 19.

Dr. Robertson Smith has well brought out the singularity and elevation of the Hebrew view in contrast with that of the other Semitic and Aryan nations, in his *Religion of the Semites* (Burnett Lectures). "The idea of absolute and ever-watchful Divine justice," he says, "as we find it in the prophets, is no more natural to the East than to the West, for even the ideal Semitic king is, as we have seen, a very imperfect earthly providence; and, moreover, he has a different standard of right for his own people and for strangers. The prophetic idea that Jehovah will vindicate the right, even in the destruction of His own people of Israel, involves an ethical standard as foreign to Semitic as to Aryan tradition" (p. 74).

Again: "While in Greece the idea of the unity of God was a philosophical speculation, without any definite point of attachment to actual religion, the Monotheism of the Hebrew prophets kept touch with the ideas and institutions of the Semitic race, by conceiving of the one true God as the King of absolute justice, the national God of Israel, who, at the same time, was, or rather was destined to become, the God of all the earth, not merely because His power was world-wide, but because, as the perfect ruler, He could not fail to draw all nations to do Him homage" (p. 75).

Again : "The Hebrew ideal of a Divine Kingship that must one day draw all men to do it homage, offered better things than these, not in virtue of any feature that it possessed in common with the Semitic religions as a whole, but solely in virtue of its unique conception of Jehovah as a God whose love for His people was conditioned by a law of absolute righteousness. In other nations, individual thinkers rose to lofty conceptions of a supreme Deity, but in Israel, and in Israel alone, these conceptions were incorporated in the conception of the national God. And so, of all the gods of the nations, Jehovah alone was fitted to become the God of the whole earth" (pp. 80, 81).

Kuenen writes thus of the universalism of the prophets : "What was thus revealed to the eye of their spirit was no less than the august idea of the *moral government of the world*—crude as yet, and with manifold admixture of error (?), but pure in principle. The prophets had no conception of the mutual connection of the powers or operations of nature. They never dreamed of carrying them back to a single cause, or deducing them from it. But what they did see, on the field within their view, was the realisation of a single plan—everything, not only the tumult of the peoples, but all nature likewise, subservient to the working out of one great purpose. The name 'Ethical Monotheism' describes better than any other the characteristics of their point of view, for it not only expresses the character of the one God whom they worshipped, but also indicates the fountain whence their faith in Him welled up."—Hibbert Lectures, pp. 124, 125.

"So far," says Mr. Gladstone, "then, the office and work of the Old Testament, as presented to us by its own contents, is without a compeer among the old religions. It deals with the case of man as a whole. It covers all time. It is alike adapted to every race and region of the earth. And how, according to the purport of the Old Testament, may that case best be summed up ? In these words : It is a history first of sin, and next of Redemption."—*Impregnable Rock of Holy Scripture*, p. 87. See the whole chapter on "The Office and Work of the Old Testament in Outline."

I may add a few words of personal testimony from Professor Monier Williams, on the comparison of the Scriptures with the Sacred Books of the East. "When I began investigating Hinduism and Buddhism, I found many beautiful gems ; nay, I met with bright coruscations of true light flashing here and there amid the surrounding darkness. As I prosecuted my researches into these non-Christian systems, I began to foster a fancy that they had been unjustly treated. I began to observe and trace out curious coincidences and comparisons with our own Sacred Book of the East. I began, in short, to be a believer in what is called the evolution and growth of religious thought. 'These imperfect systems,' I said to myself, 'are interesting efforts of the human mind struggling upwards towards Christianity. Nay, it is probable that they were all intended to lead up to the one true religion, and that Christianity is, after all, merely the climax, the complement, the fulfilment of them all.'

" Now, there is unquestionably a delightful fascination about such a theory, and, what is more, there are really elements of truth in it. But I am glad of this opportunity of stating publicly that I am persuaded I was misled by its attractiveness, and that its main idea is quite erroneous. . . . We welcome these books. We ask every missionary to study their contents, and thankfully lay hold of whatsoever things are true and of good report in them. But we warn him that there can be no greater mistake than to force these non-Christian bibles into conformity with some scientific theory of development, and then point to the Christian's Holy Bible as the crowning product of religious evolution. So far from this, these non-Christian bibles are all developments in the wrong direction. They all begin with some flashes of true light, and end in utter darkness. Pile them, if you will, on the left side of your study table, but place your own Holy Bible on the right side—all by itself, all alone—and with a wide gap between."—Quoted by Joseph Cook in *God in the Bible* (Boston Lectures), p. 16.

Note G—p. 15

Origin of the Old Testament View— Relation to Critical Theories

MANY feel that from the peculiarity of Israel's religion referred to in last note the need will arise sooner or later for recasting the whole critical view of the development. The more rich and wonderful the religious development of the age of the prophets is shown to be, the more will it be felt necessary to postulate something in the earlier stages to account for this development—the more natural and life-like will Israel's own account of its history appear [1]—the more impossible will it be found to explain the presence of such a development of religion at all apart from the fact of supernatural Revelation.

As it is, there is a growing acknowledgment among the critics of the most advanced school, that, date the books when we may, the religion can only be explained by Revelation. I quote from three recent works.

---

[1] Cf. Robertson's *Early Religion of Israel* (Baird Lectures). An able criticism of some of Professor R. Smith's positions in *The Religion of the Semites* appeared in the *Edinburgh Review*, April 1892.

H. Schultz, in his new edition of his *Alttestamentliche Theologie*, 1889, thus writes : " The Old Testament religion is thus only to be explained out of Revelation ; that is to say, out of the fact that God raised up to this people men, in whose original religious and moral endowment, developed through the leadings of their inner and outer life, the receptivity was given for an absolutely original comprehension of the self-communicating, redeeming will of God towards men, the religious truth which makes free—not as a result of human wisdom or intellectual effort, but as an irresistible, constraining power on the soul itself. Only he who explicitly recognises this can do historical justice to the Old Testament" (p. 50).

R. Kittel, in his recent valuable *Geschichte der Hebräer*, 1888–92, also based, though discriminatingly, on the results of the later criticism, thus sums up on the question : " Whence did Moses derive his knowledge of God ? " " The historian stands here," he says, " before a mystery, which is almost unique in history. A solution is only to be found if in that gap a factor is inserted, the legitimacy of which can no more be proved by strict historical methods. There are points in the life of humanity where history goes over into the philosophy of history, and speculation must illuminate with its retrospective and interpreting light the otherwise permanently dark course of the historical process. Such a case is here. Only an *immediate contact* of God Himself with man can produce the true knowledge of God, or bring man a real stage nearer to it. For in himself man finds only the world, and his own proper *ego*. Neither one nor the other yields more than heathenism : the former a lower, the latter a higher form of it. Does the thought flash on Moses that God is neither the world nor the idealised image of man, but that He is the Lord of Life, of moral commands, exalted above multiplicity and the world of sense, and the Creator, who does not crush man, but ennobles him ; so has he this knowledge, not out of his time, and not out of himself—he has it out of an immediate Revelation of this God in his heart."—*Geschichte*, i. pp. 227, 228.

Alex. Westphal, author of an able French work, *Les Sources du Pentateuque, Étude de Critique et d'Histoire*, 1888–92, is another writer who uncompromisingly accepts the results of the advanced critical school. But he earnestly repudiates, in the Preface to the above work, the idea that these results destroy, and do not rather confirm, faith in Revelation, and even builds on them an argument for the historic truthfulness of the early tradition. He separates himself in this respect from the unbelieving position. " Truth to tell," he says, " the unanimity of scholars exists only in relation to one of the solutions demanded, that of the literary problem. . . . The position which the scholar takes up towards the books which he studies, and his personal views on the history and the religious development of Israel, always exercise, whether he wishes it or not, a considerable influence on the results of his work. However, we may be permitted to affirm, and hope one day to be able to prove, that the reply to the historic question belongs to evangelical criticism, which, illuminated by the spirit of Revelation, alone possesses all the

factors for the solution of this grave problem. . . . Far from being
dismayed by the fact that the plurality of sources involves profound
modifications in our traditional notion of the Pentateuch written by
Moses, we should rather see in it a providential intervention, at the
moment when it is most necessary, a decisive argument in favour of
the primitive history."—*Les Sources*, i. Preface, p. 28.

Note H—p. 16

Nature and Definition of Religion

In strictness these Lectures ought to have included a treatment of
the general question of religion as preparatory to the consideration
of the specific Christian view. Christianity involves a "Weltanschauung," and it belongs to the type "religious." It ought therefore to be shown in what distinctively a religious "Weltanschauung"
consists, and how the Christian view is related to the general conception. This, again, would involve an inquiry into the general
nature of religion; in order, on this basis, to show how a "Weltanschauung" necessarily originates from it. A few notes are all that
can be attempted here, in addition to what is said in the text of
various portions of the Lectures, and in Appendix to Lecture III.

The main question is as to the general character, or essential
nature, of religion, as a means of understanding how a "Weltanschauung" springs from it.

I. It may be remarked that this question is not answered—

1. By an abstract *definition* of religion. Much has been written
on the definition of religion.[1] A prior question is, In what sense do
we speak of definition? Do we mean to include in our definition of
religion only the common elements in all religions; or do we propose to define by the idea of religion, as that may be deduced from
the study of the laws of man's nature, seen in their manifestation on
the field of history, and most conspicuously in the higher religions?
The fault of most definitions is that, aiming at a generality wide
enough to embrace the most diverse manifestations of the religious
consciousness,—the lowest and most debased equally with the most
complex and exalted,—they necessarily leave out all that is purest
and most spiritual in religion—that which expresses its truest
essence. They give us, in short, a logical *summum genus*, which may
be useful enough for some purposes, but is utterly barren and un-
profitable as a key to the interpretation of any spiritual fact. On
the other hand, if we take as our guide the idea of religion, we may
be accused of finding only one religion which corresponds to it—the
Christian; and in any case the definition will leave outside of it a
vast variety of religious phenomena. What is wanted is not a

---

[1] For a summary view of these definitions, and examination of them, see Max
Müller's Gifford Lectures on *Natural Religion* (1888), and Nitzsch's *Evangelische Dogmatik*, i. pp. 46–109 (1889).

logical definition which will apply to nothing from which its marks are absent, but such a comprehension of the inner principle and essential character of religion as will enable us to discern its presence under forms that very rudely and imperfectly express it.[1]

2. By exclusively *psychological or historical methods* in the treatment of religion. These are the methods in vogue at the present day in what is designated "The Science of Religions." I call a theory psychological which seeks to account for the ideas and beliefs which men entertain regarding their deities by tracing them to psychological causes, without raising the question of how far these ideas and beliefs have any objective truth. Psychology deals with the empirical—the given. It observes the facts of the religious consciousness—groups and classifies them—seeks to resolve the complex into the simple, the compound into the elementary—notes the laws and relations which discover themselves in the different phenomena, etc. In doing this, it performs a necessary service, but its method is liable to certain obvious drawbacks.

(1) If religion is a necessity of human nature, springing by an inner necessity from the rational and spiritual nature of man, this method can never show it. Psychology can only show what is, not what must or should be. Its function is ended when it has described and analysed facts as they are. It does not reach inner necessity. From the persistency with which religion appears and maintains itself in human nature, it may infer that there is some deep and necessary ground for it in the spirit of man, but it lies beyond the scope of its methods to show what that is. Its line is too short to reach down to these depths.

(2) It is a temptation in these theories to aim at an undue simplicity. This is a fault, indeed, of most theories of religion, that they do not do justice to the multiplicity of factors involved in religion, but, laying hold on one of these factors, exalt it to exclusive importance at the expense of the rest. Religion is a highly complex thing, blending in itself a multitude of elements readily distinguishable,—hopes and fears, belief in the invisible, the feeling of dependence, the sense of moral relation, desire for fellowship, emotions of awe, love, reverence, surrender of the will, etc.,—and I suppose no definition of it has ever been constructed which did not leave out some of its extraordinarily varied manifestations. Theories, therefore, err which attempt to deduce all religious sentiments and ideas from some one principle, *e.g.*, Hume, from man's hopes and fears; Tylor, from the animistic tendency in human nature; Spencer, from ghost-worship; Feuerbach, from man's egoistic wishes— "What man would have liked to be, but was not, he made his god; what he would like to have, but could not get for himself, his god was to get for him" (Strauss); others from Totemism, etc.[2]

---

[1] See a good treatment of this subject in Kaftan's *Das Wesen der christ. Rel.* (1881), pp. 1–5; cf. also Caird's *Philosophy of Religion* (pp. 314–317), and Note B., "On the possibility of discovering in the 'essence of religion' a universal religion," in Conder's *Basis of Faith*, p. 438.

[2] Cf. on some of these theories, Note A. to Lecture III.

(3) It is a common error of these theories to study religion chiefly
as it presents itself in the lowest, poorest, crudest manifestations of
the religious consciousness ; and to suppose that if they can explain
these, all the higher stages of religious development can be explained
in the same way. This is much the same as if a botanist, wishing
to exhibit the essential characteristics of plant life, were to confine
his attention to the lowest order of plants, and even to the most
dwarfed, stunted, and impoverished specimens of these.

(4) It is a further weakness of psychological theories that they
move solely in the region of the subjective. They occupy themselves with psychological causes, and with the ideas and fancies to
which these give rise ; but have nothing to teach us of the object of
religion—neither what the true object is, nor whether a true object
is to be known at all. Their function is ended when they have
described and analysed facts ; they claim no right to pass judgment.
They have, in other words, no objective standard of judgment. Yet
the question of the object is the one of essential importance in
religion, as determining whether it has any ground in objective
truth, or is only, as Feuerbach would have it, a deceptive play of
the human consciousness with itself.[1]

(5) Finally, even the higher class of psychological theories form a
very inadequate basis for a true conception of religion. Schleiermacher, *e.g.*, explains religion as the immediate consciousness of the
infinite in the finite, and of the eternal in the temporal ; Max Müller
as the perception of the infinite,[2] etc. But if we ask in Kantian
fashion, How is such an immediate consciousness—feeling or perception — possible ? what view of man's nature is implied in his
capacity to have a consciousness, or feeling, or perception of the
infinite ? we are driven back on deeper ground, and come in view
of a rational nature in man which transforms the whole problem.[3]

The same criticisms apply in part to the *historical* treatment of
religion. This, like the psychological, has its own part to play in
the construction of a philosophy of religion ; its help, indeed, is of
untold value. By its aid we see not only what religion is in its
actual manifestations ; not only get an abundance of facts to check
narrow and hasty generalisations ; but we find a grand demonstration of the universality of religion. Yet the historical treatment,
again, like the psychological, does not furnish us with more than the
materials from which to construct a theory of religion. If the historical student, in addition to recording and classifying his facts, and
observing their laws, passes judgment on them as true or false, good
or evil, his inquiry is no longer historical merely, but has become
theological or philosophical.

3. Our question is not answered by explaining religion out of the
necessity which man feels of *maintaining his personality and spiritual
independence* against the limitations of nature. This, as shown in
Note A., is the Ritschlian position, and the passages there quoted

---

[1] Cf. Max Müller, *Natural Religion*, p. 56.
[2] Cf. *Natural Religion*, pp. 48, 188.
[3] See Appendix to Lecture III.

illustrate how Ritschl and his followers develop a "Weltanschauung" from it. Its value lies in the recognition of the fact that religion contains not only a relation of dependence, but a practical impulse towards freedom ; and in this sense the Ritschlian mode of representation has extended far beyond the limits of the school. Thus Pfleiderer (otherwise a sharp critic of Ritschl) says : "There belongs to the religious consciousness some degree of will, some free self-determination. And what this aims at is simply to be made quite free from the obstructing limit and dependence which our freedom encounters in the world" (*Religionsphilosophie*, i. p. 323, Eng. trans.). "In the religious 'Weltanschauung,'" says Lipsius, "there is always posited on the part of man the striving to place himself in a practical relation to this higher power on which he knows himself and his world to be dependent, in order that through this he may further his well-being against the restrictions of the outer world, and victoriously maintain his self-consciousness as a spiritual being against the finite limitations of his natural existence" (*Dogmatik*, p. 25). Réville says : "Religion springs from the feeling that man is in such a relation to this spirit that for his well-being, and in order to gratify a spontaneous impulse of his nature, he ought to maintain with it such relations as will afford him guarantees against the unknown of destiny" (*History of Religions*, p. 29, Eng. trans.).[1] In its Ritschlian form, this theory is open to very serious objections. Professing to account for religion, it really inverts the right relation between God and the world, making the soul's relation to the world the first thing, and the relation to God secondary and dependent ; instead of seeking in an immediate relation to God the first and unique fact which sustains all others.[2] While, further, it may be conceded to Ritschl and his followers that the primary motive in religion is practical (though not prior to the immediate impression or consciousness of the Divine in nature, in the sense of dependence, in conscience, etc.), it must be insisted on that the practical motive is such as can originate only in beings with a rational nature,—*i.e.* reason underlies it.[3] Had this been kept in view, it would have

---

[1] Kaftan, on the other hand, finds the root-motive of religion in the infinity of the "claim on life" inseparable from our nature, which this world is not able to satisfy. "Generally the claim on life (Anspruch auf Leben) lies at the foundation of religion. That this claim is not satisfied in the world, and further through the world, is the common motive of all religions" (*Das Wesen*, p. 67, cf. 60). But whence this "claim on life"? Why this striving after an infinite and "überweltlichen" good? What view of man's nature is implied in the possibility of such strivings? These are questions which Kaftan does not answer, but which a true theory of religion should answer.

[2] See criticism of this theory of religion in Pfleiderer's *Die Ritschl'sche Theologie*, p. 17 ff., and in Stählin's *Kant, Lotze, und Ritschl*, pp. 238–250 (Eng. trans.) ; and A. Dorner's *Das menschliche Erkennen*, p. 221.

[3] See further, Appendix to Lecture III. On the other hand, Hegelianism would have us view religion as but a lower stage in the progress to pure philosophical thought. I have not discussed this theory in the text, as it does not represent any immediately reigning tendency. With Hegel the idea is everything. Religious truths are but rational ideas clothed in a sensuous garb. It is the part of philosophy to lift the veil, and raise the idea to the form of pure

helped to prevent the strong division which this school makes between religious and theoretic knowledge.

II. The rational self-consciousness of man being posited as the ground-work, we may with confidence recognise the following as elements entering into the essence of religion, and connecting themselves with its development :—

1. There is first the sense of absolute dependence, justly emphasised by Schleiermacher (*Der christ. Glaube*, sect. 4). But this alone is not sufficient to constitute religion. Everything depends on the kind of power on which we feel ourselves dependent. Absolute dependence, *e.g.*, on a blind power, or on an inevitable fate or destiny, would not produce in us the effects we commonly ascribe to religion. With the sense of dependence there goes an impulse to freedom. The aim of religion, it has been justly said, is to transform the relation of dependence into one of freedom. This involves, of course, the shaping of the idea of the Godhead into that of personal spirit.

2. Equally original with the feeling of dependence, accordingly, is the impulse in religion to go out of oneself in surrender to a higher object—the impulse to worship. The idea of this higher object may be at first dim and indistinct, but the mind instinctively seeks such an object, and cannot rest till it finds one adequate to its own nature. Here, again, the rational nature of man is seen at work, impelling him to seek the true infinite, and allowing him no rest till such an object is found.

3. Another directly religious impulse is the desire that is early manifested to bring life, and the circle of interests connected with it, under the immediate care and sanction of the Divine. This, which has its origin in the sense of weakness and finitude, is apparent in all religions, and brings religion within the circle of men's hopes and fears.

4. As moral ideas advance,—and we do not here discuss how this advance is possible,—the ground is prepared for yet higher ideas of God, and of His relations to the world and man. There has now entered the idea of a moral end ; man also has become aware of the contradictions which beset his existence as a being at once free, and yet hemmed in and limited on every side in the attainment of his ends ; not to speak of the deeper contradictions (within and without) which beset his existence through sin. It is here that the idea of religion links itself with the moral "Weltanschauung" of Ritschl, Lipsius, Pfleiderer, and others, who find the solution of these antinomies in the idea of a teleological government of the world, in which natural ends are everywhere subordinated to moral ; which, again, implies the monotheistic idea of God, and faith in His moral

thought. Religion gives the "Vorstellung," or figurate representation ; philosophy gives the rational conception, or "Begriff." The distinction is explained by Hegel in the Introduction to his *Geschichte der Philosophie*, vol. i. pp. 79–97. A fuller exposition is given in his *Religionsphilosophie*, vol. i. pp. 20–25. From this theory the reaction was inevitable which led to the repudiation of the metaphysical in theology altogether. One of the most delicate tasks of theology is to adjust the relation between these opposite one-sidednesses.

government, and out of which springs the idea of a "kingdom of God" as the end of the Divine conduct of history.

It does not follow, because this conception, or rather that of the Father-God of Christ, is the only one capable of satisfying man's religious or moral aspirations, that therefore man has been able to produce it from his own resources. Even if he were able, this alone would not satisfy the religious necessity. For religion craves not merely for the idea of God, but for personal fellowship and communion with Him, and this can only take place on the ground that God and man are in some way brought together—in other words, on the basis of Divine Revelation or manifestation.

III. We may perhaps test the statements now made, by applying them to two cases which seem at first sight to contradict them, viz. Buddhism, and the Comtist "Religion of Humanity"; for in neither of these systems have we the recognition of a God. Are they, then, properly to be accounted religions?

1. Buddhism *is* a religion, but it is not so in virtue of its negation of the Divine, but in virtue of the provision it still makes for the religious nature of man. Buddhism, as it exists to-day, is anything but a system of Atheism or Agnosticism; it is a positive faith, with abundance of supernatural elements. It may have begun with simple reverence for Buddha,—itself a substitute for worship,—but the unstilled cravings of the heart for worship soon demanded more. Invention rushed in to fill the vacuum in the original creed, and the heavens which Buddha had left tenantless were repeopled with gods, saints, prospective Buddhas, and still higher imperishable essences, ending in the practical deification of Buddha himself. Buddhism has all the paraphernalia of a religion,—priests, temples, images, worship, etc.[1]

2. In like manner, Comte's system has a cult, in which the sentiments and affections which naturally seek their outlet in the direction of the Divine are artificially directed to a new object, collective humanity, which man is bid adore as the "Grand Être," along with space as the "Grand Milieu," and the earth as the "Grand Fétiche"! There is the smell of the lamp in all this, which betrays too obviously the character of Comtism as an artificial or "manufactured" religion; but if it receives this name, it is because there is an application of Divine attributes to objects which, however unworthy of having Divine honours paid to them, are still worshipped as substitutes for God, and so form an inverted testimony to the need which the soul feels for God.[2]

[1] On Buddhism, see Monier Williams's "Duff Lectures" (1889); and on its relation to- religion, Carpenter's *Permanent Elements of Religion* (1889), Lecture III.; Conder's *Basis of Faith*, Note A.; Hartmann's *Religions-philosophie*, vol, ii. p. 5; Kaftan's *Das Wesen*, p. 41, etc.

[2] On Comtism as a religion, see Caird's *Social Philosophy of Comte* (pp. 47–55; and chap. iv.); Carpenter's *Permanent Elements*, Introduction, 25, 49; Conder's *Basis of Faith*, Lecture I.; Spencer's "Retrogressive Religion" in *Nineteenth Century*, July 1884. On modern substitutes for Christianity generally, see an excellent treatment in Bruce's *Miraculous Elements in the Gospels*, Lecture X.

Note I—p. 17

Undogmatic Religion

THE type of view described in the text is too common to need further characterisation. I add one or two illustrations.

"To leave the religious idea in its more complete indeterminateness," says Renan, "to hold at the same time to those two propositions: (1) 'Religion will be eternal in humanity'; (2) 'All religious symbols' are assailable and perishable'; such, then, will be, if the opinion of the wise could be that of the majority, the true theology of our time. All those who labour to show, beyond the symbols, the pure sentiment which constitutes the soul of them, labour for the future. To what, in fact, will you attach religion, if this immortal basis does not suffice you?"—*Fragments Philosophiques*, p. 392.

Réville says: "If religions are mortal, religion never dies, or we may say, it dies under one form only to come to life again under another. There is then underneath and within this multicoloured development a permanent and substantial element, something stable and imperishable, which takes a firm hold on human nature itself." —*History of Religions*, p. 3 (Eng. trans.).

M. Réville is a distinguished member of the Liberal Protestant party in France, whose programme was summed up thus in their organ, *L'Émancipation*: "A Church without a priesthood; a religion without a catechism; a morality without dogmatics; a God without an obligatory system."

Note J—p. 19

Aesthetic Theories of Religion

THE theories which ascribe to the ideals and beliefs of religion only an imaginative, poetic, or æsthetic value, constitute a large family. In Christian theology the tendency found a representative in the beginning of the century in De Wette, whose "æsthetic rationalism" is explained and criticised by Dorner (*Doctrine of the Person of Christ*, v. pp. 51–58, Eng. trans.) and Pfleiderer (*Development of Theology*, pp. 97–102). On the side of materialistic science, the best-known representative is Fr. A. Lange, author of the *History of Materialism* (1875), whose positions are yet more fearlessly carried out by his disciple Vaihinger: "We ought to have, and may have, a theory of the world (or religion), but we must not believe in it theoretically; we must only allow ourselves to be practically, æsthetically, ethically influenced by it." See this theory explained and acutely criticised in Stählin's *Kant, Lotze, und Ritschl*, pp. 92, 110 (Eng. trans.); and in Pfleiderer's *Religionsphilosophie*, ii. pp. 173–175. From the idealistic side, this view, again, is represented by Vacherot in his *La Metaphysique et la Science* (1858) : " God is the idea of the world, and the world is the reality of God." His theory is criticised at length by Caro, in his *L'Idée de Dieu*, chap. v., and in Renan's *Fragments Philosophiques*, pp. 267–324. Finally, Feuerbach, from the atheistic side, regards the idea of God as a mere illusion—the projection by man of his own *ego* into infinity. See his *Wesen des Christenthums* (translated).

Professor Seth has said of this class of theories as a whole : " The faith bred of ignorance is neither stable, nor is it likely to be enlightened. It will either be a completely empty acknowledgment, as we see in the belief in the Unknowable, or it will be an arbitrary play of poetic fancy, such as is proposed by Lange for our consolation. Our phenomenal world, says Lange, is a world of materialism ; but still the Beyond of the Unknowable remains to us. There we may figure to ourselves an ampler and diviner air, and may construct a more perfect justice and goodness than we find on earth. The poets, in word and music and painting, are the chief interpreters of this land of the ideal. To them we must go if we would restore our jaded spirits. But we may not ask—or if we do, we cannot learn—whether this fairy land exists, or whether it has any relation to the world of fact. To all which it may be confidently replied, that such an empty play of fancy can discharge the functions neither of philosophy nor of religion. The synthesis of philosophy and the clear confidence of religion may both, in a sense, transcend the actual data before us, and may both, therefore, have a certain affinity with poetry ; but the synthesis is valueless and the confidence ill-timed if they do not express our deepest insight into facts, and our deepest belief as to the ultimate nature of things."—*Scottish Philosophy*, pp. 178, 179.

Note K—p. 26

Religious and Theoretic Knowledge

A. DORNER states the distinction as it appears in recent theology and philosophy thus : " It has recently been sought in manifold ways, under a stimulus derived from Kant, to find an essential distinction between theoretic knowledge, and a knowledge which does not extend our knowledge of objects in the least, but stands solely in the service of purely subjective interests. This latter has only the significance of expressing in any given case the worth of the object for the subject; these notions have nothing whatever to do with the knowledge of truth, but only with practical interests ; therefore our knowledge is not furthered through any of these notions, but they are only the means for the attainment of subjective ends. Shortly, knowing is placed here at the service of another mental function, and on this account produces, not objective knowledge, but only representations (Vorstellungen), which are formed in a foreign interest, but are perfectly indifferent as to whether they also

extend our knowledge — help-representations we may call them,
formed in order by their means to reach other ends. Should reference be made to truth, this would still in nowise have anything to
do with knowledge ; the truth of such representations would be
measured solely by this, whether with their help one does or does
not attain the wished-for end,—irrespective of whether these representations were in themselves mere phantasies or not. Just for this
reason is all metaphysical worth refused to such notions, *e.g.* æsthetic
or religious."—*Das menschliche Erkennen*, "Die auf Werthurtheile
ruhenden Begriffe," pp. 170, 171.

The kindredship of this view to the "æsthetic rationalism" referred to in last note is greater than is sometimes acknowledged ; in
one disciple of the school, Bender, it becomes indistinguishable from
it. (See his *Das Wesen der Religion*, 1886.) It should, however, be
remarked that Kaftan has severed himself from the extreme
positions of this school, and has sought in his various works to find
an adjustment between faith and theoretic knowledge which will
avoid the appearance of collision between them. He expressly lays
down the proposition that "there is only *one* truth, and that *all*
truth is from God "; acknowledges that faith-propositions have their
theoretic side, and that "in the treatment of the truth of the Christian religion it is the theoretic side of these which comes into consideration "; explains that "truth" in this connection means simply
what it does in other cases, not subjective truth, but "objective"—
"the agreement of the proposition with the real state of the case,"
etc. (*Die Wahrheit*, pp. 1–7.) Most significant of all is his statement
in a recent article that he has abandoned the expression "Werthurtheile" altogether, as liable to misunderstanding. "I have," he
says, "in this attempt to describe the knowledge of faith according
to its kind and manner of origin, avoided the expression 'Werthurtheile,' although I have earlier so characterised the propositions of
faith (in which the knowledge of faith is given). They are theoretic
judgments, which are grounded upon a judgment of worth, which
therefore cannot be appropriated without entering into this judgment of worth which lies at their foundation."—"Glaube und
Dogmatik," in *Zeitschrift für Theol. und Kirche*, i. 6, p. 501.

Cf. further on this distinction, Stählin's acute criticism in his
Kant, Lotze, und Ritschl, pp. 157 ff. (Eng. trans.) ; Hartmann in his
Religionsphilosophie, ii. pp. 1–27 ; Lipsius in his *Dogmatik*, pp. 16–93.
Hartmann and Lipsius deal at length with the distinction and rela-
tions of the "religious" and the "theoretic" "Weltanschauung."

NOTES TO CHAPTER 2

Note A—p. 41

The Central Place of Christ in His Religion

THE unique and central place of Christ in His religion, different from that of other founders of religion, is attested by writers of the most varied standpoints.

Hegel says : "If we regard Christ in the same light as Socrates, we regard him as a mere man, like the Mahometans, who consider Christ to have been an ambassador from God, as all great men may generally be called ambassadors or messengers of God. If we say no more of Christ than that He was a teacher of mankind, and a martyr for truth, we express ourselves neither from the Christian point of view, nor from that of true religion."—*Phil. d. Rel.* ii. p. 287.

Schelling says, in his *Phil. d. Offenbarung* : "The principal content of Christianity is, first, Christ Himself ; not what He said, but what He *is*, and did. Christianity is not, in the first place, a doctrine ; it is a thing, something objective ; and the doctrine can never be anything but the expression of the thing."—Quoted by Pfleiderer, *Religionsphilosophie*, ii. p. 16 (Eng. trans.).

Dorner bears witness to the valuable service of Schelling and Hegel in overcoming the older rationalism, and introducing a profounder treatment of the Christological questions.—*Doctrine of the Person of Christ*, v. pp. 100, 138 (Eng. trans.).

De Wette says : "The *personality* of Jesus, His life and death, and faith in Him, constitute the *centre of Christianity*. The spirit of religion became personal in Him, and, proceeding from Him, exerted an influence upon the world, which stood in need of a new religious life, in order to regenerate it."—*Vorles. über die Religion*, p. 444 (quoted by Hagenbach).

Pfleiderer thus sums up the views of Vatke, a post-Hegelian : "All the streams of the world's history issue in the kingdom of God, which is the will of God in its concrete development to a moral commonwealth. Providence here acts as an actual spirit through all persons and deeds, through which the idea of the good becomes more real, especially through the creative world-historical persons, among whom Christ occupies a unique position as the centre-point of history, as the Revealer and the Reality of the archetypal idea, as the love of God grown personal."—*Religionsphilosophie*, ii. p. 268 (Eng. trans.).

On the views of Biedermann and Lipsius, see the *Christliche Dogmatik* of the former, ii. pp. 580–600 (" the central dogma of the Christian principle"), and the *Lehrb. d. Dogmatik* of the latter, pp. 535–538. " In its dogmatic utterances on the Person and work of Christ," Lipsius says, " the Church expresses the consciousness that its existence has its historical foundation in the Person of Jesus, not merely in the sense which would be suitable to all other religions having personal founders, but in the sense that the Person of Christ is the archetypal representation of the Christian idea, and therefore the authoritative pattern for all time to come ; and that His work forms the permanently sufficient, therefore the creative, basis for the constantly progressing realisation of that idea in the common and individual life of Christians."—*Dog.* p. 537.

Ritschl says : " The Person of the Founder of Christianity is the key to the Christian 'Weltanschauung,' and the standard for the self-judgment and moral striving of Christians." — *Recht. u. Ver.* iii. p. 193 (3rd ed.). Cf. the comparison with Moses, Zoroaster, Mahomet, and Buddha, in pp. 364, 365.

Kaftan emphatically says : " In the question of the Godhead of Jesus Christ, the discussion turns, not on one proposition among others which a Christian recognises and confesses, but upon the central point of the entire Christian confession of faith."—*Brauchen wir ein neues Dogma ?* p. 52.

Hartmann, too, in his *Krisis des Christenthums*, treats this doctrine as the central matter, and discusses it in his first section under the heading, " The Christian Central Dogma and its inevitable Dissolution." Cf. Preface to 3rd ed. of his *Selbstzersetzung d. Christenthums*.

It is needless to adduce instances from writers of a more orthodox tendency.

Note B—p. 44

The Defeat of Arianism

" THE Christian doctrine has been accused," says a writer in the *Church Quarterly Review*, " of being the result of the base intrigues of imperial politics, and to one who resolutely looks only at the details of much of the controversy, such a judgment might seem natural, while a close acquaintance with the Byzantine Court will not make its odour more pleasing. But to a wider view, such a judgment is impossible. The decision of the Council of Nicæa was the result of the free play of the theological ideas of the time ; for Constantine—caring little about the result, though caring very much for unity—wisely left to the Council a free hand ; but its decision may very well have been owing to the influence of a sovereign who threw his whole weight on the side which he saw was prevailing. Arius was condemned by an overwhelming majority, but the decision of the Council was not sufficient to stamp out opinions which had a natural hold on a large section of the Church. So the reaction was obliged to spread. Arianism survived for fifty years; with the help of imperial patronage it even obtained an unreal supremacy. But it had no basis of truth, and was naturally hostile to Christianity. As long as it was established, it continued to exist; orthodoxy was oppressed and persecuted, but orthodoxy increased. As soon as the balance of the temporal power swung round, orthodoxy became supreme, and Arianism vanished from the Empire as if it had never existed. It had more than a fair chance, but had no basis of truth. Orthodoxy had a terrible fight with odds against it, but in the end it was completely victorious."—*Church Quart.*, April–July 1888, pp. 462, 463.

Harnack's judgment on Arianism is equally severe. "Only as cosmologists," he says, "are the Arians monotheists; as theologians and in religion they are polytheists. Finally, deep contradictions lie in the background: a Son, who is no Son; a Logos, who is no Logos; a Monotheism, which does not exclude Polytheism; two or three *Ousias*, who are to be worshipped, while still only one is really distinguished from the creatures, an indefinable nature, which first becomes God when it becomes man, and which still is neither God nor man. . . . The opponents were right; this doctrine leads back into heathenism. . . . The orthodox doctrine has, on the contrary, its abiding worth in the upholding of the faith, that in Christ God Himself has redeemed men, and led them into His fellowship. . . . This conviction of faith was saved by Athanasius against a doctrine which did not understand the inner nature of religion generally, which sought in religion only teaching, and ultimately found its satisfaction in an empty dialectic."—*Grundriss d. Dogmengeschichte*, i. p. 141; cf. the *Dogmengeschichte*, pp. 217–224.

In his recent lectures on *The Incarnation* (p. 91), Mr. Gore directs attention to two striking passages from Thomas Carlyle and Thomas Hill Green to the same effect as the above. Mr. Froude writes of Carlyle: "He made one remark which is worth recording. In earlier years he had spoken contemptuously of the Athanasian Controversy,—of the Christian world torn to pieces over a diphthong. . . . He now told me that he perceived Christianity itself to have been at stake. If the Arians had won, it would have dwindled away to a legend."—*Life in London*, ii. p. 462. See Green's view in *Works*, iii. p. 172.

On the later history of Arianism in England, and its transformation into Unitarianism, see the valuable Appendix by Dr. P. Fairbairn to Dorner's *History of the Doctrine of the Person of Christ*, vol. v. pp. 337–466.

Note C—p. 45

Modern Unitarianism

THE completeness with which modern Unitarianism has divested itself of every trace of the supernatural will be seen from the following extracts.

Dr. Martineau, criticising Mr. Greg's *Creed of Christendom*, writes : " The education and habits of a refined and devout Unitarian family gave him the theory of life from which his independent thoughts set out. Outside observers, both sceptical and mystical, have always upbraided that theory as a weak attempt to blend incompatible elements and settle the contradictions of the world by a hollow compromise, while not denying its correspondence with a certain equilibrium of understanding and character. It may be described as essentially natural religion, enlarged and completed by a supernatural appendix. The whole of its theism, and half of its ethics, were within the reach of the human reason and conscience ; but of the inner and higher range of morals,—spiritual purity, forgiveness of injuries, love to the unlovely,—the obligation was first impressed by the Christian Revelation. And the life beyond death, vainly pursued by the dialectic Plato, and claimed by the rhetoric of Cicero, became an assured reality with the Resurrection of Christ. The universe was a mechanical system of delegated causality, instituted for beneficent and righteous ends, and, for their better attainment, not excluding fresh intercalary volitions at special crises. . . . The former of these conceptions it cost Mr. Greg but little to modify or even to sacrifice," etc.—*Nineteenth Century*, February 1883.

What even Mr. Greg desires to retain of reverence for the spiritual perfection of Jesus, Mr. F. W. Newman, in *his* review of the volume, regards only as an amiable weakness, in total inconsistency with Mr. Greg's own principles of treatment of the Gospels. See passage quoted in Note F. to Lecture I. (from *Fortnightly Review*, vol. xiv.).

In his *Loss and Gain in Recent Theology* (1881), Dr. Martineau sets himself explicitly to state the position of present-day Unitarianism ; and the two gains he principally notices are : " the total disappearance from our branch of the Reformed Churches of all external authority in matters of religion " (" the yoke of the Bible follows the yoke of the Church," p. 9) ;[1] and, second, " the disappearance of the entire Messianic theology." " As objective reality, as a faithful representation of our invisible and ideal universe, it is

---

[1] The late Principal Cairns observes on this : " It is important to remark how completely his admission bears out the whole contention of writers of the school opposite to his in the Socinian controversy, that the tendency of Unitarian doctrine and criticism was to abrogate the authority of Scripture, and reduce it to the level of human literature. This allegation was vehemently resisted in their day by the Polish brethren, who often put on Scripture a non-natural sense rather than seem to invade its authority ; and in more recent

gone from us, gone, therefore, from our interior religion, and become an outside mythology. From the Person of Jesus, for instance, everything official, attached to Him by evangelists or divines, has fallen away ; when they put such false robes on Him, they were but leading Him to death. The pomp of royal lineage and fulfilled prediction, the prerogative of King, of Priest, of Judge, the advent with retinue of angels on the clouds of heaven, are to us mere deforming investitures, misplaced, like court dresses, on the 'spirits of the just,' and He is simply the Divine Flower of humanity, blossoming after ages of spiritual growth—the realised possibility of life in God. . . . All that has been added to that real historic scene, —the angels that hang around His birth, and the fiend that tempts His youth ; the dignities that await His future,—the throne, the trumpet, the assize, the bar of judgment ; with all the apocalyptic splendours and terrors that ensue, — Hades and the Crystal Sea, Paradise and the Infernal Gulf, nay, the very boundary walls of the Kosmic panorama that contains these things, have for us utterly melted away, and left us amid the infinite space and the silent stars " (pp. 14, 15).

"Time was," says the Rev. J. W. Chadwick, of Brooklyn, "when Christianity was universally regarded by Unitarians as a supernatural revelation, attested by signs and wonders, promulgated by One who, even if purely human, was endowed with certain supernatural gifts, and perpetuated in a literature—the New Testament—whose writers were miraculously restrained from all erroneous statement, whether of doctrine or fact. These views are no longer held in their entirety by Unitarians. . . . There are to-day few Unitarians, if any, who believe in any of the New Testament miracles, from the birth of Jesus to His Resurrection inclusive, in the proper sense of the word miracles—violations of natural laws."—In a recent paper, *Why I am a Unitarian.*

Note D—p. 47

Concessions of Ritschlians on the Person of Christ

IN this school, as stated in the Lectures, the attribution of Divinity to Christ is regarded as a simple *religious* judgment—a judgment of value—with no metaphysical meaning behind it. It simply expresses the value which Christ has to the believer as the Revealer of God to him in His grace and truth, and tells us nothing of what Christ is in Himself. How Christ came to be what He was, or what lies

---

times, by Priestley and Belsham, and other controversialists. It will be remembered that in the earnest debate between Moses Stuart and Channing on the Trinity, the former urged the latter, by the example of Continental rationalism, no longer to profess unlimited submission to Scripture, but to escape insuperable critical difficulties which arose on his side, by openly denying its claims to be a judge in controversy."—Art. in *Catholic Presbyterian,* November 1888.

in the constitution of His Person behind this Revelation, it is no part of the business of theology to inquire. This is the original Ritschlian position, but it is significant that Ritschl's followers feel the need of some modification of it, and have already made several significant concessions. "It is increasingly recognised," as I have stated elsewhere, "that we cannot stand simply dumb before the Revelation which it is acknowledged we have in Christ, and refuse to ask who this wonderful Person is that bears the Revelation, and whose personal character and relation to the kingdom of God is so unique. We cannot rest with simply formulating the value of Christ to us ; we must ask what He is in Himself. . . . The mind will not stay in the vagueness of expressions about Christ's 'Godhead,' to which the suspicion constantly attaches that they are mere metaphors. Thus, in spite of their wishes, the Ritschlians are forced to declare themselves a little further, and it is significant that, so far as their explanations go, they are in the direction of recognising that metaphysical background in Christ's Person against which at first protest was entered.[1]

Thus, in a remarkable passage in his *Der Verkehr des Christen mit Gott*, Herrmann says : "It may be unavoidable that this wonderful experience should excite in us the question, how a man can win this importance for us. And it appears to me as if, for all who wish to go back on this question, and follow out the representation of a union of the Divine and human natures in Christ, the Christological decisions of the ancient Church still always mark out the limits within which such attempts must move " (p. 46, 1st ed., 1886).

In his earlier work, *Die Religion im Verhältniss zum Welterkennen und zur Sittlichkeit*, Herrmann had expressed himself, if possible, still more decidedly. "I have certainly the conviction," he says, "the grounds of which I do not need to state here further, that faith in Christ was led in a natural progress to the representation of a pre-existence of Christ, and indeed of a personal, and not an ideal, pre-existence. The assumption of a so-called ideal pre-existence seems to me unjustified. It is still clearly the Person of the exalted Lord, whose worth for the Church and for the kingdom of God is expressed by saying that He did not come into being under earthly conditions as we have done, but that, independently of the world, which represents the perfectly dependent sphere of His Lordship, He *is*. This thought finds, in the expression of a personal pre-existence of the Lord, an expression very full of contradictions indeed, but still the only one which stands at our command, which, therefore, must also have its salutary truth. The contradiction will be removed, if once a solution is found of the problem of time, in which we now view our existence. . . . Faith is led to this, to regard the Redeemer, whom it knows as the Revelation of God, as pre-existent."—*Die Religion*, etc., pp. 438, 439 (1879).

Yet more positively do Bornemann, in his *Unterricht im Christen-thum* (1891), and Kaftan, in his various works, demand a real "Godhead" of Christ, though still with much criticism of "the

---

[1] Art. on "The Ritschlian Theology," in *The Thinker*, August 1892.

old dogma,"¹ and the repudiation of all speculative or metaphysical theologising.

The former says : " Faith in the Godhead of Christ is in a certain sense the sum of the whole gospel ; the aim and the whole content of the Christian life. Its marks are the same as those of the Godhead of the heavenly Father."—*Unterricht*, p. 91.

Kaftan's views are most fully exhibited in his *Brauchen wir ein neues Dogma ?* (1890), (" Do we need a New Dogma ?").

In a section of this pamphlet, under the heading, "What think ye of Christ ?" he says : " Many will object that all has no basis and no guarantee of truth, if it is not established that Jesus has His origin and the beginning of His earthly life from above, and not from below. And in this lies something, the truth of which cannot be gainsaid. At least, it is in my view also a consequence we cannot refuse of faith in the Godhead of the Lord, that He, that His historical Person, stands in a connection of nature with God perfectly unique and not capable of being repeated. We know not how we can call a man ' God,'—the word is too great and too weighty,—if we do not truly mean that the eternal God Himself has come to us in Him, and in Him converses with us. . . . Do we believe in the Godhead of the Lord, then we believe also in His origin from above, out of God."—*Brauchen wir*, etc., p. 58. Cf. the statements in his original work, *Das Wesen*, etc., pp. 308 ff. (1st ed.).

This movement cannot fail to go further, and work itself into clearer relations with the old dogma which it condemns.²

Note E—p. 48

The Weakness of Deism

THE weakness of Deism as a logical system is universally conceded. "Deism," says M. Réville, "in sound philosophy is not tenable. It establishes a dualism, a veritable opposition, between God and the world, which stand opposite to and limit each other. . . . A reaction, in fact, was inevitable. It was necessary that it should be at the same time philosophical and religious, and should come to the satisfaction of the needs that had been misunderstood and suppressed. In philosophy Deism could no longer hold up its head against the objections of reason. In religion, every one was wearied of optimism and of empty declamations. Deism removed God so far from the world and from humanity that piety exhausted itself in the endea-

¹ The contrast between the " old " and the " new " is expressed by Kaftan thus : "The eternal relation of Jesus Christ to the Father is in the old dogma the peculiar and whole object of the doctrine ; it accords with evangelical Christianity, on the other hand, to know His Godhead in its living present relations to us and to our faith" (*Brauchen wir*, etc., p. 54). But this is not an absolute opposition, nor are the standpoints necessarily exclusive.

² Wendt, on the other hand, in his *Inhalt der Lehre Jesu*, refuses to see in Jesus anything but an ethical Sonship (pp. 450-476).

vour to rejoin Him in the icy heights of heaven, and ended by
renouncing the attempt."—*La Divinité de Jésus-Christ*, pp. 163, 171.

Again : "The eighteenth century little imagined that natural
religion, the religion which humanity was bound to profess in this
age of idyllic virtue, in which *le contrat social* had been elaborated
before it was corrupted by the artifices of priests and kings, was
nothing else but philosophic Deism. It did not perceive that this
pretended natural religion was merely an extract subtly derived
from Christian tradition, the fruit of a civilisation already old and
artificial, already saturated with criticism and rationalism, quite the.
opposite of a religion springing up spontaneously in the human
mind still influenced by its primitive traditions."—*History of Religions*, p. 14 (Eng. trans.).

Professor Seth has said : "Deism does not perceive that, by
separating God from the world and man, it really makes Him
finite, by setting up alongside of Him a sphere to which His relations are transient and accidental. The philosopher to whom the
individual self and the sensible world form the first reality, gradually
comes to think of this otiose Deity as a more or less ornamental
appendage in the scheme of things. In France, the century ended
in atheism ; and in cosmopolitan circles in England and Germany,
the belief in God had become little more than a form of words."—
From Kant to Hegel, p. 24.

"The philosophic rationalism of the vulgar *Aufklärung*," says
Hartmann, "appeared with the claim to set up in place of the dis-
esteemed historical religions a self-evident 'natural religion' or
'religion of reason' for all men, the content of which was first a
shallow Deism, with its trinity of ideas of a personal God, personal
immortality, and personal freedom of will ; but already in the
circles of the French Encyclopædists this spiritless Deism had
struck over into an equally spiritless materialism."—*Religionsphilosophie*, ii. p. 24.

Note F—p. 49

Weakness of Modern Liberal Protestantism

THE modern Liberal Protestantism in Germany, Holland, Switzerland, and France, which, while discarding the supernatural in history,
still retains the name Christian,—nay, claims to be the true Christianity, purified and brought into harmony with the "modern"
spirit,—meets with scant mercy at the hands of those who have gone
further, who ruthlessly strip off the veil which disguises its essential
rationalism. Pfleiderer and Réville may be named as well-known
representatives. The party, while claiming the right to criticise
and reject every article of the creed, would retain the traditional
forms of worship, and delight, even, to clothe their conceptions in
the familiar forms of the traditional dogmatics. It is thus that a
service of the "moderns" is described by one of their own number.

"Only put yourself," says this witness, "in the position of those who had never received any other teaching, for example, than that Jesus was born of the Virgin Mary, and suddenly heard their pastor speak on some Christmas Day of 'simple parents of the man of Nazareth,' or on Easter Sunday of 'the delusion of the early Christians that Jesus has returned to earth from the grave.' . . . Yet such preaching was actually heard. . . . The Church listened, thought it over, thought it over again, and finally a large number of her members accepted the new teaching" (quoted by Wicksteed, *Eccl. Instit. of Holland*, p. 59). It is the glaring inconsistency of this position which is remorselessly satirised by writers like Strauss and Hartmann, and the thing which gives their strictures sharpness is that there is so much truth in them.

There was a time when Strauss also wrote : "But we have no fear that we should lose Christ by being obliged to give up a consider- able part of what was hitherto called the Christian creed ! He will remain to all of us the more surely, the less anxiously we cling to doctrines and opinions that might tempt our reason to forsake Him. But if Christ remains to us, and if He remains to us as the highest we know and are capable of imagining within the sphere of religion, as the Person without whose presence in the mind no perfect piety is possible ; we may fairly say that in Him do we still possess the sum and substance of the Christian faith" (*Selbstgespräche*, p. 67, Eng. trans.). But in his *The Old Faith and the New*, Strauss later faced the ques- tion, "Are we still Christians ?" with a bolder look, and gave it the uncompromising answer, "No." He goes over the articles of the Apostles' Creed one by one, and shows that every one of them is taken by the "modern" theologians in a non-natural sense. He invites his reader "to assist in thought at the cycle of festivals in a Protestant church, whose minister stands on the ground of present- day science, and see whether he can still be uprightly and naturally edified thereby." He pictures the statements that such a minister would be compelled to make at Christmas, at the Epiphany, at Good Friday, at Easter and Ascension Day ; compares them with the book he reads, the prayers he uses, the sacraments he admini- sters ; and shows how completely the whole thing is a ludicrous pretence. His conclusion is : "If we do not wish to escape difficul- ties, if we do not wish to twist and dissemble, if we wish our yea to be yea, and our nay, nay,—in short, if we would speak as honourable, upright men,—we must confess, we are no longer Christians."—*Der alte und der neue Glaube*, pp. 12–94.

Hartmann is even more severe on the unchristian character of the modern Protestant Liberalism in his *Selbstzersetzung des Christenthums* (chaps. vi. and vii.). "We ask," he says, "what right the Protestant Liberals have to call themselves Christians beyond the fact that their parents have had them baptised and confirmed. In all ages there has been one common mark of the Christian religion—belief in Christ. . . . But we have seen that the Liberal Protestants cannot believe in Christ as either Luther, or Thomas Aquinas, or John, or Paul, or Peter, believed in Christ, and least of all as Jesus believed

in Himself, for He believed Himself to be the Christ—the Messiah"
(pp. 64, 65).

Apart, however, from criticisms of opponents, which may be
deemed unfair, it is a fact that, through all its history, Protestant
Liberalism has found it exceedingly difficult to maintain itself on the
platform even of Theism, not to speak of that of Christianity. Its
tendency has been constantly "downgrade," till either it has ended
in open rejection of Christianity, or has been displaced by more
positive forms of belief. Strauss's case is not a solitary one. A
parallel is found in the career of Edmond Schérer, the inaugurator
of the modern Liberal movement in Switzerland and France, who,
beginning with the most uncompromising traditional orthodoxy,
went on, according to M. Gretillat, to the progressive repudiation
of all the fundamentals of Christian belief, religious and even moral,
up to the point of absolute scepticism. The party of Liberal Christianity initiated by him, of which Réville is a surviving representative, had, according to the same authority, " only a fleeting existence,
and its name, to speak in popular language, soon disappeared from
the handbill"[1] (article on "Theological Thought among French
Protestants" in *Presbyt. and Ref. Review*, July 1892). In Holland,
too, the "modern" school is seen running a remarkable course. Its
originator, Scholten, was at first, like Schérer of Geneva, quite
conservative. Then he passed to a view of Revelation and of Christianity not unlike Pfleiderer's. His "thoughts, however, were not
expounded with perfect distinctness in the beginning. They were
too much clothed in the old orthodox forms, and had too large an
admixture of conservative elements for this. Scholten himself lived
in the honest conviction of having discovered the reconciliation of
faith and knowledge, of theology and philosophy, of the heart and
the intellect. He was able also to impart this conviction to others.
Soon the gospel was proclaimed with enthusiasm from many pulpits.
. . . Among his followers the illusion was well-nigh universal, that
the reasonableness of the faith and of the doctrine of the Reformed
Church had been established." This confidence received a rude
shock when, in 1864, Scholten himself declared that, while formerly
believing that he found in the Scriptures, rightly expounded, his
view of the world, he was no longer of that opinion. "He now
begins to recognise that between his ideas and those of the Bible
there is no agreement, but a deep chasm. . . . The results soon
showed themselves. The illusion had been dispelled; faith and
enthusiasm suffered shipwreck. Some ministers, like Pierson and
Busken Huet, resigned the office and left the Church. Others felt
dissatisfied with the monism of Scholten. . . . A whole group
of modern theologians broke loose from Scholten's system, and
sought a closer alliance with Hoekstra. . . . Some adherents of this
tendency went to such an extreme in the avowal of these ideas, that,
with a degree of justice, an 'atheistic shade' of modern theology
began to be spoken of."—Professor Bavinck, of Kampen, in *Presbyt.
and Ref. Review*, April 1892.

[1] It was replaced by newer Ritschlian tendencies.

Professor Bavinck thus sums up on the development in Holland : "In casting a retrospective glance at the three tendencies described up to this point, we are struck with the tragic aspect of this development of dogmatic thought. It is a slow process of dissolution that meets our view. It began with setting aside the Confession. Scripture alone was to be heard. Next, Scripture also is dismissed, and the Person of Christ is fallen back on. Of this Person, however, first His Divinity, next His pre-existence, finally His sinlessness, are surrendered, and nothing remains but a pious man, a religious genius, revealing to us the love of God. But even the existence and love of God are not able to withstand criticism. Thus the moral element in man becomes the last basis from which the battle against Materialism is conducted. But this basis will appear to be as unstable and unreliable as the others."

Note G—p. 52

Christianity and the Idea of Progress

"THE hopeful view of human history," says Professor J. Candlish, "according to which there is to be expected a gradual progress in an upward direction, and an ultimate state of goodness and happiness, was entirely foreign to the ideas of the ancient world. Its philosophers and poets either regarded the course of mankind as a continual degeneracy from a golden age in the past, or as a vast cycle in which there was a continual return or reproduction of the same events and states of things. . . . The idea of the perfectibility of mankind, and of the gradual and steady improvement of the race in the course of time, which has been so largely used by those who reject Christianity, and which enables them to make light of the supernatural grounds of hope for the world that Christians cherish, was entirely strange to the pre-Christian ages ; and though it may be due in part to the progress of science, yet is much more to be ascribed to the promises and truths of Revelation. At least it may be said with truth that Christianity, and more particularly the Christian idea of the kingdom of God, furnishes the only solid ground for such hopes of mankind. . . . In modern times the discoveries of science in its investigation of the works of creation have tended to awaken in men's minds a similar hopeful spirit, so that the gradual and sure advance of mankind to perfection has been accepted almost as an axiom or self-evident truth by many who do not accept the religious basis on which it rested in Israel. But it may be doubted whether, apart from a belief in God as the Creator of the universe, and at the same time the God of grace and salvation, there is any solid foundation for such a hopeful view of the world's history. The rise and prevalence of pessimistic views in modern times serves to show this ; and some of those who are most sanguine about the prospects of mankind, apart from Revelation and Christianity, acknowledge frankly that there can be no certainty of this on a merely natural basis, and that possibly after all we may have to fall back into Pessimism."—*The Kingdom of God* (Cunningham Lectures, 1884), pp. 38–42.

See on this subject the careful history of the idea of progress in Flint's *Philosophy of History*, pp. 28-42 ; and the valuable remarks in Hare's *Guesses at Truth* (referred to also by Dr. Candlish), pp. 305–348 (1871). Cf. Leopardi's (and Hartmann's) three stages of human illusion, in Caro's *Le Pessimisme*, pp. 39–49.

Note H—p. 53

The Prevalence of Pessimism

" It is a singular phenomenon," says Luthardt, " that in our time, in which so much complaint is made of the decay of philosophical study and interest, a definite philosophical system has attained a popularity which is almost without precedent in earlier systems ; and a philosophical work has had a success which usually falls only to the lot of the most spirited literary works, and to romances. I refer to the philosophy of Pessimism and to the work of E. von Hartmann, *The Philosophy of the Unconscious*."—*Die mod. Welt.* p. 183.

Caro observes : " We can now understand in what sense, and how far it is true that the disease of Pessimism is a disease ' essentially modern.'[1] . . . How strange this revival of Buddhistic Pessimism, with all the apparatus of the most learned systems, in the heart of Prussia, at Berlin ! That three hundred millions of Asiatics should drink in long draughts the opium of these fatal doctrines which enervate and act as a soporific on the will, is already sufficiently strange ; but that a race, energetic, disciplined, so strongly constituted for knowledge and for action, at the same time so practical, a rigorous calculator, warlike and stern, certainly the opposite of a sentimental race,—that a nation formed of these robust and lively elements should give a triumphant welcome to these theories of despair divulged by Schopenhauer,—that its military optimism should accept with a sort of enthusiasm the apology for death and for annihilation,—it is this which at the first view seems inexplicable. And the success of the doctrine is not confined to the banks of the Spree. The whole of Germany has become attentive to this movement of ideas. Italy, with a great poet, had outstripped the current ; France, as we shall see, has followed in a certain measure ; she also, at the present hour, has her Pessimists."—*Le Pessimisme*, pp. 25, 26.

---

[1] Martensen remarks of modern Pessimism that " a Pessimism like it, though it be far from Christian, can only be found in the Christian world, where the infinite craving of personality has been awakened."—*Christian Ethics*, i. p. 178 (Eng. trans.).

".There can be no question," says Karl Peters, "that Schopenhauerism is for the time the dominating tendency in our fatherland.
One needs only to consult Laban's book-list to be convinced of the
fact ; our whole atmosphere is, so to speak, saturated with Schopenhauer's views and ideas. . . . Hand in hand with the colossal
forward development of our race in all departments goes the fact
that the sorrow of earthly existence is felt to-day more keenly than
ever by the masses. A decided pessimistic current goes through
our time."—*Willenswelt*, pp. 109, 244.

Pessimism, according to Hartmann, is the *deeper* mood of humanity
—its permanent undertone (*Selbstzer. d. Christ.* p. 96).

Note I—p. 56

Transition From Pessimism to Theism— Hartmann and Karl Peters

It is a remarkable circumstance that Pessimism also should end by
recognising the need of religion, and in its own way should be found
seeking to provide for that need. The new religion, Hartmann
thinks, will represent the synthesis of the religious evolution of the
East and of that of the West—of the pantheistic and of the monotheistic evolution : only resting on that which is the indispensable
presupposition of all religion, "the Pessimism of positive Christianity." He describes it as "a Pantheism, and indeed a pantheistic
Monism (with exclusion of all Polytheism) ; or impersonal immanent
Monotheism, whose Godhead has the world as its objective manifestation, not outside of, but within itself" (*Selbst. d. Christ.* pp. 93, 97,
121). The basis of this new religious system is elaborated in the
second part of his *Religionsphilosophie*, entitled *Die Religion des
Geistes*. A simple reference to the table of contents in this work
will show in how extraordinary a fashion it is attempted to take
over the whole nomenclature of Christianity into this new philosophical religion. First the human side of the religious relation is
treated of, often very suggestively. Then it is treated of in its
double-sided aspect—Divine and human—under the following
headings—(1) Grace and Faith in General ; (2) The Grace of
Revelation and Intellectual Faith ; (3) The Grace of Redemption
and Faith of the Heart ; (4) The Grace of Sanctification and
Practical Faith. The object of religion in turn is considered in a
threefold aspect—(1) God as the Moment overcoming the Dependency of the World ; (2) God as the Moment grounding the
Dependency of the World ; (3) God as the Moment grounding the
Freedom of the World (Freedom in God, the righteousness of God,
the holiness of God). Man is considered—(1) as in need of
Redemption ; and (2) as capable of Redemption. The process of
salvation itself is exhibited in a threefold light—(1) The Awakening
of Grace ; (2) The Unfolding of Grace ; (3) The Fruits of Grace (!).

Yet God, endowed with all these attributes, wise, omniscient, gracious, righteous, holy, etc., is still regarded as impersonal and unconscious. Is not Hartmann chargeable with the same fault which he seeks to fasten on the Protestant Liberals, of trying to profit by the respect which is paid to the Bible while teaching a totally different doctrine ? (*Selbst. d. Christ.* p. 62).

Karl Peters is undoubtedly right, when he says of the systems both of Frauenstadt and of Hartmann, that they represent the transition to Theism without knowing it. In Frauenstadt's system, he remarks, "the world in its totality is no more identified with the world-Ego, and we have, without being aware of it, gone over from Pantheism to Theism." Criticising Hartmann, he comments on "this absolute, unconscious, all-wise idea, an omniscient wisdom, which embraces all, and only knows not itself," and argues that in principle Theism is involved in Hartmann's doctrine. "Here," he says, "we reach the kernel of the whole criticism. I maintain, namely, positively, that the Philosophy of the Unconscious represents the transition from Pantheism to Theism. . . . As in Schopenhauer we have the transition from an idealistic to a realistic, so in Hartmann there is executed the transition from a pantheistic to a theistic 'Weltanschauung.' The former indeed believed himself to stand on quite the other side, and no doubt the latter also thinks that he is planted on the opposite bank. But as Schopenhauer could not prevent the historical development from growing beyond his standpoint, so Hartmann will seek in vain to guard himself against such a breaking up of his system. . . . Ed. v. Hartmann's Unconscious is an almighty and all-wise Providence, raised above the world-process, which comprehends and holds within itself the whole world-development."—*Willenswelt*, pp. 148, 268, 272.

Note J—p. 57

Materialism in Germany

THE descent from an overstrained idealistic Pantheism to materialistic Atheism in Germany—through Feuerbach, Stirner, Ruge, etc.—is matter of notoriety. The following extract from an able article on "Lotze's Theistic Philosophy," in the *Presbyterian Review*, vol. vi. (1885), will illustrate the length to which things went in that direction :—

"The one-sided opposition of Empiricism to Idealism developed into dogmatic Materialism. From the 18th September 1854, when Rudolf Wagner delivered at Göttingen his famous address on 'The Creation of Man and the Substance of the Soul,' the Materialistic conflict raged in Germany for a couple of decades with unabated vigour. Taking up the gauntlet which Wagner had thrown down, Karl Vogt entered the lists with 'Köhlerglaube und Wissenschaft,' flaunting, amidst satire and ridicule, in the face of his opponent, who had declared himself content with the simple religious faith of the collier, the now famous sentence that 'thought stands in about the same relation to the brain, as gall to the liver or urine to the kidneys.' A flood of writings, more or less popular in style, followed, and a sort of religious propaganda was made of the gospel of Materialism, while a fierce crusade was waged against everything claiming to be superior to matter, or a 'function' of matter. The hostility against religion was pronounced and bitter. The creed preached was Atheism, naked and unashamed. Matter is held to be eternal; physical and chemical forces are the only ultimate agents; the world exists, Vogt tells us, 'without organic substance, without a known Creator, nay, without a leading idea.' Hellwald expressly announces that the task of science is 'to destroy all ideals, to manifest their hollowness and nothingness, to show that belief in God and religion is deception'; while Büchner, who is ever, if possible, a little more audacious than the rest, sums up the matter as follows: 'Theism, or belief in a personal God, leads, as all history shows, to monachism, and the rule of priests; Pantheism, or belief in an all-pervading God, leads, where it is in the ascendancy, to contempt of the senses, denial of the Ego, to absorption in God, and to a state of stagnation. Atheism, or philosophical Monism, alone leads to freedom, to intelligence, to progress, to due recognition of man—in a word, to Humanism.' . . . The progress of Materialism was rapid. Büchner's *Force and Matter*, the 'Bible of German Materialism,' passed, within twenty years from its first appearance (1858), through no less than fourteen editions, and was translated into almost every language in Europe. The scientific camp was said to be materialistic almost to a man. The common people, among whom this way of thinking was frequently allied with the political tenets of social democracy, were, and are still to-day largely leavened by the infection. The philosophical chairs in the Universities were feeble to resist it. . . . Materialism in Germany is no longer as strong as it was; good authorities express it as their opinion that, as it grew, so also is it waning 'rapidly'" (pp. 652–655).

See also the sketch of the German atheistic parties in Lichtenberger's "History of German Theology in the Nineteenth Century" (*Histoire des Idées religieuses en Allemagne*), pp. 360–70 (Eng. trans.); and Christlieb's "Modern Doubt and Christian Belief" (*Moderne Zweifel am christlichen Glaube*), pp. 138–140 (Eng. trans.).

Note K—p. 63

The Reasonableness of Revelation

EWALD has said, much in the spirit of the passage quoted from Pfleiderer: "How, then, should not He answer the earnestly perseveringly questioning spirit of man—He of whose spirit man's is but a luminous reflection and an enkindled spark, and to whom in his searching and questioning he can draw near quite otherwise than to the visible things of creation."—*Revelation: its Nature and Record* (Eng. trans. of first vol. of *Die Lehre der Bibel von Gott*), p. 18.

Dr. Walter Morison works out in a very ingenious way the argument for the probability and reasonableness of Revelation from the analogy of nature. Rebutting the objection that the modern conception of nature "is altogether against the idea of any interference by Revelation from Heaven with the closely linked order existing in nature," and permits "only evolution from within of coiled-up energies," he remarks : "In whatever way—whether by evolution or otherwise—the system of nature which we see around us, and of which we are a part, has come about, that system of nature supplies no presumption against there being a direct Revelation of religious truth ; on the contrary, its actual testimony, rightly understood, is in favour of that supposition. What may be called direct revelation is found to be one of the common phenomena of nature or the system of things. As soon as we pass into that region in our world where there is need for communication between individuals possessed of intelligence in any degree, we find 'revelation' to be the law. There is direct utterance. Even the inferior animals are continually telling out by their many voices, 'none of which is without signification,' their various feelings. Wherever there is what may be called individuality, with power of feeling and volition, there utterance or communication exists ; it being part of the order of nature that there be connecting bond of speech between such as possess any faculty for understanding and fellowship. And when we ascend in our observations to the region of human life as social, we perceive a corresponding development of the powers noticed in the inferior creatures. Everywhere over society we observe *speech* of some sort ; communication in a direct way from one to another ; a constant immediate *revelation* of inward thought and feeling going on. There is really nothing more familiar in the economy of human life than this phenomenon of direct communication from mind to mind, sometimes by look and sight, usually by words. . . . There is another world, then, besides this tongueless one of inorganic nature ! There is in the universe this fact, that between individuals capable of it, direct revelation is constantly going on. Where there are beings that require a medium of intelligent communication between them, there we perceive some sort of speech to exist. And hence it is not a suggestion *primâ facie* opposed to the analogy of nature, at all events, which is offered when it is asked whether there may not be some direct personal and articulate utterance made by God to man. Is there to be eternal silence between these intelligences, these kindred natures, with their mutual capacity for love and communion ? Are all creatures in the universe that have any measure of intelligence, or are even sentient, capable of telling out directly what is in them ; and have they the means and the appetency thereto ? Can man commune with man through the high gift of language ? And is the Infinite Mind and Heart not to express itself, or is it to do so but faintly or uncertainly through dumb material symbols, never by blessed speech? Is there no ' Word of God'? To give a negative answer here would be at least to go against the analogy of nature. All beings that we know possessed of any intelligence,—such beings generally, we can at all events say, —and especially the members of the human family, speak to each other in some direct way, make an immediate revelation of what is within them ; and one of the strongest presumptions, surely, is this, that a Personal God, in whose image man was made, would, in His dealings with man, if sufficient occasion called, express Himself in a similar direct manner ; in other words, give a Revelation ! "—*Footprints of the Revealer*, pp. 49–52.

Note L—p. 64
The Ritschlian Doctrine of Revelation

THE Ritschlian theologians found everything on positive Revelation. This is their distinctive position, and their merit as a protest against a one-sided intellectualism and idealism. They will not allow even of the possibility of any knowledge of God outside the Revelation of His grace in Jesus Christ.[1] Natural theology and theoretic proofs for the existence of God are tabooed by them. A few remarks may be made here on this theory by way of further explanation and criticism.

I. On the theory itself :—

1. As regards the *nature* of this Revelation, the Ritschlians are agreed that it comes to us solely through the self-presentation of Christ in His historical manifestation. He is the only vehicle of Revelation recognised by them. It is not a Revelation through doctrine, but through the felt presence of God in Christ, and through the living and acting in which Christ exemplifies to us the right relation of sonship to God, and makes manifest the character and purposes of God, as these bear on our salvation and well-being.

2. As regards the *content* of this Revelation, its central point is found in the design of God to found a kingdom of God on the earth, and to gather men into it, and induce them to make its ends their own, through the right knowledge of His character, and their acceptance of the right relation of sonship to Him. All Christ's work— His doing and dying—has this for its aim. His unity with God in His world-purpose is a feature in His Divinity ; the significance of His death is, that it guarantees to us supremely the reality of that religious relation to God into which He invites us in His Gospel.[2]

---

[1] See this position slightly modified in the *second* edition of Herrmann's *Verkehr*, p. 49. Herrmann's general views on Revelation are stated ·in his Giessen Lecture on *Der Begriff der Offenbarung* (1887). Kaftan discusses the subject in his *Das Wesen*, etc., pp. 171–201.

[2] Kaftan, however, views the kingdom of God as belonging. not to this world, but the next.

3. As regards the *proof* of this Revelation, the Ritschlians are obviously in a difficulty, since proof means that a thing is shown to be objectively true (apart from our subjective thoughts about it), while yet it is a cardinal principle with them that religion moves only in the sphere of value-judgments, *i.e.* judgments on the relation of things to our states of pleasure and pain. They cannot, however, refuse the demand for proof that this which they present as Revelation from God is really such, and not a subjective illusion of our own minds. And here—

First, and negatively, they reject, as inappropriate to religion, all merely historical evidence, or proof from objective facts, as miracles, or the resurrection of Christ (which it is doubtful if most of them accept as objective fact).

Second, and positively, the proof alleged is of two kinds :—

(1) Immediate—consisting of the irresistible impression (Eindruck) which Christ makes on the soul historically confronted with Him, compelling the acknowledgment that God is with Him. This is the theme on which the changes are incessantly rung by Professor Herrmann in his recent writings.

(2) Scientific—consisting in showing the correspondence which exists between Christianity and the religious needs of man, as these may be deduced from the consideration of his nature and history ; otherwise, the agreement of Christianity with the practical postulates of religion. This is the sort of proof which Ritschl hints at when he says : " Its representation in theology will, therefore, come to a conclusion in the proof that the Christian ideal of life, and no other, altogether satisfies the claims of the human spirit to a knowledge of things " ; *i.e.* yields a practically satisfying view of the world (*Recht. und Ver.* iii. p. 25, 3rd ed.) ; and which is undertaken in detail by Kaftan in his *Wahrheit d. Christ. Religion* (though on different fundamental lines from Ritschl's).

II. On this view I would offer the following brief criticisms :—

1. It is to be observed that this basing of everything by the Ritschlians on positive Revelation *does not harmonise well with the premises of the school.*

·(1) It does not consist well with their fundamental position that religion moves solely in the sphere of value-judgments. For if we really get out to objective Revelation, we have clearly broken through this magic circle of value-judgments, and are in the domain of judgments of fact and truth. Or is our judgment that this is a Divine Revelation itself also only a value-judgment ?

(2) The theory of Revelation does not consist well with the Ritschlian theory of knowledge. For Ritschl is thoroughly at one with Kant in the view that the theoretic reason can give us no knowledge of God, or proof of His existence. We are thus driven back on practical postulates, or " Vorstellungen," beyond which, as it would seem, even Revelation cannot raise us, for Revelation cannot take us outside the essential limitations of our faculties.

2. It is to be observed, further, that this theory has no proper answer to give to the question of *the nature of Revelation.* With its

general avoidance of the speculative, it gives us no distinct specifica-
tion of what precisely this term means, or how much it is supposed
to cover. Enough that we receive from Christ the impression that
—in some undefined sense—God is with Him, and in Him is drawing near to us; this is to us (subjectively) the Revelation, and
nothing else is of importance. Yet it is very obvious that multitudes of questions may arise just at this point as to the character,
degree, purity, limits, reliableness, and authority of this Revelation,
which Ritschlianism gives us no help to answer. We cannot but
ask, *e.g.*, respecting a Revelation mediated to us in this way through
the consciousness of another human being—How did it originate?
What did Revelation mean to Him, the original recipient? Was it
a really supernatural act? or partly supernatural and partly natural,
with a correspondingly mixed result? How is such a Revelation
even possible, since, according to another part of the theory, there is
no direct (mystical) communication between the soul and God?[1] Is
there not large room left here, which the Ritschlians (*e.g.* Wendt)
are not slow to avail themselves of, for distinction and criticism
even in the contents of Christ's own consciousness and utterances?
Are we not in danger of coming back to the view that in the last
analysis Christ's religious conceptions do not differ in origin or
character from those of any other great religious genius?

3. It is again to be observed that the character of this system
compels it *to limit very greatly the contents of the Revelation.* Ritschlianism is, as said, essentially a system of religious positivism. It
starts with *data* of experience,—the direct impression made on us
by Christ, and the experimental knowledge we have of His power
to give us deliverance and freedom,—and beyond this it declines to
go. All in the Christian system which it regards as transcendental
or metaphysical—however guaranteed by words of Christ or His
Apostles—it refuses to inquire into, or sets aside as of no importance to faith. The pre-existence of Christ, *e.g.*, His supernatural
birth, His heavenly reign, the constitution of His Person, the
Trinity of the Godhead, the eschatological doctrines, are thus swept
aside. It has no doctrine of objective Atonement, but only one of
subjective reconciliation. Other great doctrines of Scripture are
either absent, or have a large part of their meaning taken from
them.

4. Finally, it is difficult to avoid the conclusion that, while the
members of this school profess to derive their theology from positive
Revelation, *what really governs their construction is,* not the objective
Revelation, but *their particular theories of religion, and their ideas of
what is necessary for the realisation of man's practical ends.* Every
one of the members of this school has his theory of religion independently determined (the theories, however, widely differing
from each other), and agreement with this theory is not only employed for the *proof* of the Revelation, but is also the standard,
practically, of what is accepted or rejected in its contents. The
Revelation, in other words, does not come with *authority*, but rather

---

[1] Cf. Herrmann's *Verkehr des Christen mit Gott.*

derives its authority from its agreement with the practical postulates, which are previously established on quite other grounds. This is true of all the leading members of the party—Ritschl, Herrmann, Kaftan, etc, So far as relates to the proof of Revelation, it is not easy to avoid the appearance of moving in a circle. *E.g.*, in Kaftan's *Wahrheit*, while the test of the truth of the Revelation is its agreement with the practical postulates above referred to, these in turn are supposed to be confirmed by the fact of the Revelation, and thus proved to be no subjective illusion. I would not press this too far, since the argument from agreement with rational and moral postulates is in itself a sound one, and the only objection that can be raised is to the particular way of stating it, and the exclusive use made of it.[1]

---

[1] In Kant's hands, as is well known, this method was employed to eviscerate the gospel of all peculiar supernatural content, and to reduce it to a nucleus of moral notions.

NOTES TO CHAPTER 3

Note A—p. 75

Primitive Fetishism and Ghost-worship

THE theory of a gradual ascent in religion from a primitive Fetishism through Polytheism to Monotheism, made familiar by Auguste Comte, and repeated with unquestioning faith by writers like Mr. Clodd and Mr. S. Laing, receives scant countenance from the best recent authorities. Certainly, no case has been found in which it is possible to trace historically such an evolution. I cite a few statements and opinions on the subject, and on the rival theories of Ghost-worship, Totemism, etc.

Principal Fairbairn, speaking of this class of theories in general, says: "They assume a theory of development which has not a single historical instance to verify it. Examples are wanted of people who have grown, without foreign influence, from Atheism into Fetishism, and from it through the intermediate stages into Monotheism; and until such examples be given, hypotheses claiming to be 'Natural Histories of Religion' must be judged hypotheses still."—*Studies in the Philosophy of Religion*, p. 12.

Mr. Max Müller, speaking as an expert, condemns the theory of a primitive Fetishism. He says: "If it has never been proved, and perhaps, according to the nature of the case, can never be proved, that Fetishism in Africa, or elsewhere, was ever in any sense of the word a primary form of religion, neither has it been shown that Fetishism constituted anywhere, whether in Africa or elsewhere, the whole of a people's religion. Though our knowledge of the religion of the negroes is still very imperfect, yet I believe I may say that, wherever there has been an opportunity of ascertaining, by long and patient intercourse, the religious sentiments even of the lowest savage tribes, no tribe has ever been found without something beyond mere worship of fetishes. . . . I maintain that Fetishism was a corruption of religion in Africa, as elsewhere; that the negro is capable of higher religious ideas than the worship of stocks and stones; and that many tribes who believe in fetishes cherish at the same time very pure, very exalted, and very true sentiments of the Deity."—*Is Fetishism a Primitive Form of Religion?* Lecture II. p. 105 (Hibbert Lectures).

In his more recent Lectures he reiterates this view : " If one con siders," he says, " what Fetishism really is, namely, the very last stage in the downward course of religion, this attempt to make a little-understood superstition of some modern negro tribes the key to the religion of Greeks and Romans, nay of the most civilised nations of the world, is perfectly marvellous."—*Natural Religion*, p. 159.   Again : " Fetishism, from its very nature, cannot be primitive, because it always presupposes the previous growth of the Divine predicate.   As to the Fetishism of modern negroes, we know now that it represents the very lowest stage which religion can reach, whether in Africa or any other part of the world ; and I know of no case, even among the most degraded of negro tribes, where remnants of a higher religious belief have not been discovered by the side of this degraded belief in amulets, talismans, and fetishes. The idea of De Brosses and his followers, that Fetishism could reveal to us the very *primordia* of religious thought, will remain for ever one of the strangest cases of self-delusion, and one of the boldest anachronisms committed by students of the history of religions."—*Ibid.* pp. 219, 220.

Mr. Herbert Spencer passes the same judgment.   Repudiating Mr. Harrison's theory of an original Fetishism, he says : " An induction, based on over a hundred examples, warrants me in saying that there has never existed anywhere such a religion as that which Mr. Harrison ascribes to 'countless millions of men,' during 'countless centuries of time.' . . . I have shown that, whereas among the lowest races, such as the Juángs, Andamanese, Fuegians, Australians, Tasmanians, and Bushmen, there is no Fetishism, Fetishism reaches its greatest height in considerably advanced societies, like those of ancient Peru and modern India. . . . And I have remarked that, had Fetishism been conspicuous among the lowest races, and inconspicuous among the higher, the statement that it was primordial might have been held proved ; but that, as the fact happens to be exactly the opposite, the statement is con-clusively disproved."—*Nineteenth Century*, xvi. pp. 8, 9.

This also is Pfleiderer's opinion : " In presence of these facts, the 'evolution theory,' as hitherto stated, which finds the beginnings of religion in Fetishism and Animism, appears to me to be as much wanting in evidence as it is psychologically impossible."—*Religions-philosophie*, iii. p. 16 (Eng. trans.).

But then Mr. Spencer's Ghost theory, which he (and now also Dr. Tylor) propounds as a substitute for that of a primitive Fetishism, meets with an equally decisive rejection at the hands of Mr. Harrison, Max Müller, and other influential writers.

" I shall say but little about Mr. Spencer's Ghost theory," says Mr. Harrison; " I have always held it to be one of the most unlucky of all his sociologic doctrines, and that on psychological as well as on historical grounds. . . . It is certain that the believers in the Ghost theory, as the origin of all forms of religion, are few and far between.   The difficulties in the way of it are enormous.   Mr.

Spencer laboriously tries to persuade us that the worship of the sun and the moon arose, not from man's reverence for these great and beautiful powers of nature, but solely as they were thought to be the abodes of the disembodied spirits of dead ancestors. Animal worship, tree and plant worship, Fetishism, the Confucian worship of heaven,—all, he would have us believe, take their religion entirely from the idea that these objects contain the spirits of the dead. If this is not 'persistent thinking along defined grooves,' I know not what it is."—*Nineteenth Century*, xvi. pp. 362, 363.

Max Müller subjects the theory to an historical examination in his Lectures on *Anthropological Religion*, and rejects it as based on totally mistaken data. "Granting even," he says, "that there are races whose religion consists of ancestor worship only, though, as at present informed, I know of none, would that prove that the worship of nature-gods must everywhere be traced back to ancestor worship ? . . . If a pleader may tell a judge that he has been mis-informed as to facts, surely we may claim the same privilege, without being guilty of any want of respect towards a man who, in his own sphere, has done such excellent work. I make no secret that I consider the results of Mr. H. Spencer's one-sided explanation of the origin of religion as worthy of the strongest condemnation which a love of truth can dictate."—Lecture V. pp. 132, 133.

See also the examination of this theory in Pfleiderer's *Religions-philosophie*, iii. pp. 12–16.

M. Renouf has said : "If from pre-historic we pass to historic times, we at once meet on Egyptian ground with an entire system of notions wonderfully (indeed almost incredibly) similar to those entertained by our Indo-European ancestors. There is, however, no confirmation of Mr. Herbert Spencer's theory, that the rudi-mentary form of all religion is the propitiation of dead ancestors. If the Egyptians passed through such a rudimentary form of religion, they had already got beyond it in the age of the Pyramids, for their most ancient propitiation of ancestors is made through prayer to Anubis, Osiris, or some other gods."—Hibbert Lectures, p. 127.

Totemism, or belief in descent from animals worshipped as Divine, is another phase of explanation of the origin of religion which also meets with little favour from the authorities. "Totem-ism is one of those pseudo-scientific terms," says Max Müller, "which have done infinite harm to the study of mythology."— *Anthropological Religion*, p. 408. See his remarks on it in this work, pp. 121–124 ; and in *Natural Religion*, p. 159. A careful examina-tion of Professor W. R. Smith's theory of Totemism, as applied to the Semitic religions, may be seen in an article already referred to in the *Edinburgh Review* for April 1892 (art. "Semitic Religions "). M. Renouf remarks on another advocate of the Totem theory : "Many of you have probably read Mr. M'Lellan's articles on the 'Worship of Animals and Plants.' In order to show that the ancient nations passed through what he calls the Totem stage

which he says must have been in pre-historic times, he appeals to
the signs of the Zodiac. . . . Mr. M'Lellan is here more than half a
century behind his age," etc.   And a note adds : "All Mr.
M'Lellan's statements about the ancient nations are based on equally
worthless authorities."—Hibbert Lectures, pp. 29, 30.

Max Müller, Pfleiderer, Réville, and others reject all these
theories, and find the commencement of religion in the worship of
the greater objects of nature—such as mountains, rivers, the sun, the
sky, etc.   But if the other theories begin too low, does not this begin
too high, on the supposition that man started as a savage, and that
there was no primitive Revelation ?   May not the advocate of
Fetishism reply that man must be already far on in his career of
development before this grander style of worship, which demands a
highly evolved imagination, is possible to him ?   And is this view
historically supported, any more than the others ?   Do not the facts
point to a higher origin for man, and to a purer primitive perception
of the Divine than these theories allow ?   See next Note, and Note
F. to Lecture V.

Note B—p. 88

Old Testament Monotheism

Two mutually destructive theories are held by naturalistic critics as
to the origin of Hebrew Monotheism.

The *first* is that of Renan, who traces it to a "Monotheistic
instinct" said to be inherent in the Semitic race.   "The Semitic
consciousness," he says, "is clear, but lacks breadth ; it has a
marvellous comprehension of unity, but cannot grasp multiplicity.
MONOTHEISM sums it up, and explains all its characters."—*Hist.
générale des Langues sémitiques*, p. 5.   See this theory explained in the
work cited, and in the more recent *Histoire du Peuple d'Israel*,
I. chap. iv.   It is a theory which scarcely requires discussion, so
palpably contrary is it to all the facts.   Cf. in regard to it, Max
Müller's essay on "Semitic Monotheism," in vol. i. of his *Chips from
a German Workshop* ; Baethgen's *Beiträge zur semitischen Religionsgeschichte* ; Godet's *Biblical Studies on the Old Testament*, p. 68 (Eng.
trans.) ; and an able article in the *Edinburgh Review* (April 1888).

The *second* theory is that of Kuenen and the newer school of
critics (though it had many older representatives), viz., that the
Israelites began as polytheists and idolaters like their neighbours,
and only gradually attained to an "Ethical Monotheism " such as
we find in the prophets.   This theory, therefore, is the precise
reverse of the former.   See it explained in Kuenen's Hibbert
Lectures ; in Wellhausen's *Prol. to the Hist. of Israel* (Eng. trans.) ;
and in Professor Robertson Smith's *Old Testament in the Jewish
Church*, and *Religion of the Semites*   The arguments by which it is
supported are plausible, yet, when carefully looked into, are found
to be much more specious than solid.   The most sifting examination

is that of Baethgen, in the work above cited, *Beiträge zur sem. Religionsgeschichte.* See also König's *Hauptprobleme d. altisrael. Rel.* ; Robertson's *Early Religion of Israel* (Baird Lectures) ; and Schultz's *Alttest. Theol.* pp. 159–167 (1889). A good discussion of Hebrew Monotheism is found also in Vigouroux's *La Bible et les Découvertes modernes*, pp. 1–86, " La Religion primitive d'Israel " (1881). Baethgen sums up the results of an exhaustive inquiry, first, into the general character of Semitic Polytheism ; and, second, into the question, " Whether, as Kuenen and others maintain, Israel's faith in God was really, in the older and middle periods of its history, distinct in nothing from that of related tribes ? " in the following words :—" The historical investigations of both parts lead to the result that Israel's faith in God was from the oldest times specifically distinct from that of the related tribes ; and the contention that the Old Testament Monotheism has originated out of Polytheism, in the way of natural development, is proved on closer examination to be untenable."—Preface.

A strong argument against the development theory in question may be drawn from the results of the newer Pentateuch criticism itself. It is surely a remarkable circumstance that, not only in the time of the prophets, but in the documents J and E, originating in the early days of the kings (perhaps earlier), and embodying independently the oldest traditions of the nation, the history already rests on a completely Monotheistic basis, and expresses (*e.g.* in the call of Abraham) the clear consciousness of the nation's universal mission and destiny. In the documents referred to, *e.g.*, we have as fundamental, underlying ideas, the creation of the world by Jehovah, the unity of the human family, the destruction of the whole race by a flood, a covenant with Noah embracing the earth, a new descent and distribution of mankind from one centre, the recognition of Jehovah as the God of all the earth, etc. Schultz, in his *Alttestament. Theologie*, also lays weight on these considerations, though with some preliminary qualifications and explanations that the Monotheism involved is a " religious " and not a " metaphysical " Monotheism. "In the old songs," he says, "alongside of the expression, ' who is like Jehovah ? ' there stands clearly the other, ' no God besides Jehovah, no rock besides our rock ' (Ps. xviii. 32 ; 1 Sam. ii. 2). According to the Book of the Covenant, Jehovah has chosen Israel precisely because all the world is His (Ex. xix. 5), therefore not at all because He, as a particular God, was bound to this land and people. Psalms such as the 8th, 19th, and 29th praise Him who has made heaven and earth, in whose holy palace the sons of God stand serving. In B and C [the J and E of the ordinary nomenclature], the same Jehovah who is the covenant God of Israel is likewise the Creator of the world, the God of the patriarchs, whom also, as a matter of course, the non-Israelites own as God, the God of the spirits of all flesh (Gen. ii. 4 ff., iv. 3, 26, xii. 17, xxiv. 31, 50, xxvi. 29 ; Numb. xvi. 22, xxvii. 16). He proves Himself in His miracles and in His majesty the Judge and the Destroyer, the world-ruler in Egypt, Sodom, and

Canaan. In fact, therefore, the other Elohim step back as no-gods,
who are not able to determine the course of the world. He alone is
a God who can call forth faith, love, and trust. He will reveal His
glory also to the heathen world, and He will not rest till it fills the
whole earth (Ex. xv. 2). . . . But a people which itself worships
only *one* God, and regards this God as the world-creator and the
controller of all world destiny, is for that reason monotheistic. . . .
A God whose rule is not bound to the land and people in which
He is worshipped is no more a mere national God. Thus the
particularism of the God-idea in Israel has already become only
the sheltering husk under which the pure Monotheism of the Old
Testament could unfold itself and mature."—Pp. 166, 167.

Note C—p. 95

Kant on the Cosmological Argument

KANT characterises this argument as a perfect "nest" of dialectical
assumptions.—*Kritik*, p. 427 (Eng. trans. p. 374). Yet it might be
shown that the objections he takes to it depend almost exclusively
on his theory of knowledge—*e.g.*, that the mind is confined to
phenomena ; that the law of cause and effect has no application
except in the world of phenomena (though Kant himself applies it
in positing an action of things *per se* on the sensitive subject, and
introduces a " causality " of the noumenal self, etc.).[1] The same
remark applies to the " antinomies " or self-contradictions in which
the mind is said to involve itself in every attempt at a theoretic
application of the cosmological "Idea." The "antinomies" are
rather to be regarded as rival *alternatives* of thought, which, indeed,
are contradictory of each other, but which do not stand on the same
footing as regards admissibility. Rather they are of such a nature
that the mind is found to reject one, while it feels itself shut up to
accept the other. *E.g.*, The world has either a beginning in time or
it has not. The alternative here is an eternal retrogression of
phenomenal causes and effects, or the admission of an extra-
phenomenal First Cause—God. But these do not stand on the
same footing. The mind rejects the former as unthinkable and
self-contradictory (see Lecture IV.) ; the latter it not only does not
reject, but feels a rational satisfaction in admitting. Again, there is
the antinomy between natural causation and freedom of will. But
this is only an antinomy if we hold that the law of causation
applicable to physical phenomena is the only kind of causation we
know—that there may not be rational, intelligent causation over and
above the physical and determinate. Something here also depends
on the definition of freedom.

[1] Cf. Dr. Stirling's *Philosophy of Theology*, pp. 315, 316 : " The entire
' nest ' may be said to be a construction of his peculiar system."

Note D—p. 98

Kant on the Teleological Argument

KANT says : "This proof deserves always to be mentioned with respect. It is the oldest, clearest, and the most suited to the common reason of mankind. It enlivens the study of nature, even as it derives from this its own existence, and draws from it ever new strength. It brings ends and purposes into a region where our observation would not of itself have discovered them, and furthers our natural knowledge through the guiding thought of a special unity, whose principle lies outside of nature. This knowledge reacts upon its cause, namely, on the idea which occasions it, and raises faith in a highest Author of the universe to an irresistible conviction. It would, therefore, be not only a thankless, but also a vain task, to attempt to detract in any measure from the *prestige* of this argument." But he goes on to say : "Although we have nothing to object to the rationality and utility of this procedure, but have much rather to recommend and encourage it, we are nevertheless unable to assent to the claims which this mode of proof may make to demonstrative certainty," and then proceeds to state his objections to it.—*Kritik*, p. 436, 437 (Eng. trans. p. 383).[1] These, however, as observed in the text, seem more in the direction of limiting its application, than of altogether denying its cogency. The view which obtains in the Kritik of Judgment, that the idea of design has only regulative and not theoretic validity,[2] is not dwelt on in the Kritik of Pure Reason. It is not always noticed, besides, that, intermediate between full theoretic demonstration and mere opinion, Kant has a form of conviction which he calls "doctrinal faith,"—distinct from moral faith,—the characteristic of which is that it is an expression of modesty from the objective point of view, but of assured confidence from the subjective ; and that he places the doctrine of God's existence in this region.—*Kritik*, p. 561 (Eng. trans. p. 500). On Kant's service to this argument by his demonstration, in the Kritik of Judgment, of the necessity of applying the teleological conception to nature, see Dr. Bernard's valuable Introduction to his recent translation of this work (1892), and cf Professor Caird's *Philosophy of Kant*, ii. pp. 406–562.

Note E—p. 99

Schools of Evolution

IT is well to recognise the fact that evolutionists do not constitute a homogeneous party ; and that, while there is a growing disposition

---

[1] The references are to Meiklejohn's translation, but the translations are independent.

[2] Cf. Caird's *Philosophy of Kant*, pp. 477, 489, 526.

to acknowledge the reality of Organic Evolution, there is likewise a
growing tendency to question the sufficiency of the causes by which
Mr. Darwin sought to account for it.

1. From the first there has been an important section of evolutionists, represented by such names as Owen, Mivart, Asa Gray,
G. H. Lewes, Dana, and J. J. Murphy (in his *Habit and Intelligence*),
who, with differences among themselves, held that the rise of species
could not be accounted for by the Darwinian hypothesis of Natural
Selection acting on fortuitous variations.   The tendency in this
school was to seek the causes of evolution within, rather than without, the organism.   Most of them were theistic evolutionists—*i.e.*
they held that the development of organisms could not be explained
without the assumptions of intelligence and purpose.   Not all who
opposed the Darwinian hypothesis were of this class.   Mr. G. H.
Lewes, *e.g.*, writes : " At each stage of differentiation there has been a
selection, but we cannot by any means say that this selection was
determined by the fact of its giving the organism a superiority over
rivals, inasmuch as during all the early stages, while the organ was
still in formation, there could be no advantage occurring from
it. . . . The sudden appearance of new organs, not a trace of which
is discernible in the embryo or adult form of organisms lower in the
scale—for instance, the phosphorescent and electric organs—is like
the sudden appearance of new instruments in the social organism,
such as the printing press and the railway, wholly inexplicable on
the theory of descent, but is explicable on the theory of organic
affinity " (!).—*Physical Basis of Mind*, pp. 110, 117.

2. Important differences exist between Mr. Darwin and his
fellow-worker in the same field, Mr. A. Wallace, involving a distinction of principle on two vital points.   (1) Mr. Darwin's own views
underwent considerable modifications in the direction of recognising
that Natural Selection is not an all-sufficient explanation, and that
more must be allowed to forces interior to the organism.   See his
Descent of Man, p. 61 ; and cf. Mivart's *Lessons from Nature*, viii., ix.,
and the articles of Spencer and Romanes cited below.   He specially
supplemented it by the hypothesis of Sexual Selection.   These alterations on the theory Mr. Wallace rejects, repudiating Sexual Selection, and maintaining the hypothesis in the form in which Mr.
Darwin abandoned it.   (2) Mr. Darwin held his theory to be all-
inclusive, embracing man as well as the lower animals ; Mr. Wallace
holds that there are provable breaks in the chain of evolution, and
that man, in particular, has a distinct origin.   See Lecture IV.

3. Yet more significant is the recent tendency to revolt against
the authority of Mr. Darwin, and to recognise the existence of large
classes of phenomena which Natural Selection does not explain.
This change of front in recent discussions on Darwinism is too
marked to escape notice.   I take one or two examples which may
show the drift of opinion.

Mr. G. J. Romanes, who as late as 1882 wrote a book on *The
Scientific Evidences of Evolution*, in which Mr. Darwin's theory
received uncompromising support, afterwards wrote in 1887 : " The

hypothesis of Physiological Selection (his own view) sets out with an attempted proof of the inadequacy of the theory of Natural Selection, considered as a theory of the origin of species. This proof is drawn from three distinct heads of evidence—(1) the inutility to species of a large number of their specific characters ; (2) the general fact of sterility between allied species, which admittedly cannot be explained by Natural Selection, and therefore has hitherto never been explained ; (3) the swamping influence, upon even useful variations, of free intercrossing with the parent form."— "Physiological Selection," in *Nineteenth Century*, January 1887. The effect of Mr. Romanes's heresy was to arouse "a storm of criticism" from the orthodox Darwinian party.

Mr. Herbert Spencer has published two papers on "Factors of Organic Evolution," in which, while still according an important place to Natural Selection, he very greatly restricts its field of action. The articles, he says, "will perhaps help to show that it is as yet far too soon to close the inquiry concerning the causes of Organic Evolution."—P. 75. In a subsequent article in the *Nineteenth Century*, he thus delivers his soul : "The new biological orthodoxy behaves just as the old biological orthodoxy did. In the days before Darwin, those who occupied themselves with the phenomena of life passed by with unobservant eye the multitudinous facts which point to an evolutionary origin for plants and animals ; and they turned deaf ears to those who insisted upon the significance of these facts. Now that they have come to believe in this evolutionary origin, and have at the same time accepted the hypothesis that Natural Selection has been the sole cause of the evolution, they are similarly unobservant of the multitudinous facts which cannot rationally be ascribed to that cause, and turn deaf ears to those who would draw their attention to them. The attitude is the same ; it is only the creed that has changed."— *Nineteenth Century*, February 1888.

In a well-written and appreciative Essay on Charles Darwin in "The Round Table Series," the same criticism is passed upon the theory that from the standpoint of biology too much stress has been laid on Natural Selection. "Natural Selection obviously can never be the cause of modifications in any given individual. . . . Natural Selection cannot cause an iota of modification in structure. . . . In the case of Human Selection, not the least modification in an organism can be produced by the process of selection itself. The modifications somehow produced in the animals selected are transmitted to the offspring ; but the cause of modification lies elsewhere than in selection ; and it is largely due to man's own modification of the environment. . . . It would undoubtedly have been better had Darwin omitted Natural Selection as a modifying agent altogether."—Pp. 22–26.

Even Professor Huxley sounds a wavering note : "How far Natural Selection suffices for the production of species remains to be seen. . . . On the evidence of palæontology, the evolution of many existing forms of animal life from their predecessors is no longer an hypothesis, but an historical fact; it is only the nature of the physiological factors to which that evolution is due which is still open to discussion."—Art. "Evolution" in *Ency. Brit.*

4. Yet more deep-reaching is the controversy between the older Darwinian and Spencerian schools on the one hand, and the newer school headed by Prof. Weismann on the other, on the subject of the transmissibility of acquired characters. According to Mr. Spencer, "either there has been inheritance of acquired characters, or there has been no evolution."—*Cont. Rev.*, March 1893, p. 446. But this Weismann, Lankester, and others absolutely deny. See controversy between Mr. Spencer and Prof. Weismann in *Cont. Rev.* for 1893; and cf. Weismann's *Papers on Heredity* (trans. 1889), Einer's *Organic Evolution*, Thomson's *Study of Animal Life*, chap. **xx.**, etc.

Good general criticisms of the Darwinian theory may be seen in Mivart's *Genesis of Species*, Murphy's *Habit and Intelligence*, Elam's *Winds of Doctrine*, Bouverie Pusey's *Permanence and Evolution* (1882), Van Dyke's *Theism and Evolution*, Professor Schurman's *Ethical Import of Darwinism*, Principal Dawson's *Modern Ideas of Evolution*, Martineau's *Study of Religion*, Iverach's *Christianity and Evolution*, etc.

Note F—p. 103

Kant on the Ontological Argument

KANT holds firmly to the invalidity of all inference from the idea of God to His reality; but here also it is to be noticed that he allows to his "Ideal of Pure Reason" an important part in Natural Theology. If theoretic reason cannot prove, neither can it disprove the objective reality of this ideal of a supreme Being; and given a proof, or a conviction, from any other quarter (from the Practical Reason, or a "doctrinal faith" from design), it is of the highest utility in correcting and purifying our conception of this Being. "For," he says, "though Reason in its merely speculative use is far from competent to so great an undertaking as to reach the existence of a supreme Being; yet it is of very great service in correcting the knowledge of such a Being, provided this can be drawn from some other source; in making it consistent with itself, and with each intelligible view of things; and in purifying it from everything which would contradict the notion of a primary Being, and from all mixture of empirical limitations. . . . The supreme Being, therefore, remains for the merely speculative use of Reason a mere Ideal, though one free from error, a notion which completes and crowns the whole of human knowledge, whose objective reality cannot indeed by this method be proved, but also cannot be disproved; and if there should be a Moral Theology which can supply this defect, the hitherto only problematic transcendental theology will show its indispensableness in the determination of its notion, and the unceasing criticism of a reason often enough deceived by sense, and not always in agreement with its own ideas. The necessity, infinity, unity, existence apart from the world (not as world-soul), eternity without conditions of time, omnipresence without conditions of space, omnipotence, etc., are pure transcendental predicates, and therefore the purified conception of the same, which every theology finds so necessary, can be drawn from transcendental theology alone."—*Kritik*, pp. 446, 447 (Eng. trans. pp. 392, 393).

Note G—p. 105

Rational Realism

THIS argument is well stated by Pfleiderer in the following words : "The agreement, therefore," he says, "of the ideal laws of thought, which are not drawn from the outer world, and the real laws of being, which are not created by our thought, is a fact of experience of the most incontrovertible kind ; the whole certainty of our knowledge rests on it. But how are we to account for this agreement ? There is only one possible way in which the agreement of our thought with the being of the world can be made intelligible : the presupposition of a common ground of both, in which thought and being must be one ; or the assumption that the real world-ground is at the same time the ideal ground of our spirit, hence the absolute Spirit, creative Reason, which appears in the world-law on its real, in the law of thought on its ideal side. The connection of thought and being, subject and object, in the finite and derivative spiritual being, points back to the unity of the two in the infinite Spirit as the ground and original type of ours. This is the meaning of the 'ontological' argument, as indicated even in the word. We may find it anticipated even in Plato, in the thought that the highest idea, or the Deity, is the cause both of being and of knowledge ; and Augustine follows him in this, frequently and in a number of turns of thought, tracing back our faculty of knowing the truth to the fact of our participation in God, who is the substantial truth, the unchangeable law both of the world and of our thought. In modern times this thought forms the foundation and corner-stone of speculative philosophy."—*Religionsphilosophie*, iii. p. 274 (Eng. trans.).

The germs of this theory are found in Leibnitz, Herder, Goethe, and most of the deeper thinkers. It is the thought which underlies Mr. Green's *Prolegomena to Ethics*. Professor Samuel Harris, of Yale College, makes it the ground of his *Philosophical Basis of Theism* ; and it largely influences current thought.

NOTES TO CHAPTER 4

Note A—p. 122

The Creation History

THE rights and wrongs of the reconcilability of the creation narrative in Gen. i. with modern science have recently been discussed anew by Mr. Gladstone and Professor Huxley in the *Nineteenth Century* (vols. xviii. and xix.). I do not enter into this discussion. But if the one disputant imports into this early narrative more than it will bear, the other surely does less than justice to it when he brackets it "with the cosmogonies of other nations, and especially with those of the Egyptians and the Babylonians," as essentially of the same character with these.

I content myself with quoting on this point the tribute to this ancient narrative by Haeckel, surely an unprejudiced witness, in his *History of Creation*. He says : "The Mosaic history of creation, since, in the first chapter of Genesis, it forms the introduction to the Old Testament, has enjoyed, down to the present day, general recognition in the whole Jewish and Christian world of civilisation. Its extraordinary success is explained, not only by its close connection with Jewish and Christian doctrines, but also by the simple and natural chain of ideas which runs through it, and which contrasts favourably with the confused mythology of creation current among most of the ancient nations. First, God creates the earth as an inorganic body ; then He separates light from darkness, then water from the dry land. Now the earth has become habitable for organisms, and plants are first created, animals later ; and among the latter the inhabitants of the water and of the air first, afterwards the inhabitants of the dry land. Finally, God creates man, the last of all organisms, in His own image, and as the ruler of the earth. Two great and fundamental ideas, common also to the non-miraculous theory of development, meet us in the Mosaic hypothesis of creation with surprising clearness and simplicity—the idea of separation or *differentiation*, and the idea of progressive development or *perfecting*. Although Moses looks upon the results of the great laws of organic development (which we shall later point out as the necessary conclusions of the Doctrine of Descent) as the direct actions of a constructing Creator, yet in his theory there lies hidden the ruling idea of a progressive development and a differentiation of the originally simple matter. We can therefore bestow our just and sincere admiration on the Jewish lawgiver's grand insight into nature, and his simple and natural hypothesis of creation, without discovering in it a so-called Divine Revelation."—*Hist. of Creation,* i. pp. 37, 38 (Eng. trans.).

The grounds on which Haeckel concludes that it cannot be a Divine Revelation are—(1) the geocentric error that the earth is the central point in the universe; and (2) the anthropomorphic error that man is the premeditated end of the creation of the earth,—neither of which "errors" need greatly distress us. For the rest, the creation narrative certainly goes back on early tradition,[1] and is not a scientific *précis*, written in the light of the latest discoveries of modern geology. Yet it is possible to hold that the Spirit of Revelation is active in it, not merely making it the vehicle of general religious ideas, but enabling the writer really to seize the great stadia of the creation process, and to represent these in such a way as to convey a practically accurate conception of them to men's minds. Modern science may supplement, it is astonishing how little it requires us to reverse of, the ideas we derive from this narrative of the succession of steps in creation, assuming that we deal with it fairly, in its broad and obvious intention, and not in a carping and pettifogging spirit. The dark watery waste over which the Spirit broods with vivifying power, the advent of light, the formation of an atmosphere or sky capable of sustaining the clouds above it, the settling of the great outlines of the continents and seas, the clothing of the dry land with abundant vegetation, the adjustment of the earth's relation to sun and moon as the visible rulers of its day and night, the production of the great sea monsters and reptile-like creatures (for these may well be included in "she-ratzim") and birds, the peopling of the earth with four-footed beasts and cattle—last of all, the advent of Man—is there so much of all this which science requires us to cancel? Even in regard to the duration of time involved,—those *dies ineffabiles* of which Augustine speaks,[2]—it is at least as difficult to suppose that only ordinary days of twenty-four hours are intended, in view of the writer's express statement that such days did not commence till the fourth stage in creation, as to believe that they are symbols. Delitzsch defends the symbolic interpretation in his *New Commentary on Genesis,* p. 84 (Eng. trans.).

---

[1] Modern criticism would bring down the age of this narrative to the Exile, and explain its origin by late Babylonian influence; but Dillmann and Delitzsch have shown strong reasons for rejecting this view, and for regarding the tradition as one of the oldest possessions of the Israelites.—Cf. Delitzsch's *New Com. on Gen.* pp. 63–66; and Whitehouse in Introduction to Eng. trans. of Schrader's *Keilinschriften,* i. pp. 18, 19, on Dillmann.

[2] "Of what fashion those days were," says Augustine, "it is either exceeding hard or altogether impossible to think, much more to speak. As for ordinary days, we see they have neither morning nor evening, but as the sun rises and sets. But the first three days of all had no sun, for that was made on the fourth day," etc.—*De Civitate Dei,* xi. 6, 7. Cf. *De Genesi,* ii. 14.

Note B—p. 127

Evolution in Inorganic Nature—The Nebular Hypothesis

THIS famous hypothesis of Kant and Laplace is frequently spoken of as if it had become an established fact of science ; and it forms an integral part in most sketches of the process of cosmic evolution (as in Strauss, Spencer, Clodd, etc.). Yet so far is it from being established, that the objections to its sufficiency seem to multiply and strengthen as years go on, and many eminent men of science reject it altogether.

Mr. R. A. Proctor, in an article on the "Meteor Birth of the Universe," contributed to the *Manchester Examiner and Times*, May 29, 1888, thus speaks of it :—

"The nebular theory of Laplace has long held a somewhat anomalous position. Advanced by its distinguished author as a mere hypothesis, in days when the word 'hypothesis' had still its proper significance (as shown in Newton's saying, 'Hypotheses non fingo'), it had from the beginning a fascination for most minds, which led to its acceptance as if it had been a veritable theory. Yet it has never been accepted as a theory by one single student of science who has possessed adequate knowledge of physics, combined with adequate knowledge of astronomy and mathematics."

After sketching the theory, he proceeds : "The nebulous speculation of Laplace is open to two most serious objections. In the first place, as I have already pointed out, a vaporous mass of enormous size, and of the exceeding tenuity imagined, could not possibly rotate in a single mass in the manner suggested by Laplace. In the second place, some of the most characteristic peculiarities of the solar system remain altogether unaccounted for by this speculation, ingeniously though it accounts for others."

These objections are then developed. Mr. Proctor's rival theory is that of "Meteoric Aggregation." See, further, his *More Worlds than Ours*, chapter on "Comets and Meteors."

A searching examination of this theory, embodying the views of M. Babinet, may be seen in Stallo's *Concepts of Modern Physics* (International Library), pp. 277–286.

Sir Robert S. Ball, Professor of Astronomy at Cambridge, says of it : "Nor can it be ever more than a speculation ; it cannot be established by observation, nor can it be proved by calculation. It is merely a conjecture, more or less plausible, but perhaps in some degree necessarily true, if our present laws of heat, as we understand them, admit of the extreme application here required, and if also the present system of things has reigned for sufficient time without the intervention of any influence at present unknown to us."—*The Story of the Heavens*, p. 506.

Note C—p. 127

The Hypothesis of Cycles

THE idea of an eternal succession of cycles of existence—of alternating periods of dissolution and renovation — of the destruction of worlds, and continual birth of new worlds from the ruins of the old —could not but present itself early to the minds of speculative thinkers whose theories did not admit of a beginning of the world in time. We find it in Brahmanism, in some of the early Greek philosophies, among the Stoics, and it has been frequently revived in modern times as an alternative to the doctrine of creation.

Zeller says of the Greek Anaximander: "The assertion which ascribes to Anaximander an infinity of successive worlds seems borne out by his system. . . . Plutarch, indeed, expressly says of Anaximander that from the Infinite, as the sole cause of the birth and destruction of all things, he considered that the heavens and the innumerable worlds arise in endless circulation; and Hippolytus speaks to the same effect. . . . Cicero, too, makes mention of innumerable worlds, which in long periods of time arise and perish; and Stobæus attributes to Anaximander the theory of the future destruction of the world. . . . The same theory of a constant alternation of birth and destruction in the universe was held by Heraclitus, who approaches more closely to Anaximander than to any of the ancient Ionian physicists, and also most probably by Anaximenes and Diogenes. We have reason, therefore, to suppose that Anaximander also held it."—*Pre-Socratic Philosophy*, pp. 259, 260.

This theory was revived by Kant in his *Theory of the Heavens* in 1755,[1] and was adopted from him by Strauss (in his *Glaubenslehre* and *Der alte und der neue Glaube*, pp. 153–160). Vatke and others also held it.

Mr. Spencer, with all his profession of nescience about origins, adopts this theory, as in reason he is compelled to do if he advocates evolution, and yet refuses to admit a beginning in time.—*First Principles*, pp. 519–537, 550, 551.

There is a fascination and grandeur in this conception of endless cycles of existence,—of new worlds perpetually rising from the ashes of the old,—but it is a theory which cannot be maintained.

1. Philosophically, it involves all the difficulties which, in discussing the cosmological argument, we saw to inhere in the notion of an endless succession of causes and effects. This, as respects the past (*regressus in infinitum*), is a supposition which is not simply inconceivable, but which reason compels us positively to reject as self-contradictory.

2. Scientifically, it seems disproved by the doctrine of the dissipation of energy, and of the tendency of the material universe to a state of final equilibrium. This doctrine is stated

---

[1] Kant, however, held a beginning. See Strauss's criticism of him in passage cited.

by Sir William Thomson (now Lord Kelvin) in the following
terms :—

"(1) There is at present in the material world a universal tendency to the dissipation of mechanical energy.[1]

"(2) Any restoration of mechanical energy, without more than
an equivalent of dissipation, is impossible in inanimate material
processes, and is probably never effected by material masses, either
endowed with vegetable life, or subjected to the will of an animated
creature.

"(3) Within a finite past, the earth must have been, and within
a finite period of time to come the earth must again be, unfit for the
habitation of man as at present constituted, unless operations have
been, or are to be, performed which are impossible under the laws
to which the known operations going on at present in the material
world are subject."—Paper "On a Universal Tendency in Nature
to the Dissipation of Mechanical Energy," in *Phil. Mag.*, ser. iv.
vol. x. p. 304 ff. Cf. Tait's *Recent Advances in Physical Science*, p.
146 ; Stewart and Tait's *The Unseen Universe*, pp. 93, 94, 126–128,
211–214 (5th ed.) ; and Jevons's *Principles of Science*, ii. p. 483.

Mr. Spencer himself admits that, as the outcome of the processes
everywhere going on, we are "manifestly progressing towards omnipresent death,"—that "the proximate end of all the transformations
we have traced is a state of quiescence."—*First Principles*, p. 514.

Stewart and Tait say : "The tendency of heat is towards equalisa-
tion ; heat is *par excellence* the communist of our universe, and it
will no doubt ultimately bring the present system to an end."—
Unseen Universe, p. 126.

Professor Huxley says of astronomy, that it "leads us to contemplate
phenomena, the very nature of which demonstrates that they must
have had a beginning, and that they must have an end, but the very
nature of which also proves that the beginning was, to our conceptions of time, infinitely remote, and that the end is as immeasurably
distant."—*Lay Sermons, Addresses*, etc., p. 17 ("On the Advisableness
of Improving Natural Knowledge").

Cf. on the cycle of hypothesis, Flint's *Philosophy of History*, pp.
30–35 ; Dorner in criticism of Vatke, *Person of Christ*, pp. 122, 123 ;
and Chapman in criticism of Spencer, *Pre-Organic Evolution*, pp.
179–190.

Note D—p. 130

Eternal Creation

ORIGEN'S views are stated in his *De Principiis*, Book i. 2, iii. 5, etc.
In the former passage he argues that God would not be omnipotent

---

[1] Professor Proctor says that only the two hundred and twenty-seventh
part of the one millionth of all the heat from the sun reaches any planet ;
the remainder passes into space and is lost.

if He had not eternally creatures on which to exercise His power. In the latter he deals with the objection : " If the world had its beginning in time, what was God doing before the world began ? For it is at once impious and absurd to say that the nature of God is inactive and immovable, or to suppose that goodness at one time did not do good, and omnipotence at one time did not exercise its power " ; and gives for answer : " Not then for the first time did God begin to work when He made this visible world ; but as, after its destruction, there will be another world, so also we believe that others existed before the present came into being. . . . By these testimonies it is established both that there were ages before our own, and that there will be others after it."—Ante-Nicene Library, trans. pp. 28, 255. Origen's view of eternal creation is thus that of an eternal succession of worlds.

That profound mediæval speculative thinker, John Scotus Erigena, held the doctrine of an eternal creation. See the sketch of his system in Ueberweg's *Hist. of Phil.* i. 358–365.

Rothe's views are contained in his *Theologische Ethik*, i. secs. 40–52 (a special discussion of the point in sec. 52, pp. 193–204, 2nd ed.), and his *Dogmatik*, pp. 138–160. His theory turns on the notion that in positing his I, God must also, by a necessity of thought, posit his not-I, which is identified by him with pure matter, and is the product of an eternal act. This is the act of creation proper, and is beginningless ; and from it is to be distinguished the *world*, which is the product of finite development, and has its existence in space and time—has therefore a beginning in time. " What has been created in time," he says, " that has naturally a beginning ; but as undoubtedly has that which was created when there was not time no beginning. For a beginning can only be spoken of where there is time. The world is consequently in no way without beginning (as little in a spatial as in a temporal reference), and nothing belonging to the world is."—*Theol. Ethik*, pp. 198, 199.

Rothe's pure matter is almost identified by him with space and time.

The idea of a beginning of God's creative activity, Schleiermacher thinks, places Him as a temporal being in the domain of change.—*Der christ. Glaube*, i. pp. 200, 201.

The views of Lipsius may be seen in his *Dogmatik*, pp. 292, 293. " It is only a sensuous representation," he says, " to lead back creation upon a single act now lying in the past, or to speak of a ' first beginning ' of creation ; rather is the total world-development, so soon as it is viewed religiously, to be placed under the notion of creation, consequently to be regarded as without beginning or end." —P. 293.

Dorner solves the problem by the supposition of a temporal world standing midway between two eternal ones. " Just, therefore," he says, " as we have no right to say that this law of succession, and this progress from imperfect to perfect, must continue for ever, . . . so also we have no right to say that this world, tangible to sense and subject to temporality, cannot have been preceded by a world of pure spirits (although spirits not yet subject to laws of historical progress), which are withdrawn in the first instance from all relation of succession, and exist in the simultaneity of all their constituent elements, and in this character surround the throne of God,—a kingdom of which it cannot be said that a time was when it was not, not merely because no time was ere it was, but also because for it there was no time, no succession or becoming. This world can only be brought under the standpoint of time by reference to the succeeding world. From this point of view it appears a preceding one, already belonging to the past. Thus, midway between the eternal world of the end, in which temporal existence merges, and the world of the beginning standing in the light of eternity, may lie, like an island in a broad ocean, the present world bound to temporal existence."— *System of Doctrine*, ii. p. 33 (Eng. trans.).

Lotze teaches " that the ' will to create ' is an absolutely eternal predicate of God, and ought not to be used to designate a deed of His, so much as the absolute dependence of the world upon His will, in contradistinction to its involuntary ' emanation' from His nature." —*Outlines of the Phil. of Religion*, p. 74 (Eng. trans.).

The authors of *The Unseen Universe* hold that the present visible universe, which had a beginning and will have an end, is developed out of an unseen and eternal one. "We are led," they say, " not only to regard the invisible universe as having existed before the present one, but the same principle drives us to acknowledge its existence in some form as a universe from all eternity."—*Unseen Universe*, p. 215 ; cf. pp. 94, 95.

The theory of an eternal creation is contested, on the other hand, by Van Oosterzee (*Dogmatics*, pp. 303, 304, Eng. trans.), Gretillat (*Théologie Systématique*, iii. 392–397), Müller (*Christ. Doct. of Sin*, i. pp. 224–227, Eng. trans.), etc.

The difficulties which attach to such theories as Rothe's and Dorner's, which only shift the problem from the absolute beginning to the beginning of the temporal developing world, are pointed out by Müller in his criticism of the former : " Do not the difficulties supposed to be involved in a beginning of the world return now as really insoluble, because, while denying its beginning, we have to allow the fact of its eternal creation, and to believe that God, having left it as it was for a limitless period, barely existing as *materia bruta*, at length began at some definite time to think of it and ordain it, *i.e.* to begin to develop it towards the goal of its becoming spirit. And if the beginning of the world involves a transition from non-creation to creation inconsistent with God's unchangeableness, have we not here also a transition on God's part from inactivity to action equally inadmissible, because in this case God's Revelation of Himself in outward activity becomes a necessity of His nature ?"—*Christ. Doct. of Sin*, p. 226 (Eng. trans.).

Note E—p. 131

Eternity and Time

THIS difficult problem has exercised the minds of thinkers in all ages.

Augustine has profound thoughts on the subject in his *De Civitate Dei*. "For if eternity and time be well considered," he says, "time never to be extant without motion, and eternity to admit no change, who would not see that time could not have being before some movable thing were created? . . . Seeing, therefore, that God, whose eternity alters not, created the world and time, how can He be said to have created the world in time, unless you will say there was something created before the world whose course time did follow? . . . Then, verily, the world was made with time and not in time (mundus non in tempore sed cum tempore factus est), for that which is made in time is made both before some time and after some. Before it is time past; after it is time to come; but no time passed before the world, because no creature was made by whose course it might pass."—Book xi. 6.[1]

Rothe goes deeply into the question in his *Theologische Ethik*, i. pp. 193–204 (2nd ed.); and Lotze discusses it with suggestiveness and subtlety in his *Microcosmos*, ii. pp. 708–713.

The following remarks in Dorner are in consonance with a suggestion in the text: "When, therefore, the world comes into actual existence, actual time comes into existence. The actual world is preceded by merely possible time; of course, not in a temporal sense, else must time have existed before time, but in a logical sense. From the point of view of actual time, merely possible time can only be *mentally represented* under the image of the past; and the same is true of the eternal world-idea, and God's eternity in relation to the world's actual existence."—*System of Doctrine*, ii. p. 30 (Eng. trans.).

Dr. Hutcheson Stirling has also his thoughts on this difficulty. "It is easy," he says, "to use the words, the predicates that describe what we conceive to be eternal; as, for example, in the terms of Plato to say that the eternal, 'what is always unmoved, the same, can become by time neither older nor younger, nor has been made, nor appears now, nor will be in the future, nor can any of those things at all attach to it which mortal birth has grafted on the things of sense'; but how to bring into connection with this everlasting rest the never-resting movement of time—that is the difficulty." I confess that his suggestion that "time may be no straight line, as we are apt to figure it, but a curve—a curve that eventually returns into itself," does not seem to me greatly to relieve the difficulty.—*Phil. and Theol.* p. 105.

[1] Augustine, however, in these remarks does little more than reproduce Plato in the *Timæus*. See the striking passage, Jowett's *Plato*, iii. p. 620 (2nd ed.).

Note F—p. 135

Man the Head of Creation

THIS thought of man as the crown and masterpiece of creation—the goal of its developments—finds the most varied expression in writers of different schools. I cite a few illustrative instances.

Kant finds man to be "not merely like all organised beings, an end of nature, but also here on earth the *last end* of nature, in reference to whom all other natural things constitute a system of ends." —*Kritik d. Urtheilskraft*, p. 280 (Erd. ed.).

It is the key-thought of Herder's *Ideen zur Philosophie der Geschichte*, that man is the connecting link between two worlds; on the one hand, the highest of nature's products, crowning its ascent from plant to animal, and from lower to higher grades of animal life, till finally it rests in him; and, on the other, the starting-point of a new order of spiritual existences. "All is bound together in nature; one condition strives towards another, and prepares the way for it. If, therefore, man closes the chain of terrestrial organisations as its highest and last member, he likewise begins, just on that account, the chain of a higher order of creatures, as the lowest member of it; and thus is probably the middle-link between two systems of creation, intimately connected with each other."—*Ideen*, Bk. v. 6.

It is virtually Herder's thought which Dr. H. Stirling reproduces when he says : "There is a rise from object to object. The plant is above the stone, and the animal above the plant. But man is the most perfect result. His supremacy is assured. He alone of all living creatures is erect; and he is erect by reason of the Divinity within him whose office it is to know, to think, and to consider. All other animals are but incomplete, imperfect, dwarf, beside man." —*Phil. and Theol.* p. 137.

That man is the apex of the evolutionary movement is, of course, recognised by all, though not necessarily with acknowledgment of final cause. Professor Huxley, in his *Man's Place in Nature*, says : "In view of the intimate relations between man and the rest of the living world, and between the forces exerted by the latter and all other forces, I can see no excuse for doubting that all are co-ordinated forms of Nature's great progression from the formless to the formed, from the inorganic to the organic, from blind force to conscious intellect and will" (p. 108); and Professor Tyndall, in his Belfast Address, describing how in the *Primates* the evolution of intellect and the evolution of tactual appendages go hand in hand, says : "Man crowns the edifice here." And Mr. Wallace regards man as not only placed "apart, as the head and culminating point of the grand series of organic nature, but as in some degree a new order of being."—*Nat. Selection*, pp. 351, 352.

Mr. Fiske may be quoted, who says suggestively : "The doctrine of evolution, by exhibiting the development of the highest spiritual human qualities as the goal toward which God's creative work has from the outset been tending, replaces Man in his old position of headship in the universe, even as in the days of Dante and Thomas Aquinas. That which the pre-Copernican astronomy naïvely thought to do by placing the home of Man in the centre of the physical universe, the Darwinian biology profoundly accomplishes by exhibiting Man as the terminal fact in that stupendous process of evolution whereby things have come to be what they are. In the deepest sense it is as true as it ever was held to be, that the world was made for Man, and that the bringing forth in him of those qualities which we call highest and holiest is the final cause of creation."—*Idea of God*, Introd. pp. 20, 21. Cf. also the chapters on "Man's Place in Nature as affected by Darwinism," and "On the Earth there will never be a Higher Creature than Man" in his *Man's Destiny* (1890).

I quote further only the following sentences from Kaftan : "The end of nature, of its history and its development, can be sought only in humanity, in the fact that 'man is the crown of the creation.' We men can find or discover nothing in the whole world environing us which can be put in comparison with man and his spiritual life, still less which surpasses him. . . . We must on this account form the idea of an end of the natural development, and then what scientific knowledge offers in particulars advances to meet this thought. For this idea would have no support if it were not upheld by the conviction of an end pertaining to man and to his history. That the development of the natural world has its end in man, becomes a rational thought, first of all, when I can speak in turn of an end to which the world of humanity itself has regard."—*Wahrheit*, etc., p. 418.

Note G—p. 148

Mind and Mechanical Causation

IT is well to see clearly what this "gradual banishment from all regions of human thought of what we call spirit and spontaneity," which Professor Huxley speaks of ("On the Physical Basis of Life"), involves ; and the matter could not be much better put than it is by Mr. Kennedy in his Donnellan Lectures on *Natural Theology and Modern Thought*. He calls attention to the way in which this theory must, if true, affect our belief about the agency of God and the agency of the mind of man. "For the latter, the agency of the human mind," he says, "it leaves no room whatever. It tells us that, in attributing the railways and steamships and cotton-mills of the present day to the fertile mind of man, we have been making a mistake as great as that of the insane astronomer in Swift's satire, who had persuaded himself that it was his watchful care which guided the movement of the planets. The railways, steamships,

and cotton-mills would have been constructed all the same, though
we had no minds at all; just as the stars would have remained in
their proper places, though the attention of the astronomer had
been withdrawn from them. It was the boast of Comte that, to
minds familiarised with the true astronomical philosophy, the
heavens now declare no other glory than that of Hipparchus,
Kepler, Newton, and all those who have contributed to the ascertainment of their laws; but if the doctrine of Automatism be true,
it is the direct contrary of this which results; it is the glory of
Hipparchus, Newton, and Kepler which is irretrievably destroyed.
For the mind of Hipparchus was not the agent which made known
to man the Precession of the Equinoxes; nor were the thoughts of
Newton the cause of the writing of the *Principia*; nor did those of
Kepler cause the enunciation, either by pen or voice, of the laws
which bear his name. These philosophers were merely conscious
automata; and had they been unconscious automata, the result
would still have been the very same" (pp. 75, 76). This is no
travesty of the doctrine, but a serious presentation of the results of
the views advocated by Professor Huxley in his paper, "The
Hypothesis that Animals are Automata" (*Fortnightly Review*,
November 1874, pp. 575, 576). "It seems to me," says this distinguished scientific teacher, "that in men, as in brutes, there is no
proof that any state of consciousness is the cause of change in the
motion of the matter of the organism. If these positions are well
based, it follows that our mental conditions are simply the symbols
in consciousness of the changes which take place automatically in
the organism; and that, to take an extreme illustration, the feeling
we call volition is not the cause of a voluntary act, but the symbol
of that state of the brain which is the immediate cause of that act.
We are conscious automata," etc. It is difficult to see what place is
left for virtue or responsibility in such a theory of man as this!

Note H—p. 149

Mind and Cerebral Activity

THIS subject is discussed with great care in Professor H. Calderwood's *The Relations of Mind and Brain*, with the result that a
series of facts are established which I do not remember seeing
brought out as convincingly anywhere else. The chief value of his
book lies in the proof which it leads of the following positions,
which I set here in order, with reference to passages in which they
are discussed :—

1. That the primary function of the brain is to serve, not as an
organ of thought, but as an organ of sensory-motor activity (pp.
196, 290, 302–307, 2nd ed.).

2. That, as demonstrated by experiment, by far the greater part
of the brain—if not all—is monopolised for sensory-motor work,

leaving little, if any, of it to be employed for other purposes (pp. 302, 361).

3. That in the comparison of animals there is no fixed ratio between degree of intelligence and complexity of brain structure—a highly developed and convoluted brain finding its chief explanation in "the much more complex muscular system to be controlled" (p. 149). "Advance in intelligence and advance in complexity of brain structure do not keep pace with each other; they are not correlated so as to harmonise" (p. 148). The dog, *e.g.*, with a brain less elaborate in its convolutions, shows a higher degree of intelligence than the horse, with a more ample and complicated series of foldings in the convolutions of the grey matter. A number of leading cases are examined in detail in Chap. v. "Comparison of the Structure and Functions of Brain in Lower and Higher Forms of Animal Life" (pp. 123 ff.). Cf. pp. 260, 261.

4. That the view that special cells are appropriated to mental functions,—as, *e.g.*, the "mind-cells" of Haeckel (pp. 298–303), or the memory-cells of Professor Bain (pp. 356–364),—is not borne out, but is discredited by physiology. As against Haeckel, it presents "a cumulative body of evidence adverse to the hypothesis that human intelligence can be attributed to the giant pyramidal cells abounding in the fourth layer of the brain. All available evidence favours the conclusion that these giant cells are motor cells largely concerned in the functions of co-ordination of related intra-cerebral movements. It thus seems warrantable to infer that such co-ordinated movement takes rank as the highest function of brain. In accordance with this view is Dr. Ferrier's conclusion as to the frontal regions in the human brain, based on the whole range of experiments under electro-motor excitation, "that they are 'inhibitory motor-centres' such as may be associated with an exercise of attention" (pp. 302, 303). As respects Bain's theory, "the known laws of cerebral activity do not favour such calculations as are suggested by Professor Bain. The space appropriated for the sensory and motor functions includes a great part of the mass of cellular tissue" (p. 360, see proof in detail). Generally, "physiology does not discover any new function in the higher part of the system, except more detailed ordination" (p. 297). "We must regard equally the frontal and the occipital regions of the grand central organ as concerned with sensory-activity and correlated motor-activity" (p. 316).

5. That the true relation of mind and brain lies in the dependence of the former on the latter in sensory functions, and in the use made by the former (involved in all forms of mental activity) of the brain's motor functions. The following is an enumeration of forms of brain action which must be considered as generally attending on the more ordinary mental exercises: "(1) Action of the special senses, and of the more general tactile sense; (2) action of the muscles concerned in the management of these senses, and specially of the organs of sight; (3) co-ordination of sensory and motor apparatus required for use of the senses; (4) action of sensory centres consequent on use of imagination (p. 357), in part a renewal of sensory impressions,

or a movement of sensory cells consequent upon stimulus which imagination supplies; (5) sensory and motor action consequent upon the stimulus coming from mental emotion, such as weeping, facial expression of sadness or sympathy . . . all these phases of brain action, as they involve active use of brain energy, imply transformation of energy, consequent waste of brain substance, and inevitable sense of exhaustion. . . . First, there is large use of both sensory and motor apparatus in connection with all the ordinary forms of intellectual activity. Second, all thought proceeds, to a large extent, by use of language, and thus seems to involve activity of the cells concerned with the acquisition and use of language and speech. Third, concentrated thought makes a severer demand upon all the forms of brain action connected with ordinary thought, and so quickens and increases the exhaustion of nerve energy" (pp. 412–415). This defines the sense in which the brain is the organ of mind, and shows that it is not the organ of mind in the same sense in which it is a sensory-motor organ (p. 315).

6. That while the mind is thus manifoldly correlated with brain action, not only are mental-facts, as the highest authorities admit, absolutely distinguishable from brain-facts (pp. 292, 293, 314, 315); but the mental phenomena in man (even in sensation and consciousness of succession in sensations, in memory, language, still more in the higher mental functions, self-regulated voluntary activity, intellectual activities, thought on ultimate questions of existence, etc.) transcend brain action altogether, and are non-interpretable through it (pp. 304–307, 366, 367, 385–396; Chap. xv. "The Higher Forms of Mental Activity"). "Mind transcends all the sensibilities of our organism. The whole range of our thoughts,—as we interpret events under the law of causality, form conceptions of rectitude, and represent to ourselves a scheme of the universe as a whole,—transcends all the functions of the nerve system. Known facts are in accordance with this duality; paralysis of a cerebral hemisphere may leave intelligence unaffected; though high intellectual life involves good brain development, high brain development does not necesarily involve a distinguished intellectual life; but the more highly educated a man is, so much the more does his life transcend what his bodily functions can accomplish" (p. 307).

The result reached is—"that the intelligence of man, as known in personal consciousness, is of a nature entirely distinct from sensory apparatus, its functions being incapable of explanation in accordance with the laws of sensory activity. . . . The facts of consciousness lead to the conclusion that mind is a distinct order of existence, different in nature from the nerve system, differing in the mode of its action from the mechanical action of sensory apparatus, and capable of interpreting the rational sensibilities of our organism, so as thereby to discover a rational order in things external, or adaptation of related things in nature to rational purpose" (p. 307).

In establishing these positions, Professor Calderwood at the same time refutes certain others, viz. :—

1. The theory which identifies mind with brain action (pp. 313, 314).

2. The theory which supposes that there is an exact correspondence between the mental and physical facts,—or that, as Bain and Spencer put it, they are but two sides of the same thing (pp. 293–296). "That there is an absolute harmony involving a parallelism or correspondence, and making an exact equation of both organic and non-organic activity in all cases, it is quite impossible to maintain" (p. 316).

3. The theory that mental phenomena can be translated into the language of brain changes, or expressed in terms of the motions, groupings, or electric discharges of the latter (pp. 314, 315).

4. The view that mind does not act on the brain series to alter or modify it—"that action and reaction of nerve tissue carries the explanation of all that belongs to human life" (pp. 326–343). "It was inevitable that a theory reducing all human action to the play of nerve force should be propounded" (p. 336); but "(1) There is neither anatomical nor physiological evidence in support of the theory. . . . (3) The facts relied on as auxiliary to the theory do not in reality support it. . . . (4) The facts to be explained—voluntary control of muscular activity under guidance of intelligence— do not manifest resemblance to the known facts of nerve action, but present a decided contrast" (pp. 328, 329).

Note I—p. 152

Schleiermacher and Immortality

In his earlier writings Schleiermacher undoubtedly speaks slightingly of personal immortality, and Dr. Martineau enlarges on this as if it were his whole view.—*Study of Religion*, ii. pp. 355–360. But in his *Der christliche Glaube* he takes much more positive ground. In sec. 157 he distinguishes between "propositions of faith" and "propositions received on testimony," which, though their truth is not directly deducible from the contents of the Christian consciousness, are yet so intimately bound up with the credit of Christ and His witnesses, that we cannot refuse to accept them. Such, *e.g.*, is the Resurrection of Christ Himself, which, as shown in an earlier section (sec. 99), is not directly involved in faith, but yet is to be received on testimony. It is not otherwise, in Schleiermacher's view, with immortality. Here also he takes the ground that personal immortality is not a doctrine so bound up with faith that a man cannot conceivably be a Christian, and yet deny it. For if there is an irreligious denial of personal immortality, there may also, he holds, be a denial of it springing from a worthy and indeed a religious motive. "If, therefore," he says, "any one in good faith should maintain that Christ's words on this subject are to be taken figuratively, and not in their strict sense, and on this account should not attribute personal immortality to himself, faith in Christ, as such an one conceives of Him, certainly remains possible"; though, as he proceeds to explain, it would involve a complete transformation of Christianity if such a mode of interpretation should ever be established in the Church, or should be laid at the foundation of Christian faith (sec. 157, 2).   But this is purely a hypothetical case. For in these consequences to Christianity, says Schleiermacher, "it is already implied that we do not presuppose that such an interpretation can be made in good faith."   It can be maintained "that faith in the continuance of our personality is bound up with faith in the Redeemer" (*ibid.*).   He rejects all the natural arguments for immortality (sec. 158, 1), but he thinks it indubitable that Christ Himself taught His own immortality, and that of believers as united with Him in fellowship of life ; and this conviction is therefore given to us as part of our faith in Christ (sec. 158, 2).   It must, however, be admitted that this is an exceedingly weak ground on which to rest so weighty an article of faith ; for assuredly faith will not long retain a doctrine for which it experiences no religious need, and which finds no support in the facts of human nature.

NOTES TO CHAPTER 5

Note A—p. 165

Defects in Creation: An Argument Against Theism

LUCRETIUS already uses this argument. Even were he ignorant, he says, of the primordial causes of things, he could venture to affirm from the faultiness of the universe that it was not the work of Divine power.

> "Quod si jam rerum ignorem primordia quæ sint,
> Hoc tamen ex ipsis cæli rationibus ausim
> Confirmare aliisque ex rebus reddere multis,
> Nequaquam nobis divinitus esse paratam
> Naturam rerum ; tauta stat prædita culpa."
> —*De Rerum Natura*, v. 195–199.

Seneca held a view akin to Mill's.[1] Among his queries are these : "How far God's power extends ; whether He forms His own matter, or only uses that which is given Him ; whether He can do whatsoever He will, or the materials in many ways frustrate and disappoint Him, and things are formed badly by the great Artificer, not because His art fails, but because that on which it is exercised proves stubborn and intractable."—*Quæst. Nat.*, Book i. Preface.

Mr. Rathbone Greg seems in the end of his life to have come round to the views of Mr. Mill. "Thoughtful minds in all ages," he says, "have experienced the most painful perplexities in the attempt to reconcile certain of the moral and physical phenomena we see around us with the assumption of a Supreme Being at once all-wise, all-good, and almighty." These difficulties, he thinks, are wholly gratuitous, and arise out of the inconsiderate and unwarranted use of a single word—*omnipotent*. Only grant that the Creator is "conditioned,—hampered, it may be, by the attributes, qualities, and imperfections of the material on which He had to operate ; bound possibly by laws or properties inherent in the nature of that material,"—and "it becomes possible to believe in and to worship God without doing violence to our moral sense, or denying or dis-

---

[1] Mill's views are indicated in the text. They are further discussed by me in two papers in *The Theological Monthly* (July and August 1891) on "J. S. Mill and Christianity."

torting the sorrowful facts that surround our daily life."—Preface to
Enigmas of Life (18th edition).

The Pessimists, of course, lay stress on what they consider the
evil and defects of nature, as proving that it cannot have proceeded
from an intelligent cause.   Hartmann is quoted by Strauss as saying
that "if God, before creation, had possessed consciousness, creation
would have been an inexpiable crime ; its existence is only pardonable as the result of blind will."—*Der alte und der neue Glaube*,
p. 223.

Comte and Helmholtz have urged the defects of nature as dis-
proving design.   See their views criticised in Flint's *Theism*, Lect.
viii. ; Janet's *Final Causes*, p. 45 (Eng. trans.) ; Kennedy's *Nat.
Theol. and Modern Thought*, pp. 130-134 ; Row's *Christian Theism*,
chap. ix., etc.

Mr. S. Laing urges the undeniable existence of evil in the world
as a fact irreconcilable with that of an almighty and beneficent
Creator, and takes refuge in an ultimate law of "polarity," *i.e.*
dualism.—*A Modern Zoroastrian*, pp. 170–183 (see next note).

Maudsley writes : "The facts of organic and human nature, when
observed frankly and judged without bias, do not warrant the argument of a supreme and beneficent artificer working after methods of
human intelligence, but perfect in all his works ; rather would they
warrant, if viewed from the human standpoint, the conception of an
almighty malignant power that was working out some far-off end of
its own, with the serenest disregard of the suffering, expenditure,
and waste which were entailed in the process."—*Body and Will*, pp.
180, 181.

There is much that is exaggerated, jaundiced, and subjective in
these complaints, but they point to the existence of great and terrible
evils in the world, which Theism must boldly face, and do justice to
in some way in its view of the world.

Note B—p. 175

Dualistic Theories of the Origin of Evil

THE hypothesis of two principles in the universe finds classical
expression in the Zoroastrian religion.   Cf. on this Ebrard's *Christian Apologetics*, ii. pp. 186-232.   Mr. S. Laing makes an attempt at
a revival of the theory in his book, *A Modern Zoroastrian*, under the
name of "a law of polarity."   He would have us "devote ourselves
with a whole heart and sincere mind to the worship of the good
principle, without paltering with our moral nature by professing to
love and adore a Being who is the author of all the evil and misery
in the world as well as of the good " ; and holds that a great deal of
what is best in Christianity "resolves itself very much into the worship of Jesus as the Ormuzd, or personification of the good principle,

and determination to try to follow His example and do His work" (pp. 179, 180).

There is a deceptive simplicity in this idea of dividing off the good and evil of the world into different departments, giving all the good to a good principle, and all the evil to an evil principle, which may impose for a moment on the mind, yet the slightest reflection should suffice to show the crudeness and untenableness of the hypothesis.

In respect of *physical evil*, no such sharp division into good and evil is possible. Rather the terms are relative, and what is good in one relation is evil in another. Good and evil are often simply questions of degree ; the susceptibility to pleasure is involved in the susceptibility to pain, and *vice versâ*. Thus the same nerve which feels pleasure feels pain ; the one susceptibility is involved in the other. Pleasure and pain shade into each other by insensible gradations. If, *e.g.*, I approach my hands to the fire, I feel a grateful warmth ; if I bring them nearer, I am scorched. It is the same sun which fructifies the fields in one part of the world, and burns up the herbage or smites with sunstroke in another. On the hypothesis in question, the sun's heat would belong in the one case to the good, in the other to the evil principle ; so with the fire, etc.

In respect of *moral evil*, a self-subsisting evil principle is an impossible abstraction. Moral evil is a term which has no meaning except in relation to character and will ; and a character or will cannot be evil, unless along with the evil there is some knowledge of the good.[1] Natural forces, as heat and electricity, are neither good nor evil, for there is no knowledge. Bound up, therefore, with the evil principle, there must be some knowledge of the good, else it would not be evil. But a principle which participates in the knowledge of the good cannot be originally or essentially evil, but can only have become such through its own choice. Evil, in other words, has no reality, save as the negation or antithesis of the good, which is its necessary presupposition. Abstracted from knowledge of the good, the so-called evil principle sinks to the rank of a mere nature principle, of which neither good nor evil can properly be predicated. This is ultimately the reason why in dualistic systems natural and moral evil always tend to be confounded.

Note C—p. 176

Hegel's Doctrine of Sin

HEGEL's view, as stated in his *Religionsphilosophie*, may be briefly summed up thus :—

---

[1] "By its very essence," says Mr. Bradley, "immorality cannot exist except as against morality ; a purely immoral being is a downright impossibility."— *Ethical Studies*, p. 210.

1. Evil exists by a *metaphysical necessity.* "The notion must realise itself. . . . Man is essentially spirit; but spirit does not arise in an immediate way. It is essential to spirit to be for itself, to be free, to oppose itself to naturalness, to raise itself out of its state of immersion in nature, to set itself at variance with nature, and first through and by this variance to reconcile itself with nature, and not only with nature, but with its own essence, with its truth." —Vol. i. p. 268.

2. As respects his *original condition,* man exists first in a state of pure naturalness. It is hardly correctly named even a state of innocence, for innocence implies moral ideas, whereas this is a state "in which there is for man neither good nor evil; it is the state of the animal, of lack of knowledge, in which man knows nothing of either good or evil, in which what he wills is not determined either as the one or the other; for if he does not know evil, neither does he know good. . . . In truth, that first state of mere existence in unity with nature is not a condition of innocence, but of rudeness, of appetite, of barbarism generally."—Vol. i. p. 269.

3. As respects man's *essential nature* in this state, two opposite definitions are to be given—Man is by nature good; and man is by nature bad. To affirm "that man is by nature good, is essentially to say that man is spirit in himself, is rationality; he is created with and after the image of God. . . . The other statement arises from what has been said, that man must not remain as he is immediately, but must transcend his immediateness. . . . His-being-in-self, his naturality is the evil. . . . He is evil for this reason, that he is a natural being. . . . The absolute demand is that man shall not remain as a mere natural being,—not as mere natural will. Man has indeed consciousness; but he can, even as man, remain a mere natural being, in so far as he makes the natural the aim, content, and determination of his will."—Vol. ii. pp. 258–260.

4. That through which the transition is effected from the natural to the moral state is *knowledge.* With the awakening of consciousness, man recognises that he is not what he ought to be; hence arises the sense of sin, the pain of discord, of contradiction with himself. As the Bible has it, man becomes evil by eating of the tree of knowledge. "In this representation lies the connection of evil with knowledge. This is an essential point. . . . Man's nature is not what it should be, and it is knowledge which acquaints him with this and sets before him the fact of his being as he ought not to be. . . . It is not that consideration (knowledge) has an external relation to evil, but the consideration itself is the evil. Man, since he is spirit, has to proceed to this opposition, in order to be altogether for himself," etc.—Vol. ii. pp. 263–265.

It is the annulling of this self-diremption in man—represented as an essential stage in his development—which constitutes, accord-ing to Hegel, the atonement.

Note D—p. 179

Ritschl's Doctrine of Guilt

SEE a searching examination of Ritschl's doctrine on this subject in Dorner's *System of Doctrine*, iv. pp. 60–72 (Eng. trans.). Cf. also Pfleiderer's *Die Ritschl'sche Theologie*, pp. 63, 69, 70; Bertrand's *Une nouvelle Conception de la Redemption*, pp. 256–273; Stählin's *Kant, Lotze, und Ritschl*, pp. 210–212, 227.

All these writers agree that the logical effect of Ritschl's doctrine is to reduce guilt to a subjective illusion. This is borne out by the following particulars of his system :—

1. By the denial to God of everything of the nature of punitive justice. In so far as the sinner's guilty fears lead him to represent God as angry with him, or as visiting him with punishment, he is tormenting himself with needless apprehensions. Punitive justice is a conception borrowed from the sphere of civil right, and has no application in the sphere of the Divine. He teaches expressly that "external evils can only be reckoned as Divine punishments from the point of view of the subjective consciousness of guilt."—*Recht. und Ver.* iii. pp. 346.

2. By his doctrine of reconciliation. Reconciliation is defined as the removal of the separation which has come to exist between man and God in consequence of sin; and as it is the consciousness of guilt which keeps sinners far from God, pardon consists essentially in the removal of this guilt-consciousness (iii. p. 52). But this is not to be understood as if in this removal of guilt anything objective took place. Rather Christ's work was, as Dorner expresses it, "to reveal God to us as fatherly love, and scatter the gloomy terrors of an angry God and a punitive justice"; "to give deliverance from these erroneous notions of God's retributive and specially punitive justice, which interfere with Divine communion." — *System of Doctrine*, iv. p. 71.

3. The doctrine of guilt is attenuated on another side by Ritschl's view that all existing sin is sin committed in ignorance. It is on this ground that he declares it pardonable. But here again pardon does not mean the laying aside of any real displeasure on the part of God, but solely the removal of the sinner's (groundless) guilty fears. The one sin which Ritschl exempts from pardon is that of definitive unbelief—a problematical transgression which he thinks we have no reason to suppose ever existed. Here Ritschl's doctrine falls into an obvious inconsistency. He holds that if such a sin did exist, the one way the Divine Being could deal with it would be by annihilating the sinner. But surely this would be an exercise of punitive justice, if anything is ; yet Ritschl denies that punitive justice resides at all in God. On the whole, there is good ground for Dorner's charge, that "no clear, connected doctrine respecting punishment, God's punitive justice, moral freedom, and guilt, is to be found in Ritschl" (iv. p. 67).

Note E—p. 184

Alleged Primitive Savagery of Mankind

THE hypothesis of man's original savagery rests on certain unproved assumptions.

I. So far as it is a deduction from the law of evolution, it rests on the unproved assumption that man has developed by slow gradations from the condition of the animal. See on this the passages quoted in footnote to the Lecture, p. 182.

II. As respects existing savages, the hypothesis—

1. Rests on the unproved assumption that the state of existing savages represents (or most nearly represents) that of primitive man.[1] Of late, says Max Müller, there has been a strong reaction in the study of uncivilised races. "First of all, it has been shown that it was certainly a mistake to look upon the manners and customs, the legends and religious ideas, of uncivilised tribes as representing an image of what the primitive state of mankind must have been thousands of years ago, or what it actually was long before the beginning of the earliest civilisation, as known to us from historical documents. The more savage a tribe, the more accurately was it supposed to reflect the primitive state of mankind. This was no doubt a very natural mistake, before more careful researches had shown that the customs of savage races were often far more artificial and complicated than they appeared at first, and that there had been as much progression and retrogression in their historical development as in that of more civilised races. We know now that savage and primitive are very far indeed from meaning the same thing."—*Anthrop. Religion*, pp. 149, 150.

Evidence is constantly accumulating, that behind the existing condition of savage races there stood a state of higher culture and civilisation. *E.g.* Dr. Tylor says: "Dr. Bastian has lately visited New Zealand and the Sandwich Islands, and gathered some interesting information as to native traditions. The documents strengthen the view which for years has been growing up among anthropologists as to the civilisation of the Polynesians. It is true that they were found in Captain Cook's time living in a barbaric state, and their scanty clothing and want of metals led superior observers to class them as savages; but their beliefs and customs show plainly traces of descent from ancestors who in some way shared the higher culture of the Asiatic nations."—*Nature*, 1881, p. 29. Tylor's own pages furnish ample evidence of similar retrogression of the African and other tribes.—*Primitive Culture*, pp. 42, 43. On the extinct civilisations of Mexico and Peru, the mound-builders of the Mississippi Valley, and other evidences of earlier culture in America, see Réville's Hibbert Lectures, 1884, *The Native Religions of Mexico and Peru*; Dawson's *Fossil*

[1] Of course, from the evolutionist point of view, even savage life, as Tylor points out, would be "a far advanced condition."—*Prim. Culture*, i. p. 33.

Men and their Modern Representatives; Argyll's *Unity of Nature*, pp. 429–437.

A fact of the greatest importance here is that pointed out by the Duke of Argyll, viz. that the degraded races of the world are those farthest from the centres of distribution of population. "It is a fact," he says, "that the lowest and rudest tribes in the population of the globe have been found, as we have seen, at the farthest extremities of its larger continents, or in the distant islands of its great oceans, or among the hills and forests which in every land have been the last refuge of the victims of violence and misfortune."—*Unity of Nature*, p. 426. See for illustrations, chap. x. of this work.

Whately's statement stands yet unoverturned. "Facts," he says, "are stubborn things; and that no authenticated instance can be produced of savages that ever *did* emerge unaided from that state is no *theory*, but a statement, hitherto never disproved, of a matter of *fact*."—Exeter Hall Lecture on the *Origin of Civilisation*.

2. It overlooks the higher elements which exist even in the present condition of savages. See these brought out as respects the African tribes, on the basis of Waitz's *Anthropology*, in Max Müller's Hibbert Lectures, 1878, *On the Origin and Growth of Religion*, pp. 106–113.

III. As respects prehistoric man, the main points are noticed in the Lectures.

1. Here, again, the assumption is unproved that these cave-men, etc., on whose rudeness the argument was founded, represented primitive man, and were not rather a degradation of an earlier type. Against this assumption is the fact of their distance from what seem to have been the original centres of distribution of the race, combined with the very different spectacle which mankind presents as we approach these centres. On the argument based on the antiquity of prehistoric man, see Note G., and cf. Reusch's *Nature and the Bible*, ii. pp. 265–366 (Eng. trans.).

2. Many erroneous inferences may be drawn from stone implements and the like as to the intellectual and moral calibre of the people using them. See on this the most suggestive treatment in Sir Arthur Mitchell's *Rhind Lectures* on "Past and Present," and "What is Civilisation?" (1876 and 1878).

3. The greatest civilisations of antiquity do not show traces of an earlier period of barbarism. These civilisations certainly did not spring into existence ready-formed, but there is nothing to indicate any such slow rise from an antecedent state of savagery as the modern hypothesis supposes. This is peculiarly the case with the oldest civilisation—that of Egypt. "In Egypt," says Canon Rawlinson, "it is notorious that there is no indication of any early period of savagery or barbarism. All the authorities agree that, however far we go back, we find in Egypt no rude or uncivilised time out of which civilisation is developed."—*Origin of Nations*, p. 13.[1] The same writer says of Babylon: "In Babylon there is more indication

---

[1] On some supposed traces of prehistoric man in Egypt, see Dawson's *Egypt and Syria*, pp. 128–136.

of early rudeness. But, on the other hand, there are not wanting
signs of an advanced state of certain arts, even in the earliest times,
which denote a high degree of civilisation, and contrast most curi-
ously with the indications of rudeness here spoken of " (*ibid.* p. 14).
This progress of discovery in ancient Babylonia has carried back
civilisation, and a high development of the arts (as of writing), to a
quite unthought-of antiquity (*e.g.* at Nipur).

Note F—p. 184

Early Monotheistic Ideas

IT has been shown (Note A. to Lecture III.—Primitive Fetishism
and Ghost Worship) that man's earliest religious ideas were not his
poorest. It may now be affirmed that his earliest ideas were in
some respects his highest—that the consciousness of the one God
was with him in the dawn of his history, and has never been wholly
extinguished since.

Ebrard, after an exhaustive examination of ancient religions, thus
sums up: " We have nowhere been able to discover the least trace of
any forward and upward movement from Fetishism to Polytheism,
and from that again to a gradually advancing knowledge of the one
God ; but, on the contrary, we have found among all peoples of the
heathen world a most decided tendency to sink from an earlier and
relatively purer knowledge of God."—*Christ. Apol.* iii. p. 317 (Eng.
trans.).

The ancient Egyptian religion was at heart monotheistic. M. de
Rouge says : " The Egyptian religion comprehends a quantity of
local worships. . . . Each of these regions has its principal god
designated by a special name ; but it is always the same doctrine
which reappears under different names. One idea predominates,
that of a single and primeval God ; everywhere and always it is one
substance, self-existent, and an unapproachable God." (Quoted by
Renouf, p. 90.) This, he says, was the doctrine of the Egyptians in
the earliest period. M. Renouf confirms this statement. " It is
incontestably true," he testifies, " that the sublimer portions of the
Egyptian religion are not the comparatively late result of a process
of development or elimination from the grosser. The sublimer portions are demonstrably ancient ; and the last stage of the Egyptian
religion, that known to the Greek and Latin writers, heathen or
Christian, was by far the grossest and most corrupt."—Hibbert
Lectures, p. 91.

The early Babylonian religion was polytheistic ; but here also the
monotheistic consciousness breaks through in the exalted predicates
applied to the great gods by their respective worshippers. Each god
seems at first to have been worshipped by its own city as supreme—
the moon-god at Ur ; the sun-god at Sippara ; Anu, the sky, at
Erech ; Ea, the deep, at Eridu ; Nebo at Borsippa, etc   Thus the

moon-god was celebrated as the "lord and prince of the gods, whc in heaven and earth alone is supreme"; Nebo, in the belief of his worshippers, was the supreme god, the creator of the world ; Anu, the sky-god, became a supreme god, the lord and father of the universe, then "the one god" into whom all the other deities were resolved ; Asshur developed peculiarly exalted traits. "We can, in fact," says Professor Sayce, "trace in him all the lineaments upon which under other conditions there might have been built up as pure a faith as that of the God of Israel."—Sayce's Hibbert Lectures, 1887, p. 129 ; cf. pp. 116, 160, 191, etc. Others go farther, and see in Ilu = Heb. *El*, "the Babylonian supreme deity," cf. Schrader, *Keilinschriften*, i. p. 11 (Eng. trans.) ; and conclude, with Duncker and Lenormant, that the Babylonians in the earliest times worshipped one god, El, Ilu. (In Ebrard, ii. p. 330.)

The religion of the Vedas in India, in like manner, is purer than the later Hindu developments, and points back, through philology, to an earlier stage still, when the Polytheism of the Vedas was as yet non-existent. "Behind the Homeric poems," says Dr. Fairbairn, "and the Vedas, and the separation of the Iranic-Indian branches, lies the period when Celt and Teuton, Anglo-Saxon and Indian, Greek and Roman, Scandinavian and Iranian, lived together, a simple, single people. . . . Excluding the coincidences natural to related peoples developing the same germs, we find two points of radical and general agreement—the proper name of one God, and the term expressive of the idea of God in general. . . . A name for God had thus been formed before the dispersion. . . . The result is a Theism which we may name individualistic."—*Studies in the Phil. of Religion*, pp. 22–29 ; "The younger the Polytheism, the fewer its gods," p. 22.

Ebrard says : "Immediately after the separation of the Iranians and Indians, that is, during the first Vedic period, the consciousness was fully present among the Indians that the Adityas did not represent a multitude of separate deities in a polytheistic and mythological sense, but only the fulness of the creative powers of the one God, and that the holy God, and that in each of these Adityas it was always the one God who was worshipped. And the farther back we go into the past, the more distinct do we find the consciousness among the Indians. In the second, the Indra period, it dwindles away, and gives place to a polytheistic conception."—*Christ. Apol.* ii. pp. 213, 214. He finds the common root of the Indian and Iranian religions in "a primitive Monotheism, or Elohism, as we might call it, since there is no real distinction between the Elohim and the Adityas" (p. 214).

The Iranian religion in the form in which we find it in the Zend-Avesta (Zoroastrian) is dualistic ; but the conception of Ahura-Mazda, as we find it in the earlier portions, is so exalted that it may almost be called monotheistic. It unquestionably springs from the common Aryan root indicated above.

Herodotus has the striking statement that the ancient Pelasgi, the early inhabitants of Greece, gave no distinct names to the gods, but prayed to them collectively. "They called them gods, because they had set in order and ruled all things." But as for the special names attached to them, and the functions severally assigned to them—all this, he thinks, goes no farther back than Homer and Hesiod. "These framed a theogony for the Greeks, and gave names to the gods, and assigned to them honours and arts, and declared their several forms" (ii. 52, 53). Max Müller does not hesitate to say, following Welcker : "When we ascend to the most distant heights of Greek history, the idea of God as the Supreme Being stands before us as a simple fact."—*Chips*, ii. p. 157. This strain of Monotheism in the religion of the Greeks is never absolutely lost, but reappears in the beliefs of the philosophers, the Orphic mysteries, and the lofty conceptions of the great tragic poets.

Plutarch, in like manner, tells of the early religion of the Romans, that it was imageless and spiritual. Their religious lawgiver, Numa, he says, "forbade the Romans to represent the deity in the form either of man or of beast. Nor was there among them formerly any image or statue of the Divine Being ; during the first one hundred and seventy years they built temples, indeed, and other sacred domes, but placed in them no figure of any kind ; persuaded that it is impious to represent things Divine by what is perishable, and that we can have no conception of God but by the understanding."—*Lives*, on Numa. The legendary form of the tradition need not lead us to doubt that it embodies a substantial truth.

On this subject see Ebrard's *Christian Apologetics* ; Loring Brace's *The Unknown God* ; Pressensé's *The Ancient World and Christianity* (Eng. trans.) ; Vigouroux's *La Bible et les Découvertes modernes*, iii. —"On Primitive Monotheism" ; Rawlinson's Tract on "The Early Prevalence of Monotheistic Beliefs," in *Present Day Tracts* (No. 11), etc.

Note G—p. 185

The Antiquity of Man and Geological Time

IN illustration of the tendency in recent science greatly to restrict the period formerly claimed for man's antiquity, the following passages may be cited from an able article on the Ice Age in *The Edinburgh Review* for April 1892, based on Dr. Wright's *Ice Age in North America, and its bearings on the Antiquity of Man* (1890).[1]

"The Falls of Niagara," says this writer, "indeed constitute of themselves, in Dr. Wright's apt phrase, 'a glacial chronometer.' Much trouble has been bestowed upon its accurate rating ; and repeated trigonometrical surveys since 1842 afford so sure a basis for calculation, that serious error in estimating, from the amount of work done, the time consumed in doing it need no longer be appre-

[1] Dr. Wright's conclusions are reproduced in his *Man and the Glacial Period*, in the International Scientific Series, published since this note was written (1892).

hended. . . . The average rate of recession, arrived at through careful weighing of these and other analogous facts, is five feet per annum, or nearly a mile in a thousand years. Hence from seven to eight thousand years have elapsed since the foam of Niagara rose through the air at Queenston ; and the interval might even be shortened by taking into account some evidences of pre-glacial erosion by a local stream, making it probable that from the whirlpool downward the cutting of the gorge proceeded more rapidly than it does now. The date of the close of the Glacial Epoch in the United States can scarcely then be placed earlier than 6000 B.C. . . .

"Their testimony does not stand alone. . . . Pre-glacially, it [the Mississippi] followed a wide bend from Minneapolis to Fort Snelling ; now it flows straight across the intervening eight miles to its junction with the Minnesota. On its way it leaps the Falls of St. Anthony ; and the rate of their retreat since 1680, exactly determined from the observation of Father Hennequin, proves them to be about eight thousand three hundred years old. This second glacial timepiece accordingly, which, owing to its more southerly position was started earlier than the first, gives substantially the same reading. . . . The ravines and cascades of Ohio, studied by Dr. Wright, agree with the two great Falls in giving a comparatively recent overthrow of the ice *régime.* The unworn condition of the glacial deposits, the sharpness of glacial groovings, above all, the insignificant progress made by the silting up of glacial lakes, testify as well, and in some cases quite definitely, to a short lapse of time.

"But if the Ice Age in America terminated—as we seem bound to admit—less than ten thousand years ago, so, beyond question, did the Ice Age in Europe. There is no possibility of separating the course of glacial events in each continent. The points of agreement are too many ; the phenomena too nearly identical in themselves and in their sequence. Elevation and depression of continents, the formation, retreat, and second advance of the ice-sheet, the accompaniment of its melting by tremendous floods, the extermination of the same varieties of animals, the appearance and obliteration of Palæolithic man, all preserved identical mutual relations in the Old and New Worlds. . . . The point has an important bearing upon the vexed question of the antiquity of man," etc.—*Edinburgh Review,* April 1892, pp. 315–319.

The same view was advocated by Mr. P. F. Kendall in a paper prepared by Mr. Gray and himself on "The Cause of the Ice-Age," read in the Geological Section of the British Association, August 4, 1892. He said : "Another fact of great importance bearing upon this question was the exceedingly recent date of the glacial period. It was the custom of geologists not long ago to talk about the glacial period as perhaps a quarter of a million years ago, or, at all events, to make a very liberal use of thousands and hundreds of thousands of years. But now it was found that all the physical evidence was in favour of a very recent departure of the ice. They could, for instance, put the date of the commencement of the great cut of the Niagara Falls at the close of the glacial period, and other like evidence in America pointed clearly to the recency of the departure of the ice." — *Scotsman* Report, August 5. The remainder of the paper was an examination of the theories of the late Dr. Croll, Dr. Wall, and Mr. Warren Upham, and the exposition by the authors of a theory of their own connected with the variability in the heat of the sun.

Sir Archibald Geikie, in his President's Address at the same meeting of the British Association, while himself putting in a plea for longer periods on the ground of the geological record, grants that the recent drift of physical science has been enormously to reduce the unlimited drafts on time formerly made by geologists. Lord Kelvin "was inclined, when first dealing with the subject, to believe that, from a review of all the evidence then available, some such period as one hundred million years would embrace the whole of the geological history of the globe. . . . But physical inquiry continued to be pushed forward with regard to the early history and antiquity of the earth. Further consideration of the influence of tidal rotation in retarding the earth's rotation, and of the sun's rate of cooling, led to sweeping reductions of the time allowable for the evolution of the planet. The geologist found himself in the plight of Lear when his bodyguard of one hundred knights was cut down. 'What need you five-and-twenty, ten, or five?' demands the inexorable physicist, as he remorselessly strikes slice after slice from his allowance of geological time. Lord Kelvin, I believe, is willing to grant us some twenty millions of years, but Professor Tait would have us content with less than ten millions."—Report of Address. One argument of Professor Geikie for lengthening the time is the extreme slowness with which, on the evolution hypothesis, the changes in species have been brought about—a very distinct *petitio principii*. It is worth while in this connection to note his admission : "So too with the plants and the higher animals which still survive. Some forms have become extinct, but few or none which remain display any transitional gradations into new species."

Professor Tait's own words are : "I daresay many of you are acquainted with the speculations of Lyell and others, especially of Darwin, who tell us that even for a comparatively brief portion of recent geological history three hundred millions of years will not suffice.—*Origin of Species*, 1859, p. 287. We say : So much the worse for geology as at present understood by its chief authorities ; for, as you will presently see, physical considerations from independent points of view render it utterly impossible that more than ten or fifteen millions of years can be granted."—*Recent Advances in Physical Science*, pp. 167, 168. "From this point of view we are led to a limit of something like ten millions of years as the utmost we can give to geologists for their speculations as to the history even of the lowest orders of fossils " (p. 167).

See further on this subject Dawson's *Origin of the World*, and *Fossil Men and their Modern Representatives* ; Reusch's *Nature and the Bible*, ii. pp. 265–366 ; and Wright's *Man and the Glacial Period*, in the International Scientific Series.

Note H—p. 198

The Connection of Sin and Death

RITSCHL agrees with the modern view in dissolving the connection between human death and sin. Paul, indeed, he grants, affirms this connection; but the mere fact that this thought was formed by an apostle does not make it a rule for us (*Recht. und Ver.* iii. pp. 341, 342).

An able article appeared in the *Revue de Théologie* (Montauban), July 1882, on "Physical Death and Sin," by M. Charles Ducasse, which may be referred to as in agreement with, and confirmatory of, the positions taken up in the Lecture. The writer speaks of the problem created by the appearance of death in the world before sin. Before the appearance of man on the earth, death reigned; death was the law even of the organic world. He shows that from the first death entered into the Divine plan for the lower creation—is implied in what the Bible says of the reproduction of plants and animals, in the command given to Adam, etc. But he finds no contradiction in the thought that a new order of things should enter with man. Man forms part of nature. The roots of his organism penetrate into the past of other beings, and of the material world. But is man only a superior animal? Does not a new kingdom appear in him? The terminating point of the organic world, is he not equally the point of departure of the world of spirit, of reason, of morality? He is the bond of union between the world of nature and the Divine world. Why, then, should it not have been precisely his vocation to spiritualise matter, and lead it up to the conquest of new attributes? What hinders us from affirming that man was placed here to acquire corporeal immortality, and that, if he had not sinned, he would have been able to graft eternal life in his body on changeable and transient matter? This view, he thinks, agrees with both Scripture and science. Impartial science brings out the almost complete identity of our organism with that of the animals, but it establishes not less decisively the originality of our mental being, the superiority of our faculties of reason. The human kingdom constitutes in its eyes a kingdom by itself. There is, then, nothing improbable in the supposition that originally and in the plan of God the conditions of death for man were different from those for animals. The actual death of man would still in this view be the consequence of his sin; and this is in full accord with the Biblical teaching.

See also a suggestive treatment of this subject in Dr. Matheson's *Can the Old Faith Live with the New?* pp. 206-218.

NOTES TO CHAPTER 6

Note A—p. 220

The Doctrine of Pre-existence

THE more recent theology admits the application of the notion of pre-existence to Christ in the New Testament, but explains it out of current Jewish modes of thought on this subject. See on this Harnack's *Dogmengeschichte*, i. pp. 69–93, 710–719; Baldensperger's *Das Selbstbewusstsein Jesu*, pp. 85–92 (2nd edition); Bornemann's *Unterricht im Christenthum*, pp. 92–96, etc. According to these writers, the conception of pre-existence was a current one in the Rabbinical schools and in apocalyptic literature. Not only distinguished persons, as Adam, Enoch, Moses, but distinguished objects, as the tabernacle, the temple, the tables of the law, were figured as having had heavenly archetypes, *i.e.* as pre-existent. Various causes are assigned for this mode of representation :—

1. There is the desire to express the inner worth of a valued object in distinction from its inadequate empirical form, which leads to the essence being hypostatised, and raised above space and time (Harnack).

2. There is the conversion of an "end" into a "cause"—this specially in the case of persons (the Messiah), peoples (Israel), a collective body (the Church). "Where something which appears later was apprehended as the end of a series of dispositions, it was not unfrequently hypostatised, and made prior to these arrangements in point of time; the conceived end was placed in a kind of real existence before the means through which it was destined to be realised on earth, as an original cause of them."—Harnack, pp. 89, 90.

3. There is the thought of predestination, which leads to an ideal pre-existence being realistically conceived as an actual one (Baldensperger).

This category, existing in Jewish circles, was, it is thought, simply taken over and applied to Christ, believed in as the Messiah, risen and exalted to heaven. In this way, Harnack thinks, the first Christians "went beyond the expressions developed out of the Messianic consciousness of Jesus Himself respecting His Person, and sought notionally and speculatively to grasp the worth and absolute significance of His Person " (p. 90).[1] "The thought of pre-existence," says Bornemann, " was not supernaturally communicated to the apostles, nor was formed for the first time by Paul, nor generally was unusual in that time ; but we have to do here with a self-evident application to Jesus of an attribute already firmly established in Judaism as belonging to the Messiah."—*Unterricht*, p. 93. In short, the predicate of pre-existence was only one of several ways which the early Church took to express its sense of the abiding worth and felt mystery of the Person of Jesus. Bornemann mentions three of these—1. The supernatural birth ; 2. The thought of pre-existence ; 3. The incarnation of the eternal Divine Word of Revelation—"ideas," he says, "subsisting independently of each other, and alongside of each other, as distinct but disparate attempts to ground the mystery of the life of Jesus in its Divine origin" (p. 92).

It appears from this that the application of the category of pre-existence to Jesus was a mere deduction of faith on the part of the first disciples—the application to Him, as Bornemann says, of one of " the religious and philosophical notions and forms of 'Vorstellung' generally current in that time,"—and is therefore of no normative value for the Church to-day. I presume that not one of the writers I have quoted holds that Christ really pre-existed as the apostles thought He did. Before we accept this view, we would require to be satisfied of several things :—

1. That this Rabbinical mode of representation was really so widely current as is alleged, and that it was indeed the source from which the apostles derived their belief in Christ's eternal pre-existence.

2. That this belief had not its origin in very distinct utterances of Christ Himself, proceeding from the depths of His Divine self-knowledge (John viii. 58, xvii. 5, etc.).

3. That there is a true analogy between the New Testament conception of Christ's pre-existence and this Rabbinical notion. The Jewish notion, according to Harnack, was that "the earthly things pre-exist with God just as they appear on earth, with all the material properties of their being" (p. 710). They do not exist eternally—at least the Law (which was exalted most highly of all) did not (two thousand years before the creation of the world, the Rabbis said). But Christ (1) exists from eternity ; (2) as a Divine Person with the Father ; (3) one in nature and glory with the Father ; (4) His Divine nature is distinguished from His humanity which He assumed in time ; (5) His appearance on earth is the result of a voluntary act of self-abnegation and love—an ethical act. It is only confusing things that differ to pretend that the Rabbinical absurdities alluded to explain a Christian doctrine like this.

4. Many special facts testify against the sufficiency of this explanation.

(1) The support sought for it in the New Testament is of the most flimsy character, *e.g.* Gal. iv. 26 ; Heb. xii. 22 ; Rev. xxi. 2.

---

[1] On Harnack's distinction between the Jewish and Hellenistic forms of this notion, see the criticism by Baldensperger in his *Das Selbstbewusstsein Jesus*, 2nd ed. p. 89.

(2) It is admitted that "the representations of a pre-existent Messiah in Judaism were in no way very widespread" (Harnack, p. 89), and that they do not appear in all the New Testament writings. In truth, the writings in which they do appear are not specially the Jewish ones, but those in which scholars have thought they detected most traces of Hellenistic influence.

(3) It is plain that in the writings in which they do appear, these Jewish modes of thought were not dominant. Paul, *e.g.*, regards believers as eternally chosen and foreordained in Christ to salvation; but he does not attribute to them any such pre-existence as he ascribes to Christ. On this hypothesis, he ought to have done so.

I cannot therefore accept this new theory as adequate to the facts. Nor do I believe that the apostles were left simply to their own gropings and imaginings in this and other great matters of the Christian faith. I take it as part of the Christian view that they were guided by the Spirit of Revelation into the truth which they possessed, and that their teachings laid the foundations of doctrine for the Church in all time.

Note B—p. 228

Philo and the Fourth Gospel

THE most diverse opinions prevail as to the extent to which the Fourth Gospel and other books of the New Testament have been influenced by the Alexandrian philosophy—some, like Harnack and Weiss, denying its presence altogether; others, like Pfleiderer, seeing its influence in John, Hebrews, Ephesians, and Colossians, etc. It will put the matter in a clearer light if we look briefly, first, at Philo's own philosophy, and at the sources from which it was derived.

The three main sources of Philo's philosophy were Platonism, Stoicism, and the Old Testament.

1. From Plato, the chief contribution was the theory of ideas—of an ideal or noetic world in the Divine mind, after the pattern of which this visible world was made (cf. the *Timæus*). It is to be observed, however, that there is not the slightest indication in Plato that this idea of the world was conceived of as a personal agent, or as anything else than an attribute of the Divine mind, in which it resides like a plan in the mind of an architect.[1]

2. The indebtedness of Philo to Plato is very obvious; but it is not from Plato that Philo derives the term Logos. He obtains this term from the Stoics. By the Logos, however, the Stoics as little as Plato understood a distinct hypostasis in the sphere of the Divine—a second Divine Being. The Logos, with the Stoics, is simply the

---

[1] The "ideas," however, are also regarded as the immanent forms or essences of things, which become what they are through "participation" in them,—a point of contact with the Stoical doctrine noted below.

Divine Reason itself—that eternal Divine Reason which is immanent in the universe, and in substance is one with it (fire).
There was a further doctrine which the Stoics held, however, which
is of great importance for the understanding of Philo. Together
with their fundamentally pantheistic conception of the all-pervading
Divine Reason, they held that this Reason develops or manifests
itself in a multitude of powers or forces, called also λόγοι. This is
the famous Stoical doctrine of the λόγοι σπερματικοί—the Logos-
seeds or powers (δυνάμεις) which develop themselves in particular
things. The theory is very different from Plato's ; yet the step was
not great to identify these seed-like λόγοι of the Stoics—the immanent rational principles of things—with the "ideas" of Plato,
which also in their own way were active powers or principles.
Here, then, we have another premiss of the theory of Philo. Philo
takes over this doctrine of the Stoics bodily,—identifies their active
λόγοι with the "ideas" of Plato,—identifies them, further, with the
Old Testament angels and Greek demons,—and gathers them up,
finally, as the Stoics also did, into the unity of the one Logos.

3. But Philo went a step further. It is the peculiarity of his
theory that this Logos is distinguished from God Himself as the
absolute and highest Being—is hypostatised—projected, as it were,
from the Divine mind, and viewed, though in a very wavering and
fluctuating way, as a personal agent.[1] Now, where did Philo get
this last conception ? Not from Platonic or Stoical philosophy—
not from Greek philosophy at all. He got it from the same source
whence he derived his immovable Monotheism, his firm faith in
Divine Providence, his doctrine of angels, etc.,—from the Old
Testament. The Old Testament also has its distinction between
God in His hidden and incommunicable essence and God as
revealed ; and has its names for this Revelation-side of God's nature
(His name, glory, face, word, angel of Jehovah, etc. Cf. Oehler's
Theol. of the Old Testament, pp. 181-196 ; Newman's *Arians*, pp. 92,
153). There is, in particular, the doctrine of the (personified)
Divine Wisdom in the Book of Proverbs. These germs did not lie
without development on the soil of Judaism, as seen in the curious
doctrine of the Memra, or word of Jehovah, in the Targums (cf.
Edersheim's *Jesus the Messiah*, i. pp. 47, 48 ; ii. pp. 659-664—
Appendix on "Philo of Alexandria and Rabbinic Theology")—the
Memra being a distinct hypostasis whose name is substituted for
Jehovah's ; and that they were developed on Greek soil is evidenced
by the apocryphal Book of Wisdom, in which we have, as Schürer
points out, nearly all the elements of Philo's doctrine already
present (*Hist. of Jewish People*, Div. ii. vol. iii. p. 232). We cannot
err, therefore, in attributing Philo's doctrine of the hypostatic Logos
to the same Old Testament source.

Once this is granted, many things are clear. The predicates with

---

[1] It is a point on which opinions differ as to whether Philo's Logos was
conceived of as a personal agent—was hypostatised (see Drummond's *Philo
of Alexandria*, which upholds the negative) ; but the above seems the preferable view.

which Philo clothes his Logos—those of Creator, High-Priest, Arch-
angel, Intercessor, etc.—are plainly drawn over upon it from the
Old Testament. But it is also clear how Philo's doctrine should
become in a certain way a preparation for the gospel. Comparing
his view with that of the Gospel of John, we see, indeed—notwithstanding assertions to the contrary—a fundamental contrast. The
evangelist has his feet on a fact which he seeks to interpret ; Philo
moves throughout in the region of speculation. An incarnation
would conflict with the first principles of his philosophy. The
whole substance of the doctrine in the Fourth Gospel is different
from Philo's speculations. Even in their respective conceptions of
the Logos, John and Philo are at variance ; for Philo means by
Logos the internal Reason, never the spoken word ; while John
means the word uttered, spoken. His view is in accordance with
the Palestinian, not with the Greek conception. I cannot therefore
but agree with Harnack when he says : "John and Philo have little
more in common than the name" (*Dogmengeschichte*, i. p. 85). Even
the term Logos does not occur after the Prologue. But suppose the
resemblances had been greater than they are, would this necessarily
have been to the prejudice of the Gospel ? I cannot see it ; for it
has just been shown that the one peculiar thing in Philo's theory,—
that which brings it into relation with the Gospel,—viz. its hypo-
statisation of the Logos, is precisely that feature which he did not
get from Greek philosophy, but from the Old Testament. It was a
very different thing for one whose mind was stored, as Philo's was,
with the facts of the Old Testament Revelation, to come in contact
with the suggestive teachings of Plato, from what it would have
been for another with no such preparation (cf. Newman's *Arians*,
pp. 91, 92). Philo, working with these ideas, struck out a theory
which is not unchristian, but goes forward rather to meet the
Christian view, and find its completion in it. That there is a
Divine Reason in the universe, and that this universal Logos is none
other than He who is the life and light of men, and who in the fulness of time became flesh,—this is not less Christian teaching
because Philo in some respects was in accord with it. John, if we
assume him to have heard of this doctrine of Philo's, had no reason
to reject it so far as it went. It harmonised with the truth he held,
and furnished a fitting form in which to convey that truth.
Whether even this much of Alexandrian influence is present in the
Gospel, it is not easy to determine. Meanwhile, it is only doing
justice to this great Jewish thinker to see in him an important link
in the providential preparation for Christian conceptions—even if
we do not go further, and speak of him with Pfleiderer, as "the last
Messianic prophet of Israel, the Alexandrian John the Baptist, who
stretches out a hand to John the Evangelist" (*Religionsphilosophie*,
iii. p. 176, Eng. trans.).

On Philo's philosophy, and his relation to the Gospel, the works
of Siegfried, Drummond, Zeller, Schürer, Edersheim, Harnack,
Pfleiderer, Hatch (Hibbert Lectures), Martineau (*Seat of Authority*),
Godet, Dorner. etc., may be consulted.

Note C—p. 233

The Resurrection of Christ and the Reality of His Divine Claim

IF the premisses of the Christian view are correct as to Christ's claim to be the Son of God, and as to the connection of sin with death, it was impossible that He, the Holy One, should be holden of death. The Prince of Life must overcome death. His resurrection is the pledge that death shall yet be swallowed up in victory.

On the other hand, the denial of Christ's resurrection leads to a subversion of His whole claim as unfounded.[1] If historically real, the resurrection of Christ is a confirmation of Christ's entire claim ; if it did not happen, this alone negates it. The resurrection is thus an integral part of the Christian view. In this respect also—as well as in its bearings on our justification—we may say : " If Christ hath not been raised, your faith is vain ; ye are yet in your sins " (1 Cor. xv. 17).[2]

It is only what might have been anticipated, therefore, when we find the advocates of the modern view—those who refuse Christ's claim—emphatic in their denial of the resurrection, and unceasing in their efforts to demolish the evidence of it. It is more surprising to find writers who claim to be upholders of the true Christianity playing fast and loose with this fact of the Gospel, and doing their best to belittle the importance of it for Christian faith. I refer particularly to the attitude of certain writers of the Ritschlian school. It is extremely doubtful if leading representatives of this school, as Harnack and Wendt, accept the resurrection of Christ in the literal sense at all. Harnack expressly avers that there is no satisfactory historical evidence of the resurrection of Christ. He goes further, and pours contempt on the attempt to find such evid· ence. He not merely argues—what all will admit—that a faith in Christ based on mere historic evidence is no true faith ; but he scouts the idea of being dependent on historic evidence at all. Such evidence, if we had it, would give us, he thinks, no help. Faith must be perfectly independent of evidence coming to us through the testimony of others. "To believe on the ground of appearances which others have had, is a levity which will always revenge itself through uprising doubt." This is professedly an exaltation of faith ; but it directly becomes apparent that faith is not intended to give us any guarantee of the physical resurrection—that, in truth, this part of Christianity is to be given up. The Christian "has nothing to do with a knowledge of the form in which Christ lives,

---

[1] On the same principle that in a hypothetical syllogism the denial of the consequent leads to the denial of the antecedent. If Christ was the Divine Son, He could not be holden of death. If He was holden of death, His claim to be the Divine Son is refuted.

[2] The resurrection has a constitutive place in the Christian view in connec· tion with Redemption ; but into this I do not enter here.

but only with the conviction that He is the living Lórd." The
determination of the form was dependent on the widely differing
general representations about a future life, resurrection, restoration,
and glorification of the body, which prevailed at that particular
time (see the whole note, *Dogmengeschichte*, i. pp. 75, 76). Wendt
speaks in quite similar terms. Christ's sayings on His own resurrection are interpreted as conveying only the idea that "Jesus
would after the briefest delay be awakened from death to the
heavenly life with God"; and the Church misinterpreted them in
applying them on the ground of "appearances which were held by
them as certain facts of experience to a literal bodily resurrection"
(*Die Lehre Jesu*, ii. p. 543). One would like to know how much
objective reality Wendt is disposed to attribute to these "appearances." To Herrmann also the exaltation of Christ is "a thought of
faith," indemonstrable through historical evidence. It is an ill
service to name the resurrection to us living to-day as a fact likely
to convince unbelievers. "For it is related to us by others"
(*Verkehr*, 2nd edition, p. 239).[1]

This minimising of the importance of the historical resurrection on
the part of Ritschlian writers accords only too well with the general
subjectivity of the school. A theory which resolves religion wholly
into "judgments of value," or, as Herrmann prefers to call them,
"thoughts of faith," has clearly no room for an objective fact like
the resurrection. A view which lays the whole stress on the impression (Eindruck) produced by Christ's earthly life, has no means of
incorporating the resurrection into itself as a constitutive part of
its Christianity. It remains at most a deduction of faith without
inner relation to salvation. It is apt to be felt to be a superfluous
appendage. It might almost be said to be a test of the adequacy of
the view of Christ and His work taken by any school, whether it is
able to take in the resurrection of Christ as a constitutive part of it.
I cannot therefore but regard the Ritschlian position as virtually a
surrender of faith in Christ's resurrection. The attempt to set faith
and historical evidence in opposition to each other is one that must
fail. Since it is implied in Christ's whole claim that death cannot
hold Him,—not merely, as with the Ritschlians, that He has a
spiritual life with God, faith would be involved in insoluble contradictions if it could be shown that Christ has not risen; or, what
comes to the same thing, that there is no historical evidence that
He has risen. It may be, and is, involved in our faith that He is
risen from the dead; but this faith would not of itself be a sufficient
ground for asserting that He had risen, if all historical evidence for
the statement were wanting. Faith cherishes the just expectation
that, if Christ has risen, there will be historical evidence of the fact;
and were such evidence not forthcoming, it would be driven back

---

[1] Bornemann seems to hold a literal resurrection, but regards it as insoluble
whether Christ really appeared in the body to His disciples, "or whether
those appearances rested on a miraculous working of the Person of Jesus on
the *souls* of the disciples," *i.e.* were subjective impressions; and treats the
question as indifferent to faith.—*Unterricht*, p. 85.

upon itself in questioning whether its confidence was not self-delusion.

In harmony with this view is the place which the resurrection of Christ holds in Scripture, and the stress there laid upon its historical attestation (1 Cor. xv. 1–19). I cannot enter here into detailed discussion of the historical evidence. The empty grave on the third day is a fact securely attested by the earliest traditions. The undoubting faith of the first disciples in the resurrection of their Lord, and in His repeated appearances to themselves, is also beyond question. Baur and most candid writers acknowledge that something extraordinary must have happened on that third day to lay a basis for this faith, and to change their despair into joyful and triumphant confidence (see Baur's *Church History*, i. p. 42, Eng. trans.). The hypothesis of imposture has now no respectable advocates. The idea of a "swoon" finds little support. The "vision-hypothesis," which would reduce the apostles to the level of hysterical women, is inexplicable out of psychological conditions, and has been refuted almost to weariness (see good remarks on it in Beyschlag's *Leben Jesu*, in his chapter on the Resurrection, i. pp. 406–450). The attempt to make it appear as if Paul believed only in a visionary appearance of Christ, can hardly convince anybody. In all these discussions the alternative invariably comes back to be—conscious imposture, or the reality of the fact. This is the simplest explanation of all of the narratives of the resurrection—that it really took place. As Beyschlag says: "The *faith* of the disciples in the resurrection of Jesus, which no one denies, cannot have originated, and cannot be explained otherwise than through the *fact* of the resurrection, through the fact in its full, objective, supernatural sense, as hitherto understood" (p. 440). So long as this is contested, the resurrection remains a problem which the failure of rival attempts at explanation only leaves in deeper darkness.

For a good statement and criticism of the various hypotheses, see Schaff's *Hist. of the Church*, i. pp. 172–186; Godet's *Defence of the Christian Faith* (Eng. trans.), chaps. i. and ii. (against Réville); and Christlieb's *Moderne Zweifel*, Lect. VII. (Eng. trans.).

NOTES TO CHAPTER 7

Note A—p. 270

Recent Theories of the Trinity

Some examples may be given of recent theories of the Trinity which seem defective from the Christian point of view. Of these, three classes may be named :

I. *Speculative Theories*, which do not start from the basis of Christian facts, but are the products of *a priori* deduction. These theories are abstract, speculative, cosmological, with little relation to distinctively Christian interests. The typical example here is Hegel's, in his *Religionsphilosophie*, ii. pp. 223–251. Hegel speaks of an immanent Trinity in God—a Trinity of God's being before or outside of the creation of the world. He does not disdain even the name " persons,"—" person, or rather subject,"—speaks of Father, Son, and Spirit. Yet this Trinity is little more than the play of pure thought with itself in the element of highest abstraction : thought eternally distinguishing itself from itself, and as eternally sublating that distinction. The Father is the pure abstract idea ; the Son is the element of particularity in that idea; the Spirit is the sublation of this in individuality. The distinction is only ideal, does not become real till the passage is made into the actuality of the finite world. Here Hegel is careful to remind us that, though in the domain of science the idea is first, in existence it is later—it comes later to consciousness and knowledge (p. 247). This Trinity has therefore no existence prior to the world or independently of it ; it is simply potentiality and basis. [Hegel's own formula for his immanent process is—" God in His eternal universality is this : to distinguish Himself, to determine Himself, to posit another to Himself, and again to annul this distinction—therein to be in Himself, and only through this act of self-production is He Spirit " (p. 237).] The supreme abstraction of all this is very evident. The names of Christian theology are retained, with no agreement in content. What possible resemblance has " the idea in its abstract universality " to the Father in the Christian conception ? Yet Hegel's treatment contains many profound and suggestive thoughts. In consonance with this speculative mode of thought are the theories which make the world, or the idea of the world, the mediating factor in the Divine self-consciousness.

II. *Impersonal Theories*, which recognise an immanent distinction in the Godhead, but one only of potencies, of momenta in the Divine life, of modes of existence, therefore not a true personal Trinity. Thus Schelling (whose "potencies," however, become personal later in the world-process),[1] Rothe, Beyschlag, etc. This view lies near akin to Sabellianism. *E.g.*, Rothe's distinctions of nature, essence, and personality have nothing to do with the Biblical distinctions of Father, Son, and Spirit, which he takes to relate only to the sphere of Revelation. A recent example of this type of theory is afforded by F. A. B. Nitzsch in his *Lehrbuch der evangelischen Dogmatik* (1892). Nitzsch holds that we are compelled to postulate, not simply a Trinity of Revelation, but a Trinity of essence (ii. p. 442). But it is a Trinity of potencies, principles, modes of subsistence (pp. 439–446), not persons. A Trinity of persons, he thinks, would be Tritheism (p. 444). He grants that the Scripture teaches the personality of the Spirit, in part also of the Logos (pp. 440, 444). But this representation cannot be dogmatically used (p. 444). The personality of the Son lies in the human nature (p. 441), and the Spirit is not a person, but a principle. It is, however, a Divine nature, in the strict sense of the word ; is not to be interchanged with the holy disposition or religiously-elevated state of feeling of man,[2] but is considered as an objective, real Divine power, which is essentially equal with God (p. 439). Nevertheless, when we go on to ask what this threefold mode of subsistence in the Divine nature is, we find it difficult to distinguish it from a Trinity of Revelation. God as Father is God in Himself in distinction from His relation to the world ; the Logos is the Revelation principle in God ; and the Spirit is the principle of the Divine self-communication (pp. 445, 446). Christ is the one in whom this Revelation finds its highest expression ; in this sense He is the Incarnation of the Logos, and has "Godhead." "This expression," he tells us, "is quite in place " (p. 514). It is evident (1) that this so-called ontological Trinity is barely distinguishable from an economical or Sabellian one ; (2) that Christ has not real Godhead—is, in truth, purely man, only the highest organ of Divine Revelation ; and (3) that the Trinitarian doctrine sought to be established is awkward and confused, and has

---

[1] Pfleiderer remarks on Schelling's Trinity—"The interpretation of the three potencies by the three persons of the Church's doctrine of the Trinity, and the more than bold exposition of dogmatic formulæ and passages of Scripture, we may pass by as a mere *hors d'œuvre* without value for philosophy. Orthodoxy could feel no gratitude to our philosopher for his deduction of a triple Divine personality which only began with the creation, and was only to be fully realised at the conclusion of the world-process. The Trinity arrived at is that of Montanism or Sabellianism, rather than that of the Church."—*Religionsphilosophie*, iii. p. 21 (Eng. trans.). A good criticism of Beyschlag's Trinitarian view may be seen in Dorner, *Syst. of Doct.* iii. pp. 258–260.

[2] Pfleiderer explains the Holy Spirit rationalistically as "the arrival of the Divine reason at supremacy in our heart."—*Religionsphilosophie*, iii. p. 305.

little relation to the scriptural doctrine. It is made to rest primarily on God's relation to the world (p. 442), and not on the facts of Redemption. Its representation of "God in Himself" as the Father has nothing in common with the New Testament idea of Fatherhood. Then the personality is made to reside only in the first principle. God as Father is personal; the other two potencies (Logos and Spirit) are not personal. Further, in this Trinity there is no room for the Son. The Divine second principle is named "Logos," not "Son,"—the Son comes into being with Jesus Christ. We have, therefore, the contradiction of an Eternal Father without an Eternal Son; the Logos is not the Son of the Trinitarian formula. The first and third members in this formula are truly Divine—one personal, the other impersonal; the middle member is personal, but not truly Divine. The ordinary doctrine of the Trinity may be difficult, but it certainly is more coherent and less contradictory than this of Nitzsch's, which seems to originate rather in a desire to keep in touch with ecclesiastical phraseology, than in any real need arising out of its author's Christology or Pneumatology.

Dr. Dorner is a powerful defender of the Godhead of Christ, yet it is doubtful whether in his later views he has not surrendered the only basis on which this doctrine can be consistently maintained. In his *History of the Doctrine of the Person of Christ*, Dr. Dorner proceeds on the view (or seems to do so) of a Trinity of personal distinctions (cf., *e.g.*, his remarks on Hegel's theory in vol. v. p. 150). In his *System of Doctrine*, on the other hand, he abandons this ground, and falls back on a Trinity of impersonal modes—momenta in the constitution of the one Divine Personality. The Hypostases are to be thought of as "the eternal points of mediation of the Absolute Divine Personality"—as "intermediate between attributes and Egoity and Personality" (i. pp. 382, 383, Eng. trans.); as "not of themselves and singly personal," but as having "a share in the one Divine Personality in their own manner" (p. 448). As against a view which would make the Divine Hypostases "three severed subjects, with separate self-consciousness, and divided self-determination," this has perhaps its truth. But Dr. Dorner evidently so regards these momenta of the Divine Personality that neither is the Father a Person, nor the Son a Person, nor the Spirit a Person; but the three constitute together the One Personality, or Divine self-consciousness. There is not such a distinction between Father and Son as could be expressed by the pronouns I and Thou. The strained character of this construction is seen in the attempt to retain the names Father and Son for these internal modes of the Divine self-consciousness. It is not, it is to be observed, the completed Personality who is the Father, and the historical Christ who is the Son; but Father is the name for the first "point of mediation," Son for the second point, Spirit for the third, in the one self-consciousness. But how, it may be asked, can an impersonal moment in a process be described as Father, or how can an impersonal principle be described as Son?

In accordance with this view, Dr. Dorner does not admit that a personal Divine Being became incarnate in Christ, but only that a principle incorporated itself with the humanity derived from the virgin (iii. p. 163). "God as Logos, as that special eternal mode of being of the Deity, unites Himself perfectly and indissolubly with Jesus, and this may be said to have become man in Him, because as Logos He has His being, His perfect Revelation in this man, and has become a living unity with this man" (iii. p. 303). Christ is not simply human or simply Divine, but the Divine and human natures coalesce to form a "God-human Ego" or personality (pp. 308, 309). Here, again, one cannot but feel that Dr. Dorner's theory leaves the Divinity of Christ in an exceedingly ambiguous position. He is constantly objecting to the orthodox doctrine that it imperils the integrity of the humanity of Christ—makes it unlike ours. But what of his own theory of Christ's peculiarly constituted Personality? Either it must be held that this union of the Divine principle with His humanity is akin in character to that which takes place in every believer—in which case his ground is taken away for asserting a sole and exclusive Divinity for Christ; or it ceases to be a truly human person (as, on the other hand, it is not a Divine Person), and can only be thought of as a *tertium quid*, a peculiar product of the union of Divine and human factors. The Church doctrine at least avoids this ambiguity by saying boldly—it is a Divine Person who appears in humanity,—one who submits Himself to the conditions of humanity, yet in origin and essence is eternal and Divine. It is difficult to see how, on Dr. Dorner's view, Christ should be a truly Divine being; but if He is so—and there can be no mistake about Dr. Dorner's earnestness of conviction on the subject—the conclusion cannot be avoided that, as in the theories of Rothe and Beyschlag, a new Divine Person has since the Incarnation been added to the Godhead. There was but one Divine Personality before—not the Father, but the one God, constituted through the three "modes"; there is now a second, as the result of the Incarnation of one of these modes—true God and Man. Surely the mere statement of such a view is sufficient to show its untenableness.

III. *Neo-Sabellian Theories*, which resolve the Trinity into *aspects* of the Divine in the process of its self-manifestation or Revelation. The ground is abandoned of an immanent or ontological Trinity, and the names Father, Son, and Spirit are taken but as expressions for the phases of the Divine self-manifestation in nature or grace. Schleiermacher inclines to this view (*Der christ. Glaube*, sects. 170–172), and we have seen that theories like Rothe's and Nitzsch's tend to pass over into it. The Ritschlian theologians have no alternative but to adopt it. It is a view which will always have a certain popularity, seeming, as it does, to evade metaphysical subtleties, while giving a plausible, easily apprehended interpretation of the Trinitarian formula. Its simplicity, however, is all upon the surface. The moment it is touched with the finger of criticism, its inadequacy is revealed.

The forms of these Neo-Sabellian theories are as varied as the

minds that produce them. We may distinguish, first, certain
popular forms. The old Sabellianism confined itself to the stadia
of Revelation (the Father in the Law, the Son in the Incarnation,
the Spirit in the Church). In modern times we have a wide
variety of triads—God as Creator, Redeemer, and Sanctifier; God
in creation (Father), in Christ (Son), in the inward fellowship of
believers (Spirit); God in nature (Father), in history (Son), in
conscience (Spirit); God in Himself (Father), as revealed (Son), as
the principle of inward communion (Spirit), etc. A common
feature in nearly all these triads is the identification of God as
Creator with the Father; or again, God in His absolute, self-
enclosed being, is viewed as the Father. But it cannot be too often
repeated that it is not peculiarly as Creator that God, in the
Christian view, is revealed as the Father. Creation is not the
Revelation of God's Fatherhood. It is in Christ only that the
Fatherhood of God is perfectly revealed (Matt. xi. 27). We know
the Father through the Son. Still less does Fatherhood, in the
Christian sense, denote God in the depths of His absoluteness. The
truth in these views is that the Son is the principle of Revelation
in the Godhead; that the Father, apart from the Son, is undisclosed
and unrevealed. But that to which the Son leads us back in God
is a true Fatherhood of knowledge, love, and will. The second
criticism to be made on these theories is that they do not give us a
truly Divine Trinity of Father, Son, and Spirit. Whether the Son
is identified with the "world," or with "humanity," or with
"Christ," the second member of the Trinity is not Divine as the
first and third are. It is not God who is the Son, but the (non-
Divine) Son reveals God. This, it may be observed, is a principal
distinction between the ancient and the modern Sabellianism. The
old Sabellianism sought to hold by a real Godhead of Christ, though
it failed in doing so. It was the same God, according to it, who in
the old dispensation revealed Himself as Father, who afterwards
became incarnate as Son, and who later was manifested as the Holy
Spirit in the Church. The defects of this view were glaring; for if
the phases were, as the Sabellians held, successive, then the one God
ceased to be Father before He became Son, and had ceased to be
Son before He became Spirit. Then Father and Son are terms
without meaning. But, further, in ceasing to be Son, the Divine
must be supposed to have left the humanity of Christ. Thus the
reality of the Incarnation is again denied.[1] We have only a
temporary union of the Godhead with the man Christ Jesus. In
the Neo-Sabellianisms, on the other hand, the Person of Christ is
regarded as Divine only in a figurative and improper way, *i.e.* as
the bearer of a Divine Revelation, or in an ethical sense; and the
successive phases of the Divine self-manifestation are not regarded
as necessarily sublating each other; *i.e.* God remains Father, while
revealed as Son, while manifested as Spirit.

Kaftan's view of the Trinity in his *Das Wesen der christ. Religion*

---

[1] Or reduced to a mere theophany. Ancient Sabellianism spoke of an
absorption even of the humanity of Christ.

does not rise above a Trinity of Revelation or manifestation. "The Christian believes in God," he says, "the supra-terrestrial Lord of the world, who was from the beginning, and is in eternity. He believes in the Godhead of Jesus, the historical Founder of our religion, in whom God has revealed Himself, through whom God has entered into that relation to mankind which from eternity He had in view. He believes in a power of the Divine Spirit in the history of mankind which, since the appearance of Jesus Christ, and more precisely since His resurrection from the dead, has come to its perfection in Christendom, and which transplants the man, who allows himself to be possessed by it, into the blessed fellowship of the Divine life. But still it is *one* God in whom he believes. . . . How can this be otherwise brought to a single expression than by designating the Christian faith in God as the faith in a three-one God? The Christian has and knows God only through Christ in the Holy Spirit" (p. 388). "Understood in a Christian sense, God is personal Spirit; as such we find Him in the historical personal life of Jesus Christ; as such we believe in Him ruling in history: this is the signification of the Christian faith in the three-one God" (p. 390, first edition). This is a much higher position than the ordinary Ritschlian one [note the emphatic assertion of Christ's resurrection from the dead, and the connection of this with the mission of the Spirit]. The crucial point is the affirmation of Christ's Divinity. Now, whatever this means to Kaftan, it is certain it does not mean the entrance into time of a pre-existing Divine Being; nor would he allow the inference to a personal distinction in the Godhead as the ground of the Incarnation (p. 391). His Trinitarian doctrine, therefore, does not mean more than that God has a super-earthly mode of being, that He has revealed Himself historically in Jesus Christ, and that He has wrought since as a spiritual power in the hearts of men. He refuses, indeed, to admit that this is a mere economical Trinity. The Revelation, he says, expresses the essence. But Sabellianism never denied that there was that in God which determined the modes of His self-revelation, or that to this extent they expressed His nature. Kaftan's midway position is untenable. Either he must deal earnestly with the "Godhead" of Christ, which he so strenuously maintains, and then he can hardly avoid moving back on personal distinctions; or, holding to his modal view of the Trinity, he will find it increasingly difficult to regard Christ as truly Divine.

Note B—p. 276

Dr. Martineau As a Trinitarian

DR. MARTINEAU advocating Trinitarianism is a veritable Saul among the prophets. Yet this is the drift of his striking essay (first published as late as 1886) on "A Way Out of the Trinitarian Controversy." The object of the essay is to find a way of reconciling the differences of Unitarians and Trinitarians, which Dr. Martineau thinks might be accomplished if parties only came better to understand each other. He says, with great truth, "Religious doctrine may be only theory to the critic, but it is the expression of fact to the believer—fact infinite and ever present, the vital breath of every moment, deprived of which the soul must gasp and die. . . . It is from the depth of such natures that theology and churches arise ; and if you would harmonise them when they seem discordant, you must descend into the depths ; you must feel their truth ere you criticise their errors, and appreciate their difference before you can persuade them that they are one. . . . To feel charity towards a sin, you must understand the temptation ; towards a sorrow, you must know its depths ; towards an erring creed, you must appreciate its meaning and its ground" (Essay ii. pp. 526, 527). In this spirit he aims at setting forth what he conceives to be the truth about the Trinity.

The intention is excellent, but the success of the attempt must be pronounced doubtful. It is, however, exceedingly interesting as coming from Dr. Martineau. For his thought leads him to recognise a certain real Trinitarian distinction in God ; and, so far as one can judge, he does not object even to Trinitarians speaking of these distinctions as in a sense personal. The gist of his view is expressed in the following passages : "God then, as He exists in Himself ere He at all appears,—God alone with the void,—God as a still presence, —a starless night, a dumb immensity of intellect, is intended by the First Person in the received creed. Let now the silence be broken, let the thought burst into expression, fling out the poem of creation, evolving its idea in the drama of history, and reflecting its own image in the soul of man ; then this *manifested* phase of the Divine existence is *the Son*. . . . The one fundamental idea by which the two personalities are meant to be distinguished is simply this—that the first is God in His primeval essence,—infinite meaning without finite indications ; the second is God speaking out in phenomena and fact, and leaving His sign whenever anything comes up from the deep of things, or merges back again. . . . Respecting the Third Person in the Trinity, and the doctrine of the Holy Spirit, . . . the separation of His personality from the others, as not proper to be merged in them, is founded on a feeling deep and true, viz. that the human spirit is not a mere part of nature. . . . We are persuaded of something diviner within us than this—akin in freedom, in power, in love, to the supreme Mind Himself. In virtue of this prerogative, we have to be otherwise provided for, in our highest life, than the mere products of creative order ; we need, not control, simply to be imposed and obeyed, but *living communion*, like with like, spirit with spirit. To open this communion, to bring this help and sympathy, to breathe on the fading consciousness of our heavenly affinity, and make us one with the Father and the Son, is the function, truly of a quite special kind, reserved in the doctrine of the Church for the Holy Ghost. What God is in Himself ; what He is as manifested in the universe and history, brought to a focus in the drama of Redemption ; what He is in communion with our inner spirit,—these are the three points of view denoted by the ' Persons' of the Trinity " (pp. 332, 334, 335). The "Eternal Sonship" he connects with the doctrine of eternal creation. The most paradoxical part of the essay is where he seeks to prove that the Unitarians, while imagining they were worshipping the "Father," have all the while been worshipping the "Son" —that the Father "is really absent from the Unitarian Creed " (p. 536).

After the remarks in last note, it is not necessary to say much in criticism of this theory. It is, after all, only a modal theory—the substituting of "phases " and "points of view" for the orthodox "Persons." The distinction of " Father" and "Son " is that of the hidden and the revealed God ;' and the "Son" has His *raison d'être* in the existence of a world. There is no room for a special Incarnation. The "Son " is manifested in Jesus not otherwise than He is manifested in all history—only in higher (or highest) degree. But it has already been pointed out that this identification of the "Father" with God in Himself, "dormant potency," "still presence," "dumb immensity of intellect," has no resemblance to the Christian idea of the Father. Dr. Martineau goes here on an altogether wrong track. His theory does not express the Christian facts.

NOTES TO CHAPTER 8

Note A—p. 299

The Germ Theory of Justification

This subtle theory of justification, according to which the mani-foldly imperfect believer is accepted on the ground of his germinal holiness,—" for in the first moment," as Schleiermacher says, " the whole development is implicitly given" (p. 105),—is not without many advocates. Its phraseology is found in some who are far from wishing to remove the ground of acceptance from the doing and suffering of Christ ; and it finds favour with others who reject this objective ground, and need another explanation.

Dr. M'Leod Campbell finds this view in Luther, whose doctrine he expounds thus—" secondly, because this excellent condition of faith is in us but a germ—a grain of mustard-seed—a feeble dawn, God, in imputing it as righteousness, has respect unto that of which it is the dawn—of which, as the beginning of the life of Christ in us, it is the promise, and in which it shall issue" (*Nat. of Atonement*, p. 34 (4th ed.)). There is no doubt that some of Luther's expres-sions in the *Commentary on Galatians* give colour to this statement. *E.g.* "Wherefore Christ apprehended by faith, and dwelling in the heart, is the true Christian righteousness, for the which God counteth us righteous, and giveth us eternal life" (on ii. 16). "We conclude, therefore, upon these words, 'It was imputed to him for righteous-ness,' that righteousness indeed beginneth through faith, and by the same we have the first-fruits of the Spirit ; but because faith is weak, it is not made perfect without God's imputation. Wherefore faith beginneth righteousness, but imputation maketh it perfect unto the day of Christ. . . . For these two things work Christian righteousness : faith in the heart, which is a gift of God, and assuredly believeth in Christ ; and also that God accepteth this imperfect faith for perfect righteousness, for Christ's sake, in whom I have begun to believe" (on iii. 6). No one can doubt, however, taking the general drift of the Commentary, that in Luther's view the sole objective ground of the sinner's pardon and acceptance is the cross and righteousness of Christ.

In a similar way Martensen expresses himself—" For faith is like the grain of mustard-seed, a small, insignificant but fructifying seed corn, which contains within it the fulness of a whole future. In His gracious contemplation God beholds in the seed corn the future fruit of blessedness ; in the pure will, the realised ideal of freedom" (*Dogmatics*, p. 392). Yet Martensen is emphatic in declaring—"The evangelical Church teaches that Christ alone, received by faith, is the Righteousness of man ; and thus she leads man back from what is imperfect and multifarious to ONE who is Himself perfection ; she brings him back from his wanderings in the desert to the pure Fountain where freedom springs from grace ; to the holy centre where God looks upon man, not in the light of the temporal and finite, but in the light of Christ's eternity and perfection" (p. 393).

There is no question of the truth of the view in itself that, as Martensen further says, "Justifying faith cannot possibly exist in the soul in a dead or merely stationary condition, but that, like the living, fruit-bearing seed corn, it contains within itself a mighty germinating power, which must necessarily beget a holy development of life" (p. 393), and that God sees in this germinal holiness all that is to proceed from it, and even, if we please, imputes to the believer anticipatively the yet future result. But confusion is introduced if we confound or exchange this with the sinner's justification. The imputation in question is not in order to acceptance, but is a mode of contemplating the fruition of holiness in *persons already accepted*. It is an act of the Divine complacency in and towards believers already justified and adopted on the sole and all-sufficient ground of Christ's work done on their behalf.

This view, translated into their own peculiar phraseology, is naturally the one adopted by idealistic writers who treat of religion. Kant led the way here when, in rationalising the doctrine of justification, he represented it as meaning that, for the sake of our faith in the moral good, we are already held to be what, while on earth, and perhaps in any future world, we are no more than about to become (*Religion innerhalb der Grenzen der bloss. Vernunft*, Bk. II. sec. 3). I quote two illustrative passages from Mr. Bradley and Mr. T. H. Green.

"Justification by faith means," says Mr. Bradley, "that, having thus identified myself with the object, I feel myself in that identification to be already one with it, and to enjoy the bliss of being, all falsehood overcome, what I truly am. By my claim to be one with the ideal, which comprehends me too, and by assertion of the non-reality of all that is opposed to it, the evil in the world and the evil incarnate in me through past bad acts, all this falls into the unreal ; I being one with the ideal, this is not mine, and so imputation of offences goes with the change of self, and applies not now to my true self, but to the unreal, which I repudiate and hand over to destruction. . . . Because the ideal is not realised completely and truly *as* the ideal, therefore I am not justified by the works, which issue from faith, *as* works ; since they remain imperfect. I am justified solely and entirely by the ideal identification ; the existence of which in me is on the other hand indicated and guaranteed

by works, and in its very essence implies them."—*Ethical Studies,*
pp. 293, 294.

Mr. Green says : "We most nearly approach the Pauline notion
of imputed righteousness when we say that it is a righteousness
communicated in principle, but not yet developed in act."—Paper
on Justification by Faith, in *Works,* iii. p. 202.

In the former of these extracts (as also in Mr. Green's own view)
we are away from the historical Christ altogether, and have to deal
only with "ideals," in relation to which we pass an act of judgment
on ourselves in accordance with the metaphysical truth of things,
and there is neither room nor need for a special justifying act of
God.

NOTES TO CHAPTER 9

Note A—p. 325

Renan's Eschatology

HARTMANN'S theory of cosmic suicide by the concurrent decision of the race is bizarre enough, but it is outdone by the extraordinary eschatology sketched by M. Renan in his *Dialogues et Fragments Philosophiques*, which, apparently, though he heads the section "Dreams," it is not his intention that we should take otherwise than seriously. It is a curious further illustration of how every theorist feels the need of some kind of eschatology, as well as of the lengths to which credulity will go in minds that deem themselves too wise to accept Revelation. In Renan's view, the great business in which the universe is engaged is that of organising God.[1] God as yet only exists in ideal; the time will come when He will be materially realised in a consciousness analagous to that of humanity, only infinitely superior (p. 78). The universe will culminate in a single conscious centre, in which the conception of personal Monotheism will become a truth. An omniscient, omnipotent being will be the last term of the God-making evolution (*l'évolution déifique*); the universe will be consummated in a single organised being—the resultant of milliards of beings whose lives are summed up in his—the harmony, the sum-total of the universe (pp. 125, 126). The climax of absurdity is reached in the notion that the personal Deity thus realised proceeds, now that he has come into existence, to raise the dead and hold a general judgment! M. Renan may be allowed here to speak for himself—"Yes, I conceive the possibility of the resurrection, and often say to myself with Job, *Reposita est hæc spes in sinu meo.* If ever at the end of the successive evolutions the universe is led back to a single, absolute being, this being will be the complete life of all; he will renew in himself the life of beings who have vanished, or, if you will, in his bosom will revive all those who have ever been. When God shall be at once perfect and all-powerful, that is to say, when scientific omnipotence shall be concentrated in the hands of a good and just being, this being will wish to resuscitate the past in order to repair

[1] This is not among the "Dreams," but among the "Probabilities" (pp. 78, 79).

its innumerable injustices. God will exist more and more ; the
more he exists, the more just he will be. He will attain to this
fully on the day when whoever has wrought for the Divine work
shall feel that the Divine work is finished, and shall see the part
he has had in it. Then the eternal inequality of beings shall be
sealed for ever," etc. (pp. 435, 436). Comment on such "dreams" is
needless. Yet the spinning of such theories by a cultured intellect
which has parted with its faith is not without its lessons.

Note B—p. 327

The Gospel and the Vastness of Creation

An interesting article on the subject treated of in the Lecture is
contributed to the *Contemporary Review* for April 1889, by the late
Prof. Freeman, under the title—" Christianity and the 'Geocentric'
System." The article is full of suggestive and acute remarks.
Prof. Freeman states the objection in its full strength. "It is
unreasonable, it is urged, to believe that such a scheme as that of
Christianity, implying such awful mysteries and so tremendous a
sacrifice, can have been devised for the sole benefit of such an
insignificant part of the universe as the earth and its inhabitants"
(p. 541). He does not, however, think there is much in it. "If it
is meant," he says, "not merely as a rhetorical point, but as a
serious objection, it really comes to this : we cannot believe that so
much has been done for this earth as Christianity teaches, because
this earth is so little ; if this earth were only bigger, then we might
believe it. . . . Surely nobody ever believed or disbelieved on this
kind of ground. An objection of this kind is a rhetorical point, and
nothing more" (p. 542). As a rhetorical point, nevertheless, he
grants that it is telling, and proceeds to deal with it for what it is
worth. He points out, first, how little the change from the
"geocentric" view has done to alter the general tenor of our
thoughts and feelings. It is not the case that the "geocentric" view
led man to take an exaggerated view of his own importance. On
the contrary, the sight of the starry heavens, even when looked at
with "geocentric" eyes, has always been to make one feel his little-
ness (Ps. viii.). "The truth is that the objection attributes to
scientific theories a great deal more practical influence than really
belongs to them. Whether the earth goes round the sun, or the sun
goes round the earth, does not make the least practical difference to
our general feelings, to our general way of looking at things. . . .
We are all 'heliocentric' when we stop to think about it, . . . but
I suspect most of us are 'geocentric' in practice. That is, we not
only talk as if the sun really rose and set, but for all practical
purposes we really think so. . . . Nobody really accepts or rejects
the Christian religion or any other religion, merely through thinking whether the sun is so many thousands or millions of times

bigger than the earth, or whether it is only the size of a cart-wheel, or, at the outside, about the bigness of ˌPeloponnesus " (p. 544). Next, he touches the question whether we have any reason to suppose that other worlds are inhabited. "Astronomers do not even attempt to tell us for certain whether even the other members of our own system are inhabited or not. . . . I believe I am right in saying that they tell us that Mars is the only planet of our system where men like ourselves could live ; that, if the other planets are inhabited, it must be by beings of a very different nature from ours" (p. 545). But the peculiar part of his argument, developed with great ingenuity and force, is a working out of the idea that it is, after all, quite in accordance with analogy that our world should be a very small one, and yet should play a most important part in the universe. Here the analogies of his own science of history furnish him with abundant illustration. "If it should be true that our earth does hold a kind of moral place in the universe out of all proportion to its physical size, the fact will be one of exactly the same kind as the fact that so small a continent as Europe was chosen to play the foremost part in the world's history, and that so small a part of Europe as Greece was chosen to play the foremost part in Europe" (p. 558). Incidentally, in developing this argument, he refers to the fact noted in the Lecture, that the past history of our own world takes away in large part the force of the argument from the vast empty spaces of creation. " Here both the certain facts of geology and the less certain doctrine of evolution, instead of standing in the way of the argument, give it no small help. . . . We know that our own world remained in this seemingly useless and empty state for untold ages ; there is therefore at least no absurdity in supposing that other worlds, some or all of them, are in the same state still. . . . The past emptiness and uselessness of the whole planet, the abiding emptiness and seeming uselessness of large parts of it, certainly go a long way to get rid of all *a priori* objection to the possible emptiness and seeming uselessness of some or all of the other bodies that make up the universe " (p. 548).

A lengthy and valuable note on the subject will likewise be found in Dorner's *History of the Doctrine of the Person of Christ*, vol. v. pp. 265–270. Dorner reviews, with his usual thoroughness and learning, the opinions held by others, but finds nothing to shake his confidence in the Christian view. " Concerning our planet, as compared with a thousand others, we must say that it is the Bethlehem amongst the rest, the least city amongst the thousands in Judah, out of which the Lord was destined to proceed" (p. 267). He reminds us that Steffens and Hegel, like Whewell, "regard our planetary system as the most organised spot of the universe ; the earth, this concentrated spot on which the Lord appeared, as its absolute centre, which both Hegel and Becker designate the Bethlehem of worlds " (p. 269).

Ebrard likewise discusses the objection in his *Christian Apologetics*, i. p. 253 (Eng. trans.). Fiske, in his little book on *Man's Destiny*, is another who refers to it. Chap. i. is headed "Man's Place in

Nature, as affected by the Copernican Theory." He concludes—
"The speculative necessity for man's occupying the largest and most
central spot in the universe is no longer felt. It is recognised as a
primitive and childish notion. With our larger knowledge we see
that these vast and fiery suns are after all but the Titan-like *servants*
of the little planets which they bear with them in their flight
through the abysses of space. . . . He who thus looks a little deeper
into the secrets of nature than his forefathers of the sixteenth century, may well smile at the quaint conceit that man cannot be the
object of God's care unless he occupies an immovable position in the
centre of the stellar universe" (pp. 16, 17).

Among the Ritschlians, the question is touched on by Ritschl,
Recht. und Ver. iii. p. 580 ; and by Kaftan, *Wahrheit*, pp. 562, 563
(Eng. trans. ii. pp. 399–401).

Finally, I may refer to the beautiful treatment of the higher and
more spiritual aspects of the subject by Dr. John Ker in his sermon
on "The Gospel and the Magnitude of Creation" (*Sermons*, p. 227).

Note C—p. 341

Alleged Pauline Universalism

The two strongest passages in favour of Pauline universalism are
undoubtedly 1 Cor. xv. 21–28 and Eph. i. 10, yet the ablest exegetes
concur that in neither can Paul be held to teach the doctrine of
universal salvation. With this view I cannot but agree. It is easy
to read such a meaning into certain of Paul's universalistic expressions, but an unbiassed study of the passages and their context
makes it plain that it is far from the apostle's intention to affirm any
such doctrine. As respects 1 Cor. xv. 21–28, we have first the statement—"For as in Adam all die, even so in Christ shall all be made
alive" (ver. 22). But to affirm that in Christ all shall be made alive
is a very different thing from affirming that all shall be made alive
in Christ. And that the latter is not the apostle's thought is made
evident from the next verse, which declares that this making alive
of those that are Christ's takes place at His coming. "Each in his
own order : Christ the first-fruits ; then they that are Christ's, at
His coming" (ver. 23). This making alive, therefore, is the making
alive at the resurrection at the Parousia. But no universalist maintains that at *that* period "they that are Christ's" embraces all
humanity. The subsequent clauses are not more decisive. "The
last enemy that shall be abolished is death" (ver. 27) ; but here
again it is foreign to the context to suppose that Paul has in view
any other abolition of death than that he has been speaking of
throughout the chapter, viz. its abolition at the resurrection. The
putting down of all (rival) rule, authority, and power (ver. 24), the
putting all His enemies under His feet (ver. 25), the subjection of
all things to the Son (vers. 27, 28), do not naturally suggest recon-

ciliation or conversion, but rather forcible subjugation—the destruction of all hostile authority and influence. In this sense, accordingly, must be interpreted the final expression—the strongest of all—"that God may be all in all." Meyer observes—"Olshausen and De Wette find here the doctrine of restoration favoured also by Neander, so that ἐν πᾶσι would apply to *all creatures,* in whom God shall be the all-determining One. . . . The fact was overlooked that ἐν πᾶσι refers to the members of the kingdom hitherto ruled over by Christ, to whom the condemned, who, on the contrary, are outside of this kingdom, do not belong, and that the continuance of the condemnation is not done away even with the subjugation of Satan, since, on the contrary, the latter himself by his subjugation falls under condemnation" (*Com. in loc.*). Weiss similarly says : "Even the context of this passage excludes any referring of it to a restitution of all things (*Apokatastasis*), for the dominion which God henceforward wields immediately can be no other than that which Christ has received and given up to Him ; and that does not consist in this, that all hostile powers are destroyed or converted, but in this, that they have become powerless, and are subject to His will."—*Biblical Theol.* ii. p. 73 (Eng. trans.).

The second passage, again, Eph. i. 10, speaks of a summing up of all things in Christ as head (I agree with Weiss that there is no need for weakening or denying the force of the composite word) in the dispensation of the fulness of the times—a truly wonderful and comprehensive expression. The τὰ πάντα here is in itself quite general,—all created things and beings,—and might therefore quite well suit a universalistic sense. But, first, the τὰ πάντα is limited by the succeeding clause,—"the things in the heavens, and the things on the earth,"—which excludes the demoniacal powers, certainly not conceived of as "things in the heavens" ; and, next, it is a question whether the annulling of the divided state of "things on earth" is effected by the conversion of hostile powers, or not rather by their subjugation, and separation from the holy part of the creation. This is a question to be determined by Paul's general mode of thought, and Meyer and Weiss agree that such an idea as the final conversion of the unbelieving and the demons is not within his view. "With the Parousia," says Meyer, "there sets in the full realisation, which is the ἀποκατάστασις πάντων (Matt. xix. 28 ; Acts iii. 21 ; 2 Pet. iii. 10 ff.) ; when all antichristian natures and powers shall be discarded out of heaven and earth, so that thereafter nothing in heaven or upon earth shall be excluded from this gathering together again. . . . The restoration in the case of the devils, as an impossibility in the case of spirits radically opposed to God, is not in the whole New Testament so much as thought of. The prince of this world is only judged" (*Com. in loc.,* and Remark 2, on the Doctrine of Restoration). "A bringing back of the world of spirits hostile to God," says Weiss,—"which, moreover, is considered as definitely bad,—is as far away from the Biblical view as is also a need of Redemption on the part of the angel world, and therefore the author felt no need to guard his expressions against either of

these thoughts. . . . Enough that they by their subjection to Christ
are stripped of any power which can hurt the absolute dominion of
Christ" (*Biblical Theol. of N. T.* ii. pp. 107, 109).

The one thing which would be really decisive in favour of a
universalistic interpretation, would be some passage from Paul (or
any part of the New Testament), which explicitly affirmed that
fallen spirits or lost men in eternity would ultimately repent and
be saved; but *no such expression can be found.* Dr. Cox has no
scruple in telling us that those condemned in the judgment will
yet, after a remedial discipline, all be brought to repentance, to
faith; will be restored to God's Fatherly love, etc. If this is the
Scripture doctrine, why do Christ and His apostles never explicitly
say so? Why do they not use expressions as clear and unmistak-
able as Dr. Cox's own? Why only these general expressions, of
which the application is the very question in dispute? The ancient
prophets, *e.g.,* had no difficulty in making clear their belief that a
day of general conversion would come for sinful and rejected Israel.
Why does Jesus, or Paul, or John not tell us as plainly that a day
of general forgiveness and restoration will come for all God's back-
sliding children—that those whom they describe as perishing and
destroyed, and under wrath, and undergoing the second death, will
yet be changed in their dispositions, and made sharers of God's
eternal life? It is not simply that this is not declared of *all,* but it
is not, in one single utterance, declared of *any*; and while this is
the state of the case scripturally, universal restoration, however
congenial to our wishes, must be held to be a dream in the air,
without solid basis in Revelation.

What many passages do teach is the complete subjugation of those
found finally opposed to Christ; and in this way the restoration of
a unity or harmony in the universe, which involves the cessation of
active, or at least effective, opposition to Christ's rule. What may
be covered by such expressions,—or what yet unrevealed may in
future ages be disclosed,—who can tell?

Reference may be made to a careful study of the whole New
Testament teaching on this subject in a series of papers by the Rev.
Dr. Agar Beet in the *Expositor,* vol. i. (4th series), 1890.

INDEX

ACKERMANN, Madame, 70.

Acosmism, 266, 368.

Agnosticism, alternative to Christian view, 47–51; tends to Pessimism, 51; involves a negation, 80–1; Mr. Spencer's, discussed, 81–6; truth in, 12, 85; Agnostic systems, 367; controversy on, 373.

Antiquity of man, bearings on Christian view, 184–5; Boyd Dawkins on, 185; in relation to geological time, 444–6.

Argyll, Duke of, on primitive man, 441.

Arianism, defeat of, 44–5, 390–1; Harnack on, 391; Carlyle on, 391.

Astronomical objection to Christianity, 323–8, 468–70; Professor Freeman on, 468–9.

Atoms, structure of, 126; creation of, 126; Herschel on, 126–7.

Atonement, *see* Redemption. Meaning of word, 288.

Augustine, on cognisability of God, 85; on the Trinity, 268, 271; on eternity and time, 427.

BAETHGEN, on Old Testament Monotheism, 412–3.

Baldensperger, on claims of Jesus, 218; on self-consciousness of Jesus, 254–5; on pre-existence, 448–9.

Ball, Sir R. S., on planets, 325; on nebular hypothesis, 422.

Baring-Gould, S., 12.

Baur, A., on "Weltanschauung," 365–6.

Beyschlag, his Christology, 220; on "Godhead" of Christ, 236, 240, 261; on sinlessness of Christ, 231; on self-consciousness of Christ, 249–51; on Second Advent, 334; on glorification of Christ, 335; on modern views, 373.

Biedermann, his Theism, 59; on Revelation, 61; his Christology, 41; on "Heavenly Man" theory, 220; on the Trinity, 269.

Böhme, Jacob, quoted by Hegel, 54; on existence of evil, 190, 194; on the Trinity, 270.

Bornemann, on "Godhead" of Christ, 394; on pre-existence, 448; on resurrection of Christ, 454.

Bradley, F. H., on moral end, 177; on dualism, 437.

Browning, R., on immortality, 157, 159; on evil, 191.

Bruce, Professor A. B., on Kenotic theories, 243; on kingdom of God, 334, 352, 355; on modern substitutes for Christianity, 385.

Buddhism, Divinity of its founder, 217; its redemption, 288; its eschatology, 321; in what sense a religion, 385.

Bushnell, H., on Gospel picture of Christ, 229; his theory of redemption, 301–5, 316; on fate of the wicked, 337.

CAIRD, Professor E., on Comte, 6, 370, 385; on Kant, 95, 99, 132, 136, 158, 168, 415; on Kant's view of the end of creation, 108–9; on unconscious metaphysics, 370.

Caird, Principal J., on theistic proofs, 95, 97; on Materialism, 150.

Cairns, Principal J., on Voltaire, 66; on Unitarianism, 392.

Calderwood, Professor H., on mind and cerebral activity, 153, 430–3.

Calvin, on the Trinity, 267.

Campbell, J. M'Leod, his theory of atonement, 311–4.

Candlish, Professor J., on kingdom of God, 352; on Christianity and progress, 399.